W9-CSR-689

WORLD CHRONOLOGY
OF
MUSIC HISTORY

Venezia nel sec. XV (frammento).

Dalla *Venetia M D* attribuita a J. De Barbari: con l'aggiunta della cuspide del Campanile, compiuta nel 1514.

World Chronology of Music History

VOLUME I

4,000 B.C. - 1594 A.D.

Compiled and Edited by

Paul E. Eisler

Foreword by Fritz Kramer

1972 OCEANA PUBLICATIONS, INC./Dobbs Ferry, New York

Library of Congress Cataloging in Publication Data

Eisler, Paul E 1919-
World chronology of music history.

CONTENTS: v. 1. 30,000 B.C. - 1594 A.D.
1. Music — Chronology. I. Title.
ML161.E4 780'.9 72-4354
ISBN 0-379-16080-3

Manufactured in the United States of America.

To my beloved wife, Edith
and
to my earlier chronology
Judith
Paul III
Karen
and
Peter
with deepest affection

FOREWORD

The average music student, leaving school to enter life and embark on a career of his own, supposedly has a solid foundation of knowledge of the history of Eastern and Western music, both ancient and modern, and of the various musical styles and the ways to perform them. There is little doubt, however, that the sheer quantity of the material absorbed during the years of study is so overwhelming that for the young practicing musician it will take years for him to achieve true order and logic in his vision of historic perspective. There are also many professional musicians who pick up at random whatever they know about the different periods and styles of music, and the state of even their accumulated knowledge is deplorable.

The *World Chronology of Music History* is a concise survey of the art of music, especially its forms, its styles, the development of different theories, the ups and downs of music throughout the centuries and, of course, individual composers. Included, of necessity, are important highlights of what happened in other arts, what locations acquired transitory importance at any given time, and which crowned heads, emperors and kings and princes, and which theoreticians made their names known as relevant to music.

The importance of this particular *Chronology* lies in its comprehensiveness. Not only does it list the aforementioned items; it also gives literally thousands of examples of performances, premieres and — last but not least — performers. It is a gigantic undertaking. When it is complete, roughly 32,000 years of human evolution and culture will have been covered, starting with the Paleolithic Age and ending with electronic music.

Upon completion of the entire set (anticipated extent: 8-10 volumes) there will, of necessity, be added a separate index volume containing an alphabetical listing of the persons, works and events discussed in the *Chronology.*

The use of the book ought to be described. If a reader wants information about a specific time period, he will find this time period covered in chronological sequence. Should a reader wish to obtain information about a personage whom he cannot locate as to the exact time in which he lived, he may find his name listed in the Index, together with the pertinent page in the volume. The first volume, covering the ages up to the latter part of the 16th Century, will, for instance, have more to say about the Renaissance period than, let's say, about the 9th Century, the century whose only towering personage was Charlemagne, the initiator of certain chant codifications and founder of the first music schools to teach strictly Western music.

From about the middle of the 16th Century on, the material is so abundant as to require a year-by-year coverage. Let us, for example, take the year 1590. What knowledge opens up on the first Madrigal opera, on Mr. Byrd, on the "Liber Secundum Sacrarum Cantionum," on the Council of Brunswick, the popularity of lute music, the painter Zuccari, *young* Monteverdi's doings, and the violin makers in Brescia! And after having read up on the multiple facts of the year 1590, we may proceed to pages and pages of happenings in 1591, and so on. In quoting examples, the standard practice has been followed of referring to major collections of published music.

Reading about music or listening to lectures about music without listening to the music itself is definitely a profitless undertaking. It is the music itself that matters above anything else. Our author, therefore, has taken special pains to emphasize the importance of certain works by various composers which are not to be overlooked. Parallel with the emphasis on masterworks run entries of the pertinent periods in general, such as Classical Antiquity, the Middle Ages (including the Gothic centuries), the Renaissance (as far as Vol. I covers) composers up to the heavenly heights of Byrd, Orlando di Lasso, Palestrina and Victoria.

Now, *to understand music it is also necessary to have some knowledge of the forces which have conditioned the various epochs during their growth.* Music can be grasped in its very depth only if coordinated with the sum total of the art of its time of origin, with literature, painting, sculpture and architecture. The *Chronology* offers assistance even above and beyond these features by also keeping close watch over the war-and-peace-makers of different time periods, their most cunning counsellors, their most eminent philosophers.

Fritz Kramer

INTRODUCTION

The need for a work of the type presented here must be obvious at least in its more mundane aspects. I have found in my own years of study and association with students, both in music and in the more general area of humanities, that regardless of the depth of scholarship, it is impossible to retain the vast amounts of statistical information necessary to the pursuit of organized study.

In my own opinion the value of the correlated information contained in these volumes cannot be underestimated, and it would appear that on that basis a work of this type would have significant value to the period scholar as well as to the specialist in music. In the latter field there can be no questioning of the vast influence of political, sociological and geographical circumstances on a composer's life and works. An example as simple as Beethoven's composition of the "Eroica Symphony" points this out to the most elementary researcher operating at the shallowest level of sophistication. Highly sensitive and sophisticated examples show up as the depth of scholarship increases. Suffice it to say then, these volumes properly used can make the need for the chronology increasingly obvious.

The actual research, writing and organizing of the material brought severe problems into focus. First and foremost, there still exist huge areas of conflict among recognized musicologists and respected scholars. Wherever feasible it has been felt advisable to make a choice in dates, but where evidence has been inconclusive and the sources seemed of equal value in tems of reliability, they have both been preserved in the volumes and cross-indexed at the entries to as great an extent as space would permit. The reader is advised to check both the date of birth and the date of death of a composer for possible additional references; one place or the other may well contain a cross-reference. An example of this is provided by the entries on Juan del Encina on pages 157, 179, and 287. Alternate spellings have been provided where they seemed of sufficient significance to merit their inclusion, and frequently birth and death dates contain slightly different biographical information in order to conserve space and still provide maximum coverage in the brief listings in the chronology. Most of all it should be borne in mind that this reference work is designed to serve as a guide to, and not by any means as an in-depth work, on any given area in music or the allied arts.

The actual make-up of the book became increasingly difficult as the quantity of entries per year increased. In the early years, before Christ and during the first thirteen centuries after Christ, events and works were arranged in a rather loose alphabetical system based on the most essential content of the entry at hand. At all times the actual date of the event was the critical factor in determining the order. Exact dates with month and day were grouped at the start of each year. Following this group, dates for which only the month was available were entered in order of months. Entries with only the year as identification followed, and at the end of this category events, including a range in years, were placed in their proper order. Information preceded by a "circa" was arranged in the same manner, with those including a range of dates placed at the end of the entries.

Within the general framework just described, material was then divided in the following order: Births and deaths of musicians, or musically-oriented people; biographical data on musicians; performances and works; historical information of other than a musical nature; births and dates not connected with music or art; and, finally, at the end of each series, births and deaths of painters, sculptors, and architects, followed by art works with the maker's name determining the alphabetical sequence.

As is always the case with a work of this scope, many people provided assistance of immeasurable degree. My deepest thanks to Joyce Kaiden who worked side by side with me in the research, editing and typing of this volume. I am grateful for research contributions made by Cecilia Aufiero, Frances Rauscher, C. Elsie Ryan, and Melinda Scheel. For assistance in many other areas of the project, words of thanks go to Grace Bentley, Jeff Berryman, Howard Kaye, Lucinda Lewis, and Stanley Lokez. My thanks to my colleagues at the Manhattan School of Music, Dr. Fritz Kramer and Dr. Ethel Thurston for their expert counsel as well as to Don Rauscher, Justine Shir-Cliff and Ludmila Ulehla for sharing their experience with me.

The staff at Oceana has been most cooperative and helpful, Edith Ratshin in the area of publicity, and William Cowan, the editor, with whom I have spent countless hours in discussion of the format and vast problems surrounding these efforts. My gratitude is due to Philip and Fay Cohen for their confidence, encouragement, and for providing the opportunity for the entire undertaking.

Finally, a word to my wife, Edith, who complained, proofread, cheered, moaned, did research, picked up the mess, lived in a nine-room filing cabinet formerly called a home, thank you for outstanding bravery, patience, and understanding.

Paul E. Eisler

CHRONOLOGY

4,000 B.C. - 1594 A. D.

B.C.

c.30,000, Rock paintings or engravings from the Palaeolithic culture (contemporary with the last Ice Age) exist from this date to 10,000 B.C.

c.28,000, Ceiling paintings from this period exist in the Cave at Lascaux in France.

c.15,000, Painting of a Woolly Mammoth (1'8" wide) found in the Cave at Font-de-Gaume in France.

c.13,000, Painting of a Bison found in the Cave at Altamira in Spain.

c.13,000, Painting of a Reindeer found in the Cave at Font-de-Gaume in France.

c.12,000, Painting of a Reindeer and a Salmon found at Lorthet in France.

c.12,000, Painting of an Animal Group (5'6" wide) found at Lascaux in France.

c.7,000, Neolithic bone-flute unearthed in Switzerland, supplying evidence that a wind instrument with three holes existed from this period on.

c.7,000, Painting of a Group of Archers (3'10" high) found at Valltorta Gorge.

c.5,000, The beginning of the Neolithic Age in Crete.

c.4,000, During the old and middle kingdom in Egypt, instruments including clappers, sistrum, vertical flute, double clarinet types, small harps, and the popularity of harp and

B.C.(cont.)

(cont.) flute suggest a restrained type of music, performed mostly by upper classes.

c.4,000, The beginning of high culture in the Aeneolithic age, the Bronze age in the Orient.

c.3,500, Sumerians used clappers, the sistrum, vertical flute, wooden horn, drum, kithara and lute. Harp was the principal instrument.

c.3,100, The Stele of Ur-nina (1'6" wide) was carved.

c.3,000, The beginning of the Bronze Age in Crete.

c.3,000, Ancient Chinese documents place the anhemitonic pentatonic scale at this time.

c.3,000, Babylonian shepherds used lutes and pipes.

c.3,000, Numerous instruments, and an actual piece of music came from Mesopotamia, controlled by the Sumerians at this time.

c.3,000, From this time on Egyptians were aware of the concept of fourths, fifths, octaves, and unisons.

c.3,000, The ancient Egyptians made great use of polychromatic painting from this time on.

c.3,000, Sculpted Head of God Abu (full figure 30" high), Tell Asmar.

c.3,000, Texts of Sumerian writers mention ecclesiastical music.

B.C. (cont.)

c.3,000, Records indicate that in the Indus civilization there was a vertical arched harp of the type common in ancient times around the Nile and the Ganges.

c.3,000, According to Lepsius, the principle of dividing a string to obtain different pitches was used by Egyptian lutenists around this time.

c.3,000, The Stele of King Zet (Egyptian) was carved.

c.3,000, A sculpture of a Torso (from Harappa) was carved.

c.3,000, According to Tsaï-Yï, Ling Lun, the imperial music master, was sent west by Huang-Ti, beyond the Ounloun mountains to study musical practices of that region.

c.2,980 to 2,700, Sakkara, Pyramid of Zoser built.

c.2,900, Palette of King Narmer (25½" high) carved.

c.2,800, Fragment of a Harp. Made of gilt and inlaid wood, found in Ur.

c.2,700, Painting of Geese of Medum.

c.2,700, Panel of Hesire (3'9" high) carved.

c.2,700 to 2,600, Khafre, detail (5'6" high). Complete figure carved during this period.

c.2,700 to 2,600, Sphinx, Gizeh constructed during this period.

B.C. (cont.)

c.2,700 to 2,600, Statue, Kaaper, "Sheikh el Beled" (3'7" high) carved during this period.

c.2,700 to 2,600, Statues of Rahotep and Nefert (3'11" high) carved during this period.

c.2,700, Carved portrait of Hesire on a wooden door in his tomb.

c.2,700, Carved portrait head of limestone found in a tomb at Gizeh.

c.2,700, Sumerians possessed slender oboe-like instruments.

c.2,700, The well-known "Sumerian harp of Ur," a restored specimen, dates from this time.

c.2,700, Instrumentalists Playing a Vertical Flute, Double Clarinet, and Harp, with Four Singers Indicating the Melody through Hand and Finger Motions, i.e., Cheironomy. From the tomb of Nencheftkai in Sakkara.

c.2,650, Head of a King (Egyptian sculpture).

c.2,565 to 2,420, Seated Scribe (21" high), Egyptian, sculpted during this period.

c.2,500, Monument of King Naram-sin found in Susa.

c.2,500, Ranefer, statue (5'11" high) carved.

c.2,500, Sakkara, False Door of Neferseshemptah carved.

c.2,500 to 1,500, Classical Age of Sumerian art within this period.

c.2,500, Drummer, Potsherd, Sumerian relic found in Mesopotamia.

c.2,400, Gudea of Telloh (1'5" high), Sumerian sculpture of a full figure.

c.2,400, The Woman with the Scarf, Sumerian sculpture.

c.2,400, An Egyptian minister of state practised painting.

c.2,300 to 2,200, The Stele of Naram-sin (6'6" high) carved during this period.

c.2,000, The heptatonic scale appeared at this time.

c.2,000 to 1,500, Salisbury Plain, Stonehenge from this period.

c.2,000, Invaders from the North conquered Greece, and a new civilization was established.

c.2,000, The introduction of copper and the gradual evolution of bronze was essentially completed by this time.

c.2,000, In the more pretentious houses, wooden columns were employed to permit deeper rooms. When these occurred on an upper storey they were supported by square stone piers in the floor below.

c.2,000, The Cretans, by this time, did not recall their nomadic state or the circular hut. However, one might assume that early tombs (circular) indicate this tradition, due to conservatism in religious matters.

B.C.(cont.)

c.2,000, Harp player. Terra cotta plaque (Chaldea).

c.2,000 to 1,000, Babylonians used clappers, the sistrum, vertical flute, wooden horn, drum, kithara, and lute. Harp was the principal instrument during this period.

c.2,000 to 538, Mesopotamia was controlled mainly by the Babylonians and Assyrians during this period.

c.2,000, Hemitonic scale influence evidences itself in the melodic structure of the Sumatrian "Hymn of Creation." However, the scale was by this time composed of seven tones.

c.2,000, Two flutes survived from Egypt. A 95 cm. long one had finger holes at 10, 11 and 13 fifteenths of its length. The 90 cm. long one had fingerholes at 8, 9, and 10 twelfths.

c.2,000, Greece was invaded by Minyans.

c.1,900, A Wall from the tomb of Chnemhotep (Beni Hassan area) reveals inscriptions in hieroglyphics.

c.1,900, Sesostris I, Egyptian figure of seated ruler.

c.1,900, Tomb of Khnumhotep (c.28' wide) at Beni Hasan(sic).

c.1,900 to 200, Karnak, Temple of Amon Ra,was built during this period.

c.1,900, The primitive lute existed in Mesopotamia at this time. It had two strings, the standard number in this period.

B.C.(cont.)

c.1,800, Tomb of Rekhmere reveals painting of brickmakers at work.

c.1,800 to 1,600, Knossos, Palace built during this period.

c.1,800, Painting of Bull Leapers (Palace at Knossos).

c.1,800, Painting of El Bersheh, Moving a Colossus.

c.1,800, Subject Tribes brought alien music to Egypt - new harps, shrill oboes, lyres, lutes, crackling drums.

c.1,775, Stele of Hammurapi (2'4" high) was carved.

c.1,760, King Hammurapi Before the Sun God (upper portion of the Stele giving the Law Code of Hammurabi), Babylonian.

c.1,700 to 1,580, Painting of a Cat Stalking a Pheasant (1'9" high), from Hagia Triada.

c.1,600, A dagger from Mycenae, Greece (now reconstructed).

c.1,600, Sculpture of a Snake Goddess (6½" high), Greece.

c.1,600, Carved Harvester Vase (5½" wide), Greece.

c.1,600 to 1,400, The golden age of the Aegean civilization, at which time the power of Crete was at its peak.

c.1,580 to 1,090, New kingdon in Egypt. Instruments from Western Asia were introduced: double oboe types, trumpets, large harps, lyres, lutes, timbrels, drums. Change in musical style

B.C.(cont.)

(cont.) professional musicians now from lower classes, large choruses and orchestras with women playing instruments. Strong foreign influence appeared.

c.1,550 to 1,340, Strikingly modern paintings in the Theban tombs of the 18th dynasty.

c.1,500, Painted Octopus Vase (8" high), Greece.

c.1,500, Gold Cup (3" high) with relief design, from Vaphio, Greece.

c.1,500 to 1,100, Tiryns, Palace (c.480' x 310') was built during this period.

c.1,500, Conductors depicted in Egyptian wall painting from this time on were shown beating time by snapping fingers and pounding.

c.1,500, From this date on instruments appeared in Egypt, i.e. harps, zithers, oboes, cymbals, sistra.

c.1,500, Achaean invasion of Greece.

c.1,500, A copper temple instrument appeared on a tablet.

c.1,500, Lyres first appeared in Egypt along with stopped instruments and oboes.

c.1,500, Head of a Girl ("La Parisienne"), Cretan Fresco that decorated the palace of Knossos.

c.1,500, Cup-Bearer, Cretan Fresco from the Palace of Minos, Knossos.

c.1,480, Deir el-Bahri, Mortuary Temple of Queen Hatshepsut with columns 14'6" high.

c.1,475, Fresco from the tomb at Schech abd el Gurna showed musicians with harp and lute.

c.1,450, Head of Queen Nefertiti (c.1'8" high).

c.1,450, Painted wall at Thebes, Tomb of Nakht, Chapel (55"x63").

c.1,400, Fresco of Banquet Scene.

c.1,400, Chinese figure of an Owl (17 3/4" high) from Anyang.

c.1,400, Chinese Tripod Vessel, Type Ting (9½" high).

c.1,400, Chinese Wine Vessel, Type Chüeh (10"x9").

c.1,400, Painting on Sarcophagus, from Hagia Triada (figures 8½" high), Greece.

c.1,400, Painting of a Pond. From a tomb in Thebes, Greece.

c.1,400, Wall-painting of an Egyptian craftsman at work on a golden sphinx, from a tomb in Thebes, Greece.

c.1,400 to 1,200, Origins of Chinese music indicated.

c.1,400, Painters who ornamented the tombs of the Valley of Kings studied the classical authors and in some cases wrote psalms

(cont.) of a high poetical quality.

c.1,370, Limestone relief of King Amenophis IV.

c.1,360, Seated Figure of Ikhnaton (2'1" high), Egyptian sculpture.

c.1,350, Low relief from the tomb of Pa-aten-mheb showed harp player.

c.1,350, Gilt and painted woodwork from the thrones of the Pharaoh Tutankhamen and his wife found in his tomb.

c.1,300 to 1,200, Painting of Boar Hunt (1'5" wide) from Tiryns Palace.

c.1,300, Egyptian painting of a Fowler Hunting in a Marsh (2'10" high).

c.1,300, Luxor, Temple of Amon Ra, hypostyle hall. Example of Egyptian Architecture.

c.1,300, Egyptian built Karnak, Temple of Amon Ra, hypostyle hall, model. Central columns 69' high and 12' in diameter.

c.1,300, Relief of Seti I Offering to Osiris.

c.1,257, Abu Simbel, Temple of Ramses II. Egyptian sculpture (Colossi) 55' high.

c.1,250, Mycenae, Lion Gate, relief 9'6" high.

c.1,250, Full Figure of Ramses II. Egyptian sculpture (6'4" high).

c.1,250, Mycenae, Treasury of Atreus, section. Architectural relic (48'6" diameter).

c.1,200, Egyptian architecture, Karnak, Temple of Khons (105'x225').

c.1,200, The North of Europe yielded us instruments from the Baltic littoral - bronze lurer, dating from this time.

c.1,200, Chinese Beaker, Type Ku (11"x6¼").

c.1,200, The Aeolians, who had migrated from Greece to Asia Minor in this century, improved the system of Greek music by adding another tetrachord.

c.1,184, The fall of Troy.

c.1,122, The Chou dynasty.

c.1,104, The Dorian invasion of Greece.

c.1,000, The principal instruments of China's national music were mentioned at this time. They included chimes of bells or stones and longish zithers, as well as neckless instruments with silk strings.

c.1,000 to 600, The period during which the first examples of classical Greek architecture appeared.

c.1,000, Warlike tribes from Europe came to the peninsula of Greece and to Asia Minor where they defeated former inhabitants.

c.1,000 to 500, Assyrians adapted music to more secular

(cont.) uses. Influence of Egyptian music was also obvious.

c.1,000, At this time.(David and Solomon's) foreign instruments appeared; harp, double oboe type, cymbals, and sistra.

c.1,000, King David of Israel organized vocal and instrumental music for the First Temple. Professional musicians were employed.

c.1,000, From this time on, singing was heptatonic with no trace of pentatonism. Its style as a whole was logogenic, basically syllabic, and contained few ligatures and melismas. Melody followed ready-made patterns or was composed of motives rather than single notes.

c.900, King Asurnasirpal III of Assyria lived.

c.900, The poems of Homer were chanted and accompanied on the lyre.

c.885 to 860, Relief sculpture of Ashurnasirpal Storming a City, from Nimrud (3' high).

c.885 to 860, Relief sculpture of Ashurnasirpal Hunting Lions, from Nimrud (3' high).

c.885 to 860, Sculpture of Winged Bull at Palace of Ashurnasirpal, Nimrud (10'2"x2'2"x10'3" high).

c.850, Alabaster relief showed Assyrian army besieging a fortress at the Palace of King Asurnasirpal III.

c.800, In Greek painting the human form appeared again, it looked like a cardboard cut-out, angular, and conceived in purely geometric terms.

c.800, An actual Sumerian hymn concerning the creation of man existed. Both words and music were preserved and provided the oldest example of musical notation in existence. It survived on a table, dating from about 800 B.C., but the music itself was obviously older.

c.800, Pythagorean intervals were familiar to the Chinese.

c.800, A miniature showed King David playing the rota, surrounded by musicians.

c.800, The period of written history began.

c.776, The first recorded date of the Olympiad.

c.760, Cumae, the first western colony was founded by Chalcis.

c.750, Grecian Attic Vase, painted in geometric style.

c.750, Known as the Age of Homer.

c.733, Corcyra and Syracuse were founded by Corinth.

c.722 to 705, Plan of Khorsabad, Palace of Sargon in Mesopotamia (1050'x1140').

c.700, A Greek vase in the "Geometric Style" showed the Mourning of the Dead.

c.700, The Greeks learned under the influence of the Orient, how

(cont.) to draw living forms.

c.700, Greek sculpture Nikandra, from Delos (5'9"high).

c.700, Grecian painted Rhodian Vase (12¼" high).

c.700, Assyrian harpists were aware of the idea of the interval of a fifth.

c.700, The Lesbian Terpander inaugurated a classical period of National Greek Music.

c.700, Terpander completed the octave and created the Mixolydian scale.

c.700, Low relief of drum, cymbal, and zither players (Mesopotamia).

c.700 to 200 A.D., Our knowledge of ancient Greek music spans this period.

c.700, During this century Terpander and Archilochos complicated the meters in melody and the accompaniment on the lyre.

c.685, The Trombone was credited to Tyrtaeus.

c.675, Terpander's period began our definite knowledge of Greek Music.

c.675, The earliest musical personage was the Kithara player Terpander from Lesbos.

c.670, Before Terpander's time the Greek lyre had only four strings. Boethius attributed the increase to seven strings to Terpander.

B.C. (cont.)

c.668 to 626, Stone relief of Ashurbanipal Feasting, Nineveh (4'5" wide).

c.668 to 626, Stone relief of Wounded Lioness from Palace of Ashurbanipal, Nineveh (25"x40").

c.660, Archilochus (Greek) instituted technical reforms. The fast "tempo" of his trochee and iambus gave great mobility to ancient Greek music.

c.650, The Maiden from Auxerre (Greek).

c.650, The Delphic oracle during a period of unrest was supposed to have advised the Spartans to appoint the musician Terpander to pacify the city with his melodies.

c.650, Alkman introduced special partheniai (maidens' songs) for girls' choruses.

c.650, The Elamic court orchestra assisted in welcoming the Assyrian conqueror, and from indications on a relief, were aware of principles of polyphony.

c.639, Rome recognized no instrument except pipes and passed a law to "frustrate tolerance" of other instruments.

c.627, The founding of Selinus.

c.606, Pipers first appeared in Greece.

c.600 to 450, The Persian Wars.

c.600, Chinese Bell, Type Chung.

c.600, Greek statue "Apollo," in Attica (6'1" high).

c.600, Foreign music barred in Egypt. Music returned to calmer style of old kingdom. This music was influential in Greek music and theoretical progress.

c.600, Melodies existed in Yemen, Persian, and Babylonian Jewish communities that were exact counterpart to several Gregorian melodies later to appear.

c.600, Arion of Methymna founded first dithyrambic choir (50 boys and men) who performed in a circle around a piper.

c.600, Etruscan sculpture Apollo of Veii (68" high).

c.600, Stone relief from Pharsalos, Greece (2'2" wide).

c.600, Antenor, Maiden from the Acropolis, Greek statue.

c.600, Etruscans started to free themselves from Eastern influence in art but simply to come under Grecian influence.

c.600, Tarquinian statue of Horseman (Tomb of the Bulls).

c.600, Etruscan sculpture of Reclining Couple found in a tomb (79" long).

c.600, Francois Vase, black-figured style, Grecian (2'1" high).

c.600, Grecian sculpture Chares of Branchidae (4'10" high).

c.600, Vases painted in the early 6th century still showed evidence of Egyptian techniques.

c.600, The first stone temples were being built in Greece.

c.600, The monochord or single string, stretched over a sound -board and measured by moveable bridges, became the canon of musical intervals at this time determining relative scale of pitch.

c.600, The invention of the monochord was attributed to Pythagoras, but probably its use came from Egypt.

c.600, The dithyramb of Arion of Methymna underwent a bifurcation. As a choral song it developed into tragedy and on stage blended into "nomos." It was sung also by professional musicians in virtuoso performances.

c.600, Greek drama developed from dance plays which featured dithyrambs.

c.600, The beginning of the period of classical musical art.

c.600, The dithyramb which culminated in the tragedy appeared in this century.

c.600, Jubal, legendary father of music, Pythagoras, the Philosopher of Samos, and Philolaus were considered most significant by Gafurius, 15th century music theorist.

c.600. After reforms of Servien, the tuba and cornu players became an official section of the lists of Roman citizens.

B.C.(cont.)

c.600, The dithyrambs in honor of the god Dionysius were tamed in the 6th century B.C. and accepted as recognized music, and so imposed on Athenian contests.

c.597, Idelsohn was able to show that a good number of Catholic melodies still existed in the liturgy of those oriental Jews who had lost contact with the Palestinian homeland after being exiled and living in pagan surroundings.

c.590, Plan of Olympia, Heraeum (61'6" x 164'1").

c.586, Music became a part of Pythian games in Greece.

c.586, Pythian Games were won by Sakadas with composition celebrating Apollo's fight with the Dragon. A single pair of pipes was used.

c.586, The Pythic nome of the aulete Sakadas was considered to be the first important product of the aulos art, the first example of programatic music.

c.586, The lyre made its first appearance in Greek musical history.

c.580, Statue of a Youth. Found in Delphi, signed by Polymedes of Argos, in all probability represented one of the brothers Cleobis and Biton.

c.580, The founding of Acragas.

c.575, Relief of Lion on Gate of Ishtar in Babylon (6'5"x3'6").

B.C.(cont.)

c.570, Grecian sculpture of Calf Bearer (5'5" high).

c.570 to 526, Egypt's music enjoyed a last moment of brilliance during the reign of Amasis II.

c.569, The accession of Aahmes (Amasis) II of Egypt.

c.566, Organization of the Panathenaic Festival at Athens.

c.561, The accession of Peisistratus of Athens.

c.560, The accession of Croesus of Lydia.

c.550 to 530, Grecian stone relief of Perseus Slaying Medusa; Hercules and the Cecropes, from temple C, Selinus (3'9" x 4'11").

c.550 to 520, Frieze of Seated Gods, Treasury of the Siphnians, Delphi (25" high).

c.550, Grecian sculpture "Apollo," from Tenea (5' high).

c.550, Grecian sculpture Hera of Samos (6' high).

c.550, The diatonic scale was of Greek origin, introduced at about this time.

c.550 to 520, Greek statue of Nike of Delos (3' high).

c.550, Pythagoras derived tones of scale from successive pure fifths with the ratio 3:2.

c.548, The burning of the temple of Apollo at Delphi.

B.C.(cont.)

c.546, The conquest of Lydia by Cyrus of Persia.

c.540, Greek architecture: Corinth, Temple of Apollo (70'6" x 176'11").

c.540, Greek vase in the "Black figured Style" with Achilles and Ajax playing draughts. Signed by Exekias.

c.530, Grecian vase, Hercules and Antaeus, red figured style.

c.530, Grecian vase, Dionysus, black-figured style, by Exekias (12" diameter).

c.530 to 525, Grecian architecture: Delphi, Treasury of the Siphnians (20'1½" wide).

c.530, Persian architecture: Pasargadae, Tomb of Cyrus (Interior 10' x 7').

c.527, The death of Peisistratus.

c.525, Grecian painting: Hector Saying Farewell.

c.525, Aeschylus, Greek Playwright, was born(d.c.456 B.C.).

c.525 to 456, Choruses and solo voices took part in Aeschylus' dramatic works.

c.522 to 448, Pindar wrote odes in praise of victorious athletes during this period.

c.520, Etruscan painting: Male and Female Dancers at Tomb of the Lionesses, Tarquinia.

c.515, The Stele of Aristion was carved (5'9" high).

B.C.(cont.)

c.510, The fall of the tyranny at Athens.

c.500, A Renaissance took place under the Assyrian and Babylonian Empires.

c.500, Phidias was born(d.c430).

c.500, Etruscan painting of Libation Ritual, at the Tomb of the Baron, Tarquinia.

c.500, Grecian vase: The Warrior's Leave-taking. Red -figured Style, signed by Euthymides.

c.500, The power of observation of nature awakened in Greece at this time.

c.500, Artists dared for the first time in all history to paint a foot as seen from in front.

c.500, Rise in Greek drama resulted in important developments in music.

c.500, Vibrations were discovered to be the cause of sound by Lasos of Hermione, who was Pindar's teacher.

c.500 to 400, The Greeks began to organize different modes into one consistent system.

c.500, At this time the Greek chorus ceased holding the main role in tragedies.

c.500, First stationary song of the chorus from Euripides Orestes, written on papyrus, but fragmentary.

c.500, A rèbirth or renaissance occurred in Athens.

B.C.(cont.)

c.500, Greek sculpture: The Apollo of Piombino.

c.500, Sculpture of Winged Bull, from Susa.

c.500, The Greeks were tackling the complex problems of perspective and the third dimension from this date forward.

c.500, Cinerary Urn (Painted terra cotta), Tarquinia.

c.500, Greek sculpture: Victory, Paeonius (7'1" high).

c.500, Etruscan sculpture of She-Wolf (52" long).

c.500, Low relief of Aulos player from the Ludovici throne.

c.500, The Greek historian Herodotos reported that "the Egyptians have, with other curious pieces, a certain melody, which is also sung in Phoenicia, Cyprus, and elsewhere, but differently named in each of these countries."

c.499, The beginning of the Ionian Revolt.

c.495 to 485, Greek sculpture: East Pediment, Temple of Aphaia, Aegina (45' wide).

c.494, Miletus was taken by Darius of Persia.

c.490 to 430, Greek sculpture of Discobolus (discus thrower), Myron (c.4'6" high), made during this period.

c.490, First Persian invasion of Greece; battle of Marathon.

B.C.(cont.)

c.486, Stone relief of Lion Attacking a Bull, Palace of Xerxes, Persepolis (Persian sculpture).

c.486, Persian stone relief of Bactrians Leading a Camel, Palace of Xerxes, Persepolis (3' high).

c.486, Persian architecture: Persepolis, Gate of Xerxes.

c.485, The accession of Gelon at Syracuse.

c.480, Etruscan painting of Flute-Player, Tomb of the Leopards, Tarquinia.

c.480, Second Persian invasion of Greece; battles of Thermopylae and Salamis; destruction of Athens. First Carthaginian invasion of Sicily, battle of Himera.

c.480, The temples on the sacred rock of Athens, the Acropolis, were burned down and sacked by the Persians.

c.480, Painted Greek bowl showing sculptor's workshop and men at work, and a bronze foundry.

c.479, Expulsion of the Persians from Greece; battle of Plataea.

c.478, Greek sculpture of Harmodius and Aristogiton, Critius and Nesiotes(6'1"high).

c.477,The founding of the Delian Confederacy under Athens.

c.475, Lamprokles wrote, "perceiving that the disjunction of its (the Mixolydian) tetrachords should be higher up in the scale than it was almost

B.C.(cont.)

(cont.) universally supposed to be, raised it to its true position; and determined its modal structure to correspond to the octave between b and B."

c.470, The temple in Olympia was begun.

c.470, Head of the bronze statue of a charioteer from this date found in Delphi.

c.470, Etruscan painting of Female Dancer (Tomb of the Triclinium), Tarquinia.

c.470, Greek sculpture of the Birth of Aphrodite, Ludovisi Throne (4'8" wide).

c.468 to 460, Greek architecture: West Pediment, Temple of Zeus, Olympia.

c.465, Persian architecture: Persepolis, Apadana of Xerxes.

c.461, The assumption of leadership at Athens by Pericles.

c.460, Greek sculpture: Statuette from Ligurio (5" high).

c.460, Greek architecture: Paestum, Temple of Hera, interior (197' x 80'; column diameter, c.3').

c.460, Greek sculpture by Pheidias: Hercules carrying the Heavens. From the Temple of Zeus at Olympia.

c.460, Grecian vase showed the Slaughter of the Niobids, red-figured style (height of painted band 10").

B.C.(cont.)

c.457, The temple in Olympia was finished.

c.456, Aeschylus, Greek playwright, died (b.c.525 B.C.).

c.454, The transfer of the Delian Treasury to Athens.

c.450, Greek sculpture of Athena Lemnia (Phidias).

c.450, Greek painting, Cup of Hera (decoration).

c.450 to 400, The height of Athens under Pericles.

c.450, Greek architecture: A Doric Temple: the Parthenon, Athens, Acropolis. Designed by Iktinos.

c.450, Discus Thrower (Discobolos). Roman marble copy, after a bronze statue by Myron.

c.450, Greek statue of Doryphorus, Polyclitus (6'6" high).

c.450, A post classical, modern period in Greek Music existed.

c.449, Peace signed between Athens and Persia; an abortive effort to hold Panhellenic Congress at Athens.

c.448, The dedication of the Zeus Olympius by Phidias.

c.447, The beginning of the Parthenon at Athens.

c.447 to 432, Greek sculpture: Centaur and Lapith, metope, Parthenon, Athens (3'11"x4'2").

B.C.(cont.)

c.447 to 432, Greek sculpture: East Pediment, Parthenon, Athens (c.90' wide).

c.447 to 432, Greek architecture: Ictinus and Callicrates, Athens, Parthenon (101' x 228').

c.447 to 432, Athena Parthenos. Roman marble copy after a big temple statue made by Phidias between 447 and 432 B.C.

c.446 to 357, Timotheus of Miletus' dithyrambs and nomes were redundant and prolix; his melodies were light and pleasant, designed to change the austere older art. He succeeded in creating, in his nomes, a richness of color which brought universal praise from his critics.

c.440, An illustration of a Kithara appeared in a drawing on an amphora.

c.440, Grecian white-ground vase by Lekythos.

c.440, Greek painting of Bowl of the Muses.

c.438, The dedication of the Athena Parthenos by Phidias.

c.437 to 432, Greek architecture: Mnesicles. Athens, Propylaea (central portico 69' wide).

c.437, Beginning of the construction of the Popylaea at Athens.

c.431, The outbreak of the Peloponnesian War.

B.C.(cont.)

c.430, Phidias, Greek sculptor, died (born c.500).

c.430, In one of his comedies, the Attic poet Pherekrates had Music enter the stage in rags as a downtrodden woman and whimper that although once respected, modern composers, ignorant of the dignity of old and the beauty of melody, had badly dishonored and abused her.

c.429, Death of Pericles at Athens.

c.427 to 347, Passages in the Laws, Republic, Georgias, Philebos, and Timaios, of Plato set forth the ethical value of music and its place in education.

c.427, Greek architecture: Athens, Temple of Wingless Victory (17'9"x26'10").

c.427 to 347, Plato, in his Republic, placed music in the ideal state; traditional music was to be preserved, all men were to be divided into 3 choruses including young boys, young men, and men from 30-60. He placed great emphasis on ethical value of music.

c.425, The organization of the Delian Festival at Delos.

c.423, The burning of the temple of Hera near Argos.

c.421 to 405, Greek Architecture: Athens, Erechtheum built during this period.

c.421, The peace of Nicias between Athens and Sparta.

B.C.(cont.)

c.420 to 410, Stele of Hegeso was carved (4'11" high).

c.420, Greek sculpture: Tombstone of Hegeso.

c.413, The defeat of the Athenians at Syracuse.

c.410, Artists had become fully conscious of their power and influence as had their public.

c.409, Second Carthaginian invasion of Sicily; destruction of Selinus.

c.408, Greek high relief of a Goddess of Victory. From the balustrade round the Temple of Victory in Athens.

c.408, The only surviving specimen of Greek dramatic music was a very short mutilated fragment of unison melody from a chorus of Euripides.

c.404, The fall of Athens; end of the Peloponnesian War.

c.404 to 358, Persian sculpture: Double Bull Capital, Susa, Palace of Artaxerxes (10' high).

c.400, Greek painting of Actors in Satirical Drama.

C.400, The Indian Rikprātiśakhya and Rāmāyana epos gave the standard scale shadya, rśabha, gāndhāra, madhyama (middle), panchama (fifth), dhaivata, and niśāda. These are place steps, not notes.

c.400, Anchytas of Tarentum saw that there were two forms of vibrations that cause sound-stationary and progressing waves.

c.400, Timotheos of Miletos performed with four additional strings on his lyre, and the court ordered them to be snipped off.

c.400, The kithara possessed eleven strings and covered two octaves. It represented the Greek "perfect system" in its totality.

c.400, Euclid, in his writings, used the monochord to define the intervals of the ancient Greek scale.

c.400, Herakleides Pontikos developed the cryptic invective.

c.400, Phrynis, the boldest composer of his time, gave the lyre a tuning device in order to play no less than twelve harmonies on five strings.

c.400, Glaukos of Reguim and Herakleides Pontikos laid the foundations of music history.

c.400, Egyptian sculpture: Head of a Priest (4" high).

c.400, Greek statue: Niobid Chiaramonti (5'9" high).

c.400, The great temple statues of the fourth century B.C. earned their reputation more by virtue of their beauty than as works of art.

c.400, Plato's friend Archytas proposed an enharmonion of 386-50-62 cents.

c.400, Plato recommended that the ideal State be erected upon the foundation of music. Also, that any change in the

B.C.(cont.)

(cont.) traditional ways of music be resisted. He felt that any change might lead to a fatal change in the State as well.

c.400, A complete theory of rhythm and melody under the leadership of Aristotle's disciple, Aristóxenos of Tarentum, was established. Full information is not available, however.

c.400, Greek musicians, ignoring subtle differences in the structure of modes, created what they called the Perfect System using all seven modes.

c.400, Figure with temple harp (Medinet Habu). Fresco, XIXth Dynasty.

c.394, The burning of the temple of Athena Alea at Tegea.

c.390, Greek statue of a satyr, marble Faun made by Praxiteles (5'7" high).

c.390, Greek sculpture: Head from the temple of Athena ALEA, Tega. Scopas (c.10" high).

c.385, Possible birthdate of Aristophanes,Greek playwright.

c.385, Choruses and solo voices took part in Aristophanes' dramatic works.

c.384, Birth of Aristotle.

c.384 to 322, Aristotle contributed important writings on Greek music. He placed great value on the ethical merit of music.

c.384 to 322, Passages in the Metaphysics, On the Soul, and in other works of Aristotle discussed consonance, the use of music and the voice.

c.377, Foundation of the second Delian Confederacy under Athens.

c.373, Destruction of the temple of Apollo at Delphi by earthquake.

c.372 to 287, Theophrastus was opposed to the idea of attributing medical powers to music.

c.370, Greek statue of Agias by Lysippus (6'5" high).

c.356, Birth of Alexander the Great(died c.323).

c.356, Burning of the temple of Artemis at Ephesus.

c.354, Birth of Aristoxenos, Greek writer on music.

c.354, During Aristoxenos' life he wrote the Harmonics of Aristoxenos, an important early source for our knowledge of Greek musical theory. Aristoxenos was a disciple of Aristotle.

c.353, Death of Mausolus at Halicarnassus.

c.350, Greek architecture: Halicarnassus Mausoleum (c.68'x106').

c.350, Greek sculpture of Charioteer, from a frieze of the Mausoleum, Halicarnassus (2'10"high).

c.350, Harp player. Painted on

(cont.) wood.

c.350, Greek sculpture: Amazon Frieze, from Mausoleum, Halicarnassus (2'11" high).

c.350, Greek architecture: Theatre of Epidaurus (diameter 387').

c.350, Many of the most famous works of classical art were copies of statues which were created in the middle of the fourth century B.C.

c.350, Apollo Belvedere. Roman marble copy (the hands modern) of a Greek statue of this date.

c.350, Greek statue by Praxiteles: Hermes with young Dionysus.

c.350, Mourning Women, Sarcophagus, from Sidon.

c.350, Greek painting: Ulysses and the Sirens.

c.340, Grecian seated statue of Demeter of Cnidus (5' high).

c.338, Conquest of Greece by Philip of Macedon; battle of Chaeronea.

c.335, Heraclides of Pontus was a contemporary of Plato and Aristotle.

c.335, A monument was erected in honor of the winners of musical contests in the Karnaean games.

c.334, The invasion of Persia by Alexander the Great.

c.334, Greek Architecture: Athens, Choragic Monument of Lysicrates (54' high).

c.333, Alexander the Great's campaign inaugurated a cultural exchange between Greece and India.

c.331, The founding of Alexandria in Egypt.

c.330, Greek sculptured Head of Alexander the Great. Probably copy after a portrait by Lysippus.

c.330, Grecian sculpture: Alexander's Sarcophagus, from Sidon (10'5" long).

c.323, Death of Alexander the Great at Babylon(born c.356).

c.322, Death of Aristotle, Greek Philosopher(born c.384).

c.322, Indian sculpture: Asokan Capital (7'x2'10").

c.315, Demetrius of Phalerum enacts sumptuary laws at Athens.

c.310, The idea of a portrait, in the present sense, did not occur to the Greeks until late in the fourth century.

c.310, Heads of the statues usually looked much more animated and alive than in earlier works.

c.310, Etruscan sculpture: Head of a Woman. Tomb of the Ogre, Tarquinia.

c.310, Grecian sculpture: Three Tanagra Figurines.

c.307, Demetrius Poliorcetes occupied Piraeus and Athens where he and his father were proclaimed "Kings" by the Athenians.

c.306, Ptolemy Soter assumed royal title in Egypt.

c.301, The founding of Antioch by Seleucus.

c.300, Greek architecture: Priene Theater.

c.300, Corinthian Capital founded in Epidaurus.

c.300 to 300 A.D., The Hellenistic and Graeco-Roman period during which Grecian culture was amalgamated, then contaminated by, the entire eastern Mediterranean and finally destroyed.

c.300, A section of the Canon (attributed to Euclid) gave our earliest explanation of the acoustical theories of Pythagoras.

c.300, Grecian statue of Venus de Medici (5' high).

c.300, Grecian sculpted figure of Demosthenes (6'9" high).

c.300 to 200, Grecian statue carved during this period: Aphrodite of Melos (6'8" high).

c.300, Chinese architecture: Nankow, Great Wall of China.

c.300, Since the lyre and the monochord had been developed we are certain that, at this time, a stringed instrument existed as a compromise between the two.

B.C.(cont.)

c.300, The cult of Cybel, founded in the Roman empire was identified outside by the cymbals, tympanum, and Phrygian flutes used by its members.

c.286, Athens revolted against the Macedonians.

c.279, Gallic raid on Delphi; second battle of Thermopylae.

c.264, Athens was recaptured by the Macedonians.

c.257, Possible deathdate of Aristophanes, Greek playwright.

c.250, Ktesibios invented the hydraulis - a primitive organ with pipes and keyboard, water being used to provide wind pressure.

c.250, A fragment from a tragedy written at this time was discovered in a Zenon papyrus at the museum in Cairo. The piece is one of the earliest fragments among surviving examples of Greek composition.

c.250, Ptolemy Philadelphus described a procession at the court in Alexandria where participants involved included six hundred men, three hundred of them playing on golden lyres.

c.246, Ptolemy, King of Egypt, died.

c.237 to 212, Egyptian architecture: Edfu, Temple of Horus built during this period (250'x145').

c.229, Athens became independent of Macedonia.

B.C.(cont.)

c.225, Greek statue of a Dying Gaul (3' high).

c.200, Greek statue: Victory of Samothrace (6'6" high).

c.200, Head of a Faun: Detail from a Herculaneum wall painting dating from the second century B.C.

c.200, Greek sculpture: Boy with a Goose by Boëthus (2'9" high).

c.200, Grecian sculpted figure of an Old Market Woman (4' 1½" high).

c.200 to 200 A.D., Chinese sculpture of a bear carved during this period (6¼"x8¼").

c.200, A transverse flute in modern form was known in Etruria.

c.200, A short Skolion (drinking song) composed by Seikilos was found engraved on a tomb stele at Tralles in Asia Minor.

c.200, Greek music spread to Rome.

c.200, Two hymns in honor of Apollo were written.

c.200, Archaic genera was still used in Greek music, as evidenced by the two Delphic hymns.

c.197 to 159, Grecian architecture: Altar of Zeus, Pergamum (119'6"x112'3").

c.197 to 159, Grecian sculpture of Zeus Group, on the Altar of Zeus, Pergamum (7'6" high).

c.185 to 80, Indian architecture: Karli, Chaitya Hall, built during this period (124' long x 45' high).

c.174, Antiochus IV of Syria began the building of Temple of Zeus at both Athens and Lebadea.

c.170, Grecian altar carving: The Gods fighting the Giants. (from the altar of Zeus in Pergamon).

c.170, Greek musicians failed to interest the Roman populace with musical performances except when they were involved with sports events.

c.166, Rome awarded Delos to Athens.

c.150, Two Greek hymns dedicated to Apollo were engraved in stone on the Athenian treasury at Delphi.

c.150, Sculpted figure of Etruscan Orator (71" high).

c.150, In the fine arts an attempt was made to revert to archaic styles.

c.146,The destruction of Corinth by the Romans.

c.141 to 87, The Imperial Office of Music was created by Emperor Wou of China. Establishment and preservation of correct pitch was the main objective coupled with the supervision of ceremonial, foreign, aristocratic, national, and folk melodies.

c.138, The first of two Delphic

(cont.) Hymns to Apollo was one of the most concrete examples of Greek composition known.

c.128, The second of the two Delphic Hymns to Apollo was composed by Limenios, an Athenian.

c.117, Chinese sculpture of Horse Trampling Barbarian Warrior found at Tomb of Ho Ch'ü-ping, Shensi (63"x5'4").

c.116, Marcus Terentius Varro wrote De Musica, the seventh volume of his Disciplinarum libri IX. It was one of the main sources for many theoretical writers of succeeding centuries.

c.100, Roman Mosaic of The Battle of Issus between Darius and Alexander (10½' long).

c.100, A renaissance occurred in Rome.

c.100, Dionysios of Halikarnassos stated that rhythm and harmony were essentially one.

c.100, Greek statue: The Venus de Milo. Probably an imitation of a fourth-century work.

c.100, Greek sculpture: The Borghese Warrior.

c.100, Greek sculpture: Farmer Driving His Bull to Market (11"x12").

c.100, Greek sculpture: Aphrodite from Cyrene (5' high).

c.100, Sculpted figure: Archaistic Athena.

c.100, Pompeian fresco of Chorus of Bacchantes with drum, lyre, tambourine, and aulos players.

c.100, Roman wall painting at Villa Boscoreale (8' high).

c.100, Grecian sculpture, Menelaus, Orestes and Electra.

c.86, The capture of Athens by Sulla.

c.70 to 25, Indian architecture: Yakshi Shrine (Stupa #1, Sanchi, 120' diameter x 54' high).

c.63, Didymos, Alexandrian grammarian, was born.

c.55, Julius Caesar invaded Britain.

c.50, Grecian statue of a Boxer (4'2" high).

c.45, Refounding of Corinth by Julius Caesar.

c.31, The battle of Actium.

c.27, Establishment of the Roman Empire under Augustus.

c.25, Grecian sculpture, "Laocoon and his Sons." Marble group from the workshop of Hagesandros, Athenodoros and Polydoros of Rhodes.

c.16, Roman architecture: Nîmes, Maison Carree (49'x84'x56' high).

c.10, Roman sculpture, Augustus, from Prima Porta (7'3").

c.10, The final phase of

B.C. (cont.)

(cont.) Hellenic music was virtually unknown.

c.4, Seneca, Roman stoic philosopher born (died 65 A.D.).

c.4 to 65 A.D., During Seneca's life he wrote the following letter: "I heard, about midnight, a furious clamor. I asked what it was. 'Vocal exercises,' was the answer."

c.3, Pindar wrote the First Pythian Ode.

2

Ptolemy recommended his tetrachord, in the style of Pytagoras, be constructed by dividing a lute string into twelve equal parts designated by frets.

20

Philo of Alexandria was born. He represented the school of Hellenistic Judaism.

43

Under the Emperor Claudius, Britain was effectively conquered and incorporated into the Roman Empire.

49

Paul appeared at the Apostolic Council.

c.50

Architectural plan of House of Pansa, Pompeii (319'x124').

Roman architecture: House of Vettii, Pompeii, peristyle (85'x55').

(to 120) The Concerning Music was attributed to Plutarch.

58

(to 75) In the Han Dynasty three court orchestras were established, one for religious ceremonies, one for the archery of the palace, and one for banquets and the harem. A large military band also existed.

60

Emperor Nero founded periodic "holy festivals" in which music was most important.

c.60

The constitution of the Lesser Tone was demonstrated, by Didymus, unfortunately, he (cont.) placed the Lesser below the Greater. This error was corrected about 130, by Claudius Ptolemy, whose name the system carried.

64

St. Peter, of Bethsaida in Galilee, Prince of the Apostles, was the first Pope. He first lived in Antioch and then in Rome for twenty-five years, where he suffered martyrdom in the year 64.

65

Seneca, Roman stoic philosopher died (born c.4 B.C.).

67

(to 76) The Papal reign of St. Linus (born Tuscia).

70

Instrumental music disappeared in Israel. After the destruction of the Second Temple, biblical chants were still used and exerted an influence on Gregorian Chant.

c.70

Roman sculpture: Bust of Emperor Vespasianus, over life-size.

(to 80) Roman architecture: the Colosseum was built (620' by 513'x157'6" high).

(to 81) Roman architecture: Arch of Titus was constructed (43'8" wide x 47'4" high).

76

(to 88) The Papal reign of St. Anacletus (Cletus), born in Rome.

79

Pompeii was buried by an eruption of Vesuvius.

c.81
Treasures from the Temple of Jerusalem, showing trumpet players. Low relief from the Arch of Titus.

88
(to 97) The Papal reign of St. Clement (born in Rome).

97
(to 105) The Papal reign of St. Evaristus (born in Greece).

c.100
Didymos was credited with a diátonon of 204-182-112 cents in which a major whole tone 9:8 and a minor whole tone 10:9 had a ratio 81:80 or 22 cents.

India imported music from Egypt, musical maidens and pipes from Palestine, as well as musical instruments from both Palestine and Alexandria.

Seneca complained that orchestras and choruses grew to such proportions that there were more performers than spectators.

The book Perì kosmou stated "Music mixes high and low, short and long notes in different voice parts to achieve one harmony." This statement showed that the Greeks were aware of counterpoint.

Greek carving showed preparations for a gladiatorial contest, including a horn player (Amphitheater at Herculaneum).

A Greek author, wrongly called Longinus, stated that melodies were "usually" sweetened by fifths and fourths.

Epitaph of Seikilos, an example of Greek diatonic melody, was (cont.) written.

Greek wall painting: Maiden gathering Flowers (Stabiae).

Roman wall painting: Landscape.

Roman fresco: Punishment of Cupid. (Fresco from the "House of the Punishment of Cupid").

Roman frieze: Bacchante Dancing (Detail of the Frieze of the Dionysian Mysteries).

Roman frieze: Portrait of La Domina (Detail of the Frieze of the Dionysian Mysteries).

Plutarch wrote, "Our contemporaries have thoroughly neglected the finest genus, to which the ancients devoted all their eagerness. Most of them have lost the discernment of enharmonic intervals." This statement was made when the microtones of the Greek musical theory were abandoned.

Roman architecture: Segovia, Aqueduct (94' high x 900' long).

Greek painting on a sarcophagus: A painter of "funeral portraits" in his workshop, sitting by his paintbox and easel.

(to 200) Roman architecture: Nîmes, Amphitheater was built (430'x345'x70' high).

105
(to 115) The Papal reign of St. Alexander I (born in Rome).

113
Roman architecture: Forum of Trajan (920'x620').

114
The lower part of Trajan's

114 (cont.)

column was dedicated.

115

A letter sent to the Emperor Trajan by Pliny the Younger may be interpreted as referring to the practice of antiphonal singing among the Christians.

(to 125) The Papal reign of St. Sixtus I.

120

(to 124) Roman architecture: Pantheon. Portico built in 27 B.C. (interior diam. 142').

125

The Hymn to the Sun written by Mesomedes (Greek).

The Hymn to Nemesis written by Mesomedes (Greek).

(to 136) The Papal reign of St. Telesphorus (born in Greece)

130

Two Grecian Hymns to the Muse were written. One possibly by Mesomedes.

131

Indian sculpture: Bodhisattva Dedicated by Friar Bala (8'2" high).

132

Emperor Hadrian at Athens; dedication of the Olympieum.

(to 192) Tsai Yung was the author of Lute Motifs.

136

(to 140) The Papal reign of St. Hyginus (born in Greece).

140

(to 155) The Papal reign of St. Pius I (born in Aquileia).

c.150

Egyptian painting: Portrait of a man. From a mummy found at Hawara, Egypt.

Chinese painting: A reception. Detail of a relief from the tomb of Wu-liang-tse in the Province of Shantung, China.

Roman Architecture: Nîmes, Pont du Gard (length 902'x161'high).

(to c.220) Clement of Alexandria was a cultivated man, interested in music and poetry, and probably not prejudiced against instruments.

(to c.180) Pausanias wrote a description of Greece.

155

(to 166) The Papal reign of St. Anicetus (born in Syria).

(to c.222) Tertullian, born at Carthage, promoted the use of responsorial psalmody.

161

(to 180) Roman sculpture: Equestrian Statue of Marcus Aurelius was made during this period (9'10" high).

(to 180) Roman relief: Triumphal Entry of Marcus Aurelius.

162

Four Berlin fragments were written (Greek).

A Paean on the older Ajax's suicide was written.

165

"On the Dance", dialogue on Roman drama, written by Lucian described solo singing.

c.165

Justin, the widely traveled Christian philosopher, died (born 100).

166

(to 175) The Papal reign of St. Soter (born in Campania).

170

The apocryphal Acts of John, dating from before this time, imputed to Jesus and the apostles the accompanying of a hymn by a round-dance. This took place a day prior to the Passion.

c.170

Invasion of Attica by the Sarmatian Costobocs.

175

(to 189) The Papal reign of St. Eleutherius (born in Epirus)

176

(to 180) Writers have indicated that St. Cecilia was executed in Sicily under Marcus Aurelius.

c.185

(to c.254) Origen, active chiefly in Alexandria, testified to the wide use of song in worship and reconciled the old civilization of Hellas with the new Christian philosophy.

189

(to 199) The Papal reign of St. Victor I (born in Africa).

194

The "Stromata" of Titus Flavius Clemens (Clement of Alexandria).

199

(to 217) The Papal reign of St. Zephyrinus (born in Rome).

c.200

Arcadius' work on Greek Accents.

Aristides Quintilianus, Greek grammarian and author of a treatise on music which is one of the most valuable of all ancient discussions of that subject, lived in the 3rd century.

Athenaios, Greek author, lived during the 3rd century.

Roman architecture: Baalbek, Round temple (64' extreme diam.)

A fragment on the Berlin Papyrus of the Paiàn o paiàn is the only example of paeans that has survived.

Catholics in Europe welcomed the organ in their churches.

One source of Christian melody was Hellenic music. Among the relics, we have one from Oxyrhynchos in Egypt, a Christian hymn written on papyrus.

St. Clement of Alexandria wrote: "We need one instrument: the peaceful word of adoration, not harps or drums or pipes or trumpets."

Roman wall-painting: The Three Men in the Fiery Furnace, found in Priscilla Catacomb.

Egypto-Roman paintings: Funerary portraits of many persons were painted at this time.

Qaudentios confirmed that diatonic was the only genus sung in his time.

c.200 (cont.)

Indian sculpture: Head of Buddha. Found in Gandhara, northern India.

Chinese relief: Gautama (Buddha) leaving his home.

The Golden Age of historical musicology.

Chinese architecture: House Model (4'4" high).

Chinese sculpture: Visit of Mu Wang to Hsi Wang Mu, Tomb of Wo Liang Tzu, Shantung.

Nikomachos' Enchiridion stated that in pre-Orphic times the Greeks tuned their lyres in ground tones, fourth, fifth, and octave, and in post Orphic times to Terpander they had heptads only no octaves.

Roman architecture: Orange, Theater (stage wall 121' high).

The Hymn from Oxyrhynchos was written in Egypt.

Egyptian-Roman period: Portrait of a Boy, from the Faiyûm (lower Egypt).

Claudius Ptolemy in the 2nd century made use of the monochord to define the intervals of the ancient Greek scale.

Ptolemaic School submitted to the rule of simple mathematical ratios (for singers).

Tertullian wrote of vigils, lauds, and vespers being used in the Carthaginian Church.

Roman Architecture: The Theater of Marcellus.

205

(to 270) Among neo-Platonists referring to music was Plotinos.

211

(to 217) Rome, Baths of Caracalla.

Mani was born. He was familiar with Greek thought, was a poet -musician as well as a spiritual leader.

Clement of Alexandria died. He headed the Alexandrian catechetical schools where hymns originated.

217

(to 222) The Papal reign of St. Callistus I (born in Rome).

222

(to 230) The Papal reign of St. Urban I (born in Rome).

224

(to 241) Investiture of Ardashir, Nagsh-i-Rustam.

226

(to 641) Seleucides dynasty, in Persia which inaugurated a nationalistic anti Greek feeling in music.

c.229

St. Cecilia was executed in Rome, according to most writers. (under Alexander Severus).

230

Censoriaus alluded to the introduction of this alternative EdC accordatura when he credited the Cretian Chrysothemis the sixth string or synemmenos.

230

(to 235) The Papal reign of St. Pontian (born in Rome).

233

(to 304) Porphyry, a pupil of Plotinos.

235

(to 236) The Papal reign of St. Anterus (born in Greece).

236

(to 250) The Papal reign of St. Fabian (born in Rome).

242

(to 272) Persian architecture: Ctesiphon, Taq-i-Kisra.

245

(to 256) Moses striking water from the rock. Wall-painting from the synagogue in Dura-Europos (Mesopotamia).

250

Christian Hymn from Oxyrhynochos (Greek) written.

251

(to 253) The Papal reign of St. Cornelius (born in Rome).

253

(to 254) The Papal reign of St. Lucius I (born in Rome).

254

(to 257) The Papal reign of St. Stephen I (born in Rome).

257

(to 258) The Papal reign of St. Sixtus II (born in Greece).

c.257

(to c.337) Gregory the Illuminator was responsible for the Hellenizing or Catholicizing of Christianity in Armenia.

259

(to 268) The Reign of St. Dionysius (place of birth unknown).

c.260

Saxon raids on Roman Britain began.

(to c.340) Eusebios, bishop of Caesarea in Palestine, author of the Ecclesiastical History, disapproves of the use of instruments, even the Kithara.

267

The invasion of Attica by the Herulian Goths.

269

(to 274) The Papal reign of St. Felix I (born in Rome).

275

(to 283) The Papal reign of St. Eutychian (born in Luni).

283

(to 296) The Papal reign of St. Caius (born in Dalmatia).

284

(to 305) Spalato, Palace of Diocletian.

296

(to 304) The Papal reign of St. Marcellinus (born in Rome).

c.298

(to 373) St. Athanasios, patriarch of Alexandria, exerted himself towards keeping the singing of the psalms from becoming overelaborate.

c.300

Daily vigils were instituted in the Egyptian monastic communities, started by Pachomius.

The Chinese painter Ku K'ai-chi lived at this time.

Euclid tried to find the exact mathematical ratios of the intervals on the calibrated

c.300(cont.)

(cont.) string of the monochord.

A Schola Cantorum was founded at Rome by St. Sylvester I. The establishment of this and similar institutions in other places was for the purpose of improving the singing in the northern areas particularly.

It was claimed by Pellegrini, in his "Museum Historico-Legale" that the mass "Papae Marcelli" was not written by Palestrina and dedicated to his patron Marcellus II, but rather by St. Marcellus I, at the beginning of the 4th century.

(to 1453) Under the heading "Byzantine art" came all the works produced from 300 to 1453 within the orbit of the Christian state that succeeded Rome and of which the influence extended to the Middle East, Italy, the Balkans, and Russia.

Zosimos of Panopolis (now Akhmim) was an alchemist in Egypt, who flourished at this time. He was credited with research from which highly reputable modern scholars have been able to make deductions.

St. Chrysostom advocated the expulsion of instrumental music and the reign of vocal music by decrying the "lifeless strings of David's harp as compared to the living strings of a singing congregation."

Indian architecture: Bodhgaya, Mahabodhi Temple (180' high).

Plainsong passion - deacon recited mass; words of Christ sung to Gospel tone.

c.300

In the primitive church it was customary to sing a psalm while the people were receiving communion. It was therefore referred to as "communio." The psalm "O taste and see" was therefore sung in churches at Jerusalem and Antioch.

Grecian sculpture: Apollo Belvedere (7'4" high).

The employment of instruments in churches as accompaniment for singers dated from the 4th century, when St. Ambrose (Biship) brought them into the cathedral services at Milan.

Artorius became a Celtic leader.

(to 400) Chant appeared in the first, fourth, and fifth centuries, troparia, or inserts between the recitation of psalms.

(to 500) The Angles and Saxons invaded England.

Psalm-Tones were sung by early Christians and handed down by oral tradition. St. Ambrose, in the 4th century, collected and codified a series of chants, protected by church authority. This chant (Ambrosian) still exists and is used in the Milan Cathedral.

303

Armenia became the first country to adopt Christianity as a state religion.

308

(to 309) The Papal reign of St. Marcellus I (born in Rome).

309

(to 310) The Papal reign of

309(cont.)

St. Eusebius (born in Greece).

310

(to 313) Roman architecture: Basilica of Constantine, Rome (195'x265').

c.311

Emperor Constantine established the Christian Church. By the edict of Milan he assured Christianity a permanent position in the state.

(to 314) The Papal reign of St. Meltiades (born in Africa).

(to 314) During the pontificate of St. Meltiades, Rome already had 40 Christian basilicas.

312

Roman architecture: Arch of Constantine built.

314

(to 335) The Papal reign of St. Sylvester I (born in Rome).

c.317

(to 367) The Egyptian abbot Pambo deplored the use of music but admitted to its popularity.

320

(to 600) Indian architecture: Ajanta, Cave XIX (32'wide by 38'high).

(to 600) Indian architecture: Aihole, Durga Temple (84' by 36'x30'high).

(to 600) Indian sculpture: Buddha Preaching in Deer Park (5'3" high).

323

(to 337) Roman architecture: Santa Costanza, Rome (Dome diameter 70').

324

Transfer of the Roman capital to Byzantium (Constantinople).

328

Constantine the Great founded New Rome - Constantinople.

c.330

(379) St. Basil, the successor of Eusebios as Bishop of Caesarea, wrote the liturgy of St. Basil. It is still used in the Eastern Rite.

Death of the Syrian Iamblichos, who studied with Porphyry at Rome.

St. Frumentius, a Phoenician, became the first Bishop of Ethiopia.

(to 390) S. Gregory Nazianzen was the first churchman who described the History of the Passion in dramatic form.

333

(to 397) The Te Deum laudamus often attributed to Saint Ambrose, Bishop of Milan, was introduced but not composed by him.

c.335

(to 414) Niceta of Remesiana was the composer of the Te Deum.

336

(to 336) The Papal reign of St. Marcus (born in Rome).

337

(to 352) The Papal reign of St. Julius I (born in Rome).

340

St. Ambrose, Bishop of Milan, was born(died 397).

340

(to 397) St. Ambrose was the creator of the Latin Hymn as known today and used iambic dimeter.

(to 397) St. Ambrose felt that women, although to be silent in the congregation would "do well to sing their psalm."

c.340

(to 420) St. Jerome, author of the standard Latin translation of the Bible - the Vulgate - acted as advisor to Pope Damasus.

345

(to 407) St. John Chrysostom ("the golden-mouthed," 345-407), a famous Greek Father was Bishop of Constantinople. He attested to the popularity of psalm-singing in the East.

350

The Laodicean Council defended the proper singers against the undesirable ones.

(to 430) The use of the Pneuma was traced to antiquity, certainly as far as the age of St. Augustine (350-430).

c.350

The monks and bishops brought antiphonal psalmody into the Church where it spread among the secular clergy. The main proponents of this technique were the two Antiochian monks, Flavian and Diodorus. They were in Syria, Basilius, Nicaea and Palestine.
St. John Chrysostom was active in Bysantium as well.

Chinese painting: Admonitions of the Imperial Preceptress, Ku K'ai-chih (10" high).

352

(to 366) The Papal reign of Liberius (born in Rome).

354

Christmas was observed in Rome.

St. Augustine was born (died 430).

(to 430) Writers referred to what may have been part-music.

359

Roman sculpture: Christ with St. Peter and St. Paul. From the sarcophagus of Junius Bassus.

c.360

The Introduction to Music by Alypios. His tables of Greek alphabetical notation provided us with about forty scale systems, each with eighteen notes.

Alexandrian Alypios was written. The work makes possible the decipherment of Greek music.

363

A Greek epigram, attributed to Emperor Julian the Apostate, conveyed particulars on a 4th century organ.

366

Hilary of Poitiers, who died in 366, was familiar with Syrian hymnody while he was exiled to the far east. When he returned he translated Oriental hymns into Latin and added some of his own to them. Isidore of Seville called him the first Latin hymn writer.

(to 384) The Papal reign of St. Damasus I (born in Spain).

(to 384) Damasus I introduced the liturgical Order of

366(cont.)

Jerusalem into the Roman Catholic Church. Roman liturgy became highly organized.

367

The Council of Laodicea prohibited the participation of both instruments and congregations in the liturgy. Dancing was also eliminated.

c.373

St. Ephraim whose hymn-texts are among the oldest still in liturgical use was the principal Syrian hymn composer.

c.375

St. Ambrose used only four Modes, those beginning and ending on the notes D,E,F, and G.

380

(to 381) The Laodicean Council in the fifty-ninth canon reasserted strong prohibitions because Heterodox, folk-song hymnody was popular and influenced the hymns.

382

The Roman Council, presided over by Pope Damasus, officially introduced antiphonal singing to the liturgy.

384

Western instruments were established in China.

Ambrosian chant was completed and formalized.

(to 399) The Papal reign of St. Siricius (born in Rome).

385

Bishop Ambrose, in a letter of the year 385, employed the word "missa" to describe the eucharistic sacrifice.

385

The Aquitanian pilgrim Etheria described the service of worship in Jerusalem and said it included vigils, lauds, tierce, sext, nones, and vespers. Offices consisted of Psalms, antiphons, hymns, responses and collects. She also mentioned boy choristers.

c.386

(to c.457) Theodoret, bishop of Cyrrhus, mentioned a strange form of antiphonal psalm-singing. It was used at a monastery by both Greeks and Syrians. Both languages were used and verses were repeated antiphonally.

387

St. Augustine was baptized by St. Ambrose.

c.389

St. Patrick was born (died 461).

c.393

An obelisk, built by Emperor Theodosius, showed an organ with bellows instead of hydraulic mechanism which had been used prior to this type.

Theodoret, Greek church historian and biblical scholar, was born (died 457).

Theodoret referred to musical organs as being furnished with pipes of copper or of bronze.

The last Olympiad was held. The games were suppressed by Theodosius the Great.

395

The invasion of Greece by Alaric and the Goths; Eleusis was destroyed.

396

St. Ambrose was made Bishop of Hippo (now Bona, Algeria).

397

St. Ambrose died (born 340).

399

(to 401) The Papal reign of St. Anastasius I (born in Rome).

c.400

Indian Sculpture: Colossal Buddha, Bamian (175' high).

The beginning of Japanese music.

Byzantine architecture: Kalat Seman, St. Simeon Stylites (315'x318').

Coelius Sedulius wrote the Christmas hymn, "A solis ortus."

The Epiphany hymn "O Lux beata" was written.

Chinese sculpture: Colossal Buddha, Yunkang (32' high).

"Rector potens, verax Deus," "Rerum Deus tenax vigor," "Aeterne Rex altissime," were written.

The distinction between "Lord, have mercy on us" and "Christ, have mercy on us" came from a dualistic interpretation of the incarnation of Christ.

Greek sculpture: Portrait of an official from Aphrodisias.

Introits were introduced to the Proper Chants.

Ammianus Marcellinus died. He described the barritus (barbarian war song) as a soft hum which built to a great crescendo until at last it (cont.) thundered like waves breaking on rocks.

The ancient Latin hymn, "Veni redemptor gentium" was written by St. Ambrose.

Stéfano Landi's Sant' Alessio described the fate of a Roman at this time.

Claudian, the poet, left a passage describing an organist's performance in his poem "De Consulati F. Mallii Theodori."

(to 800) The art of psalm singing developed during this period.

401

(to 417) The Papal reign of St. Innocent I (born in Albano).

c.405

The Latin hymn writer Prudentius was under the influence of classical poetry. He was partly Spanish in his background.

c.406

Chinese art: Husband reproving his wife. Detail on a silk scroll after a work by Ku K'ai-Chi.

c.410

The "Nunc Dimittis" was mentioned in the Apostolical Constitutions.

Aurelius - Prudentius wrote hymns for private devotions (Spanish).

412

Proclus, the last important teacher among the Greek Neoplatonists, was born (died 485).

417

(to 418) The Papal reign of St. Zozimus (born in Greece).

418

(to 422) The Papal reign of St. Boniface I (born in Rome).

c.420

St. Jerome mentioned an organ at Jerusalem.

Sedulius wrote "Crudelis Herodes," and "A solis ortus cardine."

422

(to 432) Antiphonal singing was officially accepted during the Papal reign of Celestine I (422-432). It had come from the Service of the Hours and was used in the Introit.

(to 432) The Papal reign of St. Celestine I (born in Campania).

c.424

Byzantine art: The Good Shepherd, a painting in the Mausoleum of Galla Placidia, Ravenna.

425

Roman architecture: Nave, Santa Sabina (central aisle 43' wide).

430

St. Augustine died (born 354).

c.430

(to 438) A young Persian king, Bahram Ghur, went to the town of Al-Hira, Mesopotamia, to study Arabian music.

432

(to 440) The Papal reign of St. Sixtus III (born in Rome).

432

(to 440) Pope Sixtus established a monastery for daily practice of psalmody.

c.440

Byzantine architecture: Tomb of Galla Placidia, Ravenna (49'x41').

(to 461) The Papal reign of St. Leo I, the Great (born in Tuscany).

(to 461) Pope Leo the Great founded a monastery for the daily practice of psalmody. The monastery carried the names of St. Peter and St. Paul.

c.450

Sporadic raids on Roman Britain had grown to ruthless conquest and permanent settlements.

According to Julianus, a Spanish Bishop, the organ was in common use in the churches of Spain.

The Litany was sung at Vienne, in France.

American Indian sculpture: Stela 14, Piedras Negras, Classic Maya (c.9' high).

American Indian sculpture: Stela, Copán, Classic Maya.

c.451

A number of hymnodists at the time of the Council of Chalcedon were known.

Jacob of Serugh, Syrian hymn writer was born (died 521).

At the Council of Chalcedon the condemning of Monophysite Doctrine as heresy lead to the separation of the Armenian

c.451(cont.)
Church from the Greek.

457
Theodoret, Greek church historian and biblical scholar, died (born c.393).

Persian bronze sculpture: Peroz I Hunting (dia. 8½").

461
St. Patrick died (born c.389).

(to 468) The Papal reign of St. Hilary (born in Sardinia).

(to 468) St. Hilary founded a School in Rome for the education of Choristers.

468
(to 483) The Papal reign of St. Simplicius (born in Tivoli)

c.478
Ambros mentioned that Frottole existed at this time and that the song of the cicada and the meowing of a cat were imitated.

c.480
Boethius, author on music, philosopher, and mathematician was born (died c.524).

483
(to 492) The Papal reign of St. Felix III (II), born in Rome).

Justinian, hymn composer, was born (died 565).

485
Proclus, Greek Neoplatonist, died (born 412).

c.485
Cassiodorus, a writer on musical subjects was born. He was in the service of Theodoric (cont.) and Athalaric (died c.580).

491
(to 518) The Papal reign of Anastasios I.

492
(to 496) The Papal reign of St. Gelasius I (born in Africa)

496
(to 498) The Papal reign of Anastasius II (born in Rome).

498
(to 514) The Papal reign of St. Symmachus (born in Sardinia).

c.500
The power of observation of nature in Greece disappeared around this time.

In the list of ratios given by Boëthius, the term proportio sesquialtera signified numbers having the ratio of 2:3.

The monochord, described in the musical bible of the Middle Ages, (the five books De Musica) in which Theodoric's chancellor Boethius gave a last résumé of ancient theories of music.

Chants of the Ordinary (Kyrie, Sanctus, Gloria, Agnus Dei, Credo) came into the liturgy and became the Ordinary Mass.

Chinese sculpture: Winged Lion (on the road to the tomb of Prince Hsiao Hsiu) near Nanking.

American Indian Sculpture: Figure, Hopewell Culture.

c.500(cont.)

Peruvian pottery: Clay vessel in form of head of one-eyed man. Excavated in the valley of Chiama, Peru.

In ancient Welsh works, "to play upon the harp" was expressed "to sing upon the harp" - Canu ar y Delyn. The same expression was used in regard to the Crwth, an old Welsh instrument, popular in Britain to such an extent that some historians referred to it as a national instrument.

"Audi, benigne Conditor," and "Beati nobis gaudia" were composed at this time.

The Arabs became acquainted with the Persian lute before their conquest of the country, and an Arab musician sent to the Persian King to learn singing and performance on the lute, brought it to Mecca.

An antiphon "Da pacem Domine" was composed.

During the sixth century, during Etrurian prosperity, its "joie de vivre" provided a freedom that was lacking in Greek art.

Monasteries were the only remaining centers of culture in Western Europe.

Byzantine architecture: Kalb Louzeh, Basilica (nave and aisles 50' wide).

Byzantine architecture: Tourmanin, Basilica.

Islamic sculpture: Throne of Maximianus (47" high).

Roman mosaic: Christ and Saints.

Chinese sculpture: Empress as Donor, relief, Pin Yang Cave, Lungmen (6'4"x9'1").

Islamic sculpture: Sarcophagus of Theodore (39½"x81").

Japanese sculpture: Kwannon, Horyu-ji Temple (6' high).

(to 1000) Grecian Indian sculpture: Anthropomorphic Urn, Monte Alban - Zapotec (26½" high).

c.504

Mayan sculpture: Head of the Death-god. From a Maya altar. Copan, Honduras.

c.510

Boëthius was counsellor to Theodoric but later executed by him on the charge of treasonable acts.

c.512

Boëthius authorized the use of the first fifteen letters of the Roman Alphabet, for certain special purposes.

514

Cassiodorus, who was consul of Rome under King Vitigas the Goth, described the organ of his day.

(to 523) The Papal reign of St. Hormisdas (born in Frosinone).

c.515

The earliest record of the Oktoechos was a reference to a song collection and was found in the Plerophoriai by John, Bishop of Maiuma (now El Mineh) in the port of Gaza.

c.520

Roman mosaic: The Miracle of the Loaves and Fishes, from the Basilica of St. Apollinare Nuovo.

Death of Hygelac, uncle of Beowulf and his predecessor as King of the Geats. He was an historic chieftain.

Byzantine art: Procession of the Virgin Martyrs.

521

Jacób of Serugh, Syrian hymn writer, died (born c.451).

523

(to 526) The Papal reign of St. John I (born in Tuscany).

c.524

Boëthius, author on music, philosopher, and mathematician, died (born c.480).

In Boethius the culmination of ancient musical science of the Occident was reached.

c.526

Byzantine art: The Taking of Christ.

(to 530) The Papal reign of St. Felix IV (III), born in Samnium).

Byzantine architecture: Ravenna, San Vitale (dia. 112')

Early Christian mosaic: Emperor Justinian and His Attendants.

529

Important rules concerning boy lectors were passed at the second council of Orange.

c.530

Justinian was active as a hymn composer.

St. Benedict did not order the use of "Nunc Dimittis" during his reign.

The Gloria Patri was to be used after each psalm as ordered by St. Benedict.

Byzantine architecture: Early Christian Basilica: S. Apollinare in Classe, Ravenna.

(to 532) The Papal reign of Boniface II (born in Rome).

St. Boniface arranged a series of Chants for the whole year.

531

The second Council of Toledo set regulations concerning boy lectors.

532

(to 537) Greek architecture: "Anthemius of Tralles and Isidorus of Miletus" Constantinople.

c.532

Early Christian mosaic: The Sacrifice of Abraham, San Vitale, Ravenna.

533

(to 535) The Papal reign of John II (born in Rome).

535

(to 536) The Papal reign of St. Agapitus I (born in Rome).

c.536

The final separation of the Armenian Church from the Greek.

c.536 (cont.)
(to 537) The Papal reign of St. Silverius (born in Campania).

537
(to 555) The Papal reign of Vigilius (born in Rome).

540
The founding of a monastery in Vivarium by Cassiodorus.

c.546
Byzantine mosaic: Empress Theodora and Her Court, San Vitale, Ravenna.

Byzantine mosaic: Emperor Justinian and His Court, San Vitale, Ravenna.

c.547
Byzantine mosaic: The Empress Theodora and Her Attendants, San Vitale, Ravenna.

549
Byzantine architecture: Ravenna, Sant' Apollinare Nuovo.

c.550
King Arthur reigned.

556
(to 561) The Papal reign of Pelagius I (born in Rome).

561
(to 574) The Papal reign of John III (born in Rome).

565
Justinian, hymn composer, died (born 483).

c.570
Isidore of Seville, noted writer on music was born (died 636).

c.570
"Pange lingua gloriosi," and "Vexilla Regis prodeunt," were written by Venantius Fortunatus.

575
(to 579) The Papal reign of Benedict I (born in Rome).

576
A Nestorian Synod forbade the use of tambourines and castanets during funerals.

577
(to 590) Under the protection of Pope Pelagius II (577-590), the Benedictine Fathers established themselves near the Lateran Basilica, and opened Schools for the preparation of Candidates for the Holy Orders. They settled in Rome to escape Lombard invaders.

578
Roman architecture: San Lorenzo, F.L.M., presbytery (central aisle 36' wide).

Women, previously admitted, were excluded from choirs, except in convents.

579
(to 590) The Papal reign of Pelagius II (born in Rome).

c.580
Cassiodorus represented the end of antique musical science in the Occident.

Cassiodorus, writer on musical subjects, died (born c.485).

An organ existed "in the most ancient city of Grado," in a church of the nuns.

581

Seven Orchestras were in China, one from Kaoli, one from India, one from Buchara, one from Kutch or East Turkistan. Musicians from Cambodia, Japan, Silla, Samarkand, Paikchei, Kachgar & Turkey played in the groups.

585

When Gregory was named arch deacon in Rome, good singing and beautiful voices stimulated respect for musical talent.

589

The Council of Toledo objected to dancing during the Church Services.

590

(to 604) The Papal reign of St. Gregory I the Great (born in Rome).

(to 604) During the time Gregory I was Pope he collected and codified the best chants being used in the church and called them Gregorian Chant.

(to 604) During his Papacy, Gregory I was credited with establishing the Scola Cantorum. However, little question exists that it had been founded considerably earlier.

(to 604) Gregory I added to the four Authentic modes four newly derived modes, thereafter referred to as Plagel modes.

(to 604) Gregory the Great, who was chosen Pope in 590, discovered that the second half of the scale, H to P, was a repetition of the first, A to H and abolished the last eight letters. He then used the (cont.) first seven again, indicating the lower octave by capitals and the upper octave by small letters.

595

The Concilium Romanum was held and Gregory decreed that deacons were to sing only the Gospel and that the rest of the music in the service would be by subdeacons, or clerics.

c.595

According to Isidore, Bishop of Seville (c. 595), the oldest harps had seven strings, and the shepherds' pandean pipes had seven reeds. This indicated that the ancient scale had seven sounds.

596

The "Antiphonarium" was introduced in England by St. Augustine, who brought it there. He also brought Roman singers to teach the method of performing it. Gregory I sent him on this mission with over forty assistants.

598

Ethelbert converted to Christianity. Canterbury became the chief center of Roman influence in England.

599

St. Leander, Archbishop of Seville, who died in 599, "composed many pieces to sweet sound."

600

Bishop Venantius Fortunatus said that Burgundians and Franconians were unable to tell the cackling of geese from a swan's song.

c.600

Ethelbert, King of the Jutish Kingdom of Kent, established his authority over all south-eastern England as far north as the Humber and as far west as the Severn.

Japan became familiar with Buddism as well as ceremonial Chinese and Indian music, and dances which were converted to Japanese style and called Bugaku.

Marcianus Capella described lyres that were large as sedan chairs.

Hassan ikn-Thãbit visited the court of an Arabian monarch where he saw 10 singing girls, 5 of them Byzantines, singing songs of their country to the accompaniment of the barbat, and 5 others from Al-Hira. They had been presented to King Jabala by Iyas ikn-Qakisa, they sang songs of their native land.

The organization of the Proper of the mass was established in the seventh century and its sections have hardly ever been newly composed for the liturgy.

"Te lucis ante terminum," and "Iste Confessor" were written during this period.

An Eisteddfod was held at which King Cadwaladr presided.

Organum was probably used in the church.

Gregorian chant was cultivated in England and Germany.

Romanesque manuscript: The Book of Durrow.

The Chant appeared in the 7th century as Kontákia. These were lengthy odes consisting of a short proem and many stanzas with refrains.

According to the Venerable Bede, the harp was played in Britain and it was customary to hand it from one to another at entertainments.

The singing of Hungarians elicited comment from several contemporaries. Theophilactus (7th century) mentioned their hymns to the earth.

The parish church of St. Paul, which now stands on the old site of the Monastery at Jarrow, has been much restored. The walls of the chancel were built at this time.

The abbeys of Luxeuil and Corbie in France were active centers of culture at this time.

Japanese sculpture: Bodhisattva in Meditation, Chugu-ji Nunnery. Horyu-ji Temple (5'2" high).

Japanese sculpture: Shrine of Lady Itachibana, Golden Hall, Horyu-ji Temple.

(to c.700) Organs were first introduced into the services of the church.

(to c.700) The religion of the Middle East, which had replaced everything before it by this time, that is the religion of the Mohammedan conquerors of Persia, Mesopotamia, Egypt, North Africa and Spain, was even more rigorous than Christianity had been.

c.600(cont.)

(to c.700) The monasteries of Northumbria were great centers of learning in England. In one of them at Jarrow the Venerable Bede wrote his great "Ecclesiastical History of the English People."

(to c.700) There were two main centers of culture: the British Isles and Merovingian Gaul.

(to c.700) Japanese sculpture: Yakushi, Yakushi-ji Temple, Nara (7'4" high).

(to c.850) Indian architecture: Elura, Kailasa Temple was built (200'x100'x100' high).

(to c.900) Early MSS with Visigothic neumes contained non-liturgical laments as well as historical texts (written in Latin).

(to c.900) Early Christian manuscript: Joshua Roll; Angels Appearing to Joshua before the Walls of Jericho.

604

(to 606) The Papal reign of St. Sabinianus (born in Tuscany).

607

(to 607) The Papal reign of St. Boniface III (born in Rome)

608

(to 615) The Papal reign of St. Boniface IV (born in Marsi)

c.609

The Crwth or Crowd, the oldest stringed instrument played with the bow, was first mentioned in some elegiacs, written by Venantius Fortunatus, Bishop of Poitiers.

610

(to 641) Sergios, patriarch of Constantinople during the reign of Heraklios, wrote a celebrated Akathistos Hymn showing some similarity to the odes of Romanos.

614

St. Gall, an Irish hermit,built his cell in the forest which then was on the site of a future monastery. Pilgrims later went to his cell. Ultimately it was transformed into a regularly organized Benedictine monastery where many musicians were involved.

615

(to 618) The Papal reign of St. Deusdedit (Adeodatus I), born in Rome.

c.618

(to c.907) The Tang Dynasty brought court orchestras to their highest position.

619

(to 625) The Papal reign of St. Boniface V (born in Naples)

c.619

(to 629) A free translation into Syriac of a collection of hymns originally written in Greek by Severos of Antioch and others. Paul, Bishop of Edessa, was credited with the work.

625

(to 638) The Papal reign of Honorius I (born in Campania).

629

Sophronios was Bishop of Jerusalem.

c.630

Edwin, King of Northumbria,

c.630(cont.)
extended his authority over nearly all of England. The sole exception was the tiny Kingdom of Kent.

631
Johannes, Bishop at Saragossa, died. He had composed considerable music for the church.

636
Isidore of Seville died. He had mentioned music to a considerable extent in his encyclopedic writings. He had succeeded his brother Leander as archbishop (born c.570).

639
Conantius, Bishop of Palencia, died. He had contributed to the Chant.

640
Bishop Aldhelm was born (died 709).

St. Gall died.

(to 642) The Papal reign of St. John IV (born in Dalmatia).

(to 640) The Papal reign of St. Severinus (born in Rome).

641
Bilal ikn-Riyah, the earliest muezzin, died.

(to 652) The reign of King Chindasvinthus. At the time of his death a manuscript appeared containing a lament on his death.

642
(to 649) The Papal reign of St. Theodore I (born in Greece).

645
St. Germanos was born(died 745).

649
(to 655) The Papal reign of St. Martin I (born in Todi).

650
The Council of Cavaillon was indignant because of obscene songs which were heard at religious celebrations.

c.650
Missionaries having arrived from the Continent, all of England had become Christian. Sussex was the sole exception.

Penda, King of the Mercians, established a brief overlordship in England. He was replaced by Oswy, King of Northumbria.

The organ was invented.

American Indian ceramic: Peruvian Water Jug, Mochica (11½" high).

(to 730) St. Andrew of Crete was the chief proponent of the Canon.

(to c.750) Most popes were Byzantine or Oriental.

654
(to 657) The Papal reign of St. Eugene I (born in Rome). He was elected during the exile of St. Martin I, who had endorsed him.

657
(to 672) The Papal reign of St. Vitalian (born in Segni).

St. Eugenius died. He had contributed to the Chant.

c.657
The reign of Queen Reciberga. A manuscript at Madrid

c.657(cont.)

contains a lament on her death.

664

Following the Synod of Whitby the Christian Church in England was firmly established. It brought on advances in English civilization.

c.666

Pope Vitalian introduced the organ at Rome. It was for the improvement of the singing of congregations.

The claim that a pneumatic organ was adopted to improve congregational singing in Rome has been described as not authentic.

667

St. Ildefonsus died. He contributed to the Chant.

669

Theodore of Tarsus arrived in Canterbury with his friend Hadrian. He had been raised to archbishop.

c.669

Putta became Bishop of Rochester.

c.670

Pre-Romanesque architecture: Brixworth, Church (nave 30' wide).

c.670

Bishop Aldhelm, who wrote Anglo-Saxon poems and set them to music, was the earliest writer of Medieval times to mention part-song.

672

(to 676) The Papal reign of St. Adeodatus II (born in Rome).

(to 676) China sculpture: Colossal Vairocana Buddha, Lungmen (85' high).

(to 676) Chinese sculpture: Guardians, Lungmen (50' high).

c.672

(to 735) A tract, Musica Theoretica, was attributed to the Venerable Bede (c.673-735), it contained passages showing how to obtain simultaneous consonances on the monochord. Its authenticity was dubious.

673

The Venerable Bede was born (died 735).

c.675

Jacob of Edessa revised the translation of a collection of hymns written by Severos of Antioch and previously freely translated into Syriac by Paul, Bishop of Edessa.

English missionary, Boniface, was born.

676

(to 678) The Papal reign of St. Donus (born in Rome).

678

(to 681) The Papal reign of St. Agatho (born in Sicily).

680

At the age of 7 the Venerable Bede began his education in the school of the Benedictine monastery of Wearmouth in what is now the county of Durham.

Wynfrith (St. Boniface) was born in Devonshire. He was the principal person to spread Roman chant throughout Germany.

c.680
John (Johannes), Archcantor of the Papal Chapel, was sent to England by Pope Agatho. He became a teacher at Wearmouth Monastery and brought it to fame as a center of plainchant.

682
(to 683) The Papal reign of St. Leo II (born in Sicily).

684
(to 685) The Papal reign of St. Benedict II (born in Rome).

685
(to 686) The Papal reign of John V (born in Syria).

c.685
The Monastery at Jarrow was built.

686
(to 687) The Papal reign of St. Conon (birthplace unknown).

687
(to 701) The Papal reign of St. Sergius I (born in Syria).

690
St. Julian died. He contributed to the Chant.

691
(to 1022) Islamic architecture: Jerusalem, Dome of the Rock (98' high).

c.695
St. Germanos was an important contemporary and successor of the canon-writers.

700
(to 1000) American Indian architecture: Nunnery (189'x33'6") and Temple (160'x240'x80' high) built at Uxmal.

(to 1000) American Indian ceramic: Peruvian Water Jug, Nazca (6" high).

c.700
Indian architecture: Barabudur, Great Stupa (100' high).

The development of Plainsong Passion, text solemnly declaimed on a fixed tone; words of Christ sung to Gospel Tone with inflections and cadences.

Japanese sculpture: Bonten, Hokkedo, Todai-ji, Temple, Nara (6'7" high).

Indian sculpture: Saiva Trinity, Hindu Temple, Elephanta (12' high).

Chinese sculpture: Adoring Buddha from Tunhuang (4' high).

Organum was already in use.

Japanese architecture: Nara, Yakushi-ji Temple, Pagoda.

Japanese architecture: Toshodai-ji, Lecture Hall.

Japanese sculpture: The Priest Ganjin, Toshodai-ji Temple, Nara (2'8" high).

Bishop Aldhelm mentioned organa but did not use the term to refer to instruments. He did, however, claim that Anglo-Saxons gilded the front pipes of their organs. He also considered the organ as "a tool of heathenish enticement."

Tempo and intensity were denoted by Romanian letters.

Romanesque manuscript: Book of Kells.

c.700(cont.)

The troparia and the kontákia were dropped in favor of the kanon, or cycle of nine hymns. The same melody (heirmós) was repeated in each of the stanzas.

Romanesque manuscript: Book of Lindisfarne.

The use of the organ was appreciated, and the art of its manufacture was known in England.

Romanesque manuscript: British Gospel Book.

Though letters rarely appeared in writing, the degrees of the scale were named after them.

Romanesque manuscript: Irish Gospel Book.

"Somno refectis artubus" was written at this time.

Northumbrian manuscript: The Lindisfarne Gospel.

Northumbrian manuscript: The Echternach Gospel.

Scriptoria were numerous and manuscripts were decorated in a less heirachic, and more realistic style than in the British Isles.

(or c.800) Though not included by Pope Gregory, the Ionian and Hypo-ionian Modes were in existence by this time.

(to c.900) Islamic architecture: Cordova, Mosque (38' high).

701

(to 705) The Papal reign of St. John VI (born in Greece).

705

(to 707) The Papal reign of St. John VII (born in Greece).

708

(to 708) The Papal reign of St. Sisinnius (born in Syria).

(to 715) The Papal reign of St. Constantine (born in Syria)

709

Bishop Aldhelm died (born 640).

711

The Moorish invasion started when Tariq landed at Tarifa.

713

(to 756) A court orchestra (female) entertained Emperor Ming Huang and his mistress. Pairs of instruments including lutes, flutes, oboes, mouth organs, harps, zithers, hourglass drums, and metallophones were accompanied by a clapper and a large drum.

c.714

Pepin the Short was born. He was a member of the Carolingian Dynasty and ruled France (died 768).

715

(to 731) The Papal reign of St. Gregory II.

c.720

The heroic poem of "Beowulf" was composed somewhere in the northern part of England.

731

(to 741) The Papal reign of St. Gregory III (born in Syria)

(to 741) Benedictine monks performed the Office at Rome after their return to Monte Cassino during the reign of

731(cont.)

Gregory III (731-741).

735

The Venerable Bede died (born 673).

741

(to 752) The Papal reign of St. Zachary (born in Greece).

742

Charlemagne, King of France (Carolingian Dynasty) and Emperor of the West was born (died 814).

743

(to 744) Islamic frieze: Mschatta.

c.744

Pepin the Short, Charlemagne's father, perceived that an organ would be an important aid to devotion.

745

St. Germanos died (born 645).

747

The Council of Glasgow in order to avoid confusion in the sacred texts forbade priests to speak either softly like secular poets or tragically like actors.

A quotation from the text of the Council of Glasgow described a system of notation.

c.750

Cynewulf lived in Northumbria.

Northumbrian manuscript: St. Luke (from a Gospel manuscript).

Organ-making was introduced in France.

751

(to 768) The reign of Pepin the Short (Carolingian Dynasty), ruler of France.

752

(to 757) The reign of Stephen II (III), born in Rome. After St. Zachary died, a Roman priest named Stephen was elected but died before his consecration as Bishop of Rome. To avoid historical confusion, the true Stephen II is listed as Stephen II (III), the true Stephen III as Stephen III (IV) etc.

753

Alcuin, writer on music, was born (died 804).

754

After a meeting between Pepin the Short and Pope Stephen II in 754, a great effort was made to organize the Gallo-Frankish churches.

St. John of Damascus, Syrian theologian, died.

755

Pre-Carolingian miniature: Letter I in the Form of a Human Figure with an Eagle's Head, so-called Sacrementary of Gellone.

757

(to 767) The Papal reign of St. Paul I (born in Rome).

The earliest evidence of the organ in western Europe. The Byzantine Emperor Copronymos sent one to King Pippin of France. It was possibly the result of a request by the latter.

759
St. Theophanes, hymnwright of the school of the Studion (the famous monastery at Constantinople) was born (died c.842).

c.760
St. Kosmas of Jerusalem, a strong exponent of the canon, died.

764
Wynfrith (St. Boniface) died.

768
(to 772) The Papal reign of St. Stephen III (IV), born in Sicily.

(to 814) The reign of Charlemagne, King of France (Carolingian Dynasty) and Emperor of the West.

c.770
Paulus Diaconus (Paul the Deacon) wrote a Hymn, Ut Queant Laxis, the Festival of St. John the Baptist.

Pre-Carolingian miniature: St. Matthew (Salzburg).

772
(to 795) The Papal reign of St. Adrian I (born in Rome).

774
Charlemagne sent monks to Rome for vocal instruction, these monks were installed in monasteries.

c.775
Egbert, ruler of England and Great Britain, was born (d.839).

778
Louis I (the Debonair), King of France (Carolingian Dynasty) and Holy Roman (cont.) Emperor was born (died 840).

c.780
Small letters were found among the more usual Neumae.

(to c.890) The literary culture of Northumbria, and the resulting poetic activity were crushed by the Danish invasions which began before the end of the 8th century, and reached their peak in the latter part of the 9th century.

781
The baptism of Pepin the Short at Rome.

c.781
Carolingian miniature: Christ. Gospel-Book of Charlemagne, Diocese of Mainz.

c.783
Cynewulf, Bishop of Lindisfarne, died.

787
An account probably by the Monk of Angoulême asserted that the cantores sent from Rome by Charlemagne taught their Frankish colleagues in arte organandi. The entry appears to have been added at a later date.

790
Pope Hadrian sent two experienced singers to the north. They brought copies of the antiphonal. One, Petrus, reached Metz; the other, Romanus, remained at St. Gall, when he became ill, and headed the school for ecclesiastical singers.

c.790
Carolingian miniature: St. Luke.

c.790(cont.)

Gospel-Book of the Benedictine Abbey of St. Maximinus at Treves.

791

Zalzal of Bagdad died. He attempted to enlarge the semitone at the cost of the neighboring whole tone and assimilated them by taking a quarter tone from the whole tone and adding it to the semitone: 204-90-204 became 204-147-147 cents.

794

Charlemagne presided over the Synod of Frankfort.

795

(to 816) The Papal reign of St. Leo III (born in Rome).

c.795

The melody, "Morva Rhuddlan," was composed by Caradoc's Bard.

c.796

(to 804) Pre-Romanesque architecture: Charlemagne's Chapel at Aachen was built (48' int. diam.).

c.800

Charlemagne was crowned emperor by the Pope in Rome.

Italian fresco: Crypt of St. Germain, Auxerre, France.

Chinese painting: Amitabha Paradise, Cave, Tunhuang.

Pre-Romanesque architecture: Oviedo, Santa Maria de Naranco (interior 16'6" wide).

The Monastery at Jarrow was destroyed by Danish marauders.

The earliest complete manuscript with neumes.

Gregorian chant was cultivated in Gaul.

Fixed melodic chants were developed in Jewish music.

A miniature in the Utrecht Psalter shows a celestial concert with hydraulic organ (for two players) as well as trumpet and harp players.

The liturgy of the Eastern Church was brought to Bohemia by two missionaries, Cyril and Methodius.

Various versions of the liturgy of western Christianity, which had existed up to this time, were found in the Roman churches, Ambrosian and/or Milanese churches, as well as in Mozarabic and Gallican churches in France.

The earliest sequences we know of made their appearances in monasteries in France.

Notation was preponderantly "neumatic" at this time.

Organum was described at this time but, apparently, had existed in folk music long before. In Iceland it is still part of the folk music tradition.

Book binding from this time has relief showing church choirs.

Organs were common in England at this time.

"Gloria, Laus, et Honor," dated from this time.

Chinese relic: Notes on a Deerskin drum, Nan Cho.

c.800(cont.)

The earliest description of the portable mediaeval harp was found in Gerbert's "De Cantu et Musica Sacra," from a manuscript at the St. Blaise Monastery in the Black Forest area. There was also an early attempt there to make a set of chimes with small suspended bells tapped with a hammer.

Charlemagne decided that twelve Modes were sufficient for general use.

The handbook "Musica Enchiriadis" was written.

The Utrecht Psalter showed an early Frankish organ.

Roman church musicians protested the "Bestial" singing of the Franconians, claiming they destroyed melodies through tasteless rough singing.

The Latin text of Veni Creator Spiritus was written and has been ascribed to Charlemagne.

Roman painting: St. Matthew. From a Gospel manuscript, probably painted at Aix-la -Chapelle.

The church that Charlemagne had built at Aix-la-Chapelle was a close copy of a famous church that had been built in Ravenna about 300 years earlier.

Through the authority of Charlemagne the organ achieved a position of dignity.

Charlemagne received an organ from Caliph Haroun Alrashid. It was constructed by an Arabian organ maker and the Emperor had it installed at his (cont.) church in Aix-la -Chapelle.

(to 900) The Danes invaded England and laid waste to the land.

(to 900) The Sequence was introduced into the Liturgy during this period.

(to c.900) Eight Medieval church Modes came into general use: Dorian, Phrygian, Lydian, Mixolydian, and in each case its Hypo-equivalent.

(to c.1200) Tropes came into existence: Texts were inserted into authorized liturgical texts of Pope Gregory; the Kyrie, Gloria, Sanctus, and Benedictus dominus were troped; troped texts were set syllabically to melismas in the original chants.

(to c.1280) Polyphony was named organum. The tenor from plainsong had one or more counterpoints added to it.

802

Egbert became King of the West Saxons.

804

Alcuin, writer on music, died (born 753).

805

Interior of the church at Aix -la-Chapelle was consecrated.

c.806

Pre-Romanesque architecture: Church at Germigny-des-Prés.

c.809

The Imperial Academy of Music in Japan was made up of 28 masters of foreign styles,

c.809(cont.)
among them Cambodian and Chinese musicians.

c.810
Amalarius, mentioned the use of the "Nunc Dimittis."

Romanesque manuscript: Battle Scene in the Utrecht Psalter.

c.811
The first organ introduced in Germany was one which Charlemagne had made at Aix-la -Chapelle and patterned after the one at Compiègne.

813
The Council of Tours warned priests to be careful of things that tended to soften their souls, either visually or aurally. Manners of singing were of the greatest concern.

814
A manuscript contained a group of songs with Latin texts. The collection included a lament on the death of Charlemagne.

Charlemagne commanded the use of Antiphon in the Gallic Church; shortly thereafter it appeared in almost every Diocese.

(to 840) During the reign of Louis the Pious an exchange of emissaries occurred between Rome and the empire. Liturgical songbooks were constantly being revised so that they would conform with recent developments.

(to 840) The reign of Louis I (the Debonair), King of France and Holy Roman Emperor.

c.815
(to c.877) Johannes Scotus, an Irish philosopher and theolo-

(cont.) gian, as well as retainer of Charlemagne's grandson Charles the Bald, wrote De Divisione Naturae, which drew analogies between musical and cosmic harmony. Mention of music in parts was made but no details were included.

816
(to 817) The Papal reign of Stephen IV (V), born in Rome.

817
(to 824) The Papal reign of St. Paschal I (born in Rome).

c.820
Amalarius mentioned the Jubilate as being used in Lauds in addition to its regular position in the order of the Psalms.

Nordic woodcarving: A Dragon's Head (Oseberg, Norway).

821
St. Cecilia's house at Rome was converted to a church and her remains, as well as those of her husband and brother and several other martyrs, were moved. It was in this house that she was executed.

822
In Venice, Georgius, a monk, constructed an organ for Louis the Debonair. It was an Hydraulic organ and was installed in the King's palace at Aix -la-Chapelle.

823
Charles I the Bald, French King of the Carolingian Dynasty, was born. He later was Holy Roman Emperor as Charles II (875-877).

824
(to 827) The Papal reign of Eugene II (born in Rome).

c.825
Carolingian miniature: St. Luke. (Gospel-Book, Fulda).

c.826
The hydraulis reappeared in the West for the first time since 483. One was constructed for Louis the Pious by Georgius Veneticus.

827
(to 844) The Papal reign of St. Gregory IV (born in Rome).

(to 827) The Papal reign of Valentine (born in Rome).

828
(to 839) Egbert (Saxon) reigned in England and Great Britain.

830
In Bunting's "Ancient Music of Ireland," there is a picture of a harp with no front pillar.

c.830
Roman painting: St. Matthew. From a Gospel manuscript, probably painted at Rheims.

(to 912) Brother Notker the Stammerer, from St. Gall, composed sequences during his lifetime.

839
Egbert (Saxon) King of England and Great Britain, died (born c.775).

Charles II the Fat, French King of the Carolingian Dynasty, was born. He later was Holy Roman Emperor as Charles III (881-877)

(to 858) Ethelwulf (Saxon) reigned as King of England and Great Britain.

c.840
Hucbaldus de S. Amando, a theorist and monk, was born (Flanders). He was supposed to have written De Harmonica Institutione.

Ottfried von Weissenburg wrote an ancient "Harmony of the Gospels" in Frankish dialect. He listed the Lyre, Fiddle, Harp, and Crwth, as part of the Celestial Concert.

(to 870) A four-part motet was written: Ave miles coelestis, Ave rex patrone patriae, Ave rex. It was in honor of St. Edmund, King of East Anglia.

(to 877) Charles I, the Bald reigned as King of France (Carolingian Dynasty).

841
A manuscript contained a body of songs with Latin texts including a song on the battle of Fontenoy.

Greinald, a monk educated in Reichenau, was born(d.872).

c.842
St. Theophanes, hymnwright of the Studion School, died (born 759).

The religious value of representations of Christ, the Virgin, and the Saints in human form was recognized.

c.843
The merger of Roman-Frankish liturgical concepts had been completed by this time.

844
A manuscript contained songs with Latin texts. Included

844(cont.)
therein a lament on the death of Hugo of St. Quentin.

(to 847) The Papal reign of St. Sergius II (born in Rome).

846
Louis II the Stammerer, French King of the Carolingian Dynasty, was born (died 879).

847
(to 855) The Papal reign of St. Leo IV (born in Rome).

849
Alfred the Great, King of England and Great Britain, was born (died c.899).

850
Earliest manuscript giving rules for writing organum was written. It has been ascribed to Hucbald.

855
(to 858) The Papal reign of Benedict III (born in Rome).

856
Hrabanus Maurus, writer on music, died (born c.776).

858
(to 860) The reign of Ethelbald (Saxon) King of England and Great Britain.

(to 867) The Papal reign of St. Nicholas I the Great (born in Rome).

860
(to 866) The reign of Ethelbert (Saxon) King of England and Great Britain.

A treatise on drumming in China was written, it contained over one hundred "symphonies" (cont.) which are considered to be tālas from India.

c.860
The oldest known musician of St. Gall, Moengal or Marcellus, came from Ireland.

A monk, while fleeing from the abbey of Jumièges following its sacking by the Normans, arrived at St. Gall. He brought with him his antiphonary Notker Balbulus. One of the monks at St. Gall was inspired by this example and supplied texts for the melismas in use at St. Gall.

863
Louis III, French King of the Carolingian Dynasty, was born (died 882).

865
Robert I, French King of the Carolingian Dynasty, was born (died 923).

866
(to 871) The reign of King Ethelred I (Saxon) over England and Great Britain.

867
(to 872) The Papal reign of Adrian II (born in Rome).

870
(to 950) A Turk, Al Farābī, an islamic musicologist, adapted his doctrines to Greek patterns.

c.870
Edward the Elder (Saxon) King of England and Great Britain was born(died 924).

John the Deacon's life of Gregory the Great was written.

c.870(cont.)

Notker Balbulus developed sequences. Words and syllables were adapted to the final vowel following Alleluia and arranged in free poetry.

871

(to 899) The reign of Alfred the Great (Saxon) over the West Saxons. During his reign he was successful in checking the Danes and bringing about peace and prosperity.

872

Greinald, a monk, died (born 841).

(to 882) The Papal reign of St. John VIII (born in Rome).

874

The Arab Alkindi, an Islamic musicologist, died. He patterned his doctrines after the Greeks.

875

(to 877) Charles II reigned as Holy Roman Emperor. He had previously reigned as King of France as Charles I the Bold.

877

Charles II, Holy Roman Emperor, died. As Charles I the Bold he had been King of France prior to becoming Holy Roman Emperor (born 823).

A manuscript dating from this time at the Abbey of Fleury included a Credo apparently of native origin.

(to 879) The reign of Louis II the Stammerer, French King of the Carolingian Dynasty.

879

Charles III the Simple, French King of the Carolingian Dynasty, was born (died 929).

(to 882) The reign of Louis III, King of France (Carolingian Dynasty). He ruled jointly with Carloman.

(to 884) The reign of Carloman, King of France (Carolingian Dynasty). He ruled jointly with Louis III from 879 to 882.

c.880

The progress of Germany in making and using organs in the latter half of the 9th century, especially in the Eastern part of Franconia, was so great that Pope John VIII in a letter to Anno, Bishop of Friesingen, requested that a good organ may be sent to him and a skilled organist able to instruct the Romans.

Pre-Romanesque architecture: Lorsch, Gatehouse (33'high).

Russian mosaic: The Vision of Ezekiel, from Homilies of Gregory Nazianzus.

882

The first specimen of Old French poetry. A short song celebrating the martyrdom of St. Eulalia was written.

(to 884) The Papal reign of St. Marinus I (born in Gallese).

884

(to 885) The Papal reign of St. Adrian III (born in Rome).

c.884

A Swiss nobleman named Ratpert, who was a pupil of Marcellus, and connected with the monastery

c.884(cont.)

of St. Gall, died. He wrote a Gallus-song which became a folk song.

885

Nestor's Chronicle described the singing of the Hungarians at Kiev.

(to 891) The Papal reign of St. Stephen V (VI), born in Rome.

886

(to 917) The reign of Byzantine Emperor Leo VI.

888

(to 898) The reign of Eudes (Odo) Count of Paris, French King of the Carolingian Dynasty.

c.890

The confederation of Finno -Ugrian and Turkish tribes (of Central Asiatic origin) occupied the Middle Danube Basin. Elements of their folk music have been reconstructed through comparative study.

891

(to 896) The Papal reign of St. Formosus (born in Portus).

892

Regino became abbot of the Benedictine monastery at Prüm.

893

(to 923) The reign of Charles III, the Simple, French King of the Carolingian Dynasty. He was King in spite of opposition by Eudes.

895

King Athelstan (Saxon) was born (died 939).

896

(to 896) The Papal reign of St. Boniface VI (born in Rome).

(to 897) The Papal reign of St. Stephen VI (VII), born in Rome.

897

(to 897) The Papal reign of St. Romanus (born in Gallese).

(to 897) The Papal reign of St. Theodore II (born in Rome).

898

(to 900) The Papal reign of St. John IX (born in Tivoli).

899

(to 924) The reign of King Edward the Elder (Saxon) over England and Great Britain.

c.899

Alfred the Great, King of England and Great Britain, died (born 849).

900

(to 903) The Papal reign of Benedict IV (born in Rome).

c.900

A single horizontal line drawn across the parchment served as a guide for the position of the Neumae written on, above, or below the line.

The trope Hodie Cantandus (c.900) was arranged in dialogue form and led straight into the Introit of the Christmas Mass.

Byzantine painting: Byzantine Iconoclast, whitewashing an image of Christ; From the Chludow Psalter.

Tuotilo composed a trope to the

c.900(cont.)

Introit of the Christmas Mass: Quis est iste puer quem tam magnis praeconiis dignum vociferatis?

Chinese painting: Tung Yuan, Clear Weather in the Valley (1'3" high).

Pre-Romanesque architecture: Earl's Barton, Church (c.40' wide).

Quem quaerites, Easter trope telling the story of the three Marys, performed at Winchester Cathedral.

In southern Europe spacing of the neumes was started. They were placed in the modern way at different heights according to their pitches.

O admirabile Veneris idolum, a love song, was composed.

Most meters were discarded in favor of "prose."

The Church modes were compared to the modes of the ancient Greeks and given names which still exist in the language of counterpoint.

The shift to modern names was done by the monk Odo of Cluny. He ignored the secular major mode and adapted the "A"-"G" series to the Church modes, so that "A" rather than "C" was the basis of the second mode or Hypodorian. "A" was the lowest note, and "G" the octave of the Seventh or Mixolydian mode was the highest.

Letters of the alphabet had not repeated but had continued throughout the range of music, (cont.) until the modern usage was adopted.

A new note was introduced, situated one degree below the lowest A, and named after the Greek letter gamma. It was written "T."

The earliest attempt at harmony was the Diaphony or Organum. It was described by Hucbald, the Flemish monk, in a book called "Enchiridion Musicae." The authorship of the work has, however, been questioned.

The Czech song Hospodine promiluj ny ("Lord have mercy on us"), was attributed to Adalbert (second Bishop of Prague). Some feel the piece may have been composed at a later date.

Al Fārābī asserted that a scale has seven steps in the octave.

The term Nūba first referred to a group of musicians.

The bow, the bridge, and the fingerboard, were all derived from the monochord and were applied to the "Fidicula" or "Crwth."

The Sequence used on Easter Sunday was "Victimae paschali," the oldest one still in use.

The Wolfenbüttel manuscript was a collection of folk songs containing many of the oldest German secular songs.

The song "Mitten wir im Leben sind" was written at this time.

(to 950) Hucbaldus was the first to write a group of parts together in what could be considered

c.900(cont.)

a score.

(to c.1000) Liturgical drama developed as an outgrowth from Tropes. It involved the dramatic presentation of episodes from the Bible.

(to c.1000) An English manuscript showed a representation of an English fiddler with fiddle and bow. The former was the instrument that Chaucer called the Ribible, and that was known by the name (French form) "Rebec."

(to c.1125) Liége was an active musical center.

(to c.1200) Goliards (students in minor church orders who roamed Europe) wrote Latin songs, some had neumes with no staffs.

O Roma nobilis - a song in praise of Rome was written.

903

(to 903) The Papal reign of St. Leo V (born in Ardea).

904

(to 911) The Papal reign of St. Sergius III (born in Rome).

c.910

Hucbaldus invented a staff consisting of an indefinite number of lines. He wrote the syllables he intended to be sung between them.

Notker Balbulus made important literary contributions at St. Gall.

911

(to 913) The Papal reign of St. Anastasius III(born in Rome)

912

Notker Balbulus, a pupil of Marcellus, and a famous musician connected with the monastery of St. Gall, died.

c.912

(to 973) The Meistersinger attributed their origin to twelve great masters who supposedly were contemporaries under Emperor Otto I (912-973). They had performed for Pope Leo VIII as well as the Emperor Otto.

913

(to 914) The Papal reign of St. Landus (born in Sabina).

914

(to 928) The Papal reign of St. John X(born in Tossignano).

915

Regino of Prüm, who had divided music into musica naturalis and musica artificialis, died.

Tutilo, reputed to have invented tropes at St. Gall, died.

(to 921) Byzantine architecture: Achtamar, Church (total width, 44').

921

Edmund I the Deed-Doer (Saxon), King of England and Great Britain, was born (died 946).

c.921

Louis V d'Outremer, French King of the Carolingian Dynasty, was born(died 954).

922

(to 923) The reign of King Robert I (French King of the Carolingian Dynasty). He is frequently not counted in the regular succession of Kings

922(cont.)

having been elected by nobles. He was killed at the Battle of Soissons.

924

(to 939) The reign of King Athelstan (Saxon) who ruled England and Great Britain.

925

(to 988) The English prelate St. Dunstan, a skilled metal worker, erected an organ in Malmesbury Abbey. The pipes were made of brass. He was also instrumental in the installation of several other organs in England.

c.925

King Edred (Saxon) of England and Great Britain was born (died 955).

926

Heribald, a monk of St. Gall, was shocked by the Hungarians "shouting to their gods."

(to 936) The reign of King Rudolf (Raoul) Duke of Burgundy, French King of the Carolingian Dynasty.

927

Odo became abbot of Cluny.

928

(to 928) The Papal reign of St. Leo VI (born in Rome).

(to 931) The Papal reign of St. Stephen VII (VIII), born in Rome.

929

Charles III the Simple, French King of the Carolingian Dynasty, died (born 879).

930

Hucbaldus, a Monk of S. Amand sur l'Elnon in Flanders and a music theorist of renown, died (born 840).

931

(to 935) The Papal reign of St. John XI (born in Rome).

936

(to 939) The Papal reign of St. Leo VII (born in Rome).

(to 954) The reign of Louis IV d'Outremer, French King of the Carolingian Dynasty.

(to 973) The reign of Otto the Great, Roman emperor.

937

Athelstan, son of Edward the Elder, grandson of Alfred the Great, and King of the West -Saxons and Mercians, defeated the allied armies of Constantine, King of the Scots, and Olaf, leader of the Norsemen. A hundred years earlier the latter had established themselves in Ireland.

939

(to 942) The Papal reign of St. Stephen VIII (IX), born in Rome.

(to 946) The reign of King Edmund I, the Deed-Doer (Saxon) who ruled England and Great Britain.

c.940

Hugh Capet, French King of the Capetian Dynasty, was born (died 996).

941

King Lothair, French King of the Carolingian Dynasty, was born (died 986).

942

Odo, writer of music and Abbot of Cluny, died.

(to 946) The Papal reign of St. Marinus II (born in Rome).

943

King Edgar the Peaceful (Saxon) of England and Great Britain was born (died 975).

c.943

King Edwy the Fair (Saxon) of England and Great Britain was born (died 959).

946

(May 31) The Ceremonial Book of the Emperor Constantine Porphyrogenetes reported that Saracen ambassadors were received at the imperial palace. They came to negotiate the exchange of prisoners. For the event three portable organs were set up, one a golden organ to accompany the ceremonies of the Empress, and the other two, silver organs for the antiphonal performance of the polychronion, the acclamation addressed to the Emperor.

(to 955) The Papal reign of St. Agapitus II (born in Rome).

(to 955) The reign of King Edred (Saxon) over England and Great Britain.

950

Alfarabi (an Arab) was known in Christendom partly by way of borrowings from his works by the 12th-century Spaniard Domenicus Gundissalinus in his book De Divisione Philosophiae. Alfarabi drew much from Aristotle for his encyclopedia. He died in 950.

A large organ was erected at Winchester Cathedral. It was reported by Wulstan that it had 26 bellows and 400 pipes. It was installed by order of Bishop Elphege who died in 951.

(to 1050) American Indian ceramic: Pottery Bowl, Mimbres.

(to 1150) American Indian architecture: Chichen Itzá, El Castillo (102' high).

(to 1150) American Indian architecture: Chichen Itzá, Las Monjas (104'x30').

c.950

(to 1200) Early Byzantine notation appeared.

954

(to 986) The reign of King Lothair, French King of the Carolingian Dynasty.

955

(to 959) The reign of King Edwy the Fair (Saxon) over England and Great Britain.

(to 964) The Papal reign of St. John XII (born in Tusculum).

959

(to 975) The reign of King Edgar the Peaceful (Saxon) over England and Great Britain.

960

(to 1060) Considered to be the Ottonian golden century.

c.962

King Edward the Martyr (Saxon) of England and Great Britain was born (died 979).

963

Wulstan, the English poet who had described the Winchester

963(cont.)
Cathedral organ died.

(to 965) The Papal reign of St. Leo VIII (born in Rome). Confusion has existed regarding the legitimacy of claims. If the deposition of John was invalid, Leo was an antipope until after the end of Benedict's reign. If the deposition of John was valid, Leo was the legitimate Pope and Benedict an antipope.

964
(to 966) The Papal reign of St. Benedict V (born in Rome). Confusion has existed regarding the legitimacy of claims. If the deposition of John was invalid, Leo was an antipope until after the end of Benedict's reign. If the deposition of John was valid, Leo was the legitimate Pope and Benedict an antipope.

965
(to 972) The Papal reign of St. John XIII (born in Rome).

(to 975) The Concordia Regularis, instituted by Ethelwold, Bishop of Winchester, described the Quem quaeritis performance at Winchester as part of the third nocturne at Matins on Easter morning.

c.967
Louis V the Sluggard, French King of the Carolingian Dynasty, was born (died 987).

968
King Ethelred II, the Unready (Saxon) of England and Great Britain was born (died 1016).

c.968
Probably the oldest bit of (cont.) evidence enabling us to establish the presence of the lute in Europe was an ivory from Cordova.

c.970
Robert II the Pious, French King of the Capetian Dynasty, was born (died 1031).

972
Events like the marriage of Otto II to a Byzantine princess were examples of the influence of political events on the history of art.

973
(to 974) The Papal reign of St. Benedict VI (born in Rome).

974
(to 983) The Papal reign of St. Benedict VII (born in Rome)

975
(to 979) The reign of King Edward the Martyr (Saxon) over England and Great Britain.

c.975
The Orient underwent a Hellenization in music, science, medicine, mathematics and philosophy.

978
(to 1016) A manuscript Troparium, from the period of the reign of King Ethelred II, contained examples of mediaeval notation in which the position of the Neumae was expressed both with, and without the Rudimentary Stave.

979
(to 1016) The reign of King Ethelred II the Unready (Saxon) over England and Great Britain.

980

The organ of 980 in the monastery at Winchester, England had 10 pipes to each slider.

Bukharan Ibn-Sīnā, Islamic musicologist, was born (died 1037).

c.980

Illustrations from a manuscript of the Benedictional of St. Aethelwold, which was written at Hyde Abbey showed that chime bells in early times were mounted in campaniles. They had no appendages for ringing or swinging as they later did.

St. Gall monk, Ekkehard IV was born (died c.1060).

Guido d'Arezzo, writer on music and music theorist, was born (died c.1050).

983

(to 984) The Papal reign of St. John XIV (born in Pavia).

985

(to 996) The Papal reign of St. John XV (born in Rome).

986

(to 987) The reign of King Louis V the Sluggard, French King of the Carolingian Dynasty.

987

(to 996) The reign of King Hugh Capet, French King of the Capetian Dynasty.

988

Prince Vladimir was christened at Korsun (Crimea) and later married Princess Anna. He returned to Kiev with a Bulgarian Bishop, Michael, as well as many priests, and singers,

(cont.) Grecian and Slavic. They were sent to him with Anna by the Emperor and the Greek Patriarch of Constantinople.

989

The founder of the Russian state was converted to the Orthodox Church. He brought Byzantine artists to his Court to decorate the first churches as well as to teach art to pupils.

c.990

Several organs existed in Germany including St. Paul's, Erfurt's, St. James', Magdeburg's, and Halberstadt Cathedral's. They were small instruments but were viewed with amazement.

Ottonian miniature: Gospel -Book of Otto III.

The liturgy required a higher pitch on certain occasions than on others.

Poland accepted Christianity in its Western form. The country was then open to influences of Western civilization, including its music.

(to 1030) Fan K'uan, Chinese painter, was active.

(to 1100) The only secular music during this period was composed by goliards or wags.

991

The battle of Maldon was fought on the shores of a tidal river near the coast of Essex. A band of Viking marauders under Olaf Tryggvason had made a landing there.

c.993

King Edmund II Ironside (Saxon) of England and Great Britain was born (died 1016).

995

King Canute (Dane) of England and Great Britain was born (died 1035).

c.995

(to 1035) Danish poetry reached a high level of excellence during this period.

996

(to 1031) The reign of King Robert II the Pious, French King of the Capetian Dynasty. He is sometimes referred to as Robert I. He was a composer of chants.

(to 999) The Papal reign of St. Gregory V (born in Saxony).

997

The composition of the "Veni sancte spiritus" was attributed to King Robert II of France. It was frequently referred to as the "Golden Sequence" and was composed for use on Whit -Sunday.

999

(to 1003) The Papal reign of St. Sylvester II (born in Auvergne).

c.1000

According to a Welsh manuscript of the time of Charles I, Gryffudd ab Cynan, King of North Wales, held a congress, for the purpose of reforming the order of the Welsh bards. He invited several of the fraternity from Ireland to assist in carrying out the reforms. The most important of these reforms was the separation (cont.) of the professions of the bard and the minstrel. This meant that poetry and music which had been united would now be separated.

The St. Gall Cod. Lat., #393 was completed. It was a collection of folk songs.

Voces Hammerianae was the term applied to the syllables Do, Re, Mi, Fa, Sol, La, Si. This was the modern version of the series used by Guido d'Arezzo.

Composers worked on plain chant by placing a second part against a given cantus, in 1:1 counterpoint (note against note).

The position of the Precentor was established at Exeter, Salisbury, York, and Lincoln at this time.

Franco of Cologne named ligatures beginning with a breve, "ligaturoe cum proprietate;" those beginning with a long, "sine proprietate;" those beginning with a semibreve, "cum opposita proprietate;" those in which the last note was a long, "ligaturoe perfectoe;" those in which the last note was a breve, "imperfectoe."

Guido d'Arezzo used letters in connection with the solmisation of the hexachords although their presence as written characters was no longer needed.

A treatise on the construction of organs was included in a larger work on "Divers Arts" by a monk name Theophilus.

The means of gaining a fuller tone on an organ by a wide

c.1000(cont.)

mouth, and a more delicate one by a narrow mouth appeared at this time.

The distinction of long and short syllables was uncertain in the liturgy and was abandoned since notation was too vague to probe this distinction.

A few French sequences, like "Laetabundus exsultet" and "Gaudete vos fideles" existed in manuscripts. They were attractive march-like tunes, definitely in major keys and showed the characteristic leading tone a departure from the modal ideals of the Church.

Among treatises of the time was an anonymous vocabularium musicum, the earliest dictionary of music.

The mass was completed by the addition of the Gloria and the Credo sections.

A well preserved example of the Pandean Pipe appeared in a bas -relief from the Abbey of St. George de Boscherville, Normandy. It is probably the frestele, fretel, or fretian of the Ménétriers of the 12th and 13th centuries.

In Hungary, the fiddle was represented in a statue at the cathedral of Pécs.

The oldest manuscript in Poland that contained music was Gniezno Cathedral, No. 149.

French miniature: Minstrel playing the double chalumeau.

Catalonian miniature: King David and his musicians. Contained in (cont.) a Catalonian psalter.

Pictures of the "crwth trithant" appeared in manuscripts at this time.

Ma Fen, Chinese painter, was active at this time.

Romanesque architecture: Clermont-Ferrand, Notre Dame du Port (164'x85').

Romanesque architecture: Périgueux, St. Front. (main church, 185'x185').

Romanesque architecture: Vezelay, La Madeleine, nave (33' wide).

Byzantine architecture: Daphni, Monastic Church (47'x67').

Romanesque sculpture: Column: Jesus and the Samaritan at Hildesheim Cathedral.

Romanesque architecture: Poitiers, Notre Dame la Grande (58' wide x 59' high).

Romanesque embroideries: Bayeux Embroidery, Scene from Battle of Hastings (1'8½" high) and Arrival of the Normans at Pevensey (1'8½" high).

Chinese sculpture: Lohan, a glazed statue found in I-chou, China.

Saxon architecture: A tower imitating a timber structure at the church of Earls Barton, Northamptonshire.

French sculpture: Ivory tusk from the charterhouse at Portes (Ain).

c.1000(cont.)

Romanesque miniature: Constellation Figure. Aratus: "Phaenomena." Northern French School.

Chartres France: Alleluia Angelus was written, 2 part organa with contrary motion polyphonic sections.

Gregorian Chant was cultivated in Spain.

A manuscript contained "Descriptiones et Delineationes Instrumentorum Musicorum."

Egyptian Native poetry, mainly religious, was written. It was stimulated by great musical activity.

The eloquent homilies of Alfric brought the earliest period of English literature to an end.

The heroic poem of Beowulf appeared in manuscript known as "Cotton Vitellius A xv."

The single red reference line for f was in use.

Staff notation did not exist in the Orient. It was, however, brought in from the West at this time.

Music up to this time was primarily vocal and essentially melodic.

The text of Victimae Paschali was written at this time according to Rambachius.

A philosopher, known as Franco of Cologne, was noted for his knowledge of Mathematics, Alchemy, Judicial Astrology and Magic.

From this time on hundreds of sequences were written and sung.

Neumes began to be arranged above and below an imaginary line to indicate pitch and 2,3, and 4 line staffs were developing for use in Gregorian Chant.

(to c.1100) Free Organum developed to a large extent during this period under the leadership of Guido d'Arezzo.

(to c.1100) Indian architecture: Mt. Abu, Jain Temple.

(to c.1100) Gregorian Chant was generally accepted in Hungary.

(to c.1100) Accents were the earliest forms of notes used in the Christian Church, and it was not until this time that they began to be superseded by the definite notation of Guido Aretino.

(to c.1100) The songs of the Troubadours received strong impetus as a result of the awakened desire for intellectual pursuits.

(to c.1100) Many of the sequences extensively used were fine specimens written by great Hymnologists who wrote during this period of high productivity.

(to c.1100) Though inappropriate the term "Romanesque painting" served to designate what followed Carolingian and Ottonian painting.

(to 1300) American Indian sculpture: Stone Figure, Stela Bennett, Tiahuanaco (24'high).

(to c.1300) In Hungary, the subject of the charming anecdote

c.1000(cont.)

preserved in the anonymous Vita major of St. Gellért, apostle of Hungary, Bishop of Csanád, was folk song. He also served as a close adviser to St. Stephen, the King.

(to c.1400) Isaac drew upon many writers for his sequence texts. Among them were Notker, Abelard, and Adam de St. Victor whose lives spanned this period.

1001

(to 1301) During this period the court of the Kings of the House of Árpád was connected by ties of blood as well as by marriage with Byzantine, Polish, German, Italian, French, and English courts.

1002

The monastery of Basilians was founded at Grottaferrata, near Rome.

1003

(to 1003) The Papal reign of St. John XVII (born in Rome).

1004

(to 1009) The Papal reign of St. John XVIII (born in Rome).

c.1004

Edward the Confessor (Saxon), ruler of Great Britain and England, was born (died 1066).

1005

Pre-Romanesque architecture: León, San Isidoro, Panteón de los Reyes (25'x25').

1007

(to 1015) Romanesque sculpture: The Creation of Eve, Relief. St. Bernard's door, Cathedral, Hildesheim.

c.1007

(to 1014) Ottonian miniature: Christ Talking to His Disciples. Pericopes of Henri II.

1008

Berno became Abbot of Reichenau.

King Henry I, French King of the Capetian Dynasty, was born (died 1060).

1009

(to 1012) The Papal reign of St. Sergius IV (born in Rome).

(to 1019) Romanesque architecture: Tournus, St. Philibert, longitudinal section (nave 89' long).

c.1010

Ottonian miniature: The Vessels of Wrath. Apocalypse of Bamberg.

Guido d'Arezzo substituted his Hexachords for the Tetrachords of the Greek System. He was fully aware of the value of this principle, adapted it to another set of syllables, sufficiently extended to six sounds instead of four.

Two more black lines were added to the Stave; one, above the yellow line; and the other, between the yellow and red ones.

Voces Aretinae. A name given to the syllables, Ut, Re, Mi, Fa, Sol, La was used first by Guido d'Arezzo for Solmisation.

The method invented by Guido d'Arezzo, recognized the use of six syllables only - Ut, Re, Mi, Fa, Sol, La, suggested by the initial and post -caesural syllables of the

c.1010(cont.)

Hymn, "Ut queant laxis." The completion of the Octave was provided for by the use of several changes in the position of the root-syllable, ut.

Winchester Troper contained about 150 two part organa for Mass and Office.

1012

(to 1024) The Papal reign of St. Benedict VIII (born in Tusculum).

1013

Roman architecture: Florence, San Miniato, facade was started at this time (80' wide).

Hermanus Contractus, theoretician and writer on music was born (died 1055).

c.1014

The Credo was definitely established in the Roman Mass.

1015

Bronze sculpture: Adam and Eve after the Fall. On the bronze doors of Hildesheim Cathedral.

1016

King Ethelred II the Unready of England and Great Britain, died (born 968).

(to 1016) The reign of Edmund II Ironside (Saxon) over England and Great Britain.

(to 1035) The reign of King Canute (Dane) over England and Great Britain.

c.1016

King Harold I Harefoot (Dane) of England and Great Britain, was born (died 1040).

1017

Byzantine architecture: Chernigov, Cathedral of the Transfiguration (122'x126').

c.1018

King Hardecanute of England and Great Britain (Dane) was born (died 1042).

c.1020

King Harold II of England and Great Britain (Saxon) was born.

Anglo-Saxon ideas of heaven and hell were strikingly depicted in a drawing from a manuscript done at Winchester.

1022

Guido d'Arezzo was invited to Rome by Pope Benedict VIII, who had heard that he had invented a new method of teaching music.

Notker Labeo, the author of the first-known writings in German that dealt with music, died.

c.1024

Guido d'Arezzo's "Micrologus" was written.

Guido Aretinus, a Benedictine Monk from Tuscany, eliminated difficulties connected with the Tetrachords of the Greek tonal system. He proposed a new arrangement based upon a more convenient division of the scale into Hexachords - groups of six sounds, so disposed as to place a diatonic semitone between the third and fourth notes of each series, the remaining intervals being represented by tones.

(to 1032) The Papal reign of St. John XIX (born in Tusculum).

Wipo, the composer of the Easter sequence, Victimae Paschali

c.1024(cont)
Laudes was born (died c.1048).

c.1025
Bukharan Ikn-Sīnā, an Islamic musicology master, based doctrines on Greek traditions. He argued against "comparing musical ratios with the stars or with mental states, since this is the habit of those who do not keep the various sciences apart nor know what they directly or indirectly include." He defined the Arabic term "tarkib" as "an ornament in which two consonant notes mingle in the same stroke. The noblest consonances are large intervals and among these the octave and the fourth are the best."

In a letter, addressed to his friend Brother Michael, Guido spoke of the value, as an aid to memory, of the first six hemistichs of the Hymn for the festival of St. John the Baptist, "Ut queant laxis."

The invention of the Fa fictum, probably by Guido d'Arezzo.

The invention of accidentals resulted from the division of the scale into hexachords. This arrangement was generally attributed to Guido d'Arezzo (1025). It might well have been at a later date.

1027
William I, the Conqueror (Normandy) of England and Great Britain, was born (died 1087).

c.1027
Guido d'Arezzo wrote the Antiphonary.

Guido d'Arezzo was invited by Pope John XIX to demonstrate his (cont.) method.

c.1030
Guido d'Arezzo's goal was to educate singers quickly so that they could sing unfamiliar melodies by reading written notation. His work on this subject was called "Micrologus de disciplína artis músicae." He also introduced the older Oriental solmisation. He wrote in Free Organum although Strict Organum was recognized. Parallel fourths were considered pleasant and less harsh than parallel fifths.

1031
(to 1060) The reign of King Henry I, French King of the Capetian Dynasty.

1032
(to 1044) The Papal reign of St. Benedict IX (born in Tusculum). If the triple removal of Benedict IX was not valid, Sylvester III, Gregory VI, and Clement II were antipopes.

1035
(to 1040) The reign of King Harold I Harefoot (Dane) over England and Great Britain.

1036
Su Shih, Chinese author of "Miscellaneous Notes on the Lute," was born (died 1101).

1037
Bukharan Ibn-Sīnā, Islamic musicologist, died (born 980).

1040
(to 1042) The reign of King Hardecanute (Dane) over England and Great Britain.

c.1040

Mary Magdalen laments were numerous and set to music with great care and with great dramatic inflection.

(to 1050) Hermanus Contractus invented a new system of notation in which letters indicated intervals in melodies: e=equisonus, u=unison, s=semitone, t=tone, D-diatessaron, ▷-diapente. Dots were used for higher and lower pitches. He also composed many sequences while at Reichenau Monastery on Lake Constance. The best known of these were Ave Praeclara Maris Stella, Salve Regina, and Alma Redemptoris Mater. He combined sequence and antiphon and from them he created an organic and serious musical work.

1042

(to 1066) The reign of King Edward the Confessor (Saxon) over England and Great Britain.

1045

(to 1045) The Papal reign of St. Sylvester III (born in Rome).

(to 1045) The Papal reign of St. Benedict IX (2nd time), birthplace unknown.

(to 1046) The Papal reign of St. Gregory VI (born in Rome).

1046

(to 1047) The Papal reign of St. Clement II (born in Saxony).

(to 1196) Romanesque architecture: Milan, Sant' Ambrogio (length including atrium, 390'; 92' wide).

1047

(to 1048) The Papal reign of (cont.) St. Benedict IX (3rd time), birthplace unknown.

1048

Berno, writer on music, died.

(to 1048) The Papal reign of St. Damasus II (born in Bavaria).

(to 1054) The composer Bruno, Count of Egisheim in Alsace, thereafter Pope Leo IX, created a Gloria in excelsis Deo, which the Church refers to as Gloria I among the Cantus ad libitum.

c.1048

Wipo, the composer of the Easter sequence, Victimae Paschali Laudes, died (born c.1024). He was Chaplain for the German Emperor Henry III.

Guido d'Arezzo founded a school of singing at Rome. This fact is not universally accepted.

1049

(to 1054) The Papal reign of St. Leo IX (born in Alsace).

c.1050

Guido d'Arezzo, writer on music and music theorist, died at Avellano (born c.980).

Romanesque miniature: The Rain of Fire and Blood. Beatus de Liebana: "Commentaries on the Apocalypse." Abbey of St. Sever.

Romanesque miniature: Crwth player. From the Tropary of St. Martial of Limoges.

Three outstanding clerics presented the musical liturgy with such success that the Church

c.1050(cont.)
has retained them.

The "Ars Cantus mensurabilis" by Franco of Cologne was written, according to Fétis and many others, at this time. He was also credited with inventing the table of time.

(to c.1200) During this period the harmonic basis was that consonances in 1 part writing were unisons, fourths, fifths and octaves; thirds and sixths were treated as dissonances; 2nds and 7ths were used as passing tones and appoggiaturas.

1051
Mi Fei, Chinese painter, was born (died 1107).

1052
King Philip I, French King of the Capetian Dynasty, was born(died 1108).

1053
Three Greek teachers went to Kiev and introduced "8-mode singing" in Russia. They brought with them examples of church chant books, which they used in their teaching direction in Kiev, as well as Rostov, and other cities.

Japanese architecture: Uji, Byodoin Temple, Phoenix Hall.

1054
John of Damascus had become a saint in both the Greek and Roman Churches when the schism finally took place between the two in 1054. There had been trouble, however, before this date.

1055
(February) Hermanus Contractus, (cont.) theoretician and writer on music, died (born 1013).

(to 1057) The Papal reign of St. Victor II (born in Germany).

1056
King Henry III of Germany died.

c.1056
King William II Rufus (Normandy) of England and Great Britain was born (died 1100).

1057
Jocho, Japanese sculptor, died. Known for Head of Amida, Byodoin Temple, Uji (9'8"high).

Ambrosian Chant was employed exclusively at the monastery of Monte Cassino until monks under order from Pope Stephen IX substituted Gregorian.

(to 1058) The Papal reign of St. Stephen IX (X) (born in Lorraine).

1059
(to 1061) The Papal reign of St. Nicholas II (born in Burgundy).

1060
(to 1108) The reign of King Philip, French King of the Capetian Dynasty.

(to 1204) Romanesque architecture: Lucca, Cathedral (Facade 84' wide).

c.1060
St. Gall Monk, Ekkehard IV died (born c.980).

Franco, Scholasticus Leodiensis Ecclesiae flourished under the Emperor, Henry III.

c.1060(cont.)

He was credited by some (Fétis, Burney & Hawkins) with the tracts on measured music usually attributed to Franco of Cologne.

1061

In the Hungarian anti-Christian Rebellion of 1061, pagan shamans used old songs to arouse the people to murder the bishops and priests of the new, official religion.

(to 1073) The Papal reign of St. Alexander II (born in Milan).

1062

Romanesque architecture: Caen, La Trinité (79' wide).

1063

Byzantine architecture: Venice, St. Mark's (249'x168'). This cathedral was remarkably important to music history because of the antiphonal music to be composed there many years later by G. Gabrielli.

(to 1092) Romanesque architecture: Pisa, Cathedral (320'x230').

1064

(to 1077) Romanesque architecture: Caen, St. Étienne (360'x73').

(to 1196) Romanesque architecture: Milan, Sant'Ambrogio (total length 390').

1065

King Alfonso VI of Castile was born (died 1109).

1066

The Antiphonary of León was written.

(to 1066) The reign of King (cont.) Harold II (Saxon) over England and Great Britain.

The Norman Conquest brought about strong French influence on English civilization.

The Normans were to all intents and purposes Frenchmen.

French had become the polite language of England and therefore the literary language of all except exponents of Latin.

William the Conqueror was crowned King of England at London.

(to 1087) The reign of William I the Conqueror (Normandy) over England and Great Britain.

(to 1095) Chanson de Roland, the oldest and the most important "Song of deeds" was composed during this period.

(to 1500) Middle English was the language spoken in England during this period.

1068

King Henry I, Beauclerc (Normandy) of England and Great Britain was born (died 1135).

1071

The "superstition of Toledo" was suppressed in the Christian held part of Spain and the Roman Rite was substituted.

William IX, Duke of Aquitaine (seventh Count of Poitiers) the oldest known troubador, was born (died 1127). Certain sources give his date of birth as 1087.

1073

(to 1085) The Papal reign of St. Gregory VII (born in Tuscany).

1075

The oldest known copy of the Sursum Corda and Prefaces was from this date.

(to 1128) Romanesque architecture: Santiago de Compostela (308'x207').

c.1075

The first ideas of harmony derived from the species of counterpoint referred to as Discantus. This was a popular device consisting of combining two independent tunes.

1079

Abelard, chant composer, was born (died 1142).

(to 1093) Romanesque architecture: Winchester Cathedral (80'wide including aisles).

1080

The Rubenian came to rule in Lesser Armenia in 1080, after the collapse of Greater Armenia.

(to 1096) Romanesque architecture: Toulouse, St. Sernin. Transverse section through nave (110' wide).

1081

Louis VI the Fat, French King of the Capetian Dynasty, was born (died 1137).

Abbot Suger of St. Denis, a great statesman and historian as well as monk, was born (died 1151).

c.1081

Teutonic tapestry: A "Longship" (cont.) of the Viking type with dragon's heads, as used by the Normans in the Invasion of England. Tapestry from Bayeux Cathedral. On the same tapestry King Harold was pictured swearing an oath to Duke William of Normandy prior to the former's return to England.

1082

Hui Tsung, Chinese painter, born (died 1135).

1083

Franco continued in office at Liege until at least this year.

1084

(to 1108) Early Christian architecture: Rome, San Clemente. (nave and apse length 129'; nave width 35').

1085

Following recapture of Toledo King Alfonso VI made the Roman Rite obligatory there, in spite of opposition from the people.

1086

(to 1087) The Papal reign of St. Victor III (born in Benevento).

1087

(to 1100) The reign of King William II Rufus (Normandy) over England and Great Britain.

William IX Duke of Aquitaine (seventh Count of Poitiers) the oldest known troubador was born (died 1127). Certain sources give his date of birth as 1071.

1088

Islamic architecture: Isfahan, Congregational Mosque, interior of north dome.

1088

(to 1099) The Papal reign of St. Urban II (born in France).

(to 1130) Romanesque architecture: Cluny, Abbey.

1090

The writer St. Bernard was born (died 1153).

Romanesque paintings: The Virgin, and, Woman Pierced with a Lance, Known as Luxury. Crypt of the Church of Tavant.

c.1090

The advent of the Troubadours brought about a decisive change in knightly ideology.

Ut tuo propitiatus was written (organum).

The marriage of Alfonso VI of Castile to Constance of Burgundy brought an influx of French pilgrims.

Huge keys or levers began to be used for playing the organ.

The earliest organ with a keyboard was erected in the Cathedral at Magdeburg.

The verse-writers took their name from "trobar" or "trouver" and they first appeared in the southern provinces of France.

(to c.1500) Novgorod produced a number of extraordinary works - simple and powerful, brilliant in colour, supple in design, intellectual in conception.

1091

Wilhelm, Abbot of the Monastery of Hirsau in the Black Forest, author of De Musica et Tonis, died.

1095

Many of the songs of the troubadours and trouvères dealt with the Crusades. The first Crusade was proclaimed by Pope Urban II at this time.

1096

One of the earliest Troubadours, William, Duke of Guienne, joined the first Crusade.

(to 1133) Romanesque architecture: Durham, Cathedral was built (total length 469', nave 39'x72' high). The vault was completed at a later date.

1099

(to 1118) The Papal reign of St. Paschal II (born in Ravenna).

1100

(to 1135) The reign of King Henry I Beauclerc (Normandy) over England and Great Britain.

c.1100

John Cotton, a leading English theorist, may well have been named Joannes of Liége. His treatise, De Musica, included a description of the progress made in the development of free organum. His most pertinent rule stated "If the main voice is ascending, the accompanying part should descend and vice versa." He also asserted that a singer with no theoretical training was useless.

A treatise, ad organum faciendum was written by an anonymous French author.

King Stephen of Blois (Normandy), who ruled over England and Great Britain, was

c.1100(cont.)

born (died 1154).

Bagpipes were known in England.

Theogerus, Bishop of Metz, permitted the elongation of the Scale, either authentic or plagal, to a Tone above and a Tone below its normal limits.

Romanesque architecture: Florence, Baptistry (diam. 90').

Romanesque miniature: The Maries At The Tomb. Sacramentary of the Cathedral of St. Étienne, Limoges.

Martyrdom of Santa Julita (Detail of an Altar Dedicated to Santa Julita and San Quirico). Durro.

By this time popular music was performed almost entirely by roving musicians who, since they were involved with actors, acrobats and low-class women, led a disorganized life.

With the increase in the number of keys on the organ, two or three pipes were added sounding the fifth and octave to the unison.

The "Festum Asinorum" was celebrated at Beauvais and Sens.

The carol, "Prose de l'âne." was sung, at Beauvais, and Sens, on the Feast of the Circumcision from this time on.

"Belle Erembor" and "l'Enfant-Gérard" were anonymous compositions of some note.

The hymn "Christ ist uferstanden" was written.

Ireland's music and the ancient school of harp-playing enjoyed a high reputation and were praised in the writings of Brompton, Giraldus Cambrensis, and John of Salisbury.

Music of this time had no bar lines.

The guitar was popular in Europe.

The earliest written music for the guitar was that of the troubadours.

The most famous early Polish music was the monophonic composition Bogurodzica ("Mother of God"). The opening melody was the same as a Kyrie from a 12th-century Litany to All Saints.

In Bohemia, the liturgy of the Eastern Church survived until this time when it was replaced by the Roman.

A strong influence on polyphony was provided by the English "gymel" (cantus gemellus). The melody was accompanied by quasi-parallel, major and minor, thirds and sixths.

A bell maker recommended choosing any arbitrary weight of metal to start with and calling it C, then adding an eighth of this weight for D, and eighth of the new weight for E, and continuing in this manner. He did not realize that weight was not the only factor involved.

The dignity of Precentor was established at Rouen, Amiens, Chichester, Wells, Lichfield, and Hereford at this time.

c.1100(cont.)

A manuscript made use of letters with neumes.

An example of English Organum, Nobilis humilis, was composed.

Spervogel, an important composer, lived. His works were recorded in the Jena manuscript. It was secular monophonic music.

Plainsong Passion developed as more dramatic character was given to its presentation; parts of Christ, Narrator, and Crowd were sung in inflected monotone by priests. Different registers and tempos were used for the three parts.

The revolution of this century changed Europe in many ways. The increase and establishment of lay power brought about the creation of a secular army of clerks and lay officials.

The Renaissance of this time fostered Gothic art. It had germinated in physical and mental exploration, based on the principle of free inquiry.

The great master of Arthurian romance in France was Chrétien de Troyes.

The rigid and solemn arrangement of the sculptures of Arles are reflected in the spirit of many illuminated manuscripts of this time.

The century of the Crusades.

Gothic window: Annunciation, West central window, Cathedral, Chartres (41 3/8"x40 1/8").

Byzantine architecture: Athens, Little Metropolitan Church (cont.) (38'x25').

Islamic architecture: Isfahan, Congregational Mosque, northwest Iwan.

Gothic architecture: Laon, Cathedral (nave and aisles 67' wide; vaults 78' high).

Romanesque sculpture: Tympanum, St. Pierre, Moissac (18'8"wide).

Romanesque architecture: Ely, Cathedral (nave 208' long x 62' high).

Romanesque architecture: Iffley, Church.

Romanesque architecture: Saint-Gilles (porch 75' wide).

Romanesque architecture: Pavia, San Michele (facade 95' wide).

Japanese painting: Toba Sojo, Hare Chasing a Monkey. Kozan-ji Temple, Kyoto (1' high).

Japanese sculpture: Kichijoten, Joruri-ji Temple, Kyoto (2'11" high).

Liang K'ai, The Priest Hui-neng (2'6" high).

Indian architecture: Angkor Vat (Central tower, 200' high).

Romanesque fresco: Virgin (Detail of the "Wise Virgins"), from San Quirce de Pedret.

Miniature: Harp player, from the De Musica of Boethius.

Painting: The ecstasy of Gregory before the Deacon Peter.

Sculpture: Lyre player (Abbey of Cluny).

c.1100(cont.)

Painting: Guido d'Arezzo and his disciple Theodal examining a monochord (Codex 51, fol. 35 v.

Architecture: Facade of the Basilica of St. Denis.

Romanesque painting: Apostle (Detail of Mural Paintings in the Apse). Ginestarre de Cardós.

(to 1125) Romanesque painting: The Drunkenness of Noah, Nave of the Church of St. Savin.

(to 1125) Entry into Jerusalem, Church of St. Martin de Vicq, Nohant-Vicq.

(to 1130) Chinese painting: Li T'ang, Man on a Water Buffalo (10"x11").

(to c.1200) Romanesque architecture: Mainz Cathedral (interior 90' high).

(or c.1200) Mystery Plays were stylish and popular. Christmas carols trace their descent from this time.

(to c.1225) A "Gradual Cartusianum," was composed wholly in transitional neumes.

(to c.1300) Troubadours, poet -musicians from southern France, flourished.

(to c.1300) The French Rondeau was, in its oldest form, a song sung while performing a round -dance.

(to c.1300) For England, and all of western Europe, this was a time of intense intellectual activity.

(to c.1300) The vièle was a (cont.) most important instrument.

(to c.1300) Beata Viscera and Conductus with melismas were written.

(to c.1300) Monophonic conductus, Latin counterpart of Troubadour and Trouvére Poetry was being composed.

(to c.1300) Proper portion of Mass was composed as Organa.

(to c.1300) When convenience demanded the practice of changing the position of the clefs from one line to another, there was little to distinguish the notation of the 12th and 13th century from that now used for plain chaunt.

(to c.1300) The most prominent Troubadours and/or Trouvères were William, Duke of Guienne; Richard I; Pierre Rogier; Bernard de Ventadour; Bertran de Born; Arnaut Daniel; Guirant de Borneil; the Chatelain de Coucy; Blondel des Nesles; Thibaut de Champagne and King of Navarre.

(to c.1300) The prime of the troubadours was past when the Troubadour Academy of Toulouse was founded for the culture and preservation of their art.

(to c.1300) The pastorale was not to be confused with the pastourelle, which was an irregular form of poetry popular in France during this period.

(to c.1300) Sculptures: Three old men of the Apocalypse with psaltery, viol, and rebec. Chartres, Cathedral.

c.1100(cont.)

(to c.1300) Like English discant fauxbourdon used parallel thirds and sixths, but the lead melody was in the upper voice, so that the middle voice accompanied at the lower fourth, and the bass voice, at the lower sixth.

(to c.1300) In certain areas the polyphony heard in the popular music was found to function according to diverse forms and principles. The most elaborate of these was similar to the organum found in the written music of Europe during this period.

(to c.1300) This was a period of great upheaval in Bohemia.

(to c.1300) In Hungary, the "storytellers" formed an officially recognized group, supported by royal donations.

(to c.1300) The Meistersinger traced their origin to twelve great masters who theoretically were contemporaries under Emperor Otto I and sang for him and Pope Leo VIII. However, these twelve masters were really Minnesinger who lived during that period.

(to c.1300) Adam de la Halle was one of the most prominent figures in the long line of Trouvères who contributed so much to the formation of the French language.

(to c.1400) Chansons of this period were often altered in transcribing.

(to c.1450) Middle or Round Notation was used during this period.

(to c.1500) There was no (cont.) musical evidence of the use of the organ in Germany earlier than the 15th century, however, literary reports referred to its use as early as the 12th century.

(to c.1600) There was a great difference between the Gothic world and the modern world built on its ruins.

1101

Su Shih, Chinese author of "Miscellaneous Notes on the Lute," died (born 1036).

1102

(to 1121) American Indian architecture: Arizona, Montezuma's Castle.

1104

Chêng Ch'iao, Chinese author of "On the Proper Classification of Songs," was born (died 1162).

(to 1113) Candlestick of gilt bell metal. Made for Gloucester Cathedral.

1105

(to 1128) Romanesque architecture: Angoulême, Cathedral (50' wide; domes, 68' high).

1107

Mi Fei, Chinese painter, died (born 1051).

(to 1118) Brass sculpture: Reiner Van Huy: Font, St. Bartholomew, Liége (Belgium).

c.1107

(to c.1109) One of the most interesting examples of Laudes Regiae, from the Dalmation city of Zara, was of Hungarian origin.

1108

(to 1137) The reign of

1108(cont.)

King Louis VI the Fat, French King of the Capetian Dynasty.

1109

Abbot Aelred of Rievaulx, English historian, was born (died 1166).

King Alfonso VI of Castile died (born 1065).

c.1110

Romanesque sculpture: Tympanum: Last Judgment (West Portal, St. Lazare, Autun).

The French School used Transitional Organum - "Verbum Bonum" polyphonic sequence, 3 strophes of music and six stanzas of text. Note against Note.

"Mira lege" metrical song was written (St. Martial). It was not plainsong; some use of 2 notes against one; 5ths, 3rds, 4ths frequent; contrary and parallel motion.

In a French manuscript an organum for two voices on the Gregorian melody "Benedicamus Domino" was one of several examples.

Miniature: Horn, harp, viol, and bell players (from the Psalter of St. Alban's Abbey).

In Hungary, "Kürt" (horn) and "sip" (pipe) were incorporated in the names of towns.

1112

In Hungary, the singing of unauthorized chants was prohibited by the Synod of Esztergom.

(to 1152) Indian sculpture: The Bayon, Angkor Thom (Face 9' high).

1113

Sigebertus Gemblacensis wrote in 1113 (the year of his death) in "Chronicon" that in the year 1028 "Guido indicated these six sounds by means of the finger-joints of the left hand, following out the rising and falling of the same, with eye and ear, throughout a full Octave."

c.1113

The font of a church in Liége (Belgium), made at this time, provided an example of the part taken by the theologians in advising the artists.

c.1115

Les Miracles de Notre Dame, by Gautier de Coinci, was an excellent early example of the use of the Alexandrine. It appeared first in a manuscript in the "Pèlerinage de Charlemagne à Jérusalem."

The earliest notice of a monochord among musical instruments was found in Wace's "Brut d'Angleterre," "Symphonies, psalterions, monachordes."

(to 1180) Bishop of Chartres John of Salisbury was one of the earliest opponents of musical practices which stemmed from the Gothic period.

1118

(to 1119) The Papal reign of St. Gelasius II (born in Gaeta).

1119

(to 1124) The Papal reign of St. Callistus II (born in Burgundy).

1120

Albert Van Os, referred to as "Albert the Great," was the earliest known organ-builder. A

1120(cont.)

priest as well as organ-builder, he built the St. Nicholas organ at Utrecht.

Lootens wrote an account of a Dutch organ which was erected in the church of St. Nicholas at Utrecht.

c.1120

Gothic architecture: Morienval, Church, with ambulatory vault, was built.

1121

King Louis VII the Young, French King of the Capetian Dynasty, was born (died 1180).

1123

Mural: Lazarus at the Gates of Dives, San Clemente De Tahull.

1124

(to 1130) The Papal reign of St. Honorius II (born in Fiagnano).

c.1125

Romanesque mural: The Fall of Man, Maderuelo.

Composer of guitar music, Bernard de Ventadour, was born.

1126

William, Duke of Guienne, died. There is a strong possibility that the man referred to here is the same as William IX, Duke of Aquitaine.

1127

William IX, Duke of Aquitaine (seventh Count of Poiters) the oldest known Troubador, died (born 1071 or 1087).

The name Stradivari was erroneously claimed by Fétis to have appeared in the municipal ar-

(cont.) chives of Cremona.

1130

(to 1143) The Papal reign of St. Innocent II (born in Rome).

(to 1141) Jaufré Rudel, troubadour, was active during this period.

c.1130

Romanesque sculpture: Tympanum: Christ Sending Forth the Apostles (31'4" wide).

Romanesque sculpture: Tympanum: Christ in majesty surrounded by celestial musicians (from the portal of St. Peter's at Moissac).

Adam became a monk in the Abbey of St. Victor, which was located outside Paris.

1132

Romanesque architecture: Palermo, Cappella Palatina (108'x42').

(to 1144) Abbot Suger of St. Denis gave Gothic architecture impetus by completing a new west front and building a chevet.

1133

King Henry II (Plantagenet) of England and Great Britain was born (died 1189).

1135

Maimonides, Jewish philosopher, physician, and writer on music, was born (died 1204).

King Henry I Beauclerc (Normandy) of England and Great Britain, died (born 1068).

Hui Tsung, Chinese painter, died (born 1082).

1135(cont.)

Ts'ai Yüan-ting, Chinese author of a new book of music, was born (died 1198).

The Chapel Royal was mentioned in the Red Book of the Exchequer. The first reference to choristers, however, came during the reign of Henry V.

(to 1154) The reign of King Stephen of Blois (Normandy) over England and Great Britain.

1137

(to 1147) Romanesque painting: Saints Gereon, Willimarus, Gall and the Martyrdom of St. Ursula with her 11,000 Maidens (from a Calendar manuscript).

(to 1180) The reign of King Louis VII the Young, French King of the Capetian Dynasty.

1140

Santiago de Compostela wrote "Congaudeant Catholici" "Benedicamus Domino" and "Cunctipontens genitor."

"Jesu dulcis memoria" was composed by St. Bernard.

(to 1149) A French master erected a new church, the Church of the Priory of the Holy Sepulchre in Jerusalem.

c.1140

The rubric conductus was first mentioned in two manuscripts.

The Codex Calixtinus of Santiago showed strong evidence of French origin.

1142

Abelard, chant composer, died (born 1079).

1143

(to 1144) The Papal reign of St. Celestine II (born in Citta di Castello).

1144

(to 1145) The Papal reign of St. Lucius II (born in Bologna).

1145

Romanesque architecture: Cefalù, Cathedral, was begun (facade 95' wide).

(to 1153) The Papal reign of St. Eugene III (born in Pisa).

c.1145

(to c.1155) Romanesque sculpture: Tympanum: Christ in Mastery, with Symbols of Evangelists.

(to 1170) Gothic sculpture: Head of Jesse and Angel (Chartres, Cathedral).

(to 1170) Gothic sculpture: January, February, etc. (Cathedral, Chartres).

(to 1170) Gothic sculpture: King's Portal (Cathedral, Chartres).

(to 1170) Gothic sculpture: Royal, Portal. Cathedral, Chartres (20'6" high).

(to 1170) Gothic sculpture: North Portal. Cathedral, Chartres.

1147

Giraldus Cambrensis, historian of Welsh music, was born (died 1220). He was actually named Gerald de Barri and was an Englishman.

Marcabru of Gascony, troubadour, died(birthdate unknown).

1147(cont.)

The Crusade united nobility of the north and the south. Foreigners who visited the courts of Eleanor of Aquitaine's two daughters provided a liason between several provinces.

c.1150

Blondel de Nesles, poet and trouvére from Northern France, was born (died c.1200).

Romanesque architecture: Arles, St. Trophîme (porch c.40' wide).

The mathematician Gerlandus, was canon of the abbey of St. Paul at Besançon.

Romanesque painting: St. Clement; Martyrdom of St. Pancras, Church of St. Léger, Ébreuil.

Domenicus Gundissalinus, translator and propagator, was active in support of Al-Farabi's ideas.

The "Dies irae" was written by Thomas of Celano and sung in the Requiem Mass.

The term organista appeared at Chartres but carrying the meaning of clericus cantor or singing cleric.

Canon de Béthune, a prominent trouvère, was born (died c.1224).

Romanesque painting: Temptation of Christ. Church of St. Aignan, Brinay.

When Gothic style was first developed, Europe was sparsely populated by peasants, and monasteries and baronial castles were the main centers of power and learning.

Romanesque illuminated manuscript: The Annunciation (From a Swabian Gospel manuscript).

The great period of Romanesque art ended.

(to c.1185) Leonin, one of the greatest and most influential composers of organa, wrote Magnus Liber Organi de Gradali et Antiphonario (34 pieces for offices, 59 for mass) during this period.

(to c.1190) The early Minnesinger comprised three groups. The first during the period, 1150-1190, when the movement started and before French influence asserted itself.

(to c.1200) The Ars antiqua embraced this period.

(to c.1325) Generally known as the Early Gothic Period of Music.

1151

Abbot Suger of St. Denis died (born 1081).

1152

The marriage of King Louis VII of France to Eleanor of Aquitaine was annulled. She then married Henry of Anjou, founder of the Angevin line of English Kings. While in England she encouraged the troubadour movement and continued the attitude she had displayed in Aquitaine and in Northern France.

Bernard de Ventadour went to England, probably because Eleanor of Aquitaine had married Henry of Anjou.

1153

The writer St. Bernard died (born 1090).

(to 1154) The Papal reign of St. Anastasius IV (born in Rome).

1154

The Plantagenet line was founded in England by Henry II.

(to 1159) The Papal reign of St. Adrian IV (born in England).

(to 1189) The reign of King Henry II (Plantagenet) over England and Great Britain.

1155

(to 1191) Gothic architecture: Senlis, Cathedral spire (total height 250').

c.1155

The monochord, which had been used in teaching for many years, was mentioned in a poem which contained a list of instruments performed upon for practical purposes.

1156

(June 9) Frederick Barbarossa, the first Hohenstaufen to become Holy Roman Emperor, married Beatrix of Bergundy.

1157

King Richard I, Coeur de Lion (Plantagenet) of England and Great Britain, was born (died 1199). He became a noted trouvére in his own right.

1158

(to 1161) Roman architecture: Vladimir, Cathedral of the Dormitian (104'x119').

1159

(to 1181) The Papal reign of St. Alexander III (born in (cont.) Siena).

1160

(to 1220) Perotin, generally regarded as the greatest composer of discant, substituted new clausulae in discant style for discant and free rhythm sections in organa from Leonin's Magnus Liber; increased the number of parts in organa from two to three and even rarely four; and developed clausulae.

c.1160

Romanesque architecture: Benedictine Church of Murbach, Alsace.

Johannes de Garlandia attended Oxford.

1162

Chêng Ch'iao, Chinese author of "On the Proper Classification of Songs," died (born 1104).

1163

(to c.1235) The cornerstone of the Gothic cathedral dedicated to Notre Dame of Paris was laid in 1163 by Pope Alexander III. Construction continued during this period.

1164

Thomas à Becket escaped from England.

The song In Rama sonat gemitus developed from the church service.

1165

King Philip II (Philip Augustus) French King of the Capetian Dynasty was born (died 1223).

(to 1197) A manuscript at Heidelberg contained two songs by "Kaiser Heinrich," the son of Frederick Barbarossa.

1166

Aelred, Abbot of Rievaulx, one of the earliest opponents of the musical practices of the Gothic period, died (born 1109).

1167

King John Lackland (Plantagenet) of England and Great Britain was born (died 1216).

1169

Robert, Dauphin of Auvergne and later a patron of Gaucelm Faidit, was born (died 1234).

1170

The earliest lyrics in England after the Norman Conquest were those of St. Godric. He was an uneducated hermit (Saxon) who lived in a cave in Northern England. He claimed the songs were dictated to him through angelic visions. He died at this time.

Thomas à Becket remained in France until 1170, the year of his martyrdom.

c.1170

Walter von der Vogelweide, a most renowned Minnesinger, was born (died c.1230).

Jewish philosopher and physician Maimonides asserted that secular music should not be tolerated, and, especially, not when performed by a female singer.

Wolfram von Eschenbach, a Minnesinger, was born (died c.1220). He did not learn to write and dictated his most famous work, Parzival to a scribe.

1171

(to 1192) Romanesque architecture: Worms, Cathedral(438'long).

Gothic architecture: Cathedral of Tournai (Belgium) the nave completed in 1171, the towers probably in 1213.

1173

First organ installed in Magdeburg Cathedral (Germany).

1174

(to 1180) Gothic architecture: Canterbury, Cathedral, choir (180' long x 71' high).

(to 1189) Monreale, Cathedral, interior (334'x131').

(to 1191) Gothic architecture: Wells, Cathedral (facade 147' wide, nave 67' high).

c.1175

Franco of Cologne, in his treatise, Ars cantus mensurábilis, gave definite (relative) time values to the various conventional forms of ligatures.

Romanesque miniature: Annunciation of the Shepherds. (Detail of a painting of San Isidoro.) San Isidoro, Leon.

1179

St. Hildegard of Bingen, a chant composer, died (born c.1098).

1180

Neidhart von Reuenthal, secular monophonic composer, was born (died 1240). His songs of summer and winter were his most important works.

(to 1223) The reign of King Philip II (Philip Augustus) French King of the Capetian Dynasty.

c.1180

Romanesque architecture:

c.1180(cont.)

The Facade of St. Trophime at Arles (southern France).

Bernard de Ventadour was connected with Ermengarde of Narbonne.

Gaucelm Faidit, composer of guitar music, was born. He came from Uzerche in the Limousin, Provence (died 1206).

(to c.1207) Reimbautz de Vaquieras, troubadour, was active during this period.

1181

(to 1185) The Papal reign of St. Lucius III (born in Lucca).

c.1182

St. Francis of Assisi was born (died 1226).

(to c.1226) Italian hymns of Praise (lauda) originated from this period.

1183

Giraldus Cambrensis, when he returned from Ireland, wrote in his Topographia Hibernica that he had been impressed by the greater movement of Irish music when compared to Welsh.

The completion of the Cathedral of Notre Dame's choir.

c.1183

Perotin, celebrated composer of discant, was active at Notre Dame at this time.

1184

Gerald de Barri (Giraldus Cambrensis) became Court chaplain to King Henry II of England and Great Britain.

1185

(to 1187) The Papal reign of St. Urban III (born in Milan).

c.1185

Ramon V, Count of Toulouse, was Bernard de Ventadour's last patron.

1186

Romanesque architecture: Hildesheim, St. Michael's (nave 29' wide x 58' high).

1187

King Louis VIII the Lion, French King of the Capetian Dynasty, was born (died 1226).

(to 1187) The Papal reign of St. Gregory VIII (born in Benevento).

(to 1191) The Papal reign of St. Clement III (born in Rome).

c.1188

In the Gate of Glory of Master Mateo, to the church of Santiago da Compostella in Spain, several musical instruments may be seen. A guitar-shaped one represented the original vihuela, the old Spanish viol. The date (1188) was approximately one hundred years after the introduction of the instrument into Spain by the Moors.

The apse of the Church of Monreale, in Sicily, was decorated by Byzantine craftsmen.

1189

(to 1199) The reign of Richard Coeur de Lion (Plantagenet) over England and Great Britain.

1190

Friedrich von Hûsen, poet, died.

c.1190

Romanesque sculpture: Virgin and Child, School of Auvergne.

Romanesque architecture: Toro, La Colegiata.

The era of the Minnesinger was divided into three periods. The first, a period of growth and development, ended about this time.

Byzantine mosaics: Christ as Ruler of the Universe, the Virgin and Child, and Saints. (in the apse of the Cathedral of Monreale, Sicily).

Miniature: King David playing the psaltery, surrounded by bells (from the Westminster Abbey Psalter).

The "Stabat Mater," sung on the "Feasts of the Seven Dolours of Our Lady," was generally accepted as having been written at this time. It is sometimes attributed to Jacob de Benedictis.

Kiesewetter provided evidence that the tracts on Measured Music were not written by the Alchemist and Magician of Cologne or by the Scholastic of Liege, but, by still another Franco, who lived and wrote at this time.

De Coussemaker, in his Histoire de l'Harmonie au moyen âge, claimed that the author of the disputed tracts on Measured Music was another Franco, who lived in Dortmund, in Westphalia, at this time.

Veni Sancte Spiritus was written for Whit Sunday. Its form was aa bb cc dd ee, etc.

(to c.1250) The second period of the Minnesinger, and the high point of the movement revealing its greatest maturity.

1191

William Fitz Stephen mentioned a Monk of Canterbury who wrote Miracle-Plays during the reign of King Henry II, and died at this time.

(to 1198) The Papal reign of St. Celestine III (born in Rome).

1192

Adam de St. Victor, who died at this time, brought the sequence to its highest point of development.

Elvinus, who was sent to Paris by King Béla III in 1192 "ad discendam melodiam" ("to learn music") had been impressed by Perotin and his predecessors and their contributions to music.

1193

Richard Coeur de Lion was supposed to have been captured and imprisoned by Leopold, Duke of Austria, in 1193, and Blondel de Nesle, his minstrel, who was wandering through Germany, discovered the King's whereabouts and identified himself to Richard by singing a song on which they had collaborated.

1194

Gothic sculpture: Melchisedek, Abraham and Moses (the porch of the northern transept of Chartres Cathedral).

(to 1250) The Holy Roman Emperor Frederic II, who was also King of the two Sicilies, dominated Italy during this period.

(to 1260) Gothic architecture:

1194(cont.)

Chartres, Cathedral (427'long).

1195

Bernard de Ventadour, the leading poet of the troubadours, died in Toulouse (born 1125).

(to 1224) Hsia Kuei, Chinese painter, was active during this period.

c.1195

Giraldus Cambrensis, in describing Welsh music, stated that the inhabitants did not sing in unison as other people did, but rather in parts. In Wales each individual voice sang a different part.

Johannes de Garlandia, the probable author of "De Musica Mensurabili Positio" was reported as being born on this date, however, another source had him attending Oxford in 1160.

Two professional fiddlers from France appeared at the margravial court of Montferrat in northern Italy and entertained with popular dance tunes.

1198

A composition written for the New Year's Day service by Perotin, musical director of Notre Dame Cathedral, remained famous for centuries and affirmed the position of the school of Notre Dame as a leading one in music of the time.

Ts'ai Yüan-ting, Chinese author of a new book on music, died (born 1135).

It is claimed that an order from the Bishop Odo de Sully, referred to music for the New Year's Day Service, related to the (cont.) Sederunt, which was liturgically connected to that season.

(to 1216) The Papal reign of St. Innocent III (born in Anagni).

1199

Arnaut Daniel, poet-musician and trouvere of Provence, died.

King Richard the Lion-Hearted of England and a leading trouvère, died (born 1157).

(to 1216) The reign of King John Lackland (Plantagenet) over England and Great Britain.

1200

Wolfram von Eschenbach, secular monophonic composer and renowned Meistersinger, was active during this period.

(to 1304) Gothic architecture: Ypres, Cloth Hall (440'long).

(to 1350) Three part writing used open triads (1-5-8 with perfect or diminished fifths as principal consonances).

c.1200

Free rhythm was rarely found in polyphonic music after this time.

Many magnificent new cathedrals were built in France and neighboring countries, including England, Spain, and in the Rhineland portion of Germany.

Evidence indicated the sounding of trumpets in a battlefield as a signal for attack.

Most of the elements of violin -playing were already in existence at this time.

c.1200

Leaders of the Monodic School created new forms of cacophony equally as rough as those practiced by the Diaphonists of the time.

Primitive fiddles had satisfied the musical world of Europe until this time.

The violin, in all but the final shape of the resonator box and the fourth string, existed at this time and probably considerably earlier.

An improved instrument appeared in southern Europe concurrently with the musical literary movement of the Troubadours. The instrument was called "Viole" or "Vielle." It has been at times called the guitar-fiddle and was used by the Troubadours in France.

Jerome of Moravia gave written instructions for the "Rubeba" and for the larger Fidel, then just coming into use. He called it the "Viella."

The Crwth served as a link between ancient musical instruments and modern European ones. It is not known by whom the bow was first applied to these instruments. Various modifications of instruments, some plucked with the fingers or plectrum and others played with a bow, were used in Europe under various names such as Crowd, Rotte, Geige, Rebec, and Fiddle.

A French poem described the Rebec's tone as loud and harsh and as emulating the female voice.

An illustration showing the (cont.) Rebec was found in an Italian painting engraved in Peire Vidal's "Instruments à Archet."

A woodcut from the Cologne Cathedral showed the Geige.

The "Istromento di porco" existed but the only likeness that survived was in painted or sculptured representations. The earliest of such was in a manuscript of the time. It was played without a plectrum.

The "Symphonia" or "Chifonie" was the Hurdy Gurdy.

In pictures of bows from this time there was something similar to a nut and head, and quite possibly hair was used in place of the cord.

The Clavichord originated from this time.

The Shawm was shown in England in Norman carvings.

The Ochetto made its first appearance in secular music of the time.

The organ now had keys instead of the old clumsy sliders.

The use of the organ in divine service was deemed profane and scandalous by the Roman and Greek clergy.

This time yielded the earliest evidences of instrumental music but it was not yet written down.

The "Dies irae" previously given as composed c.1150 is believed by some to have been written at this time.

c.1200(cont.)

Time values provided by mensural notation existed.

Isorhythm (from 13th century ordines) implied a characteristic pattern of long or short notes which governed continuous melodies without variation.

The breve was originally the shorter of the two notes comprising the earliest measured music.

Neumes in Gregorian Chant had changed to a shape similar to the square notation used today.

The musical language of this time had gone beyond the capacity of the Franconian script and the rigid modal principles of the century.

Music was written in modal (rhythmic mode) notation.

The first rhythmic mode of this time regularly alternated long and short notes.

Odington's "De Speculatione Musices" was especially important for the study of rhythm.

Whereas Machaut's predecessors composed for the most part rigid metric forms, he freed himself from the restrictions of rhythmic modes.

Machaut was concerned not only with development of four voiced music but also with establishing the independence of the individual melodies involved therein.

Organum and trope were preserved in mensural notation, from Higini Angles, El Codex Musical de las Huelgas.

The oldest known carol written in England existed in the Norman French language in a manuscript of this time.

The gamut, extending from G to e″ included no chromatic alterations other than the flat on b and b′ .

The tendency to sharp the leading (seventh) tone to fit with the advancing major and minor modes.

Four scales or modes, usually attributed to St. Ambrose, existed before the time of Pope Gregory. These were known as the authentic modes and were named after the ancient Greek scales or modes as follows: 1. Dorian, 2. Phrygian, 3. Lydian, 4. Mixo-lydian.

The Notre Dame motet originated from this time. It was usually for three voices and in different rhythmic figures.

The terms Motetus and Motellus were constantly applied to the voice part afterwards referred to as Medius or Altus.

The tenor motet became standard at this time.

Cantus-firmus treatment was an outgrowth of the development of the basis of the 13th-century motet tenor.

The motet used the foundation of a cantus firmus, which was usually Gregorian chant.

The cantus-firmus Mass stemmed from extension of the motet principle.

The Montpellier manuscript

c.1200(cont.)

contained the largest collection of motets from Perotin to Pierre de la Croix and including Adam de la Halle and Adam le Bosse.

Dance music and motets were the most popular forms of the time.

The rondeau entered the realm of the motet.

The final refrain of the chorus of the French rondeau was anticipated at the onset.

In motet the voices moved within the same approximate range, but were in striking contrast with one another melodically.

A body of compositions based on the In seculum tenor appeared.

Ostinato tenors were used in motets. They constituted the lowest voices, but in the case of Busnois the ostinato differed in that the tenor was an inner voice.

The Hospital of the Mendicanti in Venice was founded for the reception of lepers.

Sang Schools, an old Scottish institution, started at this time.

Singing and dancing were no longer intermingled at this time.

The position of Precentor was established at St. David's and St. Paul's in London.

Walter von der Vogelweide wandered through Bavaria and its surroundings singing his own songs set from his own lyrics. This was a highpoint in folk (cont.) song, poetry and polemic.

Blondel de Nesles, poet and trouvére from Northern France died (born c.1150).

Peire Vidal was at the court of King Emeric at this time.

Sarngadeva discovered the second partial or harmonic octave in India.

Nithart's song was one of the works by the Minnesingers which was preserved.

The charming and lively secular poem "The Owl and the Nightingale" was written.

The Monk of Montaudon, a troubadour, was active at this time.

Spervogel, a Minnesinger, was active at this time.

Marchetto of Padua, a writer on music, was active at this time.

In a poem, Walter Mapes, an English Ecclesiastic, spoke of "subjecting Canons to the form of (the) Round."

The Dominican Jerome of Moravia asserted that all should sing at a medium pitch. He claimed that singing too low meant ululation and singing too high brought screaming.

In the dramas with music of the trouvéres the germ of "opera comique" was evident.

The earliest traces of the Singspiel in the German miracle-plays were developed outside the churches. The plays contained spoken words in German

c.1200(cont.)

but the singing was still done in Latin like the Passions.

The Kolendas or Noëls were peculiar to the Polish people; they were for the most part popular tunes and were sung at Christmas at home and in the streets.

The Carols "Resonet in laudibus" (Wir loben all' das Kindelein) and "Dies est laetitae" (Der Tag der ist so freundlich) came from this time. "Tempus adest floridum" was a similar selection.

The first clausulae were troped with extra Latin texts in an old St. Andrew's Music Book.

Some of the pieces in the Piae Cantiones were from this time.

The Exultet coelum laudibus supplied the basis for the tune of Psalm 19 (XVIII).

"Beata viscera" was written. It was an English polyphonic conductus.

"Hac in Anni janua" a secular polyphonic song in conductus style was written.

Laudes were monophonic and written in plainsong notation.

The score was dropped and replaced by the choirbook arrangement.

Since this time liturgical chants of the church have presented the Gospel in a rich and solemn manner.

Religious and moralizing songs developed in England.

"Worldes blis ne last" was written (English moralistic).

"Man mei longe" was written (English moralistic).

Psalm Tones (inflected monotone) were established.

The Jena manuscript, a collection of poems and music, was the earliest example of secular monophonic music.

The final development of Gregorian Chant came at this time and also its gradual deterioration began.

The polyphonic rondeaux, virelais, and ballades of this time contributed to the Binchois chansons at a later date.

Wandering players settled down in communities starting at this time and later acquired official recognition as Stadtpfeiffer (town pipers) who performed at various municipal ceremonies.

The pipers who had settled in towns felt the ignominious position of being classed with wandering vagabonds, so they formed "Innungen" (corporations for their mutual protection) in England, France, and Germany.

Gothic architecture which survived in cathedrals, such as Amiens and Salisbury, reached its highest point at this time.

Writings in English which had any literary value were sparse at this time.

Lu Hsin-chung, Chinese painter, was active. His best known

c.1200(cont.)
work was Vanavasi Gazing at a Lotus Pond (3'8"x1'4").

Chinese painting: Mu Ch'i, Persimmons (14"x15").

Japanese sculpture: Uesugi Shigefusa. Meigetsuin Temple, Kamakura (2'3" high).

Japanese sculpture: Jokei, Kongorikishi, Kufuku'ji Temple, Nara.

Japanese sculpture: Unkei, Hosso Patriarch Muchaku (complete figure 6'2" high).

American Indian sculpture: Figure with Arm Raised, Tarasca (14" high).

Gothic architecture: Carcassonne.

Indian sculpture: Buddha Nirvana with Ananda, Gal Vihara, Polonnaruva (23'high).

Indian architecture: Konarak, Surya Temple, Black Pagoda, wheel (10' high).

Indian sculpture: Dancing Siva (3'11" high).

Gothic architecture: Bourges, Cathedral, nave (120' high).

Romanesque architecture: Bamberg, Cathedral (312'x94'by 84' high).

Gothic sculpture: Annunciation. Cathedral, Bamberg.

Japanese scroll: Burning of the Palace (complete scroll 1'4"by 22'11").

French manuscript: Artists at work at a manuscript and a panel (cont.) painting. From the pattern book of Reun Monastery.

Chinese silk painting: Ma Yüan: Landscape in Moonlight.

Byzantine Altar painting: Enthroned Madonna and Child (Probably painted in Constantinople).

Artists occasionally abandoned their pattern book altogether in order to represent something that was of interest to them.

The main task of northern sculptors was work on cathedrals.

The sculptors of Strasbourg were noted for their ability to achieve a degree of lifelikeness.

France was the richest and most influential country in Europe at the time the great cathedrals were being built.

Almost all branches of art had their share in the era of great cathedrals in Europe.

Sculptured relief: Music epitomized. Section of vaulting from the east portal of the south facade of the Cathedral of Chartres.

Sculptured figures: Angels playing trumpets (Cathedral at Strasbourg, column of angels).

German manuscript: First words of the Easter Office.

(to 1276) Ulrich von Lichtenstein's songs were transcribed by a cleric. The melodies, sung or whistled to a professional musician, were set in musical notation by the latter.

c.1200(cont.)

(to c.1300) Machaut frequently had a voice repeat a rhythmic pattern (a talea); or had a voice repeat a melodic line (color). He also would have a voice repeat both a rhythmic pattern and a melodic line whether or not they coincided.

(to c.1300) Popular canons were written down and as a result received official recognition in England, Germany, and Spain.

(to c.1300) Companies of Laudesi were found in larger towns in Italy.

(to c.1300) Penitents developed the Lauda.

(to c.1300) Manessische pictures and poems (secular monophonic music).

(to c.1300) The Minim was invented by Philip de Vitry at this time or by Joannes de Muris in the 14th century.

(to c.1300) German-speaking countries occupied a position outside the mainstream of musical development.

(to c.1300) The Mysteries, Moralities, and Miracle Plays were very popular throughout Europe. They helped to familiarize the masses with the great events of History.

(to c.1300) Folklore described an ark containing a miraculous image of the Virgin as well as the words and music for the Mystery of Elche. It supposedly drifted to the Spanish coast of Elche.

(to c.1325) Secular music in (cont.) England developed rapidly.

(to c.1400) The instrument used for signalling was the trumpet.

(to c.1400) The word, citole, used by poets was derived from cistella (Latin). It referred to the small box-shaped psaltery often depicted in manuscripts of the period.

(to c.1425) The French, although great leaders in the field of music, were now receiving outside influence in the art as well as acting as a disseminator.

(to c.1445) The Minnesang lasted throughout this period.

(to c.1500) Conflicting signatures appeared and continued to appear until the 16th century.

(to c.1500) Fordun (13th cent.), Clynn (14th cent.), Polidore Virgil and Major (15th cent.), Vincenzo Galilei, Bacon, Spenser, Stanihurst, and Camden (16th cent.) wrote enthusiastically about Ireland's music and the Irish harp.

(to c.1600) Over 200,000 volumes and 800 manuscripts of church music survived from this period.

1201

King Thibaut, of Navarre, a noted trouvère was born (died 1253).

c.1202

Joachim of Floris, a monk and writer, died (born c.1145).

1203

The parson of Ossemer (near Stendal) was killed by a stroke of lightning as he was fiddling

1203(cont.)
for his parishioners to dance on the Wednesday of Whitsun-week in 1203. This was reported in the Brunswick Chronicle.

1204
Canon de Béthune, politician, soldier and statesman, was active at Constantinople in the Crusade.

Maimonides, Jewish philosopher, physician and writer on music, died (born 1135).

1205
Tannhäuser, secular monophonic composer, was born (died 1270). This date was recorded in the Jena manuscript.

1206
Gaucelm Faidit died(born c.1180).

(to 1242) Gothic architecture: Wells, Cathedral, facade (147' wide).

1207
King Henry III of England and Great Britain (Plantagenet) was born (died 1272).

Raimbault de Vaqueras died, famous troubadour and author of "Kalenda Maya."

Tannhäuser and Wolfram von Eschenbach competed in a Sängerkrieg held at the Wartburg by the Landgrave Hermann of Thuringia.

1208
The Crusade against the Albigenses was a severe setback to the troubadours.

Japanese sculpture: Unkei, Hosso Patriarch Muchaku, Kofuku-ji Temple, Nara (6'2" high).

(to 1238) The name Perotin being a diminutive for Pierre, the Petrus Succentor who was mentioned eight times in documents during these years may have referred to the optimus discantor.

1210
The mandore (mandola), a small lute, is one of the ten instruments which Guiraut de Calanson, in his Conseils aux Jongler, written at this date, said a jongleur had to be able to play.

c.1210
Evidence of the Staff of Five Lines was found in a manuscript tract, "De speculatione musices," written by Walter Odington, a Monk of Evesham in Worcestershire.

Because of the evidence of the Rota "Sumer is y-cumen in" it has been assumed that, in England, a school of musicians advanced beyond the Netherlands at the same period.

The "Ormulum" a long poem consisting of paraphrases as well as explanations of the Gospel was written.

Layamon's "Brut," a verse translation of an Anglo-French poem by Wace, was written. It dealt with the early legendary history of Britain.

There was an English part-song, a canon, or round.

1211
Guiraut de Calanson died.

(to 1290) Gothic architecture: Reims, Cathedral (towers 267' high, flank 453' long).

1212

Randal, Earl of Chester, was besieged at Rhydland Castle by the Welsh at the time of Chester fair. Robert de Lacy, who was constable of Chester, assembled pipers and minstrels who were attending the fair and he led them towards the castle. The Welsh were panic-stricken and fled at once. The earls of Chester received the title of "patrons of the minstrels" in honor of this event.

1213

Gothic architecture: The Cathedral of Tournai (Belgium). Towers completed in 1213, nave completed in 1171.

The earliest mention of the name Stradivari was in the Matricola of the Collegio Dei Notai for 1213. Subsequently it appeared often for three centuries.

1214

King Louis IX (St. Louis), French King of the Capetian Dynasty, was born (died 1270).

c.1214

Roger Bacon, English Monk and philosopher, was born (died 1294).

c.1215

Peire Vidal, Provençal troubadour, died (birthdate unknown).

At the battle of Bouvines the French charge was signalled by trumpets, as in numerous other battles, according to historians of the time.

(to 1225) Ma Lin, Chinese painter, King Chao-nü Standing in the Snow (9½"x10").

1216

Pope Innocent III died.

(to 1227) Early Christian architecture: Rome, San Lorenzo, F.L.M., nave (central aisle 36' wide).

(to 1227) The Papal reign of Honorius III (born in Rome).

(to 1272) The reign of Henry III (Plantagenet) over England and Great Britain.

(to 1272) During Henry III's reign translation of French Romances became extremely popular.

c.1216

The death of Richard the Lion-Hearted was the subject of a lament by a Provencal confrère, Gaucelm Faidit. Other sources have placed Faidit's death as early as 1206.

1218

Johannes de Garlandia was present at the siege of Toulouse and took part in the crusade against the Albigenses.

(to 1247) Gothic architecture: The interior of the cathedral of Amiens. The nave was built by Robert de Luzarches from 1218 to 1236, and the apse was completed in 1247.

1220

Giraldus Cambrensis, historian of Welsh music, died (born 1147). His real name was Gerald de Barri and he was an Englishman.

Walter Odington of Evesham wrote on the Subject of Measured Music.

(to 1230) The Saxon lawbook, "Sachsenspiegel" appeared at

1220(cont.)

this time.

(to 1248) Gothic sculpture: St. Firmin. Cathedral, Amiens.

(to 1248) Gothic sculpture: Portal of Christ: Apostles and Prophets. Cathedral, Amiens.

(to 1258) Gothic architecture: Salisbury, Cathedral (473'x230'; spire 404' high; nave 40' wide' vaults 81' high).

(to 1279) Gothic architecture: Amiens, Cathedral (interior length, 438'; nave width, 481'; vaults 139' high).

c.1220

Gace Brulé, a prominent trouvère, died.

Guiraut de Bornelh, called "Master of the Troubadours" by his collegues, died.

Adam de la Halle, poet-composer of the pastoral play Le Jeu de Robin et de Marion, was born (died 1287), see c.1230.

Wolfram von Eschenbach, a great Minnesinger, died (born c.1170).

(to 1230) Gothic sculpture: Christ (Le Beau Dieu), central portal, west facade. Cathedral, Amiens (10' high).

1221

Gothic architecture: Burgos, Cathedral (interior, 300' long; nave and aisles, 32' wide) was begun.

St. Bonaventura, composer of the Stabat Mater dolorosa, was born (died 1274).

1223

(to 1226) The reign of King Louis VIII the Lion, French King of the Capetian Dynasty.

1224

Islamic manuscript: Physicians Cutting Plant, from a Dioscorides manuscript (5"x7").

c.1224

Canon de Béthune, a prominent Trouvère, died (born c.1150).

1225

Lepers were collected at St. Gervasio e Protasio; later they were moved to the island of San Lazaro in the lagoon (1262).

"Mirie it is while sumer ilast" was written (English, secular).

c.1225

The goliards' influence decreased and the great medieval universities grew. Wandering students were replaced by residents.

Mensural notation developed from plainsong notation. The primary change was the distinguishing of the stemmed square, the longa, from the stemless square, the breve.

The earliest known music in harmony was the song "Sumer is icumen in," written at this time by John of Fornsete, a monk of Reading Abbey. It indicated long years of study.

(to 1235) Gothic sculpture: Annunciation and Visitation. West facade, Reims Cathedral (10'2" high).

Guilds and fraternities came into existence.

c.1225(cont.)

The earliest examples of hoquetus (part above the tenor in hocket) broke on the melodic line only.

Assyrian manuscript: A Monk, Frater Rufillus, writing the letter R (his table with colours and his pen-knife beside him).

Neithart von Reuenthal while he added simple country tunes changed the chivalrous, refined, and spiritual Minne. to the sexual experiences of uncouth swains.

The conductus, a polyphonic composition, evolved at this time.

(to c.1550) The old choir-book arrangements which had been the early motets had all voices written on one page. They were, however, not in score. Later the voices were spread out as a separate unit, on facing pages and continued this way to c.1550. The part-book had, however, become increasingly popular.

1226

Bar'-Ebhraja (Bar Hebraeus), Syrian scholar, was born (died 1286).

St. Francis of Assisi died (born c.1182).

(Oct. 4 to May 25, 1230) Father Thomas wrote his "Vita Sancti Francisci" between these dates.

(to 1270) The reign of King Louis IX (St. Louis), French King of the Capetian Dynasty.

(to 1625) The early English Schools of composition existed.

c.1226

A Vocal Composition was scored, by an English Ecclesiastic, probably John of Fornsete. The notes were exactly like those now in use in English Churches, and perfectly intelligible to a modern musician.

The Reading manuscript proved that regular form was known and used in England.

Coussemaker concluded that "Sumer is icumen in" must have been written at this time; and, that the "Rota" was composed, by a Monk of Reading, at a prior date. The "Sumer" canon was preserved in the Harleian manuscript.

1227

(to 1241) The Papal reign of St. Gregory IX (born in Anagni).

c.1227

St. Thomas Aquinas was born (died 1274).

1228

Stephen Langton, Archbishop of Canterbury, died.

Palästinalied by Walther von der Vogelweide was associated with the Crusade of this year.

1229

Johannes de Garlandia was invited to Toulouse to assist in the formation of the newly -founded University.

Walter de Odington or Walter of Evesham was often incorrectly identified with Walter, monk of Canterbury, whose election to the primacy was stopped by the

1229(cont.)

Pope in this year. The correct spelling of his name was Einesham or Eynsham.

(to 1232) Johannes de Garlandia taught at Toulouse University.

1230

Jordanus Nemorarius was active.

Guiraut Riquier, a troubadour, was born (died 1294).

Arisi, in his "Cremona Litterata," mentioned Galerio Stradivari as a learned orientalist.

(to 1240) The treatise Discantus posito vulgaris established a metrical modi to rule musical rhythm. They appear as 6 meters. The treatise was anonymous.

(to 1250) Bartholomaeus Anglicus' treatise was written during this period.

c.1230

Romanesque sculpture: The Death of the Virgin (the porch of the southern transept of Strasbourg Cathedral).

A system of notating measured music was described in various treatises and illustrated by examples almost all polyphonic in character.

Walter von der Vogelweide, a most renowned Minnesinger, died (born c.1170).

The first part of the epic poem Le Roman de la Rose was written by Guillaume de Lorris.

Rutebeuf, the first subjective and independent French lyric (cont.) poet of the Middle Ages, was born (died c.1280).

Adam de la Halle, a composer of part-music and trouvère melodies, as well as of the dramatic pastoral Le Jeu de Robin et Marion, an opéra comique type play with monophonic music, was born (died 1287), see c.1220.

(to 1240) Gothic sculpture: Equestrian Figure of a Knight. Cathedral, Bamberg.

1231

Folquet of Marseilles, a troubadour, died.

c.1232

Johannes de Garlandia and his colleagues were forced to leave Toulouse because of persecution by the Dominicans and others.

1234

Robert, Dauphin of Auvergne, a patron of Gaucelm Faidit, died (born 1169).

1235

The first manuscript in Bohemian notation was a troparium.

Robert Grosseteste, a philosopher, became Bishop of Lincoln.

(to 1255) Chinese painted scroll: Ch'en Jung, Nine Dragon Scroll.

(to 1283) Gothic architecture: Marburg, St. Elizabeth (67'3" high).

c.1235

Notre Dame Cathedral in Paris was completed. It was started in 1163.

1236

Philippe, Chancellor of Paris, died. The texts of many conducti in a French manuscript were ascribed to him.

The Benedictine Gautier de Coinci died. A vocal collection Les Miracles de Notre Dame contained about 30 of his songs.

1239

King Edward I, Longshanks (Plantagenet) of England and Great Britain, was born (died 1307).

1240

Neidhart von Reuenthal, secular monophonic composer, died (born 1180).

(to 1268) Gothic architecture: San Galgano, Abbey Church.

c.1240

Burney estimated the date of "Sumer is icumen in" as possibly not much later than 13th or 14th century.

Cimabue, a Florentine painter, was born (died c.1301). He was noted for his strong affinity toward Byzantine painting.

Sir Frederick Madden was of the opinion that "Sumer is icumen in" was written about this time.

Giovanni Cimabue, an Italian artist, was born (died c.1301).

Gothic art: Villard de Honnecourt. Sketchbook.

A confusing tract by a younger English contemporary of Garlandia's showed the transition toward Franconian notation very strongly.

(to c.1280) Adam de la Halle and Guillaume Machaud were the leading "Chansonniers" of this period.

(to c.1288) Adam de la Halle, an outstanding poet, was also a talented and versatile musician.

1241

(to 1241) The Papal reign of Celestine IV (born in Milan).

1242

George Pachymeres, scientist and mathematician who wrote on music, was born (died. c.1310).

1243

(to 1254) The Papal reign of Innocent IV (born in Genoa).

(to 1298) In Italy a "Commedia Spirituale" was performed for the first time at Padua and another at Friuli in 1298.

c.1244

(to c.1248) The St. Victor manuscript contains 10 two-part conducti.

1245

King Philip III the Bold, French King of the Capetian Dynasty, was born (died 1285).

Johannes de Garlandia was still residing in Paris.

(to 1248) Gothic architecture: Paris, Sainte Chapelle (Interior length 98'; 35' wide).

c.1245

Yolande d'Aragon commissioned a book of hours from an outstanding artist known incorrectly as the Master of the "Heures de Rohan."

1246

Henry III made a grant of land on the Thames to his wife's uncle, Count Peter of Savoy. A palatial residence was erected on the site.

1248

Gothic church windows: The choir of Cologne Cathedral, started at this time.

1250

Franco of Cologne said "Consonance at the beginning of every perfection."

Colmar manuscript (collection of poems and music) earliest entry (secular monophonic music).

Perrin d'Agincourt, a famous trouvère, died.

Thomas of Celano, who wrote the Dies irae for the Requium Mass, died. Its form was aa bb cc, aa bb cc, aa bbc de.

Tenor repetition continued after this date.

Pietro Cavallini, Florentine painter, was born (died 1330). Like Cimabue his affinity was strongly to Byzantine art.

The Early Motet Period ended.

c.1250

Gothic sculpture: Female Head, from Reims.

Gothic sculpture: Vierge Dorée, south transept portal. Cathedral, Amiens (10' high).

Nicola Pisano, an Italian sculptor, began to imitate the French masters and to study the methods of classical sculpture to learn to represent nature (cont.) more convincingly. Pisano worked in Pisa.

Raymond Berenger, Count of Provence, visited Emperor Frederick II at Milan and brought troubadours and jongleurs with him. This marked their first appearance in Italy.

A volume believed to be at least as old as this date contained compositions regularly scored for two Voices, on Staves of eight and nine lines.

The Monastery at Reading was not the only religious place in England where the vocal score was known at this time.

A score was transcribed by Hieronymus de Moravia on a system similar to that adopted by the transcribers of the Reading and Chaucer manuscripts.

Ritson believed that "the Reading manuscript" was from this time.

Morley claimed that the minima was used by Philipp de Vitry.

The sharp or diesis came into use at this time.

The composition of the Stabat Mater dolorosa was credited to St. Bonaventura.

Kiesewetter claimed that the "Ars Cantus mensurabilis" of Franco of Cologne was written at this time.

The strength of the motet vogue eliminated the conductus.

The introduction of a third symbol, the diamond-shaped semi -breve and the equivalent rest

c.1250(cont.)

in the form of the whole rest was at this time.

Jerome of Moravia, a Dominican friar from Paris, described 3 ways in which the vièle was tuned.

Chinese painting: Kao K'O-Kung: Landscape after Rain.

Giovanni Pisano, Italian sculptor, born (died c.1330).

The Middle English metrical romances, "King Horn," and "Havelock the Dane" stemmed from this date.

(to 1260) Gothic sculpture: Margrave Ekkehard II and Uta. Cathedral, Naumburg.

(to c.1275) The Classical Motet period.

(to 1280) Franco of Cologne was both a theorist and performing musician.

1252

Johannes de Garlandia's "De triumphis Ecclesiae" was completed.

Japanese sculpture: The Great Buddha, Kamakura (42'6" high).

(to 1284) King Alfonso of Castile and León assembled "cantigas de Santa Maria."

1253

King Thibaut of Navarre, a noted trouvère, died (born 1201).

1254

(to 1261) The Papal reign of St. Alexander IV (born in Anagni).

1255

A new organ was installed in the Cathedral at Prague.

Matthew Paris, an English historian, An elephant and its keeper. This was a drawing made from life using an elephant sent by King Louis of France (St. Louis) to King Henry IIIrd of England.

(to 1280) Lincoln, Cathedral, Angel Choir (nave and aisles c.88' wide).

c.1255

Duccio di Buoninsegna, Gothic painter and sculptor, was born (died c.1318).

Longer notes were in use in the time of Franco of Cologne.

1257

The Royal trombonists in Hungary were called buccinatores.

1259

A choir of twelve boys (bonifantes) was established at Prague.

c.1259

Fraternities of penitents were spread over Northern Italy.

1260

Marble sculpture: Nicola Pisano, Annunciation, Nativity and Shepherds. From the pulpit of the Baptistery in Pisa.

The Compagnia del Gonfalone was an organization which gave annual dramatic performances of the Passion. Meetings of the group were held in the Roman Colosseum.

Heinrich von Meissen, author or "Frauenlob" and a secular monophonic composer, was born

1260(cont.)

(died 1318).

(to 1453) The reign of the Palaiologoi over the Roman Empire.

c.1260

"Verbum supernum prodiens" was composed by St. Thomas Aquinas.

The earliest known motet with English words was Worldes blisce -Domino.

Manuscript painting:
Matthew Paris, The King and his architect (with compass and ruler) visiting the building site of a Cathedral (King Offa at St. Albans), from the life of St. Albans.

Byzantine painting: Guido da Siena, Madonna in Majesty.

The sculptor who produced the statues of founders of Naumburg Cathedral in Germany, c.1260, made it appear as if he had portrayed actual knights of his time.

c.1261

The "Lauda Sion" was written by St. Thomas Aquinas and was a masterpiece of mediaeval scholarship. It differed from the other four sequences still retained after the Council of Trent.

(to 1264) The Papal reign of St. Urban IV (born in Troyes).

1262

Lepers at St. Gervasio e Protasio were moved to the island of San Lazaro in the lagoon.

1263

Adam de la Halle retired to Douai and resumed his ecclesiastical habit.

The monks at the monastery of St. Matthias said the "Media vita" as one of a series of prayers to protect them from a new abbot (William) who had been appointed as their superior by the Archbishop of Treves.

1264

A Papal bull of St. Urban IV authorized the celebration of Corpus Christi "with songs and other demonstrations of joyfulness." This was taken as justification for elaborate celebration including masques, dances and processions by the religious guilds of Seville.

1265

Dante, the founder of the Italian language, was born (died 1321).

(to 1268) The Papal reign of St. Clement IV (born in France).

1266

The Florentine painter Giotto di Bondone was born (died 1337).

Pierre de Montreuil, the great Parisian mason-architect, died. His epitaph in the abbey-church of St.-Germain-des-Prés referred to him as "doctor latomorum."

1267

(to 1268) Roger Bacon, in his Opus Majus and Opus Tertium, recommended thorough mastery of music by theologians.

c.1267

Johannes de Garlandia was men-

c.1267(cont.)

tioned by Roger Bacon as eminent at Paris.

1268

Philip IV the Fair, French King of the Capetian Dynasty, was born (died 1314).

c.1269

Sordello, an Italian troubadour, died.

1270

Tannhäuser, secular monophonic composer, died (born 1205). This date was reported in the Jena manuscript.

(to 1285) The reign of King Philip III the Bold, French King of the Capetian Dynasty.

c.1270

Gothic painting: Tuscan Master: Head of Christ.

The second portion of Le Roman de la Rose was written by Jean de Meung.

(to 1280) Byzantine painting: Sienese School, Birth of St. John the Baptist (Altarpiece of the Life of the Saint).

(to 1285) Gothic painting: Giovanni Cimabue, Madonna Enthroned with Saints and Angels (126"x7'4").

1271

Alfred, in a tract written in Genoa, was described as an English priest serving under Cardinal Octoboni de' Fieschi.

Aluredus (Amerus Anglicus) was a noted English writer on music.

(to 1276) The Papal reign of St. Gregory X (born in Piacenza).

1272

In Hungary, Royal musicians owned the village of Gajdosbogdány which was named after the instrument gajd (oboe, or perhaps a horn).

Johannes de Garlandia was in all probability still alive.

(to 1307) The reign of King Edward Longshanks (Plantagenet) over England and Great Britain.

1274

Marchetto de Padova wrote on the subject of Measured Music.

The second Council of Lyons created several canons to halt so-called "injurious practices."

St. Thomas Aquinas, who wrote the Corpus Christi Sequence Lauda Sion, died (born c.1227).

St. Bonaventura, composer of the Stabat Mater dolorosa, died (born 1221).

c.1274

(to c.1309) The science of music must have been studied early in the University of Padua. The Marchetto di Padova, the next major writer on music after Guido d'Arezzo, confirmed this fact.

c.1275

Over 400 melodies by the famous Spanish cantígas in honor of the Virgin were written down for King Alfonso el Sabio and preserved in illuminated manuscripts.

Byzantine painting: Cimabue, The Madonna of the Angels.

Byzantine painting: The

c.1275(cont.)

Entombment of Christ (from a Psalter manuscript from Bonmont).

(to 1285) Adam de la Halle's pastoral play, Le Jeude Robin et de Marion was written.

1276

(to 1276) The Papal reign of St. Adrian V (born in Genoa).

(to 1276) The Papal reign of St. Innocent V (born in Savoy).

(to 1277) The Papal reign of St. John XXI (born in Portugal). Elimination was made of the name of John XX in an effort to rectify the numerical designation of Popes named John. The error dated back to the time of John XV.

1277

(to 1280) The Papal reign of St. Nicholas III (born in Rome).

1279

Robert Kilwardy, an eminent English writer on music and philosophy, died.

The Anonymus of St. Emmeram stated that the modes 3-5 were discarded in favor of modes 1, 2, and 6.

1280

Albertus Magnus died.

Leland stated that Odington was active at this time.

(to 1370) Gothic architecture: Exeter, Cathedral (nave 66'high).

c.1280

Giotto was an apprentice in Florence.

The Ars Cantus Mensurabilis furnished a codification of rules that remained standard for many years.

Rutebeuf, the first subjective and independent French lyric poet of the Middle Ages, died (born c.1230).

George Pachymeres' treatise on the four mathematical sciences included music.

Stained-glass window: The Fish vomits out Jonah upon the dry land (Cologne Cathedral).

Pietro Lorenzetti, Sienese painter, was born (died 1348).

1281

(to 1285) The Papal reign of St. Martin IV (born in France). The names of Marinus I and Marinus II were construed as Martin. In view of these two pontificates and the earlier reign of St. Martin I, this pontiff was called Martin IV.

1282

By Command of Philippe le Hardi, Robert II Comte d'Artois, accompanied the Duc d'Alencon to Naples to assist the Duc d'Anjou in avenging the Ve pres Siciliennes. Adam de la Halle, who had entered Count Robert's service, accompanied him on this trip and wrote some of his most important works for the French Court in Sicily.

(to 1390) Gothic architecture: Albi, Cathedral (walls 130' high).

1283

Juan Ruiz, writer of the Libro de Buen Amor, was born (died 1350).

c.1283
The Marchetto di Padova in his "Pomerium de Musica Mensurata," wrote that Franco was the inventor of the first four musical characters - i.e. - the Longo, the Double-Long, the Breve, and the Semibreve.

(or c.1284) The first performance of Adam de la Halle's "Le Jeu de Robin et de Marion" was held in Naples at the French court.

1284
King Edward II (Plantagenet) of England was born (died 1327).

c.1284
Simone Martini, Sienese painter, was born (died 1344).

1285
Guillaume de Machaut was born.

The death of Alexander III.

Hugo Spechtshart von Reutlingen, who wrote "Chronikon" a description of rites of Geissler and their songs, was born (died 1360).

Adam de la Halle's death, at Naples, in 1285, was described by his contemporary, Jean Bodel d'Arras, in "Le Gieus du Pelerin"(see 1287).

Byzantine painting:
Duccio di Buoninsegna, Virgin in Majesty (Rucellai Madonna).

(to 1287) The Papal reign of St. Honorius IV (born in Rome).

(to 1314) The reign of King Philip IV the Fair, French King of the Capetian Dynasty.

1286
Adam de la Bassée, who wrote Ludus super Anticlaudianum, died.

Bar'-Ebhraja (Bar Hebraeus), Syrian scholar, died (born 1226).

1287
Three grades of masons may be assumed by the terms on which Étienne de Bonnevil left Paris for Uppsala in Sweden. Bonnevil was "master of the church work of Uppsala," and took with him "companions and bachelors" of the art of masonry.

Adam de la Halle, poet-composer of the pastoral play Le Jeu de Robin et Marion, died (born c.1220 or c.1230).

(to 1288) Sienese art:
Duccio di Buoninsegna, Cartoons for a stained-glass window in Siena Cathedral.

1288
The Chose Tassin was mentioned by Grocheo and was traceable as a ministerallus in the service of Philippe le Bel.

The "Brotherhood of St. Nicolai" was instituted at Vienna, and Count Peter von Ebersdorff, a high Imperial official was elected to the position of "protector." The group was a musicians guild.

(to 1292) The Papal reign of St. Nicholas IV (born in Ascoli).

1289
King Louis X the Quarreler, French King of the Capetian Dynasty, was born (died 1316).

(to 1309) Gothic architecture:

1289(cont.)

Siena, Palazzo Pubblico (190' wide).

1290

Sienese art:
Duccio di Buoninsegna, Madonna with Three Kneeling Franciscans.

(to 1309) Gothic architecture: Orvieto. Cathedral facade (nave 343'x108').

c.1290

Approximately six hundred jongleurs, minstrels, and singers served at the court of Catalonia, Aragon from this time through the 14th century.

The English, Italian and Spanish used Latin terms, which were obsolete and inadequate as early as this time.

Russian icon: St. Boris and St. Gleb, Suzdal School.

Gothic sculpture: Smiling Angel, Reims Cathedral.

Johannes de Grocheo recommended that chants de geste "be sung to old people, working peasants, and low-caste men when they rested after work." This way they would hear about other's troubles and work more cheerily.

A brotherhood was formed by the merchants of London to encourage musical and poetical compositions.

Gothic sculpture:
Giovanni Pisano, Madonna and Child. Cathedral, Pisa.

Jean de Muris, author of Ars novae musice, was born(d.c1351).

Litaniae Lauretanae (Litany of Loreto) was written.

Stabat Mater, the poem written by Jacobus de Benedictis, was one of the finest examples of mediaeval Latin prose, second only to the "Dies irae" of Thomas de Celano.

(to c.1310) The earliest purely Ecclesiastical Motets were by Philip de Vitry, the Ars compositionis de Motetis was written during this period.

(to c.1350) The first period of great practical importance in the history of polyphonic music.

1291

(October 31) Philip de Vitry, French musician and author of "Ars Nova" was born in Vitry, France (died 1361, June 9).

The German Empire gave up its last possessions in the Holy Land.

1293

King Philip VI of France (House of Valois) was born (died 1350).

1294

Gothic architecture: Florence Cathedral (556' long).

Guiraut Riquier, a troubadour, died (born 1230).

King Charles IV the Fair, French King of the Capetian Dynasty was born (died 1328).

King Philip V the Tall, French King of the Capetian Dynasty, was born (died 1322).

Roger Bacon, English monk and philosopher, died (born c.1214).

(to 1294) The Papal reign of

1294(cont.)
St. Celestine V (born in Isernia).

(to 1303) The Papal reign of St. Boniface VIII (born in Anagni).

1296
The Siege of Berwick.

(to 1346) John of Luxemburg, the King of Bohemia, surrounded himself with adventurers. Guillaume de Machaut found his inspiration in these surroundings.

c.1296
(to 1300) Gothic painting: Giotto di Bondone, Miracle of the Spring. Upper Church, Assisi.

1297
The chronicle of Königssaal stated that tympana, nobla, tuba, sambuci, rota, figella, and lira were some of the instruments used at the coronation of Wenceslaus II.

Islamic manuscript: Stag and Doe, from a natural history manuscript (7½"x6¼").

1298
A "Comedia Spirituale" was performed in Friuli. Earlier (1243) one had been performed in Padua for the first time.

Pierre de la Croix was still active at this time.

c.1299
The oldest Florentine organ was built.

The Sainte Chapelle in Paris maintained its maîtrise (choir school).

1300
Birth of Guillaume de Machaut, in the village of Machault near Réthel in the Champagne area of France (died 1377). Machaut, composer, priest, and poet has been ranked at the top of the composers of this century by leading musicologists as well as performers.

At Rome, during the preparation for the great jubilee, Giotto produced the famous mosaic of the "Navicella." Its truth and dramatic intensity gripped his contemporaries.

c.1300
Ars antiqua was the name given the musical styles before 1300 by later generations.

The Ars nova was the name given to the period starting at this date.

The term punctus contra punctum (counterpoint) first appeared.

Four-part writing was fairly well established by this time.

Pedals were added to the organ.

The style of motet influence by the polyphonic trope flourished until this date. It lasted even longer in England and Avignon, but was not considered a living technique by this time.

The dot was derived from the ancient system of "measured music" (musica mensuralis). It had various functions, and appeared in four forms: "point of perfection," "point of alteration," "point of division," and "point of addition."

W. de Win(cestre) war referred

c.1300(cont.)

to as the composer of an organum repertoire in a table of contents in a lost manuscript from this time.

Walter Odington defined the rondellus as a piece in which two or three melodies were sung at the same time, each voice singing each melody through in turn. This was described in his "De speculatione musicae." The work also referred to the earliest temperament or arbitrary alteration of the scale. Odington also stated that binary rhythm was used along with ternary.

Up to this time there were no known composers of polyphonic music in Italy.

Italy began to compete with France in the arts.

The son of a small householder in Yorkshire, Richard Rolle, hermit and author, was born (died 1349).

John Kukuzeles, the hymnwright, was active at this time.

Giotto di Bondone was at Assisi.

Florentine fresco: Giotto. The Death of the Knight of Celano (Upper Church of St. Francesco, Assisi).

Florentine fresco: Giotto. St. Francis Giving His Cloak to the Poor Man (Upper Church of St. Francesco, Assisi).

Florentine fresco: Giotto. St. Francis Preaching to the Birds (Upper Church of St. Francesco, Assisi).

Giotto served as a leader among artists and helped the Florentines cultivate pride in their excellence that was accepted by the people.

From the time of Roger Bacon, Jacobus of Liége and Johannes de Grocheo, the Boethian musica mundana declined in influence and importance.

Psalm composition for several voices began much earlier with four-voiced expansion of the psalm melody in fauxbourdon style and had developed to a considerable extent by this time.

Johannes de Grocheo, a Frenchman, was the most important writer on music at this time. He wrote a treatise called "Theoria" that was of the utmost importance since it contained vast information on earlier medieval secular music. De Grocheo called the tenor "that part over which all others are constructed." He described conducti as still being performed at this time and identified the ductia as an example with fewer puncta.
De Grocheo warned against looking for church modes in secular music in the following words, "Non enim per tonum cognoscimus cantum vulgarem." He described motets as "a song composed of several parts with several texts, in which two voices at a time are consonant with each other. This type of song, however, is not suitable for the common people, because they neither sense its subtleties nor are they delighted when listening to it. But it is fitting for the educated and for those who seek the refine-

c.1300(cont.)

ments of the arts." Finally, he discussed authors who asserted that "Music is particularly agreeable because it is practiced by the angels; however, it is not within the province of a musician to talk about the song of angels unless he is a theologian or a prophet."

Musical guilds spread throughout France.

Up to this time the organ had been employed and designed for the execution of primitive accompaniment to plainsong.

Mailieder (May-songs) were written and had been for some time.

The slide trumpet later referred to as the sackbut was probably in existence at this time.

The Hydraulic organ was still in use but in the process of disappearing at this time.

Jacks or tangents were invented and introduced into use.

The four-stringed chiterna (a guitar-like instrument) became popular in Bohemia.

English versions of the Nunc Dimittis existed.

The "storytellers" in Hungary were only entertainers and/or instrumental musicians (joculatores). They still, however, maintained their earlier functions to some degree.

The "under-third" cadence appeared at this time.

Stringed keyboard-instruments became known in England.

The Koleda, which had been sung in Bohemia since the early Middle Ages, was at first an incantation song but, by this time, had become more like a beggar's song which students sang in the streets to earn money.

Bands of wind instruments were employed by cities such as Florence and Lucca.

(to c.1399) Musica falsa became the musica vera et necessaria as de Vitry had predicted.

(to c.1399) Jacopo da Bologna wrote music to Petrarch's Non al suo amante.

(to c.1399) A collection of manuscripts of church music by early Flemish and Burgundian musicians as well as songs for two, three, and four parts existed.

(to c.1399) There was little or no interest in Sacred polyphonic music in Italy.

(to c.1399) While 14th century intricacy was still at times present in Matteo, he exercised moderation in his work.

(to c.1399) The name "exaquir" was identified with "l'eschuaqueil d'Angleterre," which occurred in a poem titled "La Prise d'Alexandrie," written by Machault.

(to c.1399) The musical system of the Persians and Arabs was described by Abdul Kadir by means of an instrument similar to the monochord (the Helikon).

c.1300(cont.)

(to c.1399) The voices above the tenor were called motetus and triplum.

(to c.1399) In French and Italian manuscripts, secular music was the chief output of composers.

(to c.1399) Many collections of Italian organ music existed during this period.

(to c.1399) A more uniform treatment of the two higher parts of the motet (the triplum and motetus) emerged.

(to c.1399) An English manuscript of this period contained the earliest known polyphonic setting of the canticles.

(to c.1399) Several bowed instruments were known in Europe including lyres, the Hurdy Gurdy, and the lyra mendicorum.

(to c.1399) One of the greatest improvements in the organ was the introduction of the four remaining chromatic semitones.

(to c.1399) The name "madrigal" first came into use.

(to c.1399) The ballata was one of the principal forms of Italian poetry and music.

(to c.1399) The monochord was used (a chordophone instrument played with a bow).

(to c.1399) Italian estampies and arrangements of motets for organ developed.

(to c.1399) The development of the first Bohemian school of composition took place during (cont.) the 14th century.

(to c.1399) Composers did not permit the scanning of the text to control the rhythm of their music.

(to c.1399) Jean de Muris, a writer on music, lived.

(to c.1399) Secular music occupied the chief attention of composers during this period in direct contrast to preceding centuries.

(to c.1399) The virginal and clavichord in their facility and range of tone colors were slowly exceeded by northern made organs.

(to c.1399) The French created one of the most important art forms of the period, the chace, and the Italians followed with the caccia. Both were outgrowths of the canon.

(to c.1399) Symbolism in Machaut's music was described as characteristic of the general attitude of this period.

(to c.1399) A single, unique set of variations on a song, the Mills of Paris, appeared.

(to c.1399) The Madrigal, an Italian counterpart of the French chanson, had very little in common with its namesake of this period other than its free character and the form of its texts.

(to c.1399) Isorhythmic sequences occurred in most French music.

(to c.1399) Kings and princes of Europe instituted "chapels" which, like the Papal Chapel,

c.1300(cont.)
were staffed with excellent musicians.

(to c.1399) Italy threatened France's leadership in music, during the Hundred Years' War.

(to c.1399) The Crab canon was found in a motet by Loqueville.

(to c.1399) In a manuscript called "Marienklage" Mary sings in German.

(to c.1399) Polyphony was taken seriously enough to elaborate the voice parts in secular forms as well as in masses, motets, and conducti.

(to c.1399) The spirit of the Renaissance started to make itself felt in the music of this period.

(to c.1399) There were a number of hymns written to popular tunes in England during this period.

(to c.1399) Geisslerlieder were developed and sung by German penitents.

(to c.1399) There was a group of dilettante musicians called Cantori a liuto; and they were distinct from the Cantori a libro who were better schooled musicians.

(to c.1399) The bar line and the modern concept of "measure" were unknown to Machaut and his contemporaries, but he was certainly thoroughly familiar with the idea of regular measure in time.

(to c.1399) The intellectual and social upheaval of the time had (cont.) much in common with the era of Elizabeth in England.

(to c.1399) The language of fine literature once more reverted to English.

(to c.1399) England enjoyed a period of great literary and social accomplishment in spite of corruption in other areas.

(to c.1399) French art was known only to historians but the contributions of Italy rapidly became a part of life.

(to c.1399) The horizontal polyphony of the earlier Middle Ages gradually gave way to a vertical, harmonic conception of music. This was strongly reflected in the creation of keyboard type instruments and the beginnings of their literature.

(to c.1399) French music included elements of the English and Italian, thus giving an international color. This brought about a shift from the earlier nationalistic character of music.

(to c.1399) A woodcut from the Kreuz-Capelle in Burg Carlstein in Bohemia showed the improved Geige of this period.

(to c.1399) The Jena Minnesinger Codex, a collection of Volkslieder, stemmed from this period.

(to c.1399) Les Trois Maries was from a manuscript formerly used at the Abbey of Origny Saint Benoit.

(to c.1399) Valuable relics of Music adapted to ancient versions of the Story of our Lord's

c.1300(cont.)
Passion have survived. One example was taken from a French "Mystery of the Passion," written during this period.

(to c.1399) Desire and therefore attempts to relate the parts more closely existed.

(to c.1399) Dom Bedos stated that an organ was erected in the church of St. Cyprian, at Dijon, which not only had two manuals, but also had the choir organ in front.

(to c.1399) Dom Bedos referred to a curious manuscript as one which gave a great deal of information concerning the organ of that period.

(to c.1399) Feudalism had passed its prime in Germany and princes, prelates, and nobles were losing power which artisans and peasants were in turn gaining. From these middle classes the "Meistersinger," emerged and replaced the noble Minnesinger. The "Minnegesang" was succeeded by the "Meistersang" as a result of this change.

(to c.1399) A treatise by Prodoscimus de Beldemandis stated: "Color in music is taken by analogy with a certain rhetorical color, which is the name for repetition. Just as in rhetorical color there is repetition of similar figures."

(to c.1399) The keyboard was introduced although it is not sure just where or when. It is, however, reasonably sure that it was during this period in all probability in the area around Venice.

(to c.1399) The brief Italian "Ars Nova" inspired by Dante's example and influenced by French and German Trouvères culminated in the secular caccia and madrigal of Giovanni da Cascia (Johannes da Florentia), Jacopo da Bologna and the blind organist Francesco Landino. Italian music otherwise played a small role in European musical culture in general.

(to c.1399) A manuscript which had been the property of Giuliano de'Medici, contained compositions by seven Florentine Musicians.

(to c.1399) Hawkins mentioned an English manuscript tract, by Chilston, in the "Manuscript of Waltham Holy Cross," which gave rules and directions "for the sight of descant . . . . and of Faburdon."

(to c.1399) The intention to create a climax would be risky to claim if the culmination were not obvious to a singer or listener upon exposure to a Machaut Mass.

(to c.1399) The intricacies of medieval rhythm were proof that the idea of "measure" existed at this time. Observation of this characteristic increased sensitivity to the ageless qualities of Machaut's music.

(to c.1399) The physical audibility of complex isorhythmic structure was evidenced by the Gothic devises used by Machaut. These were effective because they were a response to the needs of man during this period.

c.1300(cont.)

(to c.1399) The "Istromento di porco" whose existence was still not established appeared in painted or sculptured representations, particularly at Florence, in the famous Organ Podium of Luca della Robbia.

(to c.1399) Japanese painting: Jizo (33¼"x14½").

(to c.1399) Koshun, a Japanese painter, flourished.

(to c.1399) Kuan Tao-sheng, Chinese painter, flourished.

(to c.1399) The painting of the 14th century, gold and blue, sentimental, preciosious, and of figures without substance was considered more pious than naturalistic, monumental art of innovators.

(to c.1399) Chinese painting: Fishes. Leaf from an album. Probably painted by Liu Ts'ai.

(to c.1399) Artistic centers influenced and moulded one another to an unparalleled extent because of the influence of the Courts.

(to c.1399) French sculpture: The Virgin of Jeanne d'Evreux from the Abbey of St. Denis.

(to c.1399) The most typical sculptures were not those made out of stone for the churches, but rather the smaller works of precious metal or ivory. In these the highest degree of excellence was demonstrated.

(to c.1399) Gothic builders were no longer content with the majestic and clear outlines of the cathedrals built in earlier (cont.) years.

(to c.1399) The works of Chaucer, with his knights and squires, friars and artisans, typified the life of the period.

(to c.1399) Paintings of likenesses from nature, and the art of portraiture developed during this period.

(to c.1399) Architects used graceful lacework and rich ornamentation in their work.

(to c.1399) Italians believed that art, science and scholarship had fourished in the classical period and that they all had been virtually destroyed by northern barbarians. They felt they should revive the glorious past and thus bring about a new era.

(to c.1425) A Prague manuscript entitled "Ein musikalischer Lehrcompendium des H. de Zeelandia." contained many fine volkslieder of the times.

(to c.1450) There were no musical examples from Spain existent at this time.

(to c.1499) Primitive beginnings of the English drama appeared during this period.

(to c.1499) Gothic architecture: Gloucester, Cathedral (length east of tower, 180'; tower 225' high; east window, 72'x38'; vaults, 86' high; cloister, 147' long x 12' wide x 18'6" high).

(to c.1499) Gothic architecture: Melrose Abbey (transept 42'6" wide).

c.1300

(to c.1499) Nicholas of Radom's music provided an example of the influence of 14th-century forms such as the ballade and madrigal on early 15th-century music.

(to c.1499) Wind-bands gradually assumed a definite design; Zinken were most important instruments.

(to c.1499) Dominants had started to give way to semitones.

(to c.1499) Renewal of interest in Gothic art was rapidly followed by a change in the values concerning the period.

(to c.1499) In isorhythmic compositions one or more voices repeated the same rhythmic group over and over without necessarily repeating the same tune. Each rhythmic group was referred to by the technical term, "talea."

(to c.1499) Although the Church dominated music during this period she was not active in subjugating music of secular nature.

(to c.1499) In this great period of polyphonic music the French school ranked very high. Actually this school included composers of northern France and Belgium.

(to c.1499) The circular soundhole was changed into crescents, and the two crescents were face to face. This continued to be the normal form of soundholes throughout this period.

(to c.1499) The different varieties of Real Fugue, perpetual, (cont.) interrupted, strict, and free, which were in use during this period were classified but this was of little practical value since students found it necessary to consult the actual works in order to properly understand the subject of fugue.

(to c.1600) Marenzio's poetic province ranged from 1300 to 1600.

(to c.1600) Many liturgical and choir books of this period as well as other musical works of interest survived.

(to c.1600) The term Musica Figurata was generally understood to indicate the Polyphonic Music of this period. The beauty of a Plain-Chaunt Cantus firmus was enhanced by the addition of an elaborate and carefully constructed counterpoint.

(to c.1900) Machaut's century was bound by aesthetic considerations that differed significantly from those generally accepted in the twentieth century.

1301

Ni Tsan, Chinese painter, was born (died 1374).

c.1301

Giovanni Cimabue, a Florentine painter, died (born c.1240). He was strongly influenced by Byzantine painting.

1303

Jehannot de l'Escurel, a composer, was executed at Paris.

(to 1304) The Papal reign of St. Benedict XI (born in

1303(cont.)

Treviso).

(to 1305) Giotto's frescoes in the Capella degli Scrovegni in Padua provided a significant measure of his greatness.

(to 1305) Florentine fresco: Giotto, Flight into Egypt. Scrovegni Chapel, Padua.

(to 1305) Florentine fresco: Giotto, Deposition. Scrovegni Chapel, Padua.

(to 1305) Florentine fresco: Giotto, Noli Me Tangere. Scrovegni Chapel, Padua.

(to 1306) Gothic painting: Giotto, The Betrayal. Arena Chapel, Padua.

(to 1306) Gothic painting: Giotto, The Bewailing of Christ. Arena Chapel, Padua.

(to 1306) Gothic painting: Giotto, Death of St. Francis. Bardi Chapel, Sante Croce, Florence.

(to 1306) Gothic painting: Giotto, Meeting of Joachim and Anna. Arena Chapel, Padua.

c.1303

A passage from Robert de Brunne's paraphrase of the Manuel de Peches by Robert Grosseteste claimed that the harp was noted for its powers in warding off evil.

1304

Ruediger Manesse , who collected Manessische Hs. of secular monophonic music, died.

1305

The Archbishop of Bordeaux was (cont.) elected to the papacy as Clement V. He left Rome for Avignon and during Machaut's life, the Popes lived in French Provence, practically as prisoners of secular power. Clement V left his Primicerius and Scola Cantorum in Rome.

(to 1314) The Papal reign of St. Clement V (born in France).

1306

The lute was mentioned among the instruments at the Feast of Westminster.

Facopone da Todi, who wrote a Stabat Mater for the Feast of the Seven Dolours, died.

c.1306

Giotto di Bondone covered the walls of a small church in Padua in northern Italy with stories from the life of the Virgin and of Christ.

Gothic wall-painting: Giotto, Faith (in the Cappella dell' Arena in Padua).

Gothic wall-painting: Giotto, The Mourning of Christ (in the Cappella dell'Arena in Padua).

1307

Persian manuscript: David Summoned to Be King (history of the world).

(to 1327) The reign of King Edward II (Plantagenet) over England and Great Britain.

(to 1814) Denmark and Norway combined to form one nation. Danish and Norwegian literature and the allied arts developed concurrently.

1308

The city of Siena commissioned Duccio to paint a large altarpiece of the Virgin, the Maestà. Detailed specifications were provided to the artist.

Duns Scotus, who taught at Oxford and at Paris, died. He felt St. Thomas wrong in claiming that a rational demonstration of God's existance and/or the immortality of the soul was possible.

(to 1311) Byzantine painting: Duccio. Transfiguration (Panel from the Back of the Maestà).

(to 1311) Byzantine painting: Duccio. St. Catherine of Alexandria (Detail from the Maestà).

(to 1311) Byzantine painting: Duccio. Adoration of the Magi (Panel from the Predella of the Maestà).

(to 1311) Byzantine painting: Duccio. Three Maries at the Tomb (Panel from the back of the Maestà).

(to 1311) Byzantine painting: Duccio. Calling of the Apostles Peter and Andrew (Panel from the Back of the Maestà).

(to 1313) The reign of King Henry VII (Hohenstaufen) over Germany.

1309

The building of the Palace of the Doges in Venice was started.

Chinese painting: Kuan Tao-sheng, Bamboo (11"x4'6").

(to 1376) The papacy suffered a great crisis through the half (cont.) -enforced, partially voluntary exile to Avignon.

c.1309

(to c.1343) Lucidarium and Pomerium were written by Marchettus of Padua.

1310

The dynasty of the Luxembourgs came to the throne.

Laudi Spirituali was a name given to certain collections of devotional music. These collections were for use by the "Laudisti" - a religious confraternity, instituted at Florence in the year 1310 and later held in great esteem by St. Charles Borromeo, and St. Philip Neri.

(to 1314) Le Roman de Fauvel was written by Gervais de Bus.

(to 1340) Under King John of Luxemburg and his son, Emperor Charles IV, Prague rapidly emerged as the cultural center of the Holy Roman Empire.

c.1310

Casella, a friend of Dante, and a native of Florence, helped launch a philharmonic society there whose members invented the Laudi Spirituali.

Russian icon: Archangel Michaël (Novgorod School).

Stringed keyboard instruments, precursors of the modern piano, developed.

Mülich of Prague, a Bohemian Minnesinger, was active at this time.

A famous song, Svátý Vaclave ("St. Wenceslaus"), was written

c.1310(cont.)
at this time.

The minima was mentioned by Johannes de Muris.

George Pachymeres, mathematician and scientist who wrote on music, died (born 1242).

"Puellae gremium" an English motet was written. It used duple rhythm, 3rds and complete triads, as well as crossing voices.

A highly respected source regarded Sumer is icumen in as the oldest known composition, ostensibly six parts and written about this time.

Following organum came the "Diaphonum" and "Descant." These purportedly led, by natural development, to the use of "Fauxbourdon" at Avignon. When the Papal Court returned to Rome after its seventy years absence from that city, the technique of fauxbourdon continued.

English manuscript painting: Christ in the Temple; a hawking party (Page from "Queen Mary's Psalter").

1311

(June 9) Duccio's Maestà was carried in a triumphal procession to the Siena cathedral. It was revered as an object of piety and as an emblem of the justifiable pride of the Sienese citizens who had commissioned this masterpiece.

The founder of the Meistersinger, Heinrich von Meissen, known as Frauenlob, came to Mainz and instituted a (cont.) guild of singers who bound themselves to observe certain rules.

1312

King Edward III (Plantagenet) of England, was born (died 1377).

An organ built in Germany for Marinus Sanutus, a celebrated Venetian Patrician, was erected in the Church of St. Raphael, in Venice.

1314

(to 1316) The reign of Louis X the Quarreler, French King of the Capetian Dynasty.

1315

Gothic painting: Simone Martini's first known work, the Maestà of 1315 (Palazzo Pubblico, Siena).

1316

(Nov. 15) King John I, French King of the Capetian Dynasty, was born and ruled for seven days at which time he died. His father Louis X had died before his birth, which accounted for his becoming King at birth.

Walter de Evesham was referred to in a list of mathematicians living at this time.

Interpolations in the Roman de Fauvel by Chaillou de Pesstain comprised an anthology of pieces. Several were contained in other manuscripts.

Zucchetto, the first known organist of St. Mark's was appointed.

The Council of Cologne forbade the singing of the Media vita against anyone without permission of the Bishop. The song was also known as "Mitten wir im

1316(cont.)
Leben sind."

(to 1322) The reign of King Philip V the Tall, French King of the Capetian Dynasty.

(to 1334) The Papal reign of St. John XXII (born in Cahors).

c.1316
(to 1325) De Vitry's Ars nova dated from this period.

c.1317
Simone Martini was probably in Naples painting a panel of St. Louis of Toulouse.

1318
Heinrich von Meissen, author of "Frauenlob," and a secular monophonic composer, died (born 1260). With his death the third group of Minnesinger ceased to exist.

Louis van Valbeke of Brabant, the supposed inventor of the organ pedal, died.

(to 1360) "Sweetest of all, sing," "Have good-day, my leman dear," and six other secular theatre songs were set as Latin Hymns by Richard Ledrede, Bishop of Ossory.

c.1318
Duccio di Buoninsegna, Gothic painter and sculptor, died (born c.1255).

The archives of St. Marks evidenced the existence of a long line of organists from this date forward when the position was held by a Venetian, Mistro Zuchetto.

1319
King John II the Good of France (cont.) (House of Valois), was born (died 1364).

Sienese painting: Ambrogio Lorenzetti, Madonna del Latte (Seminary, Siena).

(to 1348) Ambrogio Lorenzetti, Sienese painter, was active.

1320
The University of Dublin was founded by Alexander de Bicknor, Archbishop of Dublin.

The Troubadour Academy of Toulouse, known as "The Seven Maintainers of the Gay Science" was founded. At a later date it was visited by Petrarch.

Pietro Lorenzetti's "Arezzo Polyptych" was commissioned.

c.1320
Florentine painting: Giotto, Saint Francis Receiving the Stigmata (10'3 5/8" x 5'5 3/4").

In the Romance of Sir Gawayne and the Green Knight an example was found of the use of the word "touch" as an equivalent to "sound."

1321
(September 14) The ménestriers or fiddlers of France formed a brotherhood or corporation with a code of laws in 11 sections. This was presented to the Prevot of Paris, and registered at the Châtelet by him. It was called the Brotherhood of St. Julian. The head was referred to as the King of the Minstrels.

Dante, the founder of the Italian language, died (born 1265).

1321(cont.)

Johannes de Muris wrote on the subject of Measured Music.

1322

The typical German miracle-play appeared in the "Spiel von den zehn Jungfrauen" performed at Eisenach. The texts were in German.

The Strassburg City Council made a ruling that no one should play "after the third bell." Trombones, trumpets, drums, horns, and cymbals were forbidden, only shawms and soft pipes permitted.

(to 1328) The reign of King Charles IV, French King of the Capetian Dynasty.

c.1322

"Geistliche Schauspiele" first became common in Germany and Bohemia.

This date marked the start of a struggle between clergy and musicians which went on for many centuries. Pope John's denouncement of the compositions of the new school included his complaint that the sense of the sacred text was obscured.

(to c.1325) Pope John XXII passed an edict forbidding the leading tone.

(to c.1325) Pope John XXII's Papal Bull dealt with "Musica Figurata." This term was applied to Plain-Chaunt Melodies, corrupted by the introduction of forbidden intervals. Embellishments were also forbidden. The ochetto, which had been introduced into the discantus sung upon ecclesiastical plainchaunt, was similarly condemned. Practically all polyphony, including (cont.) the addition of the motetus and triplum, was banned.

1323

Musica speculativa, by Frenchman Jean de Muris, mentioned various kinds of stringed keyboard instruments. Neither the clavicembalo nor the clavichord were mentioned, but the monochord was described (four strings).

Italian painting: Simone Martini, Fogliano da Reggio.

Guillaume de Machaut became secretary, notary, and almoner to John, King of Bohemia and Duke of Luxembourg. Machaut travelled all over Europe with him.

c.1323

Florentine sculpture: Giotto and Andrea Pisano, Allegorical Bas-Relief from the Campanile in Florence.

1325

Francesco Landini (or Landino), a great organist, composer, poet, and philosopher, was born in Fiésole (died 1397, Sept. 2).

Witzlau von Rügen, secular monophonic composer recorded in Jena Manuscript, died.

The Great Bells of Ratisbon were installed (5 tons, 16cw.).

(to 1521) Aztec sculpture: Stone Figure (13½" high).

c.1325

Philippe de Vitry was the most influential composer at this time.

c.1325(cont.)

A manuscript, the Robertsbridge Codex, recorded the earliest intabulations (tablatures) of motets and estampies for keyboard instruments.

(to c.1425) Polyphony of the Italian Trecento.

(to c.1432) There is a great lack of source material about Keyboard music during this period.

1326

The short-necked lute and koboz were first mentioned in Hungary.

In a manuscript ballads and roundelays were mentioned.

Englishman, Robert de Handlo wrote on the Subject of Measured Music. He described the hocket as a passage truncated or mangled with a combination of notes and pauses.

1327

(to 1327) The reign of King Edward III (Plantagenet) over England and Great Britain. During this period he had numerous musicians in his service including five "trompettes," one "citoler," five "pipers," one "tobarett," two "clarions," one "makerer," two "fidelers," and three "waytes." Foreign musicians also frequently visited the court. The leader of the French poets and musicians was Jean Froissart.

1328

Japanese painting: Koshun, Hachiman as a Priest (32" high).

Sienese painting:
Simone Martini, Portrait of the Condottiere Guido-Riccio da (cont.) Fogliano.

(to 1350) The reign of King Philip VI (House of Valors) over France.

1329

Sienese painting:
Pietro Lorenzetti, Altarpiece of the Carmelites.

1330

Pietro Cavallini, Florentine painter, died (born 1250). His work was in the Byzantine tradition.

Simone Martini was in Assisi, where he decorated the St. Martin Chapel of the lower church.

The Confraternity, founded by 37 jongleurs and jongleresses, whose names were preserved, prospered sufficiently to enable the purchase of a site and the subsequent erection of a hospital for poor musicians. The hospital was finished in 1335 and dedicated to St. Julien and St. Genest.

(to 1331) Sienese fresco:
Ambrogio Lorenzetti, St. Francis at Siena.

(to 1339) Gothic sculpture:
Andrea Pisano, Visitation (Baptistry, Florence).

c.1330

Giovanni Pisano, Italian sculptor, died (born c.1250).

An Ecclesiastical document from Wernigerode described the use of the organ for liturgical purposes.

Walter Odington, an important English writer on music, died.

c.1330

Florentine sculpture: Giotto and A. Pisano: Allegorical Bas-Relief (Campanile in Florence).

Gothic painting: Cologne School, Presentation at the Temple.

Johannes de Muris, in a manuscript bequeathed by Christina, Queen of Sweden, to the Vatican Library, spoke of "Magister Franco, qui invenit in Cantu Mensuram figurarum." He himself was at one time regarded as the inventor of Measured Music.

John Wycliffe, the English composer, was born (died 1384).

1332

Antonio da Tempo used the word mandrialis to describe a rustic kind of pastoral poem, popular at the time.

Sienese painting: Ambrogio Lorenzetti, Story of St. Nicholas of Bari.

1333

Guillaume de Machaut became canon of Rheims Cathedral, a post he held till his death.

Clarions and trumpets were mentioned in an old ballad which described the defeat of the Scots at Halidon.

Simone Martini, a painter, returned to Siena and produced his finest work, The Annunciation.

Gothic painting: Simone Martini, Sant' Ansano Annunciation (9'10" x 8'7").

Gothic painting: Simone Martini and Lippo Memmi, The Annunciation (for an altar in Siena Cathedral).

(and 1346) Bohemia became another important centre of Gothic painting during the reign of Charles IV, as King in 1333 and Emperor in 1346.

1334

(to 1342) The Papal reign of St. Benedict XII (born in France). He was too fond of ceremonials to object to the elaborate music sung in his private chapel by twelve Choral Chaplains.

1335

Ambrogio Lorenzetti collaborated with his brother only once, on some frescoes that are lost. They had little in common as artists.

1336

A manuscript volume, which belonged to a company of "Laudisti" at the Chiesa d'Ogni Santi, at Florence, at this time, has been preserved.

1337

The Florentine painter, Giotto di Bondone, died (born 1266).

King Charles V the Wise of France (House of Valois) was born (died 1380).

King Edward III of England invaded Flanders; and for the remainder of Machaut's life, the French people lost land, life, and honor. Ironically, King Edward III was himself a Frenchman.

(to 1339) Sienese fresco:

1337(cont.)
Ambrogio Lorenzetti, Peace (Good Government Fresco).

(to 1339) Sienese fresco: Ambrogio Lorenzetti, Fortitude (Good Government Fresco).

(to 1343) Sienese fresco: Ambrogio Lorenzetti, Allegory of Good Government and Bad Government.

(to 1368) The organist Francesco da Pesaro was an important representative of the ars nova in Venice.

(to 1433) The Hundred Years' War between France and England halted French leadership in European music.

1338
Robert Caveron was "Rois des ménétriers" of the "Confrérie of St. Julien."

c.1338
The chronicle of the town of Königssaal stated that people everywhere, even unaccomplished musicians, sang in sixths, approximating the practice of fauxbourdon.

1339
Simone Martini met Petrarch in Avignon.

1340
Approximately 400 players performed at the court of Mantua.

Machaut's life was not well documented but it is known that he sold a horse at this time.

c.1340
The greatest of Middle English poets, Geoffrey Chaucer, was born (died 1400).

The concept of expressing of note values by different shape notes was credited by some writers to De Muris, but this was certainly in error.

The earliest German version of the Gregorian Passion with "divided roles" appeared in a Silesian manuscript.

The Northern Italian composer Johannes Ciconia was born at Liége(died 1411).

Florentine sculpture: Andrea Pisano: A Sculptor at Work (relief on the Florentine Campanile).

Florentine fresco: Maso di Banco or Giottino, A Miracle of St. Sylvester (c.8'11" by 14'6 3/4").

Gothic painting: Simone Martini, Christ Carrying the Cross (tempera on canvas (11 3/4" x 7 7/8").

1342
Sienese painting: Pietro Lorenzetti, The Nativity of the Virgin (tryptych).

Sienese painting: Ambrogio Lorenzetti, The Presentation at the Temple.

(to 1352) The Papal reign of St. Clement VI (born in France).

1344
Simone Martini, Sienese painter, died (born c.1284).

Sienese painting: Ambrogio Lorenzetti, The Annunciation.

(to 1362) Girard of Orleans, a painter, was active.

1346

King John of Bohemia, although blind, was led into the battle of Crécy "assez avant pour n'en plus revenir." His glorious death for French aristocracy caused Machaut to search for another royal patron. At this same battle, clarions and trumpets were used by the English army. A Guillaume de Machaut was reported killed during the battle.

Bishop Jan Kempa, who died at this time, was probably the oldest Polish composer known by name.

1347

The use of drums was described in the passage in Froissart (Bk. I. Pt. i. chap. 322) which stated that in the year 1347, Edward III and his company entered Calais "à grand foison de menestrandies, de trumpes, de tambours, de nacaires, de chalemies et de muses." This was a large military band that accompanied the King of England in spite of England's reputed unmusicality.

(to 1348) A very interesting composition in the Llibre Vermell was a monodic piece, the oldest known surviving example of its kind with music of a "Dance of Death." This was a strange and mysterious outgrowth of the period of the Black Death.

(to 1380) The "Limburg Chronicle" was comprised of Volkslieder which apparently were in vogue during this period. Knights' and monks' songs were also included in the collection.

c.1347

Lippo Memmi, a Sienese painter, had been a collaborator of Simone Martini.

1348

A psalter painted by Orcagna, himself a musician, looked just like an Arabic Kanun. The work was contained in his "Trionfo della Morte" (at Pisa).

Charles founded the first university of Central Europe in Prague. Musical mensural theory and the principles of consonance were taught there according to the doctrine of Johannes de Muris.

The Pietà at San Giovanni in Bragola, was founded by Fra Pierazzo d'Assissi as a succursal to the Foundling Hospital at San Francesco della Vigna.

Pietro Lorenzetti, Sienese painter, died (born c.1280).

(to 1349) A terrible epidemic of bubonic plague, known as the Black Death, swept western Europe. A famine occurred and the Chronicle of Froissart estimated that "the third part of the world perished" as a result of the two scourges.

1349

Machaut was concerned by the catastrophes surrounding him. In the opening section of Le Jugement dou Roy de Navarre, an allegoric poem he wrote expressed his feelings which were genuinely sad.

Richard Rolle, the Hermit, died near Hampole, in Yorkshire.

Copin du Brequin was "Rois des

1349(cont.)

ménétriers" of the "Confrérie of St. Julien."

The Geisslerlieder were linked with the plague.

The penitential mania was rampant in Germany during the plague.

William of Occam, who died at this time, stated that religious dogmas could not be supported on rational grounds, and that, therefore, they could be accepted only as deliberate acts of faith.

1350

(February 15) Petrarch, while he lived in Padua, wrote a long letter to de Vitry, in which he paid tribute to the French "musician" whom he considered the "greatest, the only poet of his period."

Jacopo da Bologna, Landini's teacher, was active at this time.

Juan Ruiz, writer of the Libro de Buen Amor, died (born 1283).

An organ with twenty-two keys was made by a monk at Thorn, Poland.

Italian painting: Orcagna, musician-painter, "Coronation of the Virgin."

King John I of Aragon, one of Spain's most ardent early patrons of music, was born (died 1396).

(to 1364) The reign of King John II the Good over France.

(to 1400) Rondeau, virelai, and (cont.) ballades were the principal musical forms.

(to 1400) The period of invention and development of the monochord.

c.1350

Gothic painting:
Francesco Traini, Triumph of Death, Campo Santo, Pisa. This painting was partially destroyed in 1944.

Almost all of Machaut's motets were written at this time.

The expedient of placing soundholes back to back was from this time.

Two big battles between the English and the French were fought at this time. The French were the losers in both.

Oswald von Wolkenstein's polyphonic pieces, and also Münch von Salzburg's, represented the beginnings of a tradition that was to lead German secular vocal music for more than a century. They were early examples of polyphonic settings of German lieder, but very primitive.

Machaut's Mass was the earliest known complete polyphonic setting of the ordinarium missae. It contained six movements and was polyphonically coherent.

Boccaccio invented a rhyme pattern later referred to as ottava rima: abababcc.

The cabinet picture (the easel picture) first appeared in France.

One Master Bertram was working in Hamburg.

c.1350(cont.)

English literature emerged completely from its long eclipse and burst into full glory exemplified in the works of one of England's greatest poets, Geoffrey Chaucer.

The popularity of the Ochetus began to wane.

Keyed stringed instruments were probably invented at this time.

Many curious forms of notation were noticeable in Fra Angelico Ottobi's Calliopea leghale.

The house of Gonzaga ruled over the city as well as the duchy of Mantua, and over the Margraviate of Montferrat from this time.

An important manuscript from this time contained 81 compositions (now at Chapter library, Ivrea).

The musical string of the Egyptians, Greeks and Romans was gut. Wire was practically unknown to them, since the art of wire-drawing was perfected about 1350, at the same time that keyed instruments with strings, such as the clavichord, harpsichord and/or virginal came into existence. Music wire was first drawn in 1351 at Augsburg.

"Angelus ad Virginem" was written. It was an example of English descant and fauxbourdon.

The time of development of 3 part writing of consonances.

(to 1370) Music showed influence of Machaut in the use of short phrases, rhythmic motives, chords, and 4 parts.

(cont.) Music was rapidly becoming more complex.

(to 1400) Gothic architecture: The "decorated" style was exemplified by the west front of Exeter Cathedral.

(to 1425) English vocal polyphony, as preserved in English manuscripts, revealed little structural advance over French music from previous years.

1351

Simon Tunsted's treatise "De Quatuor Principalibus Musice" was written while he was Regent of the Minorites at Oxford.

Gothic architecture: Gloucester, Cathedral, choir (East window, 72'x38'; vaults, 86' high).

Philip de Vitry became Bishop of Meaux.

(to 1412) Gothic architecture: Gloucester, Cathedral, cloister (147' long x 12' wide x 18'6" high).

c.1351

Jacopo da Bologna became the teacher of Francesco Landini.

Johannes de Muris, author of Ars novae musice, died (b.c1290).

1352

(to 1353) In the Decameron of Boccaccio there is a story of one Dion, who when asked to sing, said he would if he had a cembalo. The date of this quotation (1352-1353) has created problems among musicologists as to what instrument was meant.

(to 1362) The Papal reign of

1352(cont.)

St. Innocent VI (born in France).

1356

The battle of Poitiers.

Joachim Schund, one of the oldest known organ builders, made the organ of St. Thomas's at Leipzig.

1357

Count Hugo von Montfort, a prominent figure in the political disturbances of his period and a composer of some note, was born (died 1423). His music was written by his minstrel, Burk Mangolt.

1358

Heinrich von Mügling, a minnesinger, left Prague.

The fiddle was first mentioned in Hungary.

1359

Chaucer fought with the English army in France and was taken prisoner near Rheims. Machaut was then living there and was a canon of the cathedral.

1360

Hugo Spechtshart von Reutlingen, who wrote "Chronikon," a description of rites of Geissler and their songs, died (born 1285).

Italian painting: Portrait of Jean le Bon, King of France (26"x17¼").

Edward III of England presented an echiquier to his captive, King John of France.

c.1360

Andrei Rublev, Moscow artist, was born (died c.1430).

Gentile da Fabriano, Italian painter, was born (died c.1427).

According to Praetorius, the organ at Halberstadt had a twenty-two note complete chromatic scale.

Gothic painting: French School (Girard d'Orléans). Portrait of King John the Good.

1361

(February 23) The Halberstadt Cathedral organ, built by Nicholas Faber, a priest, was finished.

(June 9) Philip de Vitry, whose major work was "Ars Nova," died at Meaux (born 1291, Oct. 31).

Burgundy returned to the French crown when Duke Philip of Rouvre died.

1362

An English statute of 1362 ordered that pleading in the courts of law should be in English rather than in French from this date.

Old songs and ballads frequently had a chorus or motto for each verse. In the language of the time this was called a Burden or Bob. One of the oldest and most popular was "Hey troly loly lo," quoted in "Piers the Plowman," and in other early songs.

Chinese painting: Ni Tsan, Landscape (1'x1'8").

(to 1370) The Papal reign of St. Urban V (born in France).

c.1362

One version of "Piers the Plowman" was written.

1363

King John II conferred the duchy of Burgundy on his fourth son, Philip the Bold, a younger brother of the future Charles V.

Johannes Gerson, French scholar, was born (died 1429).

Seami Motokiyo, Japanese author of a collection of aesthetic treatises on music and musician training, was born (died 1443).

1364

Ite, Missa est was added to the mass, performed at the Coronation of Charles V.

Francesco Landini was awarded the laurel crown at Venice for his poetry by Peter the Great, King of Cyprus.

Machaut's Mass was on the basis of very limited evidence, described as having been composed for the coronation of Charles V. The high musical value and historical significance of this work may well have been contributory to the association with the coronation.

Ralph Higden, English chronicler and monk of the Benedictine Order, died.

The University of Cracow was founded and became an important center for musical studies.

(to 1380) The reign of King Charles V the Wise (House of Valois) over France.

(to 1380) During the reign of Charles V the lands under his rule cultivated music with great vigor.

c.1364

An inventory of the Cathedral Library at Treviso mentioned a "liber pro organis."

1365

An Ecclesiastical document recording the foundation of the chapter house of St. Stephen at Vienna ordered that on all important festivals the whole Office was to be sung by professors and students of the University, organ accompaniment was included.

1366

Taddeo Gaddi, a Gothic painter, died.

Hubert van Eyck, Flemish painter, was born (died 1426).

1367

King Henry IV Bolingbroke (House of Lancaster) of England, was born (died 1413).

The long lines of powerful portraits with large heads and sumptuous drapery which hang on the walls of the Chapel of Karlstyn were by Theodoric of Prague who was apparently also very active at Hamburg.

King Richard II (Plantagenet) of England was born (died 1400).

1368

Islamic sculpture: Granada, The Alhambra, Court of the Myrtles (120'x75').

King Charles VI the Well -Beloved of France (House of Valois) was born (died 1422).

(to 1644) It was not until the Ming period that the notes which form the interval of the half step were eliminated and trans-

1368(cont.)

formed the scale into pentatonic anhemitonic (without semitones) by discarding the F-sharp and the B.

1369

Jean Vaillant's Dame doucement was written (Chantilly manuscript).

Simon Tunsted, a French musician, died in a nunnery of St. Clara, at Bruisyard, Suffolk.

c.1369

Chaucer chose to write his "Book of the Duchess" in English.

1370

John Dunstable was born in Bedfordshire, England (died 1453, December 24), see 1435.

According to some sources Guillaume Dufay was born at Chimay. A majority of musicologists place the date at c.1400 (died 1474, Nov. 27).

(to 1378) The Papal reign of St. Gregory XI (born in France).

(to 1390) Music became extraordinarily complex rhythmically; long syncopated passages, cross rhythms, augmented sixths and fifths were frequent occurrences.

(to 1417) The Church schism resulted in the setting up of two rival popes and, in fact, later three.

(to 1430) The First Flemish School of composition.

c.1370

The Aberdeen School existed at this time. Its pupils were the same as those who attended the (cont.) grammar school. Both vocal and instrumental music were taught.

Chaucer wrote "Legende of Good Women."

The black and red forms of the notes of Measured Chaunt were gradually discarded and they were replaced by white notes.

Hermann der Münch von Salzburg translated into German verse psalm passages that served as grace at meals. Benedicite! Allmächtiger Gott became the most famous.

Marenzio set a text by Franco Sacchetti to music. The caccia "Passand con pensier per un boschetto had been previously set to music for two voices by Nicolò da Perugia.

(to 1380) The anonymous Echecs amoureux, written by a French dilettante, included the names of many instruments, as well as other information of a musical nature.

1371

The Great Bells of Frankfort were built (6'4" dia., 5 tons).

c.1372

(to c.1385) The activities of composer Johannes Ciconia took him to Liége.

1373

(to 1378) Geoffrey Chaucer was sent to Italy on business by the King.

(to 1415) With the advent of Jan Huss a new era started in Czechoslovakian history and consequently in the history of that country's music.

c.1373

(to c.1450) John Lydgate wrote the "Reson and Sensuallyte."

1374

Ni Tsan, Chinese painter, died (born 1301).

c.1374

Nanni di Banco, Italian sculptor, was born (died 1420). His best known work was a statue of St. Luke at the Florence Cathedral (80" high).

Jacopo della Quercia, Italian sculptor, was born (died 1438). Major work, Baptismal Font, San Giovanni, Siena.

c.1375

(or c.1379) Master of Flémalle (Robert Campin), Netherlandish painter, was born (died 1444).

Reginald Liebert wrote the earliest known polyphonic setting of Ordinary and Proper Mass.

A setting of the credo was written by Bartholino of Padua.

The French ballade was in mensural notation after Johannes Wolf, Schrifttafeln.

The En atendant of Selesses illustrated the extreme rhythmic complexity of music of this time.

One of the finest English metrical romances was "Sir Gawain and the Green Knight."

Jacopin Selesses wrote Ballades.

From the rituals of the medieval Church, both religious and secular dramatic forms in the vernacular developed in England by this time.

The rhythmic intricacies of Busnois went beyond the use of hemiola but they were not as complex as works common at this time.

Enchiquier, a stringed keyboard instrument, was used.

A Breslau manuscript showed the penetration into the Empire's eastern section by French music.

The art of composition owed a great deal to the intense love of music which prevailed in the Low Countries at this time.

King of Aragon, John I, wished to employ a famous Burgundian organist. He spared no expense in obtaining his portable organs and his "book in which were written the estampies and other pieces he played."

King John I of Aragon, who was related to the French reigning house by two marriages, established a Chapel Royal like the Papal Chapel at Avignon, in both its repertory and its personnel which was Franco-Netherlandish.

1376

Jean Lefevre de Ressons referred to "grosses bombardes" as "nouvelles."

Bass shawms (somewhat like our modern baritone oboes) were mentioned as something new. They resembled a baritone oboe.

1377

(April) Guillaume de Machaut died as a canon of Rheims (born c.1300). Charles V was still alive at the time of Machaut's death (born 1285).

Pope Gregory XI returned to

1377(cont.)
Rome, and brought his Choir with him.

Dufay migrated to Rome when Pope Gregory XI restored the Papal Court there.

A large number of foreigners infused the Pontifical or Sixtine Choir. Many of these were Spanish and had superior voices.

Islamic architecture: Granada, the Alhambra, Court of the Lions (92'x52').

Islamic architecture: Granada, the Alhambra, Hall of the Two Sisters (c.26'x26').

Filippo Brunelleschi, a Florentine architect, was born (died 1446).

(to 1399) The reign of King Richard II (Plantagenet) over England and Great Britain.

(to 1529) Gothic architecture: Ulm, Cathedral (tower, 528' high).

c.1377
Oswald von Wolkenstein, German composer who initiated polyphonic music in Germany, was born (died 1445).

A version of "Piers the Plowman" was written.

John Gower wrote the "Mirour de l'Omme."

1378
Chaucer went to Italy.

Lorenzo Ghibert, a Florentine sculptor, was born (died 1455).

The Choristers of St. Paul's (cont.) performed Miracle-Plays regularly. These were judiciously supervised by the church.

(to 1389) The Papal reign of St. Urban VI (born in Naples).

(to 1417) The "Great Schism of the West" was the severest blow to the papacy in history, probably brought on to a great extent by the exile to Avignon.

1379
Magister Záviš received the degree of Bachelor of Arts from the University of Prague.

c.1379
Gothic painting: Master Bertram, Christ's Entry Into Jerusalem (Panel From Altarpiece of Christ's Passion).

(to c.1386) Slovakian sculpture: Peter Parler the Younger: Self-Portrait (in Prague Cathedral).

(to c.1456) Dubrovnik records showed that the city hired Albanians, Germans, Greeks and Italians to play bagpipes and trumpets and probably other instruments.

1380
Jan van Eyck, Flemish painter, was born (died 1440), see c.1390.

Dufay was appointed as a singer in the Papal choir from this date, possibly through 1432 according to Baini.

Froissart in the Chronicles related that at the coronation of Charles VI there were "more than thirty trumpet players whose play was marvelously clear."

John of Gaunt, brother of Edward the Black Prince and a

1380(cont.)

very powerful noble in England, set up a court of minstrels at Tutsbury (Stafford).

(to 1396) Jan of Jenštejn, a composer, was Archbishop of Prague.

(to 1400) Claus Sluter, the sculptor, worked at Dijon.

(to 1422) The reign of King Charles VI, the Well -Beloved (House of Valois) over France. Although he was intermittently insane he made sure that music was cultivated during his rule.

(to 1450) The period of Guillaume Dufay, the founder of the older Flemish school.

c.1380

Gothic sculpture: Claus Sluter, Madonna; Wall of Moses (5'8" high) Chartreuse de Champmol.

Gothic painting: Master of the Trebon, Altarpiece. Resurrection.

(to 1385) French manuscript: The psalter adorned with delicate "grisailles" by André Beauneveu.

1381

The Peasants' Revolt in London.

After the death of Count Peter of Savoy, the Savoy Chapel Royal came into Queen Eleanor's control, who passed it on to her son, Edmund of Lancaster. The Lancastrian branch of the Royal family held it until 1381, when, owing to the unpopularity of John of Gaunt, the palace was ransacked by insurgents led by Wat Tyler.

c.1381

John Gower wrote "Vox Clamantis."

1382

Magister Záviš became Master of Arts at the University of Prague.

1384

John Wycliffe, the English composer, died (born c.1330).

Margrave William instituted weekly performances of a Marian Mass, accompanied by organ, in Leipzig.

Philip the Bold acquired a book of motets from a Jehan Macon, a singer at the Sainte Chapelle in Paris.

1385

John Trevisa translated Ralph Higden's "Polycronicon" into English.

c.1385

Geoffrey Chaucer finished "The Parliament of Fowls; Troilus and Criseyde."

1386

(July 9) Fifteen hundred Swiss peasants were victorious at Sempach over an army of about 5,000 men commanded by Duke Leopold III of Austria.

A second manual and couplers were added to organs.

Cambrai had ten vicaires and six boys.

Gothic architecture: Milan Cathedral was begun (facade, 219' wide; nave, 54' wide x 157' high).

Gothic architecture (secular): Bodiam Castle (175'x178'; towers 60'4" high).

1386(cont.)

Froissart reported the use of trumpets, clarions, and "toutes manières d'instrumens" on a special occasion at a church in Ghent.

Geoffrey Chaucer was elected a Member of Parliament for the shire of Kent. This indicated that he was a landowner in the county.

c.1386

Donatello, the Florentine sculptor, was born (died 1466).

Geoffrey Chaucer began "The Legend of Good Women" which he never finished.

1387

John the First, King of Aragon, had heard and wanted to own an "exaquir," a keyboard stringed -instrument.

Geoffrey Chaucer began "The Canterbury Tales" which he never finished.

Fra Angelico (Giovanni di Fiesole), the painter of Fiesole, was born (died 1455).

King Henry V (House of Lancaster) of England, was born (died 1422).

Jean Caumez was "Rois des ménétriers" of the "Confrérie of St. Julien.

c.1387

A version of "Piers the Plowman" was written, containing an illumination of note, the Sin of Pride.

1388

Froissart mentioned an organ "mélodieusement joué" at a church at Orthez.

King John I wrote to his brother-in-law Philip the Bold, Duke of Burgundy, and described an exaquier as "like an organ which sounds with strings."

1389

Francesco Landini was mentioned in the Romanza "Il Paradiso degli Alberti" by Giovanni da Prato.

(to 1404) The Papal reign of St. Boniface IX (born in Naples).

(to 1409) The Papal Choir was comprised almost entirely of musicians from Liege.

1390

John Gower wrote his "Confessio Amantis" in English.

Chartres had thirteen heuriers.

The Flemish sculptor, Claus Sluter, became Ymagier to Philip the Bold. Among his works were Philip's Tomb and the Well of Moses, with statues of the prophets.

(to 1400) Music returned to a more lyrical, less complex style, which led toward the Burgundian School.

c.1390

Masses written with counterpoint were sent to Rome from the Netherlands.

There were regular schools of music at Colmar, Frankfurt, Mainz, Prague, and Strassburg.

The hymn Gaude felix Ungaria was written in honor of St. Elizabeth of Hungary. The composer was a Dominican from Kassa and he used a troped melody from a Gregorian antiphon.

c.1390(cont.)

Since numerous organs had two manuals and a pedal keyboard they had characteristic and colorful solo stops. Among these were flute and trumpet and they were used against the bell-like uniform mass of mixtures.

The breve, as well as several other notes, was originally written in black, the more modern white notes drawn in outline were introduced by Dufay about this time.

Jan Van Eyck, Netherlandish painter, was born (died c.1441).

Icon-painting: St. George.

Icon-painting: Novgorod School, The Prophet Elijah.

Byzantine artists were still being summoned to Russia and Russian artists used their work as models.

(to c.1400) Gothic painting: Austrian School, Holy Trinity.

(to c.1420) Spörl's Song-book, a collection of Volkslieder, was written.

(to c.1425) Some songs with Flemish texts were on the periphery of the mainstream of musical composition.

(to c.1500) The name "Perpendicular" was used to describe the character of buildings in England whose decorations used straight lines and angles far more than arches of the previous period of "decorated" tracery.

1392

Sassetta (Stefano) di Giovanni, Italian painter, was born (died 1450).

Jehan Portevin was "Rois des menetriers" of the "Confrérie of St. Julien."

1393

(to 1402) Gothic sculpture: Claus Sluter: The Prophets Daniel and Isaiah (from the Moses Fountain near Dijon).

(to 1437) James I of Scotland enjoyed a thoroughly English education which equipped him both as a poet and musician.

1394

J. Asproys was among the singers with the antipope at Avignon.

(to 1427) The fiddle and the lute figured in documents during this period.

1395

The performance of any chansons concerned with the schism were prohibited.

(to 1403) Gothic sculpture: Claus Sluter, Madonnas (left and right portals, Chartreuse de Champmol, Dijon).

c.1395

Antonio Pisanello, Italian painter, was born (died c.1455).

Gothic painting: French or English School. Wilton Diptych: Richard II of England Presented to the Virgin by His Patron Saints.

1396

Jean Alain was in the service of the Duke of Lancaster.

1396(cont.)

King John I of Aragon, an ardent Spanish patron of music, died (born 1350).

The Münch's activities in profane music were encouraged by his presence at the court of Archbishop Pilgrim of Salzburg, a devotee of the arts. He died at this time.

Pierre d'Ailly, the former chancellor of the University of Paris, became Bishop of Cambrai. He appeared to be a man of musical sensibility and certainly helped to stimulate cultivation of the arts.

Michelozzo, Florentine architect, was born (died 1472).

(to 1398) Magister Záviš was in Rome.

(to 1419) Jean Malouel, French painter, was active during this period.

c.1396

King Alfonso the Magnanimous, of Aragon, was born (died c.1458).

Names of French lutenists became known at this time. Henri de Ganiere, "joueur de viele et de lus" received a gift from Duke Louis of Orleans.

1397

(September 2) Francesco Landini, celebrated blind organist, died and was buried at San Lorenzo in Florence. He was strongly influenced by French art forms and this movement spread throughout Italy soon after his death(born 1325).

Paolo Uccello (Doni), Italian painter, was born (died 1475).

450 players performed during the Reichstag at Frankfurt.

Japanese architecture: Kyoto, the Golden Pavilion.

Angelo, Abbot of St. Maria de Rivaldis, held the title of Maestro della Cappella Pontificia.

Andrea del Castagno, Italian painter, was born (died 1457). His birth is given by some sources as 1423.

1398

John Gower was married, probably for the second time.

Notre Dame (in Paris) had seventeen or eighteen clercs de matines.

1399

Guillaume Ruby was mentioned in the Rouen archives as having played the organ there.

Grenon became canon at Saint Sépulcre in Paris.

(to 1413) The reign of Henry IV Bolingbroke (Lancaster) over England and Great Britain.

c.1399

Rogier Van Der Weyden, Netherlandish painter, was born (died 1464).

1400

Guillaume Ruby was in the Royal Chapel of Charles VI.

The portative organ developed into a good sized church organ.

Alessandro Stradivari was mentioned as an orientalist. Costanzo Stradivari, a monk of the order of Umiliati, wrote a

1400(cont.)

treatise on the natural philosophy of Aristotle.

Antonio Squarcialupi, blind Italian organist, was born (died 1480),see 1417.

Johannes Brasart, German composer, was born (died 1470).

King Richard II (Plantagenet) of England died (born 1367).

Geoffrey Chaucer died (born c.1340).

Jacopo, founder of the Bellini workshop, was born (died 1470).

Luca della Robbia, an Italian sculptor, was born (died 1482).

(to 1410) The richly illuminated Ellesmere manuscript of the "Canterbury Tales" was done.

(to 1413) The reign of the Doge, Michele Steno.

(to 1450) A publication was based on 11 manuscripts in Bodleian Library, Oxford, containing works of Power, Dunstable and Childe, examples of Early Bodleian Music.

(to 1821) The period of Late Byzantine Notation.

c.1400

Gilles Binchois, regarded as one of the foremost Burgundian composers, was born at Mons in Hainut (died 1460). He was first a soldier and later a chapel singer for Duke Philip the Good, of Burgundy.

Baude Cordier, author of Rondeau "Amans Ames" and Rondeau "Belle Bonne," was born.

Guillaume Dufay, a foremost Burgundian composer, was born in Chimay (Hainut), Burgundy (died 1474, November 27).

Richard Hoppin in a paper to the American Musicological Society in Austin stated that in the generation after Machaut (c.1400) the taleae were carefully built and clearly defined so that the structural "repetitions can scarcely have been missed by even the dullest listener."

Ugolino d'Orvieto, Italian theorist, was active.

Matteo da Perugia, Italian composer, was born.

Both the clavichord and the harpsichord were known at this time.

The first reference to the word "dulcimer" in literature in the English language was found in the poem "The Squyr of Lowe Degre."

Manuscrit d'Apt, a compilation of composers, included Philippe de Vitry and Tapissier.

In England, the carol was no longer danced in cultivated society, and became a simple polyphonic form.

The "point of addition" belonged to the tempus imperfectum, the rhythm being duple instead of triple.

Art-lovers competed for "ouvrages de Lombardie" the latest fashion at this time.

Domenico Veneziano, Italian painter, was born (died 1451).

c.1400(cont.)

Conrad Witz, German-Swiss painter, was born (died c.1445).

Stefan Lochner, German painter, was born (died 1451), see c.1410.

Luis Borassa, painter, was the head of a famous workshop in Barcelona.

Art in different parts of Europe developed on similar lines up to this time.

French painting: Attributed to Jean Malouel, Grande Pietà Ronde.

German painting: Master of the Virgin of Benediktbeuren, Virgin and Child.

Starting with Giotto (1300) and Masaccio (1400), Florentine artists cultivated their tradition with pride, and their excellence was recognized by people of taste.

An anonymous love song, Otep myrrhy ("A bouquet of myrrh") was composed.

The early history of the clavichord and of the chromatic keyboard prior to this time is obscure.

Catalan painting: Luis Borrassa, Scourging of Christ.

The beginning of German panel -painting was closely allied with political and social conditions in the country.

New discoveries by the artists of Italy and Flanders created a stir throughout Europe.

Florentine masters of painting and sculpture were starting to (cont.) change the formulas and methods that had been handed down to them.

(to c.1420) A group of artists in Florence deliberately set out to create a new art and to break with the ideas of the past.

(to c.1425) The field of notation progressed in both mensural script and instrumental tablatures.

(to c.1425) Little valid information concerning performance practice of sacred polyphony was available from this period.

(to c.1425) Composers generally preferred to use the Gloria text for canonic treatment.

(to c.1430) In sacred music, an opening upper-voice duo was quite usual.

(to c.1430) Jean Vaillant taught music in Paris.

(to c.1430) Secular music received the most attention from composers.

(to c.1430) Well defined phrase formation was a chief characteristic of music of this period.

(to c.1430) The relationship of text and music was in some cases quite carefully treated.

(to c.1430) Complete settings of the Ordinary of the Mass started to appear for the first time since Machaut's work of great excellence.

(to c.1430) The technique of paraphrasing plainsong material by elaboration in the highest voice was used with great

c.1400(cont.)
success during this period and assumed mounting importance in later Renaissance music.

(to c.1430) The signature took precedence over the previously prevailing ♮ ♮ ♭.

(to c.1450) Some of the earliest examples of music for carols came from this period.

(to c.1450) The "Lehrcompendium" of H. de Zeelandia contained very fine Volkslieder from this period.

(to c.1450) Organs were used in the Coronation Cathedral in Székesfehérvár (Alba Regia) and in Löcse (= Levoča) during this period.

(to c.1450) Organ music flourished in Hungary.

(to c.1450) The villota dated back to this period according to some sources.

(to c.1450) England threatened French leadership in music during the Hundred Years' War.

(to c.1499) This century witnessed the rise of a wealthy new bourgeoisie.

(to c.1499) The strange names of songs were almost enough to reflect the vigorous, turbulent life in Florence at this time.

(to c.1499) Polychoral part -music existed in Italy during this period.

(to c.1499) Funeral Hymn on Notker's Antiphon "Media Vita In Morte Sumus" was composed.

(to c.1499) Two organs appeared in the Magdeburg Cathedral.

(to c.1499) The first definite records to be found of Palestrina's family were from this period.

(to c.1499) The three methods (rhythmic) of presenting a plainsong cantus firmus were in the "free" rhythm, augmented to a great degree in the Mass in the mannered rhythm of 15th century popular polyphony, found in fauxbourdon-influenced pieces and in the equal-note structure of these responses.

(to c.1499) Polyphonic Lamentations were composed in Europe starting during this period.

(to c.1499) In the York records of this period mention was made of "the large organ in the choir," and "the organ at the altar."

(to c.1499) The "Histoire générale de la Musique," showed Fétis under most favorable light.

(to c.1499) According to M. Danjou, treatises by Gulielmus Monachus written during this period stated that faux-bourdon was held in equal esteem in England and France.

(to c.1499) The "Feste Musical," one of the earliest forms of the musical drama in Italy, were produced at the Ferrara theatre.

(to c.1499) Puppet-plays, in England and Italy, were called "fantoccini." They were popular with all classes during this period.

c.1400(cont.)

(to c.1499) L'Homme Armé, a French Dance Tune, was supposedly written during this period.

(to c.1499) Examples of 15th-century dance music survived in the Italian dance treatises.

(to c.1499) The Polonaise was supposedly introduced by Henry III. It was very stately and came from the Pavane and Passomezzo popular at the French court during this period.

(to c.1499) "Salve Regina" was treated in the Motet Style with excellent effect.

(to c.1499) The Quaver, originally called Chroma or Fusa, sometimes Unca (a hook), was probably invented some time during this period.

(to c.1499) The earliest known instances of Retrograde Imitation were found among the works of the Flemish composers, who used their ingenuity not only with the device itself, but also upon Inscriptiones heading the Canons.

(to c.1499) The G,F, and C Clefs were used on a variety of Lines.

(to c.1499) The number of notes in a single group was often considerable; and their duration was governed by many complicated rules.

(to c.1499) To avoid having the first-entering voice begin with a rest, Clemens extended the first note of his tenor backward to fill the measure.

(to c.1499) A few of the melodies in Clemen's Souterliedekens (cont.) were found in two manuscripts.

(to c.1499) In the Mass, Sur le pont d'Avignon, Certon treated the well-known tune, from some earlier chanson setting.

(to c.1499) Pierre de la Rue's "Ista est" melody was greatly admired and used.

(to c.1499) In Italy, the viol was used independently as well as in mixed ensembles.

(to c.1499) Philippe Bassiron, a native of the Netherlands, lived and was active during this century. He was a contemporary of Josquin des Pres.

(to c.1499) Squarcialupi, the organist, lived in Florence where Isaac likewise played organ at a later date.

(to c.1499) There was little surviving instrumental music from Italy at this time. Its importance, however, was such that it should not be underestimated.

(to c.1499) Musicians called themselves Meistersinger and were described by the same title.

(to c.1499) Spanish literary sources had many references to instruments, their makers, and performances, however, little instrumental music survived.

(to c.1499) Spanish instrumental ensemble-music certainly must have included settings of the Spagna melody, probably of Spanish origin.

(to c.1499) The earliest known

c.1400(cont.) examples of the pavane superseded the basse danz.

(to c.1499) Spanish music continued to be strongly influenced by surrounding nations.

(to c.1499) The group of boys known as the seises were officially called niños cantorcicos ("boy choristers") and were established at Seville.

(to c.1499) Native Spanish names were numerous among early musicians in Iberia.

(to c.1499) Most theoretical works written or copied in Spain were based on convention or lack of knowledge. Toward the end of the century, a brilliant and revolutionary treatise of Ramos de Pareja appeared and was a major contribution.

(to c.1499) In Spanish literature, considerable antique poetry and poetry from the time of the "troubadours" was supposed to be sung. Among these the famous cancioneros, large miscellaneous collections of songs, containing large numbers of canciones, invenciones, motets, preguntas, villancicos and ballads.

(to c.1499) Most Portuguese epic-romances were of Spanish origin, and started to appear during this period.

(to c.1499) Three of Johannes Cornago's compositions with Spanish words appeared in a collection, the Cancionero de Palacio.

(to c.1499) The art of lute making spread from Spain (cont.) throughout Europe. The earliest masters were from north of the Pyrenees in the Tyrol and Bavaria. From there they made their way to all countries.

(to c.1499) Pietro Bono, the most famous lutenist, was attached to the court of Ferrara. He was later sent to Buda by Queen Beatrice's sister, Eleonora (wife of Hercules I), so that his music might help the queen to recovery from illness.

(to c.1499) Heinrich von Lauffenberg, systematically and deliberately set his sacred works to secular tunes.

(to c.1499) Stoltzer's style was an outgrowth of German style.

(to c.1499) German players were sought in many lands. German instrumentalists played at the courts of Burgundy, Ferrara, at Lyons and Venice.

(to c.1499) Many compositions from France and the Low Countries were in German manuscripts. They were, however, often in garbled and anonymous versions and occasionally the original text was replaced by a German one.

(to c.1499) German-speaking countries were not actually in the mainstream of musical development. This was strongly evidenced by the fact that their composers were writing sacred polyphonic music rather than secular music.

(to c.1499) Compositions honoring the Virgin became quite numerous.

c.1400(cont.)

(to c.1499) In Hungary, borrowed Gregorian melodies appeared in the mystery plays. The Latin and German mixed texts were preserved.

(to c.1499) Construction of instruments with corner-blocks, in varied sizes, was contemporary with the development of polyphonic choral music in Germany and the Netherlands.

(to c.1499) Several of Hoffhaimer's pieces, similar to those in the 15th-century Liederbücher, were constructed in sections with simultaneous cadences in all voices, rather than in the smoothly flowing, unified manner typical of the Netherlandish style.

(to c.1499) Palestrina's polyphony was so inimitable and of such a high quality that his name was given to the School as if he had lived in the 15th century and inaugurated it.

(to c.1499) The row of sharps was doubtless due to the necessity for transposition, and the row, complete and accurate, appeared in pictorial representations of the period.

(to c.1499) The invention of the bind was not possible to place but its use was to give rhythmic variety to counterpoint.

(to c.1499) Maitre Jacques Barbireau, a celebrated French musician, was active.

(to c.1499) Examples of the point and the black notes, were found not only in works of this time, but later even in those (cont.) of Palestrina and of his contemporaries.

(to c.1499) Franco-Burgundian court banquets were accompanied by elaborate diversions including pantomime and music. The slight trend toward dramatic unity was not successful.

(to c.1499) In Poland, the Church provided instruction in sacred music.

(to c.1499) The earliest known musical treatise of Polish Origin was the Musica of Magister Szydlovita.

(to c.1499) Polish music in its earlier period, up to this time, was basically Gregorian Chant, there were no remnants of pre-Christian music.

(to c.1499) The Speciálnik, a manuscript of Hradec Králové, contained Mass sections and motets on Latin texts. They were written for three to five voices ad aequales.

(to c.1499) All music was banned in Bohemia, except monophonic songs which were typical of the Hussite art.

(to c.1499) Mülich of Prague's music was found in the Colmar manuscript. Two tunes and four poems were preserved.

(to c.1499) The plays that carried on the tradition of the liturgical drama and mystery play of the Middle Ages grew to greater and greater proportions until some of them required a few days for a full performance.

(to c.1499) The complex techniques of the period frequently

c.1400(cont.)
obscured the material that it paraphrased.

(to c.1499) Manuscripts of this period were frequently haphazardly done.

(to c.1499) The Requiem Mass prior to this time had always been sung in plainsong.

(to c.1499) The term "Missa" was used not only to designate an ordinary but also for a cycle for the Proper.

(to c.1499) Several chant-books presented special sets that were of quite some interest.

(to c.1499) Certain works with liturgical texts were classified as motets.

(to c.1499) Secular music, though still important, did not hold the position of leadership that it had in the previous century.

(to c.1499) A few monophonic lauds survived from this time.

(to c.1499) Ballade, chanson, rondeau, virelai basically remained the same as they had been during the two preceding centuries.

(to c.1499) The way the tenor was used in La belle se siet was similar to the technique used in "motet-chansons."

(to c.1499) When space was great enough to place one voice clearly above the other the sharply contrasting melodic character of each melody was not as obvious as when the voices were in the same musical space.

(to c.1499) "Chapels," instituted by the kings and princes of Europe became progressively more fashionable during this period.

(to c.1499) The leadership of the Burgundian court was clear, however, some other centers of French civilization also showed interest in music.

(to c.1499) A new cadence of four chords evolved and gradually became one of the chief cadential formulas.

(to c.1499) The "under-third" cadence was common.

(to c.1499) Although most modern writers have used the term "Netherlandish" for years, "Netherlands," meaning "Low Countries," had no official meaning as such during the period involved.

(to c.1499) A manuscript was found at Naples containing six anonymous Masses. One stanza of the secular text had also been recorded.

(to c.1499) The sacred cantus firmi were slowly replaced by popular melodies of the chansons. This reflected the newly found desire to mix celestial and mundane things.

(to c.1499) An early 15th-century manuscript contained four of Dunstable's compositions (Liceo Filarmonico of Bologna).

(to c.1499) Five masses that could definitely be credited to Dufay belonged to the cantus-firmus type and were extremely important.

(to c.1499) It slowly but grad-

c.1400(cont.)

ually became common for the motet, basically not a liturgical form, to use Biblical texts. The motet was used mainly at solemn occasions, either sacred or secular.

(to c.1499) An Italian manuscript (at the Marciana in Venice) contained five anonymous two-part laude, each composed by "a humble Franciscan" who was also responsible for the text.

(to c.1499) A manuscript collection of Astronomical Treatises (the Bodleian at Oxford) survived this period.

(to c.1499) The same music was played everywhere: in church, at balls, and at middle-class weddings.

(to c.1499) A vellum roll of Early English carols, from this period, contained a copy of the Agincourt Song (Trinity College Library).

(to c.1499) The words of many Christmas carols from this time survived and were published in several collections.

(to c.1499) The name echiquier appeared in the "Chanson sur la journée de Guinegate," a poem of the time.

(to c.1499) The Dresden Minnesinger manuscript was a miscellaneous volume in which there were mystical hymns to the Virgin by Michael Behaim.

(to c.1499) Scottish popular music, although it surely existed, has not survived to any degree.

(to c.1499) The Stabat Mater probably was sung to a melody in the thirteenth Mode, known also as "Comme feme."

(to c.1499) Compositions from the Netherlands School in strict contrapuntal style came to Italy and began to be of slight influence, but Italian secular songs continued to be light in content.

(to c.1499) In the York cycle manuscript, five short pieces from the Weavers' play, The Appearance of Our Lady to Thomas, have survived.

(to c.1499) English keyboard music is lacking even though the organ was apparently in wide usage.

(to c.1499) Led by Conrad Celtis, musicians began to set the odes of Horace to music for four voices. They scanned them metrically, in long and short syllables.

(to c.1499) Abraham Jordan and his son of the same name belonged to an ancient family at Maidstone. The older Jordan was an organ builder. He moved to London, where he made fine instruments and prepared his son for the same profession.

(to c.1499) The highly developed musical art in England antedated the early Italian School.

(to c.1499) The Basse danse was the only stylized dance known.

(to c.1499) Martin le Franc's Champion des Dames appeared during this period.

(to c.1499) Richard Cutell, an

c.1400(cont.)
English musician, was the author of a treatise on counterpoint. A fragment of it was preserved (the Bodlean Library, Oxford).

(to c.1499) The statutes of Eton College ordered the scholars to sing an antiphon before leaving school in the afternoon and, later, to say the Lord's Prayer in church and to sing an antiphon before an image of the Virgin.

(to c.1499) Chansons were arranged for organ and independent preludes were composed.

(to c.1499) Copies of the Ars Cantus mensurabilis of this period were preserved in Milan and London.

(to c.1499) The Hymn O Salutaris Hostia was sung between the Sanctus and Agnus Dei by this period.

(to c.1499) The practice of beating time, as it is still done, was proved, by the traditions of the Sistine Choir, to be at least as old as this period and quite possibly considerably older.

(to c.1499) The viéle (medieval fiddle) came into general use, especially in England.

(to c.1499) Great improvements in the spring box, keys, pedals, wind-supply, and other features of the organ were from this period. Keys were reduced in size and pedal ranks were invented. Pipes increased to sixteen and in some cases thirty two feet, and created the need for enlarging several parts of organs, especially the bellows. The fauxbourdon came into use.

(to c.1499) The Great Bells of Gloucester were build (diam. 5'8½", weight 3 tons, 5 cw.).

(to c.1499) Examples of the introduction of the half swinging chimes were carefully recorded.

(to c.1499) In England, the function of the "waits" had become more musical, and ensembles of varied instruments and singing were used.

(to c.1499) At this time a structural difference was made between bowed and plucked instruments.

(to c.1499) No European bowed instrument, except the Marine Trumpet, a direct descendant of the Greek monochord, rested on the ground during actual playing.

(to c.1499) Corner-blocks and larger sized bowed instruments appeared, and as large fiddles could only be conveniently built by use of cornerblocks, it was concluded that the two inventions were correlative.

(to c.1499) Johannes Tinctoris, composer and musicologist, lived during this period and was claimed to have been born at Nivelles in Brabant. The latter was highly controversial. Among his major contributions were treatises, "De Origine Musicae," and "Diffinitorum Terminorum Musicorum." He did not mention the ochetus in the latter work which indicated its decline in importance. He indicated his contempt for unnecessary signs such as the "Point" by referring to them as "Puncti Asinei" (Ass'es Points).

c.1400(cont.)

(to c.1499) Spataro, a maker of scabbards, was one of the earliest Italian writers on music and a disciple of Pareja.

(to c.1499) Loyset Compère, eminent contrapuntist, was a chorister, canon, and chancellor at the Cathedral of St. Quentin.

(to c.1499) English composers on the continent were representative of only limited aspects of English music.

(to c.1499) The degrees of Bachelor and Doctor of Music were in existence at this time.

(to c.1499) Olivier Basselin, a song-writer, died at Vire during this period.

(to c.1499) An illustration from a painting by Filipino Lippi showed a "stromento di porco" strung vertically, an unusual method, more like a harpsichord or grand piano.

(to c.1499) Instruments were illustrated in a "Dance of Death" print during this period.

(to c.1499) The spirit of adventure, which existed in art during this period, marked the major break with the Middle Ages.

(to c.1499) Art splintered into numerous schools. Almost every city or small town in Flanders, Germany, and Italy had its own "school of painting."

(to c.1499) A decisive change in the history of art was caused by the discoveries and innovations of Brunelleschi's generation in Florence. This brought (cont.) Italian art to a higher plane, and separated it from the development of art in other parts of Europe.

(to c.1499) The goals of northern artists were not much different from those of the Italians. Their methods, however, differed greatly.

(to c.1499) The Renaissance was victorious in Italy but the north remained faithful to the traditions of the Gothic period.

(to c.1499) The problems and achievements of Florentine art were expressed in their noblest form in the work of the century's outstanding genius, Leonardo da Vinci.

(to c.1499) Sienese art never completely abandoned the International Gothic style which had been at its height in c.1400.

(to c.1499) It became clear that Sienese art had been marked by Simone Martini's manner. During Martini's lifetime Pietro Lorenzetti had followed a completely different trend, but Martini's style was the predominant one.

(to c.1499) Martin Schongauer was a great and famous master of engraving who lived in Colmar (Alsace), sometime during this period.

(to c.1499) German woodcut: German School, St. Dorothy.

(to c.1499) American Indian sculpture: Silver Alpaca, Inca (c.8" high).

(to c.1499) Islamic architecture:

c.1400(cont.)

Meshed, Shrine of Imam Rida, the Old Court.

(to c.1499) Romanesque sculpture: Virgin and Child - Notre Dame de Grasse.

(to c.1499) Japanese painting: So-ami, Chinese Landscape Screen.

(to c.1499) Chinese architecture: Peking, Palace, Grand Ancestral Shrine (210'x150'x90' high).

(to c.1499) Gothic architecture: Batalha, Santa Maria da Victoria.

(to c.1499) Gothic architecture: Venice, Ca d'Oro (69' wide).

(to c.1499) The introduction of the art of printing was a momentous event of this period.

(to c.1499) The morality play presented a theme of moral and spiritual struggle by means of allegory and did not deal with Bible stories or legends concerning saints. This period was its zenith.

(to c.1499) Although English literature slowed in its progress it did not suffer a severe break as it had between the Anglo-Saxon and Middle English periods.

(to c.1499) England became wasted in the struggle for the crown among the descendants of the sons of Edward III.

1401

Tomaso Masaccio, Italian painter, was born (died 1428).

F. Bartholomaeus Pisanus stated that the Dies Irae was written (cont.) by Frater Thomas, who came from Celanum; and that it was sung in Masses for the Dead.

King Charles VI founded a "Court of Love," a kind of literary society. The members occupied themselves with music and poetry much as the trouvère had.

Grenon became sub-deacon and deacon at Saint Sépulcre in Paris.

(to 1402) Italian sculpture: Florenzo Ghiberti, Sacrifice of Isaac (21"x17½").

1402

(to 1416) French painter, Pol Malouel, known as Pol de Limbourg, was active.

c.1402

Giovanni di Paolo, Italian painter, was born (died c.1482).

1403

King Charles VII of France (House of Valois) was born (died 1461).

The crozier given by William of Wykeham to New College, Oxford, has in it the figure of an angel playing the bagpipe.

Venice' reign as a musical center started with the founding of a singing school at the cathedral.

(to 1408) Grenon instructed choirboys at Laon.

1404

Leone Alberti, Italian Renaissance sculptor and architect, was born (died 1472).

The Minstrel-Laws of Eberhard von Minden were written.

1404(cont.)

The earliest definite mention of the clavichord was in Eberhard Cersne's "Rules of the Minnesingers," included with the monochord and the clavicembalo.

A German poem, Der Minne Regeln, mentioned the clavichordium and the clavicimbalum among the instruments of courtly love (see previous entry).

Ambros' earliest mention of the clavicymbalum was in a manuscript at this date.

Philip the Bold died and one of his musicians was Perrinet de Fontaines. Under the name of Pierre Fontaine he was known as a composer of chansons.

(to 1406) The Papal reign of St. Innocent VII (born in Sulmona).

(and 1419) Philip's son and grandson, John the Fearless and Philip the Good, succeeded to the duchy of Burgundy in 1404 and 1419. They added the Franche-Comté, the rest of what is now Belgium, the Provinces of Zeeland, Friesland, and North and South Holland, the counties of Bar-sur-Seine, Mâcon, and Auxerre, and the towns of Abbéville, Amiens, and Saint -Quentin. These additions were made by conquest, marriage and purchase.

c.1404

Fontaine served the three dukes of Burgundy.

1405

Foliot was a choirboy at Notre Dame.

(to 1410) French painting: (cont.) Anonymous, Miniature from the "Livre de Chasse" of Gaston Phoebus: Between Field and Forest.

c.1405

Hans Rosenblut in Nürnberg wrote Shrove Tuesday plays.

(to c.1430) Master Francke, German painter, was active.

1406

Venice conquered Padua.

Claus Sluter, Gothic sculptor, died.

Sano di Pietro, Sienese painter, was born (died 1481).

Fra Filippo Lippi, Italian painter, was born (died 1469).

The municipality of Basel forbade jugglers to wear trousers.

(to 1415) The Papal reign of St. Gregory XII (born in Venice).

1407

(April 24) The new constitution of the "Confrérie of St. Julien des ménétriers" received the sanction of Charles VI, and it was ruled that no musician might teach, or exercise his profession, without having passed an examination, and been declared "suffisant" by the "Roi des ménestrels" or his deputies.

The vocal and instrumental musicians of the "Confrerie of St. Julien," separated from the mountebanks and tumblers who had previously been associated with them.

Earliest figures giving particulars as to the cost of making

1407(cont.)

an organ in England were in the Precentor's accounts of Ely Cathedral.

Russian architecture: Manassia, Church.

(to 1457) Lorenzo Valla, author of a treatise on "Elegant Latin," hoped for the re-establishment of the Roman Language.

1408

John Gower, English poet, died (born c.1325).

Statutes for the regulation of the conduct of choirboys at Notre Dame in Paris required the choirmaster to teach the boys "plain chant and counterpoint," and stated that he might add a few "decent déchants" but musical practices "must not prevent the boys from learning their grammar."

Grenon arrived at Cambrai to teach grammar.

Prosdocimus de Beldemandis, professor and philosopher at the University of Padua, defended the originality and value of Italian music in his Tractatus Practice de Musica Mensurabili Ad Modum Italicorum.

A valet de chambre of John the Fearless was called upon to take part in the divine service. He was in all probability the composer Tapissier.

A notarized document from this date gave Martini and Reyneau legal rights to Forestier's volume called De Motets e de Ballades. Forestier, prior to his death, had loaned the book to Poblet Monastery in (cont.) Tarragona but the Abbot there refused to return it.

(to 1428) None of Gentile da Fabriano's frescoes survived. All his works at Brescia, Venice and Rome were lost.

c.1408

Florentine sculpture:
Nanni di Banco: Stonemasons and sculptors at work on bricklaying, drilling, measuring and sculpting.

1409

Nicolas Malin, the master of the choirboys at Cambrai Cathedral, in search of talent, visited Béthune, Douai, and Lille.

Trebor was serving at the court of Aragon under Martin I.

French manuscript illumination: Jacquemart de Hesdin, "Grand Heures."

c.1409

The Schütz family belonged to the aristocracy of Nürnberg.

1410

Fernando Estéban, Sacristan of the Chapel of St. Clement in Seville, wrote a book Reglas de canto plano é de contrapunto é de canto de órgano.

Conrad Paumann, German organist and composer of Fundamentum organisandi, was born at Nürnberg (died 1473).

Robert Campin was Rogier van der Weyden's teacher. He became a citizen of Tournai, at this time.

Richard Loqueville, the composer, was in the service of Duke Robert of Bar. He played and

1410(cont.

taught harp to the duke's son. He also instructed the choirboys of the chapel in the art of chant.

German painting: Upper Rhine Master, Garden of Paradise.

(to 1415) French painting: Anonymous, Portrait of a Lady (this had at one time been attributed to Pisanello).

(to 1418) Lists of singers of the Papal Choir included the names of musicians from northern France.

c.1410

Zacherio, the composer, was born.

An incomplete manuscript at Lucca, of which fragments exist at Perugia, was an important source for early secular pieces with Italian words.

Adrian Pieterez, the earliest known organ-builder in Belgium, was born at Bruges.

The major accomplishment of northern French polyphony was not to introduce novel elements but rather to bring about a fusion of English sonority, French form, and Italian canon.

Flemish painting: Jan van Eyck, Virgin and Child with Saints and a Donor (19 1/16" x 24½").

Flemish sculpture: Hubert and Jan von Eyck, Singing Angels (from the Ghent Altar).

Magister Záviš died.

German painter Stefan Lochner was born (died 1451), see c.1400.

Enguerrand Charanton (Quarton), French painter, was born (died c.1461).

Piero della Francesca, Italian painter, was born (died 1492).

Oswald von Wolkenstein adapted several French compositions to German texts.

Prayer book illustration: Paul and Jean de Limbourg, May (Page from a Book of Hours painted for the Duke of Berry).

(to 1420) The Master of St. Veronica was the first Cologne artist to reach a truly high standard.

(to 1420) German painting: "The Paradise Garden," attributed to a master of either the upper or Middle Rhineland.

(to 1440) The Caronici manuscript contained 325 pieces in three parts, a few in two and four parts. Included were chansons, motets, and mass movements.

1411

(December) Johannes Ciconia, the composer, died in Padua.

Johannes Ciconia was a canon at Padua (born c.1340).

(to 1414) There were Serbs, like the "trumbeta" Dragan from Prizren, and Croats from Zagreb, like the tubicen Nicolaus de Zagabria who served as instrumentalists in Dubrovnik.

1412

Grenon served the Duke of Burgundy.

John the Fearless, when he took

1412(cont.)

John the Fearless, when he took four choirboys over from his uncle, the Duke of Berry, also had Grenon as their leader.

c.1412

A profile portrait of King Louis II in brocaded garments has been preserved.

1413

Loqueville succeeded Malin.

A motet, "Stirps Mocenigo," was composed for the elevation of the doge by Antonius Romanus.

(to 1418) Loqueville taught music at Cambrai Cathedral.

(to 1422) The reign of Henry V (Lancaster) over England and Great Britain.

(to 1434) A manuscript from Cyprus was of great interest in illustrating the widespread French influence of the time.

1414

(November) The Council of Constance opened. It continued for four years. The Papal choir visited Germany during this time. There is a remote chance that Dufay and Dunstable attended the Council. At any rate the Council resulted in a change in attitude by German composers and a willingness on their part to at least try to set sacred Latin texts to music in an impersonal spirit.

Antonio Romano was the composer of a motet on the election of Doge Tommaso Mocenigo.

c.1414

Jaume Huguet, Spanish painter, was born (died 1492).

(to 1460) Guillaume Dombet or the Master of the Aix Annunciation, Spanish painter, was active.

1415

(October 25) The army of Henry V faced a well-equipped enemy ten times its size at Agincourt. The English victory included the capture of Charles, Duke of Orleans and his imprisonment in the tower of London as a prisoner of state. The famous song celebrating the victory, "Deo gratias Anglia," was composed at the time and truly belonged to the minstrels. After the disaster the French culture went into temporary eclipse. The Great Schism came gradually to an end.

Guillaume Ruby was listed among the musicians attached to the Burgundian Court.

John the Fearless employed Grenon, Fontaine, Guillaume Ruby and Richard de Bellengues.

c.1415

Dieric Bouts, Netherlandish painter, was born (died 1475).

Wenceslaus of Prachatitz prepared a compendium of Muris's writings.

Tinctoris was aware of a break between the music of this time and the music of the preceeding period.

The largest source of native English music was the Old Hall Manuscript.

Large manuscripts were set on a lecturn for all choristers to sing plainchant from. These manuscripts began to be re-

c.1415(cont.)
positories of part-music.

Lucas Maler, or Laux, as he inscribed his name on his instruments (lutes), lived in Bologna.

Muscatblut, a composer of Meistersinger songs, was active.

Lobkowitz, a noble and distinguished Austrian family, was founded by Nicholas Chuzy von Ujezd and derived its name from a place in Bohemia.

Faenza, a manuscript of this time, contained a large collection of keyboard transcriptions of vocal music by outstanding French and Italian composers, even Machaut and Landini. There were also included organ-mass sections which, because of their mature art, were probably Italian in origin.

Netherlandish painting: Anonymous, Portrait of John, the Fearless.

(to c.1444) Henri Bellechose, French painter, was active.

1416
French miniatures: The Limbourg Brothers, "Très Riches Heures du Duc de Berri."

Italian sculpture: Donatello, St. George, Tabernacle (82" high).

Duke Jean de Berry, noted art patron, died. He was the brother of Charles V.

French painting:
Henri Bellechose, Last Communion and Martyrdom of St. Denis.

In an attempt to heal the schism in the Church, King Sigismund, of Bohemia, Germany, and Hungary visited England.

Michel Behaim, the first important Meistersinger and adventurer, was born (died 1474). He was a singing burgher rather than a knight.

(to 1458) Reyneau continued his service into Alfonso V's reign at the Aragonese court.

c.1416
Piero Della Francesca, Italian painter, was born (died 1492).

1417
(November) The Council of Constance elected Martin V, pope, thereby ending the schism.

Bartholomaeus was organist at Magdeburg Cathedral.

An organist, Césaris, obtained a small organ from Yolanda of Aragon, Queen of Sicily, for use at the Cathedral at Angers.

When the Emperor Sigismund attended the Council of Constance a Te Deum was performed with organ accompaniment.

Antonio Squarcialupi, Florentine organist, was born (died 1480). The Squarcialupi Codex was named after him, see also 1400.

(to 1431) The Papal reign of St. Martin V (born in Rome).

c.1417
The Eya dulcis-Vale placens of Tapissier existed.

1418
(April) The Council of Constance closed.

1418(cont.)

Estienne Grossin became chaplain at St. Merry in Paris.

Loqueville died at Cambrai.

Grenon returned to Paris.

English singers were acclaimed at the Council of Constance and the qualities that characterize English musical style began to flourish in Burgundy and France.

Organ pedals received the important addition of a stop of independent pedal-pipes, and "Pedal Basses" started. They were destined to add much dignity and majesty to the general sound of an organ.

(to 1434) Renaissance architecture: Brunelleschi, Florence, Cathedral, dome (total height, 367').

c.1418

Henry Abyngdon, English ecclesiastic and musician, was born (died 1497, September 1).

1419

According to the Fabric Rolls of York Minster, John Couper, a carpenter, received "For constructing the ribs of the bellows, xii ^{d}."

At York Cathedral the instrument was referred to as "The organ," or "The great organ" from this date.

Philip the Good, whose court at Dijon, Burgundy was the center of intellectual and artistic activity, was born (died 1467).

(to 1421) Guillaume Legrant was one of the pope's singers during these years.

1420

Nanni di Banco, Italian sculptor, died (born c.1374). He was known for his statue of St. Luke at Florence Cathedral (80"high).

John Pyamour was commissioned to gather boys for the Chapel Royal in England.

Jehan Boissard called Verdelet, was "Roi des ménestrels."

Benozzo Gozzoli, Italian painter, was born (died 1497).

Sesshu, Japanese painter, was born (died 1506).

Italian composer, Nicola Zacharia, became a papal singer.

It was noted that in the summer of 1420 a "Guillaume de Fays" was in the service of St. Germain l'Auxerrois at Paris.

Dufay's Vasilissa ergo gaude was written prior to August 20. It was an introit written for the departure of Cleofe Malatesta for Greece to marry the Emperor's son. The upper two voices are in unaccompanied canon and after the canon finishes, all four voices continue isorhythmically with two taleae.

Dufay was in Italy for a period of time.

The Old Hall Manuscript was published. It contained 148 pieces in three volumes.

(to 1423) The Papal Chapel became an important music center and attracted musicians from all over Europe.

1420(cont.)

(to 1424) Florentine painting: Tomaso Masaccio, Virgin and Child with St. Anne. The Madonna, Jesus and the angel on the right all reflected the great authority in the work that was attributed to this artist. His career at Florence was startling to an area still preoccupied with Gothic traditions.

(to 1427) Pierre Fontaine was a member of the Papal Choir during these years.

(to 1432) Zacherie was a member of the Papal Choir.

(to 1480) Seven Trent Codices during this period contained over 1600 pieces by 75 French, German, Italian, English and Burgundian composers.

c.1420

Johannes Okeghem, one of the foremost of the second generation of Netherlandish composers, was born, probably at Termonde in East Flanders (died c.1495).

Composer Firmin Caron was born.

Kiesewetter provided an example of four-part counterpoint by Dufay, written at this time.

Jean Fouquet, French painter, was born (died 1481).

International Gothic painting: Gentile da Fabriano, Virgin and Child.

Choruses apparently had taken no part in the performance of polyphonic music prior to this time.

Dufay listened to and studied (cont.) much old Italian music during this time when he stayed in Italy.

(to 1430) Netherlandish painting: Robert Campin, The Merode Altarpiece (29 3/8" high, 58½" wide).

(to 1450) During this period paintings continued to have embossed gold backgrounds, decorative outlines and flowers. They were close to miniatures and metalwork. Only in Tuscany and Flanders were the artists able to escape the spell of "gold, color, and prettiness."

(to c.1450) King Alfonso the Magnanimous of Aragon, was a patron of the arts who was active in spreading the influence of the Renaissance. He had conquered Naples.

(to c.1480) The huge repertory of the Trent Codices included a few works by men active during this period. However, English music declined gradually from this time on until during the years 1460 to 1480 there was none included.

1421

(January 19) Tra quante regione by Hugho de Lantins was written in honor of Cleofe Malatesta when she married Theodore Palaiologos at Mistra near Sparta.

King Henry VI of England (Lancaster) was born (died 1471).

Niccolo Pizzola, Italian painter, was born (died 1453).

Renaissance architecture: Brunelleschi, Florence, Foundlings Hospital (180'wide).

1421(cont.)

Estienne Grossin became clerc de matines at Notre Dame.

(to 1424) Grenon taught music at Cambrai.

1422

Prosdocimo di Beldomando, a musical theorist, was Professor of Astrology at Padua, a post which carried an annual stipend of 40 silver ducats.

Conrad Witz was in Cologne at this time.

John, Duke of Bedford (John Dunstable), became regent of France.

Mass was held in Prague in the Czech language. All portions were retained as was not the case with the Taborites.

(to 1461) The reign of King Henry VI (Lancaster) over England and Great Britain.

(to 1461) The corporation of minstrels at Beverly in Yorkshire helped during the reign of Henry VI to finance the construction of a church, which bore the inscription "Thys pilor made the meynstrils."

(to 1461) The reign of King Charles VII (House of Valois) over France.

c.1422

Stephan Lochner, German "realist" painter, was active in Cologne.

1423

Hugo von Montfort, a composer, unusual in that the music was written by his minstrel Burk Mangolt, died (born 1357).

Jacques Vide was first mentioned as a valet de chambre at the court of Burgundy.

Dufay's Resveillés vous, et faites chiere lye was written.

John, Duke of Bedford (John Dunstable) married the Duke of Burgundy's sister.

Christoforo da Feltre (Christoforus de Monte) wrote a motet on the election of Francesco Foscari.

Antonio da Cividale del Friuli (Antonius de Civitate Austrie) composed a motet dedicated to Giorgio Ordellafi (of Faenza) and his wife.

King Louis XI (House of Valois) of France was born (died 1483).

Andrea del Castagno, Italian painter, was born (died 1457). Some sources give his birth as 1397.

German woodcut: St. Christopher Bearing the Infant Christ.

International Gothic painting: Gentile Da Fabriano, Adoration of the Magi.

1424

James I had organs installed in churches in Scotland.

Binchois was at Paris in the service of William de la Pole, the Earl (later Duke) of Suffolk. The latter was married to Chaucer's granddaughter and was a musician as well as poet.

Pisanello, the Italian painter, was at Mantua.

Hamburg's greatest painter was

1424(cont.)

Master Francke who painted an altarpiece for the Johanniskirche at this date.

(to 1428) Foliot (Philippe de la Folie) was in the papal choir and was at the Burgundian court (Philip the Good).

(to 1442) Gothic secular architecture: Venice, Ducal Palace (c.260' long).

1425

(July 12) Je me complains was given this date in the Oxford manuscript.

Binchois became a priest.

"I Have Set my Hert," a two -part piece in conductus style, was written.

Grenon brought four French choirboys from Cambrai. They were included on the list of papal singers.

Parisina (the heroine of Byron's poem) and her lover, Hugo, were beheaded by order of Nicholas.

In Dubrovnik, the authorities abrogated the old custom whereby on the eve of the feast of St. Blaise (the patron of the city) men and women danced in the cathedral, accompanied by fistulatores (pipers).

Jan van Eyck was at the court at Bruges both as painter and valet de chambre to Philip the Good. He was on several occasions given diplomatic missions, most often to Portugal.

Pisanello was at Venice with Gentile da Fabriano.

Renaissance architecture: Brunelleschi, Florence. San Lorenzo, Nave (250' long by 95' wide x 69'6" high).

Alesso Baldovinetti, Italian painter, was born (died 1499).

Uccello served his apprenticeship in the workshop of the gold-and-bronzesmith Ghiberti. At the age of twenty-eight (1425), he was called to Venice to make mosaics for St. Mark's.

(to 1427) Grenon was at Rome as a singer in the Papal Choir.

(to 1438) Italian sculpture: Jacopo della Quercia, The Creation of Adam (34½"x27½").

c.1425

The continued influence of the conductus was evident in the two-part song, I Have set my Hert so hye.

Two manuscripts from this time contained a large repertoire of monodic and polyphonic compositions by Wolkenstein.

Jan van Ockeghem was given the title "Prince of Music" in Flanders. He was later (1495) given the title at Tours.

Tinctoris, it has been said, would have divided medieval and Renaissance music with this date.

Italian painting: Masaccio, Expulsion from the Garden (6'9" x 2'11"), Brancacci Chapel, S.M. del Carmine, Florence.

Italian painting: Masaccio, The Tribute Money (19'8"x8'4"), Brancacci Chapel, Florence).

c.1425(cont.)

Masaccio, The Holy Trinity with the Virgin and St. John (Santa Maria Novella, Florence).

(and c.1430) The earliest sources of German organ music were a Sagan manuscript (c.1425) and a manuscript by Ludolf Wilkin of Winsem (c.1430).

(to c.1450) Dufay dominated the field of composition during this period.

1426

Dufay was still employed by the Malatesta family.

Dufay's motet Apostolo glorioso-Cum tua doctrina-Andreas was composed.

The text of Adieu ces bons vins de Lannoys (in Canonici misc. 213) indicated that Dufay may have held some post at Laon.

The introduction of the full chromatic scale in organs was completed by this time.

Concerning the introduction of the chromatic keyboard, Hubert van Eyck painted the S. Cecilia panel of the famous Ghent altar-piece, in which there appeared a Positive organ depicted with the chromatic division of the keyboard.

Emperor Sigismund granted as "an act of special grace" the town of Augsburg the privilege of maintaining a corps of "towntrumpeters and kettledrummers." This grant continued during the next century and was extended to include most other free towns. The importance of these corps from a musical viewpoint was limited.

Hubert van Eyck, Flemish painter, died (born 1366).

Gentile da Fabriano, Italian painter, worked in Siena.

(to 1427) Masolino collaborated with Masaccio on paintings in the Brancacci Chapel in Florence.

(to 1428) Guillaume Dufay served as the Maître de Chapelle in Cambrai.

(to 1428) Florentine fresco: Masaccio, St. Peter Distributing Alms, Fresco detail (Brancacci Chapel, S. Maria del Carmine, Florence).

(to 1428) Florentine fresco: Masaccio, St. Peter Healing The Sick, Fresco Detail (Brancacci Chapel, S. Maria del Carmine, Florence).

(to 1428) Florentine fresco: Masaccio, St. Peter paying the Tribute Money, Detail from the Fresco of the Tribute Money (Brancacci Chapel, S. Maria del Carmine, Florence).

(to 1428) Florentine fresco: Masaccio, Christ and the Apostles, Detail from the fresco of the Tribute Money (Brancacci Chapel, S. Maria Del Carmine, Florence).

1427

Cardinal Louis Aleman sent a leave-of-absence from Bologna to the chapter of St. Gery at Cambrai, where Dufay was serving as deacon and indicated thereby that Dufay was in Italy.

Bronze sculpture: Ghiberti, Baptism of Christ (Gilt bronze relief from a font in Siena,

1427(cont.)

S. Giovanni).

Bronze sculpture: Donatello, Herod's Feast (Gilt bronze relief from a font in S. Giovanni, Siena).

c.1427

Gentile da Fabriano, Italian painter, died (born c.1360).

Antonio Rossellino, Italian sculptor, was born (died 1479).

Italian painting: Masaccio, The Holy Trinity, The Virgin, St. John and Donors (wall-painting in Sta Maria Novella, Florence).

1428

(December 20) Gualterius Liberth, represented in the Oxford manuscript, appeared as Gualterus Liberti on the register.

(January) The list of papal singers on this date was the first that omitted Fontaine. It was also the first to eliminate Grenon and five of the six French choirboys whom he had in his charge.

(December) Dufay's name appeared in the list of singers in the Papal Choir.

Tomaso Masaccio, Italian painter, died (born 1401).

Jacques Vide was Philip the Good's secretary.

The Gualterus Liberti who was in the Papal Choir may have been Walter Frye.

Philip of Luxemburg paid tribute to Cambrai cathedral by saying, (cont.) "It surpasses all others and may well serve them as a model, with the beauty of its chant, the magnificence of its lighting, and the delightful clangor of its bells." This quotation was from a letter from Philip to the chapter at Cambrai.

Fra Angelico's earliest known work; the Fiesole altarpiece, was apparently painted at this time when the painter was forty years old.

Desiderio da Settignano, Italian sculptor, was born (died 1464).

(to 1437) Actually Guillaume Dufay was a member of the Papal Chapel in Rome for nine years, including a two-year interruption. This was conclusively indicated by archives of the Pontifical Choir. He was a Laic in 1428 and then again in 1433, 1435, and 1436. By the latter year his name was first on list of the twelve singers. Dufay's northern Gothic style gradually adapted to the spirit of the Italian Renaissance.

1429

Gentile Bellini, Italian painter, was born (died 1507).

Antonio Benci, known as Pollaiuolo, Italian painter, was born (died 1498).

Jan van Eyck, Philip the Good's painter, visited Portugal.

Johannes Gerson, French scholar, died (born 1363).

Gacian Reyneau was active at Barcelona.

Gacian Reyneau died.

c.1429

Dufay composed the mass, Missa Sancti Jacobi.

Renaissance architecture: Brunelleschi, Florence, Pazzi Chapel (Interior 59'9"x35'8").

1430

Johannes Okeghem, one of the foremost Flemish composers, was born in Flanders. His birth has also been claimed to be c.1420 (died c.1495).

Jakob Obrecht, an important representative of the Flemish School and probably later a pupil of Ockeghem's, was born (died 1505), see c.1450.

Binchois composed a motet, Nove cantum melodie, for the birth of Antoine, son of Philip the Good.

Organ pipes as long as 30 feet were reported. Their range must have been below the lowest string of a modern piano.

Philip the Good married Isabella of Portugal. This was his third marriage.

Christine de Pizan, the poet, died.

Giovanni Bellini, an Italian painter, was born (died 1516).

(to 1431) Sienese painting: Sassetta, the Virgin of the Snow.

(to 1436) Thomas Damett was canon at Windsor.

(to 1440) Florentine painting: Fra Angelico, Coronation of the Virgin.

(to 1450) Tai Chin, Chinese (cont.) painter, was active during this period.

(to 1451) Guillaume Ruby was still at the Burgundian court in the employ of Philip the Good.

(to 1480) The best-known composers of the Second Generation of Netherlanders were Okenheim, Hobrecht, Caron, Gaspar, two De Fevins (brothers). These men were most active during this period.

(to 1495) This period was known as the later Burgundian School.

(to 1600) According to Hans Moser, Dr. E. Reinhardt of Berlin was preparing a work of several volumes on the Schütz family and their mercantile relations during this period.

c.1430

Andrei Rublev, Moscow artist, died (born c.1360).

Martin Schongauer, German painter, was born (died 1491).

Italian sketch: Pisanello, Monkey. Leaf from a Sketchbook demonstrated the new interest in representing nature in an accurate fashion.

The earliest documents of fauxbourdon were Italian and from this time.

Dufay wrote a hymn cycle for the whole year for the Papal Choir. It contained twenty-two hymns.

Burgundian music, and particularly the songs, served to remotivate the musical art of Italy.

c.1430(cont.)

Hans Memlinc, Flemish painter, was born (died 1494).

Antonello da Messina, Venetian painter, was born (died 1479).

Cosimo Tura, Ferraran painter, was born (died 1495).

(to 1432) Italian sculpture: Donatello, David (62¼"high).

(to 1440) O celestial lume by Bartolomeo Brolo was written. It was a rondeau in Italian style.

(to c.1460) Binchois served the Burgundian court.

(to c.1480) The Second Period of major importance in the history of Polyphonic Music.

1431

(December 17) At the coronation of Henry VI the King was described in three ways, each "with a ballad."

Guillaume Malbecque and Jean Brassart joined the Papal Choir.

Lucas Moser, a painter from Rottweil, added a discouraged inscription to his altarpiece (Tiefenbronn). He felt that working in the town where Conrad Witz had been born and was painting and producing his greatest masterpieces was pointless.

Andrea Mantegna, Paduan painter, was born (died 1506).

(to 1432) Arnold de Lantins served in the Papal Chapel for a few months.

(to 1433) Pisanello completed Gentile da Fabriano's frescoes (at Venice).

(to 1438) Italian sculpture: Luca della Robbia, Singing Gallery, or Cantoria (c.18'6" over-all length).

(to 1443) A Council on south -west German art was held at Basle.

(to 1447) The Papal reign of St. Eugene IV (born in Venice).

c.1431

Johannes Regis, Netherlandish composer, was born (died 1485).

1432

(May 6) The altarpiece, "Adoration of the Lamb," by Hubert and Jan van Eyck was formally exposed to view in the church of St. Jean-Baptiste at Ghent. The Church is now the Cathedral of St. Bavon.

Organ music was still written in an archaic two-voiced style. This was made obvious by a manuscript of the time from Windsheim, Germany.

A hundred years after the first apparent attempt at keyboard tablature in England similar notation turned up in Germany.

The keyboard of the organ shown in the Van Eyck altarpiece at Ghent was very nearly completely chromatic.

The rout of San Romano occurred when Florentine troops won one of the frequent battles between Italian factions.

Flemish painting: Jan Van Eyck, The Righteous Judges and the

1432(cont.)

Knights of Christ (Wings from the Ghent altar).

(to 1435) Flemish painting: Rogier van der Weyden, the Annunciation (33 7/8 x 36¼").

(to 1511) Gothic architecture: Rouen, St. Maclou, facade (75' wide).

c.1432

Italian sculpture: Donatello, Niccolo da Uzzano (c.18½"high). It is not a certainty that this is Donatello's work, but generally assumed to be.

Flemish painting: Jan van Eyck, Madonna of Chancellor Rolin (26"x24½").

1433

(August) Dufay's name remained on the list of the Papal Choir up to this time.

Jacques Vide's name disappeared from records of the Burgundian court.

Dufay's Supremum est mortalibus extoled the virtues of peace. It was composed when Eugene IV and Sigismund signed a treaty reconciling their differences. This treaty led to the crowning of the latter as Holy Roman Emperor.

Netherlandish painting: Jan van Eyck, Man in a Turban.

(to 1438) Italian sculpture: Donatello, Singing Gallery (10'17" x 18'8").

c.1433

Dufay composed the ballade, C'est bien raison, in praise of Nicholas III of Ferrara, (cont.) Marquis of Este. The latter had relations with both Burgundian and French courts.

Fra Giocondo, Italian architect, was born (died 1515).

1434

Pope Eugene IV was compelled to flee to Florence.

Duke Amadeus VIII of Savoy resigned in favor of his son Louis.

Joannes de Tinctoris, composer and musicologist, was born at Nivelle in Brabant (died 1511).

Netherlandish painting: Jan van Eyck, The Marriage of Giovanni (?) Arnolfini and Giovanna Cenami (?).

Netherlandish painting: Jan van Eyck, portrait of Arnolfini and his wife standing together in a room.

Netherlandish painting: Jan van Eyck, The Betrothal of the Arnolfini.

(February to 1435, March) Dufay was in the employ of the Court of Savoy.

(to 1436) Netherlandish painting: Jan van Eyck, Virgin and Child with Canon van der Paele.

(to 1600) This period was sometimes termed the Early Neapolitan School of composition.

1435

A major source reported: John Dunstable (John, Duke of Bedford), major composer of the first generation of Netherlanders, died in France (born c.1370). General con-

1435(cont.)

sensus tends to favor 1453 as the correct year of his death.

A few early printed works and several manuscripts including seven missals with illuminations of high quality, were preserved from this date.

The Council of Basle banned songs in the Czech language.

In Bohemia, musicians were looked upon as ungodly people. On this premise they were not permitted to receive Communion.

Philip the Good imported two blind viol players, Jehan Fernandes and Jehan de Cordouval. They reputedly came from the Hispanic Peninsula.

Andrea di Cione, Italian painter and sculptor, known as Verrocchio, was born (died 1488).

(June, to 1437, June) Dufay's name reappeared in the list of Papal singers.

(to 1465) The Regensburg School of St. Emmeram and the Paumann circle at Nuremberg flourished.

(to 1507) Molinet, a Burgundian court poet, was familiar with the chief musicians of his time.

c.1435

Florid counterpoint started its development.

Dufay wrote the motet, Ecclesie militantis-Sanctorum arbitrio -Bella canunt-Ecce nomen Domini-Gabriel, for the election of Eugene IV as pope.

Dufay's Salve flos tusce gentis -Vos nunc etrusce-Viri mendaces, hailed the city of Florence and its young women.

Netherlandish painting: Rogier van der Weyden, The Descent from the Cross (Altar-painting).

P. Lombardo, Renaissance architect, was born (died 1515).

Italian sculpture: Lorenzo Ghiberti, Creation of Man ("Gates of Paradise," Baptistery, Florence).

Michael Pacher, German painter, was born (died 1498).

Friedrich Herlin, German painter, was born (died 1500).

Nicholas Froment, French painter, was born (died c.1484).

German painting: Conrad Witz, Synagogue (Panel from the Heilspiegel Altarpiece).

(and c.1444) Conrad Witz's work comprises only two altarpieces - the one called the "Heilspiegel" Altarpiece (Mirror of Salvation), and the altarpiece of St. Peter.

1436

(March 25) The Florentine duomo, Santa Maria del Fiore, was consecrated by the pope. Dufay composed his four-part motet, Nuper rosarum flores, for the event and it was performed during the ceremony.

Burgundian account books listed Fontaine as a member of the chapel choir.

The Papal Chapel in Rome number-

1436(cont.)

ed not over nine singers, but grew to 24 members by the end of the century.

Dufay was appointed canon of Cambrai Cathedral.

Dufay's most famous "State" motet was probably commissioned by the City of Florence. It still had the old instrumental tenor based on a liturgical melody. There were also two canti on different but closely related texts, Salve flos Tuscae and Vos nunc Etrusca. Dufay added a contra in the style of the time and used it to complete chordal consonances. The contra obviously gave him the third note of triads when combined with the other two voices.

Pope Eugene IV left Florence for Bologna.

International Gothic painting: Pisanello, Princess of Trebizond.

Certain art-historians have considered that all the works of the artist known as the Master of the Osservanza in that convent were early works of Sano di Pietro.

Florentine fresco: Uccello, "Portrait of Sir John Hawkwood." This was Uccello's first dated fresco.

(to 1449) The inventive but confused art of Vecchietta (frescoes in the sacristy of the Hospital) provided Sienese painters with still another source of inspiration.

c.1436

Francesco del Cossa, Ferraran painter, was born (died 1478).

Pisanello was at Verona.

1437

Dufay was occasionally in Cambrai prior to this date.

Binchois was chaplain at a church in Mons.

Dufay entered the church and became Canon at Cambrai.

The organ at the cathedral of Pécs was first mentioned.

Florentine fresco:
Fra Angelico, Annunciation (Convent of S. Marco, Florence).

Florentine fresco:
Fra Angelico, Christ Mocked (Convent of S. Marco, Florence).

(to 1443) Sienese painting: Sassetta, the polyptych of St. Francis (at Borgo San Sepolcro).

(to 1450) Dufay spent seven years of this period in Savoy.

1438

Dufay composed a three-part motet, Magnanimae gentis laudes.

Jacopo della Quercia, Italian sculptor, died (born c.1374). His best known work was the Baptismal Font at San Giovanni, Siena.

Melozzo da Forli, Umbrian painter, was born (died 1494).

Flemish painting: Jan van Eyck, St. Francis Receiving the Stigmata (5"x5 3/4").

(to 1440) As a young man Piero della Francesca worked on frescos at Sant' Egidio with Domenico Veneziano at Florence.

1438(cont.)

(to c.1454) Dufay spent part of these years at Cambrai.

(to 1460) Duke Albert III was a great patron of the arts.

(to 1532) American Indian architecture: Tampumachy, Stone architecture.

1439

Duke Amadeus VIII assumed an active role as antipope Felix V.

Johann Urban was the Cantor at St. Thomas School at Leipzig.

The group of boys known as the "seises" was organized at Seville. It came as a result of activity taken by the dean of the cathedral and was sanctioned by Pope Eugene IV.

The dances of the seises were performed before the Blessed Sacrament.

Netherlandish painting:
Jan van Eyck, Portrait of Margaret van Eyck.

(to 1445) Alesso Baldovinetti worked with Piero della Francesca on the frescoes of Sant' Egidio.

c.1439

Juan del Encina, a most distinguished composer and poet during the reign of Ferdinand and Isabella, was born (died c.1529), see also c.1468.

1440

Hartmann Schedel, German doctor and historian, was born (d.1514).

Antoine Busnois, a leading composer of the Burgundian School, was born (died 1492).

The range of voices was usually within an octave in Burgundian musical style. The men's parts were in the high register and the tenor provided an excellent counterpoint.

"Il Conversione di S. Paolo" was sung in Rome.

Jan van Eyck, Flemish painter, died (born 1380), see c.1441.

Pisanello was at Milan.

Flemish painting:
Rogier van der Weyden, Deposition (7'x8'5").

Andrea del Castagno, Italian painter, came to Florence.

(to 1445) Florentine painting:
Fra Angelico, Lamentation (Convent of S. Marco, Florence).

(to 1449) Dufay composed Supremum est and Fulgens iubar -Puerpera pura - Virgo post partum.

(to 1449) The cantus firmus in Dufay's motets was moving up from its position in the lowest voice. The Missa Caput, which appeared to be one of the oldest of his cantus-firmus Masses was composed early in this period.

(to 1480) The seven Trent Codices (#87 to #93) were compiled at Trent, which was under control of the Germans.

(to 1490) One of the great musical centers of Europe was in Hungary at the court of King Matthias Corvinus.

c.1440

Gaspar van Weerbecke, later a pupil of Ockeghem, was born.

c.1440 (cont.)

Thomas de Walsingham said in a manuscript treatise of this time, "of late a New character has been introduced, called a Crotchet, which would be of no use, would musicians remember that beyond the minim no subdivision ought to be made."

John Shirley made a collection of compositions by Chaucer, Lydgate, and others.

John Hothby supposedly settled in Florence. His Calliopea legale was his major work.

The poem "Le Champion des Dames," by Martin le Franc and dedicated to the Duke of Burgundy, contained references to Dunstable.

Evidence of interest in keyboard instruments in the North was asserted in the illustrated treatise by Henry Arnaut, a Netherlander.

Ramos de Pareja, Spanish theorist who helped to lay the foundation for our harmonic system, was born at Baeza, near Jaén (died 1492).

Hugo van der Goes, Netherlandish painter, was born (died 1482).

Veit Stoss, German painter and sculptor, was born (died 1533).

Italian painting: Giovanni di Paolo, The Presentation in the Temple (15½" x 18¼").

Fra Angelico was a friar of the Dominican order.

German painting: Stefan Lochner, The Virgin in the Rosebower.

Italian painting: Pisanello, A (cont.) Princess of the Este Family (16 7/8" x 11 3/4").

Rueland Frueauf the Elder, German painter, was born (died 1507).

1441

Luca Signorelli, Italian painter, was born (died 1523).

(to 1442) Martin le Franc's poem was dedicated to Philip the Good. It was comprised of approximately twenty four thousand verses.

c.1441

Jan van Eyck, monumental Netherlandish painter, died (born c.1390), see c.1380.

International Gothic painting: Pisanello, Portrait of Lionello d'Este.

1442

Dufay received the degree of Magister in artibus, and Baccalareus in decretis, from the Sorbonne in Paris prior to this date.

Joannes Gallicus was active at the court of Mantua after this date.

Constans de Languebroek served Philip the Good from this date forward.

King Edward IV of England (House of York) was born (died 1483).

Pisanello was at Venice.

Andrea del Castagno painted his first frescoes in Venice, in the Church of San Zaccaria.

(to 1458) Gothic architecture:

1442 (cont.)

(to 1458) Gothic architecture: Burgos, Cathedral Towers (275' high).

1443

Brassart was cantor principalis to Emperor Frederick III.

Seami Motokiyo, Japanese author of a collection of aesthetic treatises on music and musician training, died (born 1363).

King Alfonso V ("el Magnánimo") of Naples established a court where music and literature were strongly cultivated.

Pope Eugene IV returned to Rome.

Gothic architecture: Bourges, Jacques Coeur House (Facade c.150' long).

(June 24 to 1444, June 24) Johannes Ockeghem was one of twenty-five singers who served on the cantoris side at Our Lady in Antwerp. Twenty-six singers on the decani side provided the psalmody.

(to 1445) Uccello designed cartoons for the windows of Florence Cathedral.

(to 1452) Donatello was at Padua during this period.

(to 1500) The first Baron von Teschky was elevated to the rank by Albrecht, Duke of Saxony. The title was granted as a result of an act of heroism which saved the baron's life.

1444

King Henry VI created the chapel post of Master of the Children. John Plummer, probably the Polumier whose motets appeared in collections of the time, (cont.) became the first Master appointed by this royal patent.

Okeghem resigned his position at Antwerp and entered the service of the King of France.

Donato Bramante, Florentine architect, was born. He was later commissioned by Pope Julius II to build a new St. Peter's Church in Rome where the old Basilica had stood (died 1514).

Swiss painting: Conrad Witz, Christ Walking on the Waves (From an altar painting).

Sano di Pietro was a conscientious and skillful Sienese artist. His style was typical of the Sienese artists of the time. None of his works painted prior to this date, when he was 38, have survived.

Bramante, a Renaissance architect, was born (died c.1514).

Swiss painting: Conrad Witz, Miraculous Draft of Fishes (51"x61").

Robert Campin (Master of Flémalle), Netherlandish painter, died (born c.1375).

Sandro Botticelli, Italian painter, was born (died 1510).

Petrus Christus became a citizen of Bruges.

(to 1445) French painting: Jean Fouquet, Portrait of Charles VII.

(to 1459) Renaissance architecture: Michelozzo, Riccardi Palace (plan, 225'x190'x80'high).

c.1444

German painting: Conrad Witz, Deliverance of St. Peter (Wing of Altarpiece).

Sienese painting: Sano di Pietro, St. Bernardino Preaching in the Campo at Siena (Siena Cathedral).

1445

Oswald von Wolkenstein, German composer and minnesinger who initiated polyphonic music in Germany, died (born c.1377).

Some major sources gave this year as that of Josquin Des Prés' birth. Others placed it at c.1450. He was born in Hainut, Burgundy (died 1521,August 27).

Heinrich Finck, German composer, was born in Bamberg or Transylvania (died 1527,June 9).

Sir Thomas Malory was a member of Parliament from Warwickshire.

French painting: Guillaume Dombet or the Master of the Aix Annunciation, The Prophet Jeremiah (Right wing of Annunciation Triptych.

French painting: Guillaume Dombet, Annunciation (Center Panel of Triptych).

(April 15 to 1459, September 22) The catalogue of the organists of St. Marks (given in von Winterfeld's "Gabrieli") contained the name of "Bernardo di Stefanino Murer," as having held the post during this period.

(to 1450) Italian sculpture: Donatello, Equestrian Monument of Gattamelata (11'x13').

(to 1450) Dufay was a member of the Chapel of the Duke of Burgundy.

(to 1450) After his return to Florence, Andrea del Castagno showed his full ability in the frescoes he painted for the refectory of the Monastery of Sant' Apollonia.

(to 1511) The Prophenium to Tinctoris' "Proportionale" was the chief basis for the high esteem in which Dunstable's musicianship was held.

c.1445

Gaspar van Weerbecke, Burgundian composer, was born at Oudenarde.

Adam von Fulda, German theorist and composer, was born at Fulda.

Conrad Witz, German-Swiss painter, died (born c.1400).

Pietro Vannucci, known as Perugino, Italian painter, was born (died 1523).

(to 1450) Italian painting: Andrea del Castagno, The Last Supper (c.28½' wide).

1446

Dufay was at the Burgundian court on a diplomatic mission.

Leonardo Giustiniani, poet of the ballata, O rosa bella, died.

Filippo Brunelleschi, A Florentine architect, died (born 1377).

Gothic architecture: The "Perpendicular" style, King's College Chapel, Cambridge was started.

(to 1448) Johannes Ockeghem was

1446(cont.)
(to 1448) a chorister, in the chapel of Duke Charles of Bourbon.

c.1446
Dufay composed Moribus Virgo.

Netherlandish painting: Petrus Christus, Portrait of a Lady.

Netherlandish painting: Portrait of a Donor and his Wife.

1447
(November 24) Henry Abyngdon succeeded John Bernard as subcentor of Wells.

After Jehan Pullois underwent a trial period, Duke Philip declined to use the services of this respected composer.

Fontaine's name was omitted from the Burgundian account books.

Palestrina was rebuilt.

Jean Fouquet went to Rome where he painted the Pope.

(to 1455) Renaissance architecture: Alberti, Rimini, San Francesco (Facade 97'wide).

(to 1455) The Papal reign of St. Nicholas V (born in Sarzana.

(to 1468) Jehan Pullois was a member of the Papal Choir.

c.1447
(to 1461) Enguerrand Charton (or Quarton), French painter, was active.

1448
Adam Ileborgh's Tablature of (cont.) 1448 was published. The first preludes in idiomatic keyboard style were included in the work.

Chu ch'üan, Chinese musicologist who wrote a treatise concerning flutes, died.

A manuscript of preludes by Adam Ileborgh, rector of a monastery in Stendal, Germany, was preserved.

After judging Robinet de la Magdalaine (Robert le Pele) for all of Easter week,
Duke Philip engaged him as a singer. His reputation was excellent in Rome and Rouen.

German organ tablature showed the use of a double pedal.

One German organ tablature was remarkable since it contained the first bar-lines.

(to 1491) Barbireau was choirmaster at the Church of Our Lady in Antwerp.

(to 1491) Maître Jacques was choirmaster and teacher of the boys at the cathedral of Antwerp until his death.

c.1448
Italian sculpture: Desiderio da Settignano, Bust of a Little Boy (10 11/32"x9 3/4"x5 7/8").

1449
Grenon was known to be at Cambrai.

Abram et Isaac Suo Figluolo was sung at Florence.

Domenico Ghirlandaio, Italian painter, was born (died 1494).

1449(cont.)

The Great Bells of Cologne were installed (wt. 6 tons).

Netherlandish painting: Petrus Christus, St. Eligius Weighing the Wedding Rings of a Bridal Couple.

Niccolo Pizzolo and Andrea Mantegna worked together on the Eremitani Church in Padua. After Pizzolo's death Mantegna continued on the cycle of "The Life of St. James."

Lorenzo de'Medici, highly ranked among Italian Renaissance poets, was born (died 1492).

Paul Hoffhaimer, German organist and composer, was born (died 1537), see 1459.

(to 1489) Simon Marmion, Franco-Flemish painter, was known.

c.1449

Netherlandish painting: Rogier Van Der Weyden, Sacrament of Marriage (Detail of the Altarpiece of the "Seven Sacraments").

1450

The manuscript collection of the Trent Codices contained musical adaptations of the antique verse meter.

The term, Lilt, was of Scottish origin, but it was used in Ireland. It was apparently derived from the bagpipe. One type of bagpipe was described in the "Houlate" (an ancient allegorical Scottish poem), as the "Liltpype."

"The great Eisteddfod of Carmarthen," was held with the (cont.) King's sanction in that locality.

The pupils of Domenico of Piacenza, dance master at Ferrara, carried his art all over Italy.

A chair of music was created at Bologna through the influence of Nicholas V. This was despite protest by mathematicians that music belonged in their field.

The Locheimer Liederbuch was written at this time and provided an early example of secular music in Germany. It contained forty-four songs set to German texts.

The beginnings of the Spanish Villancico form came at this time.

Music from this time was contained in the Cancionero Musical along with later works.

The Bass part was added to music from this time forward.

From this date on there were complete settings of the Ordinary.

"Tappster, dryngker," a three part drinking song with textless passages, was written.

Instrumentalists serving at royal courts were frequently mentioned at this time. The bagpipers, drummers, pipers, and lute-players of the King of Bosnia were especially prominent.

The musical style of the Burgundian School included four part writing with the contratenor moving into the altus and bassus. Music was written for

1450(cont.)

four part mixed voices.

Sumiaki Toyohara, Japanese court musician and author of encyclopaedia on musical instruments and their origin, was born (died 1524).

Venetian printer Aldus Manutius, who printed the first editions of many Greek and Latin classics including Aristotle's Poetics, was born (died 1515).

Loyset Compére, French composer, was born (died 1518).

Nicolo Burzio, Italian composer, was born (died 1518).

Rogier van der Weyden went to Rome.

Sassetta (Stefano) di Giovanni, Italian painter, died (born 1392).

Nuno Goncalves was appointed royal painter in Portugal.

Master Stephen's "Virgin of the Rosary," was painted at Cologne.

(to 1452) Netherlandish painting: Rogier van der Weyden, "Last Judgment."

(to 1525) The Flemish School of Composition flourished.

(to 1550) The Basse Danse, a ceremonial court dance in duple meter, was common at this time.

(to 1550) Willaert held a high position among Flemish masters. Their leadership of the musical world was remarkable and supreme during this period.

(to 1600) During this period (cont.) Meistersinger guilds flourished in all important German towns and cities.

(to 1600) The manufacture of the viol in many varieties was chiefly done by German lute -makers.

(to 1621) The Vereeniging Voor Noord-Nederlands Muziekgeschiedenis was the literary branch of the National Society for the Advancement of Music. It was organized for the purpose of collecting and publishing materials for the musical history of the Dutch Netherlands during the period extending from Obrecht to Sweelinck.

c.1450

Josquin des Prés was born in the province of Hainaut, possibly in Condé, where he ultimately died (1521). He was recognized as the innovator of a new Mass, motet, and chanson. His writings for several simultaneous voices and handling of polyphony was the height of Burgundian accomplishments. Certain sources gave his birth as 1445 but generally this year (1450) is recognized as more accurate.

Certain sources maintained that Obrecht was born at this time, possibly in Bergen Op Zoom or Sicily. General consunsus has set his birth at 1430 (d.1505).

Heinrich Isaac, a most versatile composer, was born in Flanders (died 1517). His capacity for assimilating international styles was remarkable.

Arnolt Schlick, German organ composer and lutenist, was born

c.1450(cont.)
(died c.1527), see also c.1460.

Thomas Stoltzer (Stolzer), German composer, was born (died 1526), see c.1470.

Walter Lambe was one of the earliest composers whose manuscript compositions are in existence.

Stylistic traits of the German polyphonic lied style developed from this time to the Reformation.

Arnoul Greban composed his Mystère de la Passion.

White notes for the minim and all larger note values, although no longer new, were generally adopted both in France and Italy.

Pierluisci Palestrina was born (died 1522).

Arnold de Lantins, French composer and Papal Chapel singer, was active at this time.

Hugo de Lantins, French composer, was active. There is no evidence that he was related to Arnold de Lantins.

England's position as a leading musical nation was largely due to accomplishments found in the music of Dunstable, who introduced his own music to the continent.

William Newark, an early English Tudor composer who had a fine reputation, was born (died 1509). He was never well-known because of lack of modern publication.

Juan de Anchieta, a musician at the court of Ferdinand and Isabella, was born (died 1523).

Pierre de la Rue was born in Picardy (died 1518).

Stopless mixture organs were still being built in Italy.

English elements had come into use in French music.

The first school of music at Naples was founded by John Tinctor.

The three-part drinking song, Tappster, dryngker, fylle another ale, was composed.

Abbot Whethamstede of St. Albans presented an organ to his church which cost him fifty pounds including installation. This was a monstrous sum at the time.

A three-part song Go Hert Hurt with Adversite was composed.

Egerton manuscript #3307 was one source which described developments of the time in England.

Three of Dufay's Masses, based on Caput, Saint Gothard, and Se la face ay pale showed the characteristic of the four-part Mass of the time.

Glad and blithe mote ye be was an interesting English version of the Laetabundus, an eleventh century sequence.

A popular tune, "Mein mut ist mir betrübet gar," was the first selection in a song collection compiled by a citizen of Nürnberg.

c.1450(cont.)

Lutes at this time normally had eleven strings and all except the highest pitched one were double-stings (courses). The two strings of a course were tuned to the same pitch, so lutes were usually referred to as six-stringed.

Two English examples of the setting of the Passion "turba" choruses were recently discovered in a manuscript at St. George's Chapel in Windsor. One of the examples was imperfect.

Fontenelle mentioned a "Mystery of the Passion" which was produced by the Bishop of Angers. It apparently had so much Music of a really dramatic character that it could be described as a Lyric Drama.

Ambros, in the second volume of his "Geschichte der Musik," placed the Reading Manuscript at this time.

The Madrigal was said to exist in the Low Countries as early as this date. It was already well known to the Netherlanders as a Polyphonic Song, frequently very elaborate in construction, and at all times composed in strict conformity with the laws of the old Church Modes.

Sir Thomas Malory was involved in acts of violence and disorder which ultimately led to his imprisonment for a long period.

The Kingdom of Naples was more deeply affected by Flemish painting than any other part of Italy.

The invention of printing, (cont.) which took place in Germany, had an enormous effect on the future development of art and other areas.

Stefan Lochner, German painter, worked in Cologne.

Dieric Bouts, a contemporary of Petrus Christus, settled in Louvain.

Andrea del Castagno was commissioned to produce a series of "Famous Men and Women" for the Villa la Legnaia (near Florence).

Gerard David, Netherlandish painter, was born at Oudewater, near Gouda (died 1523).

Hieronymus Bosch, Netherlandish painter, was born (died 1516).

Martin Schongauer brought German painting to a position of dignity.

Florentine painting: Baldovinetti, Madonna and Child.

Florentine painting: Andrea del Castagno, Cumaean Sibyl (Villa Legnaia, Florence).

Florentine painting: Andrea del Castagno, Petrarch, Boccaccio (Villa Legnaia, Florence).

Florentine painting: Andrea del Castagno, Virgin, St. John (Refectory of St. Apollonia, Florence).

Florentine painting: Domenico Veneziano, St. John In The Wilderness.

Florentine painting: Uccello, The Rout of San Romano.

c.1450(cont.)

French painting: Fouquet, Book of Hours.

French painting: Fouquet, Estienne Chevalier, treasurer of Charles VII of France, with St. Stephen.

French painting: Fouquet, Virgin and Child (Right Part of Melun Diptych).

French painting: Fouquet, Self-Portrait (Enamel).

Persian manuscript: The Persian Prince Humay meets the Chinese Princess Humayun in her garden.

(to c.1499) John Hothby (Otteby), an English Carmelite monk, lived the greater part of his life in the Carmelite monastery at Ferrara and was famous for his skill and knowledge in the science of music.

(to c.1499) This period was considerably more productive for Spain than the first half of the century in the field of composition.

(to c.1499) Guillaume Crespel, a Belgian musician, was active during this period.

(to c.1499) Bernard "the German" was organist at St. Mark's in Venice. He was credited with inventing organ pedals.

(to c.1499) Founders of the Flemish School who cultivated forms of imitation were concerned with concealing the solutions of their Enimme or Aenigmatical canons.

(to c.1499) Many books of the later half of the 15th century (cont.) were illustrated with woodcuts.

(to c.1499) Information concerning English music was rather limited during this period, however, it increased as the first sources of Tudor music began to appear.

(to c.1510) German painting: Master of the St. Bartholomew Altarpiece, St. Bartholomew Between St. Agnes and St. Cecilia.

(to c.1525) A peculiar practice of inserting a flat before "f" existed at this time. Musical context made it clear that it did not mean to lower the note.

(to c.1525) Obrecht, in his "Missa Je ne demande," used five different time-signatures at the beginning of a single staff. This was typical of the Music of this period.

(to c.1550) Composers enjoyed combining Mode, Time, and Prolation with great complexity until the time of Palestrina. Then the practice slowly disappeared.

(to c.1599) The form of ligatures varied greatly in Polyphonic Masses.

(to c.1599) Humanist circles experimented in metrical writing.

(to c.1599) Many of the great musicians of this period were pupils of Maitre Jacques Barbireau.

(to c.1599) The Sharp displaced the Natural and was used to raise a B which would otherwise c.1450(cont.) have been sung as B^b.

(to c.1599) Dynamic signs were unknown to the polyphonists of the time. Tempo and expression markings were similarly unknown.

(to c.1599) Apparently music played a greater role in life than surviving texts of the Rappresentazioni stated.

(to c.1599) Organs and instruments called "vihuelas" were frequently mentioned.

(to c.1599) The largest body of German monophony in the period was the music of the Meistersinger.

(to c.1599) German monophonic music of the time was divided into three main classes: liturgical music, secular music, and a category that was a compromise between the two. In the latter category, the music was secular in style but the texts were religious.

(to c.1599) Composers of this period manipulated their subjects and answers to conform with the principles of the system of hexachords.

(to c.1599) Although the Meistersinger did not use instruments, considerable evidence existed of their widespread use throughout German-speaking countries during this time.

(to c.1599) Music was cultivated in Bohemia but its development was limited.

(to c.1599) A battle was fought over the admission of (cont.) polyphony into the Church in Bohemia. Eventually the polyphonists emerged the victors.

(to c.1599) Barbireau's most famous work was Een vroylic wesen, a three-part song.

(to c.1599) There was a practice of alternating plainsong and polyphony sometimes followed in the 15th century and usually followed in the 16th century.

(to c.1599) Polyphonic composers rarely presented their works to the performer in score.

(to c.1599) German dances, similar to French, were either solemn and slow or consisted of wild jumps and leaps.

(to c.1599) Staves of four, five, or six lines were used.

(to c.1599) A few of the songs of the Meistersinger became Volkslieder during this period.

(to c.1599) In Modern Music, the semibreve retained several characteristics that distinguished it in this period.

(to c.1599) The antiphon of Hermannus Contractus, upon which many pieces of medieval polyphony were based, continued to inspire composers in this period.

(to c.1599) The clavichord was in general use.

(to c.1599) Examples of the Missa Sine Nomine were found among the works of des Prés, Palestrina, and other composers.

(to c.1599) All the devices of

c.1450(cont.)
the Netherlandish techniques were existent in compositions of the sixteenth century in Italy.

(to c.1599) A large collection of Noenioe, or Funeral Motets, by the greatest composers of this period have been preserved.

(to c.1599) When a piece had a fifth part it always corresponded exactly, in range, with one of the other four. For this reason it was impossible to describe it as First or Second Cantus, Altus, Tenor, or Bassus.

(to c.1599) In the "Enimme," or AEnigmatical Canons, an Inscription was usually substituted for the presa, although in many cases even this was lacking, and the singer was left to his own devices.

(to c.1599) Composers frequently substituted a mixture of black and white notes for the Points of Augmentation, Alteration, and Division.

(to c.1599) "Gelobet seyst du," was composed with words by Martin Luther. Six verses were added to a 15th-century translation of Gregory the Great's "Grates nunc omnes," a Christmas sequence.

(to c.1599) Franciscans, who utilized the primitive lauda in order to promote their folklike religious ideas, were some of the most renowned English authors of carol texts.

(to c.1599) There were a number of amorous songs accompanied on the lute written during this (cont.) period. Dalmation moralists, including Marko Marulić, and the archbishops of Split, ruled that members of the cloth might not change clothes at night and wander through dark streets singing love songs, accompanied on the lute or another instrument.

(to c.1599) A "consort of viols" was a quartet, quintet or sextet or sometimes another number of stringed instruments which performed in concert.

(to c.1599) In the part-books of the period, four voices were usually mentioned by the names; Cantus, Altus, Tenore, and Bassus.

(to c.1599) Traces of Canti popolari were found in Italian compositions of this period. Very few survived in their original form but Willaert's "Canzon di Ruzante" was one that did.

(to c.1599) Secular music was music composed for the Church but it had a separate sphere of its own. This was indicated by the vaux-de-ville (vaudevilles), and airs-de-couer which were collected and published in the 16th century, although they probably were written in the preceding century.

(to c.1599) A collection of In Nomines in 4 and 5 parts, by English composers, survived from this period.

(to c.1599) Tablature was a method of notation for the Lute, but occasionally used by violists, and composers for other instruments of similar character.

c.1450(cont.)

(to c.1599) In Göttingen, Germany, at the University, collections of 145 musical works of this period have been assembled. Many of them are quite rare.

(to c.1599) Werlin's Song-book, a collection which contains many thousand melodies to sacred and secular words, has been preserved.

(to c.1599) The Antegnati family of Brescia was among the earliest of famous organ-builders. By the end of this period they had built more than 400 instruments.

(to c.1599) Evacuatio was a term used to indicate the substitution of a "void" or open -headed note for a "full," or closed one; in other words substitution of a minim for a crotchet.

(to c.1599) The virginal at this time was a set of individual tone-producing units, such as the C key with the C strings and the D key with the D strings.

(to c.1599) Most Masses were named after some melody, liturgical or secular, and that melody was played in long notes in the tenor part and acted as a support for all the sections of the Mass.

(to c.1599) Although there was little from the 15th century, there were voluminous instrumental tablatures for both the vihuela and organ in the 16th.

(to c.1599) The early anonymous basse danz melody, La Spagna, (cont.) served as the cantus firmus for a 15th-century piece. It reoccurred in various 16th century works from various countries, but seldom in the highest voice.

(to c.1599) A great deal of the polyphonic music printed in the early 16th century actually was written during the latter portion of the previous century. Sources for art forms of that period included early prints, in addition to manuscripts.

(to c.1599) There was scarcely a town of any magnitude or importance throughout Germany which did not have its own Meistersinger.

(to c.1599) A volume (manuscript) of old English songs for 2,3 and 4 voices by composers of this period was preserved. It formerly belonged to Robert Fayrfax and afterwards General Fairfax. On his death it passed to the hands of Ralph Thoresby of Leeds.

(to c.1599) L'Homme Armé, Lome Armé, or Lomme Armé was the name of an old French Chanson. That melody used by some of the leading composers as the cantus firmus of a certain kind of Mass - called the "Missa L'Homme armé"- was well-known. They embellished the tune with as many learned and elaborate devices as possible. The regularity of phrasing was rather more typical of the 16th than the 15th century.

(to c.1599) The 35th Cantique (Ecclus xxiv) of Jan Fruytier's Ecclesiasticus was set to a French 15th-century dance called L'homme armé. This was not the

c.1450(cont.)

same as the song of the same name often used as a theme for entire masses by composers of this period.

(to c.1599) Bihzad, Islamic artist, worked during part of this period.

(to c.1699) A disease known as Tarantism swept through southern Italy during these years. It apparently was a kind of hysteria, like the St. Vitus dance epidemic in Germany at an earlier date. The only cure was said to be the continued exercise of dancing the Tarantella; but the real cause of the disease was thought to be the bite of the spider. Later experiments showed that its bit was no more poisonous than a wasp's sting.

(to c.1699) The spirit and power of Volkslieder were felt in every branch of music.

(to c.1799) The passion for academic institutions was so vehement in Italy that there was hardly a town which did not have at least one, while larger cities contained several.

(to c.1799) The Viol, invented in the 15th century, passed out of general use in the 18th. Actually it remained in one form, the bass viol, but all the other sizes disappeared or were replaced.

1451

(January 14) Franchino Gafori or Franchinus Gafurius, a priest and a writer on music, was born at Lodi (died 1522). He was thought to be the first public professor of music.

The archives of the Cathedral of Cambrai contained a record of 60 scuta, given to Dufay as a "gratification," in this year.

The ambassadors of Ladislaus V visited Germany and France with trumpet corps in their retinue.

Stefan Lochner, German painter, died (born c.1400 or c.1410).

Domenico Veneziano, Italian painter, died (born c.1400).

(to 1455) Renaissance architecture: Alberti, Florence, Rucellai Palace (69' high).

c.1451

(to 1452) Netherlandish painting: Rogier Van Der Weyden, St. Mary Magdalene (Wing of the Braque Triptych).

1452

Conrad Paumann's Fundamentum organisandi was published. It contained, for the most part, short instructive examples designed to illustrate and teach the principles of composition.

The "Locheimer Liederbuch" appeared. It was a collection of volkslieder.

Felsöbánya, Hungary received an organ as a gift from Governor John Hunyadi.

King Richard III (House of York) of England was born (died 1485).

Leonardo da Vinci was born in a Tuscan village (died 1519).

(to 1453) Umbrian painting: Piero della Francesca, Solomon Receiving the Queen of Sheba.

(to 1459) Umbrian painting:

1452(cont.)

Piero della Francesca, Finding of the True Cross.

(to 1459) Umbrian painting: Piero della Francesca, Story of the True Cross: Proving the True Cross.

1453

(December 24) British composer and astronomer, John Dunstable, died in Walbrook, England (born 1370). He was buried at St. Stephen's in Walbrook and was referred to as the guiding master of English music.

(May) Constantinople fell to the Turks.

The Middle Ages came to a close in this year.

The Great Bells of Danzig were built (wt. 6 tons).

Johannes Ockeghem was a chorister in the Royal Chapel. After this date he spent most of his life in France as a conductor for the King.

Niccolo Pizzola, Italian painter, died (born 1421).

Several sources gave this date as German painter Martin Schongauer's birth, however, consensus put the date as c.1430(died 1491).

c.1453

Spanish court music: The four-part "Lealtat, O lealtat" lauded Miguel Lucas de Iranzo, Constable under Henry IV of Castile.

1454

(February) The Banquet of the Oath of the Pheasant was held (cont.) at Lille.

Dufay's relations with Cambrai became progressively closer.

French painting: Enguerrand Charton, Coronation of the Virgin (Hospice de Villeneuve-Les-Avignon).

(to 1455) Italian sculpture: Donatello, Mary Magdalen (74" high).

(to 1495) Johannes Ockeghem had the honor and distinction of acting as first chaplain and composer to three successive Kings of France-Charles VII, Louis XI, and Charles VIII.

c.1454

Bernardino Pinturicchio, Italian painter, was born (died 1513).

1455

Adrian Pieterez built an organ at Delft, and it remained in the new church. It has been restored so often that little or nothing of his work remains.

Composer Johannes Cornago, a Franciscan, was sent to Rome by the King of Spain.

Fra Angelico (Giovanni di Fiesole), the painter of Fiesole, died (born 1387).

Lorenzo Ghibert, a Florentine sculptor, died (born 1378).

International Gothic painting: Mantegna, St. James on the way to his execution (From a wall-painting formerly in the Eremitani Church, Padua.

Antonio da San Gallo, the Elder, Renaissance architect, was

1455(cont.)
born (died 1534).

(to 1456) Antonio Pisanello, Italian painter, died (born c.1395).

(to 1458) The Papal reign of St. Callistus III (born in Jativa).

(to 1478) Henry Abyngdon, English organist, became Master of the Children in the Chapel Royal in England.

(to 1485) The War of the Roses ended the active musical culture of England.

c.1455

The famous Gutenberg Latin Bible was printed at Mainz.

Vittore Carpaccio, Venetian painter, was born (died 1526).

Antonio Pisanello, Italian painter, died (born c.1395).

Franco-Flemish painting: Anonymous, Man with Glass of Wine.

French painting: Fouquet, Saint Martin and the Beggar (6¼"x4 5/8").

Italian painting: Piero della Francesca, The Dream of Constantine.

Italian sculpture: Desiderio da Settignano, Tomb of Carlo Marsuppini (c.91" long).

Italian painting: Paolo Uccello, The Battle of San Romano (72"x125").

Netherlandish painting: (cont.) Rogier van der Weyden, Portrait of a Lady.

1456

Slatkonia, bishop and Hungarian court chapel-master to Maximilian I, was born.

Ercole de' Roberti, Ferraran painter, was born (died 1496).

French painting: Master of 1456, Portrait of a Man, called the Portrait of 1456.

Sienese painting: Sano di Pietro, Madonna with Calixtus III.

Italian painting: Uccello, The Battle of San Romano (5'10 7/8" x 10' 3/8").

(to 1459) Italian painting: Mantegna, Calvary (26 3/8" by 36 5/8").

(to 1497) A Kyriale prepared for Carlo Pallavicino, Bishop of Lodi, contained a whole series of ordinary sets.

c.1456

Netherlandish painting: Rogier van der Weyden, Portrait thought to be of Antoine, "Grand Batard" of Burgundy.

1457

The first known printed book meant to include music was the Psalterium, which was printed by Johann Fust and Peter Schöffer, associates of Gutenberg at Mainz. The book was in large black letter type on vellum.

John Roose, a Brother of the Order of Preaching Friars, repaired one of the organs in York Minster.

1457(cont.)

Larger kettle drums, struck by riders on horseback in the retinue of some Polish political mission, marked the first appearance of these drums in western Europe.

Many early printed books of rarity, including a copy of the Mainz Psalter of this time, have been preserved.

Robert Morton, an English musician, became a singer in the chapel.

Hayne van Ghizeghem's name first occurred in the archives when Constans was paid for taking charge of "un jeusne filz appelé Hayne van Ghizeghem.

King Henry VII of England (House of Tudor) was born (died 1509).

Andrea del Castagno, Italian painter, died (born 1397). Some sources give his birth as 1423.

Andrea Mantegna executed a superb altarpiece for San Zeno, Verona. It acted as a manifesto for the new art in the stronghold of the international Gothic style.

(to 1468) 572 players and choir singers and 195 apprentices were received at King Setjo's Korean court.

c.1457

Filippino Lippi, Italian printer, was born (died 1504).

1458

Dufay visited Besancon, since he had been asked to function as arbiter in a musical debate (cont.) held there.

Johannes Regis was at Soignies.

Mapheus Vegius died.

(to 1464) The Papal reign of St. Pius II (born in Siena).

c.1458

Giovanni Spataro, an Italian scholar and musician, was born (died 1541). He was a pupil of Bartolomé Ramos de Pareja.

King Alfonso V the Magnanimous of Aragon, died (born c.1396).

Lorenzo di Credi, Italian painter, was born (died 1537).

French painting: Fouquet, "Grandes Chroniques de France," an illuminated book.

1459

The second edition of the Mainz Psalter was printed.

Paul Hoffhaimer, German composer, was born in Radstadt, near Salzburg (died 1537).

Conrad Celtes, German humanist and Latin poet, was born (died 1508).

Florentine painting: Benozzo Gozzoli, Journey of the Magi (Fresco Detail, Palazzo Medici, Riccardi, Florence.

(to 1472) Josquin de Prés was a singer at the Milanese duomo.

c.1459

French painting: Fouquet, the Munich "Boccaccio," an illuminated book.

1460

Binchois, Burgundian master of

1460(cont.)

vocal music, died at Soignies (born c.1400).

The Glogauer (Berliner) Liederbuch, early example of German secular music, was published. It contained 180 sacred songs, 65 German songs, instrumental dances including "O rosa bella" (Senfl).

Dunstable was mentioned in "Le Champion des Dames" of Martin Le Franc.

The registers of Cambrai Cathedral showed a Johannes Tinctoris as having been connected with its musical organization.

Ockeghem's lament on the death of Binchois was composed.

Fauxbourdon apparently reached England at this time.

The Intronati were particularly interested in the cultivation of every sort of scenic representation.

Joos van Wassenhove (Justus of Ghent) became a Master at Antwerp.

Flemish painting influenced Piero della Francesca's own manner and style.

(to 1467) Portuguese painting: Nuno Goncalues, St. Vincent Polyptych.

(to 1469) A motet of Robert Morton reappeared, adapted to a German text and in a German manuscript.

(to 1469) The Tidal Law interrupted the classical trends of (cont.) the Renaissance. It was concerned with aesthetic reversals from time to time.

(to 1469) Some printers provided red staff lines so that only notes needed to be added.

(to 1469) The Schedelsches Liederbuch was written by Hartmann Schedel, a doctor and historian, while he was a student at Leipzig and Padua, and conceivably also at Nürnberg. The book has also been known as the Münchener, Waltersches and Jüngeres Nürnberger Liederbuch.

(to 1469) The growing influence of a northern type of painting appeared in Florence.

(to 1490) Ferrara became a focal-point for different artistic styles and an important center where brilliance and originality predominated.

(to 1520) No German organ tablatures survived from this period.

c.1460

Arnold Schlick, German composer of Spiegel der Orgelmacher und Organisten, was born (died c.1517), see also c.1450.

Paulus Paulirinus wrote Tractatus de musica.

Dunstable's chanson "Puisque m'amour" was arranged for organ.

Part-book notation, in which each voice had its own book, came into existance with the Glogauer Liederbuch.

Many of the early Bohemian songs contained a chorale. An

c.1460(cont.)

example was the middle of the well-known "War Song of the Hussites."

The most comprehensive German collection of organ music was the Buxheimer Orgelbuch. It contained over 250 selections.

Thomas Linacre, founder of the Royal College of Physicians in London, was born (died 1524).

The Cologne School of Painting was under Netherlandish influence.

Geertgen Tot Sint Jans, Netherlandish painter, was born (died c.1490).

Andrea Solario, Italian painter, was born (died 1520).

French painting: Avignon School, Pietà.

Italian painting: Giovanni Bellini, Pietà.

Italian painting: Piero della Francesca, Constantine's Dream (Wall-painting in the Church of St. Francesco, Arezzo).

Italian architecture: Alberti, A Renaissance Church, St. Andrea in Mantua.

Italian painting: Piero della Francesca, The Resurrection (9'6"x8'4").

Florentine painting: Domenico Veneziano, Portrait of a Young Woman.

Book illustration: Tavernier, Dedication page to "The Conquests of Charlemagne."

(to 1480) In Spain, and later in France, the steps in the basse danz became ordered. In Italy all dance compositions were individual creations from the choreographic point of view.

(to c.1520) In an earlier version, Quand ce vendra was an example of the non-quartal style. This was evident in a small body of works of this period.

1461

A branch of the Confraternity at Paris was set up at Amiens.

Joannes Okeghem was mentioned as head of the chapel in this year of Charles VII's death.

The "Liber Niger Domus Regis," the earliest known record on the subject, stated that during Edward IV's reign there was a well-established Chapel Royal.

The four-part Der pfoben swancz, was drawn upon by later composers, but under the name of Barbingant.

(to 1483) The reign of King Edward IV (House of York) over England and Great Britain.

(to 1483) The reign of King Louis XI (House of Valois) over France.

c.1461

Enguerrand Charanton (Quarton), French painter, died (born c.1410).

1462

King Louis XII, the Father of the People, of France (House of Valois), was born (died 1515).

Piero di Cosimo, Italian pain-

1462(cont.)
ter, was born (died 1521).

Netherlandish painting:
Dieric Bouts, Portrait of a Man.

German painting:
Friedrich Herlin, Group of Female Donors.

c.1462
Independent pedal organs were used on the continent of Europe.

Gilles Mureau became an heurier at the Cambrai Cathedral.

Juan de Anchieta, a leading Spanish sacred composer, was born in the Basque town of Azpeitia(died 1523), see c.1450.

1463
The phrase "ye players at ye orgenys" came into use.

Henry Abyngdon was the earliest to receive the Mus. Bac. Degree from Cambridge. Another early graduate was Thomas Seynt Just.

Johannes Regis apparently became magister puerorum of the Church of Our Lady in Antwerp.

Dufay's Missa Ecce was composed and was copied for the Cambrai choir.

Thomas Saintwix received the degree of Doctor of Music.

1464
An excellent bass part-book was written at this time but appeared in a manuscript written by John Sadler in 1575.

The Bohemian-Moravian Brethren, founded at this time, encouraged (cont.) popular singing. They were of Hussite origin.

"Ave Regina Coelorum" was composed by Dufay.

Körmöczbánya (Kremnica or Kremnitz) had a church organ at this time.

Desiderio da Settignano, Italian sculptor, died (born 1428).

Rogier van der Weyden, Netherlandish painter, died (born c.1399).

(to 1466) Niccola Fabri, Governor of Rome, held the title, Maestro della Cappella Pontificia.

(to 1468) Netherlandish painting: Dieric Bouts, the "Last Supper" (altarpiece of "The Sacrament") was painted for the Church of St. Pierre, Louvain, where it has remained since.

(to 1471) The Papal reign of St. Paul II (born in Venice).

c.1464
Quentin Massys, Flemish artist, was born at Louvain (died 1530).

Venetian painting:
Giovanni Bellini, Four triptychs painted for the Church of the Carità.

French painting: Stone-masons and the King (From an illumination of the Story of Troy by Jean Colombe).

1465
(May) Henry Abyngdon was appointed "Master of the Song" of the Chapel Royal in London. The position carried an annual

1465(cont.)

salary of forty marks.

Robert Cornyshe, English pre madrigal composer of secular part songs, was born (died 1523).

Robert Morton was granted a leave-of-absence by Philip, the Good in order to serve the Count of Charolais, who would become Charles, the Bold.

Okeghem was chapel master at Paris.

Conrad Peutinger, a great humanist, diplomatist, political scientist, and patron of music, was born (died 1547).

The four-part Lealtat! O lealtat, previously mentioned here as c.1453, was attributed to this date by a major source. Regardless of date it was representative of a body of courtly music that was not preserved.

Venetian painting: Gentile Bellini, Lorenzo Giustiniani.

Florentine fresco: Benozzo Gozzoli, Life of St. Augustine.

Venetian sculpture: Laurana, Christ Blessing.

Hans Memlinc became a citizen of Bruges.

(to 1466) Umbrian painting: Piero della Francesca, Battista Sforza and Federigo da Montefeltro.

(to 1468) Florentine painting: Uccello, Legend of the Jew and the Host.

(to 1470) Florentine painting: Antonio del Pollaiuolo, Battle of Ten Naked Men.

(to 1495) The Trent masters and circle of the Buxheimer Orgelbuch were active.

c.1465

Busnois's motet In hydraulis was composed in honor of Ockeghem. The latter was praised as the greatest among court singers of France.

Robert Fayrfax, English Tudor pre madrigal composer of secular part songs, was born (died 1521).

Florentine print: Fresco Painting and colour grinding (showing the occupations of people born under Mercury).

Gil Vicente, Portuguese dramatist, was born (died c.1536).

1466

(June 14) Ottaviano dei Petrucci, the first printer of mensural music, was born at Fossombrone (died 1539). A collection of polyphonic music was his first effort.

Henricus Arnaut of Zwolle, who died at this time, was a physician and astrologer to Philip the Good. Later he served Charles VII and Louis XI and wrote a treatise describing in detail the structure of several keyboard instruments, among them the harp, lute and organ.

The Bohemian baron, Leo von Rozmital (brother-in-law of the King of Bohemia) visited England and other countries as part of a pilgrimage

1466(cont.)

"for the sake of piety and religion."

In the treatise of Henricus Arnaut of Zwolle there was an organ design.

Johannes Cornago was chief almoner to Ferrante, son and successor to Alfonso V.

Donatello, the Florentine sculptor, died (born c.1386).

c.1466

(to c.1499) A Mass, "Officium Auleni," probably by Johannes Aulen, was composed during this period.

(to c.1499) Agricola and Isaac, composers, were employed by Lorenzo the Magnificent in Florence.

(to 1519) Two major frottole composers, Cara and Tromboncino, were employed at the Court of Francesco II. They were part of the impetus in the rise of the Italian Madrigal.

1467

(May 1) A letter to Dufay from Antonio Squarcialupi, organist of Santa Maria del Fiore at Florence, was written. The latter was the owner of the Squarcialupi Codex, a major source of trecento music. The letter stated that Dufay had sent singers from Cambrai to Piero de' Medici and that they had been well received both by Piero and his organist.

Antonius Busnois was employed as a Singer in the Chapel of Charles the Bold, Duke of Burgundy.

Hayne van Ghizeghem was a singer and valet de chambre to Philip the Good. When the Duke died he remained to serve Charles the Bold.

Philip the Good, whose court at Dijon, Burgundy was an intellectual and artistic center, died (born 1419). At the time of Philip's death he employed Constans de Languebroek, Gilles Joye, and Robert Morton as musicians.

(to 1477) Charles the Bold, Duke of Burgundy, whose court at Dijon was an intellectual and artistic center, ruled during this period.

1468

Sir Thomas Malory was imprisoned again, this time on a charge of sedition.

The slide-trumpet, a kind of trombone, was known as a sackbut.

A tenor part-book composed at this time was preserved in a manuscript by John Sadler in 1591.

Hayne van Ghizeghem entered military service for Charles the Bold.

"The March of the Men of Harlech" was claimed by Llwyd, the "Bard of Snowdon," to have been composed during the siege of Harlech Castle.

Flemish painting: Dieric Bouts, The Last Supper (71"x59").

(to 1484) Florentine painting: At Pisa, Gozzoli painted frescoes in the Campo Santo.

c.1468

Traxdorff, of Mainz, made an organ for the church of St. Sebald at Nuremberg. It had an octave of pedals and as a result of this he has been referred to as their originator.

Juan del Encina, Spanish composer, was born in or near Salamanca (died c.1529)see c1439.

(to 1470) Franco-Flemish painting: Anonymous, Portrait of Margaret of York, Wife of Charles the Bold.

(to 1523) William Cornyshe, a great favorite of Henry VIII, was a musician, dramatist and actor who produced interludes and pageants at the court.

1469

The list of men who bore the title of Maestro della Cappella Pontificia included fourteen ecclesiastics, of whom all except the last, were Bishops.

In the "Fabrick Rolls of York Minister," the following entry occurred, "To brother John for constructing two pair of bellows for the great organ, and repairing the same, 15s. 2d."

The Rule of Lorenzo de' Medici began.

Fra Filippo Lippi, Italian painter, died (born 1406).

c.1469

Cosimo Tura and a group led by Francesco del Cossa and Ercole de Roberti worked on decorations for the Palazzo Schifanoia, including astrological frescoes and scenes of court life.

Leonardo da Vinci was apprenticed (cont.) to Verrocchio.

(and 1470) Ockeghem travelled in Spain.

(to 1471) Johann Steinwert of Soest was active as a singer at Cassel, the capital of the Landgrave Hessia.

(to 1534) Juan del Encina had sixty-eight compositions published in the Cancionero Musical de los Siglos XV y XVI.

1470

Martin Klotsch was the Cantor of the St. Thomas School at Leipzig.

Robert Morton was raised to the status of a chaplain.

Ockeghem's Requiem was almost certainly composed later than Dufay's since a scribe is known to have made a copy of the latter's at this date.

Johannes Brasart, German composer, died (born 1400).

A certain Ulrich Schütz acquired citizenship in Chemnitz at this time.

King Edward V (House of York) of England was born (died 1483).

King Charles VIII of France (House of Valois) was born (died 1498).

Jacopo, Venetian painter and founder of the Bellini Workshop, died (born 1400).

Netherlandish painting: Memlinc, Martyrdom of St. Sebastian.

(to 1471) King Henry VI (Lancaster) reigned again over

1470(cont.)

England and Great Britain. He had previously ruled from 1422 to 1461.

(to 1472) Florentine painting: Sandro Botticelli, Judith and Holofernes.

(and 1474) Alexander de Alamania was in Florence.

(to 1479) A new wave of native composition occurred.

(to 1507) The best known master of the Salzburg School, Frueauf the Elder, divided his time between Salzburg and Passau.

c.1470

Pietro Bembo, a Venetian nobleman and scholar, was born (died 1547).

Carpentras, a Netherlands composer, was born(died 1548).

Fernando de Contreras, Spanish composer, was born (died 1548).

Robert Johnson, Scottish composer, was born (died 1554).

Francisco de Peñalosa, Spanish composer, was born in Toledo (died 1528).

Thomas Stoltzer, German composer, was born in Schweidnitz (Silesia)(died 1526). This major source also gave his birth as c.1450 and it was so recorded here.

Gian Angelo Testagrossa, Mantuan composer and teacher of Francesco Canova da Milano, was born (died 1530).

The invention of the pedal was usually attributed to Bernhard, (cont.) organist to the Doge of Venice; but evidence indicated that they were known earlier.

Buxheimer Orgelbuch was published. It contained two hundred and fifty pieces.

Johannes Tinctoris' treatise Expositio Manus was written.

John Hamboys (Hanboys) Mus. Doc. and a distinguished musician was active at this time.

Permeation by the tenor, achieved great importance in the works of Josquin. It developed at this time.

Gerardus of Lisa, a musician, set up one of the first printing presses in Italy.

Renaissance architecture: Alberti, Mantua, Sant' Andrea, started at this time (300'x171').

Italian sculpture: Andrea del Verrocchio, Putto with Dolphin (27" without base).

Venetian painting: Giovanni Bellini, "Milan Pietà."

Netherlandish painting: Hugo van der Goes, Fall of Man.

French painting: Fouquet, "Antiquités Judaiques."

German woodcut: The good man on his death-bed (illustration for the "Art of Dying Well" printed in Ulm).

Pietro Aron, Italian theorist, was born (died c.1545).

Galeotto del Carretto, Italian lyric poet, was born (died 1531).

1471

(March 14) Sir Thomas Malory died (birthdate unknown).

(December) Galeazzo Maria Sforza, Duke of Milan, wrote to King Matthias Corvinus of Hungary and recommended Pietro da Vienna ex Alamania, a cousin of one of his singers named Alexander. The Duke also sent his chapel-master to England to recruit good English singers.

When the Duke of Milan went to Florence he took with him 40 players of "high" instruments.

After leaving the monastery at Ferrara, John Hothby apparently took up residence at Florence where he was held in great esteem.

Albrecht Dürer, German painter, was born (died 1528).

Nuno Goncalves, Portuguese painter, died (birthdate unknown).

(to 1472) The Magister Rainaldus who was found at Rieti (between Rome and Perugia) was possibly Raynaldino.

(to 1473) Netherlandish painting: Dieric Bouts, Justice of Emperor Otto.

(to 1484) Des Prés was a singer in the Sistine Chapel at Rome.

(to 1484) The Papal reign of St. Sixtus IV (born in Savona).

(to 1484) The Cappella Sistina manuscript 51 was from this period.

c.1471

The prologue to the Rappresentazione di San Giovanni e Paolo was written by Lorenzo de' Medici.

Poliziano wrote Orfeo with incidental music by Germi for Cardinal Gonzaga. It was the first play with musical obbligato and started a chain of festive events throughout central Italy at Ferrara, Florence, Mantua, Rome and Venice. The music, since lost, was for a chorus of Dryads and Bacchantes and a prayer of Orfeo. The title role was performed by Baccio Ugolini.

1472

(April 24) The Musicians' Company of the City of London was established and patented under the great seal of England in the ninth year of the reign of Edward IV.

(January) Alexandro was in the service of Galeazzo Maria Sforza, Duke of Milan.

(April) The Duke of Milan wrote a letter and indicated that Gaspar van Weerbecke was a cleric of Tournai. He sent him to the Franco-Netherlandish area to secure singers to serve at Milan.

Hayne van Ghizeghem appeared at the siege of Beauvais.

Records showed that an unnamed Mass by Caron was copied at Cambrai for use by the choir.

The Mystère de Saint Louis included examples of plainchant. A performance of the work lasted three days.

A children's instrumental group

1472(cont.)
was functioning at Ferrara.

Bartolomé Ramos, Spanish theoretician, left Salamanca.

Leone Battista Alberti, Italian Renaissance sculptor, died (born 1404).

Lucas Cranach, the Elder, German painter, was born at Cronach in Franconia (died 1553, October).

Michelozzo, Florentine architect, died (born 1396).

(to 1522) Henry Bredemers, organist, was in the service of Charles V. His father traveled to England, Germany and Spain and influenced both contemporary musicians and musical taste.

c.1472
Gilles Mureau became a canon.

Petrus Christus, Netherlandish painter, died (birthdate unknown).

(to c.1483) The earliest pastoral drama, Poliziano's "Orfeo," was performed at Mantua sometime during this period.

1473
Gafori went to Mantua for a time and then on to Verona.

Conrad Paumann, German organist and composer, died (born 1410).

The oldest example of Block -printing was a book with Gregorian notes printed at Augsburg by Hans Froschauer.

The earliest attempt to depict actual music in print appeared in the Collectorium super Magnificat of Charlier de (cont.) Gerson, printed at Esslingen by Conrad Fyner.

Pope Sixtus IV had the Sistine Chapel built.

German painting:
Martin Schongauer, Madonna in a Rose Garden.

Umbrian painting: Perugino was possibly the painter of panels on the "Life of St. Bernardino."

Antoine de Févin, composer of Missa Mente tota, was born (died 1515)see c.1480 and c.1512.

Giacomo Fogliano, Italian frottolist and composer, was born (died 1548).

(to 1494) Jacotino, a singer born in Picardy, was active at the Milanese court. He was one of three or four musical Jacotins who existed within a period of eighty years.

c.1473
The terminus a quo by Tinctoris was probably not earlier than this date.

1474
(April 14) The Farandole was customarily danced at all great feasts in towns of Provence. This included the feast of Corpus Domini, or the "Coursos de la Tarasquo," which were founded by King Réné on this date.

(June 10) In a complimentary letter Galeazzo Maria gave Alexander de Alamania, the musician, a leave in recognition of years of service to continue his career elsewhere.

(July 8) Dufay's will was

1474(cont.)
written on this date.

(July 15) Eighteen "cantori de camera" and twenty-two "cantori de capella" were named in a Milanese register. Almost all of them came from either Flanders or Picardy.

(November 27) Guillaume Dufay, the leading composer of the Burgundian School, died (born c.1400). He held the post of canon at Cambrai Cathedral at this time, see 1370.

Ockeghem wrote the first polyphonic piece on the Lamentations of Jeremiah.

Diabolic ensembles were heared in a Mystery of the Incarnation, played at Rouen in this year.

Some evidence indicated that Obrecht was a singer in the service of Hercules I at Ferrara, but it is not conclusive.

The highest yearly salary paid to a papal singer was 36 ducats.

Des Prés was on the register of the chapel of Galeazzo Maria Sforza.

Loyset Compère had served as a choirboy at Saint Quentin and was now on the register at Milan along with Martini.

One of the first important Meistersinger, Michel Behaim of Heidelberg, died by assassination (born 1416).

The oldest known dictionary of music was that by the Flemish musician Johannes Tinctoris. Its title was "Terminorum (cont.) musicae Diffinitorium." It was probably printed with the type of Gérard de Flandre.

Possibly Des Prés' El grillo e buon cantore alluded to Carlo Grillo, a singer of Galeazzo Sforza, Duke of Milan.

An extract from the accounts of the Lord High Treasurer of Scotland stated "gevin at the Kingis command iijo Septembris, to John Broun, lutare, at his passage our sey to leue (? lere, i.e. learn) his craft . . . . v.li.

Lucas Fernández, Spanish composer and imitator of Encina, was born at Salamanca (died 1542).

Netherlandish composer Antoine de Févin's father was alderman at Arras.

Johannes Regis, Burgundian composer, became a priest and went to Mons.

The Satires of Poggio, a humanist writer, appeared (Facetiae).

Castile and Aragon were united under King Ferdinand and Queen Isabella.

The Gonzaga family of Mantua gave Mantegna the opportunity to show his skill when he decorated the Camera degli Sposi for the ducal pair.

Umbrian fresco painting: Melozzo da Forli, Portrait of Platina.

Ferraran painting: Cosimo Tura, the "Roverella Altarpiece."

1474(cont.)

(to 1476) Italian painting: Gherardo di Giovanni, The Annunciation and Scenes from Dante's Divine Comedy (from a missal).

(to 1516) The reign of King Ferdinand and Queen Isabella, a period during which many distinguished Spanish musicians were at the court. It also was a period of colonial expansion for Spain. The court especially favored sacred music and this period was known as "el siglio de oro" ("the golden age").

c.1474

Erasmus learned music from Jacob Obrecht while a choir-boy at Utrecht Cathedral.

Evidence indicated that Tinctoris' "Terminorum musicae diffinitorium" was printed at Naples.

(to c.1484) Tinctoris completed the following treatises while at Naples: Tractatus de notis et pausis; Tractatus de regulari valore notarum; Liber imperfectionum notarum musicalium; Tractatus alterationum; Scriptum super punctis musicalibus and Complexus effectuum musices.

1475

Robert Morton, English composer, died (birthdate unknown).

At the wedding of Costanzo Sforza and Camilla of Aragon at Pesaro two antiphonal choruses of sixteen singers each performed as well as "organi, pifferi, trombetti ed infiniti tamburini."

Johannes Martini was in the service of Duke Hercules I of Ferrara, a patron of music. He received a monthly increase of 2 ducats over what he had previously been earning.

The instrument was now referred to as "An organ."

The best-known combination of sacred words and secular music was the song "Innsbruck, ich muss dich lassen," set in 4 parts with the melody in the upper part. This structure was unusual at the time.

The Terminorum musicae diffinitorium, written by Tinctoris.

Michelangelo Buonarroti, Italian painter, was born (died 1564).

Serlio, Renaissance architect, was born (died 1554).

Dieric Bouts, Netherlandish painter, died (born c.1415).

Paolo Uccello (Doni), Italian painter, died (born 1397).

Fouquet became painter to the King.

Leonardo da Vinci established himself as an independent painter.

Italian painting: Antonello da Messina, The Crucifixion (23½"x16 3/4").

Italian painting: Antonello Da Messina, A Condottiere (13 3/4" x 11").

Florentine painting: Antonio Pollaiuolo, The

1475(cont.)

Martyrdom of St. Sebastian.

(to 1476) Netherlandish painting: Hugo van der Goes, The Portinari Children.

(to 1476) Netherlandish painting: Hugo van der Goes, Shepherds.

(to 1476) The name of Alexander de Alamania appeared in the accounts of Cambrai Cathedral.

(to 1564) Roman architecture: Antonio da Sangallo the Younger and Michelangelo, Rome, Farnese Palace, court (81'x81').

c.1475

Antonius Divitis (Van Rijecke, Le Riche, etc.), Burgundian priest and singer, was born at Louvain (date of death unknown).

Louis van Pulaer, French composer, was born at Cambrai (died 1528).

Conrad Rupsch, German mass composer, was born (died 1530).

Bartholomaeus Tromboncino, a composer of frottole, popular songs of the day, was born in Verona (died 1535).

Busnois's Missa L'Homme armé, written at this time, was later quoted by Tinctoris and Ramos. Busnois, Ockeghem, Obrecht and others were leading representatives of the school immediately preceding des Prés.

The possibility existed of a connection between the harpsichord and the psaltery preserved in the church of the Certosa, near Pavia, built (cont.) about this time.

The invention of the sign for chromatically raising a note, the sharp, was credited to Josquin des Pres.

Jean Mouton, French composer, was born in Haut-Wignes (died 1522).

Tinctoris' Proportionale Musices was completed at Naples.

The first English printer, William Caxton, set up a printing press at Westminster.

Mathis Gothardt-Neithardt, known as Mathias Grünewald, German painter, was born (died 1528).

Joachim Patinir, Netherlandish painter, was born (died 1524).

Friedrich Herlin, an artist influenced by Rogier van der Weyden, worked in the town of Noerdlingen.

The great Flemish artist Hugo van der Goes, was active at this time.

Venetian painting: Giovanni Bellini, the Pesaro altarpiece.

Florentine painting: Sandro Botticelli, Portrait of a Man with a Medal.

Netherlandish painting: Memlinc, The Mystic Marriage of Saint Catherine (10 5/8" by 5 7/8").

Italian painting: Antonio del Pollaiuolo, The Rape of Deinira (21½"x31 5/8").

c.1475(cont.)

Italian sculpture:
Antonio Pollaiuolo, Hercules and Antaeus (18" high).

German engraving: Schongauer, Holy Night.

Umbrian painting: Signorelli, Scourging of Christ.

Renaissance painting:
Leonardo da Vinci, Virgin.

(to c.1499) Two actual settings of the Passion, both anonymous, one St. Matthew, the other St. John, were preserved at Modena.

(to c.1499) The only large collection of monophonic secular pieces was in the Rostocker Liederbuch.

(to c.1499) The last quarter of the century was an important period for music theory.

(to c.1499) Adam von Fulda, German theorist and composer, was most active.

(to c.1499) Dutch painting:
Geertgen Tot Sint Jans, The Raising of Lazarus (50"x38 1/8").

1476

(April 26) The earliest known example of music printing from movable type was the Roman Missal produced by Michael Zarotus at Milan.

(November 6) Tinctoris' Liber de natura et proprietate tonorum was completed at Naples.

(October) A Missal printed by movable type, which used Roman-style (square) notes, was produced by Ulrich Han (Hahn) (cont.) at Rome. The work was done with double printing, the lines printed first in red and then the notes in black.

The Duke of Alba paid Johannes Wreede a sum of money for teaching singing to three Negro boys.

The Zeuner Tantz ("Gipsy Dance") was danced by royal guests at the wedding of Matthias Corvinus and Beatrice of Aragon at Buda. The music was preserved by Hans Newsidler.

Galeazzo Maria Sforza, Duke of Milan, was assassinated. Bona of Savoy became regent during the minority of the heir, Gian Galeazzo.

Beatrice of Aragon, daughter of King Ferrante, became Queen of Hungary as a result of her marriage to King Matthias Corvinus.

Caxton's printing press was established in London.

Florentine painting:
Botticelli, Fortitude.

French painting:
Nicolas Froment, The Burning Bush (Central Panel of a Triptych), Cathédrale Saint-Sauveur, Aix-En-Provence.

Renaissance architecture:
Fra Giocondo, Verona Palazzo del Consiglio (116'wide by 56' wide).

Netherlandish painting:
Hugo van der Goes, Adoration of the Shepherds (8'1"x10').

c.1476

Tinctoris' Diffinitorium musicae was written at Naples.

1477

(January 5) Charles the Bold, Duke of Burgundy, died and the Burgundian chapel descended to his daughter, Mary of Burgundy. She married Maximilian of Austria who later became Emperor Maximilian I.

(October 11) Tinctoris's Liber de arte contrapuncti was completed at Naples. In it he stated, "There is no music worth hearing save only the last forty years."

An entry in the Burgundian court accounts indicated that Pierre de la Rue was in the service of the Court.

Gafori settled in Naples and while there he debated with Tinctoris and other well-known musicians.

According to Michaelis, Ulrich Schütz built a hammer factory and acquired dye plants, mills and other property.

After the Battle of Nancy the duchy was united with the crown.

(to 1483) Jean Mouton was a choirboy at Notre Dame at Nesle (near St. Quentin).

(to 1488) Raynaldus Odenoch de Flandria, who was a singer at the Treviso Cathedral, may have been Raynaldino.

(to 1489) German sculpture: Veit Stoss, Altar of the Church of Our Lady, Cracow.

c.1477

Nicole de la Chesnaye wrote La Nef de Santé.

(to 1488) A major source attributes Glogauer (Berliner) Liederbuch to this period. It was a three volume manuscript with the titles, "Discantus," "Tenores," and "Contratenores," and was the earliest known example of writing in part-books. Other sources have placed its publication at 1460.

1478

Henry Abyngdon became Master of St. Catherine's Hospital in Bristol.

Baldassare Castiglione, theorist and the author of Libro del Cortegiano, was born (died 1529).

Jehan Pullois, Burgundian composer, died (birthdate unknown).

Franchino Gafori went to Naples with Adorno, the fugitive doge.

Chaucer's "Canterbury Tales" was printed by Caxton in London.

Gian Giorgio Trissino, author of the first poetic drama in Italy, was born (died 1550). He adhered to classical rules and in his Sophonisba included some blank verse.

Sir Thomas More, the author of Utopia, a classic description of an ideal state, was born (died 1535).

Botticelli was asked to paint the hanged anti-Medici conspirators.

Francesco del Cossa, Ferraran painter, died (born c.1436).

1478(cont.)

(to 1480) Netherlandish painting: Memlinc, The Three Kings and their Suite.

(to 1486) Gilbert Banastre was Master of the Children for the Chapel-Royal in England.

c.1478

Italian painter, Giorgio Barbarelli, known as Giorgione, was born (died 1510).

Jan Gossaert, Netherlandish painter, known as Mabuse, was born (died c.1533).

Florentine painting: Botticelli, Primavera.

Italian painting: Leonardo da Vinci, Portrait of Ginevra Benci.

1479

Han Pang-chi, Chinese author of Yüan lo's book of music, was born (died 1555).

Hoffhaimer became court organist to Archbishop Sigmund at Innsbruck.

Obrecht became choir director at Bergen op Zoom.

Jacob Godebrye became Chaplain at Antwerp.

Des Prés was at Milan in the service of Cardinal Ascanio Sforza. The latter paid his musicians poorly, although he was a music lover Des Prés alluded to the Cardinal's parsimony in some of his works.

In a painting by Memlinc at St. John's Hospital at Bruges, the keyboard of a ruler was (cont.) pictured with the upper keys in twos and threes. The upper keys are light colored and placed farther back.

Johannes Cochlaeus was born (died 1552). He was magister at the University of Cologne and later, when a professor of music, wrote on the choral music of his time. He was a great opponent of Luther.

Antonello da Messina, Venetian painter, died (born c.1430).

Antonio Rossellino, Italian sculptor, died (born c.1427).

Sienese painting: Sano di Pietro, St. Peter Curing Petronilla.

Florentine sculpture: Verrocchio, Monument to Colleoni, Venice was started at this time (13' high).

Diego Sánchez de Badajoz, Spanish dramatist whose works used music, was born (died 1550).

1480

Antonio Squarcialupi, famous organist after whom the Squarcialupi Codex was named, died (born 1400 or 1417).

Heinrich Isaac succeeded Antonio Squarcialupi at Florence Cathedral.

Franchino Gafori wrote "Theoricum opus armonice discipline" while in Naples. He also wrote on the subject of measured music.

Variety was added to the musical texture of the carol. Prior to this time carols were

1480(cont.)

set in triple measure a2 or a3. The parts moved in parallel thirds and sixths as in earlier gymels.

Arnold de Bruck, a Protestant composer, was born at Bruges, Netherlands (died 1554). Some sources gave his birthdate as c.1500.

Adrian Willaert, Venetian school composer, was born in Bruges, Netherlands (died 1562).

Des Prés was a singer in the Papal choir.

Dunstable was mentioned in a manuscript preserved in the Escorial, written at Seville.

Gafori wrote "Theoricum opus musicae discipline" which was published in Naples by Francisco di Dino. All of his treatises were preserved including those he wrote while in Milan.

Sancho de Paredes, a chamberlain to Queen Isabella, apparently possessed a manicorde or clavichord with tangents.

N. Perotto wrote "Cornucopia" in Venice.

Bernardo Yeart's name appeared on a list of singers in the Royal Chapel. He was a Catalonian theorist and composer.

Mensural note-shapes were printed for the first time in Grammatica brevis by Franciscus Niger, published at Venice by Theodor von Würzburg.

On the earliest organs, the (cont.) keys were 3 to 6 inches wide, and were struck with the closed fist. After 1480, the octave was narrower but still measured about two inches more than on the modern keyboard. Attempts at fingering in the modern sense were out of the question.

Pope Sixtus IV proposed the formation of a "cappella musicale" in connection with the Vatican and to be distinct from the Sistine Chapel.

The Venetian Republic sent Gentile Bellini to paint Sultan Mohammed II.

Botticelli produced the "St. Augustine" in perspective in the Church of the Ognissanti.

The King of Naples provided enough Holland linen for Giovanni di Giusto, a painter, to trace a map of the world.

Lorenzo Lotto, Italian painter, was born (died 1556).

Palma Vecchio, Italian painter, was born (died 1528).

Italian painting:
Filippino Lippi, Vision of St. Bernard.

Netherlandish painting:
Memlinc, the "Sibyl Sambetha."

Margaret of Austria, granddaughter of Charles the Bold, was born (died 1530).

(to 1490) The earliest example of polyphonic Passions, both in Italian and English manuscripts, were anonymous.

(to 1520) Antoine Brumel,

1480(cont.)

Burgundian composer, was active.

(to 1520) The Third Netherland School of composition was during this period.

(to 1530) The violin gradually started to replace the viol.

(to 1568) The German Polyphonic Schools of composition were during this period.

c.1480

Hugh Aston, a Tudor composer of note, was born (died 1522). He wrote a "hornpype" which was an early example of variations with a drone bass.

Sebastian de Felstin, Polish composer, was born.

Antoine de Févin (Févim), composer and singer known as Glareanus "felix Jodoci aemulator," was born at Arras (died c.1512).

Pedro de Gante, missionary and musician, was born in Flanders.

Nicolas Gombert, Netherlandish composer, was born, probably in southern Flanders (died c.1556).

Tylman Susato, music printer and composer, was born at or near Cologne(died c.1561).

Hans Folz of Worms wrote Shrove Tuesday plays at Nürnberg.

Obrect composed Tsat een Meskin.

An organ was build in the church of St. AEgidien, at Brunswick.

An anonymous treatise written in Spanish mentioned Dufay, Dunstable, Ockeghem, and others.

Tasti scavezzi (split keys) provided slightly different pitches for notes now considered "enharmonic," D sharp and E flat; G sharp and A flat.

Johannes Tinctoris was choirmaster at the court of Ferdinand of Aragon in Naples.

The villota, similar to the frottola, enjoyed great popularity.

Albrecht Altdorfer, German painter, was born (died 1538).

Dosso Dossi, Italian painter, was born (died 1542).

Enrique de Egas, Renaissance architect, was born (died 1534).

Richafort, described by Ronsard as a Des Pres pupil, was born (died 1548).

Italian painting:
Melozzo Da Forli, Angel (Detail of a fresco).

Italian painting:
Domenico Ghirlandaio, An Old Man and His Grandson (24½"x18").

Italian painting:
Domenico Ghirlandaio, The Last Supper (c.25'7" wide).

Flemish painting:
Hugo van der Goes, The Death of the Virgin.

French painting: Master of Moulins, The Nativity and a Donor, Cardinal Jean Rolin.

Ferraran painting:
Ercole de' Roberti, Portrait of Ginevra Bentivoglio.

Ferraran painting:

c.1480(cont.)

Ercole de' Roberti, Madonna.

Umbrian painting: Signorelli, The Sacristy of Loreto.

(to 1500) Master of Moulins, French painter, was active.

1481

(December 22) Robert Wydow obtained the presentation to the vicarage of Thaxted and resigned from this presentation on the same date.

Constans de Languebroek, musician employed by Philip the Good, died.

Johannes Regis was again at Soignies and became a canon there, in which post he remained until his death.

Ottavio Scotto, music printer and publisher, was in Venice from this date on.

The first printed volume was soon followed by missals by Jörg Reyser, Würzburg printer, and by Octavus Scotus, a Venetian.

Gaspar van Weerbecke arrived in Rome to become a member of the Papal Choir.

Lodovico il Moro usurped the power of Bona of Savoy.

Jean Fouquet, French painter, died (born c.1420).

Peruzzi, Renaissance architect, was born (died 1536).

Sano di Pietro, Sienese painter, died (born 1406).

Botticelli adopted a "modern" (cont.) style in "Scenes from the Life of Moses" (on the walls of the Sistine Chapel in Rome).

Leonardo da Vinci left Florence to serve . Lodovico il Moro, Duke of Milan.

Piero della Francesca's influence was noticeable in the frescoes at the Sistine Chapel.

Signorelli worked with the best Florentine artists, including Perugino, on decorations for the Sistine Chapel.

(to 1499) Leonardo da Vinci was in Milan during this period and painted the "Madonna of the Rocks."

(to 1499) Renaissance architecture: P. Lombardo, Venice, Santa Maria dei Miracoli.

(to 1509) Renaissance architecture: P. Lombardo, Venice, Palazzo Vendramin.

c.1481

Mateo Flecha, the Elder, Spanish madrigalist, was born in Prades, Tarragona(d.c.1553).

1482

In England, a payment was made for "mending of organys."

Busnois left the Burgundian Chapel.

Musical as well as choreographic intermedi were provided for Niccolò da Correggio's Cefalo.

Franchino Gafurio was made chapel-master at the cathedral in Milan and public professor of music in that city.

In the first edition of

1482(cont.)

Higden's Policronicon (printed by Caxton) a space was left for the filling in of musical characters by hand.

Ramos de Pareja wrote De Musica Tractatus sive Musica Practica and thereby laid the foundation for our harmonic system. It was published at Bologna.

The Veni Creator Spiritus was introduced in La Vie et passion de Mgr. Sainct Didier.

The first school for music instruction in Italy was founded in Bologna by Pope Nicholas V. Bartolommeo Ramis Pereja, a Spanish music theorist, came from Salamanca to head the school.

Mary of Burgundy died and Emperor Maximilian I acted as guardian for their children, Philip the Handsome and Margaret of Austria. He also became regent of the Low Countries while Burgundy was returned to French rule.

Hugo van der Goes, Netherlandish painter, died (born c.1440).

Luca della Robbia, Italian sculptor, died (born 1400).

The "flamboyant" Gothic style was evident in the Court of the Palace of Justice (formerly Treasury), Rouen.

Gothic architecture: Valencia, La Lonja (118'x70').

(to 1485) The press of del Tuppo at Naples was idle.

(to 1492) Paduan painting: Mantegna, cartoons for "The (cont.) Triumph of Caesar," Hampton Court.

c.1482

Giovanni di Paolo, Italian painter, died (born c.1402).

1483

(May 8) Eloy d'Amerval's French and Latin motets based on the liberation of Orleans by Joan of Arc were performed. It was the 54th anniversary of the original Thanksgiving procession.

(November 10) Martin Luther was born at Eisleben (died 1546). His contribution to music through Protestantism was immeasurable. He himself was trained in Gregorian chant and then went on to develop the unison chorale with German words in order to reach the people. He wrote thirty-six hymns, played flute and lute, and sang alto in polyphonic music performed in his home.

Hans Buchner of Württemberg, German organist and composer, was born at Ravensburg (died 1538). He was a pupil of Hofhaimer.

Beatrice's gipsy musicians "qualli sonano di lauto" ("who played the lute") were active in Hungary.

The Bishop of Castella, papal envoy at the Hungarian court, described the King's singers with great respect and rated them higher than those of the Papal Choir.

Antoine Brumel became heurier of the Cathedral at Chartres.

Jakob Butzbach was organist at Cassel.

1483(cont.)

Gower's "Confessio Amantis" was printed by Caxton.

Gerard David settled at Bruges.

Raphael (Sanzio), Italian painter of highest renown, was born (died 1520).

(to 1483) The reign of King Edward V (House of York) over England and Great Britain.

(to 1485) The reign of King Richard III (House of York) over England and Great Britain.

(to 1486) Florentine painting: Domenico Ghirlandaio, decorations for the Sassetti Chapel in the Santa trinità in Florence.

(to 1487) Italian painting:, da Vinci, Head of an Angel.

(to 1498) The reign of King Charles VII (House of Valois) over France.

(to 1507) Vaqueras was a singer in the Papal Chapel. He may have been the same person as Bertrandus who sang at St. Peter's in 1481-1482.

(to 1520) Italian painting: Raphael, Ecstasy of St. Cecilia.

c.1483

German painting: Michael Pacher, St. Wolfgang and the Devil.

1484

Gilles Joye, Burgundian composer, died (birthdate unknown).

Scaliger, writer of Poetices, was born (died 1550).

Johann Spangenberg was born (died 1550).

Ulrich Zwingli, pre-Calvanist churchman and opponent of Luther, was born (died 1531).

Des Prés, who had been in Milan, Ferrara, and Rome, supposedly spent time in Paris at the court of Louis XII.

Ercole I, Duke of Ferrara, had a fine theatre opened in Ferrara, one of the best in Italy.

Hoffhaimer was court organist at Innsbruck.

Isaac stayed in Innsbruck for a short time.

In Italy, the second academy to be founded for the cultivation of music was at Milan. It was instituted by Lodovico Sforza, Duke of Milan.

Ockeghem travelled in Flanders.

The Flemish picture of St. Cecilia, in Holyrood Palace, showed a short octave organ keyboard.

Ulrich Schütz was a member of the town council of Chemnitz.

An Hungarian hymn to the Virgin by Andreas Vásárheli was preserved.

The second edition of Canterbury Tales was published by Caxton.

Niklaus Manuel Deutsch, German painter, was born (died 1530).

Sanmicheli, Italian architect, was born (died 1559).

1484(cont.)

Umbrian painting: Signorelli, Madonna with Saints.

(September to 1485, November) Obrecht was active at Cambrai Cathedral.

(to 1492) The Papal reign of St. Innocent VIII (born in Genoa).

(to 1494) Marbriano de Orto was a singer in the Papal Chapel during the time when Prioris was there.

c.1484

Isaac arrived in Florence.

Tinctoris' De inventione et usu musicae was completed at Naples.

Hans Baldung (Grien), German painter, was born in the Strasburg vicinity (died 1545).

Nicholas Froment, French painter, died (born c.1435).

Florentine fresco: Botticelli, A Lady and Four Allegorical Figures (6'11½"x9'3 3/4").

(to 1489) Russian architecture: Moscow, Cathedral of the Annunciation (79'x125'x138').

(to 1494) Des Prés remained in Rome and Ferrara during this period. He was attached to the House of Sforza.

1485

Clement Janequin, French chanson composer and part of "Paris" school, was born (died 1560).

The following was listed in the York records of 1485: "To John Hewe for repairing the (cont.) organ at the altar of B.U.M. in the Cathedral Church, and for carrying the same to the House of the Minorite Brethren, and for bringing back the same to the Cathedral Church. 13s.9d."

The earliest printed collection of Laudi Spirituali was from this time.

Galeotto Marzio heard travelling musicians singing epics at the court of Matthias Corvinus. At dinner "musici et citharoedi" sang in the vernacular, "in lyra." These epics were tales of national deeds.

The modern period of English history began with the coronation of Henry VII.

The victory of Henry Tudor at Bosworth Field was at this time.

Sir Thomas Malory's "Morte Darthur" was printed by William Caxton.

Joos van Cleve the Elder, Flemish painter, was born (died 1540).

Antonio da Sangallo the Younger, Renaissance architect, was born (died 1546).

Florentine painting: Botticelli, Madonna of the Magnificat.

Florentine painting: Domenico Ghirlandaio, Adoration of the Shepherds.

Paduan painting: Mantegna, St. Sebastian.

(to 1486) Florentine painting: Botticelli, frescoes of the Villa Lemmi.

1485(cont.)

(to 1486) Florentine painting: Botticelli, the altarpiece of St. Barnabas.

(to 1490) Florentine painting: Domenico Ghirlandaio, fresco of "The Story of St. John the Baptist."

(to 1509) The "proverb" inscribed on a wall of the Manor House of Leckingfield, Yorkshire, was probably from the time of Henry VII. It contained a reference to the virginal earlier than Virdung.

(to 1509) The reign of King Henry VII (House of Tudor) over England and Great Britain.

(to 1525) The compositions of the first forty years of the Tudor era were almost entirely large scale works in three types of liturgical forms: the ordinary of the mass, votive antiphon, and the magnificat.

(to 1553) During the reigns of Henry VII and Henry VIII, social and political ballads were plentiful. Among the best -known works of the period were "The Westron wynde," "The three Ravens," "John Dory," and "The King's Ballad." The latter was composed by Henry VIII himself.

c.1485

John Redford, English organ composer, was born (died 1545).

Adam Rener, Netherlandish composer, was born(died 1520).

Jean Clouet, French painter, was born (died c.1540).

Sebastiano del Piombo, Italian painter, was born (died 1547).

Tiziano Vecellio, known as Titian, Italian painter, was born in Codore, Southern Italy (died 1576).

Venetian painting: Giovanni Bellini, St. Francis in Ecstasy (48½"x55").

Venetian painting: Giovanni Bellini, Transfiguration (45 1/4" by 59 2/3").

Florentine painting: Botticelli, Mars and Venus.

Italian painting: Leonardo da Vinci, Unfinished portrait of a Musician.

Italian painting: Leonardo da Vinci, The Virgin of the Rocks (74 5/8"x74 1/4").

(to 1541) Hans Kotter, German composer and student of Hoffhaimer, was born (died 1541).

1486

Angiers wrote "Mystery of the Passion," a Medieval mystery drama with simple plainsong.

Loyset Compère became chantre ordinaire to Charles VIII. Later he was appointed canon and chancellor at Saint Quentin.

The music for Dafne, produced in this year, was by Giampietro della Viola. The work was an ecloghe or farse.

The Schütz coat of arms was established for the two brothers, Ulrich and Hans, by Emperor Frederic III. It was possibly associated with the monastic burial privilege.

The term sonata comes from

1486(cont.)
this time.

William Wotton, "Orkyn maker," built a "pair of organs" for Magdalen College, Oxford, for £ 28.

Jacopo Sansovino, Florentine architect, was born (died 1570).

Andrea del Sarto, Italian painter, was born (died 1531).

(to 1487) Venetian painting: Giovanni Bellini, the St. Job altarpiece.

(to 1493) Laurence Squire was Master of the Children for the Chapel Royal in England.

(to 1494) Des Pres was in the Papal Choir during this period, although there were short interruptions.

(to 1496) Renaissance architecture: Bramante, Rome, Palazzo Cancelleria (295'x80').

(to 1498) The town council of Chemnitz appointed Ulrich Schütz chief burgomaster.

(to 1519) The reign of Emperor Maximilian I.

(to 1556) Martin Agricola was cantor at Magdeburg in Saxony.

c.1486
Florentine painting: Sandro Botticelli, The Birth of Venus (79"x110").

1487
Gilbert Banestre, the successor to Henry Abyngdon, died. He had been the teacher of composers of the late fifteenth century. He wrote a five-part motet com-

(cont.) memorating the union of the two roses of Lancaster and York.

Johann Gramann, German composer, was born (died 1541).

John Hothby, English scholar and musician, died (birthdate unknown).

Aretini published a book by Guido.

Block-printing was employed for the musical portions of books such as Burtius' "Musices Opusculum" printed at Bologna by Ugo de Rugeriis. It was the first known complete printed part composition.

Sword dances were mentioned as being part of the celebration of Corpus Christi in Seville.

A Gloria Patri in Gothic plainsong notation was preserved in manuscript.

Marbriano de Orto became a canon at Comines.

Pontano authorized Tinctoris to go to France and Burgundy to procure singers for the King.

Johannes Stokhem was a singer in the Papal Choir at the same time as young Gaspar van Weerbecke and des Pres.

The troubadours came from Provence which later became the southeastern part of France.

After the first attempts of double-printing, an Italian invented a single-printing process from wooden blocks into which the page was cut as a

1487(cont.)

whole as in woodcut picture books.

Florentine painting: Botticelli, Madonna with the Pomegranate.

Netherlandish painting: Memlinc, Portrait of Martin Van Nieuwenhove.

(to 1488) Josquin probably spent brief periods in Florence and Modena.

c.1487

Tromboncino was with the Gonzagas.

William Wotton agreed to build an organ for Merton College. It was to be completed by 1489.

1488

Henricus Glareanus, a great music scholar, was born (died 1563). His real name was Loris or, Latinised, Loritus.

Florentine sculpture: Andrea del Verrocchio, Equestrian monument of Bartolommeo Colleoni was completed (begun in 1479).

Andrea del Verrocchio, Italian painter and sculptor, died (born 1435).

Georg Rhaw, printer, composer, and teacher at the University of Leipzig, was born (died 1548). At one time he was Cantor at the Thomasschule.

"Flores musice," a clavecin collection, was published.

Court records described entertainments, such as on Twelfth Night. A statement read, "at (cont.) the Table in the Medell of the Hall sat the Deane and thoos of the Kings Chapell, whiche incontynently after the Kings furst Course sange a Carall."

M. Fetis claimed that Isaac was still, or once more, in Florence for a long period after this date.

Isaac composed music for the religious drama "San Giovanni e San Paolo," written by Lorenzo de' Medici. It was used for performance within the Medici family circle.

The monophonic religious song, Jezusa Judasz przedal, with words by Wladyslaw of Gielniów, was produced.

Obrecht was succentor at St. Donatian in Bruges.

Obrecht wrote Mille quingentis, a motet lamenting the death of his father Willem. In the motet it was stated that he, Obrecht himself, was born on St. Cecilia's day (November 22).

Wenssler and Kilchen (Basle) produced the "Agenda parochialium."

Queen Beatrice of Hungary wrote to her brother-in-law the Duke and stated that she was searching for an organist, Messer Paolo. He was purportedly serving the Archduke of Austria, Sigismund, and she called on Hercules to help her to procure his services.

James III of Scotland, who died in this year, endowed a Chapel Royal at Stirling. He sent musicians abroad to study.

1488(cont.)

Andrea del Verrocchio, Florentine painter, was active until his death (born 1435).

Hieronymus Bosch, Netherlandish painter, was an established master by this time.

Lorenzo de' Medici sent Filippino Lippi to Rome.

Venetian painting: Giovanni Bellini, The Frari Triptych.

Islamic manuscript: Bihzad, King Darius and Herdsman (from a Bustan manuscript).

Islamic manuscript: Bihzad, Sultan Hussein Mirza Revealing (from a Bustan manuscript).

Florentine painting: Botticelli, Coronation of the Virgin.

Florentine painting: Domenico Ghirlandaio, The Adoration of the Magi (in the Spedale degli Innocenti).

(to 1496) In Paris, Michel de Toulouze printed L'Art et instruction de bien dancer. It carried no author's name.

(to 1496) Renaissance architecture: Valladolid, Colegio de San Gregorio.

c.1488

Covarrubias, Renaissance architect, was born (died 1564).

1489

(July 1) In the accounts of the Lords High Treasurers of Scotland the following entry appeared "to Wilzeam, sangster (cont.) of Lithgow for a sang bwke he brocht to the King be a precept, x.li."

(October 1) Robert Wydow resigned from the presentation to the vicarage of Thaxted.

(December 24) Giovanni Martini was still in Ferrara.

(September) Beatrice of Hungary, after her organist died, asked the duke to send "Zohane Martino per indurre (persuade) messer Paolo."

Juan de Anchieta became chaplain and cantor to King Ferdinand and Queen Isabella.

Marbriano de Orto became dean of St. Gertrude at Nivelles.

Tarantism was mentioned in Niccolo Perotto's "Cornucopia Linguae Latinae."

Gaspar van Weerbecke remained in the Papal Choir up to this time.

Florentine painting: Sandro Botticelli, Annunciation.

Netherlandish painting: Hans Memling, Shrine of St. Ursula, Martyrdom of the Virgins.

(to 1490) Raynaldino may be the Raynaldus Francigena referred to as magister cantus at Padua.

c.1489

Antonio Allegri, Italian painter known as Correggio, was born (died 1534).

Netherlandish painting: Hans Memlinc, Shrine of St. Ursula, Arrival at Cologne.

1490

(April 19) In the accounts of the Lords High Treasurers of Scotland the following item appeared, "To Martin Clareschaw and ye toder ersche clareschaw at ye kingis command, . xviij.s."

(August 20) Francesco d'Ana was second organist at St. Mark's Cathedral.

(September 2) Martini wrote to Isabella d'Este and informed her that her father, the Duke, wished him to come and teach her singing.

(February) Isabella d'Este, at the age of 16, married Francesco Gonzaga.

(March) Maximilian, probably with Hoffhaimer, visited Sigismund at Innsbruck.

Claudin de Sermisy, French chanson composer, was born (died 1562), see also c.1490.

Fridolin Sicher, a Swiss organist, was born (died 1546). He became a pupil of Buchner and organist at St. Gall.

Huang Tso, Chinese author of Canons of Music, was born (died 1566).

Atalante, who had been taught the lute by da Vinci, was sought for the leading part in Orfeo when it was performed before the Duke of Mantua at this time.

Barbireau visited Buda as special envoy for Maximilian. He was received with all the respect due a composer with his reputation.

Emperor Maximilian I took over the Archbishop's musical establishment at this time. Hoffhaimer went into the imperial service and remained there for many years.

Adam von Fulda wrote the treatise, De musica.

Okeghem resigned from his position as treasurer of the church of St. Martin's at Tours.

Des Prés was at the court of Louis XII in Paris.

Johannes Prioris, a Netherlander, was organist at St. Peter's.

Ladislaus Szalkai, singer and theorist, studied at the Augustinian monastery at Sárospatak.

Johannes de Tinctoris left Italy and returned to Nivelle.

Fra Urbano, a Venetian organ builder, constructed the famous organ for St. Mark's. He continued to build organs for at least forty years more.

Gaspar van Weerbecke returned to Oudenaerde where he received a great reception as well as a gift of wine.

A copy of the "Agenda Ecclesie Moguntinensis" from this date was preserved.

Matthias died in this year and the Royal Chapel in Hungary was disbanded. His successor, Wladislaus II Jagiello, King of Bohemia, brought his own musicians to Buda.

A spinet bearing the inscription "Alessandro Pasi Modenese," and

1490(cont.)

with this date was preserved.

Jean Cousin, a French painter, was born (died 1560).

(to 1498) Vittore Carpaccio's first great work, the "Life of St. Ursula," showed the progress and development in his painting.

(to 1504) A large choir book was preserved which, according to Wooldridge, was from this period.

(to 1510)Hoffhaimer's best work was supposedly done during this period.

(to 1520) Fayrfax was less florid than his contemporaries and showed a great awareness of the concept of symmetry.

(to 1526) The Hungarian court's personnel during the reign of the last two Jagiello Kings was under financial stress and the grandeur of this great Renaissance court was suddenly ended. Music, however, remained an essential part of court life.

c.1490

Marco Antonio Cavazzoni, Italian composer, was born at Bologna (died c.1570).

Sixtus Dietrich, early Protestant liturgical composer, was born (died 1548).

Costanzo Festa, an early madrigal composer of the Roman school, was born (died 1545).

Joh. Hähnel (called Galliculus and Alectorius), Protestant composer, was born.

Leonhard Kleber, Swabian composer and student of Hofhaimer, was born at Gröppingen, Württemberg (died 1556).

Robert Johnson, English composer, was born (died c.1560).

Francesco da Milano, a Spanish lute virtuoso and composer of note, was born (died c.1566).

Pierre Moulu, possibly a student of des Pres, was born (date of death unknown).

Ludwig Senfl, sacred composer and student of Isaac, was born in Zürich (died 1555 or c.1556).

Sermisy, a composer of chansons, masses, and motets, was born (died 1562), see also 1490.

William Cornyshe was master of the children of the Chapel Royal in England. He succeeded Gilbert Banestre at this time.

Allez regretz, a chanson by Hayne van Ghizeghem, became famous. Nicole de la Chesnaye used it in his La Condamnation des banquets as a dance for the characters.

The morality play was a product of English religious drama. It was filled with allegorical personification of good and evil, also the traditional art of the minstrels, and, games and sword dances. The Feast of Fools and of the Boy Bishop, became the interlude.

English music did not follow the trends of music in Europe, rather a conservative but capable school of composers developed.

c.1490(cont.)

Street songs developed into fróttola, strambotta, and villanella. Simultaneously, Flemish composers started to write madrigals which developed from the fróttola.

Voice parts appeared in the style of a fugue, with successive entries with the same motive in each section of a piece. After the initial entry however the voices were free to continue in their own way.

The increased use of imitation and the increase of the total compass came simultaneously.

Some makers of cembali and other keyboard instruments were now known by name and reputation.

A Mass, based on Verbum bonum for two choirs, each with four parts, helped make the transition from early polyphonic writing for antiphonal choirs to the compositions of Willaert. The aforementioned mass was credited to Ruphinus.

The seises were active and performed the Song and Dance of the Sybil and the Dance of the Shepherds in the Mozarabic rite. Cardinal Ximenez de Cisneros attempted to revive the old ritual and made it possible to establish a school for the Toledan seises. This school was headed by Cardinal Silíceo.

Ockeghem was generally regarded as the leader of the Netherlandish School of composition that flourished at this time.

The writing and production of Poliziano's Orfeo showed the direction of the new trends of the time.

The organ grew rapidly in importance, both in church and home music.

Polyphonic writing gradually shifted from an emphasis on melodic contrast to one on range.

Secular polyphony began to use existing melodies. Among them were De tous biens plaine, and an anonymous rondeau, J'ay pris amours a ma devise. The latter appeared in the Dijon manuscript and seven other sources.

The large amount of Spanish manuscripts at this time reflected the political stability that existed in Spain after the union of Castile and Aragon under King Ferdinand and Queen Isabella.

"Everyman," the most famous of the morality plays, was written.

Renaissance architecture: Amadeo (and others), Pavia, Certosa, facade (125'wide, 100' high in center).

Venetian painting: Giovanni Bellini, Allegory in Purgatory (29"x47").

Geertgen Tot Sint Jans, Netherlandish painter, died at Haarlem (born c.1460).

Netherlandish painting: Memling, Angels. Detail of an altar.

French painting: Master of Moulins, Portrait of A Young

c.1490(cont.)

Princess.

Italian painting: Perugino, The Virgin appearing to St. Bernard.

Umbrian painting: Signorelli, School of Pan (painted for Lorenzo de' Medici).

(to 1495) French painting: Master of Moulins, St. Mary Magdalene and a (female) Donor(20 7/8"x15 3/4").

(to c.1499) An upright virginal (spinetta) owned by a Count Correr was made during this period.

(to c.1499) Robert Fairfax was the leading musical figure of England.

(to 1500) Paduan painting: Andrea Mantegna, The Lamentation (27"x32").

(to 1510) German painting: Master of the St. Ursula Legend, The Angel Appearing to St. Ursula.

(to c.1520) The Fróttola was in popular secular form in 3 or 4 parts and in chordal style.

(to c.1520) William Pasche, English composer, was active.

1491

(June 28) King Henry VIII of England (House of Tudor) was born (died 1547). He was a composer of secular part songs.

(August 21) An item appeared in the accounts of the Lords High Treasurers of Scotland, "to iiij Inglis pyparis viij unicorns, vij li. iiij.s."

Maitre Jacques Barbireau, Netherlandish sacred composer, died at Antwerp (birthdate unknown).

Aurelio Brandolini, improvisator and writer on music, died (birthdate unknown).

Pietro de Fossis, a French Walloon, reorganized the chapel of St. Marco and remained there until his death. He was arbitrary and dictatorial as Maestro di Capella(died 1527).

Joannes Ghiselin, Netherlandish composer also known as Verbonnet, was at the court of Ferrara (also in 1503 and 1535).

Missals of Arras proved the use of the Dies irae in France.

Obrecht remained succentor at St. Donatian in Bruges until this date.

Obrecht was elected chapel -master in Antwerp cathedral.

The organ at Hagenau in Alsace had the earliest tremulant. It was an interrupting device that produced slow vibrations in connection with other stops and gave a sentimental sound to the instrument.

Bartoloméo Ramos, theoretician, was probably still living at Rome.

Giovanni Spataro, writer and pupil of Ramos, wrote Honesta defensio.

William Caxton, English painter and publisher, died.

Martin Schongauer, German painter, died (born c.1430 or 1453).

1491(cont.)

Quentin Massys, Netherlandish painter, settled at Antwerp.

Florentine painting: Ghirlandajo, The Birth of the Virgin (Wall-painting in the church of Sta. Maria Novella, Florence).

(to 1493) Raynaldus de Odena or de Honderic, who sang in the Papal Choir during this period, may have been Raynaldino.

(to 1526) The earliest choirmaster mentioned in the archives of St. Mark's in Venice was Pietro de Fossis who served during this period, at the end of which he died.

c.1491

Robert Carver, Scottish monk and composer, was born (date of death unknown).

1492

(November 17) Pierre de la Rue was engaged as a singer by Maximilian.

(October) Crispin van Stappen became maestro di cappella at the Cathedral in Padua.

Antoine Busnois, a leading Burgundian composer, died (born 1440). At the time of his death he was Rector Cantoriae at St. Sauveur at Bruges.

Ramos de Pareja, Spanish theorist who helped to lay the foundation for our harmonic system, died (born c.1440).

Clemens of Piotrków was canon of the Cathedral at Gniezno. While there he formulated a plan for compiling a new antiphonary at Cracow. He was supported in this undertaking by (cont.) Cardinal Jagiello, son of King Casimir IV.

Juan del Encina wrote and directed a Christmas eclogue on the theme of the Nativity. It was produced at the court of the Duke of Alba.

Finck was in the service of the Polish king (also in 1501, 1506).

Block-printing was used for the musical portions of books including Franchinus Gafforius' "Practica Musicae," published at Milan.

Franchinus Gafforius' "Theorica Musica" was printed at Milan. In it there was an engraving of an organist playing an early clavier of the period. It had the broad keys. At this same date his "Theoricum Opus harmonicae disciplinae" was published, also in Milan.

Heinrich Isaac set Politian's lament on the death of Lorenzo, "Quis dabit capiti meo aquam," to music. Politan also wrote another lament titled "Quis dabit pacem."

Documents contained facts concerning Johannes Martini.

Ratdolt produced a missal, probably while at Augsburg.

Pierre de la Rue served at the court of Burgundy.

Crispin van Stappen became a singer at Sainte Chapelle in Paris.

Tinctoris was living at Rome.

Lorenzo de' Medici, highly

1492(cont.)

ranked among Italian Renaissance poets, died (born 1449).

Ferdinand and Isabella conquered Granada and drove the last of the Moors from Spanish land. The Spanish Church was now released from isolation.

Jaume Huguet, Spanish painter, died (born c.1414).

Piero della Francesca, painter, died (born c.1410 or c.1416).

(to 1494) Pinturicchio decorated the apartments of Pope Alexander Borgia in the Vatican.

(to 1499) Renaissance architecture: Bramante, Milan, Santa Maria delle Grazie (102' wide across transepts).

(to 1503) The Papal reign of St. Alexander VI (born in Jativa).

c.1492

Bernard van Orley, Netherlandish painter, was born (died 1542).

1493

(November 12 and 1502 December) The Privy Purse Expenses of Henry VII listed a payment, "to one Cornyshe for a prophecy in rewarde, 13s. 4d." and in the Privy Purse Expenses of Henry's Queen Elizabeth of York, under date December 1502, a similar amount for "setting of a carralle upon Christmas day."

(November 19) Robert Wydow was appointed rector of Chalfont St. Giles, in Buckinghamshire.

Juan de Anchieta became maestro de capella to John.

A Josquin was paid by the court of Lorraine in the spring and summer of this year.

Godefridus was the best tibia -player of his day and served Emperor Frederick III.

Carlo di Lounay appeared again in the service of Pietro de' Medici. His singing was much admired.

Conrad Peutinger became secretary to the senate of Augsburg.

Rosenberger built a still larger organ than his former work at Nuremberg for the Bamberg Cathedral.

Spanish musicians went to Italy and when they returned described some viols as tall as themselves, evidently double-basses.

Viva el gran Re Don Fernando, a barzelletta, probably first sung at Naples, was included in a Roman publication. It celebrated the Spanish conquest of Granada.

The Great Bells of Munich (diam. 7'3", wt. 6 ts. 5 cw.).

German painting: Albrecht Durer, Self Portrait ($22\frac{1}{4}$"x$17\frac{1}{2}$").

(to 1509) William Newark was Master of the Children in England. In his last three years in the position he was given the additional duty of superintending and devising musical entertainments for Christmas festivities at court.

1494

(January 6 and c.1523) The singing of Mass was initiated in San Domingo and other musical activities in Mexico followed around 1523. The enthusiasm and success of missionaries was largely responsible for this.

Hans Sachs, cobbler and composer from Nürnberg, was born (died 1576). He raised the art of the Meistersinger to a high plane, a fact influenced to some degree by political events as well as the reformation. He, himself, composed over four thousand songs and two hundred plays.

The fall of the House of Medici and the rise to power of the House of Savonarola, forced Isaac to leave Florence.

A book by Mauburnus was published by Petrus Os.

Obrecht was a chaplain.

Serafino dall'Aquila, a strambatti poet, served at Mantua.

Polizano's "Orfeo" was produced at the theatre in Mantua.

Francis I, King of France (House of Valois), was born (died 1547).

Emperor Maximilian I maintained the Burgundian chapel until Philip assumed it.

Lodovico il Moro became duke of Milan.

Charles VIII's first expedition in France resulted in direct contact with the refined civ- (cont.) ilization of the area.

Antonio Correggio, Italian painter, was born (died 1534).

Melozzo da Forli, Umbrian painter, died (born 1438).

Domenico Ghirlandaio, Florentine painter, died (born 1449).

Hans Memlinc, Netherlandish painter, died at Bruges (born c.1430).

Jacopo Carrucci, known as Pontormo, Italian painter, was born (died 1556).

(to 1499) Des Prés was choir master at Cambrai Cathedral.

(to 1514) Renaissance architecture: Enrique de Egas, Toledo, Hospital of Santa Cruz (facade c.65' wide).

c.1494

Choruses of dramas, tragedies, and school plays were set to music.

Tinctoris' "Diffinitorium musicae" was printed.

Lucas Van Leyden, Netherlandish painter, was born (died 1533).

1495

(July 5) The battle of Fornovo on this date was mentioned in Et que feront povres gendarmes.

Lorenz Lemlin, a lied composer of the Heidelberg School, was born (date of death unknown).

Leonhard Paminger, German Protestant composer, was born (died 1567, May 3).

Charles VIII of France took his

1495(cont.)

chapel choir and court musicians with him on his campaigns through Italy.

Guillermo Despuig (Guillermus de Podio) published an "Ars musicorum" at Valencia. It was a fine example of a Spanish incunabulum and contained a musical illustration for which the staves were printed. The notes were put in by hand.

Matteo di Giovanni, an Italian painter who died at this time, painted the first trombone in modern form. The only difference was a less expanding bell.

The first known attempt at music-printing in England was Higden's Policronicon. It was printed by Wynken de Worde at Westminster.

Georgius Kleng added pedals to the organ at Halberstadt.

Johannes Tinctoris' knowledge impressed Trithemius enough for the latter to admit him into the Cathalogus illustrium virorum Germaniae . . . Tinctoris was the only musician in the group and had come from service to Ferrante.

Giovanni Battista Rosso, French painter and pupil of Michelangelo, was born (died 1540).

Carlo Crivelli, Paduan painter, died (birthdate unknown).

Cosimo Tura, Ferraran painter, died (born c.1430).

Florentine painting: Botticelli, Calumny.

(to 1498) Renaissance painting: Leonardo Da Vinci, The Last Supper (Wall-painting in the Refectory of the Monastery of Sta Maria delle Grazie, Milan).

(to 1525) Maximilian I and Frederick the Wise surrounded themselves with musicians of such note as Finck, Fulda, Hofhaimer, Isaac and Stoltzer.

(to 1525) Marco Cara, frottolist and composer, was in Mantua.

c.1495

Lupus Hellinck, Netherlandish composer, was born (died 1541).

Jaquet of Mantua, French sacred composer and "Doppelmeister," was born (died c.1559).

Ockeghem died at Tours (born c.1420). He was given the title "Prince of Music" and had been given the same title earlier at Flanders(see also 1430).

John Taverner, Tudor composer, English master of Franco-Flemish polyphonic style, was born (died 1545, October 25).

Brescia was a center for the making of lutes and viols from this date on.

Conrad Celtes, German humanist, suggested beatless music which was written for the next forty years.

Des Pres' Nymphes des bois was a lament on the death of Ockeghem.

A painting from this date existed showing St. Cecilia playing upon a Positive Organ, which showed the lower keys and pipes of a GG short octave manual.

c.1495(cont.)

Both Bartolomeo Tromboncino and Marco Cara, composers and frottolists, were active at Queen Isabella's court.

Marinus Van Reymerswael, Netherlandish painter, was born (died 1567).

Jan van Scorel, Netherlandish painter, was born near Alkmaar (died 1562).

Venetian painting: Vittore Carpaccio, Life of St. Ursula.

Icon painting: The Entombment.

French painting: Attributed to the Master of Moulins, Portrait of a Praying Child.

1496

(October 7) A contract was drawn between the Town Council of Aberdeen and Robert Huchosone, sangster, "who obliges himself by the faith of his body all the days of his life to remain with the community of the burgh, upholding matins, psalms, hymns." The council also appointed him master of the Sang(sic) School.

Johann Walther, German music publisher and composer, was born at Cola, near Jena (died 1570). He was a friend of Luther's and greatly involved with the Reformed Church.

Robert Fayrfax was mentioned as a "Gentleman of the Chapel Royal."

Gafori's "Practica Musicae" was published in Milan. It was a work of major importance, covering many aspects of musical practice. The following were of (cont.) major importance: comparison of the semibreve to a man's pulse at rest, that is MM 60-80; discussion of thorough temperament of keyboards by way of shortening the fifths; statement that the rest "was invented to give a necessary relief to the voice, and a sweetness to the melody; for as a preacher of the divine word, or an orator in his discourse, finds it necessary oftentimes to relieve his auditors by the recital of some pleasantry, thereby to make them more favorable and attentive, so a singer, intermixing certain pauses with his notes, engages the attention of his hearers to the remaining parts of his song." Gafori further asserted the "large" as an oblong white note with a tail descending on the right hand side; which form it has retained unchanged. He described the division of the minim into halves and quarters, greater and lesser semiminim quoting from Prosdocimus de Beldemandis. They were written in black and white. He mentioned Dunstable and gave the tenor of one of his settings of "Veni Sancte Spiritus." Generally his treatise covered all the information he felt a student needed to acquire.

Flemish musicians came to Spain starting at this time.

Arithmetica et Music by Le Fèvre was published.

The churchwardens' accounts of St. Mary's, Sandwich, contained the following item: "1496. Payd for mending of the lytell organys, iijs. ivd." "Item, for shepskyn to mend the grete organyse, iijd."

1496(cont.)

At Seurre, before a play started, musicians marched through the streets playing both hauts and bas.

An influx of Flemish musicians followed the marriage of the Infanta Joanna to Archduke Philip the Fair of Austria.

Clément Marot, French poet and son of Jean Marot, was born (died 1544).

The first volume of Encina's poetic works contained eight plays.

Ercole de' Roberti, Ferraran painter, died (born 1456).

Gerard David, Netherlandish painter, married a wealthy girl.

Paduan painting: Mantegna, Madonna of Victory.

Ferraran painting: Cosimo Tura, The Annunciation and St. George.

(to 1500) Italian painting: Perugino, St. Mary Magdalene.

(to 1506) Pierre de la Rue was in the service of Philip the Handsome from this date until the latter's death (1506).

c.1496

Venetian painting: Giovanni Bellini, The chapel of St. Mark's in Venice.

The first school of music was founded at Naples by Tinctoris.

1497

(March 27) Robert Wydow was installed Canon and Confrater of (cont.) Comba II at Wells Cathedral.

(April 10) An item in the accounts of the Lords High Treasurers of Scotland read as follows: "to John Hert for bering a pare of monicordis of the kingis fra Abirdene to Strivelin (Stirling), ix.s."

(September 1) Henry Abyngdon, English ecclesiastic and musician, died (born c.1418).

(September 1) Robert Wydewe succeeded Henry Abyngdon as subcentor of Wells.

Michel de Boteauville, French poet, set up arbitrary rules for determining quantity in French syllables. He then produced a poem following these rules.

Antoine Brumel was a member of the choir at Laon.

Crispiaenen, a singer, was mentioned in the records of the Confraternity at Our Lady at 's-Hertogenbosch.

Gafori's "Musice utriusque Cantus practica" was published in Brescia.

Johannes Grashof, organist, was at Magdeburg Cathedral.

Heinrich Isaac became court composer to Emperor Maximilian I at Vienna. He remained there until his death and enjoyed a comfortable and generous existence.

Lilium Musice plane, by Keinspect, was published by J. Schäffler.

1497(cont.)

Benozzo Gozzoli, Italian painter, died (born 1420).

Umbrian painting: Signorelli, The Life of St. Benedict.

German painting: Dürer, Dürer's Father.

John Heywood, court virginalist to King Henry VIII of England, was born (died 1587).

(to 1505) Luther probably had access to the works of the great Netherlandish composers, Isaac, Obrecht, and Ockeghem, or perhaps the Germans, Finck and Fulda.

(to 1509) John Dygon, composed the three-part motet "Ad lapidis positionem," printed in Hawkins' History. He was Prior of St. Augustine's Abbey, Canterbury.

c.1497

Hans Holbein the Younger, German painter, was born (died 1543).

(to c.1500) Matthaeus Pipelare of Louvain was choir director of the Illustrious Confraternity of Our Lady at 's-Hertogenbosch.

1498

(May 25) A petition from Petrucci to the Signori of Venice requested the exclusive privilege of printing music for voices, lute and organ, the agreement to be valid for a twenty year period. He was granted the privilege and exercised it until 1511.

Des Prés composed "La sol fa re mi."

Franco Gafurio's De harmonica musicorum instrumentorum was published in Milan.

Francisco de Peñalosa became a singer in the service of King Ferdinand.

The invention of music printing from moveable type came from this year.

Adam Rener was a choirboy for Maximilian I.

After Savonarola's fall (1498) the carnival returned, but in more sober form.

Johannes Tauler, a medieval German mystic, wrote and was published from this date forward.

Missals of Tournai indicated the use of the Dies irae in France.

Sir J. Graham Dalyell, Scottish writer, said: "Neither the form nor the use of the whistle (guhissil) is explicit. It is nowhere specially defined. In 1498 xiiij s. is paid for a whussel to the King . . . . Cornpipe, Lilt-pipe, and others are alike obscure."

King Charles VIII died (born 1470).

Antonio Benci, known as Pollaiuolo, Italian painter, died (born 1429).

Michael Pacher, German painter, died (born c.1435).

Martin Van Heemskerck, Netherlandish painter, was born (died 1574).

Gerard David was commissioned

1498(cont.)
to paint scenes representing justice.

German painting: Albrecht Dürer, The Apocalypse (Four Horsemen).

German woodcuts: Albrecht Dürer, The Apocalypse (various woodcuts).

(to 1499) French painting: Master of Moulins, Virgin and Child with Angels.

(to 1500) Antoine Brumel was maître des enfants and canon at Notre Dame in Paris.

(to 1515) Antonius Divitis (Antoine Le Riche) a French composer and colleague of Mouton, was singer in the chapel of Louis XII.

(to 1515) The reign of Louis XII the Father of the People (House of Valois) over France.

c.1498
A form of Litany with English words had existed.

Edward Hall, barrister, historian and author of Hall's Chronicle, was born(died 1547).

1499
(September 21) Robert Wydow was made one of the residentiary canons at the vicarage of Chew Magna, in Somersetshire.

Jean Cornuel, Burgundian composer also known as Verjust, died (birthdate unknown).

Archives indicated that Des Pres was at Ferrara in the service of Hercules I.

Carlo di Lounay was supposedly (cont.) once more in the service of Isabella d'Este. This was indicated by a letter he wrote to her from Bologna in which he asked forgiveness for having taken a book of hers.

The first Italian organ with two manuals was built at Rome.

According to Schlick, double semitones were tried in the organ, however they failed because of the difficulty involved in playing.

Gaspar van Weerbecke returned to the Papal Chapel.

Lodovico il Moro was expelled from Milan by King Louis XII of France.

Alesso Baldovinetti, Italian painter, died (born 1425).

German painting: Albrecht Dürer, Portrait of Oswald Krel.

Italian painting:
Leonardo da Vinci, The Last Supper (14'5"x28'3").

(to 1504) Signorelli's principal work was the decoration of the Chapel of San Baizio in Orvieto Cathedral. Here he painted the Last Judgment and its consequences in a noble and tragic style which probably inspired Michelangelo.

c.1499
Étienne Briard, engraver, was born at Bar-le-Duc (date of death unknown).

Jhan Geru, Netherlandish madrigal composer, was born (date of death unknown).

Palestrina's father was born.

c.1499(cont.)
Jehan Torrian, of Venice, was active.

Fragments of an Alsatian manuscript contained sections of the Ordinary of the Mass.
Lasarus Prussz was the composer of the Sanctus and Agnus Dei tunes.

The bagpipe came into favor in Scotland.

Becker, in his work, "Hausmusik in Deutschland," mentioned having a 16-part vocal canon by a Flemish composer, "on the approach of Summer." In the work there was an imitation of a cuckoo's voice, but it was incorrectly done.

Cracow became the center of musical activities in Poland.

Humanism was introduced into Germany, and one of its chief proponents there was the poet Conrad Celtes.

Minstrels disappeared and their disappearance was hastened by the invention of printing. When pedlars began to travel throughout the country with penny books and songs on broadsheets, the need for the minstrel was gone.

The motet turned to the new ideals of the period.

Because the Church refused to use them, the melodies for the strange Noëls sung at the time were lost.

Manuals in foreign organs were extended to four octaves in range, while those in England had reached almost the same range; the lowest octave was (cont.) either a "short octave" or a "broken octave."

The viol in three main sizes, Discant, Tenor, and Bass was generally used.

(to c.1510) Giovanni Animuccia, Italian composer, was born (died 1571). His work was chiefly in contrapuntal masses.

(to c.1510) The Dies irae was very rarely found, in early manuscripts in England, France or Germany; and was missing in many from this period.

(to c.1510) Many works of the early Tudor composers appeared in the great Eton manuscript from this period.

(to c.1510) At this time the clavichord was in greater use than the clavecin in England and Scotland.

(to c.1530) Alexander Agricola, a composer of monophonic chansons, was active.

(to c.1610) Petrarch, whose canzoniere appeared in approximately 167 editions during this period, was the most popular poet whose words were set by composers.

1500

(March 1) The accounts of the Lords High Treasurers of Scotland stated as follows: "to Jacob, lutar, to lowse his lute that lay in wed, ... xxxij. s. (Which means that the thriftless Jacob received his lute that lay in pawn)."

(May 25) Rober Wydow was installed as Sub-Dean and Prebendary of Holcombe Burnell,

1500(cont.)

Devonshire. He held this post until his death.

Serafino dall'Aquila, a leading poet of strambotti, died (birthdate unknown).

Philippe Verdelot, Flemish madrigal composer, was born (died c.1540 or 1565).

Alexander de Alamania entered the service of Philip the Handsome.

Antiphons written after this date were seldom based on a cantus firmus. The tenor still seemed to be composed before the bass and treble.

Jusquin d'Ascanio, composer, was identical with Josquin des Prés.

Johann Boemus, Netherlandish author, was active at this time.

Bonaventura da Brescia, Italian author, was active at this time.

Cardinal Francisco Ximenez de Cisneros tried to revive the old rite and had his own version painted.

During wedding festivities at Torgau for John the Steadfast (later elector of Saxony) a choir, directed by Adam von Fulda, sang two Masses accompanied by an organ, three trombones, a zink, and four krumhorns.

A manuscript of "Quid est proportio" was preserved. Hothby was quite old and died shortly after.

The Japanese Nō reached its peak. "It is an archaic lyrical drama . . . performed by a few masked actors in a strict unity of word melody and dance."

Michael Keinspeck, writer on music, was active.

Practically no composers of keyboard music were known by name.

Polyphonic laude were arranged for four voices.

Many cities had tried by this time to form regular musicians' associations, but only in London had the movement achieved lasting success.

The technique of the cyclic Mass, using material from an existing compositon had appeared in Europe prior to this date and was used both by Fayrfax and Taverner.

Jean Mouton was director of the choirboys at Amiens Cathedral.

Sancho de Paredes, a chamberlain to Queen Isabella, owned "Dos clabiorganos," two claviorgans or clavecins that had been "organized."

The restraint that was typical of the time placed the pavane in the forefront as it was a simple and calm dance.

Michele Pesenti, a Veronese composer and frottolist, was active at this time.

Bartolomeo Tromboncino, composer of frottole, was active at this time.

The Villancico was used as a solo song with lute or vihuela

1500(cont.)

accompaniment as well as for religious services.

The principle of the lute fingerboard was adopted by the makers of viols at this time.

Paris Bordone, Italian painter, was born (died 1571).

Benvenuto Cellini, Florentine sculptor and goldsmith, was born (died 1571).

Friedrich Herlin, German painter, died (born c.1435).

Italian painting: Perugino was at work on the Collegio del Cambio in Perugia.

Netherlandish painting: Bosch, Triptych of the Garden of Delights.

German painting: Albrecht Dürer, Portrait of a Young Man (Hans Dürer?).

(to 1504) Umbrian painting: Signorelli was completing the frescoes in the Chapel of San Brizio in Orvieto Cathedral.

(to 1506) Leonardo da Vinci lived in Florence.

(to 1529) Hans Maler, German painter, was active.

(to 1530) The first phase of the Renaissance was quiet, dignified, and reserved.

(to 1550) Jan of Lublin's tablature was probably the only one of the period that provided rules for the treatment of imitation.

(to 1550) The pavane and gal- (cont.) liarde were the most popular dances during this period.

c.1500

Martin Agricola, Protestant sacred composer, was born at Sorall in Lower Silesia (died 1556, June 10).

Giovanni Animuccia, sacred polyphonic composer of laude, was born (died 1571 or 1563).

Arnold von Bruck, German Protestant composer, was born (died 1554), see 1480.

Adrien Petit Coclicus, Flemish composer and pupil of Des Pres, was born (died 1563). He was the first to publish compositions in the new style, in a collection called Musica Reservata.

Hans Heugel, successor to Kern and great Cassel musician, was born in Deggendorf on the Danube (date of death unknown).

Luis Milan, celebrated Spanish lutenist and composer, was born in Valencia (died c.1565). He was also a respected poet.

Christobal Morales, a Spanish polyphonic composer, was born in Seville, Spain (died 1553). He was a member of the "Roman group."

Pedro Ordoñez, Spanish sacred composer, was born in Palencia (died 1550).

Francisco de la Torre, Spanish composer of keyboard dances, was born (date of death unknown).

Christopher Tye, English Reformation composer, was born

c.1500(cont.)
(died 1572).

Bach's chorale preludes represented the culmination of a development which started with Arnolt Schlick at this time. It continued through men such as Heinrich Bach, Buxtehude, Pachelbel, Redford and Scheidt.

The clavecin was made in the shape of a clavichord in Venice and called a spinet.

At the start of the sixteenth century experiments in counterpoint had produced impressive results in the English, French and Netherlandish schools of composers.

Josquin des Prés was not concerned with any problems of style. He simply studied the works of his teachers and contemporaries.

In the Sistine Chapel Choir all except three of Dufay's hymns were still performed although they had been composed seventy years earlier.

Numerous compositions by Dufay were found in rare Part-Books printed by Petrucci at this time.

Gafori's compositions survived mainly in three Milanese manuscripts of this time. They were assembled and copied at his behest and called the Gafori codices. These collections contained many sacred works by various composers active in Milan.

The hornpipe was probably danced frequently.

School children of Buda, Hungary sang at court on important holidays.

The bowed instruments descended from the Middle Ages were in a State of confusion.

Many monographs on instruments appeared at this time. They described families of bowed and wind instruments, including flutes and shawms, viols and rebecs, all sizes, treble, alto, tenor, and bass.

Lute music with the use of multiple stops started to appear at this time. They were patterned after the style of keyboard music.

John Lloyd's five-part O quam suavis was an example of the Great-Service type of Mass.

The singing of a motet in honor of the Sacrament and in connection with the transubstantiation became common practice. The insertion of a portion of Tu solus was included in the practice.

Obrecht supposedly wrote a Passion of St. Matthew (Latin version), for four voice parts in customary motet style. The narration proper, the words of Christ, or the interjections of the people were not isolated.

Flemish influence was obvious in the music of various organ composers both in Austria and southern Germany.

A manuscript contained passages of two-part organum in what could well have been composed as much as five or six hundred years earlier.

c.1500(cont.)

Polyphony started to be conceived in such a way that the voice parts were required to have sense as individual lines in addition to their position in the entire structure.

Music was produced with printed staves, but hand-written notes.

The normal tactus covered a breve, and either one of its two beats, covered a semibreve.

Organization of eight-beat units into three plus three plus two was a popular and frequent occurrence.

Two Ricercars for lute were written by Joan Ambrosio Dalza, a frottolist.

The oblong form of the Italian spinet, and the crow-quill plectra, were both in use at this time.

The only surviving vihuela was preserved from the time of Luis Milán. It is now in the Jacquemart André Museum in Paris.

A courtly dance band appeared in Martin Zasinger's "Decapitation of St. John the Baptist."

The growing influence of popular art on cultivated art was important and stimulated the creation of free verse forms.

Two textless pieces, apparently laude, appeared in a painting, St. Jerome in his Oratory by Carpaccio.

Corneille de Lyon, French painter, was born (died 1574).

Luis de Morales, Spanish painter, was born (died 1586).

The spirit of enterprise which inspired Bramante's plan for St. Peter's was typical of this period which produced so many great artists.

Netherlandish painting: Hieronymus Bosch, The Ship of Fools (22x12 5/8").

Italian painting: Raphael, The Three Graces.

Umbrian painting: Luca Signorelli, The Damned.

Umbrian painting: Luca Signorelli, End of the World.

Umbrian painting: Luca Signorelli, Self Portràit.

Italian painting: Andrea Solario, Virgin with the Green Cushion.

(to c.1520) Some of the texts used by des Prés' generation adhered to strict formalism, but poetry of this period sought greater freedom.

(to 1520) Laux Maler, a German lute maker, was active in Bologna. His reputation in the field was equal to that of the Stradivari in violins.

(to c.1525) German musical handbooks of the period by Virdung, Luscinius, Judenkünig, Agricola, and Gerle specifically described the viol family.

(to c.1525) Netherlandish painting: Anonymous (Juan de Flandre?), Girl with a Dead Bird.

c.1500(cont.)

(to c.1530) Many composers who tried to imitate the originality of des Prés were unaware of the real secret of his strength.

(to c.1559) The dance exerted an especially strong influence on chamber music in England during these years.

(to 1572) The Early French School of composition embraced this period.

(to c.1599) John Alford, an English lutenist, was active during the major portion of this period.

(to c.1599) Pierre Attaignant, a music printer in Paris, was said to have been the first printer in France to adopt moveable types, "caractères mobiles," to music printing.

(to c.1599) Ippolito Baccusi, an Italian monk and madrigal composer, was active during this period.

(to c.1599) Maestro di Capella Giuseppe Baini was a composer, exponent and representative of the old Roman school during this period. He was the first biographer of Palestrina.

(to c.1599) Clementine de Bourges was an eminent French composer during this century.

(to c.1599) William Byrd, the English composer, was a leader of the composers of all countries during this period.

(to c.1599) Jacobus Clemens (non Papa) was one of the most renowned musicians of the century. His sobriquet was to (cont.) identify him from another musician of the same name.

(to c.1599) Orazio Colombani was born in Verona and was active during this century.

(to c.1599) Clement Jannequin was a French composer by tradition and a distinguished follower and probably pupil of des Prés.

(to c.1599) Adrian LeRoy (Leroy) was a singer, lute player, and composer, but his most important accomplishments were as a printer during this period when printers were also publishers.

(to c.1599) Luzzasco (Luzzaschi) was the last representative of the pseudo-monody of the century. He provided written out accompaniments for keyboard.

(to c.1599) Alessandro Striggio was a composer of sacred and secular music and dramatic presentations. He was thought of as comparable to Principe Gesualdo da Venosa.

(to c.1599) Several lute-makers of the Tyrolese name Tieffenbrücker existed in Italy and became known as instrument makers in Padua, Lyons and Venice later in the century.

(to c.1599) Jacques Vaet, Flemish motet composer, was active during this period.

(to c.1599) Enriquez de Valderrabano, Spanish composer and vihuela player, was born in Penaranda de Duero. His career was during this century.

(to c.1599) Robert White was a

c.1500(cont.)
great English musician of the century, but little or no particulars on his life and career have been found.

(to c.1599) Zarlino exercised great influence on all theorists during this period.

(to c.1599) The courante was a popular, lively dance with jumping movements.

(to c.1599) Mazurkas became known during this century, they originated in national songs accompanied with dancing.

(to c.1599) In this century, as well as the previous one, dance manuals enriched the repertory of instrumental music to a great extent.

(to c.1599) In collections of dance tunes from this century the melodies usually consisted of two distinct divisions, the first written in common time, the second in triple time.

(to c.1599) After the Hussites, the Czech Brethren, founded by Peter of Chelčic, continued the development of religious songs.

(to c.1599) Czech Rorate chants and songs developed during this period.

(to 1599) Some motets with Czech texts, usually for three voices, were composed by Gontrášek and Tomek.

(to c.1599) The oldest musical notation of Dalmatian folk songs in the Serbo-Croatian language was during this period when several of them appeared in the idyllic epic poem (cont.) Ribanje i ribarsko prigovaranje ("The Fishing Trip") by Petar Hektorovic of Hvar.

(to c.1599) Court-music of Denmark was chiefly in the hands of Flemish musicians.

(to c.1599) Although most Middle Dutch chansons used binary rhythm, there were ternary passages in strict chordal style. These were introduced for contrast and emphasis on the text.

(to c.1599) Tunes closely related to the present-day "Swineherd's Dance" from the rural districts of Hungary have survived. They were titled Ungaresca, Ungarischer Tanz, Ungarischer Aufzug, and Heyducken Tantz ("Foot-soldier's Dance").

(to c.1599) The areas of the German-speaking countries that retained the previous faith were not musically productive from a nationalistic viewpoint.

(to c.1599) Stoltzer's and Mosto's works represented the only well known choral music composed by Hungarian composers.

(to c.1599) "Netherlands" described the area including the Netherlands and Belgium, also a portion of Northern France, extending slightly beyond Cambrai. Composers from this total locale were referred to as Netherlandish.

(to c.1599) The "Netherlands School" reduced the role of France in music, a fact that was unfair and inaccurate.

c.1500(cont.)

(to c.1599) Moscow and Petrograd had choirs whose cappella singing approached the finest standard of the century.

(to 1599) Little or nothing was known about music in Scandinavia during this period.

(to c.1599) Secular songs in Spain provided several new forms and names.

(to c.1599) The ground basses (bassi ostinati) and romantic melodies were in the popular tradition, and most Spanish composers used fragments of them in their works.

(to c.1599) Spanish music of this century kept its own national character and ancient traditions despite visiting musicians from France and Italy.

(to c.1599) This period was a golden one for Spanish music and composers of the highest rank in sacred vocal music, as well as guitar, organ and vihuela music were prolific and of high quality.

(to c.1599) It was typical of the close connexion between Spanish music and Spanish religion that the birthplace of Saint Teresa, at Alvila, the embodiment of Spanish religious spirit, was also the birthplace of Vittoria, the leading representative of Spanish music.

(to c.1599) Orphenica Lyra by Miguel de Fuenllana, was an example of the high standard of musical art in Spain.

(to c.1599) The earliest record of falsetto in Europe was in (cont.) reference to the Sistine Chapel. Spaniards at the Chapel gifted with this voice preceded that artificial class (castrati) whom alto and sometimes soprano parts were assigned.

(to c.1599) Instrumental music was in a confused state during this century.

(to c.1599) The construction of instruments in families, of three ranges, soprano, alto tenor, and bass was a development of this century.

(to c.1599) Instruments were expected to provide a variety of sharply contrasting sounds.

(to c.1599) Many literary references to stringed instruments in Spain, other than the vihuela, existed. Little or no music for other instruments survived.

(to c.1599) According to M. Viollet Le-Duc, the clavecin superseded the psaltery in France at some time during this century.

(to c.1599) The cittern was flat-backed, strung with four wire strings, and played with a plectrum, quill, or the fingers. It was standard barbershop furniture in London and used for amusement by waiting customers.

(to c.1599) "Fuenllana set Paseábase el rey moro," one of the loveliest songs for the guitar composed during this period.

(to 1599) Italian guitar music probably consisted entirely of struck chords during this century.

c.1500(cont.)

(to c.1599) Guitar music could first be published during these years.

(to c.1599) Spanish music for vihuela had been of great importance. The vihuela was a six string guitar with lute tuning. It had five round sound holes.

(to c.1599) The guitar was of little importance in Italy.

(to c.1599) Se Lo M'Accorgo, for guitar, was written by an unknown composer.

(to c.1599) An Este inventory of this period included an instromento piano e forte. It probably referred to a harpsichord provided with dynamic contrast by means of stops.

(to c.1599) The introduction of harpsichords with double keyboards was attributed by some to the great favor in which the Claviorganum, or combined spinet and organ, was held during this century.

(to c.1599) The majority of harpsichords of the period were made in Italy, primarily Venice.

(to c.1599) The virtuoso character of keyboard music of the time required skill on the part of the performer.

(to c.1599) Composers arranged choral works for keyboard instruments or lutes, with ornamentations suited to the particular instrument.

(to c.1599) Note repetitions did not play a prominent part (cont.) in English keyboard music.

(to c.1599) In Hungary, dramatic representations, interspersed with songs, were introduced by wandering minstrels and harp or cither players. The last performer in this group was the famous Tinódi ("Sebastian the Lutenist"), who died in this century.

(to c.1599) The chitarrone, like the archlute, was used in Italy along with the clavicembalo and other instruments to accompany the voice. A band of these provided music that had a nutty, slightly bitter timbre that was pleasant.

(to c.1599) The lute was the favorite German home instrument. Most writers of lute-tablatures tried to make their explanations simple enough for self-instruction.

(to c.1599) The lute was the most popular instrument in Italy, it was played by both courtier and ordinary citizen.

(to c.1599) Arnolt Schlick required a keyboard extending from F to a". German organ music also used this range until well into the 16th century.

(to c.1599) The increased skill of organists made mechanical transpositions unnecessary, and for the organ they disappeared. The harpsichord, however, still used them for two or more centuries.

(to c.1599) Italian organs were mechanically less advanced than French or German ones for a long period. This was a strange

c.1500(cont.)

fact in view of the relative importance of Italian organ music in this century.

(to c.1599) A particular type of organ used reeds and was known as the regal.

(to c.1599) Tablature was used by Organists to indicate the extended scale of the instruments. In Germany, organs increased in size and compass at a rapid rate.

(to c.1599) Many organs with extra notes were constructed.

(to c.1599) Louise Farrenc's name was perpetuated by the "Trésor des Pianistes," a true anthology of music that contained chefs-d'oeuvre of all the classical masters of the clavecin and piano from this century on to Weber and Chopin. There were even more modern works of high value included.

(to c.1599) Italian spinets almost always had 4 octaves and a semitone, but were divided into F and C instruments with the semitone E or B♮ as the lowest note.

(to c.1599) Two 16th-century spinets have been preserved in Florence by a man named Kraus.

(to c.1599) The development of the viol included the construction of instruments with sympathetic strings made of metal.

(to c.1599) An illustration from Jost Amman's "Büchlein aller Stände." showed a minstrel of this century performing on a three-stringed double bass.

(to c.1599) The term vihuela was used for both the viol and guitar families. In the 16th century tablatures, however, the vihuela de mano or vihuela commun was specified.

(to c.1599) The practice of placing soundholes back to back in the viol was prevalent at this time. This remained the distinctive mark of the viol as long as viols were made.

(to c.1599) The Antegnati were famous for their organs and also for their lutes and viols. Their reputation contributed to the high standing of Brescia as a lute-and viol-making center.

(to c.1599) A fine folio titled "A booke of In Nomines and other Solfainge Songes of v, vi, vii, and viii partes for voyles or Instruments" was preserved.

(to c.1599) Only five of the many clefs used in this period have been retained.

(to c.1599) The term hemiolia was applied by writers to certain rhythmical proportions, somewhat corresponding to the triplets of present music.

(to c.1599) A single ledger line, above or below the staff, was rarely but occasionally found in polyphonic music of the period.

(to c.1599) The rules concerning notation were very much simplified.

(to c.1599) Rhythmic elasticity continued to be one of the principal characteristics of style of the time.

(to c.1599) In the 16th century

c.1500(cont.)
both semiquavers and quavers were always printed with separate hooks.

(to c.1599) The semiquaver was found, although very rarely, in printed polyphonic music of this century.

(to c.1599) Great masters of the time were far more lenient towards hidden fifths and octaves than later theorists.

(to c.1599) In contrapuntal music of the period the need for some relief from note-against -note counterpoint inspired the sustaining of a note in one part as long as the others sounded consonant with it. In this way the dominant came into existence.

(to c.1599) The real fugue of polyphonic composers, was perfected and was of two types, limited and unlimited.

(to c.1599) Free canonical imitation was a feature of all polyphonic music of the period.

(to c.1599) Canonical writing was looked upon by composers as a display of virtuosity that commanded respect and admiration.

(to c.1599) Documents concerning vocal polyphony proved that the Italian madrigal was cultivated in Dalmatian towns by the upper classes.

(to c.1599) Leopolita, a Polish composer named Marcin Lwowczyk, drew upon non-liturgical sacred songs used in congregational singing. He rewrote them in a contrapuntal imitational style but retained a basically har- (cont.) monic texture in the style of the period.

(to c.1599) The qualities of holiness, goodness of form, and universality, which Gregorian chant supposedly possessed to the highest degree, were also present to a large degree in classical polyphony, especially that of the Roman school. It reached the highest degree of perfection in the works of Palestrina.

(to c.1599) Polyphonic music was cultivated at court and castles of the nobility and also in literary societies. These societies or fraternities were spread throughout the country. In Czechoslovakia townspeople organized these societies.

(to c.1599) Melodic independence of parts, associated with 16th century polyphony, was even more evident in polyphony of earlier decades.

(to c.1599) The "madrigal" first appeared in the collection "Madrigali de diversi musici libro primo."

(to c.1599) When strict counterpoint gave way to free part -writing, often erroneously called strict counterpoint, 16th century polyphony was replaced by that polyodic style, which was equally antagonistic toward the monodic school rapidly growing in Italy.

(to c.1599) Madrigalists and Ecclesiastical composers wrote for a greater variety of voices than was generally recognised.

(to c.1599) The Italian madrigal

c.1500(cont.)
generated repercussion and antaganism all over Europe. Italian music produced monody and opera and cultural centers of Europe, including Dalmatia, felt the domination of Italian influence in music.

(to c.1599) A work of great importance that helped establish the madrigal singing in Dalmatia was a collection of madrigals for 4 and 5 voices by Giulio Schiavetto, a musician in the service of Girolamo Savorgnano, Bishop of Sibenik.

(to c.1599) The idealistic madrigal dealt with hopeless love or nymphs and shepherds. Music for entertainment provided an authentic picture of the peoples life in Italy.

(to c.1599) The early madrigal was quite different from the 16th century version.

(to c.1599) The term madrigale cromatico referred to a madrigal in which blackened notes appeared and therefore a faster tempo was indicated.

(to c.1599) The literary madrigal was similar to the canzone, and could be described as a single stanza canzone.

(to c.1599) Pure tonal fugue existed even in this century. An excellent example was provided by Palestrina's virtually unknown madrigal, "Vestiva i colli."

(to c.1599) The madrigal and other light forms of music referred to one another and poked fun at each other with a dra-

(cont.) matic background.

(to c.1599) Several forms of secular music such as the madrigal and forms related to it were neither private nor public, but rather fell into a category halfway between.

(to c.1599) Machaut's Mass was still widely performed.

(to c.1599) The term "Missa parodia" (Parody mass) was the only one used for the Renaissance Masses during this century.

(to c.1599) A valuable collection of anthems and masses by Ashwell, Austen, Davy, Fayrfax, Lovell, Pasche, Prowett and Taverner was preserved.

(to c.1599) Some motets by Richafort were chosen as models for Parody masses. This type of mass was usually preferable to composers in this century.

(to c.1599) An anthem of this time was simply a motet with English text.

(to c.1599) Only twenty-five motets and about ten secular pieces of Pierre de la Rue were found in publications of the period. This was a miniscule amount when compared to the catalogue of des Prés' printed compositions.

(to c.1599) There was practically no stylistic difference between Catholic and Protestant motets composed in Germany.

(to c.1599) A large collection of the finest works of this century was printed and used successfully at Services in the

c.1500(cont.)
Cathedral of Regensburg by Dr. Karl Proske who was canon and kapellmeister there.

(to c.1599) The Formula of Concord was the last symbolic document of Lutheranism. It was planned as a unifying device for all the Lutheran churches in Germany.

(to c.1599) The Lutheran Church produced and/or adopted 174 contrafacta while the German Catholic Church adopted 42 during the same period of years. This fact indicated the great need for usable material in the new Church.

(to c.1599) Bach's ecclesiastical works as well as those of Handel and his predecessors were composed for the meantone system.

(to c.1599) Almost no music of this century continued in use after the Restoration of the Monarchy. At that point new material was demanded and produced.

(to c.1599) Concurrent with the growth of early 16th-century Catholic music in France and the Low Countries, some types of Protestant music developed in the French-speaking part of Switzerland.

(to c.1599) The Princes of the Roman Catholic Church had secular musicians entertain them in their palaces.

(to c.1599) The Tregians were a rich and powerful Catholic family at Golden or Volveden in Cornwall. Near the end of this century the leader of the family was Francis Tregian. His mother, Katherine, was the daughter of Sir John and Lady Elizabeth Arundell of Lanherne.

(to c.1599) Duke Giovanni Angelo was a collector of musical treasures during this period. Many manuscripts that he acquired have survived through a later collection of Cardinal Ottoboni who procured these items from the House of Altaemps.

(to c.1599) A fine collection of printed music of the 16th century survived and became the property of the Liceo filharmonico at Bologna.

(to c.1599) There were in the neighborhood of 100 In nomine compositions in England dating from this period. They were composed for varied performance media.

(to c.1599) An interesting specimen of Forkel's works was contained in a large volume of church music, scored by him. It survived in a German library.

(to c.1599) Portense Florilegium, a collection of sacred vocal music in separate parts was published in 2 volumes by Bodenschatz and contained 265 compositions.

(to c.1599) An interesting volume of theological tracts by Garson and his contemporaries survived. Some blank pages in it carry two ballads for three voices.

(to c.1599) Six folio volumes of vocal music of the period were preserved at Arnstadt,

c.1500(cont.)
Germany.

(to c.1599) A small but precious collection of printed works of the period were preserved by the Gymnasium at Brieg, Germany.

(to c.1599) A collection of seventy-six compositions from this century was preserved at Elbling, Germany.

(to c.1599) In the library at Güstrow, Germany a small but valuable collection of rare early printed musical works, chiefly of this century, have survived.

(to c.1599) A few printed works and manuscripts of liturgical works were preserved at Neisse, Germany.

(to c.1599) Difficulties of publication were probably increased by the requirement for royal sanction.

(to c.1599) Almost no music was printed in England before the "Cantiones Sacrae." There were, however, early missals by Pynson and others.

(to c.1599) Many music books systematized various kinds of ornaments in order to aid performers.

(to c.1599) Karl Proske, canon and kapellmeister at Regensburg Cathedral, collected documents sufficient to lead to the conclusion that composers of the period wrote their Music in Score, at first, but always transcribed it into separate part-books.

(to c.1599) After des Prés' (cont.) death the function of music was to further develop the style which existed in his works and those of his contemporaries. Then it was to be disseminated throughout Europe.

(to c.1599) The Cantori a liuto improvised since musical notation remained complex and difficult for all except accomplished musicians to notate.

(to c.1599) The polyphonic chanson became one of the most common forms of the period.

(to c.1599) Composers of the period were far more interested in the structural improvement of music than in having sacred compositions in particular reflect the serenity and idealistic features that should have been the goal.

(to c.1599) Improvisatory techniques were an important feature of 16th-century musical practice.

(to c.1599) Compositions referred to as "Miserere" in England, and especially those written for instruments, frequently included the melody of the psalm-antiphon "Miserere mihi" used as a cantus firmus, or sometimes they used some other device purely for the technical satisfaction achieved thereby.

(to c.1599) The problem of monody was probably best solved by the singer improvising over basso ostinato.

(to c.1599) The progress of serious compositional art up until this century had been restricted to the development of good part-writing and satisfactory harmonic progressions.

c.1500(cont.)

(to c.1599) Fauxbourdon style became prevalent in settings of the Passion, and prevented much description of situations or characters.

(to c.1599) Polychoral part-music gradually returned to great importance, especially in Venice.

(to c.1599) After the collapse of polyphony late in the century the "Stilo alla Cappella" of the 16th century lay dormant.

(to c.1599) The Responsoria were treated in polyphonic style, with great effect, not only by the leading composers of the century, but even as late as the time of Colonna, whose responsoria of the Office for the Dead, for 8 Voices, were written with great respect for the solemn importance of the text.

(to c.1599) In Collections of romanceros of the 16th century, the old ballads were reputed to have come from blind ballad-singers, who had sung them in the streets. None of the music was written, but hundreds of the ballads survived.

(to c.1599) Variations appeared in two basic forms, grounds and paraphrases.

(to c.1599) The Volta remained in fashion and, according to Larousse, it was introduced in Germany with its name changed to "Walzer."

(to c.1599) Arcadelt's treatment of dissonance was frequently unorthodox when compared with the style of Palestrina. Arcadelt taught in Italy during (cont.) this period.

(to c.1599) It was considered perfectly legitimate for Fra Lodovico Balbi, a famous choirmaster and singer, to rework the upper voices of 27 famous madrigals for four voices and to convert them into five-voiced madrigals by adding four lower voices of his own.

(to c.1599) The objection of purists to Bernacchi's fioriture as new were unfounded since the embellishments were from the 16th century, and were only developed by him and used more in the style of instrumental music.

(to c.1599) Claudin's "Jouissance vous donneray" was exceedingly popular.

(to c.1599) Clemen's Souterliedekens drew heavily from popular melodies, mostly Dutch. On rare occasions the influence of art song was evident.

(to c.1599) Richard Farrant was a Gentlemen of the Chapel Royal in England.

(to c.1599) Adam von Fulda's polyphonic lied, "Ach hülf mich leid," apparently achieved great popularity during this period.

(to c.1599) In the 16th century, the love of luxury and of rich sonority, brought Gastoldi's success which depended on the balletti for five voices and not those for three voices.

(to c.1599) Janequin's Cris de Paris was an outstanding chanson of the period.

c.1500(cont.)

(to c.1599) Luca Marenzio was constantly kept before the English public during his lifetime.

(to c.1599) S. Filippo Neri founded an Order and included the following among its rules: "the contemplation of celestial things by means of heavenly harmonics," a sixteenth-century equivalent of "the education of the soul in virtue by the movement of sounds."

(to c.1599) Palestrina's name was the leading one associated with the "reform of church music."

(to c.1599) The impossibility of comparing the value of money in the 16th century with its value today, plus the varied standard of life, prohibit the possibility of estimating Palestrina's financial position. It appeared to have been comparable to that of the average cathedral organist today. At the present cost of living his basic salary would probably have a purchasing power of between $12,500 and $15,000. He surely must have earned extra fees on many occasions.

(to c.1599) Palestrina's forty-five "Hymni totius anni" followed the vocal practice of furnishing a different setting for each odd-numbered stanza. The remaining ones and the incipit to the first stanza were not set but rather were to be sung in plainsong.

(to c.1599) Palestrina, as was usual among composers, developed some of the facets of des Pres' art, meanwhile adding (cont.) techniques that eliminated other trends that des Pres had set.

(to c.1599) Separate Parts of Palestrina's Masses, and Marenzio's madrigals were printed in Venice during the closing years of the century. Although the designs were artistic and in bold, legible type, they were quite inferior to earlier examples in execution.

(to c.1599) Palestrina directed the compilation of Guidetti's "Directorium Chori."

(to c.1599) Ambros, in writing of this period, stated "When we think of the principal works of the 16th century, these Psalms (Lassus') and Palestrina's Missa Papae Marcelli always come first to our minds."

(to c.1599) Beethoven, Brahms, Debussy, Gluck, Liszt, Mendelssohn, Mozart, Schumann, Wagner, and many other composers of lesser rank have all admitted to the great influence that the masters of this period exerted on them. Liszt in his last years aspired to being known as the "modern Palestrina."

(to c.1599) Cipriano de Rore's "Calami sonum ferentes" enjoyed particular fame during this period.

(to c.1599) Heinrich Schütz, while he adhered to the polyphonic language of the century, also restored in his music a severe and vigorous archaism.

(to c. 1599) Schütz' harmonizations of the principal psalm

c.1500(cont.)
hymns were as fine as the settings of Praetorius; of the Schein "Cantional" and Scheidt's "Görlitzer Tabulaturbuch."

(to c.1599) Schütz did not limit himself to agogically shortened and lengthened weak beats, groups of three's, or pathetic anticipations which gave German folk and church music its powerful and lively effect.

(to c.1599) Eitner named over 100 separate pieces composed by Ludwig Senfl during the first half of the century and ultimately printed in various collections.

(to c.1599) Galliarda Tamburina was written probably for guitar by an unknown composer.

(to c.1599) Thomas Tallis composed during the middle fifty years of the century. His career included all the religious upheavals of that period, and rapid and basic changes in the status and style of English church music occurred during his most productive years.

(to c.1599) Tallis' surviving music reflected the period during which it was composed. There is at least one example of almost every musical style known in the English church during the century. He achieved a fine blend of technical proficiency and emotion that placed him among the leaders of his century.

(to c.1599) Mediaeval musicians worked with a method that was so complicated that, even in that century, errors and misunderstandings were frequent. Some of them were sufficiently (cont.) serious so that Zacconi found it necessary to indicate them with a great degree of clarity.

(to c.1599) The Battell by William Byrd was a highly successful piece of descriptive music in the dance category. Whereas its musical interest was not great, the marches it contained showed an unusually strong rhythmic sense and assorted meters that gave the piece a unique quality.

(to c.1599) The reign of King Francis I over France closely paralleled the first period of the 16th-century chanson.

(to c.1599) The formula known to musicians as "Digniora sunt priora" was used by Byrd.

(to c.1599) The glosa was frowned upon by many 16th-century musicians, who felt it lowered the standards of music.

(to c.1599) German military signals generated a custom among the soldiers of inventing doggerel. Some of these rhymes were probably ancient and went back to this period.

(to c.1599) The contents of all known laude collections were comprised of part-music settings.

(to c.1599) The 16th-century ricercari was serious in nature, whereas canzoni were livelier.

(to c.1599) Details of Scotish popular music of this period were meagre.

(to c.1599) The word "vaudeville" was used by 16th century writers

c.1500(cont.)
to describe a song sung about a town and with an attractive melody.

(to c.1599) Villancicos (peasants' songs) had refrains and ritornellos. They were apparently sung as six-voiced villancicos by Puebla. However, in proportion to the amount of existent words to these songs only a small amount of their music survived.

(to c.1599) Villanesche also appeared under other names in 16th century prints.

(to c.1599) The entire first strain of Saint Anne's Tune was purportedly traceable to 16th century French chanson.

(to c.1599) The culture and wealth of Italy attracted many foreigners. They were favorably received by noble families who could afford the finest music to add adornment to their courts.

(to c.1599) The first Italian printed book that dealt expressly with 16th-century chansons was Antico's Primo Libro de la canzoni francese.

(to c.1599) Although Italian composers travelled and lived in France they did not inspire the French to imitate them by composing ricercars and canzoni a sonar, typically Italian instrumental forms.

(to c.1599) Provincial musicians were forced to acknowledge the authority of the corporation in Paris. In this century many branches were established in the important towns of France under the regular title, "Confrérie de (cont.) St. Julien des ménétriers."

(to c.1599) In the Middle Ages, when Minnesingers and Troubadours flourished even into this century, a custom prevailed that whoever created a singable verse and a new meter also composed the melody.

(to c.1599) The 16th century differentiated between works written in musica-reservata and works written in other styles even when by the same composer.

(to c.1599) Music for use in connection with dramatic or semi-dramatic productions showed a cooperation between instruments and voices.

(to c.1599) Problems of identity, some still unsolved, occurred in details concerning musicians of the period.

(to c.1599) The Ionian mode-il modo lascivo was favored by strolling singers and ballad-mongers. Scholars and musicians of the period scorned its use.

(to c.1599) The writer of a set of part books preserved in an English Library was an ardent admirer of Robert White. This collection was a highly interesting one in regard to 16th century composers.

(to c.1599) London alone was able to support an organized company of independent musicians for any length of time. Generally musicians were able to secure a respected status and regular renumeration by joining the waits.

c.1500(cont.)

(to c.1599) Sixteenth century musicians were properly recognized in the field of church music.

(to c.1599) Cremona was an important and famous music center during this period.

(to c.1599) The epidemic of Tarantism was at its peak during these years and bands of musicians travelled around the country playing music which was the only known healing medicine.

(to c.1599) Convention exercised a powerful force in music as it did in the fine arts and in poetry during this century.

(to c.1599) There were a few poems that almost every composer of the century attempted to set. Similarly, nearly every painter attempted a Madonna and Child, and almost every sculptor did a Pieta.

(to c.1599) Classical authors frequently used the word "scena" to apply to that part of a Greek or Roman Theatre which we now call the stage. The classical tendencies of the Renaissance led to similar usage in the 16th century.

(to c.1599) Latin school-dramas were presented in German-speaking countries.

(to c.1599) Shrove Tuesday plays gradually degenerated into obscene works, until Hans Sachs and Jakob Ayrer initiated a movement which resulted in reformation of the German stage. Both of the aforementioned poets used music in their plays.

(to c.1599) Mavro Vetranović, a 16th century poet, mentioned the "trumbetari" and "pifari" from "Alamannia" in a carnival song of the period.

(to c.1599) Zarlino invented ten rules that showed his concern over textual treatment and proved to be an important feature of 16th-century composition, particularly in the area of sacred and Italian secular music.

(to c.1599) In 16th-century England the two great movements, Renaissance and Reformation, were simultaneously developing.

(to c.1599) Middle English was the intermediate between the Old English of the Anglo Saxon period and the English of the 16th century. In spite of some obsolete words and constructions the latter was essentially our own modern English.

(to c.1599) When Spanish and Portuguese conquerors arrived, the Aztecs in Mexico and the Incas in Peru both ruled over mighty empires.

(to c.1599) The state of research on French 16th-century painting was so unsatisfactory that several wedding scenes, records of royal entries and some of the activities of the Catholic League, still may be undiscovered.

(to c.1599) Chu Tuan, Chinese painter, was active during this century.

(to c.1599) Sesson, Japanese painter, was active during this century.

c.1500(cont.)

(to c.1599) Spanish painting, Catalonian School, (unknown artist), Martyrdom of St. Cugat.

(to c.1599) Islamic painting: Illumination, from Hamza-namah (27"x21").

(to c.1599) Spanish architecture: Covarrubias, Salamanca, Palacio Monterey.

(to c.1599) Renaissance tapestry: School of van Orley and van Roome, Singers with open choir book and harpist (Detail from Danaë and the Shower of Gold). The man appeared to be beating the tactus.

(to 1600) The School of Composition of Bologna existed during this period.

(to 1600) The School of Composition of Lombardy, although relatively unimportant, existed at this time.

(to c.1600) Some of the most renowned harpers (harpists or minstrels) of the time were Rory Dall O'Cahan, Thomas and William O'Conallon, Gerald O'Daly, Carolan Denis Hempson, Cornelius Lyons and John and Harry Scott.

(to c.1620) The origins and development of chamber music (for strings) during this period should be considered from the historical point of view rather than the aesthetic one.

(to c.1620) The range of the alto voice was limited to notes admissible on the staff in the alto clef.

(to c.1620) Preservation of (cont.) part-books from this period was quite remarkable since many factors ruled out their survival. They passed out of service at an early date and had received daily use for so long that many were completely worn out. A final factor against their survival was the period of the Commonwealth when cathedral choirs were eliminated and church music entirely suppressed.

(to c.1625) The lute was a fashionable instrument and although a reasonable amount of music was specifically composed for this instrument a great demand existed for arrangements for lute of choral music, either sacred or secular.

(to c.1650) Gamba type viols were used for chamber music, whereas viols of the braccio family were considered street instruments. This categorization was made by Zacconi in his Prattica di musica, and was adhered to during this period.

(to c.1699) The term Accademia referred to an institution whose type flourished all over Italy. These institutions were generally founded for the promotion of art, literature and science. Six of these centers of instruction were in Bologna, five in Florence, four in Siena, two in Vicenza, and one each in Cesena, Ferrara, Padua, Salerno, and Verona. The Bologna ones were devoted entirely to music instruction, the group in Siena were directed toward musical dramatic presentations as were the two in Vicenza. The Verona Accademia was founded by Alberto Lavezzola from a combination of two rival institu-

c.1500(cont.)

tions. Bologna actually boasted a total of thirty such institutions but many were for arts and sciences other than music.

(to c.1699) The term "air" referred to a cheerful melody.

(to c.1699) Catches were immensely popular with the lower classes as was indicated by numerous allusions to "alehouse catches" in dramas of the period.

(to c.1699) Concerto was a term that denoted both "to agree" and "to compete." It was applied to different forms of instrumental and vocal music.

(to c.1699) The Madrigal and the Cantata were both very important, particularly concerning chamber-music, during this period. Both forms were, however, doomed by the rise of opera.

(to c.1699) Matassins, (Matacins, or Matachins), also called Bouffons, were dances for men in armor, popular in France at this time.

(to c.1699) The Pavane, (Pavan, or Pavin) was a slow, solemn dance, very popular during these centuries. The dance was usually coupled with the Galliarde. Many examples by instrumental composers were preserved.

(to c.1699) Trenchmore was an old English country dance, frequently mentioned by writers of the period.

(to c.1699) The cither enjoyed great popularity on the continent as well as in England.

(to c.1699) Players reputedly used clumsy fingering in which the thumb and usually also the 4th and 5th fingers were omitted.

(to c.1699) The harpsichord had not acquired sixteen foot stops, which sounded an octave lower.

(to c.1699) Instrumental ensemble music was a highpoint for English music.

(to c.1699) Leather for the tongue of the jack was found in instruments of the 16th and 17th centuries.

(to c.1699) Lutenists, "lewters" or "luters" were always included as part of the musical retinue of royalty. One such musician was usually attached to the household of noblemen and wealthy country land-owners.

(to c.1699) The term "pair of organs," was used but its interpretation has always been a confusing problem.

(to c.1699) Scheidemann was the name of a renowned family of organists in Hamburg.

(to c.1699) French, German and Italian composers used their clavecins and spinets much like organs.

(to c.1699) London was almost purely a center for the manufacture of stringed instruments. The popularity of viols resulted in the appearance of many makers of the instrument. Among the most prominent were Addison, Aldred, Bolles, Jay, Ross, Shaw,

c.1500(cont.)
and Smith.

(to c.1699) Contrapuntal treatment became more elaborate under such musicians as Stephen Mahu and Johann Kugelmann early in the 16th century. It advanced greatly in the number of voice parts as well as the general complexity throughout these years.

(to c.1699) Complicated key signatures were avoided by all composers.

(to c.1699) Notation of the period proved insufficient for the needs of the time.

(to c.1699) The study of mathematical proportions shed light on the theory and practice of music when the Greek writers were translated and studied in Italy in the 16th and 17th centuries.

(to c.1699) The ballad "The Jolly Miller" was a favorite during these centuries.

(to c.1699) The cantus firmus was a conspicuous feature in "Non nobis Domine," and many other works of the time.

(to c.1699) English poets of the period wrote new texts to old tunes and created difficulty in assigning precise dates to many ballads.

(to c.1699) Except for the influence by the Flemish School on ecclesiastical music of Portugal it escaped all foreign influences, until Italian opera came into existence and had a strong impact on all Portuguese music.

(to 1699) Political and ecclesiastical relations between the two most bigoted Catholic countries, Austria and Spain, were close and intimate.

(to c.1699) William Hawes edited the publication in score of "The Triumphs of Oriana," the famous collection of madrigals by composers of the 16th and 17th centuries.

(to c.1699) Lutheran cities continued to maintain high standards although internal political conditions, religious problems and wars made it difficult. Turkish occupation of the central part of Hungary and the Calvinist movement eliminated the remains of musical culture in other locations.

(to c.1699) Mantuan records were the most clean in their description of life during this time.

(to c.1699) "Geschichte der Orgelmusik" by A.G. Ritter provided a full description of the German "Coloristen" of the 16th and 17th centuries.

(to c.1699) Many apparently original melodies of the 16th and 17th centuries were actually well-known Volkslieder, harmonised or treated with contrapuntal devices.

(to c.1699) At the library of the Grey Friars in Berlin an important collection of works carefully arranged in parts was preserved. It provided a view of ancient vocal music by one director Bellermann, and his son, Heinrich Bellermann.

(to c.1699) Rare vocal music of

c.1500(cont.)
great importance in the musical history of Frankfurt, by Carl Israël, survived in libraries of St. Peter's Church and the local Gymnasium in that city.

(to c.1699) The Landesschule in Grimma, Germany collected about 131 works of the 16th and 17th centuries.

(to c.1699) The Gymnasium library at Heilbronn, Germany collected part-books from the period.

(to c.1699) An extremely valuable collection of music was assembled at Ritter Akademie in Leignitz, Germany.

(to c.1699) In London at the British Museum many interesting collections of early English and Italian songs, both words and music, were preserved.

(to c.1699) Many madrigals, including a fine collection of the productions of brilliant English madrigal writers, were collected at the Royal Academy of Music Library in London.

(to c.1699) The Stadtbibliothek in Lüneburg, Germany assembled collections of musical works of the period, both in manuscript and printed versions.

(to c.1699) A small but valuable collection of 16th and 17th century music was assembled at the University Library in Munich, Germany.

(to c.1699) At the Stadtbibliothek in Nürnberg, Germany 13 manuscripts and 47 printed collections of church music of the time were assembled.

(to c.1699) The Stadtkirch library in Pirna, Germany contained eight manuscripts and sixty-three printed musical works of the 16th and 17th centuries.

(to c.1699) The University library in Prague collected a few valuable early treatises in manuscript as well as printed works of the centuries in question.

(to c.1799) F.W. Ditfurth's "Volksund Gesellschaftslieder des 16ten, 17ten, und 18ten Jahrhundert." included secular songs of the period.

(to c.1799) "Harmonia Sacra" was a collection of Anthems in score selected from the most eminent masters of the period, edited and published by John Page.

(to c.1799) During the reocurring wars which devasted Ireland in these centuries, the art of music languished, decayed, and all but disappeared.

(to c.1799) The most important period in the history of Italian music was during these years. Later the country occupied a leading position but restricted essentially to opera and oratorio.

(to c.1799) The harpsichord was the most important of the group of keyboard instruments that preceded the pianoforte, and held a position analogous to that now held by the piano.

(to c.1799) Whereas modern collections of musical instruments are primarily in the nature of museums, those of the 16th, 17th, and 18th centuries were actually

c.1500(cont.)

intended for use.

(to c.1799) The spinet was a keyed instrument, with plectra or jacks, and according to Burney "a small harpsichord or virginal with one string to each note."

(to c.1799) An important collection of parts, and vocal music was collected at the Church of St. Katharina in Brandenburg.

(to c.1799) The Chetham library at Manchester collected the music of many old popular songs from these years.

(to c.1799) Musical works of these centuries were assembled at the Royal Academy of Music library at Upsala, Sweden. The collection included 191 musical works of the 16th century, 198 from the 17th century, and 120 from the 18th century.

(to c.1800) Miguel Hilarion Eslava's "Lira sacro-hispaña" was a collection of Spanish church music of the above period.

(to c.1850) Zarlino proposed that the octave should be divided into twelve equal Semitones for the lute. He advocated the practice that finally, in the 19th century, was universally adopted.

(to c.1900) The conventionalism of most musical dance forms, whether the alternation of duple and triple rhythms as in the 16th century, or of verse and refrain as in the 20th, satisfied the dancers of all centuries and of all positions in life.

1501

(February 5) Petrucci published Canti B, numero cinquanta in Venice.

(May 14) Petrucci published Harmonice Musices Odhecaton in Venice. It included compositions by Ockeghem and Busnois among others, and was actually a collection of part-music.

(June) Antonius Divitis became choirmaster at St. Donatian.

Girolamo Cardano, writer on music, was born (died 1576).

Des Prés was seen in France by the duke's agent who reported this fact to his master from Blois.

Antonius Divitis became a singer at St. Donatian.

Finck was in the service of the Polish king (also in 1492 and 1506).

Jean Mouton was director of the choirboys at Grenoble.

Ottaviano dei Petrucci first printed Music from moveable types.

The earliest known record of sortisatio occurred in the Opus aureum by the French theorist, Nicolas Wollick, at Cologne.

The important position of the chanson became obvious with the great number of publications it received in Italy and in France.

The first results of the madrigal's popularity were the publications in Venice.

(June 12 to 1504, November 28)

1501(cont.)

Chrysander gave a list of 18 works that were surely published by Petrucci during this period and 2 others that may have been.

(to 1502) Pierre de la Rue, Burgundian composer, visited Spain.

(to 1510) Pierre de la Rue was a prebend of Courtrai, and later held the same benefice at Namur. He resigned from the latter in 1510.

c.1501

The Jardin de Plaisance was published by Antoine Vérard.

(to c.1502) The degree of Doctor of Music was conferred on Fayrfax by Cambridge University.

(to c.1550) Josquin Baston, Flemish composer, was active during this period.

(to c.1550) Jean Courtois, chanson composer of the Paris school, was active during these years.

(to c.1550) Johann Kugelmann, of Augsburg, was a leading trumpet-player and contrapuntist during this period. He also held the post of Kapellmeister for Duke Albert at Königsberg.

(to c.1550) Philippe Verdelot, Flemish madrigal composer, spent considerable time in Italy, both in Venice and Florence, where he worked as a composer.

(to c.1550) Italian, French, and Spanish Singers, outnumbered Netherlanders in the Sistine Choir. Giovanni Bonnevin, Elizario Genet (surnamed Carpentrasso), Costanzo Festa, Pietro Perez, Bernhard Salinas, and Giovanni Scribano were mentioned in the list of members.

(to c.1550) The bassoon was supposedly discovered by a canon of Ferrara.

(to c.1550) Practically no music was actually composed for the virginal. Its use was for the performance of dances, popular songs, and arrangements of polyphonic vocal music.

(to c.1550) From the time of Okenheim to the middle of the century, composers apparently treated the creation of contrapuntal devices as a duty, the neglect of which was unthinkable.

(to c.1550) Most composers during these years strove to imitate des Prés but unfortunately, for the most part, copied his failings rather than his virtues.

(to c.1550) The science of hymnology began to attract a great deal of attention.

(to c.1550) Women did not take part in singing so madrigals were written for men's voices and parts composed in the soprano clef could be sung falsetto.

(to c.1550) Publications devoted to the music of one man were rare.

(to 1564) Eitner's Bibliographie der Musik-Sammelwerke described more than forty collections of motets and psalms by Isaac collected during these years.

(to c.1650) The expression,

c.1501(cont.)

"one peyre of orgynys;" continued in use up to the time of Pepys, who wrote his "Diary" in the second half of the 17th century.

(to c.1799) Free part-writing was not new but a gradual development from strict counterpoint of the 16th century through the end of the 18th.

1502

(March 28) The Privy Purse Expences of Elizabeth of York stated that on this date Robert Fayrfax was paid 20s. "for setting an Anthem of oure lady and Saint Elizabeth."

(May 9) Petrucci published Motetti A, numero trentatre A at Venice.

(May 10) Petrucci published Motetti B, numero trentatre B at Venice.

(September 21) Robert Wydow was made Seneschal, and shortly thereafter Auditor of the Chapter House.

(September 27) Petrucci published Missae Josquin at Venice.

(December 27) Petrucci published Missarum Josquin. Lib. I at Venice.

Portuguese composer, nobleman and friend of Erasmus, Damião de Góis, was born (died 1574). He composed sufficiently well to have a motet included in the Dodecachordon.

Johannes Mauburnus, author on music, died (birthdate unknown).

Luis de Vargas, a Spanish painter and musician, was born in Seville (died 1568).

Robert Cooper received the degree of Doctor of Music from Cambridge University.

Johannes Lupi, Netherlandish musician, served as organist at Nivelles.

Edward Stanley sang and accompanied himself on the virginal before the King of Scotland.

Among Agricola's most important works were two motets for three voices from a collection, "Motetti xxxiii," published by Petrucci at Venice on this date. One of them was "O quam glorifica luce" and based on a Gregorian hymn.

Des Prés' Missa L'Homme armé super voces musicales was a cantus-firmus mass, almost certainly an early work because of its complexity. It contained intricate contrapuntal techniques. Petrucci published it during this year.

Gafori's "Practica Musicae utriusque Cantus" Bernadinus Misinta de Papia appeared at Brescia.

Arcadia, by Sannazaro was published. It was a pattern for pastoral verse for this century.

Tromboncino's music was performed at the wedding celebration of Lucrezia Borgia who married Queen Isabella's brother, Alfonso d'Este, at Ferrara during this year.

Plautus' Asinaria was revived with interpolated music by

1502(cont.)

Tromboncino.

Petrucci printed a book of des Prés' masses including Missa Fortuna, Missa Gaudeamus, Missa L'Homme armé sexti toni, and Missa La Sol Fa Re Mi.

Ottaviano dei Petrucci published "Motette, A. numero trentatre" at Venice.

Petrucci, the first musical publisher, published the motets and masses of the Netherlands composers but had little to offer from Italian composers except frottole which were pleasant but inconsequential part-songs.

The earliest historical mention of the harpsichord in England was under the name of Claricymball.

In the Ordenanzas de Sevilla a compulsory examination for all instrument makers was described.

The churchwardens' accounts of St. Mary's, Sandwich, contained the following item: "1502. Paid for mending of the gret organ bellowis and the small organ bellowis, vd." "Item for a shepis skyn for both organys, ijd."

Kisszeben' in Hungary had an organ.

A musical society was established in Louvain and its statutes placed before the magistrate for sanction. The founders wanted to have the new association be under the patronage of "St. Job." The magistrate decided otherwise and placed it under the patronage (cont.) of St. Cecilia.

Four editions of Gafurius' treatises were preserved in a private library in England.

Renaissance architecture: Bramante, The Tempietto, Rome, S. Pietro in Montorio (Diameter of colonnade, 29', total height, 46').

German painting: Dürer, A Hare (Water-color painted in Vienna).

German painting: Dürer, Piece of Lawn (Water-color study, painted in Vienna).

(to 1520) Gothic architecture: London, Westminster Abbey, Henry VII's Chapel (c.75'wide).

(to 1536) Gil Vicente, composer and dramatist, who interposed vilancicos in his plays, was most active during these years.

c.1502

(to 1507) Netherlandish painting: Gerard David, Virgin and Child, St. Mary Magdalene with the Donor Madelaine Cordier.

1503

(February 10) Canti C, numero cento cinquanta was published by Petrucci in Venice.

(March 24) Missae Obreth was published by Petrucci in Venice.

(June 17) Missae Brumel was published by Petrucci in Venice.

(July 15) Missae Ghiselin was published by Petrucci in Venice.

(August 13) An item in the accounts of the Lords High Treasurers of Scotland stated:

1503(cont.)

"Item to viij Inglis menstrales be the Kingis command xl frenche crownis, . xxviij . li."

(October 1) Robert Wydow was appointed to the perpetual vicarage of Buckland Newton, in Dorsetshire.

(October 31) Missae Petri de la Rue was published by Petrucci in Venice.

(December 27) Missarum Josquin Lib. II & III were published by Petrucci in Venice.

Johannes Ghiselin, Netherlandish composer, also known as Verbonnet, was at the court of Ferrara (also in 1491 and 1535).

Ghiselin brought des Prés back to Ferrara from France.

Eight four-part songs from the collection "Canti cento cinquanta" were published by Petrucci in Venice.

Five of Antoine Brumel's masses were printed in one volume by Petrucci in Venice. A perfect copy was preserved in Berlin's Royal Library.

Kiesewetter, in "Essay on the Music of the Netherlands," printed three four-part chansons from the "Canti Cento Cinquanta" published by Petrucci in Venice. They showed decided progress from the music of Dufay's period.

Two of five compositions published by Petrucci in a collection of Masses by "Joannes Ghiselin" were found under the name of Verbonnet in other collections.

A motet, "In nomine Jesu, was published by Petrucci in the Motetti B collection with the composer listed as Gompert.

A portion of one of the Weerbecke motets was published by Petrucci in the Motetti B collection. The motet "Verbum caro factum est" was reprinted in his second collection of Laude with different words.

The best songs in Petrucci's "Canti Cento-cinquanta," published in this year, were French, German and Netherlandish.

Petrucci published "Motetti de passioni, B."

Petrucci published "Canti C no. cento cinquanta C."

Petrucci published a collection of masses by Pierre de la Rue. A copy survived and was kept at the British Museum.

There was an inventory of musical instruments which belonged to Queen Isabella. It was found at the Alcazar of Segovia and dated 1503.

Candidates for a degree in music were required to compose a rather elaborate work.

Pierre de la Rue wrote thirty-six masses of which Petrucci published five during the composer's life-time. This collection, published at Venice, was titled "Misse Petri de la Rue." A few others appeared in later collections.

A woodcut of the Virginal by Virdung showed a rectangular or oblong spinet which resembled the spinetta of 1503, described

1503(cont.)

by Banchieri in "Conclusione nel suono dell' organo" (Bologna) to have been invented by the Venetian, Spinetti.

Julius II decided to build an impressive tomb himself and discarded his idea of adding a chapel to the existing church. The church was in crumbled condition and he decided to carry out the idea favored by his predecessor Nicholas V, which was to build a new building.

Scaliger, writer of Poetics, entered his active period.

Sir Thomas Wyatt, English poet, was born (died 1542).

Angelo Bronzino, Italian painter, was born (died 1572).

Francesco Mazzola, also known as Parmigianino, Italian painter, was born (died 1540).

Jan Gossaert, Netherlandish painter, was a member of the Antwerp guild.

It was not until this date that Michelangelo started to paint.

German painting: Lucas Cranach, the Elder, "Crucifixion."

Italian painting: Michelangelo, The Holy Family.

(to 1503) The Papal reign of St. Pius III (born in Siena).

(to 1505) Netherlandish painting: Gerard David, the Wedding at Cana (37 3/4" x 50 3/8").

(to 1508) Pinturicchio, Italian painter, worked in (cont.) Siena.

(to 1513) The Papal reign of St. Julius II (born in Savona).

c.1503

Francesco d'Ana, organist at San Leonardo in Venice, died (birthdate unknown).

A manuscript, the Fairfax Book, which contained several works by Robert Fayrfax, derived its name from a former owner whose family apparently had no connection with the composer's.

(to c.1531) Fridolin Sicher's tablature (St. Gall 530) was probably written during this period.

1504

(March 23) Missae Alexandri by Agricola was published by Petrucci at Venice.

(September 15) Motetti C was published by Petrucci at Venice. In the collection there is a motet "Ut heremita solus" which although listed as anonymous is probably by Ockeghem. Crétin lists a motet with that title as being composed by Ockeghem.

Hans Buchner was organist at Constance.

In the Canti C published by Petrucci a Rosa playsant was credited to Philipon. This same work was credited to Caron in a manuscript at Florence and to Dusart in a manuscript at Rome.

Nicholas Craen became a singer at St. Donatian in Bruges.

The Liber generationis by des Prés was published. It was

1504(cont.)

a setting of St. Matthew's narrative of Jesus' geneology and an early example of a Gospel motet. This particular type of motet became popular at a late date.

The "Liber primus missae Josquin" by des Prés was published by Petrucci.

Four volumes of frottole were published by Petrucci in Venice.

A collection of five masses by Obrecht was published by Petrucci. This volume represented over two-thirds of the composer's works.

Petrucci published a new arrangement of motets with all voices in separate part books, one each for cantus, altus, tenorus and bassus.

Crispin van Stappen, Netherlandish composer and singer, received an appointment to a canonry at Cambrai.

Jehan Torrian built the organ at Notre Dame des Tables, Montpellier.

Virdung, in a letter written in this year, described a 36-part composition by Ockeghem.

William Cornyshe was in Fleet prison on what he claimed was misinformation given by an enemy of his. He wrote a poem "A Treatise between Trouth and Informacion." Some excerpts from it were quoted in an History of Music by Hawkins.

Isabella of Castile, Queen of Spain, died (born 1451). Philip the Handsome and his (cont.) wife Joanna now came to rule over Castile, Granada, and León and the result was closer ties between Spain and the Netherlands, especially in music.

Florentine poet, Giovani Battista Strozzi, was born (died 1571).

The pastoral poem was firmly established by Sannazard's "Arcadia."

Naples was a Spanish possession and the theatrical art form that flourished in Spain was brought to the Italian city and its environs.

Filippino Lippi, Florentine painter, died (born c.1457).

Francesco Primaticcio, French painter and architect, was born (died 1570).

Lucas Cranach the Elder was brought to Wittenberg by Frederick the Wise, Elector of Saxony.

German painting: Cranach the Elder, The Rest on the Flight to Egypt.

German engraving: Dürer, Adam and Eve.

German engraving: Dürer, The Nativity.

Italian painting: Giorgione, Madonna of Castelfranco.

(to 1505) Antonius Divitis left St. Donatian and became a choirmaster at St. Rombaut, Malines for these two years.

(to 1508) Petrucci published

1504(cont.)

nine collections of fróttole containing an average of sixty-four selections in each volume.

(to 1508) Raphael was in Florence during these years.

(to 1510) Works by Tromboncino appeared in publications during these years.

(to 1514) Petrucci's publication of collections of fróttole grew to eleven in number. These collections raised Italian secular music to a new prominence. Of the eleven books ten have survived.

c.1504

Jacques Arcadelt, Netherlandish madrigalist, was born (died c.1567).

A laude appeared in a painting in a large altarpiece by Lo Spagna.

The members of Vittore Carpaccio's workshop aided in the painting of a "Life of the Virgin" for the Scuola degli Albanesi.

1505

(March 22) Petrucci published Missae de Orto at Venice (five masses by Marbriano de Orto). They were based on chansons and the plainsong, Missa Dominicalis. His L'Homme armé Mass was also included.

(October 4) Robert Wydow, poet and musician to King Edward IV, died (birthdate unknown).

(November 28) Petrucci published Motetti à 5. Lib. I at Venice.

Jacob Obrecht, a leading (cont.) Flemish composer, died at the Este court (Ferrara) of the plague (born 1430). He held the post of Cantor of Ferrara at the time of his death (see also c.1450).

Among Agricola's most important known works was a volume of five masses "Misse Alex." It was published by Petrucci at Venice during this year.

Johannes Aulen, a German sacred composer, was credited with the composition of a mass, "Officium Auleni." Otherwise he was unknown except for a motet published by Petrucci at this time.

Cardinal Pietro Bembo, an Italian poet as well, wrote Gli Asolani and dedicated it to Lucrezia Borgia. It was published in 1505 and was his most significant work.

Petrucci published a book of des Prés' masses.

A Dorian plainchant setting of the hymn, Ave maris stella provided the basis for des Prés' Mass of the same name that was published in 1505.

The Missa Hercules Dux Ferrariae, by des Prés, was an early work although it was not published until 1505. It contained a rigid cantus-firmus technique. Duke Hercules I died in this year and it was dedicated to him.

Des Prés' Missa Malheur me bat borrowed from a three-part chanson credited to Ockeghem. The composition was published in 1505.

Divitis was a singer in the

1505(cont.)

chapel of Philip the Handsome.

Marbriano de Orto was a singer in the chapel of Philip the Handsome.

Petrucci published a Kyrie de Beata Virgine by Marbriano de Orto (Fragmenta Missarum).

Pierre de la Rue visited Spain for a second time.

Petrucci published Fragmenta Missarum at Venice.

Petrucci published Frottole Lib. V at Venice.

Petrucci published "Motetti libro quarto;" and, a book, for five voices, "Motetti a cinque libro primo."

Petrucci published a volume of strambotti at Venice. The poems contained an eight line text with a rhyme scheme invented by Boccaccio in the fourteenth century, abababcc.

The strambotto, Me stesso incolpo, was anonymous and contained in Petrucci's Frottole Libro Quarto.

Petrucci published Motetti Libro Quarto. Sebald Heyden's De arte canendi contained an Ave mater omnium from the Motetti collection to serve as an example of Mode II.

Alfonso I of Ferrara, brother-in-law of the Italian Duke of Sora, offerred Brumel a position as maestro di cappella for life.

Luther narrowly escaped death when lightning struck a tree near to him. He decided at (cont.) that time to enter the Augustinian monastery in Erfurt.

Albrecht AltDorfer became a citizen of Ratisbon.

Perugino, Italian painter, was invited to Mantua.

Venetian painting: Giovanni Bellini, Madonna with Saints (Altar-painting in S. Zaccaria, Venice).

Venetian painting: Giovanni Bellini, "Saint Zachariah."

Renaissance sculpture: Anonymous, Head of Christ Crowned with Thorns.

Italian painting: Lotto, Portrait of Bernardo de'Rossi.

Renaissance drawing and painting: Raphael, Leaf from a sketch-book with four studies for painting, "The Virgin in the Meadow."

(to 1515) The classical era of Venetian painting began with Giorgione. He was considered to have been the motivating factor in the dramatic change.

c.1505

Thomas Tallis, "father" of English cathedral music, was born in Leicestershire (died 1585, November 23). He was organist at Waltham Abbey, Essex and became a Gentleman of the Chapel Royal.

Jachet Berchem, Netherlandish madrigal composer, was born in Flanders (died c.1563).

Louis Bourgeois, French composer and theorist, was born in

c.1505
Paris (died c.1560).

Claude Goudimel, Flemish composer who wrote numerous masses and chansons, was born (died 1572). He worked on a musical organization of the psalter.

Robert Granjon was born (date of death unknown). He was a type-founder and printer and one of the first to introduce round notes and oval-shaped notes. He also led the suppression of ligatures and proportion signs, which had made the old style notation so difficult to read.

Sebastian Tinódi, Hungarian poet and musician, was born (died 1556).

John Tuck transcribed a manuscript collection of Treatises on Music.

The cushion dance, an old English dance, was used particularly at weddings.

The sarabande was found in Europe at this time. The dance was performed in a way that indicated that its source may have been Oriental.

Afranio, who lived at this time, was a canon at Ferrara, and was credited with the invention of the bassoon. It stemmed from a wind instrument of his called the Phagotum.

The earliest surviving examples of lute tablature, which were Italian, first appeared at this time.

The organists of note at Esztergom were Brassó, (cont.) Valentin Klein and Grimpeck.

An ingenious but complex spring soundboard was discontinued because of frequent and difficult repairs. A soundboard with sliding registers was substituted.

The viol had become stable in construction by this time in the Netherlands and parts of Italy. The classifications were treble or discant viol, tenor viol, bass viol and double bass or violone.

The invention of music-printing was more helpful to Okeghem's pupils than to the composer himself.

Petrucci published frottole, villanelle, and other forms at this time.

The use of the bar line started at this time. Its object was to facilitate the reading of compositions written in score. The various parts were correctly placed under one another. Rhythmic division was not the goal although, of course, it was a fortunate by-product.

Ligatures were in common use but were not the same as those used in Palestrina's time.

L'Araldo was the first to eliminate songs in the rappresentazione.

Obrecht's Passio domini nostri Jesu Christi secundum Matthaeum was composed.

Ockenheim was apparently still alive at this time.

c.1505(cont.)

Senfl was at the Court of Munich "in musica totius Germaniae princeps;" here came Cipriano di Rore, Trajano, Venerolo and the peerless Orlando di Lasso, "Fürst und Phönix der Musiker."

By the time the Volkslied had attained its greatest splendor songs had been composed for almost every sentimental situation and every way of life.

The "Cinquecento" was the most magnificent period in Italian art.

At this time the fate of Lombardian art was decided by Leonardo's visit to Milan and to some extent by the proximity of Venice.

Netherlandish painting: Bosch, Christ Carrying the Cross.

Italian painting: Giorgione, The Tempest (32 1/4" x 28 3/4").

Italian painting: Raphael, The Madonna del Granduca.

1506

(April 8) Petrucci published Lamentations Jeremiae. Lib. I at Venice.

(May 9) Petrucci published Lamentations Jeremiae. Lib. II at Venice.

(June 8) Agricola's name was removed from the court rolls.

(October 20) Petrucci published Missae Henrici Izak (Heinrich Isaac) at Venice. A copy was preserved at the Lyceum Library at Bologna. It contained five four-part masses, Chargé de (cont.) deul, Misericordias domini, Quant j'ay au cor, La Spagna, and Comme femme.

Petrucci published Frottole. Lib VI at Venice.

Petrucci published Tinctoris' setting of the Lamentations.

Petrucci published two volumes of Lamentations with settings by Tinctoris, Ycaert, De Orto, Francesco (d'Ana) da Venezia, Johannes de Quadris, Agricola, Tromboncino, and Gaspar and Erasmus Lapicida at Venice.

Agricola entered the service of Duke Philip of Austria who was also sovereign of the Netherlands. Agricola went with him to Castile in this year.

On a second trip to Spain, Philip the Handsome died of a fever, and, in all probability, Agricola, who was with him, died from the same malady.

Richard Ede was commissioned to compose "a Mass with an Antiphona," to be sung at the University of Oxford on the day he received the degree of Bachelor of Music.

Finck was in the service of the Polish king (also in 1492 and 1501).

A seven-volume antiphonary was compiled. Four volumes survived at Gniezno in a manuscript.

Marbriano de Orto accompanied Philip the Handsome on a trip to Spain.

Pierre de la Rue was in the service of Margaret of Austria.

1506(cont.)

Crispin van Stappen was listed as a member of the Confraternity. This was, however, not necessarily evidence that he actually served the Confraternity.

A small collection of printed music, including copies of the "Silium Musice Plane" of 1506, and Wollick's "Enchiridion" (Paris, 1512), were preserved in Cologne, Germany.

Andrea Mantegna, Paduan painter, died (born 1431).

Sesshu, Japanese painter, died (born 1420).

Dürer travelled from Venice to Bologna "to be initiated in the secret art of perspective." The quotation was from a letter to a friend named Pirckheimer.

Dürer visited Italy, for the second time.

When the group of the Laocoon was discovered in 1506, artists and art lovers were overwhelmed by the effect of this tragic group.

The decision of Pope Julius II in 1506 to pull down the Basilica of St. Peter which stood at the place where St. Peter was supposedly buried was a dramatic one. He planned to have it rebuilt in a way contrary to traditions of church architecture.

Italian painting: Lotto, St. Jerome.

(to 1511) The capitulary acts of Bruges stated that Hellinck was a choirboy at St. Donation during these years. After his (cont.) voice changed he was transferred to another position.

(to 1514) Renaissance architecture: Bramante, Rome, St. Peter's (c.560'x560').

(to 1548) The Collegium Rorantistarum was founded at King Sigismund the Elder's chapel at Cracow during his reign.

c.1506

Spanish composer Alonso Mudarra, an instrumental composer, was born (died 1580, April 1).

Italian painting: Raphael, Portrait of Agnolo Doni.

(to 1510) Italian painting: Leonardo da Vinci, Madonna and St. Anne (5'7"x4'3").

1507

Valentin Bakfark, Hungarian lutenist, was born in Brassó, Roumania (died 1576, August 15 or 22).

Melchior Newsidler, German lutenist, was born (died 1590).

Hans Schütz reputedly died in Nürnberg(birthdate unknown).

The lauda, "Sancta Maria ora pro nobis," was attributed to Cara and Tromboncino.

Nicole de la Chesnaye's La Nef de Santé was published.

Des Prés' Laudate Dominum, composed at this time, was preserved in a manuscript (#42) at the Sistine Chapel.

Sebastian de Felstin, Polish theorist, enrolled as a student at the University of Cracow in

1507(cont.)

the liberal arts area.

King Louis XII of France praised Antoine de Févin's chansons in a letter from this date.

The Gafori codices contained nineteen Weerbecke motets. Sixteen of these comprised two cycles that belonged to a special type of mass. A separate mass was also published during this year.

Isaac wrote "Imperii proceres," "Sancti Spiritus assit," and "Substinuimus pacem" for the Imperial Diet of Constance.

Prioris was maître de chapelle for King Louis XII of France.

Adam Rener served the Elector of Saxony, Frederick the Wise, from this date to his death.

Richafort was director of the Chapel at St. Rombaut, in Malines.

Crispin van Stappen remained at the Papal Chapel except for a brief visit to Padua.

A collection of odes by Tritonius was one of the first musical publications in Germany. The publisher was Öglin.

Brumel composed the earliest recorded motet setting of a psalm, differing from the settings in fauxbourdon style. It was found in a manuscript from this date.

Petrucci reprinted Frottole Lib. II at Venice.

Petrucci published Frottole Lib. VII at Venice.

Petrucci published Frottole, Lib. VIII at Venice.

Petrucci published Intabulatura de Lauto. Lib. I at Venice.

Petrucci published Intabulatura de Lauto. Lib. II at Venice.

Petrucci published the oldest known ricercari. They were composed for the lute.

Petrucci published two lute books by Francesco Spinaccino of Fossombrone.

Petrucci published a book of five masses by Weerbecke titled Misse Gaspar.

The expense of double printing was solved by Erhard Öglin of Augsburg. He printed staff and notes simultaneously, thus improving Petrucci's method.

Italian tablature was already being printed.

Emperor Maximilian appointed Margaret of Austria as Regent of the Netherlands for her brother's infant son, who would later rule as Charles V.

Gentile Bellini, Italian painter, died (born 1429).

Rueland Frueauf the Elder, German painter, died (born c.1440).

Vignola, Italian architect, was born (died 1573).

German painting: Dürer, Adam and Eve.

(to 1508) The largest known collection of polyphonic laude of the time was contained in

1507(cont.)

Petrucci's Laude Libro primo (1508) and his Laude Libro secondo (1507).

(to 1512) Italian fresco: Michelangelo, The Creation of Eve (Sistine Chapel, Rome).

(to 1514) Pedro de Escobar, Spanish musician and possible composer of two movements of the Missa de Nuestra Señora, was active during these years.

(to 1516) Dionisio Memmo held the position of organist at St. Marks in Venice.

(to 1527) Louis van Pulaer was choir director at Notre Dame Cathedral in Paris.

(to 1539) Juan Escribano was a member of the Papal Choir.

(and 1617) A small collection of early printed musical works, including the "Harmonie" by Tritonius (Augsburg, 1507) and the "Novus partus sive concertationes musicae" by Besardus (Augsburg, 1617), were preserved at Strassburg, Germany.

c.1507

Petrus Tritonius, German composer, set the odes of Horace secundum naturas et tempora syllabarum et pedum (according to the nature and time valve of the syllables and feet).

The first colophon by the printer Jodacus Badius Ascensius, of Paris, was the earliest authentic representation of a printing press.

1508

(March 15) Petrucci published (cont.) Missarum diversorum. Lib. I at Venice.

Hans Newsidler, a German lutenist, was born (died 1563).

Carpentras was in the papal choir under Julius II.

Claudin served Sainte Chapelle for a short time.

Joan Ambrosio Dalza included a few frattole in "Intabulatura di Lauto."

William Cornyshe took part in another court play, as evidenced by payment "To Mr. Kite, Cornishe, and other of the Chapell that played affore the King at Richmonte bl. 13s. 4d."

Basiron's "Messa de franza" was published.

Franchino Gafore wrote "Angelicum et divinum opus musice" in Italian at Milan.

The Cathedral Chapter at Constance commissioned Isaac's Choralis Constantinus to be the first polyphonic setting of the complete Propers of the Mass to include the whole church year.

John Mason, Bachelor of Music, was appointed clerk of Magdalen College, Oxford.

Sermisy was appointed a Royal Chapel singer for Louis XII, and became sous-maître under Francis I.

A branch of the Paris Confraternity was established at Tours.

The dances of the seises were first recorded in the archives.

1508(cont.)

at Seville Cathedral but were referred to as established practice at that date.

The first Gregorian tunes with Hungarian texts were found in Nádor Codex.

Brumel was mentioned in literary works with Agricola, des Prés and others. These works included Crétin's Déploration on the death of Ockeghem, as well as the Livre de la Deablerie by Eloy d'Amerval.

Petrucci of Fossombrone published Basiron's Missa de Franza and several other masses.

Petrucci published a volume of sixty-six laude by Innocentius Dammonis.

Petrucci published Frottole. Lib. IX at Venice.

Petrucci published Intabulatura de Lauto. Lib. IV at Venice.

Petrucci attributed three motets to Isaac in his publication Motetti a cinque.

Petrucci, at Venice, published tablatures for lute that contained the earliest pavanes.

Mouton was at his peak when Petrucci began to publish music and the edition of five masses for four voices (1508) was an early example of an entire volume devoted to the works of one composer.

Petrucci published Missarum diversorum auctorum liber primus and in the volume included Weerbecke's Missa N'as tu pas (based on an anonymous (cont.) chanson that appeared in Canti C).

Conrad Celtes, German humanist and Latin poet, died (born 1459).

Perugino, Pinturicchio, and Sodoma (of Siena) began to decorate the Vatican "Stanze." The work was finally completed by Raphael.

Raphael was invited to Rome.

Titian worked with Giorgione.

German painting: Dürer, The Adoration of the Holy Trinity. This was one of his last paintings before he devoted himself chiefly to engraving.

(to 1512) Italian fresco: Michelangelo, Daniel (in the Sistine Chapel, Rome).

(to 1512) Italian painting: Michelangelo, Isaiah (larger than life-size).

(to 1512) Italian fresco: Michelangelo, Judith (in the Sistine Chapel, Rome).

(to 1512) Italian fresco: Michelangelo, Original Sin (in the Sistine Chapel, Rome).

(to 1512) Italian painting: Michelangelo, A section of the ceiling of the Sistine Chapel in the Vatican.

(to 1513) Carpentras was at the court of Louis XII at some time during this period.

(to 1513) Italian painting: Raphael, School of Athens (18'x26').

1508(cont.)

(to 1516) Castiglione wrote Il Libro del Cortegiano.

c.1508

Diego Pisador, Spanish composer and author of Libro de Musica de Vihuela, was born (died 1557).

Italian painting: Giorgione, Three Philosophers.

(to 1510) Italian painting: Giorgione, Sleeping Venus (3'7"x5'9").

1509

(February 12) John Mason was graduated from Magdalen College, Oxford. He was then appointed chaplain and teacher of choristers.

William Newark, an English composer of the early Tudor period, died (born c.1450).

The abbot John Dygon was succeeded by John Hampton. Dygon died during this year.

Petrucci reprinted Fragmenta Missarum at Venice.

Petrucci published a rare collection of Songs with Lute Accompaniment at Venice.

Petrucci published Tenori e contrebassi intabulati, Lib. I at Venice.

Mouton composed Non nobis, Domine, to the birth of Renée, second daughter of King Louis XII of France.

Richafort was succeeded by Noel Bauldeweyn as maître de chapelle at St. Rombaut in Malines.

Because of the crushing defeat of Venice by the League of Cambrai the area became antagonistic to and unfavorable for artistic achievement.

Van Weerbecke's name remained on the roster of singers at the Papal Chapel until this date.

John Calvin, Protestant religious leader, was born (died 1564). He by no means was favorably inclined toward music.

Israel van Meckenem, Flemish painter, died (birthdate unknown). In his Feast of Herodias he showed players using drums, fifes, and oliphants.

Hans Baldung was granted citizenship rights in Strassburg for the first time.

Lucas Cranach the Elder's first Venuses, painted in Leningrad, showed a classical quality.

Grünewald, German artist, was painter to the Court of the Elector and Archbishop of Mainz, Ulrich of Gemmingen.

Lorenzo Lotto, Italian painter, visited Rome.

Netherlandish painting: Gerard David, Virgo inter Virgines.

(and 1511) Petrucci published Franciscus Bossinensis' two books of frottole by Cara, Tromboncino, and others. They were transcribed for one voice and lute accompaniment. Short preludes for the lute, called ricercari, were added. The books were described as for "tenori e contrebassi intabulati col sopran in canto figurato per

1509(cont.)

cantar e sonar col lauto."

(to 1511) Renaissance architecture: Peruzzi, Villa Farnesina, Rome.

(to 1511) Italian painting: Raphael, La Disputa.

(and 1517) Some rare liturgical printed books, including a York Manuale (W. de Worde, 1509) and a York Missal (Rouen, 1517), were preserved in Minster library at Ripon.

(to 1522) Antoine de Longueval, also known as Johannes à la Venture, was in the service of both King Louis XII and King Francis I of France as maître de chapelle.

(to 1523) William Cornysh was Master of the Children at the Chapel Royal in England.

(to 1530) Gothic architecture: Tour de Beurre, Rouen (252' high).

(to 1547) The reign of King Henry VIII (House of Tudor) over England and Great Britain. He was left a relatively small, but flourishing, kingdom by his father, King Henry VII.

c.1509

Netherlandish painting: Gerard David, Rest on the Flght Into Egypt.

(to 1513) Finck was in the service of Duke Ulrich of Württemberg at Stuttgart.

1510

Antonio de Cabezón, Spanish composer and blind harpsichordist and organist to Charles V (cont.) and Phillip II, was born near Burgos (died 1566).

Andrea Calmo, poet and comedian, was born (died 1571).

Jacobus Clemens, non Papa, a Netherlandish composer in an advanced harmonic idiom with a clear style and expressive melodies, was born, probably on the island of Walcheren (died 1557).

Andrea Gabrieli, Venetian school composer of classical madrigals, was born in Venice (died 1586). He was a pupil of Willaert(see also c.1520).

Andrea Antico, a composer, Giovanni Battista Columba, an engraver, and Marcello Silber (Franck), a printer, produced the first published collection of frottole by Antico, "Canzoni nove con alcune scelte de varii libri di canto."

Francesco Canova da Milano was at Mantua, studying under Gian Angelo Testagrossa.

According to Drayton in the "Legend of Thomas Cromwell," (Stanza 29) catches were introduced in Italy by the Earl of Essex.

In a legal document Palestrina's paternal grandfather Pierluisci was referred to as "discretus vir," indicating the excellent reputation of the family.

Pierre de la Rue was at Malines and served in the chapel of Charles who was then only ten years old.

The Bishop required Virdung to send him the "Gedicht der

1510(cont.)

Deutschen Musica."

Current frottola collections showed a trend toward more serious forms, such as the canzone, oda, and sonnet.

Luigi Tansillo, a Neapolitan poet from Venosa, was born (died 1568).

Jacopo Bassano, Italian artist, was born (died 1592). His entire family were artists.

Botticelli, Florentine painter, died (born 1444).

Giorgione, Italian painter, died (born c.1478).

An illustration in Antico's Canzoni nove portrayed four singers using a choir-book.

An angel with a lute was pictured in a painting of a "Madonna" by Vittore Carpaccio in Venice.

Leonardo Da Vinci's anatomical studies of the larynx and leg were completed.

(to 1520) Fra Ruffino Bartolucci d'Assisi was maestro at the cathedral of Padua.

c.1510

Juan Bermudo, a Spanish author and Franciscan monk, was born near Astorga, Spain (date of death unknown).

Francesco Corteccia, Italian madrigal composer, was born in Arezzo (died 1571), see c.1520.

Bartolomé Escobedo, Spanish choir-master, was born in Zamora (died 1563).

Georg Forster, German composer, was born (died 1568), see c.1514.

Johannes Lupi, a member of the "wolfpack" and therefore part of the confusion of identity problem, was born (date of death unknown). This particular Lupi was a choirboy at Cambrai until 1526.

John Merbecke (Marbeck), eminent Protestant composer, was born (died c.1585) see also 1523.

Pierre Phalèse of Louvain, Franco-Flemish composer of chansons and lute music, was born (died c.1573).

Balthasar Resinarius, Protestant composer, was born at Hessen in the territory of Meissen (date of death unknown).

William Cornyshe, Jr., an English composer, was active at this time.

Richard Davy, an English composer, was active at this time.

Benedictus Ducis (Hertoghs) was a Flemish musician and organist of the Lady Chapel in the cathedral at Antwerp. He was referred to as "Prince de la Gilde" in the brotherhood of St. Luke in Antwerp.

Dunstable formed the only link between the early English school which produced the "Rota" and the later school which provided such men as Cornysshe, Fayrfax, and Pigot.

Robert Fayrfax supposedly held an appointment as organist or chanter of St. Alban's Abbey.

Petrucci produced a few works

c.1510(cont.)
in lute-tablature in Italy at this time.

Philippe Verdelot, Flemish composer, was most active at this time.

Canzoni alla Francese were popular in Italy at this time.

Although chanson composers of Paris school dominated the French musical scene their production served as a brief, but important, stage in the development of the chanson from des Prés to Lassus.

An Eton manuscript containing carols with smooth polyphony in duple meter and voices in pairs was preserved. The motet style of the Tudor period was strongly evident.

The University of Dublin was founded by Alexander de Bicknor, Archbishop of Dublin, however it disappeared about this time.

The rejection of the Lutheran concept of music in the Reformed Church began with Ulrich Zwingli.

The use of Plain Chaunt lamentations was discontinued, in the Pontifical Chapel, in order to accomodate a polyphonic setting by Elziario Genet, known by his Italian cognomen, Carpentrasso.

The Bowed instruments were divided in two important categories, viola da braccio and viola da gamba.

A type of harpsichord came into general use, and was known as the virginal.

The success of Belgian and Dutch lutenists led to their coming to England.

The organ and the lute created a definite need for a repertoire specifically for those instruments.

The lower C was reached by Lazarino.

Covered stops were first made in Germany.

The invention of the violin was attributed to Gaspar Duiffoprugcar, of Bologna.

A manuscript preserved at the British Museum contained excerpts of several chapters of the "Secundum Principale" written by a Fellow of New College, Oxford.

The St. Gall Codex #546 contained chiefly music for the ordinary of the mass and sequences. The latter were, however, inferior to Gregorian Chant at its peak.

Nicolas Du Chemin, a French music publisher, was born (died 1576).

The Latin language was still the accepted vehicle for expressing thoughts or ideas in England.

Social and political conditions in France stimulated the growth of secular music.

Lescot, French Renaissance architect, was born (died 1578).

Venetian painting:
Giovanni Bellini, Feast of the Gods.

Netherlandish painting: Bosch, Hell (right wing of a triptych).

c.1510(cont.)

Venetian painting: Vittore Carpaccio, Two Courtesans.

Italian painting: Giorgione, Pastoral Symphony (43¼"x54 3/8").

Italian painting: Giorgione, Pastoral Concert, also known as Concert. This picture was finished by Titian.

German painting: Hans Maler, Posthumous Portrait of Mary of Burgundy.

(to c.1550) Polish composers active during this time included a group known by their initials only, such as J.S., M.H., and N.C.

(to 1630) The younger composers who were growing up in artistic central and northern Italy concentrated on the composition of music particularly written for instruments. This culminated in the period of Italian organists comparable with the early school of organists and virginalists in the Tudor period in England.

1511

This was one of various dates given for the conferring of the degree of Doctor of Music on Robert Fayrfax by Oxford University.

Osbert Parsley, English composer and a contemporary of Tallis, was born (died 1585).

Johannes Tinctoris, composer and musicologist, died (born 1434).

Giorgio Vasari, Renaissance author, was born (died 1574).

Nicola Vicentino, a prominent pupil of Willaert's and a leader in the field of chromatic madrigals, was born (died 1572).

Gonzalo Martinez de Bizcargui's Arte de canto llano" was published at Burgos.

Petrucci moved to Fossombrone.

Virdung mentioned zymbeln and glocken together.

Arnold Schlick's "Spiegel der Orgelmacher und Organisten" was published. In it he mentioned three-part playing on the pedal. This was the first work on organ construction printed in German. It was published in Mainz, Germany.

"Musica getutscht" by Sebastian Virdung was published. It was the first book on instruments and tablatures written in German. There were illustrations of instruments included, also the fingerboard of the lute. The clavicytherium (upright harpsichord) and virginal were described and the steel stringing used on clavichords also.

Virdung and Schlick, in their essays, did not mention the spinet.

The earliest German tablature dated from this time.

Schöffer printed staff and notes simultaneously.

The current idea that the name virginal referred to the "maiden Queen Elizabeth" was disproved by the fact that the term was used in a book by Virdung and referred to the

1511(cont.)
instrument.

When the Medici were restored in 1511, the carnival did not regain its frivolous quality but rather became a sombre court ceremonial. The canti carnascialeschi also lost their previous style and became more literary in character.

Luther visited Rome.

German illustration: Horn, positiv organ and singers (frontispiece from "Spiegel der Orgelmacker" by Schlick.

Ammanati, Italian architect, was born (died 1592).

Sebastiano del Piombo left Venice for Rome.

(to 1514) Italian painting: Raphael, The Mass of Bolsena.

(to 1519) The violin was not mentioned in contemporary musical handbooks which carefully described the stringed instruments of the period. For this reason it may be assumed that it was rare at that time.

(to 1520) Venetian painting: Vittore Carpaccio, The Life of St. Stephen.

1512

(July 13) At Lincoln, Henry Byrde, former mayor of Newcastle, died and was buried in the Cathedral.

(April) John Dygon was granted the degree of Bachelor of Music at Oxford.

Gilles Mureau, Flemish composer, died (birthdate unknown).

Cavazzoni left Bologna and went to Urbino.

John Dygon, an English composer of three-part motets, was awarded the degree of Bachelor of Music from Cambridge University.

Gafori's "Practica Musicae utriusque Cantus" Augustinus de Zannis de Portesio was published at Venice.

Henricus Glareanus (Févin) was crowned poet-laureate at Cologne. The honor was bestowed for a poem in honor of the Emperor which he composed and accompanied himself.

John Hessebruch was organist at Cassel.

Johannes Prioris was still active.

Schlick achieved a transposition with the organ.

Schöffer published Schlick's "Tabulaturen etlicher lobgesang und lidlein uff die orgeln und lauten" at Mainz.

Sixtus IV built a special choir chapel for St. Peter's which was set up by Julius II. It was called the Capella Julia and replaced the old schola cantorum since it prepared singers for the Sistine Chapel. It was especially for the training of Italian singers, since the papal choir had been comprised of Flemish singers and other foreigners for many years.

Singers at the Poznań Cathedral were required to adopt the Cracow tradition.

Erhard Öglin published his

1512(cont.)

first collection of songs. He was court printer to Emperor Maximilian.

The Liederbuch printed from movable type by Erhard Öglin was probably the earliest German music printed by this method. It was also the first four part collection in German. It contained works by Hofhaimer, Isaac and Senfl, among others.

A small collection of printed music was preserved in Cologne, Germany. It included "Silium Musice Plane" (1506) and Wollick's "Enchiridion" (Paris, 1512).

When Michelangelo finished his work on the Sistine Chapel ceiling he eagerly returned to his project of building the tomb of Julius II.

(to 1516) Grünewald's masterpiece was the enormous altarpiece which he painted for the Antonites of Isenheim.

(to 1520) Pietro Bembo occupied the position of papal secretary in Rome.

(to 1525) Georg Kern was singing master at Cassel.

c.1512

Antoine de Févin, composer and singer known as Glareanus "felix Jodoci aemulator," died at Blois (born c.1480 or 1473).

1513

(October 22) Petrucci, now at Fossombrone, obtained a patent from Pope Leo X for a monopoly on music-printing in the Roman states for 15 years.

Domenico Maria Ferabosco, Italian ballota composer, was born (died 1574).

Francisco de Salinas, Spanish composer and author of De Musica Libri Septem, was born at Burgos (died 1590).

Ulrich Schütz III was born at Chemnitz (date of death unknown).

Antico held papal privileges for a serious competitor of Petrucci.

Calandria, a comedy by Cardinal Bibbiena, was produced at Urbino with finely mounted intermezzi.

The "Cappella Giulia" was founded for service at the basilica.

Carpentras became maestro di cappella under Leo X who held him in high esteem.

Cavazzoni followed Bembo to Rome.

Benvenuto Cellini became a member of a band at Florence in which his father played piffara. He was at this time thirteen years old.

Jacques Champion of Liége succeeded Bauldeweyn at Malines.

Finck was at the court of Maximillian I in Augsburg.

"Lupus," according to Galilei, journeyed from the Franco -Netherlandish area to Italy. He was by this time a musician of good reputation and went because of the court of Pope Leo X.

Hall wrote: "On the daie of the

1513(cont.)

Epiphanie at night, the Kyng with a. xi. other were disguised, after the maner of Italie, called a maske, a thyng not seen afore in Englande . . . "

Mouton was a member of the chapel of Louis XII.

A famous organ existed with distinctive registers for the Martinsstift.

Isaac's early relations with the Medici were indicated by a six-part motet, Optime pastor, written for the celebration of the accession of Leo X. The latter was a son of Lorenzo, the Magnificent and had studied with Isaac at an earlier date.

The "Lament for Flodden" was written.

Petrucci published Missa Choralis at Fossombrone.

There were 4-part German songs by Virdung in the rare collection of Peter Schoeffer at Munich.

Bernardino Pinturicchio, Italian painter, died (born c.1454).

Venetian painting: Giovanni Bellini, St. John Chrysostom.

(to 1515) Leonardo da Vinci lived in Rome.

(to 1515) Italian painting, Leonardo da Vinci, Mona Lisa.

(to 1515) Italian sculpture: Michelangelo, Moses (8'4").

(to 1518) Noel Bauldeweyn received the post of maître de (cont.) chapelle at Our Lady in Antwerp.

(to 1521) The Papal reign of St. Leo X (born in Florence).

(to 1532) A collection of Hans Kotter carried the date 1513 on the title page. However, the last composition was dated 1532. The volume contained sixty-seven pieces including works by Barbireau, Buchner, des Prés, Dietrich, Hofhaimer, Isaac, Martini, and Moulu. Several of Kotter's own compositions were included as well.

c.1513

Giovanni Contino, choirmaster and possible teacher of Marenzio, was born at Brescia. Most of his productive years were spent at Trent (died 1574).

The Melody of "The Flowers of the Forest" was composed.

Italian painting: Raphael, Portrait of Bindo Altoviti.

1514

(March 1) Petrucci reprinted Missarum Josquin, Volume I and III at Fossombrone.

Hartmann Schedel, German doctor and historian, died (born 1440).

Petrucci published a second book of des Prés' masses. He had published a previous volume in 1505.

The earliest recorded of des Prés' psalms was in Book I of Petrucci's Motetti de la Corona, published in this year. The volume included Memor esto verbi tui (Psalm CXVIII 119). The volume also included

1514(cont.)

Laudate Dominum.

A four-part motet, by Antonius Divitis, "Desolatorum consolator," was included in the first book of the "Motetti della corona" published by Petrucci at Fossombrone or Venice. A conflict exists as to the location.

Six motets by Antoine Févin were included in the first volume of "Motetti della corona."

Petrucci published his eleventh collection of fróttole.

Two motets by Eleazar Genet (Carpentras) appeared in the first and third books of the "Motetti della Corona."

Andreas de Silva, in the service of the Duke of Mantua, was represented by a single motet in Motetti de la corona, Book I.

Castiglione's "Corteggiano" for soloist over chorus was composed.

Des Prés' Missa de Beata Virgine was published.

Des Prés Missa Mater Patris was published.

The Erfurt Enchiridion, a setting of the song "Aus tiefer Not," was composed.

Mouton's "Quis dabit oculis" was composed as a lament on the death of Queen Anne of Bretagne (Renée's mother).

Theoretical treatises started to appear in Poland, in printed versions. The Algorithmus Proportionum by (cont.) Henricus Scriptor (Erfurt) was published at Cracow.

Juan de Espinosa's Retractiones de los errores was published at Toledo.

Costanzo Festa's first known work appeared at this time.

Pope Leo X.'s Master of Ceremonies, Paride Grassi, stated that the Miserere was first sung to a fauxbourdon.

Morales studied at Seville cathedral.

Van Weerbecke was still referred to as "Cantor Capelle pape" at the time of his entry into the confraternity of the German Campo Santo at Rome (1514).

The title of "roi des ménestrels" was changed to "roi des ménestrels du royaume."

(to 1516) Books of masses in the Vienna library contained three by "Anthonius Fevin, pie memorie." Ambros proved that these books were written during this period.

(to 1519) Petrucci published a total of four volumes of Motets, known (from a figure engraved on the title page) as the "Motetti della Corona."

(to 1522) Penet, a cleric at Poitiers, was a singer for Pope Leo X.

(to 1522) Antonio de Ribera was a member of the Papal Choir.

(to 1574) Pedro Fernandez de Castilleja served at Seville Cathedral as "maestro de los

1514 (cont.)

moços."

c.1514

Georg Forster, Nuremberg physician, composer, and humanist, was born (died 1568), see c.1510.

Caspar Tieffenbrucker of Lyons was born (died 1571). He was a member of the famous family of instrument makers.

Donato Bramante, Renaissance architect and painter, died (born 1444).

German painting: Dürer, Portrait of his mother.

Dutch painting: Quentin Matsys, The Moneylender and his wife (28"x26 3/4").

Italian painting: Raphael, Galatea (c.7'4"x9'7").

Italian painting: Titian, Sacred and Profane Love.

(to 1516) Benedictus de Opitiis was organist at Our Lady in Antwerp during these years.

1515

(April 11) Petrucci reprinted Missarum Josquin, Lib. II at Fossombrone.

(August 11) Petrucci published Missarum Joannis Mouton Lib. I at Fossombrone.

(November 22) Petrucci published Missae Antonii de Févin at Fossombrone.

Antoine de Févin, composer of Missa Mente tota, died (born 1473 or c.1480; see also c.1512).

Aldus Manutius, Venetian printer (cont.) of first editions of Greek and Latin classics, died (born 1450).

St. Philip Romolo de' Neri, a priest highly involved in ethical matters of the period, was born (died 1595).

Caspar Othmayr, German Protestant Composer, was born (died 1553).

Clement Jannequin's "La Bataille" was written to immortalize and describe the battle of Marignan, between the French and Swiss.

Clement Marot, a French poet, wrote Epitre des dames de Paris.

Mathias' "Battaglia" was similar to Jannequin's "Bataille" except that it was based on the victory of Francis I over Swiss mercenaries at Marignano. Mathias' composition became famous in Italy and inspired the Italians in the hope that they could defeat the French.

Nachtgall's "Musicae Institutiones" was published at Strassburg.

Archduke Charles made an impressive entry into Antwerp with Maximilian, Benedictus de Opitiis wrote two works, Sub tuum praesidium and Summae laudis, o Maria in honor of the grandfather and grandson on this occasion.

The Great Bells of Brunn (5 ts., 10 cw.).

Richard Davy after several years at Oxford became chaplain to Sir William Boleyn, the grandfather of Anne (1501), and

1515(cont.)

continued with them until this date.

Des Prés remained at the court of Louis XII until the latter's death.

Des Prés probably went from the service of Louis XII to Maximilian, who acquired the Netherlands at this time.

Antonius Divitis was a member of the chapel of Louis XII of France at this time (the year of the King's death).

Benedictus Ducis, Flemish composer, left Antwerp.

Henricus Glareanus, Netherlandish composer, was teaching mathematics at Basle.

At the time of the festivities for the double wedding of Maximilian's grandson and granddaughter to the daughter and son of King Wladislaus II of Hungary at Vienna, Hofhaimer was Knighted by the King and raised to the nobility by Emperor Maximilian.

Isaac was permitted to move to Florence, although he was still being paid by Maximilian.

The first military signals handed down in notation were found in Jannequin's "La Bataille."

Dionisio Memo, a Venetian organist, was so successful that Henry granted him a prebend.

Archduke Charles, the future Charles V, appointed de Orto as his first chaplain.

Petrucci published a book of five masses containing three by Antoine Févin, "Sancta Trinitas," "Mente tota," and "Ave Maria" at Fossombrone.

Petrucci published Missarum X. Libri duo at Fossombrone.

Petrucci published a book of five Masses by Mouton.

Senfl was court composer to Maximilian I.

Claudin de Sermisy accompanied King Francis I to Italy and later lived at the court of the Duke of Ferrara.

Boemus' "Augustae Vindelicorum" was published.

Roger Ascham, English writer and scholar at the court of Henry VIII, Edward VI, Mary and Elizabeth, was born at Yorkshire (died 1568).

Charles V had been declared to be legally of age.

France moved strongly toward the Renaissance movement after Francis I ascended the throne.

As the result of a meeting between King Francis I and Pope Leo X at Bologna, musicians attached to both courts joined one another in a performance. However, details of the program were never found.

St. Theresa of Jesus was born at Old Castile, in the diocese of Avila (died 1582).

Lucas Cranach the Younger, German painter, was born (died 1586).

1515(cont.)

Fra Giocondo, Renaissance architect, died (born c.1433).

Hans Holbein the Younger was at Basle.

P. Lombardo, Renaissance architect, died (born c.1435).

Gerard David, Netherlandish painter, joined the guild at Antwerp where he met Quentin Massys.

Joachim Patenir, Netherlandish painter, settled at Antwerp and joined the guild there.

Renaissance architecture: Chenonceaux, Château.

Renaissance architecture: London, Hampton Court, Palace.

Italian painting: Raphael, Sistine Madonna.

(to 1519) Renaissance architecture: Blois, Château, Francis I wing.

(to 1520) Dürer executed woodcuts for Emperor Maximilian.

(to 1526) The most famous man who held the title of Maestro della Cappella Pontificia was Elziario Genet, of Carpentras, "Vescovoin in partibus" who was named after his birthplace, Carpentrasso.

(to 1547) The reign of King Francis I (House of Valois) over France.

c.1515

Carols in the works of Richard Pygott and others were composed in imitative counterpoint, a style that led directly (cont.) to the carol motets of Byrd.

Delorme, French Renaissance architect, was born (died 1570).

German painting: Grünewald, The Crucifixion and the Resurrection (from the Isenheim Altar).

German painting: Grünewald, St. John the Evangelist, The Virgin and St. Mary Magdalen (from the Crucifixion, Isenheim Altarpiece).

German painting: Grünewald, St. John the Baptist (from the Crucifixion, Isenheim Altarpiece).

German painting: Grünewald, Virgin (from the Angel Concert, Isenheim Altarpiece).

Netherlandish painting: Mabuse, St. Luke painting the Virgin.

Italian painting: Raphael, St. Cecilia.

(to 1520) Willaert's six-part masses included a Missa Mente tota (probably written during these years).

(to 1610) The French literary Renaissance embraced these years.

1516

(May 29) Petrucci reprinted Missarum Josquin (Lib. I and III) at Fossombrone.

(October) Ornithoparcus, German theorist, was connected with the University of Würtenburg.

John Foxe, an English author of Actes and Monuments, was born (died 1587).

1516(cont.)

Cipriano de Rore, Flemish composer of classic madrigals and pupil of Willaert, was born (died 1565).

Fra Armonio was second organist at St. Marks in Venice.

Pietro Aron, Renaissance theorist, wrote "De Institutione Harmonica," his only treatise written in Latin.

Benedictus de Opicijs was organist at Notre Dame Cathedral in Antwerp. The cathedral archives stated that he went to England in February of this year and the Chapel Royal archives showed that a Benet de Opicijs was appointed court organist to Henry VIII in March, 1516.

Ariosto wrote Orlando furioso, a 40-canto version of which was published in this year. These stanzas were used by composers to teach the musical madrigal "to express passion and ardour."

A book on music by Cochlaeus was published.

Henricus Glareanus' principal treatises on music theory included "Isagoge in musicen Henrici Glareani," which carried the dedication, "ad Falconem Consulem urbis Aventinensis," and was headed, "Basileae, anno Christi 1516, 4to. ad idus Martias."

Ornithoparcus' "Musicae Activae Micrologus" was published at Leipzig.

Ornithoparchus dedicated the second book of his Micrologus, published at Leipzig in this (cont.) year, to Jörg Brack.

A collection contained music by Richard Sampson, dean of the Chapel Royal. There were several anonymous motets in the Flemish style and one motet was signed by Benedictus de Opicijs.

A motet by Richard Sampson, Quam pulchra es, was preserved. It carried this date and contained extensive imitation, combined with clear harmonic writing, which proved to be the style of Taverner.

Tromboncino set Petrarch's "Hor che'l ciel e la terra."

Petrucci published Missarum Josquin, Liber III.

When King Ferdinand died (1516) the future emperor, Charles V, came from the Netherlands and assumed rule. He brought Netherlandish customs and an entire capilla flamenca with him and reigned as King of Spain(birthdate unknown).

Queen Mary I, Bloody Mary (House of Tudor) of England and Great Britain, was born (died 1558).

Giovanni Bellini, Venetian painter, died (born 1430).

Hieronymus Bosch, Netherlandish painter, died (born c.1450).

(to 1518) Benedictus de Opitiis was organist to King Henry VIII in England.

(to 1518) A large organ was erected at St. Mary's church in Lübeck. It had two manuals from D to A above the treble staff, and a separate pedal

1516(cont.)

down to C.

(to 1519) Jacotin Level was a singer in the Papal Chapel.

(to 1520) Heinricus (=Wolf Heintz?) was organist at Magdeburg Cathedral.

(to 1757) A Flemish family of bell founders named Van Den Gheyn was inscribed on bells in the chimes of Malines and Louvain with dates ranging throughout this period.

c.1516

Pietro Aron founded a school of music in Rome.

Francisco de Peñalosa continued in the Chapel Royal in Spain until this time.

Des Prés was appointed canon of the Collegiate Church at Condé.

Hans Judenkunig, a lutenist, published an Utilis et compendiosa introductio (Useful and Comprehensive Introduction for Lutes and Viols) in Vienna.

The Italians replaced wooden blocks with hand-engraved metal plates, still used today.

Hans Baldung painted the main altarpiece of the cathedral in Freiburg. It was finished in this year.

Italian sculpture:
Michelangelo, The Dying Slave (Marble statue destined for the tomb of Pope Julius II).

1517

(October 31) Martin Luther entered the great conflict by posting his famous Ninety-five (cont.) theses on the doors of the Würtenburg Church. Music became an important solace and inspiration to him.

(January) The Micrologus by Ornithoparcus was published at Leipzig.

Jobst von Brandt, Lutheran composer, was born (died 1570).

Heinrich Isaac, leading Netherlandish composer, died in Florence (born c.1450).

Antonio Scandello, an Italian Protestant composer who lived in Germany, was born (died 1580).

Pedro Alberch Vila (Vich) was born near Barcelona (died 1582). He was reputedly one of the finest Spanish musicians of his time.

Gioseffo Zarlino, prominent Italian theorist and pupil of Willaert, was born at Chioggia (died 1590). He succeeded de Rore as chapel-master at St. Marks in Venice, but his greatest contribution was the evolvement of the major triad from the overtone series as well as the minor triad from equal divisions of a string giving the inverted harmonic series.

Noel Bauldeweyn remained maître de chapelle at Our Lady in Antwerp until this year.

Bártfa, Hungary had an organ.

Cavazzoni was in Venice where he was employed by Francesco Cornaro, nephew of the Queen of Cyprus.

Festa became a singer in the Papal Chapel of Pope Leo X

1517(cont.)

and stayed there until his death in 1545.

Henricus Glareanus was appointed a professor of philosophy and "artes liberales" at Paris on the recommendation of Erasmus.

An Antoine de Longueval was mentioned as maître de chapelle.

Peñalosa was mentioned as a chorister in Rome in letters from Leo X. He was described as exercising his art "with great prudence and probity."

The oldest printed Italian organ music was at this time.

Antico published his Frattole intabulate da sonare organi.

William Cornysh wrote the Garden of Esperance, which was produced at this time, and described in Hall's Chronicle.

In Musice active Micrologus by Ornithoparcus, published at Leipzig in January, he set laws for strict counterpoint. Combinations of mode, time and prolation produced complicated forms which changed from era to era and presented a problem to the author. He described eight combinations of proportion, all with analogies in "modern music."

The "large" and "long" are no longer in use since they are not expressable in modern notation. A copy of this work was preserved in the library at Bonn, Germany.

Tromboncino's music for Orlando's lament, "Queste non son più lagrime che fuore" was published.

A York Missal (Rouen, 1517) and a York Manual (W. de Worde, 1509) were preserved at Ripon.

Sir Thomas More wrote "Utopia."

(to 1518) Pierre de la Rue spent the last two years of his life at Courtrai.

(and 1519) The setting of the first stanza of Petrarch's "Canzone x in vita di Madonna Laura, Se'l pensier che-mi strugge" by Carpentras and Maio in 1517 and 1519 was an outstanding work.

(to 1522) Glareanus, impressed by Mouton's music, wrote that it was "in the hands of everyone." He met the latter at court during this period.

(to 1526) Johann Walter sang in the court choir of Frederick the Wise of Saxony.

(to 1565) The Early Roman School of composition was during this period.

c.1517

Huberto Waelrant, a Flemish theorist, was born (died 1595). He introduced a system called "Bocedisation," ("Bobisation") founded on seven syllables, Bo, Ce, Di, Ga, Lo, Ma, Ni, at Antwerp. These have since been called "Voces Belgicae."

Franceso Portinaro, Italian madrigalist, was born in Padua (date of death unknown). He was associated with the Este family and with accademie in Padua.

Arnold Schlick, German composer, died (born c.1460), see also c.1527 and c.1450.

c.1517(cont.)

Henry Howard, Earl of Surrey, English poet, was born (died 1547).

Italian keyboard compositions became plentiful around this time when Antico's Frottole intabulate da sonare organi appeared at Rome.

The Epithoma utriusque musices practice by Stephanus Monetarius of Körmöczbánya (Kremnica) was published at Cracow.

German painting: Hans Baldung, Death and the Lady.

German painting: Lucas Cranach the Elder, Portrait of a Saxon Prince.

(to 1520) Two motets by Richard Sampson survived in manuscript from these years. One was a four-part Psallite felices, supposedly written in honor of Henry VIII, and a five-part Quam polchra es.

1518

Nicola Burzio, Italian composer, died (born 1450).

Loyset Compére, French composer, died at St. Quentin (born 1450).

Girolamo Falletti, author on musical subjects, was born (died 1564).

Pierre de la Rue, French composer, died (born c.1450).

Ariosto's I Suppositi was produced for Pope Leo X with intermezzi that used cornetti, lutes, organ, viols, and voices. The scenery was designed by Raphael.

A book on Gregorian chant by Ulrich Burchard was published.

Carpentras was made Bishop in partibus by Leo X.

John Charde was requested "to put into the hands of the Proctors" a mass and antiphon which he had composed and also to compose an additional five-part mass on "kyrie rex splendens."

A letter written by the composer Sixt Dietrich to the humanist Bonifaz Amerbach contained an apology for changing the music of a song "since it did not easily lend itself to quadration."

A book by Duran was published by Cromberger.

Gafori's treatise on instruments "De harmonia musicorm instrumentorum was published in Milan.

J. Charlier de Gerson's "Beschreibung Musikalischer Instrumente" was published in Basle.

Sacred works by the earlier J. Lupi were included in a manuscript preserved at Bologna.

Queen Mary of Hungary sent four lute players to the wedding of Bona Sforza to Sigismund I of Poland, the king's uncle.

Tromboncino's setting, of a poem by Michelangelo, Come haro dunque ardire was published.

Willaert went to Rome.

The four-part Nobis Sancti Spiritus was contained in a manuscript at Bologna known as

1518(cont.)

the Rusconi manuscript, by Agricola.

A marked rise of Calvinism occurred in German-speaking sections of Switzerland.

Andrea Palladio, Italian architect, was born (died 1580).

Jacopo Robusti, known as Tintoretto, Italian artist, was born (died 1594).

Grünewald, German painter, entered the service of Archbishop Albrecht of Brandenburg who was elevated to Cardinal at this time.

Italian sculpture: Stucco relief of members of Raphael's workshop plastering, painting and decorating the Loggie (Vatican Loggie).

German etching: Dürer, The Cannon.

Italian painting: Titian, The Assumption of the Virgin.

(to 1523) Italian painting: Titian was commissioned to do the mythological series "Bacchanals" by Alfonso d'Este. They showed magnificent "joie de vivre."

(to c.1545) Gothic-Renaissance architecture: The choir of St. Pierre in Caen (designed by Pierre Sohier, and built during this period).

c.1518

Carpentras became the Pope's Chapel-master.

Italian painting: Raphael, Pope Leo X with two Cardinals.

(to 1537) Renaissance architecture: Antonio da Sangallo the Elder, Montepulciano, San Biagio (c.120'x120').

1519

(October 31) Petrucci published the fourth volume of the "Motetti della Corona" at Fossombrone.

(January) Ludwig Senfl was chapelmaster at the Court of Maximilian I until the emperor's death during this year. He wrote music to the words "Quis dabit oculis nostris fontem lacrimarum" to commemorate Maximilian's death.

Thoinot Arbeau, French writer on dance forms, was born (died 1595).

Théodore de Beze (Beza), the poet, was born (died 1605). He translated the psalter and was highly respected by Calvin.

John Colet, an English professor of exegetics at Oxford and one of the leaders of the humanist movement, died (birthdate unknown).

William Grocyn, early scholar and teacher of Greek at Oxford, died (birthdate unknown).

Juan de Anchieta, Spanish sacred composer, was pensioned and retired from service by Charles V.

Carest was accepted as an apprentice painter of clavecins.

Jacques Champion of Liége left the position of maître de chapelle at St. Rombaut in Malines.

Anthony Duddyngton of London

1519(cont.)

contracted to build an organ for All-Hallows, Barking, for the sum of £50.

Encina, composer of music for pastoral plays, was ordained. He made a pilgrimage to the Holy Land, and while there celebrated his first mass in Jerusalem. When he returned to Rome he published an account of his trip.

Gallus, an organ builder in Kassa, was mentioned at this time.

Hoffhaimer became organist in the cathedral at Salzburg after Maximilian's death.

Three motets attributed to Noel Bauldeweyn were contained in Petrucci's Motetti de la Corona, Book IV. One is the O pulcherrima mulierum that was credited to Févin in another source.

Petrucci published four books in the series "Motetti de la corona," at Fossombrone.

Petrucci published des Prés' Miserere (Psalm L 51) which was written for Duke Hercules I.

Jhan Gero's earliest known work was a motet, "Benignissime Domine Jesu." It was included in the "Motetti della Corona."

Petrucci published a Postquam consummati sunt which he attributed to "Lupus."

Georg Rhaw wrote a twelve-part mass, De Sancto Spiritu, in Leipzig. It was composed and performed on the occasion of Luther's debate with Dr. Eck.

Andreas de Silva was a singer in the Papal Choir. He was referred to in the records as "our composer."

The court choir in Denmark was made up of eighteen singers.

During this year the earliest specification for an English organ appeared.

A German translation of the Bohemian-Moravian Brethren's songbook was written.

An entry in accounts of St. Mary at Hill, London, recorded the occasion for which the loan of an organ was received: "1519. For bringing the organs from St. Andrew's Church, against St. Barnabas' eve, and bringing them back again, vd."

King Henry II (House of Valois) of France was born (died 1559).

Leonardo da Vinci, Italian painter, died (born 1452).

Anthonis Mor Van Dashorst, known as Antonio Moro, Spanish style painter, was born (died 1575).

Correggio settled in Parma, where he experimented with new ideas.

German painting: Dürer, Virgin and Child with St. Anne.

Netherlandish painting: Bernard Van Orley, Portrait of the Doctor Georg Van Zelle.

(to 1520) George Rhaw was Cantor at the St. Thomas School in Leipzig.

(to 1526) Pedals were known as "player keys" in England.

1519(cont.)

(to 1528) Italian painting: Titian, Madonna with Saints and members of the Pesaro family.

(to 1590) Jhan Gero's madrigals and motets appeared in various collections printed during this period.

c.1519

Giulio Fiesco, Italian madrigalist, was born (date of death unknown).

Mensural treatises, Opusculum musices by Sebastian de Felstin and Epithoma utriusque musices practice by Stephanus Monetarius of Kremnica, Slovakia, were published at Cracow.

German painting: Grünewald, St. John the Evangelist (detail from A Crucifixion).

1520

(February 19) Senfl received a gift of 50 gulden from Charles V.

(June) Fayrfax' name headed the list of Singing Men of the Chapel at the Field of the Cloth.

(November) Senfl edited the "Liber selectarum Cantionum." This was the first book of Latin motets by German composers. The collection which contained five works by Isaac was published at Augsburg by Wyrsung. A copy has been preserved in the Littleton collection.

Adam Rener, Netherlandish composer, died (born c.1485).

Bernard Schmit the elder, "composer of the colorist school," was born (died 1590).

Welcker described the oldest clavichord he knew as having the date 1520 in the soundhole and in the four octaves on the instrument the notes D# and G# were missing.

A well-known Posaunen-macher (trombone-maker) named Hans Menschel, made slide trombones at least as well as those made in the early twentieth century.

The authenticity of any date of manufacture in a violin before this time was dubious.

It has been claimed that three violins made by Duiffoprugcar, carrying a date prior to this, were preserved.

Antico published two collections of chansons. Three of Janequin's works were included.

A des Prés' setting of the De profundis (Psalm CXXIX 130) was published and also appeared in the Dodecachordon. It was an important one because of the clefs used as well as for its music quality.

Gafori's "Apologia adversus Spatarium" was written at Turin.

Peutinger published a collection of motets for five voices at Augsburg. This was in the form of wood-engraving.

Peutinger's preface to the "Liber Selectarum Cantionum quas vulgo Mutetas appellant, sex, quinque, et quatuor vocum" showed his devotion to music. Latin motets by des Prés, Isaac, Obrecht, de la Rue and Senfl were among the composers whose words were included (see

1520(cont.)

November 1520).

Petrucci published Missae Choral III at Fossombrone.

Petrucci published Musica di messer Bernardo Pisano sopra le canzone de Petrarcha which placed "the lofty poetry of Petrarch" in a "rich garb of motet-like polyphony.

Tromboncino's music for Orlando's lament originally published in 1517 was reprinted. It was now arranged for voice and lute.

Werrecore composed the Bataglia Taliana to honor Sforza's great victory.

Willaert's earliest chansons, appearing in the Motetti novi et chanzoni franciose . . . sopra doi of 1520, indicated a close relationship with Mouton and revealed Netherlandish influence to some degree.

Fayrfax' last public appearance was as leader of Henry VIII's musical delegation at the Field of the Cloth of Gold.

Gombert formulated the final classical language and style of Netherlandish polyphony. He was a singer in the chapel choir at Brussels at this time.

Senfl completed Isaac's Choralis Constantinus at Augsburg.

Sermisy was one of the musicians present when Francis I and Henry VIII met at the Field of the Cloth of Gold.

Charles V, while still an archduke, travelled to England with (cont.) his chief musician Henri Bredeniers.

Charles V was proclaimed Emperor at Aix-la-Chapelle.

Raphael(Sanzio), Italian painter of great renown, died (born 1483).

Andrea Solario, Italian painter, died (born c.1460).

Dürer made a tour of the Netherlands during which all painters paid homage to him. He made some fine silverpoint drawings while on the trip.

(to 1521) Cavazzoni was in the service of Pope Leo X.

(to 1526) Vaet was attached to the imperial Kapelle at Vienna holding the position of chanter and probably also of court -composer. During this period he wrote a motet, "in laudem serenissimi principis Ferdinandi archiducis Austriae."

(to 1530) Many compositions were published under the title of canzone. They were actually rather more madrigals.

(to 1540) German painting: Cranach the Elder, Portrait of a Little Girl (quite possibly Luther's daughter).

(to 1557) Thomas Crecquillon, was essentially a Netherlandish chanson composer during this period.

(to 1590) The last Netherlandish School of composition was during these years.

(to 1600) "Mannerism" was assumed to describe a complex trend

1520(cont.)

which emerged during these years and was contemporary with a series of significant events including the Reformation, the Counter-Reformation and the establishment of authoritarian governments in Italy linked with Spain and the Empire.

(to 1625) The early school of anthem writing during this period included composers such as Byrd, Gibbons, Tallis and Tye.

c.1520

Girolamo Cavazzoni, Italian keyboard composer, was born (date of death unknown).

Francesco Corteccia, an Italian madrigal composer, was born in Arezzo (died 1571), see c.1510.

Mateo Flecha the Younger, Spanish madrigalist, was born at Prades (died 1604).

Miguel de Fuenllana, vihuela virtuoso and composer, was born at Madrid (date of death unknown).

Andrea Gabrieli, pupil of Willaert and successor of Merulo as organist at St. Mark's in Venice, was born (died 1586).

Vincenzo Galilei, Italian madrigal composer and father of the astronomer, was born at Florence (died 1591).

Costanzo Porta, Italian sacred composer, was born at Cremona (died 1601), see also 1530.

Bernhard Schmid the Elder, instrumental dance composer, was born (died 1590 or c.1596).

John Shepherd, a prominent (cont.) English sacred composer, was born (died c.1563). He served in the Chapel Royal during Queen Mary's reign.

Waclaw Szamotulczyk, Polish composer, was born (died 1572).

Music of Robert Carver, a Scottish monk from Scone Abbey, was preserved in Scotland's National Library.

A setting of the passion, "turba" included choruses composed by the Englishman, Richard Davy.

Johannes Lupi was an outstanding and typical representative of the chanson of this time.

Queen Mary, a pupil of the organist, Bredemers, and King Louis II were skilled instrumentalists. The Queen was a virginalist and the King, a lutenist.

Dominique Phinot, a composer of music for double chorus, was a native of southern France and northern Italy.

A two-line fragment from this date composed by Philip Pominoczky, a Minorite Priest, was the only surviving Hungarian folk-music of the time. It was noted on the inside of his Manuale cover.

The derivation of the word spinet was from spina, a thorn, mentioned in Scaliger's Poetices.

Antico apparently was at Venice where he and Ottaviano Scotto jointly released several printings.

The basse danse, a ceremonial dance of the Burgundian court,

c.1520(cont.)

was replaced by the pavane, a courtly Spanish dance.

A German manuscript of a "Spanyöler Tancz" was written at this time.

The Glogauer Book was the last large collection of German secular polyphony until this time.

The transition from the song form to the motet form was one of the greatest revolutions in musical history.

The newly developed art of printing was applied to polyphony to a large degree.

The usual range of the virginal was from F to a''' , but at the zenith of the period, it was from A to c

François Clouet, French painter, was born (died 1572).

Gothic architecture:
Compton Wyngates (facade c.120' long).

Art-connoisseurs in Italian cities more or less agreed that painting had reached the peak of perfection.

Netherlandish painting:
Joachim Patenir, Flight Into Egypt.

Netherlandish painting:
Joachim Patenir and Quentin Massys, Temptation of St. Anthony.

Italian painting:
Palma Vecchio, Portrait of a Lady.

French painting: Unknown French (cont.) master, Group of Feminine Musicians.

(to 1539) Mathias Werrecore, a Doppelmeister, wrote three villotte that Gardano published with the "Battaglia."

1521

(August 27) Josquin des Prés died at Condé, Belgium (born c.1450). At the time of his death he held the position of provost at Condé Cathedral.

Any compromise between Luther's followers and the Roman Catholic Church became impossible after this date.

Antonio Altoviti, Italian madrigalist, was born (died 1571).

Robert Fayrfax, English Tudor secular composer, died (born c.1465).

Philippe da Monte, a leading polyphonic composer, was born in Malines, Belgium (died 1603). His works included masses, motets, madrigals and chansons in prolific quantity. He had a close affiliation with Lassus and they worked together to achieve a final synthesis in the field of polyphony.

Josquin was canon at St. Gudule in Brussels as well as provost of the chapter at Condé.

Fayrfax was a member of the Chapel Royal during much of his life and his work was a culmination of the early Tudor style.

When Luther made the trip to Worms where the imperial ban

1521(cont.)

was laid upon him, he had brought his lute and played it for comfort during these difficult times.

The publication Antico's Motetti Libro quarto included Mouton's Iocundare Jerusalem.

Mouton's Christe Redemptor, O Rex omnipotens was published.

Mouton's In illo tempore (Antico's Motetti Libro quarto) used portions of the plainsong melodies "O filii" and "Victimae paschali."

Macchiavelli, in passages in his "Art of War" written for Lorenzo de' Medici, 1521, clearly stated that the drum was the commander of all things in a battle and issued the commands of the officer to his troops.

Peutinger while at the diet of Worms obtained the confirmation of the ancient privileges of the city.

Spataro's Dilucide . . . demonstratione, a book on theory, was published by Pompeana.

A book on music by Veguis was published by Mediolani and Taurini.

The oldest existing harpsichord was made by Geronimo di Bologna in Rome.

Although Virdung apparently knew very little about the harpsichord or clavicembalo, there was a fine authentic specimen of this instrument (two-unisons) made in Rome and (cont.) preserved in an English museum.

At Christmas during this year Carlstadt held the first German mass in Würtenberg.

An entry noting expenses incurred for "a pair of new organs" for the Church of St. Mary at Hill, in this year, included the cost "for bringing them home," and amounted altogether to only "xs. viijd."

Frederick the Wise, the Elector of Saxony, granted asylum to Luther at Wartburg.

At the death of Pope Leo X, a true patron of music, Adrian VI held the Papal throne for less than two years.

Piero di Cosimo, Italian painter, died (born 1462).

Lucas van Leyden was at Antwerp at this time and Dürer made a drawing of him.

German painting: Hans Holbein the Younger, Christ Entombed.

Italian painting: Lotto, St. Bernardino altarpiece (Bergamo).

(and 1525) Georg van Frundsberg, a German composer, met Luther at Worms in 1521 and gave the latter his support. After the battle of Pavia in 1525 Frundsberg composed a song "Hofgunst" which was often sung or played at officer's parties.

(to 1557) During the reign of King John III of Portugal, music and art prospered through his patronage.

1521(cont.)

(to 1565) During this period the development of the motet coincided very closely with that of the mass.

1522

(March 22) Luther left Wartburg and began to busy himself with projects for the reform of church services. The major alterations were in the musical parts of the mass and brought striking results.

(June 24) Franchino Gafori, an eminent Italian scholar, priest, and musician died (born 1451).

Hugh Aston, Archdeacon of York, Canon of St. Stephen's, Westminster, and an English composer, died (born c.1480).

Jean Mouton, French composer, died (born c.1475). At the time of his death he was a canon of St. Quentin.

Palestrina's paternal grandfather, Pierluisci, died (born c.1450).

English composer Hugh Aston or Ashton wrote a piece for virginal, "Mylady Carey's Dompe."

Gafori's "Practica Musicae" was published at Venice, probably by Petrucci.

A German mass was introduced by Kaspar Kantz, a reformer at Nördlingen, however, it was nothing more than a mechanical translation of the Roman mass into German.

There was no record of Benedictus de Opitiis after this date.

Duke Francesco Sforza's victory over the French at Bicocca was probably the inspiration for a piece published by Gardano in 1549, "Italian Battle."

The Incurabili, on the Zattere, an hospital for incurables at Venice was founded by Maria Malipiero and Maria Grimani and inspired by San Gaetano Thiene. The building was made of wood.

Andreas de Silva, Italian madrigal composer, received payment for his services from the Duke of Mantua.

Joachim du Bellay, a writer and disciple of Ronsard, was born (died 1560).

(to 1523) The Papal reign of St. Adrian VI (born in Utrecht).

(to 1524) Cavazzoni was at Venice.

(to 1525) Willaert journeyed from Rome to Ferrara and there became attached to the court of the Este during this period.

(to 1554) Bakfark took a leave of absence to reestablish connections with Prince Albert of Prussia. He travelled through France, Germany and Italy and his first lute book was published at Lyons.

c.1522

Sante Pierluigi was probably married.

Niklaus Manuel Deutsch, German painter, decided to go to the wars in Piedmont.

Italian painting: Titian, Man with a Glove.

1523

(August 30) The first teacher of music in the "New World," Pedro de Gante, arrived in Veracruz.

Juan de Anchieta, a musician at the court of Ferdinand and Isabella, died at Azpeitia (born c.1450 or c.1462).

Robert Cornyshe, English secular composer, died (born 1465).

Johannes Eccard, a Thuringian composer of Protestant music, was born (died 1611),see 1533.

Richard Edwards, an English composer and native of Somersetshire, was born (died 1566, October 31).

John Merbecke, English composer of The Booke of Common Praier Noted, was born (died c.1585).

Claudio Merulo, principal organist at St. Mark's and successor of Annibale Padovano, was born (died 1604),see 1533.

At the end of a one-line In Christi Jesu thalamo, an inscription was found which stated that the lowest portions of the melody should be sung by a bass, the middle portions by an alto, and the highest portion by a tenor.

Pietro Aron, Italian theorist, wrote Il Toscanello in Musica, his best-known treatise, at Venice.

Cavazzoni's Recerchari, motetti, canzoni, Libro I written at this time included two ricercari, two transcriptions of motets and four transcriptions of chansons.

Robert Granjon, Netherlandish composer, had his first publications issued at this date.

A major publication written by Hans Judenkünig appeared. It was published at Vienna and titled "Ain schone kunstliche underweisung." The book was an instructional work for lute and contained tablatures.

"Ach Gott vom Himmel," with words by Luther (Ps. xii. "Salvum me fac.") appeared.

The first version of "Aus tiefer Noth," with words by Luther and containing four verses (Ps. cxxx. "De profundis") was completed.

Luther wrote "Ein neues Lied," A hymn to the memory of two Lutheran martyrs, H. Voes and J. Esch. They had been burned at Brussels on July 1 of this year.

In his "Formula Missae et Communionis" of this date Luther ordained a Latin celebration for the chapters and cathedrals or any richly endowed churches. He disclosed his desire for congregational singing and objected to the singing of long graduals while he also asserted that the choice of certain hymns should be left to the priest.

Luther wrote "Nun freut euch," a hymn of thanksgiving.

Petrucci's last work was given this date and it was presumed that he died shortly thereafter.

Aron first explained mean-tone tuning as by use of pure thirds with the fifths flatted by one quarter of a comma.

1523(cont.)

Josse Carest, a clavecin-maker, was admitted to St. Luke's guild as a painter and sculptor of clavichords. Literally this was "Joos Kerrest, clavecordmaker, snyt en scildert."

At Caerwys, Flintshire, an Eisteddfod was held. Many prominent men were present at the event.

Encina was in residence at León as prior.

Mateo Flecha the Elder became a singer, and later maestro di capella, at the Lérida Cathedral.

The Italians printed first keyboard scores in modern form, with a right-and left-hand staff of five lines each and bar-lines as early as this date.

Thomas Münzer was a radical theologian who went to Thuringia and made himself pastor of Alstädt. He introduced a German church service there.

Francesco di Portalupis' name was on the oldest spinet bearing a date and it was preserved at the Conservatoire at Paris. Portalupis came from Verona.

George Rhau moved to Würtenberg where he eventually became a Ratsherr (Senator).

The appearance of the term "ricercare" was in connection with organ music and the term canzone was used in connection with instrumental music. Cavazzoni's recerchari, motetti, canzoni of this year was the work that used the terms first.

Mathias Werrecore was appointed choirmaster at the Milan cathedral.

Two young members of the Augustinian order in Antwerp were burned at the stake in Brussels. They were the first martyrs of the Reformation.

Gerard David, Netherlandish painter, died (born c.1450).

Pietro Perugino, Italian painter, died (born c.1445).

Luca Signorelli, Umbrian painter, died (born 1441).

German painting: Hans Holbein the Younger, Erasmus (18½x12½"). This work was considered by many to be his first and most expressive portrait of the man.

(to 1525) Fétis mentioned three masses, in a large folio, printed for the lecturn of a church, probably by Petrucci. The folio was sold to an unknown buyer in Rome.

(to 1534) The Papal reign of St. Clement VII (born in Florence).

(to c.1545) Senfl was associated with the musical portion of the court at Munich, Bavaria.

(to 1560) King Gustav Vasa of Sweden, who reigned during this period, was interested in music.

(to 1572) Pedro de Gante was in Mexico during these years. He was the first music teacher from Europe to be active there.

c.1523

Laux Maler, considered to be the Stradivarius of the lute, was

c.1523(cont.)

active in Bologna.

German painting: Niklaus Manuel Deutsch, Judgment of Paris.

German painting: Niklaus Manuel Deutsch, Pyramus and Thisbe.

1524

Lord Hunsdon, Byrd's patron, was born (date of death unknown).

Thomas Linacre, founder of the Royal College of Physicians in London, died (born c.1460).

Sumiaki Toyohara, Japanese court musician and encyclopedist, died (born 1450).

Martin Agricola was teacher as well as cantor in the first Protestant school at Magdeburg, a post he held until his death.

William Chell, Mus. Bac., was successively lay vicar, prebendary, and precentor of Hereford Cathedral. He graduated in music from Oxford in this year.

Wolfgang Dachstein, a Roman Catholic priest at Strassburg, adopted the Reformed principles and married. He later became vicar as well as organist of St. Thomas' Church in the same city.

A second John Dygon was Master of the Chantry of Milton in Kent, a position he apparently held until his death in this year.

Finck was at Salzburg and then retired to a monastery in Vienna.

Jobst Gutknecht published the "Acht Lieder Buch" at Nürnberg. The songs were of south German origin.

Justus Jonas, a friend and collaborator of Luther's attacked the old ritual observed in the cloisters and cathedrals "wherein the manner of the priests of Baal-the chorale is roared, not sung." He compared those priests with donkeys braying to a deaf God.

A tablature by Leonhard Kleber included pieces by Hofhaimer.

Luther attempted to put his ideas for congregational singing into practice. He created a hymn-book of his own which included seven hymn paraphrases.

In a pamphlet answering the Enthusiasts, Luther wrote "I would gladly have a German mass today, and I am going to work on it, but I should like it to be of a genuinely German nature."

Luther had long entertained the idea of a German Mass, and was occupied with the project of arranging such a service.

Luther wrote to a friend, George Spalatin, "I wish, after the example of the Prophets and ancient Fathers of the Church, to make German psalms for the people, that is to say, sacred hymns so that the word of God may dwell among the people by means of song also."

During this year many compositions appeared in which Luther made a contribution or at least was believed to have participated in their emergence.

1524(cont.)

Text by Luther:

Ach Gott vom Himmel, a hymn appeared in four collections, Ps.xi.

Christ lag in Todesbanden, a hymn later made into a cantata.

Christum wir sollen loben, a Christmas hymn by Sedulius.

Diess sind die heiligen zehn Gebot, the decalogue.

Es spricht der Unweisen, Ps.XIV, "Dixit insipiens."

Es wollt uns Gott, Ps.lxvii, "Deus miseratur."

Gott der Vater, wohn uns bei, from a XV century litany.

Gott seigelobet, from a sacramental hymn of the XVI century.

Komm Gott, Schöpfer, from the "Veni Creator."

Komm, heiliger Geist, from the "Veni sancte Spiritus" attributed to King Robert of France.

Mensch, willst du leben, abbreviated version of the decalogue.

Mit Fried und Freud, the "Nunc Dimittis."

Mitten wir im Leben sind, two verses added to a XV century funeral hymn on Notker's antiphon, "Media vita in morte sumus."

Nun bitten wir den heiligen Geist, from a XIII century Whitsuntide hymn.

(cont.)

Nun komm der Heiden Heiland, from a Christmas hymn by St. Ambrose, "Veni Redemptor."

Wär Gott nicht mit uns, Ps.cxxiv, "Nisi qui Dominus."

Wir glauben all an Einen Gott, from the creed "Patrem credimus."

Wohl dem, der in Gottesfürchte, Ps.cxxviii, "Beatiomnes."

Text and probably music by Luther:

Aus tiefer Not schrei ich zu Dir, appeared in Erfurt in the Enchiridion and in the "Geistliche Gesangbüchleyn Tenor," Würtenberg. A second version contained five verses.

Ein neues Lied wir heben an, first appeared in Enchiridion, Oder eyn Handbüchlein eynem yetzlichen Christen fast nutzlich bey sich zu haben zur stetter vbung vnnd trachtung Geystlicher gesenge vnd Psalmen, Rechtschaffen vnd kunstlich vertheutscht 1524." Printed at Erfurt.

Es spricht der Unweisen Mund wohl, appeared in the "Gesangbüchleyn" 1524.

Jesus Christus unser Heiland, from the "Enchiridion,"

1524(cont.)

from John Huss' hymn "Jesus Christus nostra salus."

Mensch, willst du leben seliglich, from the "Gesangbüchleyn."

Mit Fried und Freud ich fahr dahin, from the "Gesangbüchleyn."

Nun freut euch, liebe Christen g'mein, from the "Achtliederbuch."

Wohl dem der in Gottesfürchte steht, from the "Geistliche Gesangbüchleyn."

Fray Pedro learned the Aztec language well enough to found a school later moved to Mexico City. The school became a center of music.

Georg Rhaw established a publishing business at Würtenberg. The purpose of the firm was to provide Lutheran churches, choruses, and schools with a satisfactory printed repertoire for their musical needs. Rhaw himself had written a musical primer.

Taverner was a boy chorister at Collegiate Church at Tattershall and in this year was appointed master of the choristers.

Johann Walther was a singer in the choir at Torgau and was called to Würtenberg to assist Luther in the project of developing a German mass.

Johann Walther wrote his "Chorgesangbüchlein." It included thirty-two German and (cont.) five Latin hymns written in parts.

The Dreikönigskirche at Dresden preserved a few of Walther's printed works, including the discant and tenor parts of the Würtenberg hymnbook.

Walther wrote Wittembergisch geistlich Gesangbuch, the first polyphonic music based on Protestant chorales. It contained thirty-eight chorales with three to six parts with the melody in the tenor. The book was printed at Würtenberg.

Walther worked with Luther on the "Enchiridion," or hand-book collection, published at Erfurt.

The first Protestant hymn-book appeared, "Etlich christliche Lyeder Lobgesang und Psalm dem reinen Wort Gottes gemess auss der h. gschrifft durch mancherlay Hochgelerter gemacht, in der Kirchen zu singen, wie es den zum tail bereyt zu Wittenburg in yebung ist Witenburg, 1524."

Chorale-books with unaccompanied melodies were published in "Strassburg as well as Erfurt and Würtenberg.

Joachim Patinir, Netherlandish painter, died at Antwerp (born c.1475).

Jan Gossaert, Netherlandish painter, transferred his allegiance to Adolph of Burgundy after Philip died.

Italian architecture: Michelangelo, Florence, Laurentian Library, stairs.

(to 1525) Crispin van Stappen

1524(cont.)

was maestro di cappella at the Casa Santa di Loreto.

(to 1534) Italian sculpture: Michelangelo, Tomb of Lorenzo de Medici (width, overall, 12'9½").

(to 1534) Italian sculpture: Michelangelo, Day-Tomb of Giuliano de' Medici (c.34 5/8" high from base).

c.1524

(December 17) Evidence indicated that Palestrina was born in 1524, and very possibly December 17th since that was the feast-day of St. John the Apostle, from whom he derived his name. His actual name was Giovanni Pierluigi but he added the name of his birthplace, Palestrina, and was so known (died 1594, February 2).

German painting: Grünewald, St. Erasmus and St. Maurice.

1525

(May 15) The battle of Frankenhausen took place during the peasants' revolt.

(June 11) Luther was married to Catherine von Bora, formerly a nun at Nimptsch in Saxony.

(July 21, 22) John Mason became prebendary of Pratum minus, July 21, and of Putson minor, July 22.

(October 29) Luther started to perfect the German mass and conducted the first one on the twentieth Sunday after Trinity, at the Würtenberg Schlosskirche.

Antoine Brumel, Burgundian composer, died (birthdate unknown).

Pietro Aron's "Trattato della natura et cognitione di tutti gli tuoni di canto figurato" appeared.

Queen Beatrice of Hungary had gipsy musicians who played the cithara at her court.

Luther's German Kirchenlieder, adapted to favorite melodies of the day, both sacred and secular, were set for four, five, and six parts, with the plainchaunt in the tenor, by Johannes Walther. They were first published, as previously noted, at Würtenberg, then reprinted the following year with a special preface by Luther.

A hymn from a tune known as "Er ist das Heil" probably by Speratus was contained in Adam Dyson's hymn-book, published in Breslau. In all probability, Luther composed both music and text.

Peñalosa, singer and composer, returned to Spain.

George Rhaw opened a music -printing plant.

The Strasbourg Teutsch Kirchen amt was a collection of church songs that appeared at this time.

Verdelot was at St. Mark's in Venice.

Johann Walther was Kapellmeister or "Sängermeister" for the Elector of Saxony.

A reprint of Walther's Geystliche Gesangkbüchleyn appeared with changes and additions. (Other reprints were done in 1537, 1544, and 1551.)

1525(cont.)

William Whytbroke was a contemporary of Taverner at Cardinal College, Oxford.

The following books were published in this year: Das Strassburger Enchiridion, Das Nürnberger Enchiridion, Das Strassburger Deutsche Kirchenamt, Das Breslauer Gesangbuch, and Das Zwickauer Gesangbuch.

Lord Berners' Froissart appeared in translation in English.

The victory at Pavia truly belonged to the Emperor's Spanish general.

German woodcut: Dürer, the Painter studying the laws of foreshortening by means of threads and a frame (from the 1525 edition of his text-book on perspective and proportion).

Italian painting:
Andrea del Sarto, Madonna with the Sack.

(to 1528) Italian painting: Jacopo Pontormo, Descent from the Cross (123"x75½").

(to 1530) John Taverner was organist of Wolsey's Cardinal College. This is now Christ Church, Oxford.

(to 1545) Giorgione sought the company of cultured art-lovers in Venice. Catalogues of the main collections compiled during this period by Michiel indicated a demand for his works.

(to 1555) The early Protestant composers M. Agricola, Dietrich, Senfl, Sporer and Walther were members of the Heidelberg Liederschule.

c.1525

Claude Le Jeune was born at Valenciennes (died 1600), see also 1528.

Richard Farrant, English organist and singer, was born (died 1580, November 30), see c.1533.

Claude Goudimel, composer and native of Besancon, was born according to some sources (died 1572), see also c.1505.

Giaches de Wert, madrigalist and Doppelmeister, was born in the Netherlands (date of death unknown).

Dietrich, an important liturgical composer of early Protestantism, composed antiphons and hymns that showed his deep convictions without humanistic tendencies.

A French type cutter and printer, Pierre Haultin, simplified the printing process with a single printing technique.

In England there were isolated instances of the use of polyphony in the daily office other than in the Magnificat, the main portion of the ordinary.

The earliest source of English harpsichord music was a manuscript from this time. It contained several dance compositions.

This period began to produce small and modest versions of the ordinary, the votive, antiphon, and magnificat for use on non-festive occasions. These might be used in institutions with small choirs. There were also some polyphonic settings of the responses and hymns.

c.1525(cont.)

George Gascoigne, Elizabethan poet, was born (died 1577).

Pieter Bruegel the Elder, Netherlandish painter, was born (died 1569).

Italian painting: Correggio, Antiope Asleep.

Italian painting: Correggio, Jupiter and Antiope (74 3/4 x 48 7/8").

Italian painting: Lorenzo Lotto, Portrait of a Young Man.

Italian painting: Titian, The Entombment (58 ¼ x 84 5/8").

(to 1527) Willaert served Cardinal Ippolito d'Este at Milan.

(to 1535) Francesco Sforza was not in a position where membership in his choir was politically expedient.

(to 1555) Hermann Finck considered this to be his time when writing on musical style. His birthdate, however, is recorded as 1527.

(to 1594) A great contrast between Willaert's progressive school of Venetian composers and the simultaneous Roman school headed by Palestrina was obvious.

(to c.1600) German vocal polyphony drew on French and Netherlandish music until the Reformation. Later German composition continued to be dependent on music from other countries.

1526

Hans Judenkunig, lutenist and composer, died (birthdate unknown).

Sophonias Päminger, author on music, was born (died 1603).

Thomas Stoltzer, German composer, died. His date of birth was given both as c.1450 and c.1470 by the same major source.

Ladislaus Szalkai, Polish theorist, died at the battle of Mohács (birthdate unknown).

The name of William Crane appeared as master of the children at the Chapel Royal in England.

Divitis may have been a member of the choir at St. Peter's under the name of Antonius Richardus.

Christoffer Endel was organist at Cassel.

Gombert was associated with the Imperial chapel in several capacities from this date forward. He went to Seville with Emperor Charles V during this year.

Luther sent for Conrad Rupsch and Johann Walther. They came to Würtenberg and aided him in producing a German mass.

The idea of universal priesthood and that a believer himself, without benefit of priestly intercession, could and should approach God impelled Luther to depart from the old Latin Mass as the basis of the service. This was when he accomplished the German Mass.

Luther's translation of the

1526(cont.)

Psalms were published at Antwerp.

Christobal Morales was chapel master at Avila.

Johann Petreius, a printer and music publisher, graduated as "Magister" at Nuremberg and set up a business in that city as a printer.

On one title-page prepared this year Senfl was referred to as "Musicus intonator" for the Duke of Bavaria.

An anonymous lutenist served Governor John Szapolyai of Transylvania and, after this date, King of Hungary. This lutenist was responsible for the education of Valentin Bakfark, the great lutenist and composer in Buda.

John Taverner was musical director of Cardinal Wolsey's college at Oxford.

Johann Walther became municipal Cantor in Torgau.

Willaert was believed to have returned to Italy during this year.

A frottola included in a collection evidently became a villanella. It is still sung in Venice with the same words and melody, "Le son tre fanticelli tutti tre da maridar." The composition was part of a collection of twenty-two frottole published in Rome by Junta.

The first Low German hymnbook appeared, apparently in Magdeburg.

Both text and music of "Jesaia dem Phropheten das geschah" were probably written by Luther. This composition replaced the Sanctus in "Eine Weiss, Christlich Mess zu halten." In English it was "The Vision of Isaiah."

Senfl's "Quinque salutationes D.N. Hiesu Christi" was written at Nürnberg.

Stoltzer set several psalms, translated by Luther, to music. One of these was included in Rhaw's collection. Stoltzer was requested to do this by Queen Mary of Hungary, whom he served as court conductor as well as by Duke Albrecht of Prussia. The particular psalm was "Erzürne dich nicht."

Verdelot's first work was a motet. It was included in the "Fior de' Motetti e Canzoni" probably published at Rome in this year.

The capilla española was established by Queen Isabella of Portugal and remained as a permanent fixture at Madrid.

King Henry VIII at his court in England had drums, a fife, a harp, three lutes, three rebecs, ten sackbutts, three taborets, fifteen trumpets, and two viols. This impressive collection indicated that chamber music must have received considerable attention.

Sixteen singers were on the rolls of the Julian Choir. Its charter was later consolidated by Pope Paul III.

The Pisan harpsichord was built.

1526(cont.)

The court records of Sweden listed musician's names from this date forward.

Paolo Caliari, Italian painter known as Veronese, was born (died 1588).

Vittore Carpaccio, Venetian painter, died (born c.1455).

Hans Holbein the Younger made his first trip to England.

German painting: Dürer, The Four Apostles (painted at Munich).

German woodcut: Hans Holbein the Younger, The Husbandman (Dance of Death Series).

German painting: Hans Holbein the Younger, Portrait of Maddelena Offenburg as Laïs of Corinth.

Spanish architecture: Machuca, Granada, Palace of Charles V, court was begun at this time (102' diameter).

Italian painting: Titian, Madonna with Member of the Pesaro Family (16'x8'10").

(to 1530) Morales was maestro de capilla at Ávila Cathedral.

(to 1530) Taverner was organist at Oxford.

(to 1530) Italian painting: Correggio, Assumption of the Virgin.

(to 1550) French architecture: Chambord, Château (525'x370').

(to 1554) Gombert was in Madrid for much of this period.

c.1526

Johannes Lupi served as a choir-boy at Cambrai until this date.

Italian painting: Correggio, St. John the Baptist (study for a wall-painting).

German painting: Hans Holbein the Younger, Meyer Madonna.

Italian painting: Lotto, Portrait of a Young Man.

1527

(March 21) Hermann Finck, German theorist and grand nephew of Heinrich Finck, renowned organist, was probably born (date of death unknown).

(June 9) Heinrich Finck, German organist and composer, died at Vienna (born 1445).

(October 22) Palestrina's grandmother Jacobella Pierluigi's will was executed on this date.

(December 12) Willaert was appointed choir-master of St. Mark's at Venice by Andrea Gritti, the Doge. Willaert succeeded Pietro de Fossis. He also founded a music school at St. Mark's.

Pietro de Fossis, choir-master at St. Mark's in Venice, died (born 1491).

Palestrina's grandmother, Jacobella, died at Rome.

Annibale Padovano, Italian organist who preceded Andrea Gabrieli as second organist at St. Mark's, was born (died 1575).

A book on music by Bonaventura

1527(cont.)

da Brescia was published.

Ettich gesäng by Königsberg was published.

Jaquet of Mantua was a singer in the Cardinal's chapel there.

Leonhard Keyser, a Bavarian cleric and close friend of Luther, was tried and convicted of heresy.

It was believed by some that music collections containing many of Okeghem's works were destroyed when Rome was plundered and that his compositions at St. Martin's at Tours were similarly lost.

Willaert became cantor regis Ungariae.

Duke Albert V of Bavaria was born (died 1579, October).

The archives of the Pontifical Chapel at Rome were destroyed at the sacking of Rome under Charles V.

The town of Palestrina was again ravaged by Charles V.'s soldiers. Music of the next period was fortunate in that Pierluigi Sante (Palestrina) was at the time an infant.

The Ospedaletto was founded at St. Giovanni e Paolo in Venice. It was a poorhouse and orphanage.

Netherlandish painting: Jan Gossaert, Danaë.

Italian architecture: Sanmicheli, Verona, Palazzo Bevilacqua (77'wide x 53'high).

(to 1530) The plundering of (cont.) Rome by the soldiers of Charles V and the ultimate fall of Florence in 1530 led to the restoration of Medici control. They had been driven out three years earlier but now conditions once more were prohibitive to freedom of expression.

(to 1536) Pierre Attaignant published nineteen books containing motets by various composers, both French and foreign. During this same period Robert Ballard and Adrian le Roy also published several volumes. Attaignant also issued collections of chansons, galliardes, masses and pavanes. His publishing plant was at Rue de la Harpe in Paris.

(to 1562) Andrea Gabrieli was a pupil of Adrian Willaert, maestro di capella at St. Mark's during these years.

(to 1609) The so-called "Venetian School of composition" flourished during these years.

c.1527

Arnold Schlick, German organ composer and lutenist, died (born c.1450), see also c.1517.

The first organ built at the school of Fray Pedro was installed at this time.

1528

Francisco Guerrero, Spanish composer and choirmaster, was born at Seville (died 1599). His career and life were spent chiefly in Spain, but his compositions were well-received in France, Italy and the Netherlands where they were published.

Claude Le Jeune, court composer to the King of France, was

1528(cont.)

born at Valenciennes (died 1600). He was one of the most eminent French composers of his time.

Laux Maler, the great German lute-maker at Bologna, died (birthdate unknown).

Francisco de Peñelosa, Spanish composer, died in Seville (born c.1470).

Godescalcus Praetorius (Schulz), composer and Professor of Philosophy at Würtenberg, was born at Salzburg (died 1573, July 8).

Louis van Pulaer, French composer, died at Cambrai (born c.1475).

Martin de Rivaflecha, Spanish composer, died (birthdate unknown).

Thomas Whythorne, an English composer who frequently wrote villanellas and madrigals, was born (died c.1590).

Agricola's Musica instrumentalis deudsch was published at Magdeburg. In the work he mentioned a "Polische Geige", a special kind of instrument similar to a rebec. One of the earliest usages of the bar occurred in this work. A copy of the book was preserved in an English library.

Pierre Attaingnant began publication of French Chansons using Haultin's type. In time he published about seventy collections of chansons containing approximately two thousand selections. In the first collection, seventeen of thirty-one compositions were by Claudin.

(cont.) There was also a complete volume of Janequin's works.

Henry VIII and his contemporaries composed chansons much in the style of those published by Attaingnant.

Castiglione's "Il Libro del Cortegiano was published.

Seven chansons au luth by Claudin were included in the Chansons nouvelles published in this year.

Rhaw printed "Ein kurtz deutsche Musica."

Hercules married Renée the daughter of Louis XII and Rore later composed En vos adieux.

The Sarum hymnal was published.

Albrecht Dürer, German painter, died (born 1471).

Mathias Grünewald (Mathis Gothardt-Neithardt), German painter, died (born c.1475).

Palma Vecchio, Italian painter, died (born 1480).

Albrecht Altdorfer's fellow-townsmen wanted to make the painter burgermaster of Ratisbon.

Hans Holbein the Younger returned to Basle.

German painting: Holbein the Younger, The Artist's Wife with their Two Children.

German painting: Holbein the Younger, Anne Cresacre, Sir Thomas More's daughter-in-law (Drawing made in 1528 at Windsor Castle).

1528(cont.)

(to 1531) Cavazzoni was once more at Venice.

c.1528

Janequin's "Bird Song" appeared.

French painting: Jean Clouet, Portrait of Francois I.

German painting: Holbein the Younger, The Virgin with the family of Burgomaster Meyer.

(to 1530) Attaingnant's Trente et sept chansons was published. The volume was undated but has been placed in these years.

1529

Baldassare Castiglione, theorist and frottolist, died (born 1478).

Noel Baulduin, composer and contemporary of des Prés, died at Antwerp (birthdate unknown).

Jean de Clève, Netherlandish composer, was born (died 1582).

Jacob Godebrye, who was also known as "Jacotin," died at Antwerp (birthdate unknown).

Marbriano de Orto, composer and singer, died (birthdate unknown).

Samuel van Quickelberg, physician, humorist and writer, was born at Antwerp (date of death unknown).

Raynaldo Francigena died at Parma. He was a singer at the Church of the Steccata and was succeeded by his son, Ernoul Caussin, a composer. The man referred to as Raynaldo may well have been Raynaldino.

Pierre Certon became a clerc de (cont.) matines at Notre Dame. He barely escaped imprisonment for his dubious behavior.

Music played by cornet and five trombones was a feature of a wedding banquet at the Ferrara court.

A portrait engraved on a medal by Hagenauer of Augsburg, bore the inscription "Ludovvicus Senfel." On the back was engraved "Psallam deo meo quamdiu fuero 1529." The medal was preserved in a collection of coins and medals at Vienna.

Susato settled at Antwerp and occupied himself in the transcription of music for the chapel of the Virgin in the Cathedral.

Johann Walther founded the first informal Protestant Kantorei in Torgau on the Elbe.

William Whytbroke was ordained a priest.

An anonymous instruction book for "Manicordion (clavichord) Luc et Flutes" was published at Antwerp. It carried the title "Livre plaisant et tres utile . . . . "

"Toscanello in Musica" was published at Venice.

Two Attaingnant lutebooks started to appear. The first was "Dixhuit basses dances . . . avec dixneuf Branles . . . . The second was an instruction book, "Tres breve et familiere introduction . . . " which contained an explanation of tablature as well as the tuning of the lutes.

An early collection of chansons

1529(cont.)

was published by Attaingnant. It was dated and bore the title "Trente et une chansons musicales."

Lodovico Fogliano's "Musica theorica" (1529) approached the subject of just intonation better than Ramos' treatise had. Fogliano had a brother, Giacomo, who composed in a similar manner. The work was published at Venice.

French tablature was first printed in this year.

The galliard first appeared in prints during this year.

The Klug'sche Gesangbuch appeared.

Two hymns with texts by Luther were issued.

Herr Gott dich loben wir, from the "Te Deum."

Verleih uns Frieden gnadiglich, from "Da pacem Domine."

Two works with text and probably also music by Luther appeared.

Ein feste Burg ist unser Gott, first appeared in "Geistliche Lieder, auffs new gebessert zu Wittenberg, Dr, Martin Luther, 1529," Ps.xlvi, "Deus noster refugium."

Here Luther applied the 46th Psalm to the upheaval of his times. His fear was that because of the diet of Spires the rule of the Antichrist was nearer than the Kingdom of God and that propagation

(cont.)

of the true Word of God had been stopped.

Nun freut euch, liebe Christen g'mein, from Klug's "Geistliche Lieder (Wittenberg, 1529).

The second diet of Spires brought deep despair to Luther's followers.

Giovanni Bologna, Italian sculptor, was born (died 1608).

Jean de Boulogne, Flemish sculptor, was born (died 1608).

German painting: Albrecht Altdorfer, The Battle of Arbela.

German painting: Hans Baldung, Vanitas Music.

One of the most surprising examples of Lucas Cranach the Elder's later style was in the picture at Vienna in which he showed the Elector Frederick the Wise taking part in a stag -hunt.

German painting: Cranach the Elder, the Judgement of Paris.

German painting: Lucas Cranach the Elder, Venus in a Landscape (Panel 15x10¼").

Netherlandish painting: Martin van Heemskerck, Portrait of Anna Codde.

German architecture: Hildesheim, Butchers' Guild Hall.

Italian painting: Lotto, the altarpiece of St. Nicholas (Venice).

1529(cont.)

(1529, 1532 and 1545) Rhaw printed "Musica instrumentalis deudsch" by Agricola in three different editions.

(to 1573) Eitner's Bibliographie der Musik-Sammelwerke mentioned nearly 250 of Gombert's compositions. They were contained in over ninety different collections.

c.1529

Juan del Encina, Spanish composer, died at Leon (born c.1468 or c.1439).

Gombert was magister puerorum from this date. He accompanied the emperor on journeys from Spain to Austria, Germany, and northern Italy.

Janequin was active at Bordeaux.

Susato, the Belgian printer, set himself up in Antwerp. While there he was involved in a variety of occupations, including flutist, music copyist, publisher and trumpet player.

1530

(April) In the Privy Purse Expenses of Henry the Eighth there was an entry, "1530 (April) Item the vj daye paied to William Lewes for ii payer of Virginalls in one coffer with iiii stoppes, brought to Grenwiche iii li . . . and for a little payer of Virginalls brought to the more, tc."

Orlando di Lassus, Netherlandish polyphonic master, was born in Mons, Netherlands (died 1594).

Francesco Patrizzi, Italian composer, was born (date of death unknown).

Costanzo Porta, Italian madrigalist and pupil of Willaert's, was born in Cremona (died 1601).

Conrad Rupsch, German mass composer, died (born c.1475).

Gian Angelo Testagrossa, Mantuan composer and teacher of Francesco Canova da Milano, died (born c.1470).

Étienne Briard settled at Avignon.

Arnold de Bruck was Kapellmeister to the King of Rome (who became Emperor Ferdinand I) at Vienna.

Hans Kotter was banished from Freiburg, Switzerland for embracing Protestantism.

Luther was banned by the emperor and excluded from participation in the Augsburg Diet, an important event in the history of Christianity.

Jehan Tabourot was ordained a priest.

Taverner joined the Reformation movement and ceased writing music. He left Oxford at the same time.

Verdelot was at Florence from this date on.

Antonius Divitis' motet, "Gloria laus," appeared in the tenth book of the collection of ancient motets published by Attaignant at Paris.

Fayrfax' works included two magnificats, six masses, and twelve motets. He also composed several secular songs, two of them being included in a printed

1530(cont.)

song book. A manuscript of Fayrfax' works included seven more of his songs.

Janequin in Chantons, sonnons, trompetes provided a welcome-song for Francis I's sons' return to France from Spain. They had been held as hostages to guarantee their father's fidelity to the treaty of Madrid.

David Peblis, a Scotish composer and one of the canons at St. Andrews, set the canticle "Si quis diliget me" in five parts.

Senfl composed a motet for the Diet of Augsburg.

Verdelot's works reached France and were printed in French collections. Some of them were included in the Madrigali de diversi musici . . . .

Wynkyn de Worde produced a set of songs from which only the Bassus part survived. The book of songs was published in this year.

In the collections in the British Museum (Music Catalogue C 31b; "Book"), it was obvious that florid music was printed in England at this time.

French chanson and early French instrumental transcriptions were first published by Attaingnant. One such collection was called "Chansons und Tänze" for lute.

Blume's Enchiridion was published. It contained twenty-five hymns, eighteen of which were by Luther.

The Madrigali de diversi musici . . . contained madrigals by Festa.

Attaingnant published two volumes containing basses dances, branles, pavanes, and gaillards. These were issued in the form of part-books.

The first Polyphonic Songs that appeared in England were published by de Worde. They were in a volume of which neither Burney nor Hawkins had any knowledge. It contained an interesting collection of works, sacred, and saecular, by Taverner, and other English composers.

The Bassus Part of the collection of Songs by de Worde was preserved in the British Museum. The work is an outstanding production and is of the highest quality of any of the works printed with movable type.

A printed collection, In this boke ar cōteynyd xx sōges, ix of iiii ptes and xi of thre ptes, was an early example of music printed in England. It bore this date as that of publication.

University Library at Cracow preserved an anonymous Carmen saphicum dating from before this year. This work, in the style of Tritonius, Celtes' pupil at Ingolstadt, strove to provide music in which time-values were determined by the scansion of the Latin text.

Eleanor, wife of Francis I and brother of Charles V, had keyboard instruction from Henry Bredemers as did her brother and sisters.

1530(cont.)

Henry VIII's band at this time consisted of four lutes, two drumslades, one harp, three minstrels, three rebecs, nine sackbuts, three taborets, sixteen trumpets, two viols and one virginal.

The rigidity, restraint, and serenity of the Josquin-Raphael period had all but disappeared by this date.

Except for a brief intermission, Charles V had Margaret continue to serve as Regent of the Netherlands until her death in 1530.

Czar Ivan IV the Terrible of Russia was born (died 1584).

Margaret of Austria, granddaughter of Charles the Bold, died (born 1480).

Niklaus Manuel Deutsch, German painter, died (born 1484).

Quentin Massys, Netherlandish painter, died (born c.1464).

(to 1532) German painting: Holbein the Younger, Portrait of Erasmus (Circular).

(to 1533) French chansons appeared in Italian collections.

(to 1540) Hans Heugel worked in Cassel as an architect.

(to 1549) Complete Protestant psalters, with one-line melodies, made their appearance in Germany.

(to 1550) Early specimens of English instrumental ensemble music appeared during this period. They were instrumental (cont.) arrangements of the "In nomine" portion of the Benedictus in Taverner's Missa Gloria tibi Trinitas.

(to 1560) Cabezon composed the Obras de Musica para Tecla, Arpa y Vihuela.

(to 1560) The four voice parts of chansons were somewhat polyphonic in an unscholastic way but at times they reached a chordal structure.

(to 1565) The second phase of the Renaissance was increasingly agitated, dramatic, and free.

(to 1588) Thomas Whythorne's seventy-six Songes to three, fower, and five voyces was the only English secular collection published during this period.

c.1530

Alexander Agricola, German (?) composer, died at Castile (birthdate unknown).

Ammerback, a composer of the "Colorist" school, was born at Naumburg (died 1597).

Marco Cara, Italian frottolist and composer, died (birthdate unknown).

Geronimo Carlo, Italian motet composer, was born at Reggio (date of death unknown).

Pierre Certon, a French musician and composer, was active at this time.

Baldassare Donati, choirdirector and successor to Zarlino, was born(date of death unknown).

William Mundy, English motet composer, was born (died c.1591).

c.1530(cont.)

Juan Navarro, Spanish composer, was born in the province of Seville (died 1580).

Alessandro Romano (known also as Alessandro Della Viola), a composer and violist, was born at Rome (date of death unknown).

Pietro Vinci, chanson and madrigal composer, was born in Nicosia, Sicily (died 1584).

Robert White, an important English composer, was born (died 1574, November 11).

Etienne Briard, music engraver, was working at Avignon.

Gaspard Coste was a chorister at the cathedral of Avignon.

Jean Daniel was organist at St. Maurice in Angers.

John Redford was organist and almoner, as well as master of the Choristers, at St. Paul's Cathedral in London during the latter part of the reign of Henry VIII.

John Taverner was organist of Cardinal College, Oxford (now Christ Church).

Verdelot lived in Florence at sometime around this date.

Anthology of sacred and secular pieces, vocal and instrumental, was published in England. It contained carols by Ashwell, Couper, Gwynneth, and Pygott.

Francesco di Milano composed "La Battaglia."

Luis Milán composed El Maestro (cont.) and Fantasia.

Willaert composed a five-part mass with no title.

Italian organs retained the same structure as in the previous century, however, more registers were added starting at this time.

Many transcriptions of motets and secular pieces by Byrd, Farnaby, Philips and others employed a great deal of figuration such as used in France at this time.

Marc Duval, French painter, was born (died 1581).

F. Zuccari, Italian architect and printer, was born (died 1609).

Italian painting: Correggio, The Holy Night (Altar-painting).

Italian painting: Correggio, Jupiter and Io (5'4"x2'5").

Italian painting: Correggio's "Loves of Jupiter" was painted for the palace of Mantua.

German painting: Cranach the Elder, Three Girls.

French painting: Anonymous French master, three ladies performing a chanson.

Italian painting: Andrea del Sarto, The Assumption.

Italian architecture: Sanmicheli, Verona, Palazzo Pompei (70'3" wide x 44' high).

(to 1535) Precursors of the later virginal style included

c.1530(cont.)

a hornpype by Aston, "My Lady Carey's Dompe," and the "Short measure off My Lady Wynkfyld's Rownde." All three have been preserved in the British Museum.

(to 1536) In Willaert's Netherlandish chansons, the tenor had the cantus firmus while the other voices were in similar broad, but strongly melismatic, style. The melismas had no significance in regard to the text.

(to 1540) Taverner was writing in a florid and broad manner certainly equal to his predecessors.

(to 1540) Italian painting: Titian, Magdalene.

(to 1570) Sperindio Bartoldo alternated binary and ternary rhythms in a ricercar.

1531

Ercole Bottrigari, Italian author on music, was born (died 1612).

Guillaume Costeley, organist to Charles IX and cultivator of "Vers mesuré," was born, quite possibly in Normandy (died 1606).

Vespasiano Gonzaga, Italian madrigalist, was born (died 1591).

Corteccia was organist at St. Lorenzo in Florence.

John Merbecke was at St. George's in Windsor.

Jacques de Meyere in this year claimed that Willaert was born (cont.) at Roulers, near Courtrai. Meyere also considered that Flanders produced the greatest singers, among them "Alexander" (presumably Agricola).

Richafort was in the service of Mary of Hungary who was still active as Regent of the Netherlands.

Susato was mentioned as having taken part in a performance of masses at Antwerp in the chapel of the Virgin in the cathedral in the capacity of trumpeter.

A John Wyldebore was Master of the Hospital of St. Mary's at Strood, in Kent, up to this time when it surrendered.

Attaingnant published "Deux livres d'orgue" and also seven books for "Orgues Espinettes et Manicordians." The latter indicated that there was no difference between the music for organ and the music for stringed keyboard instruments in France or Italy. Also, no apparent stimulus to keyboard music in France resulted from these publications.

A clavicembalo bearing this date was preserved in Italy by an eminent art critic. It had five soundholes, each one with a rose inserted.

Benedictus Ducis composed an elegy on the death of Josquin.

Févin's Sancta Trinitas was published.

The fróttola apparently had its last publication at this time.

The Gutknechtsche Gesangbuch

1531(cont.)

appeared.

Dorico reprinted Janequin's Bataille.

Jacques de Meyere's Rerum Flandriacum tomi X was written. The erroneous idea that Willaert became a member of the Chapel Royal in Hungary stemmed from an error in de Meyere's work.

The Passion was sung in Germany for the first time at Strassbourg.

De Sermisy's "Jouyssance vous donneray" was included in Trente et sept Chansons published by Attaingnant.

An inventory of the "Château de Pont d'Air," in this year, mentioned "una espinetta cum suo etuy," (a spinet with its case) meaning a case from which the instrument could be removed, as was the custom at that time.

Tallis was "joculator organorum" at Dover Priory.

Michael Weisse's "Böhmisches Brüdergesangbuch" appeared.

Galeotto del Carretto, Italian lyric poet, died (born c.1470).

Sir Thomas Elyot wrote "The Book Named The Governor."

Ulrich Zwingli, pre-Calvinist religious leader and opponent of Luther, died (born 1484).

Andrea del Sarto, Italian painter, died (born 1486).

Sebastiano Luciano was known as del Piombo after Pope Clement VII had given him (cont.) the sinecure of Frate del Piombo which he greatly desired.

Italian painting: Lotto, Crucifixion.

Netherlandish painting: Jan Van Scorel, Portrait of A Student.

(to 1536) Johannes Herrmann was Cantor of St. Thomas School at Leipzig.

(1531, 1532, 1539, 1542, and 1545) A certain Magister White was hired to repair the organ in the College Chapel at Magdalene College, Oxford.

c.1531

Jacobus de Kerle, a Flemish composer often referred to as "savior of church music," was born (died 1591).

Merbecke wrote a mass for Lent, Per arva justitiae.

Alonso Sanchez Coello, Spanish painter, was born (died 1588).

1532

Jean-Antoine de Baif, musician, friend of Ronsard, and a coleader of the Pléiade, was born (died 1589).

Giovanni Guidetti, allegedly a pupil of Palestrina, was born at Bologna (died 1592).

Ludwig Hembold, a German poet who wrote in a religious vein, was born (died 1598).

Orlando di Lasso, great Flemish composer, was born at Mons in Hainut (died 1594). As a boy he served as a musical apprentice (choirboy) at St. Nicholas

1532(cont.)

Church in Mons. Although he was a Catholic his influence on Protestant music was great. His works were in great contrast to those of Palestrina, his monumental contemporary. His was a truly international outlook as opposed to the parochial and more reserved Palestrinian style(died 1594, June 14).

Adam Puschman, a composer of Meistersinger songs and a pupil of Hans Sachs, was born (died 1600).

Leonhart Schröter, a Lutheran composer, was born (died 1601).

Crispin van Stappen, singer and maestro di capella, died at Cambrai (birthdate unknown).

Pierre Certon was Clerc at Sainte Chapelle.

Ducis, a Protestant pastor in Ulm, was found neglectful of his duties and accused of beating his wife. However, he was active in the humanistic movement.

Attempts (probably unjustified) have been made to identify Benedictus de Opitiis as Benedictus Ducis whose career in Germany was during a period starting at this date.

A list from this date indicated that Susato owned two trumpets, a "velt-trompet," and a "teneur -pipe."

A house in the parish of Notre Dame, at Antwerp, carried a sign "de clavizimbele." This was the earliest appearance of the clavecin or harpsichord.

Attaingnant published a series of seven polyphonic mass books.

A Te Deum and Benedictus (in F) were attributed to Thomas Barcrofte in a manuscript collection of this date. This time was actually too early for an English setting of these hymns. It was more probable that the composer was George Barcrofte, vicar-choral and organist of Ely cathedral.

The works of the composer Carpentras were published at Avignon in Briard's characters. The publisher was Johannes Channay.

The lutenist and lute-maker Hans Gerle (Nürnberg) wrote a Musica Teusch in German for use by lutenists and violinists.

Only one printed copy of a Johannes Prioris mass survived. It was a Requiem for four voices. Other Prioris masses were preserved but in manuscript form.

Georg Rhaw's "Enchiridion musicae mensuralis" appeared. He also published "Musica figuralis deudsch" at this time.

Hans Sachs composed Klingende Ton.

Stoltzer's works were included in printed collections after this date.

Verdelot composed motets that were included in various collections by publishers from this date forward. His madrigals, however, were his most noteworthy output.

1532(cont.)

Hans Holbein the Younger returned to London.

German painting: Cranach the Elder, Venus.

German painting: Holbein the Younger, Georg Gisze, a German merchant in London.

German painting: Holbein the Younger, Portrait of Hermann Wedigh.

(to 1535) Two sketches were made by Martin van Heemskerck, a pupil of Jan van Scorel. They represented the church as Pierluigi knew it (St. John Lateran) and showed the interesting relics of the old palace of the Laterani on the east side of the Basilica. This had once been the residence of Constantine's wife, Fausta, and was given by him to the Popes, who lived there until they migrated to Avignon. The sketches were made while the artist was in Rome.

(to 1537) Carpentras produced four volumes of compositions, one each of hymns, lamentations, Magnificats and masses during this period.

(1532, 1537, 1546 and 1552) Tablatures by Hans Gerle were published at Nürnberg during the years indicated.

(to 1538) Jean Courtois composed numerous motets that were published in three volumes of motets at Lyons.

(to 1539) Gaspard Coste, composed songs and madrigals that were preserved in "Motetti del Fiore."

(1532, 1539, and 1540) A Missa Hercules dux Ferrariae mass was preserved in prints of 1532, 1539, and 1540. This was one of several that carried the name of "Lupus" as composer. The printings were from different editions of a collection published by Moderne, edited by Fr. Layolle, the Younger. The latter composed a "Missa Adieu mes amours" that was included in the volumes.

(to 1549) Jean Courtois' French songs included two songs that were included in "Trente-cinq livres de Chansons nouvelles."

(to 1555) Jacques (Jacotin) Le Bel was a singer in the Chapel Royal.

c.1532

Cornetts and Sackbuts were used at Canterbury.

Quotations were made in a letter on this date and described as coming from the Gloria of Dufay's Missa Sancti Anthonii de Padua. The communication was from the Italian theorist Giovanni Spataro to his colleague Pietro Aron.

German painting: Altdorfer, Landscape.

1533

(April) Claudio Merulo, noted Italian organist, teacher and composer, was born at Coreggio (died 1604). He held the post of first organist at St. Mark's in Venice for many years. His compositions included mainly canzone, ricercari and toccate. The latter form was his particular specialty. His teaching career was equally distinguished. (see also 1523)

1533(cont.)

Jacques Champion's brother Nicolas died (birthdate unknown). He had gone to Spain with Philip the Handsome as a member of the latter's chapel.

Gallus Dressler, a Lutheran composer of some note, was born (died c.1585).

Johann Eccard, composer of Protestant church music, was born in Thuringia (died 1611).

De Sermisy was made a canon at St. Chapelle and thereby was assured of a substantial salary.

Caspar Tieffenbrucker, instrument maker, entered his most prolific period.

Attaingnant published the Vingt et huyt Chansons musicales.

Faber's Melodiae Prudentianae was preserved in a Glasgow library.

Attaingnant published Janequin's "Sacrae cantiones seu motectae quatuor vocum."

Lanfranco's Scintille di musica was published.

Attaingnant published a collection which included "Je suis desheritée," credited to "Lupus."

The first collection of serious five-part madrigals was published.

The collection "Madrigali novi de diversi excellentissimi musici" was published.

The earliest madrigals, written by Arcadelt and Verdelot and (cont.) several Italian composers including Festa, were published at Rome.

Marot wrote bright and cheery love poems and since this date provided metrical psalm translations in French for the court of Francis I. The first of these was Psalm vi and was published in "Le Miroir de tres chretienne Princesse Marguerite."

Ornithoparcus' Micrologus was published at Cologne.

Verdelot was the chief contributor to "Madrigali Novi de diversi excellentissimi Musici."

The Vienna Song-book, a collection of Volkslieder, consisted of five part-books, with both sacred and secular words and music. It was preserved in a Viennese Library.

The recommended range for keyboard instruments was increased to include G and e''', in the Recanetum de musica aurea by Stephanus Vanneus.

Musicians pictured in Burgkmair's woodcuts included the trombone maker, Hans Neuschel of Nürnberg who died in this year. He had been summoned to Rome by Pope Leo X and rewarded for the silver trombones he had made for that Pope.

Queen Elizabeth I (House of Tudor) of England was born (died 1603).

Lucas Van Leyden, Netherlandish painter, died (born c.1494).

Veit Stoss, German painter and sculptor, died at Nürnberg

1533(cont.)

(born c.1440).

German painting: Holbein the Younger, Jean De Dinteville and Georges De Selve, French Ambassadors at the English Court.

(to 1537) Konrad Krebs during these years built the Wendelstein, which, in spite of the conciliatory influence of Dessau and Meissen, gave the general impression that those who planned it aimed to make a Ferrara out of "Town of the Heavy Beer."

(to 1549) Many of Pierre Certon's motets were included in collections published by Attaignant during this period.

(to 1584) The reign of Czar Ivan IV, the Terrible, over Russia.

c.1533

Richard Farrant, English composer, was born (died 1580).

With the onset of the Italian Renaissance, the madrigal was a logical reaction to the great development in Italian poetry of the time, initiated by Petrarch and carried to an emotional climax by Ariosto, Cardinal Bembo, Sannazaro, Tasso, Torquato and others.

As a result of the intense evolution of the Renaissance madrigal, new music became increasingly influenced by and capable of interpreting poetic words.

Gossaert, Netherlandish painter known as Mabuse, died (born c.1478).

1534

(April) Attaingnant started issuing a series of thirteen motet books, one per month.

Ludovico Agostino, choirmaster, and composer, was born at Ferrara (died 1590, September 20).

Count Giovanni Bardi of Vernio, a patron of music and head of the Florentine Camerata, was born (died 1612).

Fernando de las Infantas, contemporary with the composer Victoria, and a priest, was born in Cordova. He was at Rome for most of his life.

Lucas Osiander, court preacher in Würtenburg and a German composer who used trombones, was born at Nürnberg (died 1604).

Padre Francesco Soto, a composer of laude, was born at Lanza (died 1619, September 25).

Von Bruck was obviously in sympathy with Lutheranism. He composed music for a series of Luther's hymns, for example, "Komm Heiliger Geist," "Gott Vater wohn' uns bei," "Mitten wir im Leben sind."

Ferdinand Columbus, son of the explorer, acquired a music manuscript for his library.

Gombert became a prebend.

Jaquet of Mantua was master of the choirboy's in the Cardinal's chapel at Mantua.

A gymnasium (school) was created in accordance with the will of Julius II. He left money for masters "in musica et cantû et in grammatica."

1534(cont.)

Nürnberg became the center of the music-publishing industry in Germany.

The editions by Ott and Egenolff only supplied texts for those parts that were presumably meant to be sung.

Palestrina was supposedly enrolled in the choir-school of Santa Maria Maggiore. He was nine or ten years old at the time.

The bishop of Palestrina (Cardinal Andrea della Valle) became archpriest of the basilica of Santa Maria Maggiore in Rome. He probably took young Palestrina with him since another source stated that Palestrina was sent to Santa Maria Maggiore in Rome to serve as a choirboy.

On a title page, Ludwig Senfl was referred to as "Musicus primarius," of the Duke of Bavaria.

De Sermisy composed a St. Matthew's Passion.

Master Mathias Werrecore reorganized the chapel in the cathedral at Milan.

Antico's "Primo Libro de la canzoni francese" appeared.

Jean Courtois composed numerous motets, published in "Liber quartus: XXIX musicales quatuor etc." at Paris.

Attaignant included a work by Divitis in his collection of Magnificats published at Paris.

One magnificat by Fevin appeared in Attaignant's 5th book for 4 voices, and two of his motets were included in the 11th book, both published at Paris.

The first publication that included Mouton's Reges terrae was in this year, twelve years after the composer's death.

A Collection of Volkslieder by Johann Ott included Songs in 5 parts and was published at Nürnberg. A perfect copy of this valuable song-book was preserved in libraries at Munich and Zwickau. The original publisher was Formschneider.

Pierre de la Rue composed Missa Ave sanctissima Maria, a parody on a motet written for three voices and increased to six. It was published by Attaingnant and attributed to Verdelot.

Eighty-one pieces by Senfl in Ott's collection of 121 songs.

Senfl's "Varia carminum genera, quibus tum Horatius, tum alii egregiae poetae . . . . . harmoniis composita" was written.

The formal break between Henry VIII's England and the papacy was at this time.

Hercules II did not come to the throne until this date.

Catholic Reform started a new phase of its development when Pope Paul III assumed the pontificate and Ignatius Loyola and six others took their vows.

During Pope Paul III's reign a wall in the old building collapsed and the Sacrament-altar

1534(cont.)

in the chapel of St. Simon and St. Jude was reinstated. It was situated between the fifth and sixth columns of the old basilica and authorities proceeded to adorn it magnificently with precious gilding, marbles, and paintings.

Antonio Allegri, Italian painter known as Correggio, died (born c.1489).

Enrique de Egas, Spanish architect, died (born c.1480).

Antonio da San Gallo, Renaissance architect, died (born 1455).

Italian architecture: Antonio da Sangallo the Younger, Rome, Farnese Palace (185'x 235'; facade 185'x96'6").

(to 1535) Attaingnant published a motet series.

(and 1539) Publications of Sebastian de Felstin's Opusculum musices in these years were combined with another tract, De Musica Figurata by Martin Kromer of Biecz.

(to 1540) Italian painting: Parmigianino, La Madonna del Collo Lungo (The Madonna with the long neck).

(to 1544) Jean de Bilhon's compositions were included in several collections of church music published during these years at Leyden and Paris.

(to 1549) The Papal reign of St. Paul III (born in Rome).

(and 1550) "Primiera" was the card game of the upper classes. (cont.) There were comments concerning "Capitolo del gioco della primiera col comento di messer Pietropaulo da San Chirico" published in Venice also in, "Gioco di Primiera con una nova gionta composta per Benedetto Clario Cieco Venetiano" published in Bologna (1550).

c.1534

De Rore went to Italy.

1535

Andrea Amati was born at Cremona (died 1611). This was the beginning of the dynasty of the great violin-makers. He developed his style from da Salo. The Amati family combined with the Guarneri family and the Stradivarius family brought lasting fame to Cremona as the birthplace of the most magnificent violins.

Wilhelm Breitengraser, German lieder composer, died (birthdate unknown).

Fabritio Caroso, dancing master of Sermoneta, was born (died c.1610).

Magister Andreas Ornitoparchus (Vogelsang?), author of Musicae Activae Micrologus, an outstanding theoretical tract, and faculty member at Tübingen, died (birthdate unknown).

Alexander Striggio the elder, composer of intermezzi, was born (died 1587, September 22).

Bartholomaeus Tromboncino, frottole composer, died (born c.1475).

Giaches de Wert, Netherlandish madrigalist who spent much of

1535(cont.)

his life in Italy, was born (died 1596).

Cardinal de Cupis founded the "Cappella musicale nella protobasilica di S. Giovanni in Laterano."

An artisan, Francesco, founded Santa Maria di Loreto. He had taken orphans into his house on the Mercato and had them fed, clothed and instructed in music.

Ghiselin, Netherlandish composer also known as Verbonnet, was at the court at Ferrara (also in 1491 and 1503).

Francesco Canova da Milano was in Rome in the service of Pope Paul III. Milano taught the lute to the Pope's nephew.

Morales became a singer in the Papal Chapel Choir under Pope Paul III.

Andrea Antico's "Canzoni francesi" was written.

Silvestro di Ganassi's "La Fontegara" an early flute method appeared. It was usable for recorder or whistle flute.

"God save the king" was found in the English Bible (Coverdale, 1535).

Joseph Klug's Hymnbook contained the hymn "Ach Gott Vom Himmel" set to a tune in the Phrygian mode, which was afterwards adapted to Andreas Knöpken's Psalm "Hilf Gott, wie geht das immer zu." The hymn had previously been known in a hypophrygian setting.

Two more hymns with text by (cont.) Luther appeared:

Sie ist mir lieb, The Christian Church (Rev.xii.).

Von Himmel hoch, The Nativity (a children's hymn).

"Luther's Hymn" was first published.

Luis Milan's "El Maestro" appeared. It was the first printed tablature book in Spain.

Luis Milan's Fantasia No. 26, for guitar, was composed.

The "Villote a la Veneziana" was published.

Christian Egenolff published the Gassenhawerlin und Reutterliedlin am Main.

The proportion of native singers in the Pontifical Choir was at seven out of twenty-two. This represented a gradual increase.

The villota, as published from this date on, was a true folk dance-song from several Italian provinces.

"The Golden Book of Marcus Aurelius" was written.

Sir Thomas More, the author of Utopia, a classic description of the ideal state, died (born 1478).

The Tyndale-Coverdale translation of the Bible, which appeared at this time, ultimately became the basis for the authorized version (King James) which was published in 1611. The Coverdale Bible contained the word "ballad" as the title of

1535(cont.)

the Song of Soloman. "Salomon's Ballettes called Cantica Canticorum."

Italian architecture: Peruzzi, Rome, Palazzo Massimi (64'7" high).

(to 1536) El Maestro, the Milan book published during these years, contained villancicos, romances, instrumental fantasies, pavanes and preludes. It also gave directions for tuning as well as in the reading of tablature.

(to 1537) Northern Renaissance architecture: Designed by Jan Wallot and Christian Sixdeniers, The old Chancellery in Bruges ("La Greffe").

(to 1545) The first decade of Italian madrigals embraced these years.

(to 1565) Jacques Berchem was in the service of the Duke of Mantua. He was referred to by the Italians as Giachetto di Mantova.

(to 1567) Hans Heugel's compositions occurred during this period.

(to 1572) Francisco Ceballos, Spanish composer, was maestro at Burgos Cathedral. He died in the latter year.

c.1535

A primer by Marshall was published in England. It contained mattins (sic), laude, prime, terce, sext, none, vespers and compline, Apostle's Creed and the Lord's Prayer.

Alessandro Striggio, organist, lutenist, and composer, was a member of a noble Mantuan family(died 1587, September 22).

Bartolomeo Tromboncino, frottole composer, died (born c.1475).

Thomas Barcrofte was said to have been organist of Ely Cathedral.

The "Cappella di Musica nella basilica Liberiana" (Ste. Maria Maggiore) was founded.

The period of the madrigal's popularity started at this time when Verdelot published the first set of vocal works that bore the actual title of "Madrigali."

Italian painting: A fresco in the dome of Saronno cathedral showed a complete trio, a violin, a viola, and a tenor violin, however, each had only three strings.

(to 1540) Four books of madrigals for five-parts were published. One volume was devoted entirely to Verdelot's compositions.

(to 1545) Titian experimented with "Mannerism," very popular in Italy at this time.

(to 1551) Benedictus Appenzeller was master of the choirboys in the chapel of Mary of Hungary at Brussels. During this period he composed sacred music.

1536

Jachet van Berchem, Flemish contrapuntalist, was born (died 1600).

Mariana, writer of "Tratado contra los Juegos Publicos"

1536(cont.)

("Treatise against Public Amusements"), was born (died 1623).

Chu Tsai-yü, Chinese author of a Compendium of Music, was born (died 1611).

Bartolomé Escobedo was in the Papal Choir with Morales. The former was a judge in the controversy between Vicentino and Lusitano.

Andrea Gabrieli apparently began his musical career as a singer at St. Mark's in this year. While there, he came under the influence of Willaert, however, little definite evidence exists concerning these facts.

Palma Pierluigi, Palestrina's mother, died leaving four sons, the composer being the eldest.

Christopher Tye was graduated from Cambridge with a Bachelor of Music degree.

"Intavolatura degli Madrigali di Verdelotto da cantare et sonare nel Lauto . . . per Messer Adriano," was published in Venice.

Antico's "La Couronne et fleur des chansons a troys" appeared.

Casteliono's Intabolatura de leuto contained suites including a pavane, three saltarelli, and a toccata.

Benedictus Ducis' elegy on the death of Erasmus was composed.

Heinrich Finck's Songs in four parts were published in Nürnberg. The volume contained (cont.) fifty-five sacred and secular songs by Finck and other composers. Perfect copies have survived in Munich and Zwickau Libraries and an imperfect one at the British Museum.

A lute version of Janequin's Bataille was published.

A tochata (toccata) by Francesco da Milano and a fantasia by Marco d'Aquila appeared.

Mouton's "La, la, la, l'oysillon du boy" was published.

The first performance of "Mystery of the Acts of the Apostles" was at Bourges. It was a medieval mystery drama.

Tablatures by Newsidler were published in Nürnberg for two parts.

The "Fünff und sechzig teütscher Lieder" was published by Schöffer and Apiarius at Strassbourg.

A close resemblance to ancient Welsh notation was found in a work entitled, Musurgia, seu praxis musicae, illius primo quae Instrumentis agitur certa ratio, ab Ottomaro Luscinio Argentino duobus Libris absoluta. Argentorati apud Ioannem Schottum, Anno Christi, 1536.

An entertaining quodlibet, later called a fricassée, by the French, was published at this time. There were about fifty excerpts from popular chansons of the time, and Sermisy was represented by more compositions than any other composer.

1536(cont.)

Verdelot's first volume for four parts probably appeared, since Willaert's arrangements of twenty-two of Verdelot's madrigals for solo voice and lute were published the same year.

Book II of madrigals in four parts containing works by Festa, Verdelot, and other composers was published.

Virdung's "Musica getuscht und ausgezogen" was translated into Latin as "Musurgia, seu Praxis-Musicae," and published at Strassburg.

Willaert anticipated monody with his instrumental tablature of madrigals composed by Verdelot who lived in Venice for most of his active life.

Willaert's five Masses for four -parts were published in Venice.

Willaert at this time did not arrange all of Verdelot's madrigals for voice and lute, rather only those that had a "cantilena" with simple accompaniment. A second edition was published in 1540.

All churches in England had an English Bible by this time.

The Gardano family at Venice printed both staff and notes simultaneously for about a century and a half, starting at this time.

Since the archlute was not mentioned in Luscinius it probably appeared at a later date.

Complete Latin and German masses and also mixed ones were held in Würtenburg.

The passamezzo was a favorite selection in collections of lute music.

Henry Fitzroy, Duke of Richmond and Somerset, a natural son of Henry VIII, died (birthdate unknown).

Luther's friend, Wolfgang Musculus in his "Itinerarium" described the Würtenburg church service of the time.

Thomas Sackville, Lord Buckhurst, Elizabethan poet and writer, was born (died 1608).

Peruzzi, Renaissance architect, died (born 1481).

Italian architecture: Michelangelo, Rome, Piazza del Campidoglio, begun in this year (Museum 164' wide).

Italian architecture: Jacopo Sansovino, Venice, Library (275'longx58'high).

(to 1537) Cavazzoni was an organist at Chioggia.

(to 1539) The closing and plundering of monasteries in England occurred.

(to 1540) Wolfgang Jünger was Cantor of the St. Thomas School in Leipzig.

(to 1541) Italian painting: Michelangelo, Last Judgment.

(and 1542) The "Musurgia seu praxis musicae" by Ottomarus Luscinius (Othmar Nachtigal), dated Argentorati, Strassburg, 1536, was published and reprinted in

1536(cont.)
1542.

(and 1542) Calvin and Marot met in 1536 at the court of Ferrara, however, it was not until Marot fled to Geneva in 1542 that any communication or friendship between them developed.

c.1536
Gil Vicente, Portuguese dramatist, died (born c.1465).

French painting: Corneille de Lyon, Portrait of Clément Marot.

Italian painting: Titian, La Bella.

1537
Jacques Le Fèvre, author on music, died (birthdate unknown).

Girolamo, A Sienese academician known as "Materiale Intronato" was born (died 1586).

G.F. Guarini, a writer of intermezzi, was born (died 1612). His best known work was "Pastor fido," written in the form of simple madrigals.

Paul Hoffhaimer, German organist and composer, died in Salzburg (born 1449 or 1459).

Leonard Barre was a singer in the Papal Chapel.

Gombert went to Madrid and took twenty singers along. He apparently became choirmaster for Charles V.

Palestrina was listed among the pueri cantantes of the Cappella Liberiana at Santa Maria Maggiore in a document at this time. He was by this time eleven or twelve years old and (cont.) his voice was nearing the age of change. There were six choirboys in all and they were instructed by Gialomo Coppola.

Tallis was conductor of the choir St. Mary-at-Hill, London.

Andrea Antico's (da Montona) "Madrigali a tre voci" appeared.

Arcadelt's first madrigals appeared, one in a collection for 3 voices, published by Scotto, and one in Verdelot's Book III for four voices.

The "Provinciales" of Antonio de Arena appeared.

A few melodies from Clemen's Souterliedekens were found in a manuscript written at Zutphen.

Jean Courtois composed numerous motets, published in "Novum et insigne opus musicum" at Nürnberg.

Festa's collection for three voices was published.

Tablatures by Hans Gerle were published at Nürnberg (also in 1532, 1546, and 1552).

Luther probably composed the music and text for Vater unser im Himmel-reich, in Köphyl's Strassburg Gesangbuch (1537). It also appeared in Lotther's Magdeburg Hymn-book (1540).

Johann Petreius' first music publication was probably "Musicae, id est, Artis canendi, libri duo, autor Sebaldus Heyden. Norimbergae apud Joh. Petreium, anno salutis, 1537."

1537(cont.)

Ludwig Senfl's "Magnificat octo tonorum, à 4" appeared.

The first Catholic collection of liturgical monophony with German texts was by Michael Vehe. It was called "Ein new Gesangbuechlin geystlicher Lieder" and was published at Leipzig. It included fifty-two songs.

From this date forward various collections of Verdelot's madrigals for four, five, and six voices were published, by, among others, Gardano and Scotto. They were, however, included with other composer's works.

Book III of madrigals for four voices was published and contained works by Festa, Verdelot and other composers.

The first known volume devoted entirely to villanesche was an anonymous collection for three voices carrying this date.

A reprint of Walther's Geystliche Gesangkbüchleyn appeared with changes and additions (other reprints were done in 1525, 1544, and 1551).

The earliest surviving clavichord was of Italian origin.

Information was sent to the Council to prosecute John Hogon, who, "with a crowd or a fyddyll," sang a song with political implication using the tune "The hunt is up."

Santa Maria di Loreto was founded.

King Edward VI (House of Tudor) of England was born (died 1553).

Jane (Lady Jane Grey), recognized by some as Queen of England for nine days, was born (died 1554).

Hans Cranach, son of Lucas Cranach the Elder (German painter), died during a visit to Italy (birthdate unknown).

Lorenzo di Credi, Florentine painter, died (born c.1458).

Della Porta, Italian architect, was born (died 1604).

(to 1548) The organ tablature of Jan of Lublin was written during these years.

1538

Hans Buchner, German organist and composer, died (born 1483).

Guglielmo I, a patron of the arts in Mantua, was born (died 1587).

Arcadelt was the first to hold the office, "Maestro dei putti" (master of the boys).

Joan Brudieu and four other French singers took part in Christmas festivities in the town of Urgell, in the Pyrenees.

Compositions by Pierre Cadéac appeared in Attaingnant publications from this date forward.

Ghiselin Danckerts, a native of Tholen, Zeeland, became a singer at the Sistine Chapel.

Francesco Canova da Milano accompanied the Pope to the Council of Nice. While there, he impressed King Francis I of France with his playing.

1538(cont.)

Luis de Narvaez initiated the variation for the lute.

The composer Gaude Maria was listed as Johannes Okegus in a source from this date.

The epitaph published by Rhaw in Würtenburg stated that Agricola died near Valladolid in Spain at the age of 60. No date, however, was assigned to the event.

Francisco de Salinas visited Rome. While there, he heard da Milano improvise on a galliarde melody, however, no dance compositons by him were ever published.

Waclaw Szamotulczyk, Polish composer, studied at the University of Cracow.

Pedro Alberch Vila was organist at Barcelona Cathedral where he later became a canon.

Arcadelt's First Book of Madrigals was published at Venice.

Crespel's lament on the death of Ockenheim mentioned Agricola as a fellow-student of his during his studies with the master. The dates of his published compositions when considered with an interesting epitaph published with a collection of motets published at Würtenburg provided information for vague biographical material.

A motet by Benedictus Ducis, "Dum fabricator mundi Supplicium" was included in Rhaw's "Selectae Harmoniae . . . de Passione Domini" published in Würtenburg.

Galliculus' Passion was published by Rhaw.

Gardano published a collection "Motetti del Frutto" at Venice.

Madrigals by Ivo appeared in various early collections, the first one being Verdelot's, published in this year.

In a ceremonial motet for six voices, Jubilate Deo, which was written for the peace conference between Charles V and Francis I arranged by Pope Paul III, the quintus sang Gaudeamus repeatedly on the notes of the Gregorian Introit, Gaudeamus omnes.

Luther wrote a short treatise in praise of music. A poem on the same subject ("Frau Musika") was also written and was preserved in the Leipziger Allgemeine Musikalische Zeitung.

The tune to Ein' Feste Burg by Luther (Psalm xlvi) apparently first appeared in "Psalmen und geistliche Lieder," by Wolfgang Köphyl, published at Strassburg.

Morales wrote a cantata for the peace conference at Nice.

Luis de Narvaez, a Spanish composer of variations, wrote Delphin de Musica, a volume of tablatures. It included transcriptions of vocal works by des Prés, Gombert, and other composers, as well as Spanish folk-music. The collection was published at Valladolio in this year.

Johannes Otto, A Nürnberg printer, included the following in

1538(cont.)

the preface to the second volume of his Novi Operis Musici: "no painter could express with the aid of pencil and colors the suffering face of the Crucified more convincingly than Josquin with his music." He was describing the motet, Huc Me Sidero.

Book IV of the Parangon was published.

Ludwig Senfl's Maximilian lament "Quis dabit oculis" was published by Ott.

Walsingham, an old English song, referred to the famous Priory of Walsingham in Norfolk. It must have been composed before this date when the Priory was suppressed.

Calvin, having been expelled from Geneva, went to Strasburg and decided to follow the example of the Lutherans in Germany and compile a psalter for use in his own church. He became acquainted with congregational psalm-singing in the German language while at Strassburg. Calvin referred to his translations of Psalms 25 and 46 in a letter written during his exile from Geneva.

In the deed of surrender of St. Augustine's Abbey, which was dated July 30, Henry VIII showed that at the time John Essex was abbot and John Dygon was principal of the four priors. Apparently, Dygon's position was only inferior in rank to that of the abbot.

The printing press was first used in Hungary at this time.

Georg Rhaw's close relationship with Luther was obvious from the preface which Luther wrote for his "Symphoniae jucundae." In this preface he stated that music was of divine origin, insolubly bound to the Holy Scriptures and that it was the best means of spreading the truth, since it was in itself a divine service.

German illustration:
H. Aldegrever, Three Trumpetists from "The Wedding Dancers."

Albrecht Altdorfer, German painter, died (born c.1480).

Italian painting: Titian, Venus of Urbino.

(to 1539) John Taverner had dealings with Cromwell.

(and 1540) Some of Johann Walther's compositions were included in collections of Rhaw and Forster, "Montan -Neubers Psalmenwerk" and "Motettensammlung."

(to 1541) Lassus was in Italy.

(to 1543) Some of Arcadelt's chansons were published by Attaingnant and Moderne. These years were essentially during the composer's madrigal period.

(to 1543) Jacques Moderne published Parangon des chansons in eleven volumes.

(to 1546) Among interlude writers in England was John Redford, whose "Wyt and Science," presented at court during this time included three songs.

(to 1546) French architecture:

1538(cont.)

Serlio, Ancy-le-Franc, Château (190' wide; court 95' wide).

(to 1548) Martin Agricola's Musica instrumentalis deudsch was reprinted in various editions.

(to 1569) Gardano was a composer, printer and publisher of music in Venice during this period.

c.1538

Costanzo Festa's "Non s'incolpa la voglia" appeared in Verdelot's "Madrigali a cinque."

French painting: Anonymous master, Portrait of Charles de Cossé, First Count of Brissac.

German painting: Holbein the Younger, Thomas Howard, Duke of Norfolk (Windsor Castle).

Hans Buchner, German organist and composer, was still active.

1539

(April 24) Rubino was choirmaster at S. Maria Maggiore up to this date.

(January) Arcadelt was admitted to the Julian Chapel.

Ottaviano dei Petrucci, the first printer of mensural music, died (born 1466, June 14).

Nicolaus Selneccer, organist, composer, and theologian, was born in Franconia, (date of death unknown).

Jean Courtois was chapelmaster to the Archbishop of Cambrai when Charles V passed through on his way to Ghent. Courtois (cont.) composed a motet in 4 parts for the occassion, "Venite populi terrae," which was performed at the Cathedral.

Jaquet of Mantua became maestro di cappella of the Mantuan Cathedral of St. Peter's. He was still in the service of the Cardinals.

At the wedding of Cosimo de'Medici and Eleanora of Toledo at Florence a performance of the comedy, Il Commodo, by Antonio Landi, was presented. It was produced with intermezzi, including madrigals with texts by Strozzi and music by Corteccia.

Palestrina started his musical studies with Robin Mallapert, a French choirmaster at the Cappella Liberiana at Santa Maria Maggiore. He quite possibly continued under Firmin Le Bel.

Pedro Ordoñez became a member of the Papal Choir.

Sometime after his voice changed Palestrina served as the magister puerorum and trained the boys in the Cappella Giulia at St. Peter's.

According to Michaelis, a line of Schütz' family was raised to hereditary nobility by Emperor Charles V.

The first successful measured verse in Italy resulted from Tolomei's "Versi e Regole de la Nuova Poesia Toscana."

A certain Magister White was hired to repair the organ in the College Chapel at Magdalene College, Oxford (also in 1531,

1539(cont.)

1532, 1542, and 1545).

Zarlino spent his youth studying for the Church and was admitted to the Minor Orders at this time.

The hymn "All Lob und Ehr soll Gottes sein," first appeared.

Four books of Arcadelt's madrigals for four voices were published.

Arcadelt wrote five books of masses.

An Attaingnant collection attributed "Je suis desheritée" to Cadéac.

Two psalms by Carpentras appeared in the "Psalmorum Selectorum Tom. II." published by Petreius at Nürnberg.

Attaingnant first published the works of Clemens non Papa in a collection produced this year.

Corteccia's compositions included nine pieces for four, six, and eight voices with various instruments. They appeared in an unusual collection titled "Musiche fatte nelle nozze, etc." published by Gardano in Venice.

Corteccia, along with Festa, Masaconi, Moschini and Rampollini provided music for entertainment. This included mostly madrigals and a few instrumental pieces, all of which were published by Gardano at Venice. The event was the marriage of Cosimo I de'Medici and Leonora of Toledo.

Courtois composed several motets (cont.) published in "Fior de' Motetti" at Venice. He also had motets published in the "Psalmorum selectorum" at Nürnberg.

Des Prés' "Missa Da pacem" and "Missa Pange lingua" were published by Ott at Nürnberg.

Douen traced the origin of almost half the melodies of the complete Genevan Psalter and discovered that thirteen of them were taken from the Strassburg Psalter of this date.

Ducis was erroneously claimed as a German by some on the basis of the publication and dedication of a setting of the Odes of Horace at Ulm in this year. The dedication was to the youths of that city and it was asserted that this proved his residence in that city. In all probability the dedication was the idea of the publisher rather than the composer.

The "Missae tredecim . . . Norinbergae . . . arte Hieronymi Graphei, 1539" appeared.

An Easter Mass for four voices was partly on Christ ist erstanden and issued by Johannes Hähnel.

Hilsey's primer was published. It contained matins, lauds, prime, terce, sext, none, vespers and compline, Apostle's Creed and Lord's Prayer.

Four of Isaac's lieder were included in Förster's collection, "Ein auszug guter Teutscher liedlein" published by Petreius at Nürnberg.

1539

Isaac's mass "O praeclara," one of his greatest works, was included in the "Liber quindecim missarum" published by Petreius at Nürnberg.

Two masses, "Salve nos," and "Fröhlich Wesen," by Isaac were included in Ott's collection "Missae 13, Vocum" published at Nürnberg.

Attaignant reprinted "Ce me semblent choses perdues," which had first appeared in Book IV of Layolle's Parangon.

A Missa Hercules dux Ferrariae mass was preserved in prints of 1532, 1539, and 1540. This was one of several that carried the name of "Lupus" as composer. The printings were from different editions of a collection published by Moderne, edited by Fr. Layolle, the Younger. The latter composed a "Missa Adieu mes amours" that was included in the volumes.

"Vater unser" (The Lord's Prayer) appeared in the version with Luther's text.

Marot completed his first installment of thirty psalms, simple and in Calvinistic style. Prior to this, they had only existed in manuscript.

Moulu wrote a "Missa duarum facierum" which was included in Petreius' Liber XV missarum published at Nürnberg.

"Liber quindecim Missarum . . l Norimbergae apud Joh. Petreium, 1539." was issued.

The Missa O praeclara was pub- (cont.) lished by Petreius at Nürnberg.

Rhaw published "Von den Proportionibus;" "Rudimenta Musices."

Ruffo, a native of Verona, probably composed a Magnificat published at this time.

Rhaw published the Officia paschalia.

Two duos by Sermisy appeared in the Canzoni francese . . . , published by Gardano in Venice.

The Strassburg tunes of this time which still survived in the Genevan Psalter were those to Psalms 1,2,15,36,91,103,104, 114,130,137 and 143. Two of them, 36 and 137, kept nearly their original form and 103 remained unchanged.

The Hymn Book of Valent. Schumann appeared in Leipzig.

Willaert's motet setting of the sequence, Benedicta es coelorum Regina was not published until this date.

At the marriage of Cosimo I and Eleanora of Toledo in Florence a performance of "Intermezzi," or separate musical scenes from plays, particularly tragedies based on Greek dramas, took place. The music was by Corteccia and included 3 solos, 4 madrigals (for 4,6 & 8 voices) all with varied instrumental accompaniments.

The first time solo-singing was supposed to have occurred was this year in an Intermezzo, in which Sileno sang the upper

1539(cont.)

part of a madrigal by Corteccio. He accompanied himself on the violone, while the lower parts, representing the Satyrs, were taken by wind instruments.

As early as this date, vocal compositions were adapted to be either played on the viol or sung (buone da cantare et sonare).

Pietro Bembo was elevated to Cardinal by Pope Paul III.

Calvin's first Psalter, published at Strassburg, contained eighteen psalmes of which six were with texts, translated by Calvin himself, and the Song of Simeon, the Creed, and the Ten Commandments.

Ippolito d'Este was elevated to cardinal.

A translation of the Bible, begun by William Tyndale and finished by Miles Coverdale, was published in England as the "Great Bible," under the patronage of King Henry VIII. The title-page showed Henry VIII distributing the "word of God" to his subjects.

In spite of Henry VIII's violent procedures, the Six Articles, enacted in this year, reaffirmed the main points of Catholic doctrine.

Pope Paul III bestowed the privilege of conferring knighthood on the family of Count Francesco Sforza.

A printing press was brought from Spain and set in operation at Mexico City.

German painting: Hans Holbein the Younger, Anne of Cleves (25 5/8" x 18 7/8").

German painting: Holbein the Younger, Henry VIII.

(to 1540) Ducis' songs were included in Forster's collection of German songs published by Petreius at Nürnberg.

(to 1540) Palestrina certainly must have received a stipend for musical tuition from the choirmaster in charge at Santa Maria Maggiore while he was a choirboy. The choirmaster was Mallapert, a French musician, who resigned from the position this year (1539). He was succeeded for a short time by Fevin, following which Firmin Le Bel was appointed (1540).

(and 1540) Collections of madrigals for four voices by della Viola were published.

(and 1541) Gombart had his motets of these years accomodata for viols and wind instruments.

(to 1541) "Le Parangon des Chansons" was published by "Jaques Moderne dict Grand Jacques" at Lyon.

(to 1545) Three collections of motets by Willaert were published at Venice.

(to 1545) Berchem's madrigals, masses and motets appeared in several collections published at Venice during these years.

(to 1549) Arcadelt was in the Papal Choir in Rome.

(to 1549) Gaspard Coste com-

1539(cont.)

posed madrigals and songs that were included in "Trente-cinq livres des chansons à quatre parties" published at Paris during these years.

(to 1549) The tradition of the motet-like Netherlandish chanson carried on during the period of Janequin and Sermisy through the works of several composers. Among them was Jean Richafort as well as several others whose compositions were seldom included in Attaingnant publications during these years. Their works were, however, included in Susato's collections.

(to 1553) The position of "Maestro de' Putti" at the Cappella Giulia was successfully filled by Arcadelt, Rubino, Basso, Ferrabosco, and Roselli.

(to 1556) The five parts of the Frische teutsche Liedlein were published during these years by Forster.

(to 1556) Forster's Song-books (collections of Volkslieder) were published at Nürnberg during these years.

(to 1556) Ein Auszug guter alter und neuer teutscher Liedlien was published by Forster.

(to 1558) From 1539 on through the reigns of Edward VI and Mary and the ascent of Elizabeth to the throne in 1558, there was great uncertainty, doubt and confusion on the parts of church composers.

(to 1569) Morales' published works, dating between these (cont.) years, included magnificats, sixteen masses (in two volumes) and several motets.

c.1539

Nicholas Gomólka was probably born in Cracow (date of death unknown). He was a pupil of Hans Claus, a member of the Royal Chapel.

Coverdale published Goostly psalmes and spirituall songs after Luther, together with fifty-one melodies.
Henry VIII's aversion to Luther drove him to ban the book.

Goudimel founded a music school at Rome.

A New Interlude and Mery of the Nature of iiij Elements appeared.

Sante Pierluigi married Maria Gismondi (a second marriage).

(to 1600) The "Early Florentine School of composition" included these years.

1540

(May 11) Richard Edwards was admitted as a scholar at the Corpus Christi College of Oxford.

(December 6 and 9) A Roberto was mentioned in the archives and he has not yet been identified. However, on December 6, a name occurred that was assumed to be that of Palestrina's teacher. Firmin le Bel, the teacher in question, was at first referred to as Chaplain of S. Bernardino. On the 9th of December, he was described as choirmaster.

1540(cont.)

Giovanni Andrea Dragoni, a madrigal composer and pupil of Palestrina, was born at Meldola (died 1598 or 1594).

Marcin Lwowczyk (Martin of Lwów), known also as Leopolita a pupil of Felstin's, was born (died 1589). His compositions showed influence of both the Netherlandish and Roman schools.

Tomás Luis de Victoria, a member of the Roman group of Spanish composers and musicians, was born in Avila, Spain (died 1611). He was known in Italy as Vittoria and became one of the monumental composers of the time. He was a pupil of Morales.

Arcadelt was admitted to the college of papal singers.

Valentin Bakfark was in Italy and France. He served a Count Tournon, minister and archbishop of Béthune and later of Lyons for a short period.

Le Bel became director of the Cappella Liberiana at Santa Maria Maggiore.

Sixt Dietrich had been in Würtenburg several times and kept in constant touch with Luther.

Adrien Leroy worked with the types of Le Be (cut in 1540) in the same way as Attaingnant had done before him with Hautin's types.

According to Matthesius, a close friend, Luther loved his lute. Matthesius stated, "During the meal and after, the doctor sometimes sang and (cont.) played the lute. I sang with him."

Morales obtained a leave to return to Spain.

Palestrina apparently left Santa Maria Maggiore.

The choristers of Salisbury sang a Mary-antiphon in memory of Bishop John Waltham each day until this year.

Sermisy's style was no longer the leader in published collections after this date.

No more information about Senfl was available.

Tallis was organist at Waltham Abbey for several years before its dissolution in this year. He was relieved of his duties and given 20s for wages and 20s as a reward for his excellent service.

Tallis was high in favor with King Henry VIII before the dissolution of Waltham Abbey and, as he became older, his prestige grew until he was referred to as the "father of music."

A ricercare by Cavazzoni was included in "Musica nova" published this year.

An Attaingnant publication was issued which was particularly interesting, since it included three parody masses (two by Certon and one by Sermisy). The motets on which the masses were based were also printed in the volume.

Clemens non Papa made settings for three voices of the

1540(cont.)
Souterliedekens. They required twenty-six different combinations of voices. The composer verbally indicated in which voice the melody appeared.

Courtois composed many motets that were published in "Selectissimae . . . Cantiones" at Augsburg.

Dankerts' six-part motet "Tua est potentia" was included in the "selectissimae cantiones ultra centum."

After Petrucci's Canti C, no printed collection containing chansons by Josquin appeared until the Selectissimae . . . cantiones published by Kriesstein at Augsburg. Chansons in his now mature style were included.

Numerous motets for three voices by Antonius Divitis were included in the collection "Trium vocum cantiones centum D'" published by Petreius at Nürnberg.

Ducis' elegy for five parts, "Plangite Pierides," on the death of Erasmus, as well as an eight part "Agnus Dei," were both included in the "Selectissimae nec non familiarissimae cantiones ultra centum."

A motet by Fevin, "Descende in hortum meum," as well as a fugue, "Quae es ista," were included in the "Cantiones selectae ultra centum."

Forster's "Der zweite Teil der Kurtzweiligen guten frischen teutschen liedlein."

Gombert's six part "En l'ombre d'ung buissonet," a triple canon, and "Quine l'aymeroit," a quadruple canon, were included in the "Selectissimae."

Sebald Heyden's De arte canendi appeared.

Johann Kugelmann wrote some sacred music that was published at Augsburg.

A Missa Hercules dux Ferrariae mass was preserved in prints of 1532, 1539, and 1540. This was one of several that carried the name of "Lupus" as composer. The printings were from different editions of a collection published by Moderne, edited by Fr. Layolle, the Younger. The latter composed a "Missa Adieu mes amours" that was included in the volumes.

An arrangement of "Ein' feste Burg ist unser Gott," for three voices with the melody in the Tenor, appeared in "News Gesang, mit dreyen stimmen den Kirchen und Schulen zu nutz, neulich in Preussen durch Johann Kugelmann gesetzt," published at Augsburg. Kugelmann was Kapelmeister to Duke Albert of Brandenburg at this time.

Luther's "Vater unser im Himmelreich" was included in Lotther's Magdeburg Hymn-book. It had previously appeared in Köphyl's Strassburg Gesangbuch (1537).

Luther's "Vom Himmel hoch, da komm ich her" appeared in Lotther's Magdeburg Gesangbuch, published in this year.

Tablatures for two parts by

1540(cont.)

Newsidler were published in Nürnberg.

In the "Psautier Flamand Primitif" all the Psalms were for a single voice. All but two could be traced back to their sources in popular Flemish and French songs.

A collection of Souterliedekens was published at Antwerp. It included free metrical versions of the Psalms, set to secular melodies, mostly Flemish and North German Volkslieder and with a few French Chansons. A copy was preserved in the Royal Library at Dresden.

The "Old Hundredth" was included in "Souter Liedekens ghemaect ter eeren Gods."

A volume of Souterliedekens by Clemens, with monophonic settings, was published by Symon Cock of Antwerp.

Willaert's second setting of the Petite camusette appeared.

Wilhelm van Zuylen van Nijevelt published a collection of Psalms through Simon Cock in Antwerp. This particular edition was reprinted over thirty times.

The style of the Madrigal changed from this date on under the leadership of Flemish composers da Monte, de Rore, and Willaert, who were all ensconced in Venice.

Possibly lack of a decisive personality in his youth, combined with the stimulus of the change from monastic to secular life, made it possible for (cont.) Tallis to gradually change his style from this date on and keep in step with current trends in composition and public appeal.

All of the large forms such as the Mass (ordinary), the votive antiphon, and the Magnificat maintained their identity. However, their prominence decreased so that only a few could be placed after this date.

Scipione Bargagli, a Sienese academician, was born (died 1612).

King Henry VIII of England married Anne of Cleves.

Joos van Cleve the Elder, Flemish painter, died (born 1485).

Francesco Mazzola, known as Parmigianino, Italian painter, died (born 1503).

Giovanni Battista Rosso, French painter and pupil of Michelangelo, died (born 1495).

(to 1543) Gaspard Coste composed madrigals and songs which were included in "Le Parangon des chansons" published at Lyons.

(to 1549) The elimination of choirs in England during this decade probably helped to produce a strong revival of organ polyphony.

(to 1549) Ulrich Lange was the Cantor of the St. Thomas School in Leipzig.

(to 1549) A new trend in madrigal composition became apparent, probably from the influence of

1540(cont.)

villanesca.

(to 1550) Changes of style centered on making the text clearer and on the expression of emotion as well as pictorial content. Italian influence was the great motivator behind this development.

(to 1559) Sacred and secular composition by Werrecore appeared in publications including the Bataglia Taliana composed to honor Duke Francesco Sforza after he had won a great victory.

(to 1562) Jean Goujon, French sculptor, was active during this period.

(to 1568) The volumes of Souterliedekens were used during these years.

(to 1571) Hungarian Prince John Sigismund neglected the organ because of Protestant scruples which concerned him.

(to 1576) Nicolas Du Chemin's editions were published in Paris and included among them a seventeen-volume collection of chansons.

(to 1590) Vocal music continued to dominate the musical scene and compositional techniques in spite of the accomplishments of the Venetians led by Willaert and also of the English virginalists and Italian organists.

(to c.1599) Adam Berg, a well-known music printer in Munich, was active during this period.

(to 1605) The so-called Spanish School of composition embraced (cont.) this period.

(to 1750) Guillaume le Bé made the types for the Ballard family and they remained in use through this period of years.

c.1540

Jean Clouet, French painter, was still active up to this time.

Bolognese canon and musical theorist, Giovanni Artusi, was born (died 1613).

William Daman, a Walloon composer, was born at Liège (died 1591).

Paschal de l'Estocart, a chanson composer noted for his use of augmented sixth chords, was born at Noyon, Picardy (date of death unknown).

Giovanni Ferretti was born in Venice (date of death unknown). Some authorities claim he was born at Ancona.

Pinello di Gherardi, contemporary of Palestrina, was born (died 1587, June 15).

William Gibbons, father of Orlando Gibbons and a Wait of the town of Cambridge, was born (died 1595).

Severin Cornet, a composer referred to in a Russignol work, was born (died 1582), see 1593.

Nicholas Ludford, an English composer, died (birthdate unknown).

Jacob Regnart, Netherlandish composer, was born (died c.1600).

Annibale Stabile, composer and pupil of Palestrina, was born

c.1540(cont.)

(date of death unknown).

Philippe Verdelot, Flemish madrigal composer, died (born 1500). His date of death was given by another source as 1565.

Giovanni Contino, probably one of Marenzio's teachers, was a member of the Papal Choir.

Crecquillon became director of Charles V's chapel.

Phillipe da Monte was a music master in the service of Cosimo Pinelli in Naples. The latter was a noble of Genoese descent.

Morales became a member of the Papal Chapel, appointed by Pope Paul III.

An entry was found in the records of the town of Palestrina which said in effect, "towards this year (1540) one of our fellow-citizens, by name Giovanni Pierluigi, went to Rome to study music."

Thomas Tallis served as a Gentleman of the Chapel Royal from this date until his death.

Christopher Tye was awarded the degree of Doctor of Music by both Cambridge and Oxford University.

Cornelius Canis,
Jacobus Clemens, Jehan Le Cocq,
Thomas Crecquillon, Jean Guyot,
Pierre de Manchicourt, and
Jean Richafort all wrote polyphonic chansons and after this date composed chansons in five or more parts.

Several Italian lute books appeared.

The Peterhouse part-books were issued.

Tallis' "Ave Dei patris," which survived in an incomplete state, was composed in duple time, a technique that became more and more common until it became standard procedure from this date forward.

John and Robert Wedderburn of Dundee, Scotland, who were active at this time, probably were the authors of "Gude and Godly Ballates."

"Quanto più m'arde," a madrigal by Willaert, was published.

Compositions for more than four voices came into favor.

The Madrigal did not change the national taste for the Volkslied in Germany. The Volkslied, by the middle of the 16th century, was absorbed into the Chorale.

In Italy, reeds were introduced into the organ.

The violin differed from the viol in several ways. It had shallower sides and an arched back, rather than a flat one. The shoulders were square and the instrument was composed of curved and/or arched pieces of wood, glued together under tension on the blocks. It was first made in Italy toward the middle of the 16th century.

Jean Clouet, French painter, died (born c.1485).

French painting:

c.1540(cont.)

Corneille de Lyon, Portrait of Jacqueline de Rohan Gié.

French architecture: Primaticcio, Fontainebleu, Gallery of Francis I (165' by 20'x20').

American Indian architecture: Taos. Pueblo.

Italian painting: Titian, Portrait of a man (so-called "Young Englishman").

(to c.1560). This period produced a confused assortment of musical forms and styles.

(to 1575) Ivo de Vento, was a composer and colleague of Lassus' while the latter was at Munich. He was active during these years.

1541

(December 12) "Was fürcht'st du Feind was published. The text was written by Luther and it was taken from "Hostis Herodes impie," an Epiphany hymn by Coelius Sedulius.

(September) Calvin returned to Geneva.

Johann Gramann, German composer, died (born 1487).

Lupus Hellinck, Netherlandish composer, died (born c.1495).

Hans Kotter, German composer and organist, died at Berne (born c.1485).

Giovanni Spataro, an Italian scholar and musician, died. (born c.1458).

Louis Bourgeois followed Calvin (cont.) to Geneva. He became cantor of a church, but had a disagreement with the presbytery. They apparently would not permit him to introduce harmonised versions of the Psalms into public worship.

Jacques Buus was first organist at St. Mark's in Venice.

When Calvin returned to Geneva the Protestant movement in Switzerland found a leader quite aware of the power of music "d'esmouvoir & enflamber le coeur des hommes."

Bartolomé Escobedo returned to Spain for a visit.

Guillaume Franc settled in Geneva and obtained a license to institute a school of music.

Lassus was one of the earliest "Maestri de' Putti" ("Cappella musicale nella protobasilica di St. Giovanni in Laterano").

When Marot arrived in Geneva he became closely associated with Calvin.

Michel was organist at Magdeburg Cathedral.

Palestrina completed his service in the choir of Ste. Maria Maggiore at the end of this year. His final year coincided with le Bel's appointment and first year in office.

Tye was appointed Master of Choristers at Ely Cathedral.

John Wylbore was appointed prebendary at Rochester Cathedral.

Zarlino moved from Chioggia,

1541(cont.)

his birthplace, to Venice. He commenced his studies with Willaert at this time and was ordained a Deacon in the same year.

Agricola's "Sonntagsbuch" appeared.

Several of Compère's motets appeared in the collection "Trium vocum Cantiones," published at Nürnberg.

Dietrich wrote thirty-six antiphons, published at Würtenburg.

Giovane Domenico da Nola's "Canzoni Villanesche" appeared.

Jhan Gero's first book of madrigals appeared. His use of syncopation was notable. Thirty-two of his madrigals and motets were included in "Trium vocum cantiones centum," published by Petreius at Nürnberg.

Attaingnant started publishing Gombert's music. The first issue included a six-part Mass "Quam pulchra es," with a seven-part Agnus Dei on a cantus firmus.

A manuscript (#1872) was preserved in the Royal Library of Copenhagen, written by trumpeter Jorg Haider.

Ihan's madrigals were published.

Rhaw published "Opus de cem missarum 4 vocum" at Würtenburg. The collection included Isaac's two masses "Carminum" and "Une Musque de Biscay."

Luther wrote the text for "Christ unser Herr," The (cont.) Baptism of Christ. He also wrote the words and possibly the music for "Erhalt uns, Herr," a children's hymn directed against the Pope and the Turks.

In the "Vermahnung Zum Gebet wider den Türken" ("Exhortation to Prayer") Luther said, "I rejoice to let the 79th Psalm, "O God, the heathen are come," be sung as usual, one choir after another.

Marot's psalms appeared in a psalter published at Antwerp. Their text was the same as that published by Calvin.

Morales' first published motets appeared, in collections devoted almost exclusively to the works of Gombert and published by the latter.

Giordano Passetto, choirmaster at Padua Cathedral, composed a book of four-voiced "madrigali a voci pari" in the style of Arcadelt that was published in this year.

Gardano published a collection of six-part madrigals by Verdelot, and described them on the title page as the most divine and beautiful music ever heard.

Della Viola wrote music for Cinzio's "Orbecche."

When Cardinal Albrecht left Halle, the Cathedral Chapter seized the large organ there and had it installed in the Magdeburg cathedral.

Villanella or villanesca appeared as the title of a Neopolitan type folksong.

1541(cont.)

Domenikos Theotokopoulos, Greek painter known as El Greco, was born (died 1614).

(to 1545) De Bruck was chief Kapellmeister at Vienna during this period.

(and 1545) Rhaw published several of Rener's works including five masses which appeared in publication at these two dates.

(to 1548) French architecture: Lescot, "Lescot Wing" of the Louvre in Paris (c.175' long by 95' high).

(to 1550) The first organist at St. Mark's during these years was Jacques Buus (Bohusius, von Paus), quite possibly born at Ghent. Willaert was at this time "maestro" at the Cathedral.

(and 1556) The repertory of the court choir in Denmark included music by the same composers as the Swedish choir, including compositions by Heinrich Finck and Senfl. Two manuscripts have been preserved from the years indicated.

(to c.1557) The composer most responsible for melodic settings of the Psalter was Bourgeois. He succeeded Franc at Geneva and remained there during this period.

(and 1559) A few madrigals by a "Mathias" were printed in the madrigal books of Ihan (1541) and Arcadelt (Primo Libro, ed. of 1559).

(to 1561) Tye served as Master of the Choristers at Ely Cathedral during this period, however, quite possibly with (cont.) occasional breaks when he travelled elsewhere.

(to 1585) Merbecke was organist at St. George's, Windsor until his death (1585).

1542

(November 1) Tarquinia Molza, poetess, singer, instrumentalist and even occasional conductor, was born in Modena (date of death unknown).

(February) A psalter supposedly printed at Rome by the command of the Pope was published at Strassburg.

(November) Marot arrived at Geneva and translated nineteen more psalms and the Song of Simeon. The thirty previously published, combined with these new efforts comprised what is usually referred to as the "Cinquante Pseaumes."

Lucas Fernández, Spanish composer, died at Salamanca (born 1474).

Gasparo da Salò of Brescia, the first maker of true violins, was born (died 1609).

Johann Weimann, a composer and organist at Nürnberg, died at Würtenburg (birthdate unknown).

Cornelius Canis succeeded Gombert as magister puerorum in the service of Charles V. He composed six masses and six motets.

Cavazzoni founded a prolific school of organ composition at Venice. He personally composed ricercari, a Missa Apostulorum, Falte d'argens, and an Easter Hymn.

1542(cont.)

Corteccia was chapel-master to Cosmo I.

John Dygon might possibly have been the same person as John Wyldebore who was vicar of Willesborough at this time.

Franc became master of the children and a singer at St. Peter's. He received a salary of ten florins.

Le Jeune was only about twelve years old when the first edition of the Genevan psalter was published.

Mundy was a chorister at Westminster Abbey.

John Shepherd was Instructor of Choristers and organist at Magdalen College, Oxford.

A book by Martin Agricola was published by Rhaw at Würtenburg. It carried the title, Musica instrumentalis deudsch inn welcher begriffen ist: wie man nach dem gesange auff mancherley Pfeiffen lernen sol. Auch wig auff die Orgel, Harffen, Lauten, Geigen vnd allerley Instrumenten vnd Seitenspiel nach der rechtgegründten Tabelthur sey abzusetzen.

A chanson collection devoted entirely to Benedictus Appenzeller was published.

Arcadelt composed "Ecco, d'oro l'età" for the wedding of Margaret of Austria and the Duke of Parma.

Arcadelt's madrigal book for three voices was published.

(cont.) Arcadelt wrote both French chansons and madrigals at this time.

Bourgeois adopted seventeen tunes from the Strassburg Psalters with modifications and added twenty-two new tunes.

The first edition of the Geneva Psalter was published by Calvin.

The younger J. Lupi was referred to in an Attaingnant collection published this year: Jo. Lupi, "Chori sacre Virginis Marie Cameracensis Magistri Musice Cantiones" was the manner in which he was mentioned.

Cavazzoni published his Intavolature cioè Recercari, Canzoni, Himni, Magnificat, etc. at Venice. This marked the beginning of the great store of literature for keyboard in Italy. This publication was specifically for organ.

Ferrabosco's first book of madrigals was published at Venice.

Franc's name was known chiefly for his connection with the Geneva Psalter. The first edition of the book appeared in this year.

Ganassi's "Regola Rubertina" appeared.

A work by Thelamonius Hungarus was included in Rhaw's Tricinia.

The "Musurgia seu praxis musicae" by Ottomarus Luscinius (Othmar Nachtigal) was reprinted at Strassburg from an earlier edition in 1536.

Marot, at Geneva, published

1542(cont.)

thirty Psalms, followed by another set of fifty. The latter collection had a preface by Calvin.

Petreius published the "Deo gratias."

Tricinia . . . Latina, Germanica, Brabantica, et Gallica . . . was published by Rhaw at Würtenburg.

G. Rhaw's three-part collection of Volkslieder was published at Würtenburg. A copy has been preserved at Göttingen.

Rhaw's hymn collection was published.

De Rore issued his first book of madrigals for four voices. The work sustained its popularity for a long time.

The first edition of Rore's Primo libro di madrigali cromatici for five voices was published. De Rore also set Petrarch's "Hor che'l ciel e la terra."

Vincenzo Ruffo's Mass, published in this year, was apparently the first polyphonic mass by a native Italian to be issued. His composition appeared in a collection published by Scotto.

A book of Ruffo's motets for five voices was issued.

A manuscript bearing this date was found at the Thomasschule in Leipzig. It contained "26 canons in the 8 modes . . . " of which the first 17 were in three parts and the other nine in two parts . . . for all (cont.) equal-voiced instruments and especially zinks . . . " The manuscript was attributed to Johann Walther.

Willaert's madrigals were included in Scotto's Madrigali a quattro voci. They followed the note nere trend previously found in Festa.

Book I of Willaert's motets for six voices included three compositions that carried the name of Jachet Berchem. One was simply attributed to "Jachet."

An order was issued to the effect that a chapter of the English Bible (1536 edition) must be read after the Te Deum and Magnificat.

The chanson was transcribed into a specific type of keyboard music.

The imitative instrumental ricercar appeared at this time.

The trio of viols, tuned as directed in the "Regola Rubertina" continued to be used unchanged for a century and a half as the basis for chamber -music. Playford's "Introduction to the Skill of Musick" prescribed the same tuning.

Isabella Medici was born. She was the second daughter of Duke Cosimo I and Eleanora of Toledo (date of death unknown).

Sir Thomas Wyatt, English poet, died (born 1503).

Dosso Dossi, Italian painter, died (born c.1480).

Bernard van Orley, Netherlandish

1542(cont.)

painter, died (born c.1492).

Italian painting: Titian, Christ Crowned with Thorns.

(and 1543) Cavazzoni published two collections of organ pieces under the title "Intavolatura cioè recercari canzoni himni magnificati."

(to 1543) Silvestro di Ganassi wrote one of the earliest viol methods, the Regola Rubertina in two volumes.

(to 1543) Mundy was still a choirboy at Westminster Abbey.

(to 1544) De Rore's first three books of madrigals for five voices appeared in Venice.

(to 1546) Cyriacus Spangenberg lived with Luther.

(to 1547) Richafort was director at St. Gilles, Bruges.

(to 1547) John Shepherd was organist at Magdalen College, Oxford through most of this time.

(to 1548) Elias Mullerstedt was organist at Magdeburg Cathedral.

(to 1550) De Rore's works were published continuously during this period.

(to 1555) Delclaracion de Instrumentos Musicales was written. It contained information about instruments, methods of performance and musical practices of the time.

(and 1556) Willaert was authorized to return to Flanders on these two occasions.

(to 1557) Bourgeois was musical editor of the Genevan Psalter.

(to 1554, 1562) Including the Song of Simeon and the Decalogue, the Genevan Psalter contained 125 tunes, of which eighty-five were selected or adapted between 1542 and 1554, the rest in 1562.

(to 1572) Certon was maître at Sainte Chapelle.

c.1542

Jacob Meiland, a German Lutheran transitional composer, was born (died 1577).

Arcadelt was commissioned by a Roman banker to set music to two of Michelangelo's madrigal poems. Strangely, the composer was not enthused at the prospect.

"Trente Pseaulmes" was published, probably by Marot.

Ricercari referred to polyphonic, imitative pieces for soloists or instrumental ensembles. This form was a precursor to the fugue.

The fixed number of six strings, and tuning by fourths with a major third in the middle, was proven to be from this period by a viol method published at Venice.

1543

(July 26) Merbecke and two of his colleagues were condemned to death for heresy.

(October 5) A new Bishop, Cardinal Giammaria Ciocchi del Monte, formerly Bishop of Pavia and Archbishop of Siponto, was installed as Bishop of Palestrina.

(March) Merbecke was arrested and imprisoned for heresy.

(November) Susato's "Premier livre des chansons à quatre parties" appeared.

William Byrd, a foremost English composer, was born in London (died 1623, July 4). Byrd was essentially a composer of Latin church music, but was the most versatile of the late Renaissance composers. He was certainly eminent among the early madrigalists.

Alfonso Ferrabosco, an English composer, was born in Bologna (died 1588).

Francesco Canova da Milano, lutenist and composer, died, according to a major source (born c.1490). His death was otherwise given as c.1566.

Giovanni Maria Nanino, composer, maestro di cappella, and quite possibly a pupil of Palestrina, was born (died 1607), see 1545.

Andries Pevernage (Bevernage, Beveringen), French sacred and secular composer, was born in Harelbeke near Courtrai (died 1591).

Joan Brudieu, a French madrigalist, apparently studied for the priesthood. Most of his active life was spent in Spain.

Jachet Brumel, who was possibly Antoine Brumel's son, was organist at the court in Lyons.

Costanzo Festa was in ill health and therefore did not follow the Pope to Bologna.

Alberto Lavezzola founded a public institution for music in Verona. The effort was a combination made by uniting two rival institutions.

Merbecke was apparently arrested in 1543 as a result of a search of his lodgings that brought to light writings showing Calvinist tendencies. Henry VIII was strongly opposed to Calvinism as well as to Lutheranism. Merbecke barely escaped execution a year later.

Shepherd resigned from his position of Instructor of the choristers and organist of Magdalen College, Oxford.

Antonio da Bologna wrote one of the oldest organ tablatures in modern notation. This was preserved in a private collection in Vienna.

Cadeac's compositions were included in: "Quintus liber Motettorum" published at Lyons.

A few two-part motets by Carpentras were published by Gardano.

Cavazzoni published a volume including hymns as well as Magnificats for organ and three complete organ-masses.

Several of Clemens non Papa's works were published by Fétis.

Attaignant was still active as a printer and publisher. This date appeared on a "Livre de danceries" by Consilium.

Gardano published Festa's madrigal book, "Il vero Libro di Madrigali a tre voci di Constantio Festa."

1543(cont.)

Ganassi spoke about three varieties of violins as Viola di Soprano, di Tenore, e di Basso in the first part of his "Regula Rubertina," published at Venice.

Ganassi's "Lettione seconda . . . di sonare il Violone" mentioned pizzicato and vibrato.

A new edition of the Genevan Psalter was published.

Fourteen of Gero's madrigals appeared in the Second Book of Madrigals published at Venice by Gardano.

A five-part "Missa super Veni sponsa Christi" was attributed to "Joannes Lupi" in a Scotus publication.

Luther wrote the text and possibly the music for "Vom Himmel Kam," a Christmas hymn.

Luther wrote the text to "Der du bist drei," from "O Lux beata," an Epiphany hymn.

Narrative sections of the New Testament were set polyphonically as responses.
Balthasar Resinarius wrote a two-volume series for the year, with 118 selections for four voices included. The set was published by Rhaw at Würtenburg during this year. Its title was "Responsoriorum numero octoginta de tempore et festis . . . libri duo."

Susato published on his own from this date forward. Previously, he had worked in association with several friends.

Susato published "Premier Livre des chansons à quatre parties . . ." Eight chansons by the publisher himself were included in the collection. This was probably the first group of polyphonic chansons published in the Netherlands.

The earliest academy to survive more than for a brief period and to be concerned primarily with music was the Accademia Filarmonica of Verona, founded during this year. Nasco and Ruffo, as well as other well -regarded composers, were hired to furnish music for the institution.

The term "citole" was still in use at this date.

The earliest known perfect example of a clavichord was an Italian model.

The Council of Geneva resolved that "whereas the Psalms of David are being completed, and whereas it is very necessary to compose a pleasing melody to them, and Master Guillaume the singer is very fit to teach the children, he shall give them instruction for an hour daily."

Documents in Hungary described gipsy violinists who, oddly, beat their instruments as a dulcimer was beaten. They sang simultaneously.

The period, which has been considered by many musicologists to be the Golden Age of Polish music, was influenced greatly by the founding of the Collegium Rorantistarum by King Sigismund the Elder at the chapel in Cracow.

1543(cont.)

Hans Holbein the Younger, German painter, died (born c.1497).

Italian sculpture: Cellini, Salt Cellar of chased gold and enamel on a base of ebony (made for King Francis I of France).

(to 1549) At least four collections of madrigals published during these years contained compositions by Festa.

(to 1550) Courtois' French songs composed during this period included a canon and two songs in five and six parts published in "Chansons a 4,5, 6, et 8 parties, de divers auteurs" at Antwerp by Susato.

(to 1561) Susato published over fifty volumes of music, nearly every one of which contained some compositions of his own.

c.1543

Jakob Regnart, German song composer, was born (died c.1600).

Francisco Guerrero became a choirboy at Seville under Pedro Fernandez de Castilleja.

Coverdale's Goostly psalmes and spirituall songs was published.

John Redford's "Rejoyce in the Lorde allwayes" appeared.

1544

(May 27) The English translation of the Litany was first published, without musical notes.

(June 11) Cranmer's Litany in English was published.

(June 16) Merbecke and Cranmer's musical setting for the Litany (cont.) was published by Richard Grafton, the King's printer.

(October 7) Cranmer wrote a letter on this date to Henry VIII. The letter has unfortunately been the subject for much misquotation.

(October 23) Palestrina was appointed to the cathedral of St. Agapito in his native town as organist and choirmaster. The contract was signed on this date and described his duties as choirmaster for all occasions, organist on festivals, and instructor of boys as well as canons.

Benedictus Ducis, chanson and madrigal composer, died (birthdate unknown).

Clément Marot, French poet and son of Jean Marot, died at Turin (born 1496).

Georgius Otto, German polychoral composer, was born in Torgau (died 1618), see c.1550.

De Felstin was still alive at this date.

Jannequin was proposed for the curacy of Unverre (near Chartres).

Erasmus Lapicida (Steinschneider?), a composer published by Petrucci, was in Austria and although old and sickly still received payments from Ferdinand I.

Gonzaga took Lassus to Fontainebleau where the peace negotiations with King Francis I were in progress.

1544(cont.)

Lassus arrived in Italy.

The Duke of Milan had music played on four viols for his morning and evening entertainment.

Hieronymus Ostermayer was organist in Brassó.

Ott, in a song collection of this year, warned "not to exclude music from the services, as the uncouth jackasses, Anabaptists, and other religious enthusiasts (Schwärmer) are doing."

Palestrina remained in Rome until he received his first appointment which was at the cathedral in his native city. At this time he was about nineteen or twenty years old.

Bishop Reid founded and endowed a "Sang School" In Orkney.

Georg Rhaw wrote a preface in which he indicated that he felt his end was approaching (he lived four more years). He went on to say that he considered himself to have been fortunate to have completed his series of works in church music.

Rore dedicated a festive motet to Christoforo.

The Inn Zur Sackpfeife was taken over by the Schütz family.

Michele Varotto could hardly have been identical with the Michele Novarese mentioned in Doni's "Dialogo" in 1544. This was an error on the part of Vito Fedeli who assumed them to be identical.

Waelrant was established as a singer in the choir of the chapel of the Virgin at Notre Dame at Antwerp.

Arcadelt's madrigal book for four voices was published.

Leonard Barre composed some madrigals and motets published in a collection at Venice. His name also appeared in many manuscript compositions preserved in the library of the Papal Chapel.

Many of Certon's motets were included in the de Rore collections published at Venice in this year.

Several of Crequillon's compositions were published by Gardano at Venice.

Des Prés' Dirge in memory of his friend and teacher Okenheim was published at Antwerp.

Arcadelt's madrigals published only five or six years earlier were already considered outdated by Doni.

In Part I of Doni's Dialogo della musica, the music of several madrigals was given. It was to be sung by the interlocutors, who were four men.

De Felstin's treatise, "Directiones musicae ad cathedralis ecclesiae Premislienis usum," appeared.

Several of Ferrabosco's motets were published at Venice.

Gombert composed a "Chant des Oyseaux."

1544(cont.)

Ott's collection of "115 guter newer Liedlein" published at Nürnberg contained ten lieder by Isaac.

An arrangement of Luther's "Ein' feste Burg ist unser Gott" for four voices, with the melody in the Bass, was included in Rhaw's "Newe deutsche geistliche Gesenge cxxiii" published at Würtenburg. Another source maintained that the collection included at least four contrapuntal arrangements of the tune.

Sixteen of Morales' masses were published.

Newsidler's tablature, Ein new Künstlich Lautten Buch included a piece, "Der Polnisch Tantz." Its rhythmic construction was quite different from the type which became the norm for a Polish dance. Two separate books of Newsidler's tablatures were published at this time.

Newsidler wrote a Battle of Bafia (Pavia).

Ott's 115 Songs, in 4,5, and 6 parts, published at Nürnberg, only survived in two copies, one at the Berlin Library, and the other at the British Museum.

Johann Petreius' latest music publication was apparently "Guter, seltsamer, und kunstreicher teutscher Gesang . . . . Gedruckt zu Nürnberg, durch Jo. Petreium. 1544."

The "Italian Battle" was first published as early as this date in a collection by Petreius issued at Nürnberg.

Eight Magnificats by Rener were published.

"Newe deudsche geistliche Gesenge . . . für die gemeinen Schulen" was published by Rhaw. It included works by the leading masters of the day.

Rhaw was quite possibly the composer of the compositions indicated as anonymous in a song-book for the use of Lutheran parochial schools published in this year.

De Rore's "Primo libro di madrigali cromatici a 5" was reprinted in a second edition.

De Rore's first motet book, published at Venice, included seven works by him and sixteen composed by ten other musicians.

Schmeltzl's Liederbuch included the first large collection of quodlibets to appear in Germany. The collection was titled "Guter, seltzamer und Kunstreicher teutscher Gesang."

"115 guter newer Liedlein" was published containing sixty-four compositions by Senfl.

Only one mass by Verdelot was known. This mass, titled "Philomena," was included in a volume of five masses published by Scotto at Venice.

A reprint of Walther's Geystliche Gesangkbüchleyn appeared with changes and additions (other reprints were done in 1525, 1537, and 1551).

Johann Walther's "Cantio Septem Vocum" appeared.

King Francis II (House of

1544(cont.)

Valois) of France was born (died 1560).

Torquato Tasso, Catholic reform poet, was born (died 1595).

Cranmer's recommendation "for every syllable a note" was underscored by the issuance (perhaps in association with Merbecke) of the Litany in English set to traditional chant and conforming with the recommendation. In the same year a setting harmonized for five voices and "according to the notes used in the Kynges Chapel" was published. The litany was practically identical with that used today. The book also was concerned with the projected processional.

In England the "Rules and Ordynaunces for the Warre" were published for the French campaign of this year.

Polychoral writing already existed in Germany.

In Hungary, the martial military oboe was described as the "Turkish pipe."

The organ of the Incoronata Church in Lodi was altered by Giovanni Battista Antegnati.

(to 1545) Guillaume le Bé engraved music types for printing lines first and then notes, however, this system was found inconvenient and quickly discarded.

(and 1547) Corteccia published two books of madrigals for four voices, one in each of these two years.

(to 1551) Palestrina served at St. Agapit's in his native village. During this period he probably composed the four-part motets included in the 1563 book.

(to 1554) Lassus spent these years in service at Sicily, Milan, Naples, and Rome.

(to 1566) Giandomenico Martoretta's works appeared. He was essentially a madrigal composer.

c.1544

Merbecke was lay clerk and afterwards organist at St. George's Chapel, Windsor.

The Musica nova was apparently a reprinting of a collection published this year and dedicated to La Pecorina. No known copies of the original printing survived.

François Quesnel, French painter, was born (died 1616).

1545

(April 10) Costanzo Festa, a madrigal composer of the Roman school, died (born c.1490). His death was recorded in the archives of the Pontifical Choir.

(May 23) John Mason became treasurer of Hereford Cathedral.

(October 25) John Taverner, Tudor composer and master of Franco-Flemish polyphonic style, died (born c.1495). He was also organist at Oxford.

(November 1) Ferrante Gonzaga and Lassus landed at Palermo.

1545(cont.)

Marc' Antonio Ingegneri, sacred composer, was born in Verona (died 1592, July 1).

Bernhard Klingenstein, German sacred composer, was born (died 1614).

Luzzasco Luzzaschi, organist at Ferrara Cathedral and Frescobaldi's teacher, was born (died 1607).

Giovanni Maria Nanini (Nanino), chanson and madrigal composer and friend of Palestrina's, was born (died 1607), see 1543.

John Redford, organist at St. Paul's Cathedral during the reign of Henry VIII, died (born c.1485).

Leonard Barre was one of the musicians sent to the Council of Trent by the Pope to assist and advise in musical matters.

Coclico pursued his career in Würtenburg.

The town council of Marseilles rented a house to lutenist Barthélemy de la Croix for use as a lute-school for children.

Franc left Geneva and joined the choir at the Cathedral of Lausanne, where he remained until his death. His position at Geneva was given to Bourgeois and Guillaume Fabri. Bourgeois received a salary of sixty florins and Fabri forty, totaling the one hundred florins which Franc had received.

According to Froude a watchword of the navy as early as this date was "God Save the King," with the countersign (cont.) "Long to Reign Over Us."

Morales received permission to return to Spain and became maestro de capilla at Toledo.

The most famous publisher of lute music in the Netherlands was Phalèse, active at this time. His lute publications included foreign and native compositions.

Shepherd was reappointed Instructor of the choristers and organist at Magdalen College, Oxford.

Cardinal Silíceo started a school for the Toledan seises.

Andres Torrentes was maestro de capilla at Toledo up to the date of Morales' appointment.

Arbeau's "Orchesographie" published at Langres contained an early example of the dance tune referred to as a "Branle" or, in English, a "Brawl."

Several manuscripts in the Sistine archives as well as a book of motets by Arcadelt were published at Venice.

Agricola, in his Musica instrumentalis deudsch, mentioned a "Polische Geige" as a special kind of instrument of the rebec type (also in 1528).

Aron's Lucidario provided a list of eminent lute singers and also a number of aristocrats, clerics and city magistrates who were somewhat qualified in the art.

Val Babst's Geystliche Lieder was published at Leipzig. It contained 129 hymns. He also wrote "Das Babst'che Gesangbuch.

Bruhier's duo for basses based on L'Amour de moy was included in Secundus Tomus Biciniorum, published by Rhaw.

Calmo's comedy "La Travaglia" was written.

An eight-part motet by Dankerts, "Laetamini in Domino," included in Uhlard's "Concentus octo . . . vocum," was published at Augsburg.

The 7th book of Susato's songs, published in this year, contained twenty-four compositions by des Prés. He was the only composer represented in the book.

Dietrich wrote "Novum opus musicum," published at Würtenburg.

Dietrich's hymns appeared.

The "Dixieme livre des chansons," published at Antwerp by Susato, was preserved at the British Museum.

Ducis composed a four-part "monody" on the death of des Pres which appeared in the 7th set of French chansons in 5 and 6 parts, a work devoted to compositions by des Prés.

Two five-part motets by Ducis, "Benedic Domine," and "Corde et animo," were included in Kriesstein's "Cantiones sex et quinque vocum etc." published at Augsburg.

A motet by Ducis, "Peccantem me quotidie," appeared in the (cont.) "Cantiones octo . . . vocum" published at Augsburg.

Songs like "Eulogy of Saxon Mines," were found in Rhaw's collection (1545). They were almost surely known to Luther, and references to them appeared in Luther's famous battle hymn.

One composition by Fevin was included in the "Bicinia Gallica, etc." published by Rhaw at Würtenburg.

Gerle published a work for the lute at Nürnberg.

Gombert's "Le Chant des Oyseaux," for three voices, was published.

One of the earliest steps towards the use of English in the Services was with the issuance of the Primer of Henry VIII.

Hans Heugel's "Carolus Henricusque" in honor of Duke Henry of Brunswick appeared.

Jannequin's "La Bataille" was published at Antwerp by Susato with a fifth part added by Verdelot.

A "Postquam consummati sont," attributed to "Johannes Lupi," was reprinted by Rhaw.

The alternation of plainsong and polyphony frequently appeared in settings of the Magnificat in a volume published at Venice. The collection included sixteen settings by Morales, eight with odd- and eight with even-numbered verses polyphonically composed basically in four-parts.

1545(cont.)

The "Officia de Nativitate . . . was published.

Bicinia, Gallica, Latina, Germanica . . . Tomus Primus was published by Rhaw at Würtenburg. Secundus Tomus Biciniorum . . . also appeared under the same auspices.

Rhaw's two-part Songs were published at Würtenburg. Berlin and Vienna libraries and the British Museum have preserved copies.

Rore's second book of motets was published.

A book of Madrigals by Vincenzo Ruffo, published in this year at Venice, survived in the Fétis Library.

Villanesca collections for three voices were issued by Tomaso Cimello and by Vincenzo Fontana.

A collection of Willaert's Canzone was published at Venice.

In a letter to the King, Archbishop Cranmer mentioned certain English translations of processionals he had made. His concern was that if they were set to music there by only one note to a syllable.

The Council of Trent was convened by Pope Paul III in order to bring about Catholic reform and codify the results.

Hans Baldung (Grien), German painter, died (born c.1484).

Italian painting: Titian, The Aretino.

Roger Ascham's "Toxophilus," a treatise on the educational and patriotic advantages of archery and a handbook on the technique of the sport was written.

(to 1546) Titian visited Rome.

(and 1548) Christopher Tye received the degree of Mus. Doc. at Cambridge (1545) and in 1548 was admitted ad eundem to Oxford.

(and 1559) Settings for two and three voices of the "Je suis desheritee" melody were published in these two years respectively. Both compositions were attributed to "Jacotin."

(to 1559) Cavazzoni was a singer at St. Mark's during this period.

(to 1563) The Council of Trent considered the use of music in church. Its first move was to eliminate all tropes and sequences except five. These were: Dies Irae, Stabat Mater Dolorosa, Lauda Sion Salvatorem, Veni Sancte Spiritus, and Victimae Pascham Laudes. The Church redefined its position toward art and approved the use of printing in religious service. Palestrina was connected with the music committee within the Council. The final pronouncements of the Council of Trent were carried to all Roman Catholic communities of the world.

c.1545

Pietro Aron, Italian theorist, died (born c.1470).

Ludovico Balbi, a polyphonic composer who worked mostly in Padua, was born (died 1608).

c.1545(cont.)

Anthoine de Bertrand, a chanson composer, was born at Fontanges in Auvergne (date of death unknown).

Giacomo Gastoldi, Italian madrigalist, was born (died 1609).

Jan Willemszoon Lossy, an organist and composer, was born (died 1629).

Jacob Polonais, a Polish lutenist, was born (died 1605).

Clemens non Papa returned to the Netherlands. Nine of his chansons were included in "Huitiesme Livre . . . " published by Susato.

Some ballate from Boccaccio's Decameron had music. "Io mi son giovinetta" was first set by Domenico Maria Ferabosco.

The dedication of Vincenzo Galilei's first book of madrigals was to Bianca Capello. The composer was the father of the astronomer.

German influence was obvious in Polish music.

Tintoretto visited Rome.

(to c.1585) During this period Thomas Mulliner, choral director at St. Paul's, compiled "The Mulliner Book," an old and important keyboard source. A copy survived in the British Museum.

1546

(February 18) Martin Luther, founder of the Lutheran Faith, composer and author, died at Eisleben (born 1483, Nov. 10).

(September 26?) Bishop Bonner ordered the burning of Coverdale's "Goostly psalmes and spirituall songs," a hymnal. One copy survived.

Joachim à Burck, an early composer of Protestant church music, was born at Magdeburg (died 1610). His actual name was Moller.

Firolin Sicher, a Swiss organist, died (born 1490). He was a student of Buchner and held the position of organist at St. Gall.

Berchem was in Venice as indicated by the dedication of his madrigal collection of this year.

Bianchini was one of the earliest imitative ricercari composers.

Coclico was active at Frankfurt an der Oder.

Ferrante Gonzaga was appointed governor of Milan.

Francisco Guerrero was appointed maestro de capilla at Jaen.

Some of Borrono's compositions were included in a collection of lute music published this year.

Certon's thirty-one Psalms appeared.

"Motecta quinis vocibus, auctore Clemente non Papa" was published by Susato.

Courtois composed motets, published in "Cantiones sacrae" at Antwerp.

Giovanni Maria da Crema composed

1546(cont.)

both imitative and non-imitative ricercari from this date forward.

Lodovico Domenichi's translation of Polybius (Polibio historico Greco tradotto . . . , Venezia, was published by Giolito at Venice.

Domenichi's "Rime diverse di molti autori" was reprinted at Venice.

Tablatures by Hans Gerle were published at Nürnberg (also in 1532, 1537 and 1552).

A collection of Villanescas by Giovan Tommaso di Maio was published.

Alonso Mudarra published Tres libros de Musica en cifra para vihuela at Seville. The volumes included original compositions for four-stringed guitars, Obras para Guitarra in temple viejo and temple nuevo.

Alonso Mudarra composed a Pavana for guitar.

A madrigal book for five-voices by Parabosco was published.

Passamezzi were included in Rotta's lute-book of this year.

Nicola Vicentino published Volume I of his madrigals with explanatory directions. The purpose of the book was to restore the old Greek scales.

Susato published five books of "Cantiones sacrae quae vulgo Moteta vocant."

A letter was found which implied that the Pope's interest in the (cont.) purity of the chant went back as far as this year.

An increased appreciation for quality of performance was made obvious by a Venetian decree that provided that neither cannons or priests should interrupt performing organists. They were instructed to remain quiet and patiently await the finish of a selection.

Henry VIII granted the manor of Marcham as a fee to William Boxe, an alderman of the City of London.

Antonio da Sangallo the Younger, Renaissance architect, died (born 1485).

Italian painting: Titian "Paul III and his Nephews" (78½" x 49").

(to 1547) The "Wanley" manuscripts executed at this time included musical settings of portions of the service in English. The manuscripts were preserved in the Bodleian Library.

(and 1551) Fétis mentioned two instruments made by Andrea Amati bearing these dates. One was a rebec with three strings and the other a viola bastardo (small violin).

(and 1555) Berchem published books of madrigals for five and four voices respectively.

(to 1556) Phalèse, Susato and Waelrant published about 551 works in thirty-three motet books, mostly during these years.

(to 1560) Petrus Maessens was

1546 (cont.)

chief Kapellmeister in Vienna during this period.

c.1546

Robert Carver composed "O Bone Jesu."

A fraternity of laudesi (mostly artisans) existed. Their meetings were held in a church every Saturday, after the service of nones. They sang laude in four-parts.

1547

(April 8) The compline was sung in English at the Chapel Royal.

(June 3) Gombert dedicated a motet to Ferrante Gonzaga.

(June 12 or July 12) Palestrina married the daughter of a well-to-do citizen, Francesco de Goris. The latter had just died and left a large dowry for his daughter, Lucrezia.

(September) Glareanus' "Dodecachordon" was published at Basle. This work deals thoroughly with the subject of early counterpoint.

Lucrezia Bendidio, a female performer in music with a high reputation, was born (date of death unknown).

Cervantes, the great Spanish dramatist, was born (died 1616). He used instrumental music to quite an extent with his plays.

George de la Hèle (Helle), a madrigal composer, was born at Antwerp (died 1587).

Christofano Malvezzi, maestro di cappella to Francesco and Ferdinando de' Medici, teacher (cont.) of Peri, and madrigalist, was born (died 1597).

John Mason, English choral director and teacher, died (date of birth unknown).

Conrad Peutinger, diplomat, humanitarian, political scientist, and patron of music, died (born 1465).

The Council of Geneva admitted Louis Bourgeois to citizenship "in consideration of his being a respectable man and willing to teach children."

Coclico continued his career at Königsberg.

When Christ Church College was founded, Richard Edwards became a student there, and graduated as M.A.

Giulio Fiesco was influenced by Rore, the outstanding musical personality in Ferrara at this time.

Glareanus defined the Church modes of individual lines, but never on the basis of polyphonic composition in its complete form. He placed the beginnings of musical art almost a century before his time.

Hans Heugel became head of the court chapel in Cassel.

Sermisy and Louis Hérault shared the position of sous-maître under Francis I. They retained the post when Henry II became king.

John Sheppard held his position of Instructor of the choristers and organist at Magdalen College, Oxford until this date.

1547 (cont.)

Szamotulczyk was appointed composer to the King, a position he held until his death.

Waelrant had a school of music in Antwerp where he introduced a new method of solmisation. It was known as bocedisation or the voces Belgicoe.

Bourgeois published his "Le premier livre des Pseaulmes de David, contenant xxiv. pseaulmes. Composé par Loys Bovrgeois. Endiuersité de Musique : à scauoir familiere au vaudeuille; aultres plus musicales . . . . Lyon."

Bourgeois published his "Pseaulmes cinquante de David . . traduictz . . par Clement Marot, et mis en musique par Loys Bovrgeoys, à quatre parties, à voix de contrepoinct egal consonnante au verbe. Lyon, 1547."

Calvin's opposition to harmonization could not prevent four part settings made by Bourgeois in this year. They antedated Jannequin's.

A set of Buus ricercari were published in part-books.

Corteccia published his second book of madrigals for four voices, the first had appeared in 1544.

Corteccia's compositions included "Primo libro de' Madrigali a 5 e 6 voci." They were dedicated to Cosimo de' Medici.

The collection "La Fleur des Chansons," published at Louvain and Antwerp, contained compositions by de Castro, Clérеau, (cont.) Cornet, Créquillon, Faignent, Jacotin, Jannequin and Noé.

Tablature(s) by Simon Gintzler were published at Venice.

Othmair's "Symbola" was written.

Angelo da Picitono's "Fior angelico di musica" appeared.

Enriquez Valderrábano, a Spanish composer, wrote "Silva de Sirenas." It contained arrangements for one or two vihuelas by des Prés, Gombert, Morales, Verdelot, and Willaert.

Enriquez de Valderrabano wrote a Pavana for guitar.

Pietro Bembo, Venetian nobleman and scholar, died (born c.1470).

Edward Hall, barrister, historian, and author, died (born c.1498).

The Earl of Surrey, English poet, died (born c.1517). His actual name was Henry Howard.

Under the Protestant regime at this time, Cranmer and his committee started to work earnestly on a liturgy completely in the vernacular.

Nicholas Hillyarde, an English painter, was born (died 1619).

Sebastiano del Piombo, Italian painter, died (born c.1485).

Italian architecture: Michelangelo, Rome, St. Peter's (560'x560', height of west end 470').

Italian painting: Tintoretto, The Last Supper.

1547(cont.)

(to 1548, January 28) King Henry VIII of England and Great Britain, died (born 1491, June 28). Edward VI ascended the throne simultaneously.

(to 1549) French sculpture: Jean Goujon, Nymph (from the Fontaine des Innocents).

(to 1553) The reign of King Edward VI (House of Tudor) over England and Great Britain.

(to 1553) Tallis composed for the official English liturgy under King Edward VI.

(to 1553) Under Edward VI, Calvinism and Lutheranism were tolerated, while the Anglican Church became Protestant.

(to 1559) The reign of King Henry II (House of Valois) over France.

(to 1566) Bakfark was lutenist to the King of Poland.

(to 1579) Francisco de Montanos was maestro at Valladolid.

c.1547

Evidence revealed a Johannes Lupi who was active at Our Lady at Antwerp and died in this year.

De Rore left Venice for the court of Hercules II, Duke of Ferrara.

1548

(March 8) The Order of Communion was issued by Royal Proclamation.

(April 14) A Royal Injunction was delivered to the Dean and Chapter of Lincoln Minister.

Carpentras, composer of sacred music and important personage in the Papal service for most of his life, died (born c.1470).

Fernando de Contreras, Spanish composer, died (born c.1470).

Sixtus Dietrich, early Protestant liturgical composer, died at St. Gall (born c.1490).

Giacomo Fogliano, Italian frottolist and composer, died (born 1473).

Juan Ginés Perez, a sacred composer, was born at Orihuela (date of death unknown).

Richafort, a des Prés pupil, died (born c.1480).

Georg Rhaw, printer, composer and teacher, died (born 1488).

Bernhard Schmid the Younger, son of the Elder and a leading intabulator, was born in Strassbourg (date of death unknown).

Gonzaga was appointed governor of Milan and Lassus remained at the Lombard capital until this year when he lost his voice.

Mundy became parish clerk at St. Mary-at-Hill Church, in London.

With the influence of Charles de Ronsard, Jannequin's brother, the latter became curate of Unverre (near Chartres). He continued to live in Paris, however.

Christopher Tye was admitted ad eundem to Oxford.

Zarlino had a clavicembalo con-

1548(cont.)
structed with two sizes of all major and minor semitones.

Abondante used embellishment rather than imitation in his fantasia published in this year.

Appenzeller's double canon, Sancta Maria, embroidered on a tablecloth was given to Queen Mary of Hungary.

Calmo's "La Travaglia" was first performed.

The Cracow Tablature appeared.

The "Premier livre de chansons spirituelles composées par Guillaume Guéroult et mises en musique à quatre parties par Didier Lupi second et autres" was issued at Lyons.

A composition attributed to Henry VIII called "The Kynges Ballade" was mentioned in "The Complainte of Scotland," published in this year.

Johann Honterus' Odae cum harmoniis was published at Brassó. This was the first music ever printed in Hungary.

The collection, Madrigali di Giovanni Nasco, for five voices, was issued during this year.

Phinot, who usually avoided any sensational or unconventional textures, published five motets for two choruses of four-voices.

Thomas Sibilet's Art poétique was published.

King Edward VI of England employed a bagpiper, a drumslade, a flute, a harper, two lutenists, eight minstrels, a Welsh (cont.) minstrel, a rebec, four sackbutts, a virginal, and seven viols.

Italian painting: Tintoretto, St. Mark Freeing the Condemned Slave.

Italian painting: Veronese, Bevilacqua Altarpiece (Verona).

(to 1549) Cornelius Canis was one of four musicians at the Spanish court. The others were Crecquillon, Lestainnier, and Payen. They jointly published a motet collection dedicated to their patron.

(to 1549) French sculpture: Jean Goujon, Nymphs, Fountain of the Innocents (approx. life -size).

(and 1554) Ippolita, Gonzaga's daughter, married Fabrizio Colonna, Duke of Tagliacozzo, in Milan in 1548. In 1554, she married Antonio Carafa di Mandragone. Both Hoste and Rufilo dedicated madrigals to her in respect to her musical training.

(to 1555) Johann Walther was brought to Dresden for the purpose of organizing and directing the court Kapelle of the Elector of Saxony. He was recommended by Melanchthon and remained until 1555 when he returned to Torgau.

(and 1561) Willaert's two collections of madrigals were published at Venice.

(to 1572) Sigismund Augustus, who reigned during this period, was successor to Sigismund the Elder. He brought an outstanding group of musicians to his

1548(cont.)

court including Bakfark and some fine native Polish musicians.

c.1548

A book with no date or music was apparently printed at this time. It contained nineteen psalm translations (in verse) by Thomas Sternhold. It was described as "Certayne Psalmes chosen out of the Psalter of David and drawen into English Metre by Thomas Sternhold, Grome of ye Kynges, Maiesties Robes, London, Edvardus Whitchùrche."

François Roussel, a predecessor of Palestrina, was at the Julian Chapel and held the title of magister puerorum. He also held the position of maestro di cappella at St. John Lateran and at St. Luigi dei Francesi.

The Sternhold and Hopkins Psalter was first published in the form of a small book.

1549

(January 21) The Act of Uniformity was passed stating that the Book of Common Prayer was to be used after this date.

(November 10) At this date, the death of Paul III, an unforseen situation in the Papacy came about. The dominant Imperial and Farnese parties were at swords point and political tensions were high.

François Eustache du Caurroy, Sieur de St. Frémin, a composer and academician, was born at Gerberoy, near Beauvais (died 1609). After the academicians were disbanded he still composed musique mesurée.

Francesco Rovigo, Italian maestro, was born (date of death unknown).

Whit Sunday Publication of first Booke of Common Prayer by Edward VI.

François du Caurroy, French sacred composer, was a nobleman, cleric, and teacher.

Francesco Soriano, Italian composer who studied with Nanino and Palestrina, was born at Suriano (died 1621).

Thomas Sternhold, known for his English psalter, died (birthdate unknown). He was also Groom of the Robes to both Henry VIII and Edward VI.

Vincenzo Colombi, an Italian, built the organ at the church of St. John Lateran at Rome.

Goudimel was active as a composer of French chansons.

Palestrina's son Rodolfo was born at Palestrina (date of death unknown).

After Philip II dismissed Susato from his position at Antwerp in this year, the latter was not employed by the city again.

Nicola Vicentino opened a small private school at Rome for selected students whom he indoctrinated with his musical views.

The appendix to Barberiis' Intabulatura di Lauto contained four compositions for seven -string guitar entitled Fantasie per sonar sopra la chitara da sette corde.

1549(cont.)

Joachim du Bellay, French writer, published a manifesto, Défense et Illustration de la Langue Francaise. This was an answer to Sibilet's "Art poétique" defending Marot.

Juan Bermudo's "Libro de la declaracion de instrumentos," Vol. I, was published at Ossuna.

Bourgeois changed seventeen tunes in the Genevan Psalter and replaced eight.

Jacques Buus' nineteen motets for four-voices were published.

In Cavalli's "Il Giasone" he had a song accompanied by two violins and a bass, in a style that anticipated Handel's use of the same instruments fifty years later.

The "Psalter of David . . . ," translations by Robert Crowley, included a single setting for four-voices to be used for all 150 psalms.

A second edition of the Dodecachordon, bearing the title "De Musices divisione ac definitione," but with the same chapter headings was apparently published at Basle.

Gardano published a collection of Villotte by Mathias Fiamengo at Venice. The title of the volume was La bataglia taliana. The composer was the choirmaster at the Milan Cathedral. The composition probably celebrated Duke Sforza's victory over the French at Bicocca (1522) rather than at Pavia.

Forster's Song-books (in an imperfect copy) were preserved in (cont.) the British Museum.

Gardano published a collection of ricercari by Buus in part-books.

Gardano's publications of this year were almost an "unearthing of old music."

The first known publication of Goudimel's music was in a book of chansons published by Du Chemin at Paris, Goudimel was almost surely living in Paris at the time.

Additions were made to the Sternhold and Hopkins Psalter in a reprinted volume. Hopkins added seven and eighteen more by Sternhold, however, there was still no music included.

In the first published collection of Jannequin's psalms, only the superius, contratenor, and bassus were existent, but the tenor could be added as a result of the phrase "sur le chant ja usité."

Merbecke's work was the first musical setting of the liturgy in England permitted by the Act of Uniformity of this year.

Diphona Amoena et florida . . . J. Montanus et A. Neuber was published at Nürnberg.

The third volume of Rore's motets appeared.

Sternhold published a book of thirteen metrical psalms as well as a later collection of fifty-one psalms.

Verdelot's last works in publication appeared this year.

1549(cont.)

Willaert's Fantasie e Ricercari was published at Venice.

Compositions by Willaert and Rore were included in a publication which also contained ricercari written by the violist, Tiburtino.

Chinese composer Yuan lo's book of music was published.

Cranmer's Prayer-Book was published under authorization of the King. In the book the word "Alleluia" was included as a response for use between Easter and Trinity, whereas during the rest of the Church year it appeared in translation. The "Benedicite" was to be used during Lent instead of the "Te Deum." Later this restriction was lifted and the choice became optional. The "Deus Misereatur" was not included and the Introit disappeared although in King Edward VI's prayer-book it was to be used as an entire psalm followed by the "Gloria Patri," however, sung with no antiphon. The "Jubilate" did not appear in the Cranmer version.

English forms of Liturgy had begun to appear prior to this date.

Psalter, The English Metrical, or paraphrastic rhyming translation of the Psalms and Evangelical Hymns to be sung, dated from this year, the third year of Edward the VI's reign.

The Complaynte of Scotland was issued.

King Edward the Sixth's "First Prayer-Book" was issued.

The term vaux-de-vire (voix-de -ville) appeared in the preface to Du Bellay's "Vers lyriques."

The Sternhold-Hopkins collection was brought to Frankfurt and Geneva by Protestants driven out of England by Queen Mary. During their exile, the Anglo-Genevan Psalter appeared with a revised version of the forty-four psalms as its basis.

Charles V entered Paris.

Tommaso Garzoni, Italian author, and madrigalist, was born (died 1589).

Etienne Tabourot, French poet, was born (died 1590).

Antonio Moro's patrons, Cardinal Granvelle and the Duke of Alba, presented him to Charles V and Prince Philip when royal parties were in Brussels this year.

Italian architecture: Palladio, Vicenza, Basilica (232'x124').

(Dec. 14 and 1550, 1553) "All such psalmes of David as Thomas Sternehold late groome of y[e] Kinges Maiesties Robes didde in his lyfetime draw into English metre. Newly imprinted by Edward Whitchurch." was published. Lowndes mentioned a second edition of this work in the following year: "by the widowe of Jhon Harrington, London, 1550." A third edition appeared in 1553, again published by Whitchurche.

(to 1551) Wolfgang Figulus was the Cantor at the St. Thomas

1549(cont.)

School in Leipzig.

(to 1551) Shepherd was a Fellow at Magdalen College, Oxford.

(to 1553) Robert Parsons' First Service was published sometime during this period.

(to 1555) Bermudo's Declaración de Instrumentos Musicales was a book for students, actually a method book for instrumental students. It was published at Osuna in three editions during these years.

(to 1597) Over sixty of Goudimel's compositions were published during these years.

(to 1620) The Cathedral library at Lincoln preserved a large collection of madrigals and motets from this period, by many obscure composers.

c.1549

Spanish painting: Antonio Moro, Portrait of the Duke of Alba.

John Day, an early English musical typographer, began printing in Holborn at this time.

1550

(February 8)
Giammaria Ciocchi del Monte ascended the Papal throne as Julius III.

(March 18) According to Fétis, Johann Petreius died at Nūremberg (birthdate unknown).

(December 6) Orazio Vecchi, Italian choral-dramatist, was christened at Modena.

Diego Sánchez de Badajoz, Spanish dramatist, died (born (cont.) 1479).

Emilio de' Cavalieri, the first ballet composer, madrigalist and performer, was born at Rome (died 1602).

Jacobus Gallus, German composer and outstanding contemporary of Palestrina, was born (died 1591). He wrote masses and motets for the Catholic service. His actual name was Handl which was Latinized and made Gallus.

Jean de Guise, the first Cardinal of Lorraine, died (birthdate unknown).

Mancinus, a later contemporary of Palestrina, was born (date of death unknown).

Tiburzio Massaino, a Madrigal composer, was born at Cremona (date of death unknown).

Pedro Ordoñez, Spanish sacred composer, died in Rome (born c.1500).

Scaliger, writer of Poetices, died (born 1484).

Johann Spangenberg died (born 1484).

Thomas Szadek, Polish composer, was born (date of death unknown).

Gian Giorgio Trissino, author of Italian poetic drama, died (born 1478).

Orazio Vecchi, a choral dramatist of great significance, was born at Modena (died 1605).

Antonio Barre was an established composer of repute at Rome.

Jean Bermudo, Spanish theorist,

1550(cont.)

author of Declaración de Instrumentos Musicales, was active at this time.

Buus received a leave of absence from St. Mark's and went to Vienna.

Scipione Cerreto indicated Baccusi's exact era by stating that he had composed prior to this date.

A Rosso spinet dated 1550 and signed by Annibalis Mediolanesis was preserved.

Donato became a singer at St. Mark's in Venice.

Dunstable's name did not appear in Bale's "Scriptores Britanniae."

André de Escobar went to the West Indies where he wrote a method for the shawm.

Miguel de Fuenllana, Spanish composer of Orphenica Libra, was active at this time.

Francisco Guerrero became a singer at Seville.

The Booke of Common Praier Noted was written by Merbecke.

Merbecke received the degree of Mus. D. from Oxford.

Da Monte went to Rome.

The Antoni Patavini Spinet from this date was preserved at Brussels.

Bourgeois published "Le droict chemin de musique, composé par Loys Bourgeois avec la manière de chanter les pseaumes par (cont.) vsage ou par ruse, comme on cognoistra, au xxxiv, de nouveau mis en chant, et aussi le cantique de Siméon. Genève 1550."

The collection "Chansons anciennes" by Du Chemin appeared.

Claude Gervaise, who wrote Three Dances, was active.

R.L. Greene defined the carol as "a song on any subject, composed of uniform stanzas and provided with a burden." He stressed the fact that "the burden makes and marks the carol."

"Certayne Psalms chosen out of the Psalter of David and drawen forth into English Meter by William Hunnis. London, by the wydow of John Hereforde, 1550."

Volume I of a three volume set of Isaac's Choralis Constantinus was published by Hieronymus Formschneider at Nürnberg.

Jannequin's Le Chant des oiseaux has a point where simultaneous false relation would exist if musica ficta were applied. This has been given as evidence that the Franco-Netherlanders, at this time, used the modes in pure form in their vocal music.

Luther's Psalm 118 : 17, "Non moriar sed vivam et narrabo opera Domini" ("I shall not die, but live, and declare the works of the Lord") was written (the text and the melody) on the wall of his study, and his physician, Ratzeberger, saw it as late as this date.

1550(cont.)

Merbecke's Booke of Common Praier noted was published. It contained monophonic settings that were partly adaptations from the traditional chant, and partly Merbecke's original work. Two chants were given for the "Benedictus" viz the 5th tone with 1st ending, and the 8th tone with the 1st ending. A special chant was given for the "Deus Misereatur," however, no chant for the "Jubilate" was given. The "Gloria in Excelsis" was included but apparently not sung in the early days after the Reformation in England and received little attention from English composers. Merbecke's revision of the musical setting for the Litany was published.

The lauda in Filippo Neri's prayer chapel

Girolamo Parabosco's collected tales "I Diporti" were issued.

Andrea Patricio, from Cres, composed four madrigals for four-parts. They have survived in a collection by Antonino Barges, "Il primo libro de villote," published by Gardano.

Tallis was surely influenced by the character of the well-known Ambrosian Te Deum which Merbecke published in his prayer-book. Tallis' "Te Deum" in d minor was the composition where this fact was obvious.

Vasari wrote Vite de' più Eccellenti Architetti, Pittori, e Scultori Italiani.

Willaert's famous antiphonal psalms appeared in a collection (cont.) published at this time.

Some tablature by Rudolf Wyssenbach were published at Zürich.

The Catholic organ chorale started to decline in the Catholic countries at this time. Of the Reformed Churches, only the German branch continued the tradition.

Noble courtesans of Venice sang to the accompaniment of lute or "gravicembalo."

Harmony was already recognized in English church music at this time.

In Merbecke's prayer-book, published by Grafton of London, the four lines of the staff were continuous and not made up of small sections. They were printed in red ink, the square notes were black and appeared to be each a separate type.

The passamezzo and saltarello replaced the pavane and galliarde as popular dances from this date forward.

The ricercar was based either on one theme (monothematic) or several slow themes in succession.

At Rouen a considerable amount of "fiddles" were said to have been at public performances.

The use of the variation technique by English instrumental composers started prior to this date.

King Charles IX (House of Valois) of France was born (died 1574).

1550(cont.)

Spanish architect, Machuca, died (birthdate unknown).

Pieter Bruegel began working for Hieronymus Cock (a print publisher) as a designer in Antwerp.

Antonio Moro was sent to Portugal where he painted several portraits.

Italian architecture: Palladio, Italian 16th-century villa near Vicenza.

(to 1552) Paolo Animuccia was appointed Maestro at the Lateran when Rubino was sent to the Vatican. The former held the position for two years and was then succeeded by Lupacchini. One source claimed that Animuccia was there for five years but the "Libri Censuali" proved this premise to be incorrect.

(to 1555) The Papal reign of St. Julius III (born in Rome).

(to 1556) Nicholas Duchemin printed music at one printing during these years.

(to 1557) A John Wilbore was vicar of Minster in Thanet during this period at the end of which he resigned.

(to 1559) Ferrara took the lead in producing experimental music, primarily concerned with the projected uses of chromaticism.

(to 1559) Nasco's madrigal books containing compositions in as many as eight parts were issued during these years.

(to 1559) Petrarch's "Crudele (cont.) acerbo, inexorabil morte" was set by de Rore during these years.

(to 1559) Petrarch's Vergine bella was a favorite Counter-Reformation text after Rore had set the style during this period.

(to 1560) Quadrio mentioned three academies for theatrical music in Florence, "degl" Infocati," "degli" Immobili, "de" Sorgenti," they were founded during these years.

(to 1563) The Diary of Henry Machyn was written.

(and 1568) Donato was among the later composers of villanesche. Collections of his works in this genre were published in these two years.

(to 1575) The influence of plainsong was gradually replaced by that of modern continental styles.

(to 1583) Nine different original publications of Vincenzo Ruffo's works were mentioned by Fétis and Pougin as being from this period.

(to 1610) The Renaissance in Germany affected the culture of the upper class, mainly, and was artificially superimposed on the persisting Gothic-Nordic sentiment of the nation as a whole. This superimposed Renaissance maintained itself with a degree of purity only for a short time, actually for about sixty years.

c.1550

Giovanni Battista Ala, an Italian organist born at Monza

c.1550(cont.)

at this time, composed madrigals and canzonets. He died at the age of thirty-two.

Ippolito Baccusi, Italian madrigalist, was born (date of death unknown).

Veit Bach, a baker and the first of the monumental family of composers, was born (died 1619).

Luigi Balbi, a pupil of Porta and a composer, was born at Venice (died 1608).

Giovanni Bernardino brother and pupil of Giovanni Maria Nanino, was born (died 1623),see Nanino.

Giacomo Brignoli, Italian polyphonic composer, was born (date of death unknown).

Miguel Gomez Camargo, Spanish composer, was born at Guadalajara (date of death unknown).

Giovanni Caraccio, Italian singer, choir director, and composer was born at Bargamo (d.1619), see 1555.

Girolamo Conversi, Italian madrigalist, was born at Correggio (date of death unknown).

Giovanni Giacomo Gastoldi, an Italian madrigalist, was born at Caravaggio (died 1622). He was highly regarded for his work in related lighter forms, and was apparently Wert's assistant at the court in Mantua.

Nathaniel Giles, English organist and Mus. D., was born at Worcester (died 1633, Jan. 24).

Edward Johnson, English composer, was born (date of death unknown).

Giovanni Bernardino Nanino, Italian madrigalist, was born at Vallerano (died 1623)see c1560.

Georgius Otto, German composer and teacher of Schütz, was born (died 1618), see 1544.

Jacopo Peri, an Italian composer and singer, was born of noble parentage, at Florence (died c.1615), see 1561.He was a member of the Florentine Camerata.

Johann Berg, a music printer, born in Ghent, set up a printing office in Nürnberg at this time in association with Ulrich Neuber.

Byrd was involved in a lawsuit in connexion with his Stondon property. The case started about this year when Osborne Foster, who occupied the property at Stondon Place, bought a small piece of property called Malepardus Farm.

Cadeac was master of the choristers at Auch.

Dankerts, a native of Tholen in Zeeland, was a singer in the Papal Chapel at this time.

Des Prés' chansons experienced a strong revival at this time.

Dietrich, the German composer, lived at Constance.

Alfonso Ferrabosco, the Italian musician who settled in England, was ranked among the foremost of the Elizabethan composers.

Andrea Gabrieli composed some of

c.1550(cont.)
the earliest toccatas.

Nicolas Herman was Cantor at Joachimsthal in Bohemia.

Robert Johnson, an ecclesiastic who was active at this time, composed motets, part-songs, and virginal pieces.

The house of Ballard in Paris was established at this time by Robert Ballard and his son-in-law Adrien Le Roy.

De Rore succeeded Vicentino as maestro di cappella.

De Rore apparently left Venice for the court of Hercules II, Duke of Ferrara.

Vicentino experimented with a six manual harpsichord with thirty-one tones to the octave.

Thomas Ashwell was a cathedral musician of the period who adhered to the Roman Catholic faith. Motets composed by him were preserved in manuscripts at the Music School at Oxford.

Many French works published by Attaingnant prior to this date survived in a Flemish manuscript.

Poetry by Diego Sanchez de Badajoz was set by madrigalists in "La Farsa del Juego de Cañas" issued at about this time.

Festa's compositions were published in great number by Gardano and Scotto at Venice.

Fuerte's "Historia de la Musica Española," published at Madrid, maintained that the sarabande was invented at this time by a (cont.) dancer, Zarabanda, who according to some sources was a native of either Seville or Guayaquil. It was assumed on the basis of this evidence that the dance was named after him.

A manuscript in the collection of St. Egidi in Bártfa included Introits, and other chants by Isaac, Stoltzer, and others. The alternation of organ with plainchant and vocal polyphony was indicated in the manuscript.

A large repertoire of ensemble music such as fancies (fantasias) was preserved in the British Museum. The dates of the compositions ranged from this time on through the time of Purcell.

John Thorne, of York, was a prominent musician of the time and was mentioned by Morley in his "Introduction."

Voces Belgicae was the name given to the syllables Bo, Ce, Di, Ga, Lo, Ma, Ni, proposed by the Flemish Composer, Waelrant, as a substitute for the syllables used for the purpose of solmization by d'Arezzo.

Walther's St. Matthew's Passion appeared at this time.

The Dies irae became an established part of the Requiem Mass in France sometime after this date.

The composition of "In nomines" came into favor.

The Passion was at all times sung by only the three Deacons.

The earliest known example of a bona fide sketch, the earliest

c.1550(cont.)

rota, the earliest polyphonic motet, and the earliest example of a vocal score was the product of the English School. It was composed by Shepherd, either for testing the possibilities of a subject he planned to use as the basis for a motet, or some vocal composition, or for the instruction of a pupil.

Polyphonic vocal compositions of the highest quality were important in Dalmatian churches long before the principles of monody (17th century type) were brought into religious music.

By this time the use of clavecin instruments with jacks had become common in England, France and the Netherlands, as well as in Italy where they originated.

A seven-string guitar was being played in Italy at this time.

Experiments in chromatic music led organ builders to provide for execution of intervals smaller than the semitone.

Players of bowed instruments began to escape from the long domination of the lute and its tunings by fourths and thirds, as well as its excessive number of strings.

The earliest developments in instrumental composition, particularly for strings, dated from this time.

Rules for fingering had not yet come into existence, although double stops had already occurred.

The viol, in all its forms and sizes, reached maturity in the (cont.) areas of design and scope.

No instrument of the violin family actually existed up to this time.

Organ parts to some English anthems and services were among the earliest examples of instrumental accompaniment.

Any history of the development of instruments must examine the instruments themselves rather than deal with names. The existence, descriptions, and graphic representations, however imperfect, were the only evidence up to this time. Bowed instruments as a class by themselves had already existed for a century.

Italian influence brought chromaticism into favor among French composers.

The idea of harmony proper, as apart from polyphony, was just starting at this time.

This period witnessed a rapid move toward perfection, in many centers of technical activity, but all these gains and earlier ones were eventually forgotten when the later Roman School came into prominence.

The Italians took a strong lead in production of passamezzi.

This time was the birth date of polychoral style in Italy.

Almost nothing was known about the secular music in England prior to this time.

The theatres of Italy were frequently constructed by archi-

c.1550(cont.)

tects, such as Palladio. The melodious language of Italy combined with its fine music were the wonder and admiration of the world.

Sketches preserved in the Vatican Library made it simple to form concrete ideas comparing the precincts of old St. Peter's as they appeared at this time. These sketches were by Grimaldi, Heemskerck, and several anonymous artists.

About this time several European rulers were sent to the Netherlands for composers and singers to enhance their musical groups.

Sir Edward Dyer, Elizabethan poet, was born (died 1607).

French painting: Jean Cousin, Eva Prima Pandora.

African sculpture: Bronze head of a Negro (excavated in Nigeria).

Italian painting: Titian, Self-portrait (38"x29½").

(to 1560) Alternating points of imitation with chordal passages appeared in Richard Edwards' "In goinge to my naked bedde." The effect of European influence on English secular music before the English madrigal appeared was existant but not significant.

(to 1599) Giovanni Maria Artusi, a theorist, was born at Bologna (date of death unknown).

(to 1599) Giovanni Matteo Asola (Asula), sacred composer and madrigalist, was born at Verona (died 1609), see c.1560.

(to c.1599) Romano Alessandro, surnamed della Viola in respect to his skill on the instrument, lived during this period.

(to c.1599) Giovanni d'Antiquis, who lived during this period, was Director of music in the church of St. Nicholas at Bari in the Kingdom of Naples, as well as author of two collections.

(to c.1599) Scipione Bargaglia, a Neopolitan composer and contrapuntalist, mentioned by Cerreto, lived during this period.

(to c.1599) Kerle, a Netherlandish musician, held an important position at the Hapsburg court. Other foreign musicians were similarly engaged at that court.

(to c.1599) Johann Baptist Weber was at this time a man of property and the earliest known member of the musical family.

(to c.1599) Giaches de Wert, the Flemish composer of this period, was the subject of much confusion to his biographers.

(to c.1599) Crequillon's masses, motets and chansons appeared in all the major collections published at Antwerp and Louvain in these years.

(to c.1599) At the Allerheiligen Bibliothek in Danzig, a small collection of works of this period was preserved. The town library in the same city also had a similar collection.

(to c.1599) Vincenzo Galilei's "Il Fronimo" was especially valuable for its clarification

c.1550(cont.)
of the form of tablature employed by the Italian Lutenists, as well as their method of tuning the instrument at this time.

(to c.1599) During this time the French and Flemish Schools of Polyphony moved toward over-ornamentation and mannerisms in elaboration that might best be described as secular in orientation and quite removed from the plainsong element from which liturgical polyphonic form had evolved.

(to c.1599) Composers in looking for expression developed the madrigal to its highest possible refinement and its ultimate peak.

(to c.1599) German organ tablatures showed coloration to such an exaggerated and unimaginative degree that much of the music suffered by comparison with contemporary English, Italian, and Spanish keyboard works and even with earlier German works by Schlick and Kleber.

(to c.1599) The circle was constantly used in connection with, or replaced by, the figure "3." The rationale was the perfection of a circle and thus an analogy with the Holy Trinity.

(to c.1599) Major composers seldom wrote melodies of the short rhythmical type required for ballads.

(to c.1599) For lack of better evidence, a writer agreed with Charles Reade, quoted in Mr. Hart's book, "The Violin," that no true violin was made prior to the second half of the century, when Gaspar di Salo and Andreas Amati commenced their work.

(to c.1599) The virginal underwent great development and improvement.

(to c.1599) Youthful treble voices were gradually replaced by a new kind of adult male soprano, called the "soprano falsetto." These were imported, first from Spain, where the technique was cultivated by some strange system of training. The manner of training was never publicly revealed.

(to c.1599) Several versions of the whole book of Psalms in metre were issued, other than the Sternhold and Hopkins version.

(to c.1599) French painting: Anonymous, Diana as Huntress.

(to c.1600) The sheer numbers of madrigals composed during this period was astonishing.

(to 1700) The duration of the school of pure six-stringed viol music was about a century and a half.

(to 1750) Cremona, in Lombardy, Po, was the seat of the famous Cremona school of violin-makers for about two centuries.

(to the present) Palestrina and contemporaries employed a musical diction that was unique and may not be compared with music of later centuries or treated as a crude and elementary version of the music of the following centuries. Rather, it was the ultimate peak of the development of polyphony.

1551

(December 3) Bourgeois was thrown into prison for having "without leave" changed the tunes of some psalms. Calvin's intervention secured his release on the following day.

(September) Palestrina was appointed Master of the Boys in the Julian Choir at St. Peter's.

(September) Rubino finally retired teaching in the Cappella Giulia of the Vatican. Palestrina was appointed as his successor apparently in recogrecognition of his talent and eleven years of service.

(November) In the archives of the Cappella Giulia, Palestrina was referred to as Magister Joannes, and three boys were assigned to his charge.

Palestrina's son Angelo was born just before the composer left to return to Rome (d.1576).

Albert de Ripe, a Mantuan lutenist, died (birthdate unknown). At the time of his death tributes were received from Baif, Ronsard and others.

Johannes Wannenmacher, a Swiss composer and friend of Zwingli, died (birthdate unknown).

The firm formed by Robert Ballard and his half -brother Adrian Le Roy at this time ultimately became the publishers of Couperin's and Lully's works.

Ercole Bottrigari edited an anthology.

Buus became organist at the imperial court in Vienna.

Contino was choirmaster at the cathedral in his native town, Brescia.

Fétis mentioned an instrument made by Andrea Amati bearing this date. He also described one by the same maker dated 1546. One was a rebec with three strings, the other a viola bastardo (small violin).

In order to fight the corruption assailing the Chant, a project was drawn at the instigation of Ivan the Terrible. The plan was to form institutions to teach reading, writing, and singing, instruction to be given by the clergy.

Le Jeune was not over twenty-one years of age when all of Marot's and the first part of Beza's translations of the Genevan Psalter had already appeared.

Lassus came to Rome for his appointment.

Le Roy married Ballard's sister. The latter was already involved with music printing, and was attached to the court.

Clement Marot dedicated his version of the Psalms, published at Lyons, to his country women.

The elevation of Cardinal del Monte to the Papacy was an event of great importance to Palestrina.

St. Philip Neri lived mostly at Rome and was ordained priest there in this year. He went to live with the priests of San Girolamo della Carità.

Palestrina was Director of the Julian Choir in Rome. He was

1551(cont.)

also teacher of native singers.

Parabosco was first organist at St. Mark's in Venice.

Robartt, of Crewkerne, was an "orgyn maker," who rented organs to churches by the year. The Mayor of Lyme Regis paid him ten shillings for his year's rent in this year.

Juan Vasquez, a native of Badajoz, entered the service of Don Antonio de Zúñiga, in Andalusia, probably before this date.

Waelrant married for the first time.

In the Genevan Psalter, Bourgeois changed four tunes and substituted twelve new melodies, some for earlier ones he had composed himself.

The Fundamentbuch by Buchner was published.

Two chansons by Divitis, under the name Le Riche, were included in the collection "des plus excellentes chansons" published by Du Chemin at this time.

Gardano published the dance music collection, Intabolatura nova di varie sorte de Balli da sonare per arpichordi, Clavicembali, Spinette & Manichordi, Raccolta de diversi excellentissimi Autori.

The "Old Hundredth" was the melody adapted to Beza's version of the 134th Psalm. It was included in the first installment of psalms that he contributed to the Genevan Psalter. There were thirty-four of these which (cont.) he added at this date.

Eight of Goudimel's psalm settings in motet style were published by Du Chemin. The settings were broad in structure and polyphonic in style.

Goudimel published the earliest French musical version of Marot's psalter.

A hymnbook containing seventy-eight German and forty-seven Latin texts appeared.

Jannequin's "Le Chant des Oyseaux," for four voices, was published.

Points of similarity between French and Italian military signals would probably be disclosed in a comparison of Jannequin's "La Bataille," "La Guerre," and "La prinse et reduction de Boulogne," with Milano's "La Battaglia." The Jannequin pieces were included in du Chemin's fifth book of chansons.

Le Roy's "Briefve et facile Instruction pour apprendre la Tablature," was first published at Paris.

Susato's seven "Musyckboexkens" appeared under the title "Het ierste musyck boexken mit vier partyen daer inne begrepen syn XXVIII niewe amoreuse liedekens . . . ." Also, his "Het derde musyck boexcken . . ." which contained examples of basse dances and other dances was issued.

Vasquez's "Villancicos y canciones . . . a tres y a cuatro" was published at this time.

1551(cont.)

A reprint of Walther's Geystliche Gesangkbüchleyn appeared with changes and additions (other reprints were done in 1525, 1537, and 1544).

Valentin Balassi, a Hungarian lyric poet, was born (died 1594).

William Camden, founder of the Chair of History at Oxford, was born (died 1623).

King Henry III (House of Valois) of France, was born (died 1589).

Bruegel became a master in the Antwerp guild.

(and 1552) After Marot's death, the Genevan Psalter remained incomplete until work was resumed in this year of thirty-four additional translations by Beza, which were combined with the forty-nine by Marot already in use in a publication in 1552.

(to 1552) Ruffo taught at the Accademia Filarmonica in Verona.

(to 1554) Both texts and melodies in the Anglo-Genevan Psalter (with Kethe and Wittingham translations) drew on the French Psalter of this period. The music, was anonymous.

(to 1554) Julius III was involved with the directing of building operations for his new and pretentious villa outside the Porta del Popolo. This was the so-called "Villa di Papa Giulio." It was started in 1551 and finished three years later.

(to 1554) Palestrina was the first "Maestro della cappella (cont.) della basilica Vaticana" and held the position throughout this period.

(to 1555) A series of five volumes of music for the four -course guitar was published by Le Roy in France during these years.

(to 1555) A series of magnificats belonging to the Julian Choir dated from Palestrina's first period at St. Peter's.

(and 1560) A melody was set differently by Vasquez in the two books with these dates. Its title was De los alamos vengo, madre and it sounded very much like a folk song.

(to 1562) Beza carried on the work of Marot and musical settings of Psalms continued to appear.

(to 1564) Buus was an organist at Vienna.

(to 1564) Melchior Hager was the Cantor at the St. Thomas School in Leipzig.

(to 1566) Claude Goudimel set the rhymed psalms of the French Huguenots and the Swiss Calvinists by Marot and Beza. He produced three different settings and these ranged in style from polyphonic motets to simple fauxbourdon.

(to 1568) The firm of Leroy and Ballard published twenty books of chansons for four voices during this period.

c.1551

It was only a few months after Julius III was elevated that he sent for Palestrina and appointed

c.1551(cont.)

him master of the Julian Choir.

St. Philip de' Neri organized a society of secular priests to discuss ethnical matters in his home and later at San Girolamo.

Czar Boris Godunov of Russia was born (died 1605).

(to 1552) Coclico continued his career at Nuremberg.

(to 1561) A manuscript preserved at Treviso included sixty-five sacred works by Nasco, probably written during his years as maestro at the Cathedral. Other composers' works were also contained in the manuscript.

1552

(February 16) Le Roy and Ballard established their partnership and obtained a patent bearing this date as sole printers of music to Henry II.

(April 19) A contract was drawn between Morlaye and the printer Fezandat on this date. It stipulated that the first edition would be 1,500 copies. This large printing certainly assumed that there was no lack of amateur lutenists in France.

(July 28) An entry in the registers of the Council of Geneva clearly stated that Bourgeois had set the psalms of Beza to music that had been published the year before, and that he had also arranged those already published in previous editions of the Psalter.

(November 2) Some historians attributed the Genevan Psalter melodies to Franc. Their contention was based on a letter (cont.) written to Bayle by David Constant, professor of theology at Lausanne. In the letter it was stated that Constant had seen a certificate bearing this date and that it had been given by Beza to Franc, and that in the certificate Beza testified that it was Franc who had first set the psalms to music.

William Bathe, Irish musician, was born at Dublin (died 1614, June 17), see 1564.

Johannes Cochlaeus, professor of music at the University of Cologne and a strong opponent of Luther, died (born 1479).

Heliodoro de Paiva, a canon at the Monastery of Santa Cruz in the university town of Coimbra, died (birthdate unknown). He composed magnificats, masses, and motets.

Under the patent granted to Ballard and Le Roy by Henry II many tablatures for lute and other music were rapidly published.

Barré, a Frenchman, was listed as an altus in the Julian Chapel records of this year.

Thomas Caustun was a Gentleman of the Chapel Royal.

Franc apparently was working on a new Psalter, for he obtained a license to publish one at Geneva, since there was no press at Lausanne at that time.

Gombert was living at Tournai.

Lassus was choirmaster at St. Giovanni in Laterano.

1552(cont.)

Padovano was second organist at St. Mark's in Venice.

At first Phalèse had been a publisher who used independent printers, but he started to do his own printing this year.

Rabelais described Carêmeprenant as having toes like an "epinette organisée."

According to Michaelis: Hieronymus von Schütz died in 1552 (birthdate unknown). He had voluntarily surrendered his Chemnitz burgomastership in 1544.

Schütz owned a house in the Zeitz quarter of Weissenfels, the present Loricke house. It was one of the free houses (Freihäuser) presented by the elector to Secretary Rost in this year.

Shepherd was a Gentleman of the Chapel Royal.

Tallis's Preces, Responses and Litany, as well as his Service in the Dorian mode, were probably composed shortly after the second Prayer Book of Edward VI was issued.

A lute-book by Bakfark was published at Lyons. The Hungarian composer was at that time staying in France.

A collection of Psalms by Certon was issued.

Coclico's "Musica Reservata" was published. The work was of great significance and discussed the application of the text to its proper place and the avoidance of using long notes for (cont.) short syllables on the reverse.

Coclico's "Compendium musices" described Jannequin's teaching in great detail. The work was published at this time.

Tablatures by Hans Gerle were published at Nürnberg (also in 1532, 1537 and 1546).

Four types of sonnets were published with music by Certon, Goudimel, Jannequin and Muret.

Le Roy's "Tiers Livre de tablature de luth" was published.

Jean Maillard's mass, published at Paris, was based on a French chanson "Je suis deshéritée." The secular words were placed under the liturgical ones so that his clever manipulation of the theme would surely be noticed.

Martoretta's works appeared in a Book II of madrigals.

Volume I of Phalèse's best-known collection of lute music, the Hortus musarum, appeared.

The Libro de Musica de Vihuela was written by Pisador. It included settings of ballads and madrigals and translations of Masses by des Pres as well as motets by Morales. The volume was published at Salamanca.

Tablatures by Hans Jacob Wecker were published at Basle.

The second book of Common Prayer in England was published.

All spiritual domains were taken over by the Protestants under the treaty of Passau.

1552(cont.)

The Cantate Domino was introduced in the revision of Merbecke's "Book of Common Praier Noted," published in this year.

The "Deus Misereatur" was given as an alternative for the "Nunc Dimittis" in the revised edition of the Prayer-Book.

The "Jubilate" was added in the revised edition of Cranmer's Prayer-book, issued during the reign of Edward VI.

The Collegium Germanicum in Rome was founded by St. Ignatius Loyola under Julius III. It was considered to be one of the most distinguished places of education in Rome, and not created solely for Germans, but rather numbered amongst its members people from noble families throughout Europe.

Merbeck's setting of the Nicene Creed in the "Book of Common Praier noted" for the use of the English reformed church followed the Roman original far less closely than did most of the rest of his setting of the service. As a result of this, it was far more melodious and free.

The organ at St. Paul was silenced until Mary became Queen (1553).

The Protestant Revision was published and this was the actual birth of the Anglican Service.

The "tap-dance canaries" were mentioned first in a Spanish source from this year.

Edmund Spenser, Elizabethan poet, was born (died 1599).

Italian architecture: Palladio, Vicenza, Palazzo Colleoni (88½' wide x 59' high).

Italian architecture: Palladio, Vicenza, Villa Rotonda (80' x 80').

Italian painting: Titian, Danaë.

Italian painting: Veronese, the altarpiece of "Cardinal Gonzaga," (Mantua).

(and 1553, 1561, 1569, 1571) Luc. Lossius Psalmodia; Wittenberg, 1552. Several later editions of this work appeared, and a copy of the 1569 edition was preserved in the Library at Wernigerode. It included 429 Latin and 9 German hymns in 4 and 5 parts. Copies of the other editions survived in the British Museum.

(and 1559) Elizabeth was sufficiently prudent not to resist the re-establishment of the 1552 prayer-book, as part of the settlement of 1559.

(and 1561) After Marot's death, Beza, a good friend of Calvin, continued writing psalm-hymns. Shortly after these psalms were set to music, first by Franc in 1552, and later, in 1561, by Bourgeois.

(to 1564) Padovano was second organist at St. Mark's in Venice.

(to 1565) Porta directed the choir at the Cathedral of Osimo.

(to c.1610) The expression "musica reservata" appeared. Similar terms with the same

1552(cont.)

meaning appeared in various sources.

c.1552

Giovanni de Macque, madrigalist and pupil of Monte's, was born at Valenciennes (died c.1614).

Paolo Virchi, Italian madrigalist, was born at Brescia (date of death unknown).

Richard Farrant was admitted to the Chapel Royal.

Thomas Wright was a Gentleman of the Chapel Royal.

Sir Walter Raleigh, Elizabethan poet, soldier, and statesman, was born (died 1618).

1553

(March 25) John Day obtained a license to print "A Catechism in English with an A B C thereunto annexed." He also was permitted to publish the works of John Poynet, Bishop of Winchester, and Thomas Beacon, Professor of Divinity.

(July 6) King Edward VI of England died (born 1537).

(October 7) Cristobal Morales, Spanish polyphonic composer, died at Toledo (born c.1500).

(October) Lucas Cranach the Elder, German painter, died (born 1472).

Leonhard Lechner, a Tyrolian composer, was born (died 1606).

Luca Marenzio, a perfectionist in the field of madrigal composition, was born at Coccaglio, near Brescia (died 1599).

Caspar Othmayr, German Protestant composer, died (born 1515).

The majority of Arcadelt's chansons dated from this period, which was after the one during which he composed his madrigals.

The archives of the Court of Mantua for this year carried an account of a performance of Ariosto's "I Suppositi," the entr'actes for which were composed by Cardinal Gonzaga, Regent of Mantua during Duke William's minority.

A gamba player, Diego Ortiz, was in Naples. He gave the first examples of variations over a "basso ostinato."

Tinódi was almost surely the composer and performer of his melodies. His "patent of nobility" in this year emphasized his "ars canendi historiarumque . . . in rhythmos elegans compositio" ("art of singing and the elegant writing of historical poems in varied rhythms").

Tye published a major work in the spirit of the Reformation, the "Actes of the Apostles."

John Wylbore was appointed prebendary of Rochester Cathedral where he died this year (birthdate unknown).

Bakfark published his first lute book at Lyons.

"Dialoghi della Musica" by Luigi Dentice was published at Naples.

Faber's "Musices practicae" Volume II was issued.

1553(cont.)

A theory handbook published by Hähnel had reached its sixth printing by this time.

In a rare old work, by Macropedias, "Bassarus. Fabula festivissima," published at Utrecht, some verses were adapted to a melody not especially noteworthy for its festive character. They were presented at the end of each scene.

"Tratado - - - en la Musica de Violones" written by Ortiz. It contained some of the earliest examples of instrumental variations (for bass-viol and cembalo).

Ortiz, chapel master to the Viceroy of Naples, published a method for viols, the Tractado de glosas. It provided variations for the viol. The publication was issued at Rome.

Part II of Phalèse's the Hortus musarum, a lute collection, appeared.

"Certayne Psalmes select out of the Psalter of David, and drawen into Englyshe Metre, with notes to every Psalme in iiij parts to Synge, by F.S. Imprinted at London by Wyllyam Seres, at the Sygne of the Hedge Hogge, 1553." In the dedication, to Lord Russell, the author gives his full name, Francys Seagar.

Seven psalms by Whittingham without music were added to the Sternhold-Hopkins Psalter. A psalter by Francys Seager was also published which included nineteen versified psalms and two settings for four voices, one used for twelve psalms and the other for two.

Tye translated the first fourteen chapters of the Acts of the Apostles into metre, set them to music, and published them. They were set for four voices in a popular style.

Burchard Waldis had his rhymed Psalter published by Egenolph in Frankfurt am Main.

King Henry IV of Navarre (House of Bourbon) of France was born (died 1610).

Act of Common Council was passed.

The Book of Common Prayer was repealed and Roman worship restored.

Queen Mary (a Catholic) came to the throne determined that she would restore completely the religion still observed by the majority of her subjects.

Veronese lived in Verona until this year when he reached the age of twenty-five and moved to Venice.

Veronese worked on the ceiling of the Palazzo Ducale.

(to 1553) The reign of Jane (Lady Jane Grey) over England. Nominal Queen of England for nine days, but was not considered Queen by Rome authorities. She was beheaded in 1554.

(to 1554) Des Près was chorusmaster at St. John the Lateran Church in Rome.

(to 1554, December) Lassus assumed the position of choirmaster at the Lateran.

(to 1554) Waelrant's "Chansons" were published by Phalèse at

1553 (cont.)

Louvain.

(to 1557) Salinas served as organist at the palace of the Duke of Alba in Naples sometime between these years.

(and 1557, 1559) One of Lassus' earliest canzoni was also one of his best and was published by both Barre and Bruno in Rome (1557). The work was apparently composed in 1553, and later reprinted as the first selection in the "Secondo libro a cinque (1559). It was a setting of Petrarch's canzone, of the "six visions," on the transience of the "Standomi un giorno, solo, alla finestra."

(to 1558) Byrd published three masses (probably composed during these years) without any date or printer's name.

(to 1558) Guillaume Morlaye, a slave trader and pupil of de Ripo, collected six volumes of his teacher's works. They were published during this period.

(to 1558) Tallis composed for the Latin rite again during its restoration under Queen Mary (Tudor).

(to 1558) The reign of Queen Mary I, Bloody Mary (House of Tudor), over England and Great Britain.

(to 1560) Susato published fifteen books of "Ecclesiasticae Cantiones" or motets.

(to 1564) Johannes de Cleve sang in the choir at Vienna.

(to 1611) Johannes Eccard, a (cont.) pupil of Lasso, director of Fugger's private orchestra, later in Königsberg and Berlin, was born at Mühlhausen and active during these years.

c.1553

Edmond Hooper, English composer, was born at Halberton, Devon (died 1621, July 14).

Mateo Flecha the Elder, Spanish madrigalist, died at Poblet, Catalonia (born c.1481).

Richard Pygott, English composer, died (birthdate unknown).

Arcadelt probably returned permanently to France since the great chanson production which marked the final phase of his career began at this date. Le Roy and Ballard published these chansons promptly.

News of his parents' illness called Lassus back to his home in Flanders.

Udall's "Ralph Roister Doister" was written.

(to 1558) The Gyffard Part-Books appeared.

1554

(April 21) John Sheppard applied for the degree of Mus. Doc., but it was not indicated whether it was awarded to him.

(November 30) Cardinal Pole pronounced his formal absolution of the nation.

(December 2) Mass was celebrated with great splendour in St. Paul's Cathedral (first Sunday in Advent).

(December 25) King Philip of

1554(cont.)

Spain was still in London following his marriage to Mary.

(November) It was recorded in the archives of the Julian Choir that a payment was made to one Giovanni Belardino (sic) Pierluigi for the purchase of a first book of masses. This Giovanni Belardino was probably Palestrina's brother Bernardino who, if it was he, must have gone to Rome with his brother.

Arnold von Bruck, German composer, died at Vienna (born c.1500 or 1480).

William Inglott, an organist and virginal player, was born (died 1621, December).

Robert Johnson, Scottish composer, died (born c.1470).

Sante Pierluigi ,Palestrina's father, died (born c.1499).

The melody of the "Old Hundredth" appeared in Beza's Geneva Psalter of this year.

Byrd was senior chorister of St. Paul's Cathedral. His name apparently appeared on a petition from the choristers requesting restoration of certain rights of which they had been deprived.

Cabezón, the blind Spanish organist-composer, visited England in the entourage of King Philip II.

Marshal de Brissac brought the Milanese dancing master Pompeo Diobono to the French court. A large group of instrumentalists (violinists) led by Baldassare da Belgioioso ar-

(cont.) rived a short time later.

Escobedo returned to Spain and became maestro de capilla at Segovia.

Gonzaga employed the musician L'Hoste da Reggio as "maestro della musica." This fact made it obvious that Gonzaga had his own private chapel.

Joachim Gräff, a poet, copied Luther's motet and put it in a school drama called "Lazarus." He later wrote "I had this little piece printed because it is so short and not too well known, and used it for my drama." . . . "Non moriar sed vivam, D.M.L." The book was published at Würtenburg and there was no doubt that Luther was the composer of the music.

Guerrero became maestro de capilla at Malaga.

Moritz von Der Heyden, was organist at Magdeburg Cathedral until this date.

Claude Le Jeune's name appeared as a composer.

Musical matters at St. John Lateran, the cathedral church of Rome, were most unsatisfactory after Lassus relinquished his appointment as musical director in this year.

Lassus apparently went from Flanders to England with Giulio Cesare Brancaccio, who was attempting to secure Mary Tudor's hand for King Philip II of Spain.

Lassus was probably settled at Antwerp by the end of this year.

1554(cont.)

Lassus wrote some music in honor of Cardinal Pole at this time.

Le Maistre succeeded Walther as Kapellmeister to the Elector of Saxony.

Giandomenico Il Martoretta, a native of Calabria, made a trip to the Holy Land. He was a "dottore in musica," as well as an ecclesiastic.

Monte's long stay in Italy ended in this year. His first madrigal book for five voices, in a purely Italian style, was published in Rome, where he had gone after resigning from his position with the Pinelli family at Naples.

Navarro battled Guerrero for the position of maestro at Malaga and lost. He did, however, hold a similar position at Salamanca, Ciudad Rodrigo and at Palencia.

Neri received permission to have an oratory constructed at one side of the church at San Girolamo. Here he could hold his discussions and add sermons to them as well as the singing of laude spirituali.

The archives of the Julian Choir showed that "Belardino" who described himself as "brother to Messer Giovanni Pierluigi" bought a set of part-books of his brother's first book of masses for the Julian Choir. He arranged to have them suitably bound.

A picture of "Palestrina Presenting his Masses to Pope Julius III" appeared in the frontispiece of the first volume of masses published at (cont.) this time. It was the earliest known portrait of the composer.

Ruffo's and Nasco's entertainments were presented for the Accademici Filarmonici of Verona.

Ruffo was maestro di capella at the Verona Cathedral.

Vasquez' name appeared at the end of the license in Fuenllana's vihuela book published this year.

Waelrant, the composer, and the printer Jean Laet set up a publishing house which operated until the latter's death.

Walther was dismissed from his position as director of the court Kapelle of the Elector of Saxony and a pension was granted him.

Georg Weber was studying at Leipzig.

The "Commedia Spirituale," Abel e Caino, was written.

The actual start of the Pastoral Drama was with the performance of Agostino Beccari's "Sacrificio d'Abramo" in Ferrara. The music for this work was by Alfonso Della Viola and has been reprinted by Solerti.

Cadeac's works were included in: "Gardano's XII Missae" published at Venice.

The Certon psalms were included in Morlaye's voice-and-lute transcriptions of this year.

Fiesco's first book of four -part madrigals was already

1554(cont.)

unusually "literary" in the sense referred to by de Rore. Fiesco's entire output was dedicated to members of the Este family.

John Foxe's "Actes and Monuments" was first published.

Miguel de Fuenllana's Orphénica Lyra was published at Seville. It was a tablature book including fantasies, romances, villancicos, and transcriptions of mass movements and motets. Its subsidiary title was "Libro de Musica para vihuela."

Fuenllana's Fantasia for guitar was composed.

Andrea Gabrieli's first published madrigal appeared in a collection devoted mainly to the works of Ruffo.

Six more psalms appeared in the Genevan Psalter.

Martoretta's Book III was published.

Da Monte's first madrigal book was published at Rome by Giovanni Battista Bruno.

Pierluigi's madrigal, "Con dolce altiero," was published by Gardano of Venice in a collection described on the title-page as "Il quarto libro de Madrigali a quattro voci a note bianche." It was the first of Palestrina's madrigals to be published.

Palestrina's Missarum cum 4 et 5 vocibus, Liber Primus was published by Valerio and Aloysio Dorico at Rome. This was the first collection of (cont.) his masses to be published and it was dedicated to Pope Julius III. Although the Dorici brothers issued the volume, Palestrina, himself, bore the expense. The titles included were, "Ecce sacerdos magnus," "O Regem coeli," "Virtute magna," "Gabriel archengelus," and "Ad coenam agni providi."

Some compositions by Clemens non Papa appeared in the "Motetti del Labirinto" published at Venice.

De Rore's Latin ode for four basses "Calami sonum ferentes," was a signficant work that strongly influenced subsequent madrigal composition. It had been composed by this date.

The third book of five voiced madrigals by Ruffo appeared.

The "Commedia Spirituale," Sansone, was written.

The Cronica written by Sebastian Tinódi "the Lutenist" appeared.

A French chanson by Jacques Vaet was included in Phalèse's first book of "Chansons."

The recitative had forerunners as far back as this date in della Viola's pastoral play "Il Sacrificio."

William Chell was Precentor of Hereford at this time, but after the accession of Queen Elizabeth was dismissed from all cathedral appointments.

A Don Pedro di Lasso attended the marriage of King Philip and

1554(cont.)

Queen Mary as ambassador from King Ferdinand of the Romans.

Jane (Lady Jane Grey) was beheaded (born 1537). See other entries for her status as nominal Queen for nine days.

Richard Hooker, writer of "Of the Laws of Ecclesiastical Polity," was born (died 1600).

John Lyly, a Pioneer in developing the stylistic qualities of prose and its use in romances, was born (died 1606).

Richard Sampson, Bishop of Chichester, Coventry, and Lichfield, died (birthdate unknown).

Sir Philip Sidney, a major poet of the Elizabethan period, was born (died 1586).

Serlio, Renaissance architect, died (born 1475).

(and 1555) Geronimo Carlo published a collection of five -part motets by composers, including Clemens non Papa and Créquillon, entitled "Motetti del Labirinto," in two volumes, at Venice in these years.

(to 1555) Da Monte was a member of King Philip II's choir during the first part of the latter's marriage to Queen Mary. This was while Philip was in England.

(to 1557) Lassus was in Antwerp during this period.

(to c.1557) Monte's stay in England embraced these years.

(to 1559) Pedals were known as (cont.) bases in England.

(and 1564) Compositions by Szamotulczyk were found in collections by Montanus and Neuber in Nürnberg in these years.

(and 1567, 1569) Only three publications by Fiesco existed and were from the years indicated above.

(to 1603) About 1,150 madrigals by da Monte were published during this period.

c.1554

René de Mel, a French composer, was born at Malines (died c.1598).

Mary Nevill, a contemporary of Byrd's, was born (date of death unknown).

Fernando Franco, polyphonic church composer, arrived in the New World.

Lassus visited England.

Netherlandish painting: Pieter Bruegel the Elder, Adoration of the Magi (3'6½" by 2'8 2/3").

1555

(January 13) Palestrina was admitted to the Collegio dei Cappellani Cantori by command of Pope Julius III.

(March 23) Pope Julius III died.

(April 28) The term "musica reservata" was used by Dr. Seld in a letter to Duke Albert V of Bavaria, in a matter concerning an alto singer, Egidius Fux.

(May 13) Lassus published his first work (at Antwerp) "Primo

1555(cont.)

libro dove si contengono Madrigali Villanesche, Canzoni francesi, e Motetti a quattro voci." In the preface he stated that he had composed the works since his recent returning from Rome.

(May 23) The Sacred College met again and elected a new Pope on this date, twenty-three days after the death of Pope Marcellus II.

(June 2) Shepherd pleaded guilty to the charge of molesting a boy.

(July 1) The theory that "musica reservata" concerned ornamentation was deduced from Seld's letter in which he commented upon coloratura passages as improvised by Netherlandish singers.

(September 22) Da Monte was in London as a member of Philip II's private chapel. This was made evident by the letter from the Bavarian agent and imperial vice-chancellor, Dr. Seld of Brussels, bearing this date. He recommended da Monte to Duke Albert V as a composer and an exponent of "musica reservata."

(October 1) Palestrina was appointed choirmaster at St. John the Lateran Church. Exactly when he assumed his new duties was not clear, however, an entry in the archives of the Lateran basilica recorded payment for a "cotta (surplice) for "ms. Io. m^{o} di cappella" and it was probably a reference to Palestrina "ms. Io").

(July 18 to July 30) The choir (cont.) -attendance book of the Sixtine chapel recorded Palestrina as infirmus from July 18 to July 30, on which date he was dismissed.

(October to December) Palestrina apparently did not teach the boys at St. John Lateran, which indicated that he lived outside the precints. The evidence for this assumption derived from Chapter-accounts during this period which stated that a certain Bernardino, tenor, instructed the boys and was in charge of them.

Giovanni Caraccio, singer, maestro and composer, was born at Bergamo (died 1619)see c.1550.

Han Pang-chi, Chinese author of Yüan lo's book of music, died (born 1479).

Ludwig Senfl, Catholic sacred composer, died at Munich (born c.1490). He also wrote "Kling Klang" (Bells of Speyer).

Lodovico Zacconi, theoretician, humanist, and member of several chapel choirs in Germany and Italy, was born (died 1627).

Baini indicated that Animuccia quite possibly was Maestro at the Lateran for a temporary period just before Palestrina was appointed. One source claimed he held the position until his death.

Arcadelt entered the service of Cardinal Charles of Lorraine, duke of Guise, and went with him to Paris, where he probably died.

Barre started a printing-press in Rome. He later moved to

1555(cont.)

Milan and while there published a series of six volumes that included music by himself and other composers.

Van Berchem was organist to the Duke of Ferrara.

Bermudo described the five -course "Spanish" guitar as rare at this time even though Fuenllana had written music for the instrument.

Goudimel apparently settled in Paris.

Jannequin was described as "singer in ordinary of the King's Chapel," and later he became "composer in ordinary" to the King. He was probably the first musician to hold this title in France.

De Kerle became magister capellae at the Cathedral of Orvieto (near Rome). After a short time he became cathedral organist and town carillonneur.

Lassus was not actually known as a composer until this date.

Lassus settled in Antwerp where he rapidly assumed a position of leadership in musical circles.

Da Monte had left England to return to Antwerp.

Palestrina had started his "Papae Marcelli" Mass but put it aside because of outside committments.

Palestrina became one of the twenty-five singers in the pontifical Chapel. This was a high honor to be bestowed on a musician in Rome at this time.

A source maintained that Palestrina was expelled from the Pontifical Choir.

The oldest known keyboard instrument in England (South Kensington Museum) was the work of Rosso of Milan and carried this date.

Rosso originated the pentangular and/or heptangular model of the spinet. One of the instruments was dated 1555.

Sostrow, burgomaster of Stralsund, described the arrival of four Polnische Geiger at his city.

In a work titled "L'antica Musica ridotta alla moderna Prattica," Vicentino explicitly stated that De Muris invented all notes, from the Large to the Semiquaver.

Barre published "Primo Libro delle Muse a 5 voci, Madrigali di diversi Autori." and "Primo Libro delle Muse a 4 voci, Madrigali ariosi di Antonio Barre ed altri diversi autori." He later set up his own printing press in Rome and Milan.

Berchem published a book of madrigals for four voices. He had published one for five voices in 1546.

An enigmatic canon on a checkerboard was included in "El libro Llamado declaracio de instrumentos," by Bermudo, published at Ossuna.

Guerrero's first collection was published at Seville.

The second and third volumes of Isaac's "Choralis Constantinus"

1555(cont.)

were published by Hieronymus Formschneider at Nürnberg.

Chromaticism was first evidenced in some degree-inflection in "Cantai," the first madrigal in Lassus' Book I for five voices, published at Venice. The volume ultimately disappeared.

Lassus' first two publications appeared in this year. The first was published at Antwerp, the second at Venice. The first one was devoted only partially to madrigals, the latter completely. The first was titled, "Il primo libro dove si contengono Madrigali, Vilanesche, Canzon francesi, e Motetti . . ."

In Lassus' "Sto core mio," in his Book I, the superius and tenor of an existent composition were interchanged and combined with two new voices.

Several of Lassus' cycles were occasional compositions, for example, the early sestina that was the first selection in the Antwerp publication from this year titled "Del freddo Rheno a la sinistra riva . . . "

The first chanson in the Antwerp publication was "Las voulez vous." It showed many features typical of Lassus' best work in this genre. The greatest feature of his compositions was the great scope of expression achieved by his extraordinary musical ideas in great variety.

A setting of the Latin ode, "Alma Nemes" was included in Lassus' Antwerp publication.

It was assumed that "Villanelle d'Orlando di Lassus ed altri eccellenti Musici libro secondo," published at Rome by Dorico, a publication unknown to Vogel and Sandberger, used Lassus' name for advertisement.

Waelrant and Laet published a book of fifty of Marot's psalm versions with setting by Louys.

The British Museum preserved a single voice-part (superius) of Mouton's twenty-two motets published by Le Roy as well as a complete manuscript score of the same collection.

In Palestrina's book of madrigals, he was described on the title-page as being a member of the Papal Choir.

Palestrina's Book I for four voices was his second published work and included "Quai rime fur sì chiare." The text and music were both by Palestrina and were a tribute to Francesco Rosselli.

Several compositions by Clemens non Papa appeared in the "Liber primus Cantionum sacrarum" published at Louvain in this year.

Book I of Porta's motets was published at this time.

De Rore excelled in subtle rhythmical divisions in his chromatic madrigals. In his revolutionary motet for four bass parts "Calami sonum ferentes," published by Susato, he used "Musica ficta," i.e. accidentals, dissonant to the ecclesiastical mode and in a highly imaginative manner. In this way he anticipated the

1555(cont.)

later generation of the time of Marenzio and Gesualdo.

Rore's "Madrigali a quattro" was published.

Thomas de Sancta wrote "Arte de Taner Fantasia . . . "

Vicentino tried to restore Greek music according to its three genera, the diatonic, chromatic and enharmonic and the results of his attempts were published at Rome under the title of "L'Antica Musica ridotta alla Moderna Prattica." Two of his own motets included in the book illustrated his theories of chromaticism.

The Moscheni brothers published an edition of Werrecore's first book of motets for five voices, probably in Milan.

Willaert's book of psalms was published.

Zarlino's Instituzioni armoniche appeared.

A harpsichord with four rows of keys, an "Archicembalo," was preserved at Bologna. It was purportedly made by a Venetian, Vito Trasuntino, from a plan by Nicolo Vicentino. The latter described it in his work "L'Antica Musica ridotto alla moderna prattica" published at Rome this year.

Johann Arndt, a theologian, was born (date of death unknown).

Herman Vultejus, a famous jurist, was born in Wetter, Hessia (date of death unknown).

The political situation in (cont.) Germany after the Augsburg peace treaty which gave the Lutherans (not the Reformed) the "cujus regio ejus religio," began a long period of peace.

(to 1555) The Papal reign of St. Marcellus II (born in Montepulciano).

(to 1556) Veronese, the Italian painter, worked on frescoes for the Convent at San Sabastiano.

(to 1557) Two spinets made by Rosso of Milan survived at South Kensington.

(and 1557) Two of Pietro Taglia's madrigal books were published at Milan in these years.

(and 1557, 1559) Apparently, most of the contents of Lassus' second book for five voices, published in 1559, were already published two years earlier in the "Secondo libro delle Muse," and they antedated the contents of his first book published in 1555.

(and 1559) Porta's first sacred compositions were published by Gardano. The first book of motets for five voices appeared in 1555 and the first book of motets for four voices in 1559.

(to 1559) The Papal reign of St. Paul IV (born in Naples).

(to 1560) Palestrina was musical director of St. John Lateran Church in Rome during this period.

(to 1560) A series of magnificats at St. John Lateran dated from Palestrina's stay there.

1555(cont.)

(to 1560) In the basilica of St. John Lateran at Rome a small portable organ of the postif type was preserved. It dated from the time when Palestrina was choirmaster.

(to 1560) Byzantine architecture: Moscow, Cathedral of St. Basil was built during these years (130' x 124').

(to 1563) Apparently it was assumed that Palestrina's secular compositions were from this period since it was dubious that he would have used such themes after the Tridentine Council of 1563 and the effect of Pope Marcellus II's address on the subject of secular music.

(to 1570) Diego Ortiz, Spanish composer and theorist, was employed by the Duke of Alba as maestro of the Viceroyal Chapel.

(to 1585) The German villanellists Regnart and Scandello were active during this period.

(to 1786) A collection of South Kensington Museum included instruments of the harpsichord family dating from this period, among them one by Pascal Taskin (1786).

c.1555

Antonio Amati, violin maker from the famous family, was born at Cremona (died c.1640).

Leone Leoni, Italian madrigalist, was born (date of death unknown).

Alfonso Lobo, Spanish composer, was born at Borja (died c.1610).

Pomponio Nenna, Gesualdo's (cont.) teacher and a composer in his own right, was born (died c.1617).

Porta was a Franciscan monk as well as musician.

Hans Ruckers the Elder, Flemish keyboard-instrument maker, was born (date of death unknown).

Andrea Gabrieli's Petrarch Sestina was probably written at this time.

Jannequin was under the protection of François, Duke of Guise, from this date forward.

Lassus' sacred motet cycle, the "Prophetiae Sibyllarum," was composed at this approximate date.

The high treble and the contra -tenore were very rarely used at this time.

De Brosse, French architect, was born (died 1626).

Netherlandish painting: Peter Brueghel the Elder, Kermess.

Italian painting: Tintoretto, St. George's fight with the Dragon.

1556

(January 31) In Forster's collection of Liedlein the preface carrying this date spoke of Senfl as "L.S. seliger" (i.e. dead).

(February 21) Seth Calvisius, musician, astronomer, and chronologer, was born at Gorschleben in Thuringia (died 1615).

1556(cont.)

(June 10) Martin Agricola, Protestant sacred composer, died at Magdeburg (born c.1500).

Giovanni Cavaccio, Italian ricercar composer, was born (died 1626), see c.1556.

Giovanni Gastoldi, Italian madrigalist, was reported born at this time by one source. Others place him at c.1560 (died 1622).

Leonhard Kleber, Swabian composer and organist, died at Pforzheim (born c.1490).

Jacob Paix, German intabulator and composer of Colorist School, was born at Augsburg (died 1591).

Sabastian Tinódi, Hungarian poet and musician, died (born c.1505).

Attaignant, the publisher, died (birthdate unknown). Some compositions of Gervais' published by his firm this year were possibly edited by his widow.

Cadéac referred to himself as master of the choirboys at Auch in a publication of du Chemin's works in this year.

Rodrigo Ceballos was ordained a priest and became maestro at Cordova.

Contino was reappointed choirmaster at the cathedral in his native town of Brescia for a five-year term.

Hermann Finck wrote that singers should not vary intensity but rather sing steadily like an organ.

Hermann Finck described his great-uncle Heinrich thusly, (cont.) "he excels not only in talent but also in learning, but his style is hard."

Andrea Gabrieli was second organist at St. Mark's in Venice.

Nicolas Gombert probably spent the last years of his life in Tournai.

Francisco Guerrero visited Lisbon and presented his first book of Masses to King John III of Portugal.

Jannequin acted as curate at Unverre (near Chartres) in the south western portion of Paris.

Lassus accepted an appointment as conductor for the ducal court of Bavaria on invitation of Albert V. He went to Munich for this position.

Palestrina resumed work on his "Papae Marcelli" Mass when he took his new position at St. John Lateran.

Vasquez became a priest and served Juan Bravo who was probably Count Juan of Ureña, Salamanca. The latter was referred to as "el Santo."

Cardinal Pole was appointed by Philip and Mary to head the commission of inquiry into the state of the pensions due to the monks of the dissolved monasteries. John Wilborne was still receiving his full pension at this time.

The "Commedia Spirituale," Abram et Sara, was written.

Cadeac's works were included in "Missarum Musicalium" published at Paris.

1556(cont.)

The Cancionero de Palacio was published at Venice.

Hermann Finck in the Practica Musica asserted, "if the old composers were eminent in the treatment of difficult mensural procedures, the newer composers are superior to them in the matter of euphony and are especially eager to fit the notes to the words of the text in order to render their meaning and mood with the greatest clarity."

The Practica musica by Hermann Finck was published.

The Anglo-Genevan Psalter was first published with music at Geneva in this year. It included fifty-one psalms with a separate tune for each.

Wolf Heckel's tablatures were published at Strassbourg.

Le Roy and Ballard's "Sixième livre de chansons" was published.

Lassus' "Di Orlando di Lassus il primo libro de mottetti a cinque & a sei voci . . ." was published by Waelrant and Laet at Antwerp.

Lassus wrote music in honor of Cardinal Pole and it was published in this year.

A publication for lute by Hans Newsidler was issued at Nürnberg.

The first book of the "Ordinarium" was published in Mexico City. It was the first music published in the Western Hemisphere and was embellished with plainchant in two colors, (cont.) having red lines and black notes.

A set of four-part ricercari by Padovano was published in part-books.

Godescalcus Praetorius published "Melodiae Scholasticae" at Magdeburg. He was assisted in the work by Agricola.

A madrigal collection by Ruffo, carrying this date, was titled "Opera nuova di musica intitolata armonia celeste nella quale si contengono 25 Madrigali, pieni d'ogni dolcezza, et soavita musicale. Composti con dotta arte et reservato ordine dallo Eccellente Musico Vincenzo Ruffo."

"One and fiftie Psalmes of David in English metre, whereof 37 were made by Thomas Sterneholde and the rest by others. Conferred with the hebrewe, and in certeyn places corrected as the text, and sens of the Prophete required." was published by John Crespin at Geneva (The Anglo-Genevan Psalter).

A French chanson by Vaet was included in "Jardin musical" published by Waelrant and Laet in this year.

The volta, in which the gentleman turned and flung up his lady, was brought to the Paris Court from Provence.

Charles V abdicated, and turned the ancestral Hapsburg possessions over to his brother Ferdinand I as well as giving the Spanish holdings and Burgundian inheritance to his son Philip II. The capilla flamenca was included in the bequest to the latter.

1556(cont.)

Lorenzo Lotto, Italian painter, died (born 1480).

Maderna, Italian architect, was born (died 1639).

Jacopo Carrucci, known as Pontormo, an Italian painter, died (born 1494).

Veronese, the Italian painter, decorated the Villa Barbaro at Maser.

(to 1557) Susato published "Musyck Boexken" ("Music Books"), IV-VII, Clemens' three-part Souterliedekens or "Little Psalter Songs" were included in these volumes.

(to 1559) German architecture: Heidelberg, Castle, Ottoheinrichsbau (c.100' wide).

(to 1560) Some of Clemens non Papa's works appeared in publications of this period.

(to 1562) Coclico served at the court in Denmark both as "musicus" and singer.

(to 1566) There were no important secular lied publications after 1556 when the fifth part of Forster's collection appeared until ten years later.

(or 1573) Tallis' motet "Spem in alium (299)" was certainly an occasional piece, for some sort of state occasion. The large number of voices (forty) surely had great significance and one theory was that it was written for the fortieth birthday of a ruler, possibly either Mary (1556) or Elizabeth's (1573).

(to 1662) "Frottola" and (cont.) "villanella" were assimilated into the madrigal, or transformed into the "Falala canzonetta" and the "balletto" both by Gastoldi and Vecchi.

c.1556

Hieronymus Amati, violin maker and member of the famous family, was born (died 1630).

Johann Berg, the printer, died and the printing office in Nürnberg continued in its operation under Neuber and Gerlach.

Giovanni Cavaccio, Italian instrumental composer, was born at Bergamo (died 1626), see 1556.

Nicolas Gombert, Netherlandish composer, died at Tournai (born c.1480).

Charles Luython, a pupil of da Monte's and one of the last followers of the tradition of Lassus, was born (died 1620).

Ludwig Senfl, German-Swiss Protestant composer (although himself a Catholic) and pupil of Isaac, died (born c.1490).

1557

(April 25) Hercules II sent a copy of Rore's "Missa Praeter rerum" to Albert V of Bavaria as a gift. The latter wrote a letter of thanks on this date and expressed admiration for the work.

(September 16) Jacques Mauduit, a composer of four-part chansons mesurées, was born (died 1627).

Costanzo Antegnati, an Italian organist of high repute, was born at Brescia (died c.1620).

Jacobus Clemens non Papa, a

1557(cont.)

major Netherlandish composer, died (born 1510).

Thomas Crecquillon, Netherlandish sacred composer, died at Béthune. He also composed light chansons (birthdate unknown).

Girolamo Diruta, an Italian instrumental composer, was born (died 1612).

Giovanni Gabrieli, nephew of Andrea, was born (died 1612). This great composer represented the culmination of the Italo -Flemish and carried on in Willaert's tradition. He succeeded Mérulo as first organist at St. Mark's. Early in his career he served at Munich under Lassus and later he himself was teacher to Schütz. He was also active as an editor and was the first major composer of toccatas.

Grimald, composer of hunting songs, was active. He used the word "tarantarara."

Matthaeus Le Maistre, a Netherlandish doppelmeister, chanson and madrigal composer, died (birthdate unknown).

Samuel Marschall, English musician, was born at Tournai (date of death unknown).

Thomas Morley, eminent English organist and composer of madrigals, ballets (fa-las), and canzonets, was born (died 1603). He held the degree of Mus. Bac.

Diego Pisador, Spanish composer and vihuelist, died (born c.1508).

Cornelis Schuyt, Netherlandish madrigal composer, was born (cont.) (died 1616).

Bourgeois left Geneva and probably had no connection with the Genevan Psalter after this date. He returned to Paris.

At Antwerp, Carest headed a petition from the clavecin-makers asking to be admitted to the privileges of the guild as such, and not simply as painters and sculptors for their instruments.

Ludwig Daser held the position of "chapel-master" for several years when Lassus went to Munich.

Antonio Gardane, the printer, officially became known as Gardano after this date.

When the major portion of the Genevan psalter had already been published at this time, Goudimel was still a member of the Roman Catholic Church.

Claudio Merulo became first organist at St. Mark's in Venice. One source maintained that he only became second organist, but this was presumably inaccurate.

Nicolas Selneccer was Court preacher at Dresden.

Shepherd presented some songs to the Queen.

"Piissimoe ac sacratissimoe Lamentationes Jeremioe Prophetoe" was published in Paris by Le Roy and Ballard. It contained Carpentrasso's capo d'opera and some fine compositions by Archadelt, Festa, Févin, le Jeune, and de la Rue.

Le Roy and Ballard published a collection of three Masses by

1557(cont.)

Le Roy and Ballard published a collection of three Masses by Arcadelt. These were the only ones by him that survived. The collection was published at Paris.

Azzaivolo's "Villotte alla padoana" appeared.

Giovanni Battista Bruno published the madrigals of Lassus' "Secondo libro delle Muse."

Two lamentations by Févin, "Migrauit Juda" and "Recordare est" were included in the collection published by Le Roy and Ballard in Paris.

Attaingnant finished his publication of a series of ten volumes of dances, composed or edited by Gervaise, du Tertre, and others.

"Libro de Cifra Nueva para tecla, harpa y vihuela" (Alcalá de Henares) was compiled by Venegas de Henestrosa.

One of Lassus' five-part madrigals of this year, Fortunio Spira's sonnet, "Volgi cor mio, la tua speranza homai," contained a fine example of contrapuntal freedom.

Apparently most of the contents of Lassus' second book for five voices published in 1559 were already published two years earlier in the "Secondo libro delle Muse" and they antedated the contents of his first book published in 1555.

Le Roy wrote an instruction book for the lute that was a counterpart to the earlier one published by Attaignant (Tres

(cont.) breve . . .) Le Roy's was titled "Instruction de partir toute musique facilment en tablature de luth." The book was translated into two different versions.

A book of Masses published by Le Roy and Ballard in this year carried a dedication to Charles de Guise (second Cardinal of Lorraine). Arcadelt had served him as maître de chapelle.

Da Monte published his first book of masses at Antwerp.

Archbishop Parker's Psalter was completed.

Rore's Passion according to St. John, written for Hercules II, was published at Paris, along with other compositions.

Ruffo's collection of four Masses for five voices was published.

Francisco de Salinas' book of popular songs and ditties, some of which were hundreds of years old, appeared.

Collections from this year included Lassus' music for Tasso's "Vostro fui, vostro son, e sarò vostro . . . "

Johann Walther's "Magnificat octo tonorum" appeared.

The Imperial chapel in Brussels still referred to its six male singers as haultcontres, tailles (tenors), and basse contres. The epithets for both the alto and the basso kept the prefix "contra."

1557(cont.)

Public records of Palestrina, which would have proved the date of the composer's birth, were destroyed by the soldiers of Alva in the fire. No private documents have been discovered which compensated for this loss.

The "veglia" (evening entertainment) was one form of amusement that was left to the Intronati of Siena. This was an old and distinguished "accademie," that survived after the demotion of Siena by Cosimo I and the resulting loss of the city's independence in this year.

Czar Theodore I of Russia was born (died 1598).

The works of Sir Thomas Wyatt and the Earl of Surrey were collected in a book of songs and sonnets, published as "Tottel's Miscellany" in this year, a date which is regarded by many as the beginning of Elizabethan literature.

A fire broke out in the Palazzo Ducale and Bellini's historical pictures, which had decorated the sala del Maggior Consiglio were destroyed.

Moro entered the service of King Philip II and painted him in armor after his victory at Saint Quentin in this year.

(or 1558) The end of Clemens non Papa's life was probably spent in Ypres and Dixmude.

(to 1558) Goudimel wrote Masses and a Magnificat for Catholic service during these years.

(to 1558) Ten of the Antwerp (cont.) harpsichord makers petitioned the deans and masters of the guild to be admitted without submitting masterpieces and the chiefs of the commune consented. During the next year they were received into the guild under new conditions.

(and 1559) Woneggar, a Lithuanian, published an abstract of the "Dodecachordon" at Freiburg and Basle this year. The second edition of this, issued two years later, contained a poem by Glareanus in praise of the thirteen Federal cities of Switzerland set to music by Manfred Barbarin.

(and 1559, 1569) Filippo Azzaiuolo's three books of "Villotte alla padoana" were published at these times.

(to 1566) Le Roy and Ballard published Goudimel's psalm settings in motet style during these years.

(to 1571) Franciscus Marcellus Amsfortius, a Netherlander, served as Kapellmeister at Copenhagen.

(to 1573) Girolamo Savorgnano was Bishop of Sibenik.

(to 1584 or 1585) Merulo was first organist at St. Mark's during this period.

(to 1594) Lassus was in Munich.

(to 1612) The "Compositional Schools of Munich and Nürnberg" embraced these years.

(to 1613) The earlier works of the two Gabrielis carried this phrase on the title, "Sacrae

1557(cont.)

Cantiones, tum viva voce tum omnis generis Instrumentis cantatu commodissimae" (most convenient for the voice, as for all kinds of instruments), etc. No specific instrument was mentioned.

c.1557

Giovanni Croce, Italian sacred and secular composer, was born at Chioggia (died 1609).

Palestrina's son Iginio was born (date of death unknown).

Girolamo Parabosco, Italian madrigal composer, died (birthdate unknown).

(or 1558) Alessandro Striggio published his first volume of five-voiced madrigals.

1558

(November 17) Elizabeth became Queen of England and Great Britain.

(December 28) Hermann Finck, German theorist and great-nephew of Heinrich Finck, died (birthdate unknown).

Juan Escribano, Spanish composer and member of the Papal Choir, died (birthdate unknown).

Andrea Gabrieli was mentioned as organist at San Geremia in Venice.

Lassus married Regina Weckinger, a maid of honor at the Munich court.

Mielich painted a portrait of Rore. The composer probably posed during a short stopover in Munich during this year.

Da Monte composed a festive madrigal for the wedding of Paolo Giordano Orsini, Duke of Bracciano, and Isabella Medici.

De Neri's society of secular priests held their meetings at the oratory of San Girolamo.

De Rore returned to Antwerp to visit his parents after a brief stop in Munich.

"Merten" van der Biest joined the Antwerp Guild as one of ten clavecin makers.

De Wert began as Rore's pupil with a work for five voices.

Antonio Barre published "Secondo Libro delle Muse a quattro voci, Madrigali ariosi di diversi excellentissimi Autori, con due Canzoni di Gianetto, di nuovo raccolti e dati in luce. In Rome appresso Antonio Barre 1558."

The British Museum preserved a few pieces "written by one Raphe Bowle to learne to playe on his Lutte in anno 1558."

Several of Certon's motets were included in collections published by Phalése at Louvain at this time.

Three masses by Certon appeared.

Le Roy and Ballard published the "Proverbes de Salomon" set by Jannequin, however, only an incomplete copy survived.

Kerle's "Hymni totius anni" was published at Rome.

The first version of Marot's psalter must have antedated Goudimel's conversion to

1558(cont.)

Calvinism since Goudimel still composed and published Catholic masses as late as this year.

The need for theoretical studies for amateurs was filled by such as the Nouvelle "Instruction familière" by Michel de Menehou, which was published this year. The book was concerned with rudiments.

A lute tablature publication by Sebastian Ochsenkhun appeared in Heidelberg in this year.

Palestrina showed an interest in cycles as early as this date when he composed two of them. One was a setting of Petrarch's canzoni, "Chiare, fresche e dolci acque" and the other "Voi mi poneste in foco" included in a collection published by Barré.

Susato published "Madrigali e Canzoni francesi a 5 voci."

Clemens non Papa's death was proved by a motet on his death composed by Vaët. This was included in a work published that year at Nürnberg and titled "Novum et insigne opus . . .' tom. I."(see 1557)

Waelrant's "Il primo Libro de Madrigali e Canzoni francesi a cinque voci, Anversa, Huberto Waelrant e J. Latio, 1558." was published.

De Wert published a volume of madrigals which drew considerable attention. Shortly after its appearance de Wert was compared to famous musicians of the day by Guicciardini.

De Wert's "Cara la vita mia" was included in his first madrigal (cont.) book for five voices published this year.

De Wert's "Chi salirà per me" was first published.

Zarlino's chief work "Istitutioni harmoniche" was first published at Venice. It confirmed the use of drums and trumpets by the Italians and also stated that the part above the tenor was called the contra-tenor by some also the contralto and the alto.

Lord Hunsdon was elevated to the peerage.

No paintings by Bruegel survived that carried dates earlier than this.

(to 1562) Phaer's "Aeneid" was written.

(and 1564) De Wert dedicated his first work to Alfonso I Gonzaga in 1558 as well as another in 1564.

(and 1591) The ten books of madrigals by de Wert published at Venice during these years were reprinted several times by Gardano and contained the best of the composer's works.

(to 1603) The reign of Queen Elizabeth I (House of Tudor) over England and Great Britain.

(to 1603) The best-known ballads during Queen Elizabeth's reign were "The carman's whistle," "The British Grenadiers," "Near Woodstock Town," "The bailiff's daughter of Islington," "A poor soul sat sighing," "Greensleeves," "The friars of Orders Gray," and

1558(cont.)

"The Frog Galliard."

c.1558

Giulio Caccini (Giulio Romano) was born in Rome according to the preface of his "Nuove Musiche," in 1558 (or 1560). He was a member of the Florentine Camerata and one of the earliest opera composers (died 1640).

George Peele, Elizabethan poet, was born (died 1598).

Mathias Werrecore, motet composer, died (birthdate unknown).

Neri inaugurated religious services of a non-liturgical character about this year. He wanted to attract simple souls to whom St. Augustine's definition of hymns as "praise to God with song" could not fail to appeal.

1559

(August 13) The death of Pope Paul IV was the major event of the year.

(July) Palestrina sold four barrels of wine to the authorities of St. John Lateran for eight golden scudi.

Adam Gumpelzhaimer, German composer, was born (died 1625).

Nathaniel Giles was admitted as a chorister at Magdalen College, Oxford.

Robert Granjon, printer, left Paris for Lyons. The first work was printed by his new system at this time.

Jannequin complained in a dedication because of his "age and Poverty."

William Mundy left St. Mary at Hill Church, London.

Juan Pablos, an Italian, obtained the first license to print, the second was given to Antonio de Espinosa in this year.

De Rore returned to Venice to assist Willaert in his duties at St. Mark's in Venice.

The first two periods in his life showed Tallis' earlier Latin church music as something integral to the liturgy decorating or replacing ritual plainsong. For fifty years or more prior to this date it was not uncommon for monastic and other institutions to use an organ instead of a choir for this purpose, mainly in office hymns and antiphons.

Two madrigals by Animuccia appeared in separate volumes. One was included in a volume of Lassus' works and the other in a miscellaneous collection of several composers, both published by Gardano at Venice in this year.

A magnificat by Certon was published in a collection of eight "Canticum B.M. Virginis, etc. 1559."

Cleve's Cantiones sacrae . . . Lib. I appeared.

Two books of Dankerts' madrigals for 4,5, and 6 voices were published by Gardano at Venice.

An early and famous collection of canti carnascialeschi was made in this year by Anton Francesco Grazzini, known as Il Lasca. It was titled

1559(cont.)
"Tutti i Trionfi, Carri, Mascherate e Canti Carnascialeschi."

Settings for three voices of the "Je suis desheritée" melody were published in this year. The music was credited to "Jacotin."

Lassus' second book for five voices was published. (See entries for 1555 and 1557 for further information concerning this issue.)

Le Roy published Jannequin's works in Paris. He prefaced the collection with a sonnet written by the poet Antoine de Baïf in honor of Jannequin.

According to Fétis, Jannequin published his music to eighty-two psalms, with a dedication to the Queen of France.

In the second collection of Jannequin's psalms, published this year, only the bassus survived.

A second edition of some of Jannequin's works was published in Paris this year.

A chanson collection was published at Lyons. The volume points out the difference between "Lupus" and "Lupi Second" by assigning different works to each.

A lute-book by Jean Matelart was published.

A few madrigals by a "Mathias" were printed in the madrigal book by Arcadelt, Primo Libro, edition of 1559 (See also entry in 1541).

Selectissimorum Triciniorum (Bassus etc.) Discantus . . . J. Montanus et A. Neuber was issued at Nürnberg.

There were two contrasting phases of Tudor keyboard music. Liturgical organ music prior to this date was represented in the "Mulliner Book," whereas the Elizabethan repertory of secular pieces for the virginal was collected in the "Fitzwilliam Virginal Book" and in other collections.

Porta's first book of motets for four-voices was published by Gardano (See also 1555 entry).

Luigi Tansillo's "Vendemmiatore" was placed on the Index.

Triller's Song-book, published at Breslau, contained many volkslieder in their earliest form, however, they were arranged for several voices. Copies were preserved in the Berlin and Wernigerode Libraries.

Three fantasies in part-books by Willaert were published in this year along with other compositions.

Willaert's Mass for six voices, "Mittit ad Virginem" appeared.

Willaert's "Musica nova" signalled the start of a new art of expression, music in the service of "poetry." The volume contained madrigals and was edited by Viola, a student of Willaert's.

Konrad Wolffhart's Basel "Gesangbuch" appeared.

Francis the fourth Earl of Cumberland, was born (date of

1559(cont.)

death unknown). He was a patron of Byrd's.

There was no evidence of any extensive cultivation of church polyphony in England as a whole, except for simple forms of psalm -singing.

Cremona, along with Milan and Pavia became a Spanish possession by virtue of the Treaty of Cateau Cambrésis in 1559. It had been the center of north Italian culture since the middle of the century.

After the Treaty of Cateau Cambrésis, at which a large area of the Po River Valley fell to Spain, Mantua, the Margraviate of Montferrat, and neighbouring duchies of Parma, Ferrara and Tuscany, acquired more political and cultural importance.

The Book of Common Prayer of 1559 was the book of 1552 with few but significant changes. The restoration of vestments as provided in the 1549 book was one such change.

A harpsichord bearing this date and made by Trasuntini was mentioned by Giordano Riccati, "Delle corde ovvero fibre elastiche" and was probably made by the father.

There were enough Protestants to hold a national synod, at which a church of Calvinistic doctrine but presbyterian government was created.

The Sarum Rite was abandoned.

Sanmicheli, an Italian architect, died (born 1484).

In art as well as politics, the sixteenth century was divided in two for France by this year which marked the end of the Italian wars and the beginning of the Religious wars.

(to 1560) The reign of King Francis II (House of Valois) over France.

(to 1565) The reign of Pope Pius IV (born in Milan). He ranked highly as a "building" pontiff.

(to 1571) The most important lute manuscript of the time survived in the Folger Shakespeare Library in Washington. This book, approximately dated as given here, belonged to various owners, three of whom were contributors to a small section of lute-tablature at the beginning of the book.

(to 1584) Spanish architecture: Juan Bautista de Toledo and Juan de Herrera, Madrid, Escorial (680'x530').

(to 1695) The Chapter library at Westminster Abbey preserved a collection of early printed madrigals, English and Italian, published between these years.

c.1559

Jaquet of Mantua, French sacred composer, died (born c.1495).

French painting: Corneille de Lyon, Portrait of Marguerite of France.

(and 1701) Various instrumental bicinia (imitative ricercari) for two voices survived from these years. Four were composed by Bernardino Lupachino

c.1559(cont.)

and one by Joan Maria Tasso. They were included in a collection reprinted often during this period.

1560

(January 5) William Cobbold, Elizabethan composer, was born (date of death unknown). He was represented in the "Triumphs of Oriana."

(February 7) Tarquinia Molza married Paolo Porrino, a nobleman from Modena.

(August 10) Hieronymus Praetorius, German protestant composer, was born (died 1629).

(August) Palestrina's "Papae Marcelli" Mass was probably completed by this date.

William Brade, municipal music director in Hamburg, and other cities including Copenhagen, was born (died 1630).

The "Kettenton" of Hans Folz appeared.

Ruggiero Giovanelli, Italian madrigalist, was born at Velletri, near Rome (died 1625), see c.1560.

Clément Jannequin, French chanson composer, died (born 1485).

Romano Alessandro was admitted into the choir at the Pope's chapel in Rome.

Clementine de Bourges' husband was killed while fighting against the Huguenots.

A branch of the Confraternity of Paris was set up at Orleans.

The earliest Academy for poetry and music in Mantua was that of the "Invaghiti," founded by Gonzaga, the Duke of Mantua, and di Guastalla.

George de la Hèle was probably one of the boys Manchicourt brought from the Low Countries to Madrid when the former reorganized the Royal Chapel.

Palestrina's position as maestro di cappella at St. John Lateran terminated, according to most sources by his own resignation. His experience had been neither happy nor lucrative.

One set of Palestrina's Lamentations was finished as early as this year and used at the Lateran Basilica, where the original manuscript was preserved.

Striggio in his serenade showed his interest in the bizarre as well as a tendency to question the concept of sentimentality exhibited in the madrigals.

The anthem with English text developed from the Latin motet mostly through the work of Tallis and Tye.

Vasquez was living in Seville.

Robert White received the Mus. Bac. degree at Cambridge and was master of the choristers at Ely Cathedral.

An old manuscript preserved in a private collection revealed that Robert White was organist of Westminster Abbey "temp. 1560."

Unfortunately, none of Duke William's compositions

1560(cont.)

were found, but entries in the court accounts referred to the sending of music-paper from Venice, yearly starting at this date. This corresponded with the details of the Duke's compositions as evidenced by his letters. It further indicated that he was serious in his study of music.

A private library contained Davante's "Pseaumes de David" dated this year.

John Day's "Certaine Notes, set forth in foure and three partes, to be sung at the Morning, Communion, and Evening Praier, ... and unto them to be added divers Godly praiers and psalmes in the like forme." was published. The work contained versions of the Psalms as well as two anthems by Shepherd, "I give you a new commandment" and "Submit yourselves." Compositions by the six composers who were represented in the "Wanley" manuscript were included and this proved that some of the works pre-dated Mary's reign. The book used an improved style of typography and diminished the need for manuscript books for the choristers. Day came from Aldersgate.

The first collection of French Keyboard music, Attaingnant's "Premier livre de tablature d'Espinette, chansons, madrigals, et gaillardes," appeared at this date. It was issued by Simon Gorlier, a musician and publisher from Lyons.

Hans Heugel's "Pangite Castalides," in honor of the wedding of Count Ludwig VI of the Palatinate, appeared in this (cont.) year.

One year after the publication of the "Injunctions" Strype indicated the earliest record of the anthem's actual use, at the Chapel Royal on mid-Lent Sunday of this year, "And, Service concluded, a good Anthem was sung."

Lassus' five-part setting of Guéroult's famous "chanson spirituelle" was published by the composer.

Lassus' "Psalmi Davidis poenitentiales" was finished.

The authenticity of the "moresca" ("O Lucia miau miau"), printed under the designation "d'Orlando" in the "Terzo libro delle Villotte," was considered dubious.

A Manuale sacramentorum from this year had one hundred and seventy three numbered pages.

Barre published "Madrigali a quattro voci di Francesco Menta novamente da lui composti e dati in luce" at Rome.

Palestrina's "Crux Fidelis," and a collection of "Improperia," all for eight voices, composed this year, became rapidly well-known. Pope Paul IV, who had dismissed him, could not resist having them sung at the Vatican, and after hearing them had them added to the collection at the Apostolic Chapel.

Palestrina's madrigal "Donna bella e gentil" was published by Scoto at Venice, included in a volume of madrigals by Striggio.

1560(cont.)

Palestrina composed "Improperia" for Holy Week use.

Stefano Rossetti of Nice included a number of pieces specifically labeled "madrigali ariosi" in his first book of four-voiced madrigals composed at Schio in the Veneto.

Striggio's first madrigal book for six voices was issued.

"Susanne un jour" was published.

Tallis provided eight tunes for Day's Psalter.

Juan Vasquez' "Recopilación de sonetos y villancicos a quatro y a cinco" was published.

An edition of the Anglo-Genevan Psalter appeared in England.

Walter Haddon published a Latin translation of the 1559 Prayer Book "Liber precum publicarum."

The Improperia, after the reign of Pope Pius IV, have always been chanted (in the Sistine Chapel) to simple, but beautiful Faux bourdons. They had been adapted for them by Palestrina.

A surviving manuscript and certain publications showed that composers' music most frequently performed in Sweden after this date were Lassus and Meiland.

Archbishop Parker's Psalter "The whole Psalter translated into English metre. which contayneth an hundred and fifty psalmes," was printed at London by John Daye who lived under (cont.) St. Martyn's at Aldersgate, "Cum gratiâ et privilegio regiae maiestatis, per decennium." The book was, however, never released.

This year marked the appearance of "Psalmes of David in Englishe Metre, by Thomas Sterneholde and others; conferred with the Ebrue, and in certeine places corrected as the sense of the Prophete required; and the Note joyned withall. Very mete to be used of all sorts of people privately for their godly solace and comfort, laying aparte all ungodly songes & ballades, which tende only to the nourishing of vice, and corrupting of youth. Newly set foarth and allowed, according to the Quenes Maiesties Iniunctions. 1560."

Tallis' "Eight Tunes" were printed by John Day, at the end of Archbishop Parker's metrical translation of the Psalms at London.

Robert White received the degree of Mus. B. at Cambridge.

Joachim du Bellay, a writer and disciple of Ronsard, died (born 1522).

Ronsard wrote a preface for a book of chansons published by Le Roy & Ballard at Paris. In it he mentioned Jannequin with sufficient reverence to call him one of des Pres' celebrated disciples, but obviously considered him as a composer of a bygone age.

Ronsard's "Livre de meslanges" was published in an edition bearing this date.

1560(cont.)

Jean Cousin, French painter, died (born 1490).

Veronese, Italian painter, visited Rome.

(to 1561) Giovanni Contino's surviving works were all published during these years. They included a book of masses, a book of lamentations, and two collections of motets. One, contained Alleluia, Gradual, and Introit settings and thus indicated the interest in music for the Proper of the Mass.

(and 1561) Marenzio apparently served his apprenticeship in Brescia under Contino during these years. Contino wrote several books of church music during this period and a book of five-voiced madrigals.

(or 1561) The organ at St. Mary's received the addition of a third Manual, then called "Positiv in Stuhl."

(and 1565) A litany for four voices, by Robert Stone, gentleman of the Chapel Royal, was included in Daye's "Certain Notes . . . "

(to 1569) The poet Jean-Antoine Baïf and musicians Thibault de Courville and Goudimel adapted metrical composition from humanists of c.1500. They used a long note with a long, and a short note with a short syllable, with all voices singing every syllable at exactly the same time.

(to 1569) At least fifty years after des Prés had set the two laments of David "Planxit autem David," and "Absalom fili mi," (cont.) music of fairly expressive quality appeared in England.

(to 1569) Sweelinck followed his father, also an organist, to Amsterdam.

(to 1569) Massimo Troiano was singing alto in the chapel of Johann Jacob Fugger at Augsburg.

(to 1569) De Wert's madrigals, composed during this period, were reasonably conventional.

(to 1569) The younger generation of continental composers were barely becoming aware of the range of mood and vivid pictorialism which a mature madrigal could convey.

(to 1570) Palestrina's "Veni Creator" for six voices was composed during these years.

(and 1571) Striggio published two books of six-voiced compositions.

(to 1572) Des Prés' chansons appeared frequently in Le Roy and Ballard's Meslanges of this period.

(to 1574) The reign of King Charles IX (House of Valois) over France.

(to 1579) The quantity of Italian madrigals preserved in Elizabethan manuscripts from these years demonstrated how much Italian music had been circulated in England before English composers started to compose in the new style.

(to 1579) This was obviously a transition period in the devel-

1560(cont.)

opment of Protestant music.

(to 1590) Striggio was a major madrigalist between Rore and Monteverdi.

(and 1620) The Landesbibliothek at Cassel, Germany, preserved about 340 musical works, both printed and in manuscript. Among the former were copies of Morley and Weelkes' madrigals.

(to 1620) The English school of virginal composers dated approximately from this period.

c.1560

Felice Anerio, composer of Al Suon for lute & harpsichord, was born (died 1614), see c.1564.

Giovanni Matteo Asola, Italian composer, was born at Verona (died 1609), see c.1560.

Girolamo Belli, Italian sacred composer, was born (date of death unknown) , see c.1562.

Louis Bourgeois, French composer and theorist, died (born c.1505).

Juan Blas de Castro, Spanish madrigalist, was born (died 1631).

Giovanni Luca Conforto, Italian composer, was born at Mileto (date of death unknown).

Christian Erbach, German instrumental composer, was born at Algesheim in the Palatinate (date of death unknown).

Thomas Este, English composer, was born (died c.1624).

Giles Farnaby, English composer, (cont.) was born (died 1600).

Hans Foltz' (Folz) Kettenton appeared.

Giovanni Giacomo Gastoldi, Italian madrigal composer, was born in Verona (died 1622).

Don Carlo Gesulado, Prince of Venosa in South Italy, was born in Naples (died 1614). He was a radical composer of the "chromatic" school and his personal life has been severly castigated by historians. Evidence has pointed to some justification for this.

Ruggiero Giovanelli, Italian madrigalist, was born at Velletri, near Rome (died 1625).

Nicolas Gombert, great Flemish composer, died according to two sources (birthdate unknown). The dates of Gombert's life are quite vague (born c.1480).

Clement Jannequin, great chanson composer, was still active at this time.

Robert Johnson, English composer, died (born c.1490).

Duarte Lôbo, Portuguese composer and pupil of Manuel Mendes, was born (died 1643), see c.1565.

Giovanni Bernardino, brother of Giovanni Maria Nanino, was born (died 1623), see also c.1550.

Benedetto Pallavicino, Cremonese composer, was born (died 1601).

Peter Phillips, English composer of Bon jeur mon couer, was born (died 1633).

c.1560(cont.)

Paolo Quagliati, madrigalist, was born (died 1630).

Sabastian Raval, Spanish composer, was born (date of death unknown).

Melchior Vulpius, German Protestant composer, was born at Wasingen, in the Henneberg territory (date of death unknown).

Andrew Fekete, Hungarian lutenist, who lived in Padua, supported himself by teaching members of the Hungarian nobility who were studying at the University.

Alfonso Ferrabosco I went to Queen Elizabeth's court.

Goudimel, essentially a Protestant composer, composed works for Catholic use before he converted at this date.

Cristofano Malvezzi, an Italian canzoni composer, was born (date of death unknown). He developed theme fragments in his works.

Palestrina received the patronage of Cardinal Ippolito d'Este and was well treated by the latter for a long period of time.

German lute and viol makers maintained their important position in Italy until about 1650. They made fine instruments. Magnus Tieffenbrucker, active at this time, was a leader among them.

Guglielmo I built the church of St. Barbara, founded the ducal cappella, and finally engaged de Wert as maestro di cappella to the Mantuan court and the (cont.) church of St. Barbara.

Lassus' Penitential Psalms were composed.

Lassus' "Prophetiae Sibyllarum" was composed.

Two psalms by Tallis, "Domine quis habitabit (#246)" and "Laudate Dominum (#266)" dated from this period.

Tallis' "Hear the voice and prayer" ("a Prayer") for four voices was published in Day's "Morning and Evening Prayer and Communion."

Tallis' "If ye love me" ("the Anthem") for four voices was included in Day's "Morning and Evening Prayer and Communion," as were "I give you a new Commandment" and "O Lord Thee is all my Trust" both also for four voices.

Tallis' "Remember not, O Lord God" for four voices was published in Day's "Morning and Evening Prayer and Communion."

From surviving manuscripts as well as other printed works it may be assumed that the composers whose music was most frequently performed in Sweden at this time included, Crecquillon, Gombert, Jannequin and non Papa.

Robert Greene, Elizabethan poet, was born (died 1592).

Walter Haddon's Latin translation of the prayer-book (1552?) was published. It was titled "Liber precum publicarum" and Queen Elizabeth wanted it used in the two universities as well as in the public schools.

c.1560(cont.)

French painting: School of Fontainebleau, Venus and the Goddess of the Waters (51 3/8"x 38").

Italian painting: Tintoretto, Susunna and The Elders.

Italian painting: Veronese, Banquet Scenes (the musicians are the painter, his brother Bassano, Tintoretto and Titian).

(to 1590) Blasius Amon, German composer, was active.

1561

(March 1) In the Atti Capitolari of S. Maria Maggiore this date was given as that of Palestrina's appointment to the Basilica Liberiana, St. Maria Maggiore. He had been a chorister there twenty-four years earlier.

(August 20) Jacopo Peri, first Italian composer to write an opera, and member of the Florentine Camerata, was born in Rome (died c.1615). One source claimed he was born in Florence, see c.1550.

(September 4) Firmin le Bel became maestro di cappella at St. Luigi de' Francesi.

(September 30) Clementine de Bourges, choral composer, died (birthdate unknown).

(February) Palestrina remained at the Lateran until this time when he was transferred to a similar position at Santa Maria Maggiore. He was probably succeeded by Giovanni Animuccia.

(June) An entry in the "Comptes des recettes et depenses pour les pauvres" indicated the pay- (cont.) ment of ten florins to "Maître Pierre" for having set psalms to music.

(September) Lucrezia Bendidio, celebrated performing musician, came to Padua.

Nicolas Herman died (birthdate unknown). It was an established fact, however, that he was an elderly man.

Luis Milan, celebrated Spanish lutenist, died (birthdate unknown).

Hans Bach was mentioned as a Gemeinde-Vormund-schaftsglied at Wechmar.

Van Berchem dedicated three books of capriccios to the Duke of Ferrara.

Bourgeois was still living in Paris.

Rodrigo Ceballos became maestro at Granada.

Contino went to Mantua to enter the service of Duke Guglielmo Gonzaga.

Nathaniel Giles resigned as chorister of Magdalen College, Oxford.

The title "sonata" appeared at one of its earliest occasions in a suite by Gorzanis which consisted of a passo e mezzo and padovana.

Palestrina was appointed maestro di cappella Liberiana at Santa Maria Maggiore.

Rizzio came to Scotland in the entourage of the Ambassador from Piedmont.

1561(cont.)

Duke Ottavio Farnese of Parma returned home after a visit to Margaret of Austria. He had been accompanied by de Rore, who became his maestro di cappella.

Salinas returned to Spain.

Wert's only book of four-part madrigals demonstrated an apotheosis of homophony. He dedicated the volume to the Marquis of Pescara, then governor of Naples.

One of van Berchem's major works was a setting for four-parts of ninety-three stanzas of the "Orlando Furioso" by Ariosto, published at Venice this year. There were three volumes and they were dedicated to Duke Alfonso II of Ferrara.

The most important hymn book compiled by the Czech Brethren was published by Bishop Jan Blahoslav in this year.

Bourgeois published a volume containing 83 Metrical Psalms at Lyons.

Bourgeois' last known work in process was on melodies for the Anglo-Genevan Psalter. It was entitled "Quatre-vingt-trois Psalmes de David en musique . . . à quatre, cinq, et six parties, tant a voix pareilles qu'autrement, etc. Paris 1561."

Salvatore Essenga's second book of madrigals for five-voices published this year.

Gardano's "Terzo libro delle muse a 5" appeared.

Nine of Gero's madrigals ap- (cont.) peared in the "Madrigals for 3 Voices" published at Venice by Gardano during this year.

A set of magnificats and vesper psalms by de Kerle appeared at Venice at this time.

Milan published El Cortesano, a book which gave a vivid description of court life at Valencia in his time.

The "Missale" was published in Mexico City.

Nasco's widow published a collection (reprinted twice) which contained four-part lamentations by her late husband, two Passions and other compositions.

Antonio Scandello composed a Passion according to St. John.

Susato published three books of songs in Dutch titled "Musyck boexken," and another book apparently the second of a series of "Souter-Liedekens" (Psalter -ditties) which was of interest.

The "Old Hundredth" was included in Utenhove's Dutch Psalter ("Hondert Psalmen Davids") published by Day in London.

Vasquez' "Agenda" defunctorum was published and dedicated to Juan Bravo.

Vila's "Odarum quas vulgo madrigales appellamus . . . lib I" appeared.

A five-part madrigal by della Viola, "Non pur d'almi splendori," was published in the "Libro terzo delle Muse" by Gardano at Venice during this year.

1561(cont.)

Walther's "Ein gar Schöner geistlicher und christlicher Bergkreyen" appeared.

Walther's "Ein newes christliches Lied" was composed.

Cardinal d'Este on a delicate and important diplomatic mission to the Court of France, as Papal Legate, took his private choir and four hundred horsemen with him.

The Anglo-Genevan Psalter was enlarged to eighty-seven psalms set with sixty tunes. This year saw the publication at Geneva of its last edition.

Kethe wrote versions of twenty-five psalms for the enlarged edition of Knox's Anglo-Genevan Psalter, published in this year.

"Foure score and seven Psalmes of David in English Mitre, by Thomas Sterneholde and others; conferred with the Hebrewe, and in certeine places corrected, as the sense of the Prophet requireth. Whereunto are added the Songe of Simeon, the then commandments and the Lord's Prayer. 1561" was published at Geneva.

Nicola Vicentino, theorist as well as composer in Venice, studied with Willaert. He designed a complicated keyboard for a super-organ or super-harpsichord (arciórgano, arcicémbalo) with 31 keys for each octave on six manuals. This way it could produce various shades of the diatonic, chromatic, and enharmonic genders of the Greeks (see also 1555).

Luis de Góngora, a Spanish poet, was born (died 1627). The movement "Gongorism" in Spain carried his name.

Thomas Sackville, with Thomas Norton wrote "Gorboduc, or, Ferrex and Porrex," the first English tragedy in blank verse.

Spanish painting: Antonio Moro, Portrait of a Nobleman.

Spanish painting:
Luis de Vargas, Retablo de la Gamba, two panels in which he portrayed angelic musicians performing a four-part "Tota pulchra es," probably composed by him. The paintings were executed in a chapel of Seville Cathedral.

(to 1565) Contino was maestro di cappella at the court of Mantua.

(to 1571) A lute-book by Giacomo de Gorzanis was published during this period.

(to 1571) Palestrina held the positions as Maestro di Cappella and Maestro dei Fanciulli di Coro at the Church of S. Maria Maggiore simultaneously.

c.1561

Wolfgang Schmeltzl, German quodlibet composer, died (born c.1500).

Palestrina's "Papae Marcelli" Mass was included in Papal choir-books.

Tylman Susato, Belgian printer and composer, died (born c.1480).

c.1561(cont.)

Vicentino had an organ built by Vicenzo Colombo of Venice.

White succeeded Tye as Master of the Choristers at Ely Cathedral.

(and 1564) In the "Secondo libro a cinque" of these years, de Wert's choice of texts was far more uniform than in his first book. Contrasts of musical structure were also more evident.

1562

(February 7) Hans Sachs included the old Mailied (May-song) in his Fastnachtsspiel "Der Neydhart mit dem Feyhel," composed on this date.

(February 27) Byrd was appointed organist of Lincoln Cathedral.

(June 8) Soto entered the college of the Pope's Chapel.

(September 10) The Council of Trent outlawed many practices and was insistent on conformity but not specifying the manner of enforcement. A committee of deputies drew up a canon dealing with the music to be used at mass on this date.

(September 17) The Tridentine session made the recommendation that the church must "exclude all music tainted with sensual and impure elements, all secular forms and unedifying language." This recommendation was made so that "The House of God may in truth be called a House of prayer."

(September 20) Da Monte signed the dedication of his "Primo libro a 4" at Naples.

(November 1) The preface to Lassus' "Cantiones" was signed by the composer, and bore this date "Venetiis 1562 die 1. Nov."

(November 11) The twenty-fourth session of the Council of Trent stressed the positive values of liturgical music but left the details of enforcement and regulation in the hands of the local hierarchy.

(December 7) Adrian Willaert, major composer of the Venetian school, died at Venice (born 1480). He had also held the position of chapel master at St. Mark's in Venice.

(June) Lassus published his first book of entirely sacred music, "Sacrae cantiones, à 5."

(December) John Dowland, noted British composer, was born in Ireland (died 1626). One source placed his birth at Westminster.

Philippus Dulichius, German composer, was born (died 1631).

Pietro Fortini, Italian madrigalist, died (birthdate unknown).

Ottavio Rinuccini, celebrated poet and writer of texts for some of the earliest operas, was born (died 1621). He was a member of the Florentine Camerata.

Claudin de Sermisy, French chanson composer, died (born 1490 or c.1490).

Jan Pieterszoon Sweelinck, Dutch composer, was born in Deventer (died 1621). Although he spent much of his life in Amsterdam, he studied with Andrea Gabrieli and Zarlino. He was organist at the Oude Kerk

1562(cont.)

(Old Church) in Amsterdam for about forty years.

A pension was granted to Master Alfonso by the Queen of England. The event was proof of the presence of a noted Italian madrigalist in that country.

Signora Bendidio was already at the court of Ferrara by this date.

Byrd accepted his appointment at Lincoln Cathedral and immediately turned his attention to composing English Services and anthems.

Alfonso Ferrabosco I, later to become a friend of Byrd's, arrived in England. He was awarded a pension from the Queen.

The first of the castrati, emasculated male sopranos, entered the papal choir.

William Daman emigrated to England.

Ludwig Daser was allowed to retire with his full salary.

Donato was placed in charge of the cappella piccola at St. Mark's. It was organized this year.

Kerle entered the service of Otto von Truchsess von Waldburg, Cardinal of Augsburg, at Rome. Later he went to Germany with the Cardinal.

At this year's session of the Council of Trent there were frequent performances of Kerle's "Preces speciales pro (cont.) salubri generalis concilii." The delegates thus became favorably disposed toward contrapuntal church music.

Lassus returned to Italy (also in 1567, 1574, 1578, 1585, and 1587).

René de Mel entered the choir school of St. Rombaut, at Malines.

Da Monte's longest stay was probably in Rome by the inclusion of some of his compositions in collections published by Barre, such as "Terzo libro delle Muse a 4" issued this year.

Palestrina's sister Palma was married to a citizen of Palestrina. Her brother, as head of the family, provided the dowry.

Soto entered the Papal Choir as a singer and supposedly kept his voice until he was eighty years old.

A treatise by de La Taille "Manière de Faire des Vers en françois, comme en grec et en Latin" appeared.

During Sebastian Westcote's term as master of the Children of St. Paul's the "Tragedie of Gorboduc" was produced in the Hall of the Inner Temple on Twelfth Night. Cornets, drums, flutes, hautboys and violins were used at the performance.

The reorganization of the choir at St. Mark's and its change into the cappella grande and the cappella piccola was maintained until the time of Zarlino. The original intention

1562(cont.)

was for the new arrangement to be used only during the period of Willaert's illness.

Zarlino asserted that Merulo, Viola, and Willaert met at the latter's house. Willaert was bedridden at the time with gout but their conversation was reported in the five Ragionamenti of the Dimostrationi.

The circle of "Roman" musicians of this period were described in a publication issued by the composer and publisher Barre in the "Terzo libro delle Muse a quattro . . . madrigali arios."

An excerpt from Dante's Inferno, "Quivi sospir: pianti ed alti guai," was set by five or six composers after this date.

Des Prés' "Sacrae Cantiones" for five voices was published.

Goudimel published his "Seize Pseaumes mis en musique à quatre parties, en forme de motets" after the Genevan Psalter was finished.

Various instruction books for lute were written with examples in tablature. The oldest known to survive in England was the "Lauttenbuch" by Wolf Heckel, published at Strassburg and preserved in the Library of the Sacred Harmonic Society.

The second edition of Johann Honterus' "Odae cum harmoniis" was published.

A book of six masses by Kerle was published at Venice.

Giovanni Camillo Maffei da (cont.) Solofra wrote a manual on ornamentation.

The Ballards published "The Psalms of Marot."

Palestrina's fourth mass in the series for four and five voices was written and dedicated to Pope Gregory at the latter's request.

In gratitude for his monthly pension, Palestrina sent two motets "Beatus Laurentius," and "Estote fortes in bello," as well as a mass for six voices, "Ut Re Mi Fa Sol La." All of these were for use at the Apostolic Chapel.

Scotto's collection "I dolci e harmoniosi concenti . . . Libro Secondo, 1562" appeared.

The Preces published at Venice in this year and commissioned by Otto von Truchsess von Waldburg, Cardinal of Augsburg, included settings of ten Latin poems by Soto, Professor of Theology at Dillingen.

Thomas Tallis' "Foelix Namque. 1" was composed.

Some of Viola's works were included in a collection published by Scotto during this year.

Zarlino's "Dimostrationi harmoniche" was divided into five Ragionamenti and was written in the form of dialogues. According to Zarlino, these were reports of a conversation among friends who met at Willaert's house.

Zarlino's "Istitutioni armoniche" was reprinted at Venice (see also 1558 and 1573).

1562(cont.)

St. Barbara, the family chapel and favorite church of the Gonzaga family, was built this year.

The definitive edition of the Sternhold-Hopkins Psalter appeared and quickly became the most popular Psalm book among English-speaking Protestants. The Genevan Psalter was now completed and was to be used by the Reformed Church in England and the Pilgrims in America.

The "Whole Booke of Psalmes," by T. Sternhold, J. Hopkins, and Others," was published by John Day of Aldensgate.

At the meeting of the Council of Trent in this year decrees were issued in general terms for the purpose of suppressing undesirable features which were being introduced into Church music, especially those of secular character.

Samuel Daniel, English essayist and historian who wrote an account of the Wars of the Roses, was born (died 1619).

Sackville and Norton's "Gorboduc" was first acted and produced.

Jan van Scorel, Netherlandish painter, died at Utrecht (born c.1495).

According to one source, a group of Huguenot explorers landed near Charleston, South Carolina and sang psalms.

French painting: François Clouet, Portrait of Pierre Quthe.

Italian painting: Tintoretto, (cont.) The Findings of St. Mark's Remains.

(and 1564) The "Fitzwilliam Virginal Book" included Tallis' two largest and most important keyboard compositions, the settings of "Felix namque," dated (in manuscript) 1562 and 1564 respectively. A plain song cantus firmus was used in the old style in both compositions.

(to 1567) A list of organists was found in an organ-book at Ely Cathedral according to which White was organist there during this period and died at the end of this tenure.

(to 1587) A fine music book was written for and presented to Cardinal Ferdinando de'Medici during these years. The book included motets, psalms, three dirges on the death of Queen Anne Boleyn, some French chansons and Italian villote.

c.1562

Giulio Belli, sacred polyphonic composer, was born (date of death unknown),see c.1560.

John Bull, English composer noted for his "Parthenia," was born (died 1628).

Francis Pilkington, an English madrigal composer, was born (died 1638).

Philippe Rogier, a composer of masses and motets, was born at Arras (died 1596).

(to c.1612) The Fitzwilliam Virginal Book, copied out by Francis Tregian, contained almost 300 pieces. Practically every major English keyboard composer and all types of music

c.1562(cont.)

they composed during this period were included and the starting and final dates cover the range of the compositions included.

1563

(February 13) At the Town House of Convocation a resolution abolishing organs was considered and defeated by one vote.

(February 21) William Mundy became a Gentleman of the Chapel Royal.

(May 28) Henricus Glareanus, renowned Swiss theorist, died at Freiburg (born 1488).

(October 17) Robert Parsons of Exeter became a Gentleman of the Chapel Royal.

(October 18) De Rore succeeded Willaert in his duties at St. Mark's on the latter's death.

(November 11) Music was again considered at the twenty-fourth general session of the Council of Trent.

(February) Andries Pevernage became choir director at the Cathedral of St. Sauveur in Bruges. He only held the position until the following September, however.

(March) Two new cardinals were appointed to fill vacancies brought on by the death of Giovanni Moroni, Bishop of Palestrina, and Bernardo Navagero. They advocated monophonic music for the mass and stronger enforcement of the elimination of "scandalous noises."

(October) Pevernage went to Courtrai where he assumed the position of choir director at Notre Dame.

According to Poccianti, Paolo Animuçcia died at Rome at this time. However, the generally accepted date is 1571 (born c.1499 or c.1500).

Adrien Petit Coclicus, Flemish composer and pupil of des Prés, died (born c.1500).

Bartolomé Escobedo, a member of the Roman group of Spanish musicians, died at Segovia (born c.1510).

Hans Newsidler, German lutenist, died (born 1508).

Jean Titelouze, the renowned French organist and composer, was born (died 1633).

Corneille Verdonck, a Dutch composer, pupil of Waelrant, and disciple of Lassus, was born (died 1625).

A man named "Brouno" was organist at the St. Nikolaas-Kerk in Utrecht at this time.

Shortly after Byrd's appointment as organist at Lincoln Cathedral he was elected a Gentleman of the Chapel Royal.

Richard Edwards was appointed Master of the Children of the Chapel Royal. He succeeded Richard Bower.

De Fuenllana was chamber musician to Queen Isabel de Valois, third wife of Philip II of Spain.

Nicholas Gomólka resigned his

1563(cont.)

position at the Royal Chapel.

Kerle accompanied Cardinal Truchsess von Waldburg on his journey to Spain.

Lassus went from Antwerp to Duke Albrecht V of Bavaria (Munich). He sang tenor in the court chapel and at this date became choir director.

Vittoria entered the Collegium Germanicum.

Le Maistre was court composer at Dresden.

Bernardino de Ribera was maestro at Toledo.

Ruffo was choirmaster at the cathedral in Verona up to this date when he went to Milan.

Ruffo was appointed maestro di cappella at the Cathedral in Milan. He was considered by some sources to be the outstanding sacred composer of his time.

The organist Candius Sebastiani had been forced to write a defense of the organ.

Andrés de Villalar was appointed maestro at Cordova.

Animuccia, Florentine composer, published a collection of spirituals at Rome.

A book on music by Cardano was published.

Thomas Causton wrote some of the tunes included in the collection of psalms published by Day, "The whole Psalmes in foure parts, which may be sung (cont.) to all musical instruments."

Des Prés' "Seven Penitential Psalms of David" was issued.

A music book by Falletti was published by Beuilacqua.

Galilei's Intavolatura de lauto Madrigali e Recercate, which contained thirty-four pieces in tablature, was published at Rome. This was essentially a collection of lute transcriptions of polyphonic compositions.

Giacomini set a sonnet "Nobil coppia gradita in cui risplende" for the wedding of Paolo Giordano Orsini, Duke of Bracciano, and Isabella Medici. It was published in a madrigal book during this year.

Giacomini set the text from Petrarch's "Trionfo della fama."

Guerrero's collection of Magnificat settings of this year included one in each of eight keys, with the even-numbered verses written in polyphony for four parts.

The Vienna library (also) preserved a collection of magnificats by Guerrero, published at Louvain, by Phalesius during this year.

Barre published Lassus' third book of five-voiced madrigals at Rome in this year.

The first edition of Le Roy's Instruction de partir toute musique facilement en tablature de luth was published in this year but was lost.

Lucas Lossius' "Erotemata

1563(cont.)

musicae" appeared.

The first appearance of the tune "Old Hundredth" may have been in a French translation of the Psalms with music by Marot and Beza, published at Lyons at this time.

Palestrina's first collection of motets was published, however, no copy survived.

Palestrina dedicated a volume of "graceful motetti" to Cardinal Pio di Carpi, who had been kind to him. They were printed by the Dorici Brothers in this year.

Collections of laude that were sung by Neri's Congregation as well as others were published during his lifetime and after his death as well. One of the earliest was published at Venice. It included laude sung by groups in Florence and edited by Serafino Razzi, a Dominican friar.

A collection of madrigals for four and five voices was composed by Schiavetto and published by Scotto in Venice. It was dedicated to Bishop Savorgnano, but its quality was difficult to evaluate since the only surviving copy (at the Accademia Filarmonica in Verona) was defective.

A music book by Sparenburg was published by Horst.

The following settings by Tallis were included in Day's "Whole Psalter":

"Come, Holy Ghost, eternal

(cont.)

God" (for four voices).

"Even like the hunted hind," 5th do. (for four voices).

"Expend, O Lord," 6th do. (for four voices).

"God grant with grace," 8th do. (for four voices).

"Let God arise," 2nd do. (for four voices).

"Man blest no doubt" 1st tune (for four voices).

"O come in one," 4th do. (for four voices).

"Why bragst in malice high," 7th do. (for four voices).

"Why fumeth in fight," 3rd do. (for four voices).

Michele Varotto's six-voiced masses were published.

Della Viola composed music for Lollio's Aretusa.

De Wert's third book of madrigals was dedicated to his former benefactor in southern Italy, Consalvo Fernandes di Cordova, Duke of Sessa.

John Day printed "The whole Booke of Psalmes in foure partes," which may be sung to all Musicall Instruments," in this year. The melody was in the tenor.

Shepherd's Prayer "O Lord of Hostes" was included in "Whole Psalms . . . "

Pope Pius IV issued a "commission" to eight cardinals

1563(cont.)

authorizing them to use all means to enforce the resolution of the Council of Trent. Two of the most active of the group were Cardinals Borromeo and Vittellozzi. They requested Palestrina to compose a mass to demonstrate what music for a sacred office should be like.

The famous decree issued by the Council of Trent in this year practically eliminated most music which had been written for Latin rites up until then.

One result of the deliberations of the Council of Trent in this year was a decision to found a Roman seminary, where students could be trained for the priesthood, and to which sons of the laity might also be admitted. Palestrina was appointed the first "Master of Music" at this Seminary. His duties included the teaching of Gregorian Chant.

Michael Drayton, Elizabethan poet and historian, was born (died 1631).

Foxe's "Acts and Monuments," usually known as "The Book of Martyrs," was written.

Thomas Sackville was a contributor to "A Mirror for Magistrates" the "Induction" and "The Complaint of the Duke of Buckingham."

Orazio Gentileschi, Italian painter, member of the so-called "Caravaggio school," was born (died c.1640).

Netherlandish painting: Pieter Bruegel the Elder, the Beggars.

Netherlandish painting: Pieter Bruegel the Elder, Tower of Babel (3'8 7/8" x 5'1").

French painting: Clouet School, Portrait of Claude de Beaune.

Spanish Colonial architecture: Mexico City, Cathedral, begun 1563 (145' wide).

Italian painting: Veronese, The Marriage at Cana "The orchestra is made up of Venetian painters: Bassano, flutist; Tintoretto, viola; Titian, double-bass; and Veronese, cello.

(and 1564) Gioseppe Caimo a highly respected musician in Milan was entrusted with the composition of the festival music for the reception of the archdukes Rudolf and Ernest, when they visited Trent, Mantua. Ariosto's "Suppositi" with "concerti per intermedii" was performed there on December 18. The archdukes also visited Cremona, Piacenza, and Milan (January 5) on their way to Spain in these years.

(and 1565) "The whole psalmes in foure partes, which may be song to al musicall instrumentes, set forth for the encrease of vertue, and abolishyng of other vayne and triflyng ballades. Imprinted at London by John Day, dwelling over Aldersgate, beneath Saynt Martyns. cum gratiâ et privilegio Regiae Maiestatis, per Septennium. 1563" A second edition was published in 1565.

(to 1565) De Rore was Maestro di Cappella at St. Mark's during these years.

(to 1568) Several lute-books by Galilei were published during

1563(cont.)

this period.

(to 1572) Byrd was organist of Lincoln Cathedral during these years.

(to 1847) An interesting monograph concerned with the history of the Old Hundredth psalm-tune was published by the Rev. W.H. Havergal. It had an appendix with twenty-eight examples of the tune as harmonised by different composers between these dates.

c.1563

Jachet Berchem, Netherlandish madrigal composer, died (born c.1505).

Andreas Raselius, German composer, was born (died 1602).

John Shepherd, English sacred composer, died (born c.1520).

Baïf visited Italy.

Marc' Antonio Ingegneri, a pupil of Ruffo's, probably settled in Cremona.

1564

(February 14) Grindal, Bishop of London, wrote a memorandum, dated 14 February 1564/5 that concerned the "Varieties in Service and ye Administration used."

(April 26) William Shakespeare was born in Stratford-on-Avon and was baptized in the village church there on this date (died 1616, April 23).

(December 1) Vaet was appointed "obrister kappelmeister."

(April) Richard Farrant resigned (cont.) from the Chapel Royal when he became Master of the Children at St. George's Chapel, Windsor. He may have also been a lay vicar and organist there.

(July) Vaet's activity as a composer to the court was demonstrated by his motet "in laudem invictissimi Romanorum imperatoris Maximiliani II." The latter ascended the throne in July of this year.

(July-Sept) During these months Palestrina, at the invitation of Cardinal d'Este, directed several musical performances at the Villa at Tivoli. He apparently obtained a leave of absence from Santa Maria Maggiore since he was able to provide a replacement, an arrangement doubtless facilitated by his patron.

Gregor Aichinger, German composer, was born (died 1628).

William Bathe, an Irish writer on music, was born on Easter Sunday (died 1614, June 17). He was the son of John Bathe, a judge, and Eleanor Preston.

Girolamo Falletti, author of books on music, died (born 1518).

Lodovico Grossi da Viadana, an influential figure in the early history of the basso continuo, was born (died 1627),see c.1564.

A Protestant nobleman, Christof Harant (of Polžic and Bezdružic), was born (died 1621). He was a musician and author and wrote a motet "Qui confidunt" for six voices as well as a mass for five voices.

Hans Leo Hasler, German organist, pupil of Andrea Gabrieli, and

1564(cont.)

composer of both Catholic and Protestant sacred music, was born, possibly at Nürnberg (died 1612). He was ennobled by Emperor Rudolf II late in life. His was a direct and clear style of composition.

Duke Heinrich Julius of Brunswick, a writer of dramas, was born (died 1613).

Amish farming communities in the Pennsylvania Dutch Country still use a Protestant hymnal, or "ausbund," from this date in their services. This is the oldest book of its kind still used in the United States.

The Kapellmeister of S. Marc at Bar-le-Duc punished one of the boys until he drew blood.

William Blitheman, who was a member of the choir and master of the choristers at Christ Church, Oxford, was also a Gentleman of the Chapel Royal and an organist.

It was quite possible that a group of Huguenot explorers taught Indians in Florida to sing Psalms by Louis Bourgeois.

Gioseppe Caimo was organist at St. Ambrogio Maggiore.

John Case became a Scholar at St. John's College.

William Endel was organist at Cassel.

Richard Farrant was appointed Master of the Choristers as well as organist at St. George's Chapel at Windsor.

Flecha the Younger was in Italy.

Andrea Gabrieli became organist at St. Mark's Cathedral (according to some sources he only became second organist.

The complete Genevan psalter, harmonized in double counterpoint, was published.

The first psalm in which the psalm melody was in the superius was attributed to Goudimel. He used this technique in all except fifteen of the psalms in the collection from this year.

Le Jeune settled in Paris and was in touch with Huguenot groups.

Claudio Merulo succeeded Parabosco as first organist at St. Mark's.

Mundy became a Gentleman of the Chapel Royal.

When he became rector at San Giovanni dei Fiorentini in this year, Neri moved his meetings to the larger oratory there.

The Florentine group in Rome asked Neri to assume leadership of their congregation at this time.

Otto became a student at Schulpforta, a school with an established reputation in the history of church music.

Palestrina held the position of maestro of the concerts at Villa d'Este in Tivoli while he was the director of the Cappella Liberiana.

While still at St. Maria Maggiore, Palestrina apparently received a leave of absence from his duties there during the

1564(cont.)

three summer months. Entries supporting this fact were found in the expenses of the d'Este household for this year.

Porta was chapel-master at Osimo up to this time.

De Rore returned to Parma.

Soriano became a member of the choir at St. John Lateran.

According to Mr. Chappell in "Popular Music" the earliest mention of Trenchmore was in a Morality by William Bulleyn, published in this year.

Tye was at Wilbraham.

Victoria left the Collegium Germanicum to become choirmaster and organist at various other churches in Rome.

Antonio Barre published "Il Primo Libro di Madrigali a quattro voci di Ollivier Brassart. In Roma per Antionio Barre 1564."

Caimo published his first book of four-voiced madrigals.

Michael Deiss, musician to Emperor Ferdinand I of Germany, composed a motet for four voices for his patron as well as eight other pieces. They were published by Joannelli in his "Thesaurus Musicus."

Des Prés' pars I of Lugebat David Absalon was published by Montanus and Neuber.

The Gombert Credo was not published until this date.

Goudimel published an abridged (cont.) form of the Marot-Bèze Psalter, with musical settings in modified motet style during this year.

A collection of ten "en forme de motets" was the first published psalm collection by Le Jeune.

Lassus published two volumes of chansons, one at Antwerp and one at Louvain.

Lassus was in Munich and Le Roy and Ballard issued their first publication devoted exclusively to his works.

The oldest existing copy of Palestrina's Pope Marcellus Mass was preserved in the library of St. Maria Maggiore. The Mass also certainly existed in manuscript.

A collection of motets by Schiavetto dedicated to the Bishop Savorgnano and from this year was preserved.

The "Fitzwilliam Virginal Book" included Tallis' two largest and most important keyboard compositions, the settings of "Felix namque," dated 1562 and 1564 respectively. A plainsong cantus firmus was used in the old style in both compositions.

Vaet's compositions were included in the "Novus Thesaurus" and in the five volumes of the "Thesaurus musicus" published in Nürnberg in this year. They were all motets.

The French Mascarades were often used as part of the ceremonies for welcoming distinguished guests. When Charles IX came

1564(cont.)

to Bar-Le-Duc actors representing the four elements, the four planets and various allegorical and mythological personages appeared.

The Scottish Psalter was completed in this year and developed along with the English Psalter, during the "Anglo -Genevan period."

John Calvin, Protestant religious leader, died (born 1509).

Christopher Marlowe, English playwright, was born at Canterbury (died 1593).

Michelangelo Buonarroti, Italian painter, died (born 1475).

Covarrubias, Spanish architect, died (born c.1488).

French architecture: Delorme, Paris, Tuileries, loggia.

Tintoretto started the great cycle of the Scuola di San Rocco. He worked on this for twenty-three years.

(and 1565) Two collectionf of strophic settings of the entire Genevan Psalter for four voices by Goudimel were published by Le Roy and Ballard. The first collection was in embellished chordal style, the later one in note-against-note style.

(to 1565) A Commission of Cardinals appointed to study the use of music in the church met at Rome during these years.

(to 1565) Kerle went with (cont.) Cardinal Truchsess von Waldburg to Dillingen during these years.

(to 1567) Vaet was first Kapellmeister in Vienna during this period.

(1567 and 1583) Bartolommeo Spontone published his first set of madrigals for five voices at Venice in 1564. There were more editions of the publication in 1567 and 1583.

(and 1577) In both the 1564 and 1577 edition of the Psalter "An Introduction to learn to sing" was included. It consisted of the scale and a few elementary rules, for the benefit of the voice.

(and 1580) Le Jeune published "Dix Pseaumes de David nouvellement composés à quatro parties en forme de motets . . ." in 1564 and then in 1580. The psalms were by Marot but the music was entirely original.

(to 1585) Andrea Gabrieli held the position of organist at St. Mark's throughout this period.

(to 1594) Valenten Otto was Cantor at the St. Thomas School at Leipzig.

(to 1717) The Savoy Chapel Royal was used by the parishioners of St. Mary's.

(to 1759) A. Göhler's "Musikalienverzeichnis nach den Messkatalogen" covered this period of composition.

c.1564

Felice Anerio was, according to one source, born in Rome (died

c.1564(cont.)

1614). Generally c.1560 is the closest approximation to his date of birth.

Lodovico Grossi da Viadana, Mantuan composer in the "new style," was born (died 1627).

Leonard Schroeter became Cantor of the Cathedral of Magdeburg. He succeeded Gallus Dressler, a composer of some degree of importance.

Tasso visited Mantua.

Netherlandish painting: Pieter Bruegel the Elder, Triumph of Death (46" x 63 3/4").

1565

(June 19) Palestrina's Missa Papae Marcelli was first sung in the Sistine Chapel.

(December 25) Corteccia and Striggio composed the music for intermedi by the renowned poet Giovanni Battista Cini first performed on this date at Florence. D'Ambra's "La Cofanaria" was produced on that date with the intermedi mentioned above. The performance was in honor of the marriage of Francesco de' Medici to Johanna of Austria. The story had its basis in Apuleius' "Cupid and Psyche."

(January) Netherlandish painting: Pieter Bruegel the Elder, Hunters in the Snow.

(August) Pope Pius IV died and was eventually succeeded by Pope Pius V.

Jacques Buus, ricercare composer and organist, died, probably at Vienna (birthdate unknown).

Pierre Guédron, originator of French choral madrigals, was born (died 1621). Guédron was considered to have been influenced by Monteverdi when he accompanied Vincenzo I on his journey to Flanders.

Sigmund Hemmel, German Protestant composer, died (birthdate unknown).

In the fall of this year Cipriano de Rore, Flemish composer and pupil of Willaert, died at Parma (born 1516).

Tassoni, a writer who was interested in Scottish music, was born (date of death unknown). This was the year of Rizzio's death, but Tassoni never mentioned him in his works.

Philippe Verdelot, Flemish madrigal composer, was thought by one source to have died in this year. Generally his death date was given as c.1540 (born 1500).

Alfonso had two big halls "del Pallone" and "dei Giganti" built in his castle. One was for dramatic performances and the other for musical ones.

A perfect example of the modern violin carrying this date was built by Andrea Amati.

Bakfark escaped to Vienna by way of Breslau and became court lutenist to the Emperor.

Cavazzoni was organist at Santa Barbara in Mantua.

Contino returned to his position as choirmaster at the cathedral in Brescia.

The number of dances of the

1565(cont.)

seises was set at ten.

Danckerts was a singer at the Sistine Chapel and had remained there under the reign of five different popes, until this date.

Pierre Dubuisson, a singer, was in gratuitously granted the rights of citizenship at Geneva.

Fruytiers was living at Antwerp.

Goudimel was living in Metz, but left shortly thereafter with other Huguenots, due to hostility on the part of a new commandant. He first returned to Besançon and then went to Lyons.

Goudimel's collection of psalms from this year had seventeen psalms with the melody in the superius, the rest had it in the tenor.

The Goudimel Psalter of this year had its greatest success in Germany, as well as in other Protestant areas. The psalter was in a simple chordal style of harmonization.

La Grotte's "Je suis Amour" was probably sung as part of an intermedi during court festivals at Fontainebleau.

A commenting tenor appeared in Infantas' motet in honor of the victory over the Turks at Melilla this year.

Van Quickelberg spoke of Lassus' children, whom he must have known at a very early age, as "elegantissimi."

The simplicity of Lassus' church music at this time demonstrated (cont.) that the causes of Palestrina's revolution were not all warranted.

Two of the best sources of this time for information on Lassus' early life were Vinchant's "Annals of Hainault;" and an article by Van Quickelberg in the "Heroum Prosopographia," a biographical dictionary compiled by Pantaleon.

Marenzio associated his music with de Rore by a literal quotation from one of the latter's posthumous madrigals for four voices. The reference appeared in the seventh number of Marenzio's "Primo libro a sei."

Cardinal Pacacco, a Spanish representative at the papal court, inferred to Palestrina that the dedication of a work to King Philip II would be most pleasing to the latter.

Pope Pius IV conferred title of Composer to the Pontifical Chapel on Palestrina and granted him an honorarium of three scudi and thirty baiocchi per month.

When Palestrina's three masses written this year were submitted to the Commission of Cardinals for approval it was ordered that copies be made of them to be preserved in the archives, and, that the Missa Papae Marcelli should be transcribed in "letters of extraordinary size."

Rore was succeeded as maestro di cappella at St. Mark's by Zarlino.

Sigismund, of Hungary, rebuilt the cathedral organ, which had been destroyed in this year.

1565(cont.)

Victoria received a grant from Philip II to continue his musical studies at Rome. He entered the Collegium Germanicum, a Jesuit college founded by Loyola.

The Capella di San Marco first attained world renown under Willaert and de Rore. The latter had supervised its activities for numerous years.

Zarlino, when elected to succeed de Rore, was given great honor and respect.

Cornets and trombones were first used at St. Mark's after Zarlino became maestro di cappella this year.

The anonymous "Hor va, canzone mia, non dubitare" was included in the "Quattro libri delle Villotte" issued this year.

Asola published a collection of Introits and Alleluias (collection of music for the Proper) during this year.

Bakfark's second lute book was published in Cracow at this time. It was dedicated to Sigismund II of Poland.

A manuscript by Johann Braittenstein was preserved. It included various compositions for the Mass and Office and had German, Greek and Latin texts as well as some attempts at translations into Hebrew and Aramaic. Braittenstein was a Bavarian parish priest who collected the works for his own use.

"Il Figluolo Prodigo," an allegorical pre-oratorio type (cont.) morality work, was produced in Florence.

Jan Fruytiers, a Lutheran author, wrote the text and music for "Ecclesiasticus oft de wijse sproken Jesu des soons Syrach, etc." published at Antwerp by Selvius in this year. It was a metrical translation of the book of Ecclesiasticus. L'Homme Armé was included with a sacred text. Thirty-four melodies were taken from the Cock print.

Andrea Gabrieli's "Sacrae cantiones quinque vocum, liber primus" was published. He dedicated the work to Duke Albert of Bavaria.

Jan Kochanowski's metrical translations for Gomólka's psalms for four voices were of literary value and were dedicated to Bishop Peter Myszkowski. There was a eulogistic Latin introduction by Andreas Trzycielski, leader of the Polish dissidents that was similar to the dedication of Goudimel's psalms of 1565.

A copy of Goudimel's Psalms which was said to be unique was preserved in a private library in England.

Goudimel's psalter appeared with settings in simple four-voiced movements. The basis was the French metrical version of the Marot and Beza volume. The melody was in the tenor and the music was note against note. The book was published by Jaqui at Lyons in this year and at Paris by Le Roy. The French title was "Les Pseaumes mis en rime francoise."

1565(cont.)

Le Roy's "Missa Panis quem ego dabo" was based on a motet by Hellinck and was published at Venice with Palestrina's Mass on the same source in this year.

Homer Herpol wrote gospels for the year.

Gardano published Lassus' "Cantiones."

Lassus' "Lectiones ex propheta Job" appeared.

Lassus composed an occasional piece, the sestina, and presented it to Duke Alfonso d'Este when he went to Munich. It was published this year and bore the title "Qual nemica fortuna oltra quest' alpe."

Lassus wrote the seven "Penitential Psalms" and Duke William of Bavaria ordered them to be copied in an illuminated manuscript which became one of the most valuable relics of the 16th century. The publisher was Hans Mielich and the volume included sectional motets without the "bonding" of a cantus firmus.

Lassus wrote a bipartite wedding song for Alessandro Farnese and Maria of Portugal, "Vieni, dolc'Imeneo, vieni e infiamma." The composition ended with a literal repetition of the first ten measures of the beginning.

The Lausanne Psalter appeared under the following title: "Les Pseaumes mis en rime françoise par Clement Marot et Theodore de Bèze, avec le chant de l'eglise de Lausane (sic) 1565. Avec privilege, tant du Roy, que de Messieurs (cont.) de Geneve."

Marenzio set music to a text by Franco Sacchetti. The work was a caccia "Passando con pensier per un boschetto," and it was included in a poetic anthology of this year edited by Dionigi Atanagi, Marenzio's usual vade mecum.

This was one of several different years assigned by various sources to the completion of the Missa Papae Marcelli by Palestrina.

Most of Palestrina's purely Secular madrigals were probably composed before this date. There were about one hundred of them in all.

Primavera published his first book, "canzoni napoletane," for three voices.

The entire psalter in a version in simple counterpoint, was published at Geneva.

Tomás de Sancta Maria published a method for keyboard and other instruments, the "Arte de tañer fantasía."

The gospel songs of Matthew Seydel appeared during this year.

A few of Shepherd's compositions were included in a work entitled "Mornyng and Evenyng Prayer and Communion," published at London this year.

Striggio the Elder's Intermezzo, "Psiche ed Amore," included a list of instruments for use at its performance.

Sancta Maria's "Libro llamado

1565(cont.)

Arte de tañer fantasia assí para tecla como para vihuela . . . ." published at Valladolid in this year was devoted to the study of instrumental technique and music especially for the clavichord.

Waelrant edited, "Symphonia angelica di diversi eccellentissimi Musici, a quattro, cinque, e sei voci: Nuovamente raccolta per Uberto Waelrant, 1565."

Willaert's Psalms published in Venice in this year were preserved at the library of the Royal Academy of Music in London.

A reprint of Day's "The whole Booke of Psalmes in four partes, which may be sung to all Musicall Instruments" appeared.

The wedding of Alessandro Farnese and Maria of Portugal purportedly took place.

Ronsard's "Abrégé de l'art poétique françois" was published.

At the Roman seminary, one feature of the curriculum was an in-depth course in musical theory and liturgical music, especially plainsong. This course was probably actually instituted at this time.

Cardinal d'Este, patron of Tasso, referred to the latter as one of his "gentiluomini" in this year.

Netherlandish painting: Pieter Bruegel the Elder, The Return of Hunters (46"x63 3/4").

(to 1566) Goudimel produced another arrangement of the (cont.) psalms, this time for three, four, or more voices and in the form of motets.

(to 1566) Lassus added three more volumes of "Sacrae Cantiones" (several parts of which were scored by Commer) and his first set of "Sacrae lectiones, 9 ex prophetâ Job."

(to 1566) Palestrina having been offered the position of music master at the Roman seminary saw an opportunity to give up church work and be able to continue at the Villa d'Este. He accepted the offer and started his duties during this period.

(to 1567) Porta was choir director at St. Anthony's church in Padua.

(and 1567) Two works for lute (licensed for printing) appeared. One was a "Scyence of Lutynge" (1565), the other an "Exhortation to all Kynde of Men how they shulde learn to play of the Lute" (1567). Neither one survived, possibly because the license was not used and they were not printed.

(and 1570) Animuccia published a volume entitled "Il primo libro delle Laudi" followed by a "Secondo libro" of a more advanced character (1570).

(to 1570) Palestrina's "Veni Sancte Spiritus" was probably composed during this period while Palestrina was music master at the Roman Seminary.

(to 1570) Italian painting: Tintoretto, Portrait of the Sculptor Jacopo Sansovino.

(to 1575) Golding's Ovid was

1565(cont.)

finished during this period.

(and 1578) De Wert became acquainted with Tasso when the poet visited Mantua in both of these years.

(and 1585) Andrea Gabrieli's harmonies reflected the significant changes that occurred during this period.

(to 1590) Zarlino directed the music at the Capella di San Marco for this entire period.

(to 1594) The so-called "Later Roman School of composition" embraced these years.

(to 1596) De Wert was maestro di cappella at the court at Mantua including the Church of Santa Barbara.

(to 1600) The "Fifth Epoch" witnessed the rapid and sudden advance of the mass and the motet to ultimate perfection.

(to 1620) This period has been referred to as "The Golden Age of Ecclesiastical Music."

c.1565

Netherlandish drawing: Pieter Brueghel the Elder, The Painter and the Buyer.

Italian painting: Titian, Christ Crowned with Thorns (110" x 72").

John Danyel, English composer, was born (died 1630).

John Farmer, English composer, was born (date of death unknown).

George Kirbye, English composer, was born (date of death unknown).

Duarte Lobo, an important Portuguese composer, was born (died 1643), see c.1560.

John Heywood, an accomplished virginal player attached to the Court of Henry VIII, died at Mechlin at this time (birthdate unknown).

John Mundy, English organist, was born (died 1630).

Ingegneri's first work was actually written this year.

Albert V had an illuminated manuscript done at Munich. It included twenty-five motets by de Rore and eighty-three miniatures, including a portrait of the composer done by Hans Mielich, court painter.

De Wert was appointed choirmaster at Saint Barbara's, the private chapel of the Gonzaga family.

Italian painting: Tintoretto, Miracles of St. Mark.

1566

(January 31) Hans Heugel's ten-voiced "Colloquium hospitis et nymphae" was performed at the preliminary celebration for the wedding of the parents of Landgrave Moritz.

(March 26) Antonio de Cabezón, Spanish composer and keyboard virtuoso, died at Madrid (born 1510).

(September 3) Richard Edward's "Palamon and Arcite" was produced before Queen Elizabeth in the Hall of Christ Church,

1566(cont.)

Oxford.

(September 17) Merulo was appointed organist at Brescia.

(October 31) Richard Edwards, English composer, died (born 1523). He was also a playwright.

Domenico Pietro Cerone, Spanish composer, was born at Bergamo (date of death unknown).

William Luther, died (birthdate unknown). He held leases for various properties in Stapleford-Abbot, including Battails Hall.

Huang Tso, Chinese author of Canons of Music, died (born 1490).

Josquin Baston was still living.

Herm. Bernroder was organist at Magdeburg Cathedral.

The first musical academy at Padua was that of the "Costanti," and was founded by the nobles of the city in this year.

Cornets and trombones were played in an adjoining room to honor Ferdinand of Bavaria when he visited Ferrara.

Giovanni Macque came to Italy.

Claudio Merulo was active also as a music printer and publisher at Venice. He formed a company with a partner and their first publication appeared in this year.

Da Monte performed music with (cont.) the younger members of the grand-ducal family in Florence.

A document preserved at Toledo mentioned the "musica quoe organica dicitur."

Porta was chapel-master at Padua, and perhaps first at the cathedral. The fifty-two Introits published this year were dedicated to the Cathedral Chapter, and later to the church of St. Antonio.

Both of Palestrina's sons were enrolled as students at the Roman Seminary, but apparently later abandoned the idea of becoming priests.

The Veccias were related to Palestrina's first wife, Lucrezia. In this year he placed his nephews at the Roman Seminary.

Jakob Rudolf was organist at Magdeburg Cathedral.

Salinas was appointed to the chair of music at Salamanca. He taught there for twenty-one years.

When Sweelinck was four years old a storm of iconoclasm went from Antwerp to Amsterdam and launched a period of religious and political revolt.

De Wert accompanied his employer, Duke Guglielmo Gonzaga, to Augsburg. His mastery of improvised counterpoint created great interest and admiration.

Caimo's first book of canzonette for three voices was preserved in one part only - the "canto." It was discovered several years

1566(cont.)

ago in Cracow.

Salvatore Essenga published a volume of "Madrigali" which included a piece, probably his first essay, by Vecchi.

Andrea Gabrieli's madrigal "Ecco l'aurora con l'aurata fronte" appeared.

Gascoigne's translation of Euripides' Jocasta was produced at Gray's Inn in England. It included five "dumb shows" accompanied by somewhat elaborate music.

By this date Goudimel's Psalter had grown to eight books and contained large settings in motet style.

Guerrero's most important works were published under the title, "Liber primus Missarum F. Guerero Hispalensis Odei phonasco autore." The issue was by Du Chemin in Paris.

A lament on the death of the Duke of Guise was published.

Hans Heugel's "Generosa vivat Hassia," for six voices, was composed in honor of Landgrave Philipp.

Hans Heugel's "Inclitus Hassiaci" was composed in honor of the wedding of William the Wise in this year.

Le Maistre's "Geistlich und Weltliche Teutsche Geseng" appeared.

Merulo's first publication was a new edition of Verdelot's madrigals. It was notable for its unequivocal placing of (cont.) accidentals before the notes to be altered.

Merulo wrote music for Lodovico Dolce's "Troiane" in this year.

Two volumes of tablatures by Newsidler were published at Venice during this year.

Palestrina wrote a madrigal on the death of his friend the poet Annibale Caro.

A collection of settings of plainsong Introits for Sundays and another collection of Introits for Saints' Days, possibly by Porta, were among the earliest publications to be produced by Merulo.

Primavera published his second book of "canzoni napoletane" for three voices.

De Rore (or his printer) included a sonnet-setting by Andrea Gabrieli in the fifth book of Rore's five-voiced madrigals this year.

Scandello's "Il primo libro delle Canzone Napoletane" was published at Nürnberg at this time.

Walther's "Das christ lich Kinderlied Dr. Martin Luthers, Erhalt uns Herr, bei Deinem Wort . . . mit et lichen lateinischen und deutschen Sängen gemehret" appeared.

Zarlino's "Modulationes sex vocum" was published at Venice in this year.

King James I (House of Stuart) of England was born (died 1625).

1566(cont.)

George Gascoigne's "Jocasta," a translation from Euripides, was completed.

George Gascoigne's "The Supposes" appeared.

Netherlandish painting: Pieter Bruegel the Elder, The Numbering of the People At Bethlehem.

(and 1567) One musician who was close to Queen Isabella was Stefano Rossetto from Nizza in Florence. In these two years he dedicated two madrigal books to her.

(to 1567) Paynter's "Palace of Pleasure" was written.

(to 1572) The Papal reign of St. Pius V (born in Bosco).

(and 1584) The "Congregazione dei Musici di Roma sotto l'invocazione di Sta. Cecilia" was founded by Pope Pius V in 1566, but its existence has usually been dated from 1584, when its charter was confirmed by Gregory XIII.

(to 1600) A new building was erected for the Hospital for the Incurables at Venice, originally founded in 1522.

c.1566

Francesco da Milano, Spanish composer of villancicos and great lutenist, died (born c.1490), see also 1543.

Diego Ortiz, Spanish instrumental and sacred composer, died (birthdate unknown).

Verdelot's death was placed at this time by one source but (cont.) c.1540 seems a more accurate choice (born 1500).

Palestrina probably remained titular director of Santa Maria Maggiore until this time.

Palestrina was the first master of music at the Roman Seminary.

Praetorius included musical memoirs of Walther in his work "Syntagma Musicum." Walther had written them in this year.

French sculptor Jean Goujon died (birthdate unknown).

1567

(January 8)
Jacques (Jacob) Vaet, Flemish motet composer, died (birthdate unknown).

(March 10) The dedication of Massimo Troiano's third book of villanelle was signed at Treviso.

(May 3) Leonhard Paminger, German Protestant composer, died (born 1495).

(May 14) Claudio Monteverdi, Italian composer, was born at Cremona (died 1643). Monteverdi was the composer that provided the bridge between the Renaissance and Baroque styles. His contributions in madrigals and the beginnings of opera were immeasurable. Schütz returned to Italy during Monteverdi's lifetime to observe the new developments in music that the latter was leading.

(May 15) Claudio (Giovanni Antionio) Monteverdi was baptised at Cremona.

1567(cont.)

At Caerwys, Flintshire, an Eisteddfod was held, under a commission granted by Queen Elizabeth.

(July 30) Contino was discharged by the cathedral in Brescia because of his refusal to give vocal lessons to the clergy.

(September 12) Striggio's most famous work, the "Chatter of Women at their Washing" was published by Giulio Bonagionta. The latter signed the dedication in the first edition on this date.

(September 12) John Walker was "presented to the living" on Tye's resignation.

(December 9) The official register of the organists at Ely Cathedral began with the name of John Farrant on this date.

(April) The archives of St. John Lateran for this month and year revealed that Palestrina had returned there to assist in the Holy Week music at the church. The chapter of the institution had apparently agreed to overlook earlier differences.

(August) Palestrina resumed his duties at the Villa d'Este at this time and was a candidate for the position of music director to Maximilian II's court in Vienna. His salary demands were so great that da Monte was engaged instead.

Andriano Banchieri was born at Bologna. He was an important theorist, sacred and secular composer, and a leading composer of madrigal-comedies (died 1634).

Thomas Campion, English composer of songs with lute accompaniment, was born (died 1620).

Christoph Demantius, German composer, was born at Reichenberg (died 1643).

Nicolas Formé, motet composer, was born (died 1638). He frequently composed for double choirs.

According to Guicciardini, Verdelot had already died by this date.

Bakfark returned to his native Transylvania. He then received an estate from Prince Sigismund.

Christoforo moved to Rome and turned over the church at Trent to his nephew Lodovico.

Alfonso Ferrabosco I was accused of the murder of a foreign musician, an allegation that was harmful to his reputation.

William Gibbons was appointed as a wait at Cambridge. This fact indicated that he was a singer, instrumentalist, or perhaps both.

Alfonso I Gonzaga built a theatre.

Lassus returned to Italy (also in 1562, 1574, 1578, 1585, and 1587).

Nicholas Morgan was a countertenor and Gentleman of the Chapel Royal.

Palestrina apparently remained at Santa Maria Maggiore at least until the spring of this year. He then resigned from his position of maestro di cappella.

1567(cont.)

Striggio's journey to France possibly intensified his love of the "battaglia," the "caccia," and other descriptive fancies.

Striggio wrote the intermezzi for the "Fabii" of Lotto di Mazza. This was for the occasion of Leonora Medici's christening.

Striggio began his career as a viola virtuoso. Cosimo Bartoli praised him as such in his "Ragionamenti."

Alessandro Striggio was in England and France (Paris).

Waelrant's association with Laet terminated when the latter retired or died in this year.

The Reverendo Monsignore Lodovico Agostini of Ferrara's "Musica . . . sopra le rime bizzarre di M. Andrea Calmo, et altri Autori" was published at Milan.

A collection of Animuccia's Masses was issued at Rome. A copy was preserved in a private library in England.

Primavera and Gian Leonardo dell' Arpa apparently stimulated Giovan Domenico da Nola to new activity since after a lapse of twenty-five years he published a "Primo (sic) libro delle Villanelle alla Napolitana," for three and four voices, and included some pieces by dell' Arpa in the collection.

Baïf began translating the Psalms into vers mesurés. He also composed his Chansonnettes mesurées.

Bartoli's "Ragionamenti" of this year was devoted to instrumentalists from the time of Pope Leo X to c.1545.

William Costeley wrote songs in the "Chansons à 4 et 5 parties," published by Le Roy and Ballard in this year.

Des Prés was esteemed long after his death in many quarters. This was evident from a passage in Bartoli's "Ragionamenti accademici" published in Venice at this time.

Giovanni Ferretti produced five books of canzoni for five voices beginning with the one of this year (also in 1569, 1575, c.1573 and 1585).

Giulio Bonagionta, a prolific editor, arranged for Giovanni Ferretti's first work to be printed by Scotto. It was dedicated to a Paduan nobleman, Benedetto de' Lazzarini.

Lassus' fourth book of madrigals for five voices was published.

Lassus' first German works, the "Newe Teutsche Liedlein mit fünff Stimmen," included twelve secular and three religious songs. The book was published this year.

Lassus' collections of songs in four, five and six parts were preserved at the Royal Library in Munich (The issues included those from 1572, 1583 and 1590 as well as that of this year).

An edition of Lassus' "Sacrae Cantiones" and a collection of twenty-four magnificats were published by Gerlach.

1567(cont.)

A German Catholic hymnal "Geistliche Lieder Und Psalmen was published by Johann Leisentritt, deacon of Bautzen.

Da Monte's second book of five -voiced madrigals was "Roman" in style and content. It appeared at this time.

The first publication of Palestrina's Masses appeared. It included: "De Beata Virgine," "Inviolata," "Sine nomine," "Ad fugam," "Aspice Domine," "Salvum me fac," and "Papae Marcelli." The volume was dedicated to King Philip II of Spain. The publishers were the successors to the Dorici borthers at Rome. The volume contained engraved pictures of the Saviour, the Blessed Virgin, various saints and other religious items, however, there were also several "amorini" and portraits of gallants that inadvertently were included. The book was titled "Missarum . . . Liber Secundus."

Palestrina composed the "Missa Assumpta Est Maria."

Stefano Rossetto ended his career with a madrigal book based on and titled "Il lamento di Olimpia."

Bartolommeo Spontone published his first set of madrigals for five voices at Venice in 1564. There were more editions of this publication in 1567 and 1583.

Alessandro Striggio's "Il cicalamento delle donne al bucato" was published.

Della Viola composed music for (cont.) Argenti's "Lo Sfortunato."

De Wert's fourth book of madrigals was sponsored by Duke Guglielmo of Mantua and was dedicated to him. One of the latter's compositions opened the collection.

A copy of an order by Queen Elizabeth concerning the bestowal of a Silver Harp on the best harper survived.

The Harp was listed as Ireland's national instrument in several state documents.

Day "imprinted" "The first Quinquagene" of Archbishop Parker's metrical version of the Psalms.

Antonio Altoviti, Archbishop of Florence, was the son of Bindo Altoviti, a wealthy man. He was a violent opponent of the Medici, especially Duke Cosimo, and had insurmountable problems in attempting to assume his ecclesiastical duties in Florence until this time.

Thomas Nash, Elizabethan poet, was born (died 1601).

Marinus van Reymerswael, Netherlandish painter, died (born c.1495).

Italian sculpture:
Giovanni da Bologna, Mercury (Bronze statue).

Netherlandish painting:
Pieter Bruegel the Elder, Land of Cockaigne.

(and 1570) Pope Pius V wrote a letter to the Bishop of Lucca (1567) and alluded to the

1567(cont.)

question of eliminating all music other than Gregorian chant from the Church. He complained about some musical performances during Holy Week in Lucca. In 1570 he complained again, this time about Church music in Mexico.

(to 1574) Porta directed the choir at the Cathedral of Ravenna during these years.

(to 1590) Monteverdi spent his youth in Cremona, a period that included these years.

(to 1591) Giovanni Ferretti composed five books of "Canzoni" in five parts published in Venice during these years.

(to 1625) The reign of King James VI (House of Stuart) over Scotland (until 1603) and then as James I over all England.

(to 1643) Wagner's youth and old age were the later counterpart to the momentous change in musical life in Europe and particularly in Italy between these dates which spanned the life of Monteverdi.

c.1567

Jacques Arcadelt, Netherlandish madrigalist, died (born c.1504).

Jean Baptiste Bésard, lutenist and composer for that instrument, was born (date of death unknown).

The entire Psalter was translated into English metre by Archbishop Matthew Parker. It was printed, but never placed on sale.

A play titled "Tancred and Gismunda" was produced at the Inner Temple. Robert Wilmot and three other members of the Inns of Court wrote the drama.

Italian painting: Titian, Martyrdom of St. Lawrence.

1568

(January 8) Da Monte was summoned by Emperor Maximilian II for the position of Imperial choirmaster to succeed Vaet, who died at this time.

(April 19) Duke William of Gonzaga wrote to Pierluigi and assured him that the mass which the latter had sent to him pleased him extremely.

(May 1) It was probably because of Lassus' recommendation that Da Monte went to Vienna to become Emperor Maximilian II's Chapelmaster. Da Monte assumed his duties on this date.

(May 1) Palestrina wrote to Duke William of Gonzaga and expressed his gratitude for a gift of fifty ducats. He also, in the letter, expressed his wish to serve him perpetually.

(July 31) Scipio Gonzaga, a relative of the Duke's, wrote to the Duke as follows: "As I well Know Your Excellency's inclination for music and especially for that of Messer Palestrina, I send you two of his motets."

(September 14) William Byrd married Juliana Birley at St. Margaret's in the Close, at Lincoln.

(November 6) Massimo Troiano was in Venice.

1568(cont.)

(December 15) Palestrina wrote to the Duke of Gonzaga and apologized for the delay in setting certain motets to words chosen by the Duke.

(February) Duke William of Gonzaga married Princess Renata of Lorraine. Lassus composed music in honor of the occasion.

(February) A letter from this date provided the result of de Wert's request for a mass from Palestrina. After the many compliments he had been paid custom demanded that Palestrina inform the Duke that the mass which his "rare musician Messer Giaches" had asked for was ready and that it was being sent. Further, Palestrina stated that if it did not come up to expectation he hoped he would be permitted to try again. The Duke was simply to tell him whether he desired a long or short mass, and whether he was very particular that the words should be clearly understood.

(December) Palestrina went through a fairly serious illness. He informed the Duke of this fact when sending the motets to him at this time.

Juan Bautista Comes, sacred polyphonic composer, was born in Valencia and died there (1643).

Georg Forster, German composer, physician and humanist, died (born c.1510 or c.1514).

Thomas Ulrich, German organist who served at Wernigerode was born (date of death unknown).

Luis de Vargas, Spanish musician and painter, died at (cont.) Seville (born 1502).

John Case was awarded the degree of B.A.

Mateo Flecha the Younger came to Vienna.

Mateo Flecha the Younger was named Abbot of Tihany in Hungary.

A spinet made by Marcus Jadra (Marco dai Cembali; or dalle Spinette) at this time was preserved in Milan.

One of Lassus' motets with five cornetti and two trombones was performed at a ducal wedding in Munich. Another polyphonic composition by him (probably also a motet) was performed by an orchestra made up of eight viols, eight violins, and eight wind instruments. These facts were reported by Troiano.

At the wedding of William V to Renée of Lorraine, Lassus was in charge of the music for the festivities. He composed a motet, "Quid trepidas," for the occasion and also sang Azzaiolo's celebrated "Chi passa" accompanied by his own lute playing.

Da Monte was again in Rome at this time in the service of Cardinal Flavio Orsini.

Scipio Gonzaga, Patriarch of Jerusalem, while staying at the Villa d'Este, saw two of Palestrina's motets. They impressed him so much that he had them sent to the Duke. The result was a commission to Palestrina to compose motets to texts selected by the Duke himself (see 1568, July 31).

During this year Palestrina

1568(cont.)

fulfilled a commission, from Duke Gonzaga of Mantua, for the composition of a mass for use at Santa Barbara. This represented the beginning of a long association between the composer and the nobleman.

The Mantuan archives contained letters beginning at this time and continuing to within a short time of Palestrina's death.

Palestrina was given an opportunity to leave Rome when Emperor Maximilian II, through his ambassador, offered him the position of musical director at the court in Vienna.

Casimiri discovered entries in various church archives relating to rent for a house paid by Palestrina from this date forward.

A private music academy named "Degli Alterati" (the thirsters) was founded by seven Florentine noblemen who met at Giambattista Strozzi's home.

The Sweelinck family was living in a house on the Lange Niezel. The premises had been vacated by a Protestant who had been forced to leave the city.

Troiano became a member of the court chapel at Munich.

The Inquisition at Mons confiscated two motet books published by Waelrant.

Waelrant married for the second time prior to this date.

Robert White went to Westminster Abbey to become Master of the Choristers.

Animuccia's "Magnificat Quinti Toni" appeared.

Animuccia's two Missae de Beata virgine from which the Marian tropes were omitted appeared.

A motet by Animuccia was included in a collection of Motetti published at Venice in this year.

Baldisserra Donati's "Secondo libro a quattro" was published.

Melodies from the "Souterliedekens" were included in the "50 Psalmen Davids" by Cornelius Boskop published this year.

Joachim a Burck's St. John's Passion appeared.

"Tristis est anima mea" by Des Prés was published.

Donato published a book of villanesche (see also 1550 and 1568).

Merulo published a new edition of Festa's collection for three voices.

A collection of madrigals by Flecha the Younger was published at Venice.

Galilei's "Fronimo" was published.

Galilei's "Urania" for guitar was published.

Lassus published his "Selectissimae Cantiones à 6 et pluribus" and also the same for five and four voices.

Le Roy's instruction book for the lute was translated into

1568(cont.)

English by Alford and published in London. It was titled "A Briefe and Easye Instruction to learne the tableture, to conduct and dispose the hande unto the Lute, Englished by J.A." A cut of the lute was included.

Molino-Burchiella's great interest in music apparently led him to become a musician himself. This was indicated by the implication of a book by Merulo, "dilettevoli madrigali" for four voices, dedicated to the composer Maddalena Casulana of Vinceza and containing compositions by Antonio Molino.

Neuber published the anonymous "Deo gratias."

Palestrina's 1555 book of secular madrigals was reprinted.

Lute duets were included in Phalèse's "Luculentum theatrum musicum" of this date.

A mass by Robledo carrying this date appeared.

"Arte de Tañer Fantasia" was written by Santa Maria. It was a treatise on musical interpretation and technique for keyboard instruments.

Italianate characteristics were evident in the lieder published by Scandello in this year.

De Rore published a "Dialogo a 7" by Bartolommeo Spontone at this time.

Striggio's "Ecce beatam lucem" dated from this approximate time.

Two motets by Vaet were included (cont.) in P. Ioannelli's "Novus Thesaurus Musicus" published at Venice. The volume also contained a motet "in obitum Iacobi Vaet."

A French chanson by Vaet was included in Buchaw's "Harmonine" published this year.

Settings of nine sections of Psalm 118 included four by White dated from this approximate year.

Cardinal Giulio Feltrio della Rovero founded a boys' school at Ravenna.

The "Eighty Years" war for Spanish political and religious freedom was precipatated by the actions of King Philipp II.

Ventadour, a famous musical name, was given to a street and a lyric theatre in Paris. The name came from a village in the Limousin that became a duchy in this year ruled by Duke Gilbert de Levis, whose descendants have since carried the name of Levis de Ventadour.

Roger Ascham, Elizabethan scholar and writer, died (born 1515).

Luigi Tansillo, Neopolitan poet, died (born 1510). He was the founder of "lagrime" poetry.

The "Bishops' Bible" of 1568 was published.

Cornelis Boschop published a collection of fifty psalm settings.

Gabriel Fiamma, canon at the Lateran, published his "Rime Spirituali."

1568(cont.)

Luis de Vargas, Spanish painter and musician, died in Seville (born 1502).

Italian architecture: Ammanati, Florence, Pitti Palace (court 110' high).

Netherlandish painting: Bruegel the Elder, Peasant Dance.

Netherlandish painting: Bruegel the Elder, Parable of the Blind.

(to 1574) Felice Anerio served as a choirboy at Santa Maria Maggiore and learned the principals of counterpoint from Nanino.

(and 1574) A later parallel to Attaingnant's "Tres breve . . . introduction" was written and published by Le Roy in the form of an "Instruction de partir toute musique facilement en tablature de luth." It survived only in the two English translations published in Cordon, one in this year and one in 1574.

(and 1574) Ruffo's psalms and mass were described in the prefaces as having been written for his patron Cardinal Borromeo in accordance with the decrees of the Council of Trent.

(to 1575) Kerle served as organist at Augsburg during these years.

(and 1577) Jan Willemszoon Lossy was described as a "hoechconter" (countertenor) from Dordrecht and his salary was placed at 30 stuivers per month in this year. He was given an increase in 1577 for assisting by doubling the lower voices on his bass shawm.

(to 1580) Antonius Scandellus (Scandelli) was one of Schütz' predecessors at Dresden during these years and composed both a "Passion" and a "Resurrection."

(to 1580) Pietro Vinci was maestro di cappella at Santa Maria Maggiore at Bergamo during this period.

(and 1584) Galilei set five of Palestrina's madrigals for lute and included them in a collection of similar compositions which he published under the title of "Fronimo" through Scotto of Venice in this year and again in 1584.

(to 1584) Italian architecture: Vignola, Rome, Il Gesù (Interior 225' x 115').

(and 1589) It was probable that Andrea Gabrieli sang for members of the Accademia Filarmonica in the Petrarch sestina. The work was published by Bonagionta in this year and then reprinted as the first selection in his posthumous "Madrigali e Ricercari" for four voices in 1589. It must have been intended as chamber music.

(to 1603) Da Monte was chief Kappelmeister in Vienna.

c.1568

Giles Farnaby, English madrigalist as well as virginal composer, was born (died 1600), see c.1560.

Christoph Thomas Walliser was born at Strassbourg (date of death unknown).

Ingegneri probably settled at Cremona where he was most active.

A book on music by Päminger was

c.1568(cont.)
published by Ratisponae.

The German Psalmes of David for four to six voices by Georg Weber was published.

De Wert moved to the court of the Duke of Mantua but his life was disturbed by the apparent misconduct of his wife.

Netherlandish painting: Pieter Brueghel the Elder, A Country Wedding.

Netherlandish painting: Bruegel the Elder, Head of An Old Peasant Woman.

French painting: School of Clouet, Portrait of François de France, Count of Alençon.

1569

(January 25) Robert Parsons was drowned in the Trent River at Newark (birthdate unknown).

(February 11) John Keper of Hart Hall, Oxford, was awarded the degree of M.A.

(February 22) William Byrd was sworn as a Gentleman of the Chapel Royal, succeeding Robert Parsons.

(March 1) One of Da Monte's madrigal books from Naples carried this date, although he was back in Vienna.

(May 1) Alessandro Striggio wrote the intermezzi for the "Vedova" by Giovambattista Cini, performed on this date in the great hall of the Palazzo Vecchio in honor of a visit from Archduke Charles of Graz.

(October 28) Thomas Causton, (cont.) English Protestant composer, died (birthdate unknown).

(November 5) Farrant was reappointed a Gentleman of the Chapel Royal and Master of the Choristers.

(November 18) Byrd's son Christopher was baptized at St. Margaret's.

(May) A seven-part motet by Palestrina was published at this time. It started with a phrase that was identical with the first phrase of Saint Anne's Tune, however, after the opening section there is no further resemblance.

Giulio Cesare Barbetta, Italian lute composer, was born (died 1603).

Manuel Cardoso, Portuguese composer of masses and motets, was born at Frontiera (died 1650).

Giambattista Marini, an overly sentimental composer, was born (died 1625).

George Quitschreiber, Thuringian composer, was born (died 1638).

Du Caurroy was appointed director of the King's band in this year and continued in that position during the reigns of Charles IX, Henry III, and Henry IV.

Cavazzoni was still alive.

Alfonso Ferrabosco I protested his innocense in the murder of a foreign musician. At this time the matter was settled in his favor and he bound himself to Elizabeth's service for

1569(cont.)

life and was once more granted his pension.

Alfonso Ferrabosco I went to Italy to settle his affairs in that country.

Ferretti's contacts tended to be more and more with Rome from this time forward.

Ferretti signs a dedication at Ancona.

A spinet, signed by Annibalis Mediolanesis and carrying this date was preserved in Hamburg. It was brought there from the palace of San Severino at Cremona, Lombardy.

Cardinal d'Este was a strong patron of Palestrina's as was evidenced from the dedication to him of the volume of motets published this year.

Pevernage became permanent vicar at Notre Dame.

Porta left Padua to become chapel-master at Ravenna. He also became a teacher in the boys' school in that city founded by Giulio Feltrio della Rovero.

Robledo returned to Spain to become choir master at the older of the two cathedrals at Saragossa.

Cyriacus Spangenberg's statements in the "Cithara Lutheri," published at Erfurt in this year, were significant since he was considered to be one of the connoisseurs of mastersinging.

Striggio's intermedio "L'Amico Fido" was performed in Florence with a staging of such pomp and music of such style as to be called a forerunner of seventeenth century opera.

Striggio's "Ecce beatam lucem" was performed during this year at the marriage of Duke William of Bavaria and Renée of Lorraine. This was reported by Troiano in his "Dialoghi."

Victoria became Maestro di Capella of S. Maria di Montserrato at Rome.

Barbetta's "Gagliarda Del Passo E Mezo Detto Il Moderno" for guitar appeared.

Ferretti produced his second book of canzoni for five voices (see also 1567, 1575, c.1573 and 1585).

Ferretti's second book of five-voiced canzoni was dedicated to Giovanni Ferro.

Giulio Fiesco of Ferrara dedicated his "Musica nova," a book of five-part madrigals published this year, to Lucrezia and Leonora d'Este, Tasso's patronesses.

Nicolas de la Grotte's "Chansons de Pierre de Ronsard . . ." were published this year. It contained short chordal pieces in a simple, graceful style. Grotte was organist to King Henry III.

The first polyphonic setting of the complete psalter in German was by Sigmund Hemmel and was published in this year. It was for four parts and titled "Der gantz Psalter Davids."

1569(cont.)

Adam Berg, court publisher at Munich, published Lassus' "Cantiones aliquot à 5." It included fourteen selections. Two books of "Sacrae Cantiones" partly new were also published, all in Louvain.

Mazzone described the ruling principles of madrigal composition during this period in the introduction to his first book of madrigals for four voices published at this time.

Maddalena Casulana of Vicenza collected a number of Antonio Molino's madrigals and dedicated them to Francesco Pesaro, the "capitano" of her native town. She was a friend of the composer.

Da Monte's second book of madrigals for four voices appeared during the spring of this year.

Georg Ostermayer of Brassó left a fragmentary motet that he composed in Heilbronn in a manuscript that was found in that city.

Palestrina's second volume of masses was printed by the Dorici brothers.

Palestrina's first book of motets, for five, six, and seven voices, was published by Scotto through the Dorici brothers at Rome in this year. The collection was dedicated to Cardinal d'Este. Included therein was his six-part "Dum complerentur" and other motets that were probably composed during the summer at Tivoli. In the preface to the collection Palestrina spoke of "those who devote their gifts to light and (cont.) vain ideas."

Several compositions by Clemens non Papa's were included in the "Recueil des fleurs," published this year at Louvain.

Primavera published a book of "canzoni napoletane" for four voices.

Striggio's "Card-Game" was published.

Ivo de Vento's lieder of this year showed Italianate characteristics.

Ulrich Schütz III, Imperial Secretary at Saragossa at this time, established a foundation with 4,000 gulden, the annual interest on which, 200 gulden, was to be awarded, upon application, as a wedding gift to the female descendants of his father, Hieronymus, burgomaster of Chemnitz, or, if none existed to Hieronymus' brothers' female heirs.

Edmund Spenser was admitted as a sizar (an indigent student) to Pembroke Hall, Cambridge, the university where most of England's poets studied.

Pieter Bruegel the Elder, the eminent Netherlandish painter, died (born c.1525).

A portrait of Thomas Whythorne, painted in this year, was preserved in a private collection in England.

(to 1572) The so-called "Antwerp Polyglot Bible" was published during this period at the expense of King Philip of Spain.

1569(cont.)

(and 1572, 1575) During Palestrina's lifetime thirty six-part motets by him were published in the collections of motets from these years.

(to 1582) The names of eight Musical Representations produced during these years were mentioned by Leo Alcatius in his "Drammaturgia."

(to 1593) Palestrina especially enjoyed composing five-part motets. These and the offertories were published in 1593 and he wrote nearly two hundred such compositions between 1569 and the aforementioned date.

(to 1600) Jean de Castro composed many sets of madrigals, odes, sonnets, and sacred songs during this period.

c.1569

Du Caurroy entered the royal service.

Johann de Cleve set ten melodies of Protestant lieder and Andreas Gigler the rector at Graz set ten of the same. These were all included in a four-part collection of rhymed Gospel sermons in German, assembled by Gigler and published at about this time.

(to 1587) Ingegneri published five books of madrigals for five voices during this period.

1570

(March 15) George Bacon became rector of Newton after Tye's resignation.

(March 23) A letter from Palestrina under this date indicated that the Duke has re- (cont.) cently sent a motet and a madrigal to the composer for correction and criticism.

(August 12) On this date Don Annibale Capello wrote Duke William of Gonzaga and informed him that he would shortly send him a motet by Palestrina composed for King Philip II of Spain.

(September 2) Palestrina's motet "Domine in virtute tua" was sent to Duke William of Gonzaga on this date with apologies for the poor copy, "as no one in Tivoli could be found to do it better."

(April) Troiano and another singer, Camillo of Parma, purportedly murdered the violinist Battista Romano for revenge. They fled and were pursued by State agents with a warrant.

(May) Palestrina moved into a new house which he had bought from relatives of his friend Canon Attilio Ceci of St. John Lateran.

(June) Guillaume Franc, organist and choir director at Geneva prior to Bourgeois, died (birthdate unknown).

(November) Delmotte suggested that Lassus' visit to Paris had to do with a new Academy of music, for which Charles had issued a letter-patent of permission at this time.

Sebastián de Aguilera de Heredia, an Aragonese organist, composer and monk, died (birthdate unknown).

Jobst von Brandt, Lutheran

1570(cont.)

composer, died (born 1517).

John Cooper, English musician, was born (died 1627) and took the name of Giovanni Coperario. This was not unusual for English musicians who felt that an Italian name would help their career.

Hans Gerle, a fine lutenist, died (birthdate unknown).

Valentin Geuck was born (date of death unknown).

Caspar Hassler was probably born (date of death unknown). He enjoyed a fine reputation as an organist and clavecinist. He was the third brother of Hans Leo Hassler.

Volupius Musagetes (Wolfgang Schoensleder), author on music, was born (died 1651).

Tomás de Santa Maria, author of Arte de Tañer Fantasia, died (birthdate unknown).

Johann Walther, German music publisher and composer, died at Torgau (born 1496).

Animuccia became maestro di cappella of Neri's Oratory at San Girolamo.

A spinet made by Baffo, a Venetian, and carrying this date, was preserved at a hotel in Paris.

King Charles IX granted Baïf certain privileges in regard to an academy "de poesie et de musique." The plan, however, did not appear to include dramatic representation. Baïf in conjunction with Joachim Thibaut (cont.) (known as de Courville), joueur de lyre du roi, founded the Academie to establish a union between the two arts but it was a complete failure.

Lucrezia Bendidio was the object of persistent attentions and poetic words from G.B. Pigna, the Duke's first minister.

De Castro was at Lyons.

In all probability it was Costeley who organized the Confraternity of St. Cecilia at Evreux during this year. He was the first elected "prince."

Lassus was Knighted by Emperor Maximilian II at the diet of Spires.

A "Lorenzini del liuto" was in the service of Cardinal d'Este at this time.

Da Monte was sent on a short trip to the Netherlands to recruit musicians for the emperor's chapel choir.

Gian Domenico Montella, a Neopolitan composer of sacred music, was born (date of death unknown).

Georg Otto became a candidate for the position of cantor at the Dresden court and was rejected, however, he became the cantor at Salza.

Guglielmo I commissioned a mass and several motets from Palestrina. He greatly admired Palestrina and they carried on a voluminous correspondence at this time while he was sending his own compositions to the composer for revision and criticism.

1570(cont.)

A part-song by Scandelli was published at Dresden in this year in which the cackling of a hen laying an egg was imitated with the sounds, "Ka, ka, ka, ka, ne-ey! Ka, ka, ka, ka, ne-ey!"

Animuccia published his second book of laude. This one required more highly trained singers than his previous compositions had.

Cerone devoted an entire book to a study of Palestrina's Missa L'Homme armé, published this year.

The "Clifford Manuscript" appeared.

Corteccia's compositions included "Responsoria et lectiones hebdomadae sanctae," composed at this time.

Filippo, Duke of Flanders, dedicated his book of four-voiced madrigals to his compatriots, the Flemish students of Padua.

Andrea Gabrieli dedicated the second book of his "Madrigali a cinque" to Molino. The latter was known in Italian literary history as Burchiella. Included in the collection was the madrigal, "Vaghi augeletti che per valli e monte."

Andrea Gabrieli's "Missarum sex vocum, liber primus" was published in this year.

Guerrero's five-part "Ave, Virgo sanctissima" was published at this time.

Phalèse and Bellère published a collection of chansons devoted (cont.) to the works of Lassus, da Monte and de Rore.

Lassus' twenty-three new Cantiones for six voices, two books of chansons containing eighteen new ones and a book of twenty-nine madrigals were published at Munich, Louvain and Venice respectively. France was represented by an edition of chansons "mellange d'Orlande de Lassus" that, however, contained little new material.

Da Monte published his chansons for four and five voices, in which he was associated with Rore and Lasso. This was probably the same volume published by Phalèse and Beuere.

Palestrina's brilliant "Hexachord Mass" was published in this year.

The first publication of these Masses by Palestrina appeared: "Spem in alium," Io mi son giovinetta," "Brevis," "De feria," "L'Homme armé," for five voices, "Repleatur os meum," "De Beata Virgine," "Ut re mi fa sol la." The volume was dedicated to King Philip II of Spain. The publishers were the successors to the Dorici brothers.

A "Second libre des Chansons a Quatre et cinq Parties . . ." was published at Louvain by Phalèse, and at Antwerp, by Bellère during this year.

Primavera published his third book of "canzoni napoletane" for three voices.

The "Passio secundum Matthaeum" was published at

1570(cont.)

Nürnberg by Clemens Stephani in this year.

Alessandro Striggio's "Secondo libro a cinque" appeared.

Utendal published "Penitential Psalms and Orationes."

Middleton, the author of the "Schoolmaster," was born (died 1627).

Michael Tempest was proven guilty of taking part in the Northern Catholic Rebellion in this year.

"The Schoolmaster" by Roger Ascham was published.

Delorme, French Renaissance architect, died (born c.1515).

Francesco Primaticcio, French architect and a pupil of Romano, died (born 1504).

Jacopo Sansovino, Italian architect, died (born 1486).

English architecture: Kirby Hall, court (100' wide).

Italian architecture: Palladio, The Five Orders.

An illustration from a map of this year showed St. Peter's in the course of reconstruction.

(and 1574) Duke Guglielmo Gonzaga of Mantua sent three of his compositions to Palestrina for criticism, a madrigal and a motet in 1570, and a mass in 1574.

(and 1574, 1575) A manuscript note in the margin of a copy of Burney's History (vol.iii.p.66) (cont.) at the Royal College of Music Library in London stated that "Robert White commenced org. of West. Abbey anno 1570, and master of the choristers 1574. Died 1575."

(to 1577) Annibale Zoilo was a contralto in the choir during this period. He had previously been maestro di cappella at St. John Lateran and composed two collections of madrigals.

(to 1579) England was greatly influenced by and in awe of Italy's culture during these years.

(to 1579) Lodovico lived in Rome during this period.

(to 1579) Palestrina's interest was obviously in musical "form." He repeated musical sections with different texts, in the style of a French chanson, a practice that madrigalists of this period found objectionable.

(to 1583) Francisco Martinez di Loscos served as maestro of the Viceroyal Chapel during these years.

(to 1590) French painting: Anonymous, Lady At Her Toilet.

(to 1591) Asola published masses for three and eight voices.

(to 1600) Regnart's compositions were the most popular of German lied publications during this period.

(to c.1620) During this period organ playing in Germany was restricted almost entirely to what was known as the art of "coloring" sacred or secular melodies by the insertion of

1570(cont.)

extraneous passages, based on the same pattern, and placed between each note or chord of the melody.

(to 1657) In Heidelberg, organ playing was forbidden during these years.

c.1570

Johann Agricola, music professor at Erfurt and composer, was born at Nürnberg (date of death unknown).

John Bennet, English composer, was born (died 1615).

Erhard Bodenschatz, sacred composer, was born at Lichtenberg in the Erzgebirge (died 1638).

Marco Antonio Cavazzoni, Italian composer, died (born c.1490).

Gian Paolo Cima, Italian ricercari composer, was born (date of death unknown).

Fabio Costantini was born at Rome (date of death unknown).

Richard Dering, English sacred composer, was born (died c.1658).

The Neopolitan actor, Silvio Fiorillo, was born (died 1620). He was the first to portray the figure of Pulcinella on the stage.

Antoine Francisque, French theorist and lutenist, was born (died 1605).

The Rev. Edward Gibbons, Mus. Bac., was born (died c.1650). He was the son of William Gibbons, one of the (cont.) Waits of the town of Cambridge and the brother of Orlando Gibbons. He did, however, compose in his own right.

Anthony Holborne, English composer of "The Fruit of Love," "Heigh Ho," and "Holiday," was born (died 1602).

Robert Jones, English song composer, was born (date of death unknown).

Pacelli, a late contemporary of Palestrina's, was born (date of death unknown).

Salomone Rossi, Hebreo madrigal composer, was born (died c.1628, see also 1587.

Robert White became organist of Westminster Abbey.

Ingegneri's large output of compositions began about this time with his "First Book of four-part Madrigals."

Luzzaschi's madrigals were composed around this time.

Benedetto Serafico di Nardo, a Neapolitan, set the outbursts of Olimpia and Fiordiligi expressly calling them "lamenti."

In type of keyboard texture as well as in ornamentation the round dance or "branle" of Brabant was closely allied with psalm settings, since both originated in the area of Antwerp at this time.

Francis Kindlemarsh, a poet of the period wrote "From Virgin's womb this day did spring," a poem with four verses.

c.1570(cont.)

The term "villanesca" was dropped about this time in favor of "villanella."

Many fine instruments of the whole violin family were being made at Cremona by this time.

French painting: Antoine Caron, "Triumphs of the Seasons" series.

Spanish painting:
Luis de Morales, Virgin and Child.

(to 1593) Henry Ainsworth was a Biblical scholar at this time.

1571

(January 20) William Byrd's daughter Elizabeth was baptized at St. Margaret's.

(February 15) Michael Praetorius originally named Schulz (Schulze), a notable contributor to Protestant church music, composer and author, was born at Kreutzberg in Thüringen (died 1621).

(April 1) Palestrina became Master of the Julian Chapel.

(May 16)
Maria Domitilla Monteverdi was born (date of death unknown).

(June 7) Francesco Corteccia, Italian madrigal composer, died at Florence (born c1510 or c1520).

(October 7) After the Battle of Lepanto, on this date, Zarlino was commissioned to compose music for commemoration of the great Venitian victory.

(March) When Animuccia died, Palestrina was restored to his (cont.) old position as Maestro at the Vatican.

(March) Giovanni Animuccia, Italian sacred composer, died at Rome. One source placed his death at 1563 (born c.1499 or 1500).

(March) Palestrina remained in the service of Cardinal d'Este until the end of March of this year (see April 1 entry).

(August) Some details of Lassus' stay in Paris were included in the "Primus liber modulorum á5," published by Le Roy, at whose home he stayed during his visit to Paris at this time.

Some musicologists claim that when Palestrina resumed his duties of maestro di cappella at the Julian Chapel after Animuccia's death, he also continued Animuccia's work in Neri's Oratory.

Andrea Calmo, poet and comedian, died (born 1510).

Johann Kepler, writer on music, was born (died 1630).

Giovan Battista Strozzi, writer of madrigal texts for Corteccia, died (born 1504).

Caspar Tieffenbrucker, noted instrument maker, died (born c.1514).

Any actual history of the Académie founded by Baïf was unclear.

Bakfark retired to Padua.

Giulio Cesare Colonna became Prince of Palestrina.

1571(cont.)

William Costeley was a member of the society called "Puy de musique en honneur de Ste. Cecile" at Evreux and on occasion entertained members at his own house in Evreux.

Eccard went to Paris with Lassus.

John Farrant was organist, for various periods, at Ely, Bristol, Salisbury, and Hereford Cathedrals from this date forward.

Fernando de las Infantas went to Italy to have his compositions published and apparently had a subvention from King Philip II.

A spinet signed Benedictus Florianus and carrying this date was preserved.

Two fanatical objectors broke into the church at Frankfort am Main and seized the organ.

De la Hèle was enrolled as a student at the University of Louvain in this year and was under Royal protection.

Nicholas and Jerome Laniere were musicians to Queen Elizabeth.

Lassus was in France during the better part of this year.

Le Roy was instrumental in Lassus' acceptance at the French court.

Le Roy entertained Lassus as his house guest.

The "Le Puy de Musique" was founded at Evreux, Normandy.

Nanino succeeded Palestrina as maestro di cappella at Santa (cont.) Maria Maggiore.

Palestrina moved into a house near St. Peter's on the corner of a little street later named Calle del Palestrina. He moved in with his wife, and sons, three or four choirboys and a private pupil. He remained at this house until his death.

Palestrina was awarded the honorary title of "maestro compositore."

Palestrina composed a madrigal on the great naval victory in the Gulf of Lepanto and in it used descending octave leaps in three of the voices to illustrate the word, "impallidir."

Palestrina sent two masses, one for five and the other for six voices, to the Papal Choir as a gift.

Cesare Veccia was organist of St. Agapito.

Victoria succeeded Palestrina as maestro at the Collegium Romanum (seminary).

Agostini's "Musical Riddles" appeared.

One of the earliest examples of marked fingering was that given by Ammerbach in his "Orgel odor Instrument Tabulatur," published at Leipzig this year.

The books by Nikolaus Ammerbach included large numbers of simple dance tunes.

An anonymous treatise at Besancon was concerned with instruction in contrapuntal writing.

1571(cont.)

Corteccia's compositions included "Canticorum liber primus" published this year.

Andrea Gabrieli's "Canzoni alla francese per l'organo" was published this year.

Andrea Gabrieli published a book of "greghesche" and "giustiniane."

These years of Kerle's life spent in Germany and Bohemia were productive particularly of motets. Several collections of them appeared at this time at Nuremberg, Munich, and other German cities.

Le Roy published a volume by Lassus called "moduli" which was dedicated to King Charles IX.

Le Roy and Ballard's "Livre d'Airs de Cour miz sur le Luth" was published.

The Reverend Padre Mattia Mauro composed two books of four-and -five-voiced madrigals this year.

Antonio Molino wrote the texts for the "greghesche" published by Andrea Gabrieli. The collection was dedicated to the Provveditore delle Gambarare, Girolamo Orio.

Palestrina composed secular piéces d'occasion one of which immortalized the victory at Lepanto. It was called "Le selv' avea al Lido Eusono Il superbe Ottoman col ferro tutte Recise."

Palestrina's Second Edition of motets of 1563 was published.

Phalèse's "Liber primus" appeared.

Striggio published two books of six-voiced compositions. The second one appeared this year (see 1560).

Pompilio Venturi, a Sienese dilettante, dedicated a book of three-voiced villanelle "fatte in lode di molte Signore, et Gentildonne Romane" to Madonna Cleria.

Thomas Whythorne's seventy-six "Songes to three, fower, and five voyces" were published by John Day. The songs were polyphonic in texture and this was the second such collection.

One of Petrarch's sonnets appeared as a canzonetta in the first book of the "Napoletane" by Giovanni Zappasorgo da Treviso. There was no linguistic reminiscence or any intention of parody.

Zarlino's treatise "Dimostrationi armoniche" was published at Venice this year. It was reprinted in 1573.

Don Juan of Austria's naval victory at Lepanto took place.

Sir Robert Bruce Cotton, English literary noble, was born (died 1631).

Paris Bordone, Italian painter, died (born 1500).

Benvenuto Cellini, Italian sculptor and goldsmith, died (born 1500).

French painting: Attributed to François Clouet, Portrait of Elizabeth of Austria.

1571(cont.)

(and 1573, 1577) Utendal published three books of motets, one in each of these years.

(and 1575) Two Te Deum settings by Kerle appeared, one at each year indicated.

(to 1575) Nanini was Maestro di Cappella for the Basilica Liberiana at St. Maria Maggiore during these years.

(1575, and 1583) Elias Nicolaus Ammerbach published three tablatures, one in each of the above years. The third was actually a thoroughly revised edition of the first.

(to 1581) Palestrina's masses that appeared in the fourth book were composed during these years.

(to 1584) Impressive concerts were given under the direction of Luzzasco Luzzaschi and Tarquinia Molza. They were for the entertainment of the court at Ferrara and were well received.

(to 1586) Arnoldus de Fine served as Kapellmeister at Copenhagen during this period.

(to 1599) The Báthori princes of Hungary in this year made every effort for the old faith. Sigismund, for whom Diruta wrote his "Transiluano," was especially interested in the organ.

(to 1792) Thirteen Polish cantionales written during this period were preserved in a private library at Elbling, Germany.

c.1571

Prince Sigismund Báthori, a Polish lutenist, was born (died 1613).

Thomas Tomkins, English composer and pupil of Byrd's, was born (died 1656).

1572

(August 24) As the St. Bartholomew's Day massacre at Paris continued on this date the Huguenots at Lyons were attacked by local fanatics.

(August 24) Admiral Coligny was murdered in a room in the Rue de Bethisy in Paris.

(August 27) Claude Goudimel, Flemish composer of chansons and masses, died at Lyons (born c.1505). His birth has also been given as c.1525. His death came about through assassination after the St. Bartholomew's Day massacre.

(November 7) According to a will carrying this date Palestrina's wife Lucrezia received half of a small inheritance on the death of her sister Violante.

(December 7) Thomas Butler was elected master of the choristers and organist at Lincoln "on y[e] nomination and commendation of Mr. William Byrd." He was to share the duties with Tallis and thus succeed Byrd who was leaving.

(May) Pope Pius V died. He was buried in St. Maria Maggiore, where his tomb in the Sixtine Chapel is still intact.

(September) Don Annibale Capello wrote the Duke to the effect that he was sending him a book

1572(cont.)

of motets for use by the choir of Santa Barbara. It was a newly published volume from Scotto of Venice.

Pierre Certon, a chanson composer in the "old school" and an important church composer, died (birthdate unknown).

Cardinal Ippolito d'Este, Palestrina's patron, died.

Sir William Petre died (birthdate unknown).

Waclaw Szamotulczyk, Polish composer, died in Poland (born c.1520).

Christopher Tye, English Reformation composer, died (born c.1500).

Nicola Vicentino, a leading Italian Madrigal composer, died (born 1511).

Valentin Balassi, a renowned lyric poet, performed the Ungaresca (Ungarischer Tanz) at the imperial court.

Byrd began to share his duties of organist at the Chapel Royal with Tallis and then left at the end of the year.

John Case received the degree of M.A.

The accounts of King Charles IX of France showed a payment of 50 livres to one of the King's musicians, the money to be used to purchase a Cremona violin.

Alfonso Ferrabosco I had returned to England.

De la Hèle was appointed maitre (cont.) de chapelle at St. Rombaut, Malines.

Lassus travelled a great deal at this time and his compositional output ceased for the moment.

The Duke of Mantua promised the position of organist at Santa Barbara to Rodolf, Palestrina's son. This was certainly a decision influenced by the dedication of a motet book containing works by Rodolfo and his brother Silla to the Duke. The book had been published by the elder Palestrina and was essentially his own work.

Duke William of Gonzaga came to Rome and Palestrina almost surely was invited to see him. However, no concrete evidence supported this assumption.

Philippe Rogier was in Spain as a choirboy.

A volume of Arcadelt's chansons, edited by Goudimel, was published.

Girolamo Bargagli wrote a "Dialogo de giuochi che nelle vegghie sanesi si usano di fare."

Girolamo Conversi published his first work, a volume of canzoni alla napoletana" for five voices.

Andrea Gabrieli's "Madrigali a 5 voci, liber primus" included twenty-four madrigals and six canzoni. His setting of Petrarch's sonnet "Due rose fresche e colte in paridiso" was also contained in the book.

Lassus published a set of fifteen German songs.

A collection, dedicated to

1572(cont.)

Charles IX by Ronsard, was published in this year. It was titled "Meslanges de Chansons" and contained songs for four, six, and even eight voices, by the best-known French and Belgian masters, including des Près, Le Jeune, and Mouton.

Palestrina's First Book of Masses was published at Rome. (Roma apud heredes Aloysii Dorici, 1572) by the Dorici brothers firm. The edition was in folio style with coarse but legible type.

Palestrina's second book of motets appeared and contained one composition by his son, Angelo, as well as works by Rodolfo and Silla. He had taught all three of his sons. Included in the book, which was dedicated to Duke Guglielmo, were Palestrina's own "Gaude Barbara beata," and "Beata Barbara ad locum" written for the Mantuan church. "Domine in virtute tua" and "Laudate Dominum" also appeared. Quite possibly Gardano was also involved in the publication of the volume (Earlier motets had been issued in 1569).

Phalèse's "Een duytsch musyck boeck," a collection of chansons, appeared.

Vicentino's five-part canzone da sonare, "La Bella," appeared. Book V of his madrigals was published.

The first collection of Victoria's compositions was published with a dedication to Cardinal Otto von Truchsess von Waldburg. This volume represented most of his motets and (cont.) was issued at Venice by Gardano under the title "O Vos Omnes." The motets were for four to eight voices.

Landgrave Moritz, the son of the ruler William the Wise, was born in Cassel (date of death unknown).

Jean Girin of Lyons in a book, "Traité de la Musette" included an excellent drawing of the Shepherd's Pipe in its various forms, with the method of holding it, and thereby distinguished it from the "Cromorne" and "Hautbois."

The martial military oboe was known in Hungary under its local name "tárogató."

After the Huguenot massacre on St. Bartholomew's Day in this year, help from France was out of the question and Dutch hopes lay with Protestant England.

Angelo Bronzino, Italian painter, died (born 1503).

François Clouet, French painter, died (born c.1520).

(and 1573, 1576, 1583, and 1590) Lassus' German lieder were published in collections at the above dates.

(and 1575) More than fifty eight part motets were included in the collected edition of Palestrina's works. Only ten, however, were published during his lifetime and these were in the motet books of 1572 and 1575.

(and 1575) Della Viola's two books of Canzoni Napolitane for five voices were published at

1572(cont.)

Venice in these two years respectively.

(to 1575) Sir Philip Sidney made a tour of Italy and the Continent in an attempt to bring the German Protestant states into a confederation headed by England.

(to 1580) Palestrina's sons Rodolfo, Angelo, and Silla, as well as the composer's wife, died from epidemics during this period.

(to 1585) The Papal reign of St. Gregory XIII (born in Bologna).

c.1572

Martin Peerson, a keyboard and string composer and contributor to the Fitzwilliam Virginal Book, was born (died 1650).

Robert Granjon published music at Lyons at this time.

1573

(January 3) A letter to the Duke of Mantua from Bishop Odescalco written from Rome on this date revealed the death of Palestrina's son and brother.

(January 31) Giulio Cesare Monteverdi was born (date of death unknown).

(March 15) Hugh Bellet was "presented to the living" of Doddington-cum-March after Tye's death.

(July 8) Godescalcus Praetorius (Schulz), composer and Professor of Philosophy at Würtenberg, died (born 1528).

(October 18) A letter on this date from Annibale Capello to the Duke of Mantua stated that Palestrina had been unable to fulfill certain desires expressed by the Duke because of indisposition affecting both his head and his sight.

(December 7) John Thorne, English musician and composer, died and was buried in York Cathedral (birthdate unknown).

(January) Silla Pierluigi, Palestrina's son, died (birthdate unknown).

(January) Robert Johnson, lutenist and composer, was retained in the household of Sir Thomas Kytson, of Hengrave Hall, Suffolk.

(July) Lassus published the first volume of the "Patrocinium Musices."

Antonio Altoviti, Italian madrigalist of some renown, died (born 1521).

Christian Erbach, German composer who wrote somewhat in the Italian style, was born at Algesheim (date of death unknown).

Melchior Franck, German dance composer, was born (died 1639).

Ellis Gibbons, English composer and brother of Orlando, was born (died 1603).

Juan Pablo Pujol, a Spanish composer and choirmaster at Barcelona, Saragossa and Tarragona, was born at Barcelona (died 1626).

Sweelinck's father, known as

1573(cont.)

"Mr. Pieter," an organist in his own right, died (birthdate unknown).

John Wilbye, eminent English madrigal composer, was born (died 1638).

Cornelis Boschop (Boscoop) succeeded Swellinck's father as organist of the Oude Kerk in Amsterdam.

The renownded "Improperia" were heard during Holy Week at St. Peter's.

Palestrina's motet book of this year included exquisite views, apparently of contemporary Roman churches, villas, etc.

For a brief period the German and Roman seminaries were combined, but in this year Pope Gregory XIII reorganized the former as a separate institution, with Victoria as maestro di cappella. The composer received a commission to set the psalm "By the waters of Babylon," the setting to be used for a farewell service prior to the departure of students from their old home in the Palazzo Colonna to their new one at the Palazzo della Valle.

The first volume of Adam Berg's "Patro-cinium musices" was issued.

Venetian poet Zambo del Val Brembana's political madrigal on the naval victory at Lepanto was set to music by Ferretti at the end of his first book for six voices published this year.

Ferretti's first book of six -voiced "canzoni alla (cont.) napoletana" was issued.

The Goudimel Psalter, in a translation by Ambrosius Lobwasser, first appeared in this year.

Ingegneri's Book I of Masses for five to eight voices was published.

Keuchenthal's Hymn-book, published at Würtenburg in this year, was a very fine collection of sixteenth century melodies. A copy was preserved in the Berlin Library.

An engraving by Johann Nel showed the nine instrumentalists and five singers of the chapel of the Duke of Bavaria. It was on the lower portion of the title page of the Patrocinium Musices by Lassus, published at Munich by Adam Berg.

The term vaux-de-vire (voix-de -ville) appeared on the title -page of Le Roy's "Premier livre de chansons en forme de vau-de-ville," published this year.

The second edition of "Geist liche Lieder und Psalmen" was published this year.

Päminger's gospels for the year appeared.

A German version of the Passion was published at Würtenburg with Music for Recitative and Choruses. The introduction and finale were in four parts.

Rore's "O altitudo divitiarum" was included in the Sacrae Cantiones published at this time.

1573(cont.)

Tallis' motet "Spem in alium (299)" was certainly an occasional piece for some sort of state occasion. The large number of voices (forty) surely had great significance and one theory was that it was written for the fortieth birthday of a ruler, possibly either Mary (1556) or Elizabeth's (1573). This question raised the possibility that it was composed in 1556.

Utendal published a magnificat and three masses.

Zarlino's "Istitutioni armoniche" was reprinted at Venice (See also 1558 and 1562).

Emperor Maximilian I of Bavaria was born (died 1651).

More and more Milanese dancing masters appeared at the French Court and this increased the desire for Italian figured dances. Ultimately the influence led to the choreographic complexities of Le Ballet des Polonais produced this year.

Henry III of Anjou was elected to the Polish throne and a year later held a large reception at Cracow. The wives of the nobles marched in a procession past the throne to the accompaniment of stately music. Apparently, after this, whenever a foreign prince was elected to the crown of Poland, a similar ceremony took place and out of it grew the Polonaise which became the opening dance at court festivals.

Tasso published his famous pastoral drama "Aminta."

Tasso wrote a sonnet in Rome praising the beauty of Barbara Sanseverino, Countess of Sala. She was living there at the time with her step-daughter Leonora San Vitale.

Ben Jonson, celebrated English author and playwright, was born at Westminster (died 1637, August 6).

Edmund Spenser received his B.A. degree at Cambridge.

Michelangelo Merisi, known as Caravaggio, an Italian painter, was born (died 1610).

Inigo Jones, an English architect and pupil of the Italian theater architect Palladio, was born (died 1652). He was in the employ of King James I and designed sets for the masques produced at the English court.

Vignola, Italian architect, died (born 1507).

Italian painting: Veronese, Feast (Christ) At the House of Levi.

(and 1572, 1576, 1583, and 1590) Lassus' German lieder were published in collections at the above dates.

(to 1580) Othmayr's Opus musicum was published posthumously in four volumes during this period.

(and 1591, 1592) Two books of tablatures by Matthäus Waissel (Waisselius) were published at Frankfurt an der Oder, during these years.

(and 1595) Two sets of Sacrae cantiones by Rore were pub-

1573(cont.)

lished after his death, one in each of these years.

(and 1596) Adam Puschmann, a pupil of Hans Sachs left accounts of the Meistergesang. They bore the titles, "Gründlicher Bericht des deutschen Meistergesanges" (Görlitz 1573); and "Gründlicher Bericht der deutschen Reimen oder rhythmen" (Frankfurt a. O. 1596).

(to 1598) The Patrocinium musices was a twelve-volume collection of works by five composers. It was printed at Munich by Adam Berg during this period and contained twenty-three magnificats by Lassus, and his five-part Passion after St. Matthew. The set was under the patronage of the Duke of Bavaria.

(to 1631) John Donne, English leading metaphysical poet, was born (died 1631).

c.1573

Pierre Phalèse of Louvain, Franco-Flemish composer, died (born c.1510).

"the Earl of Oxenford made a lease for 31 years of the manor of Battylshall in the County of Essex to W. Byrde one of the gent. of her Maties Chapple to take place at the deathe of Aubrey veare Esquier or at the deathe of his Lawful wyfe."

Feretti produced his second book of canzoni for five voices (see also 1567, 1569, 1575 and 1585).

Marenzio's "Sacrae cantiones" was composed.

Primavera was active as the "maestro di cappella" to the Spanish governor of Lombardy.

Antonio Scandello's Resurrection was taken from a similar composition, Auferstehung, by Schütz.

1574

(January 1) The second volume of the "Patrocinium Musices" was published and dedicated to Pope Gregory XIII.

(April 7) Lassus received the Knighthood of the Golden Spur from Pope Gregory XIII.

(April 17) Annibale Capello wrote to the Duke and stated that Palestrina was too busy to judge the quality of a mass written by his patron in Mantua. Apparently the Duke's ambition had been motivated by praise.

(June 15) Andreas Pevernage held a position in his native town, Courtrai, until this date when he married. Soon after this he moved to Antwerp and became choirmaster at the cathedral there.

(July 21) A "tragedia" by Cornelio Frangipane was produced for King Henry III by Comici Gelosi on this date. The composer was Merulo who was a pupil of Zarlino.

(August 3) Alessandro Striggio's instrument was described in some detail in a letter written from Duke William V of Bavaria to his father Albert V.

(November 7) Robert White made his will.

1574(cont.)

(between November 7 and November 11) Robert White, an important English sacred composer, died at Westminster (born c.1530).

(November 30) Robert White's wife was buried.

(December 15) Samuel Besler, sacred composer, was born at Brieg-on-the-Order (died 1625, July 19).

(February) Palestrina's son Angelo and his wife rented a house in the Borgo (a district within the fortified Leonine City) in the Piazza delli Scarpellini.

(November) Angelo, Palestrina's first child, was baptized.

Giovanni Contino, Italian choirmaster, died (born c.1513).

Domenico Ferabosco, Italian ballata composer, died (born 1513).

Damaião de Góis, Portuguese composer and friend of Erasmus, died (born 1502).

Petrus Siculus, a Hungarian composer, wrote a "Salve Regina," which was preserved in a Liegnitz manuscript (#18).

The Canon Paul Belisonius of Pavia supposedly introduced quills. The use of leather was shown in a harpsichord made by Baffo, carrying this date.

A harpsichord with this date, made by Baffo was preserved at S. Kensington. It was the oldest one in the collection.

The Republic commissioned (cont.) Andrea Gabrieli to write music for performance at the reception for King Henry III of France on his visit to Venice. He composed several pieces for the occasion.

Jacobus Gallus was a member of the choir at the Vienna Court Chapel at this time.

Ulrich Griesetopff (who was honored as senior at the test at Gronigen) was the organist at Magdeburg Cathedral.

De la Hèle went to Tournai Cathedral but remained maitre de chapelle at St. Rombaut, Malines.

Lassus' spells of depression became more and more frequent after this date and eventually led to complete melancholia.

Lassus went on another journey to Paris.

Lassus returned to Italy (also in 1562, 1567, 1578, 1585, and 1587).

King Charles IX offered Lassus a high salary as a chamber musician but the ruler died during the year, and Lassus remained in his position at Munich.

Merulo wrote music for a pasticcio called Tragedia. It was more like a cantata than a dramatic performance, however, it was performed before King Henry III of France at Venice during his visit to that city.

Morley was appointed organist and master of the Choristers at Norwich Cathedral.

Newsidler added the F below the

1574(cont.)

bass G on the lute. This made thirteen strings in all, the highest, or Chanterelle, being a single string.

Ruffo was at the Cathedral in Pistoia.

Jehan Tabourot was made canon of Langres.

Giovanni de Antiquis' first book of "Villanelle alla Napolitana a tre voice di diversi musici di Bari," published this year, contained twenty-two pieces by composers such as Stefano Felis and Nenna. It was published at Venice during this year.

Adam Berg's third volume of the "Patrocinium musices" was published.

Giovanni Francesco Capuano's "Primo libro delle Villanelle alla Napolitana a Tre Voci, de diversi Musici di Bari" appeared.

Eccard composed twenty "Cantiones sacrae," published at Mühlhausen during this year.

Filippo Duke of Flanders dedicated a book of spiritual madrigals to two Counts Montfort of Vorarlberg who were apparently students of his at the time.

Andrea Gabrieli's first book of six-voiced madrigals appeared. It started with a musical dedication, "Rendete al Saracini Muse," to the Magnifico St. Giovanni Saracini Bolognese.

Galilei's madrigal book for three to five voices was composed.

Tablatures by Kargel were published.

Keper composed "Select Psalms in four parts."

A later parallel to Attaingnant's "Tres breve . . . introduction" was written and published by Le Roy in the form of an "Instruction de partir toute musique facilement en tabulature de luth." It survived only in the two English translations published in London, one in this year and one in 1568.

The third edition of Leroy's Instruction book for the Lute was translated into English by "F.K. Gentleman" and published this year.

John Merbecke published "The Lives of Holy Saincts."

Tablatures by Newsidler were published at Strassbourg.

Georg Otto writes a set of introits in manuscript form for the church year.

Palestrina composed magnificats for the Papal Choir on the request of Pope Gregory XIII.

Primavera published his fourth book of "canzoni napoletane" for three voices.

Jac Reynart's Villanelle were published at Nürnberg in this year. Sixty-seven songs for three voices in sonnet form were included and were very popular and widely sung during the composer's lifetime. Copies were preserved in both Berlin and Munich Libraries.

1574(cont.)

Ruffo's psalms and mass were described in the prefaces as having been written for his patron Cardinal Borromeo, in accordance with the decrees of the Council of Trent (See also 1568).

After King Henry III visited Venice he returned to France from Poland in this year. He was greeted on board the Bucentaur with a composition by Zarlino. The Latin texts for the verses were provided by Rocco Benedetti and Cornelio Frangipani.

Robert Flud, the son of Sir Thomas Flud, who was treasurer of war to Queen Elizabeth in France and the Low Countries, was born at Milgate, in the parish of Bearsted in Kent (date of death unknown).

The escacherium was still listed among other keyboard instruments.

The seniors of the Bohemian Brethren wrote to Prince Elector Frederick III of Saxony and referred to their song book as follows, "Our melodies have been adapted from secular songs, and foreigners have at times objected. But our singers have taken into consideration the fact that the people are more easily persuaded to accept the truth by songs whose melodies are well known to them."

In Scotland great attention was apparently paid by the parliament to the study of music. A statute was passed in this year "instructing the provest, baillies and counsale, to sett up ane sang scuill, for instruction of the youth in the art of musick and singing, quhilk is almaist decayit and sall schortly decay without tymous remeid be providit."

Giorgio Vasari, Renaissance author, died (born 1511).

Corneille de Lyon, French painter, died (born c.1500).

Martin Van Heemskerck, Netherlandish painter, died (born 1498).

French painting: Antoine Caron's "Astrologer studying an Eclipse" was connected with the eclipse of this year.

(and 1575) A similarity of style between the music of "Surge illuminare" and the eight-part "Jubilate Deo," composed for the opening of the Holy Door at Christmas, this year, inaugurating the Jubilee Year (1575), was understandable since both were apparently composed during the same period.

(to 1579) The Lobwasser translation of the Goudimel Psalter had more than fifty printings during these years.

(to 1586) Monsignor Antonio Boccapadule held the title of Maestro della Cappella Pontifica during this period.

(to 1589) The reign of King Henry III (House of Valois) over France.

c.1574

One of Palestrina's greatest eight-part works was "Surge illuminare" from the time of its composition at this time to present day it has been sung every year at Epiphany in the

c.1574(cont.)
Sistine Chapel.

1575

(January 21) Tallis and William Byrd obtained "Letters Patent" granting them exclusive rights for printing music and ruled music paper for twenty-one years. This was the first such patent granted and the penalty for infringement was to be forty shillings.

(February 9) Palestrina wrote to the Duke, addressing him by his newly acquired title, "Duke of Mantua and Montferrata." The title had been bestowed on the Duke by Emperor Maximilian II., and it was obvious from the nature of the letter, that Palestrina had received a commission from his patron to set a canzone to music.

(June 25) Hans Ruckers was married at Notre Dame Cathedral in Antwerp under the name of Hans Ruckaerts, to Naenken Cnaeps.

(November 20) An Agnes Tye, possibly Christopher Tye's daughter, was married at Little Wilbraham to John Horner.

(April) Robert Johnson assisted at the entertainment given in honor of Queen Elizabeth by the Earl of Leicester at Kenilworth.

(December) Palestrina's eldest son, Angelo, died at approximately nineteen years of age.

(December) Francesco Soto was a friend of St. Philip Neri, and at this time, studied music at the Oratory founded by the latter.

Annibale Padovano, second organist at St. Mark's in Venice for many years, died (born 1527).

Ivo de Vento, lieder composer and colleague of Lassus at Munich, died (birthdate unknown).

Anerio was a soprano in the Julian Chapel under Palestrina's direction.

The "Cantiones" of this year were not comparable in quality with Byrd's later and more mature works. This fact, notwithstanding, Byrd had established a fine reputation by this time.

Byrd's excellent contrapuntal skill made it possible for him to handle all types of imitative devices with ease. He seldom, however, introduced passages of any length in strict canon after this date.

Byrd was referred to as "Organist" in the Cantiones Sacrae, but since that position did not exist in the Chapel Royal, the title was an honorary one.

The Confraternity of St. Cecilia at Evreux added musical contests to its activities.

Two musical academies, "Degli Eccitati" and "Degli Atestini" were established in Este.

Jehan Facien, the elder, and Claude de Bouchardon, were oboists in the band of King Henry III at this time.

Ferretti was the choirmaster at Ancona Cathedral in the Adriatic seaport.

1575(cont.)

Giovanni Gabrieli already had established a fine reputation as a composer.

Gesualdo was studying with Pomponio Nenna at this time.

Adam Gumpelzhaimer was employed by the Duke of Würtemberg as a musician and acquired a good reputation as a composer of both sacred and secular songs.

King Henry III granted Lassus a special privilege for the publication of his works.

Nanini resigned from his position as Maestro di Cappella for the Basilica Liberiana (St. Maria Maggiore). He was succeeded by Ippolito Tartaglini.

Pope Gregory XIII authorized the founding of a Congregation of secular priests called the Congregazione dell'Oratorio in Vallicella. Neri was the leader.

Mary Nevill married Sir Thomase Fane of Bodsil.

Pacchierotto's family were driven from Siena by political troubles this year and took refuge in Pianca-stagnaio. A branch of the family later settled in Fabriano.

Palestrina composed magnificats for the Julian Choir.

Palestrina stated in the preface to his book of motets that he only agreed to publish them at the entreaty of his friends.

Fifteen hundred singers from Palestrina's native town came to Rome and sang music by their famous fellow-citizen.

(cont.) Palestrina himself conducted the chorus.

The Chapter of St. Maria Maggiore tried to entice Palestrina back offering him a larger salary.

The archbishop granted Porta's request to be moved from Ravenna to the church "della Santa Casa" at Loreto. There he succeeded Pionerio. Porta promised to publish some new works in exchange for this favor.

Ferdinand Richardson wrote a long set of Latin Elegiacs which were included with other prefatory matter in the publication of a set of "Cantiones Sacrae" by Byrd and Tallis this year.

The invention of the Regal has often been credited to an organ-builder named Roll who was at Nürnberg at this time.

Mathes Schütz was the son of Christof II by his first marriage to Margaret Weidemann from Gera at this time.

In a diary kept by Jacopo Sorranzo, the Venetian ambassador during this year, he stated that he heard "molti ottimi musici" at Dubrovnik. This indicated that the cultivation of instrumental music in that city was active.

Since Tallis selected his Latin motets for publication as late as this year it was assumed that the composer still leaned toward the Roman Church.

Tallis' compositions published this year had no bar-lines.

1575(cont.)

Simone Verovio, the publisher and engraver, arrived at Rome.

Victoria was appointed choir -master at St. Apollinaris and also ordained a priest.

Asola's collection of "Falsi Bordoni per cantar Salmi," published this year, included examples by his teacher, Ruffo.

Adam Berg's fourth volume of the "Patrocinium musices" was published.

Cosimo Bottegari edited a collection of compositions by musicians of the Bavarian court chapel that was published by Scotto. The title was "Il secondo libro de Madrigali a cinque voci."

A six-part setting of the antiphon, using both a cantus firmus and canonic treatment was included in the "Cantiones sacrae."

Byrd and Tallis published a collection of motets titled, "Cantiones quae ab argumento sacrae vocantur, quinque et sex partium." Eighteen of the compositions were by Byrd who was only thirty years old at the time. The following compositions were included:

"Aspice, Domine, quia facta" 6 voc. No. 10.

"Attollite portas" 6 voc. No. 11.

"Da mihi auxilium" 6 voc. No. 23.

"Deo Patri sit gloria" 3 pars. 6 voc. No. 12.

(cont.)

"Dies mei transierunt 2 pars." 5 voc. No. 5.

"Diliges Dominum" 8 voc. No. 25.

"Domine, secundum actum meum" i pars.

"Emendemus in melius" 5 voc. No. 4. (Kerman described this motet as "his only motet in the 1575 collection which really gives a strong personal impression.")

"Gloria Patri, qui creavit" 6 voc. No. 32.

"Ideo deprecor" 2 pars. 6 voc. No. 24.

"Laudate, pueri, Dominum" 6 voc. No. 17.

"Libera me, Domine, de morte" 5 voc. No. 33.

"Libera me, Domine, et pone. 1 pars."

"Memento homo quod cinis es" 6 voc. No. 18.

"Miserere mihi, Domine" 6 voc. No. 29.

The subject of "Non nobis Domine" appeared in one of the "Cantiones sacrae."

"O lux beata trinitas." 1 pars.

"Peccantem me quotidie" 5 voc. No. 6.

"Siderum rector" 5 voc. No. 19.

"Te deprecor supplico" 6

1575(cont.)

voc. No. 31.

"Te mane laudum carmine" 2 pars.

"Tribue, Domine" 6 voc. No. 30.

The "Recueil des plus belles et excellentes chansons en forme de voix de villes" was published at Paris by Jean Chardavoine.

Conversi's "Canzoni a 5 Voci" was published in Venice by Scotto.

Gaspard Coste composed songs and madrigals that were preserved in "Sdegnosi ardori; Musica di diversi authori sopra un istesso sogetto di parole" published this year at Munich.

Ferretti dedicated his second book of canzoni for six voices to Giacomo Boncompagni.

Andrea Gabrieli published a collection of madrigals for three voices.

Andrea Gabrieli started the "pre-monodic secular oratorio" with his music for Ariosto's "Orlando."

A copy of de la Grotte's Chansons was preserved in a Scottish library.

A second Te Deum setting by Kerle appeared. An earlier one had been issued in 1571.

Two of Lassus' madrigals were included in the second volume by Cosimo Bottrigari in Venice.

The first collection of Lassus' secular works was published at (cont.) La Rochelle.

Da Monte's sixth book of madrigals for five voices included a mixture of occasional compositions and works of high literary quality.

Da Monte's "Sonetz de Pierre de Ronsard . . . " was published at Antwerp and Louvain this year.

A setting of the "Lauda Sion" by Palestrina was published in this year by Gardano in the Third Book of Motets for five, six and eight voices.

Palestrina's thirty six-part motets were published in a collection. (See also 1569 and 1572) The volume was dedicated to Alfonso II, Duke of Ferrara.

Palestrina's motet "Hodie Christus natus est" was published.

François Regnart's four and five-part "Poésies de P. de Ronsard et autres Poëtes" was issued at Douai.

Thomas Vautrollier published the "Cantiones Sacrae" by Tallis and Byrd in London.

Included in the first publication of the "Cantiones Sacrae" were the following by Tallis:

"Absterge Domine, a 5. No.2"

"Derelinquit impius, a 5. No. 13"

"Facti sunt Nazarei, a 5. No. 22."

"In jejunio et fletu, a 5. No. 26"

1575(cont.)

"Illae dum pergunt (Hymn), à 5. No. 16."

"In manus tuas, à 5. No. 3"

"Mihi autem nimis, à 5. No. 7"

"Miserere nostri, à 7. No. 34."

"O nata lux (Hymn), à 5. No. 8"

"O Sacrum convivium, à 5. No. 9"

"Procul recedant (Hymn) à 5. No. 20"

"Sabbathum dum transisset, à 5. No. 14"

"Salvator Mundi, à 5. No. 21"

"Salvator mundi, à 5. No. 1"

"Si enim (2 da pars), à 7. No. 28"

"Suscipe quaeso. à 7, No. 27"

"Virtus, honor et potestas, à 5. No. 15"

Vecchi wrote two sonnets included in the "Quinto libro delle muse" of this year. One of them used a text by Francesco Coppetta.

The movement for Catholic Reform was exhibited in arts and letters. In the field of literature there were examples of restored church thought. "Jerusalem Delivered" by Tasso dealt with the first crusade - and numerous reactionary traits shown in the work were reminiscent of the character and (cont.) style of medieval writing.

George Gascoigne's lyrics were collected in a volume, "An Hundred Sundrie Floures bound up in one Poesie" during this year.

George Gascoigne's "The Glasse of Government" appeared.

Antonio Moro, Spanish painter (Anthonis Mor Van Dashorst), died (born 1519).

(to 1577) Nanino was maestro di cappella at San Luigi de' Francesi during these years.

(to 1578) Floris van Adrichem was organist at the St. Bavo Kerk during this period.

(to 1578) Jacobus Gallus was apparently in Bohemia, Moravia, and Silesa during these years and spent considerable time in Breslau and Prague.

(to 1579) Anerio was choirboy at St. Peter's under Palestrina throughout this period.

(to 1579) Giovanni Gabrieli was a member of the court chapel at Munich under Lassus.

(to 1579) Zacconi was a member of the court chapel at Munich under Lassus.

(to 1581) The untimely deaths of Palestrina's sons and brother obviously affected his creative output and nothing composed by him was published during these years.

(and 1581, 1589, 1594)

1575(cont.)

Palestrina's third volume of motets was reprinted by Scotto and Gardano at Venice in each of these years.

(to 1585) Fernando Franco was maestro de capilla of the Cathedral of Mexico during these years.

(to 1585) Two of Palestrina's magnificats, "Aeterna Christi munera" and "Iste confessor" were composed during this period.

(to 1589) Byrd started on the next book (1589) immediately after the publication of the "Cantiones sacrae." Almost certainly several of the works in the later book were composed shortly after 1575, but the smoothness and precision of his writing rapidly revealed a far more advanced technique.

(to 1625) Over five hundred works by Elizabethan virginalists were preserved in hand written or printed collections from these years.

c.1575

Thomas Bateson, an English madrigalist, was born (date of death unknown).

Antonio Cifra, composer, learned musician and one of Palestrina's few students, was born (date of death unknown).

Alfonso Ferrabosco II, composer of ayres, was born at Greenwich (died 1628).

Marco da Gagliano, an early composer in the opera idiom, was born (died 1642).

Domenico Micheli, madrigal composer, was born (date of death unknown).

Philip Rosseter, English composer of songs with lute accompaniment, was born (died 1623).

Willem Swart, Dutch composer, was born (died c.1640).

Thomas Weelkes, great English madrigalist who used chromatic melodic lines, was born (died 1623).

John Baldwin was appointed a lay-clerk at St. George's Chapel in Windsor Castle.

Open scores, with a separate staff for each part, returned in this year. A book of keyboard arrangements of French chansons published by Gardano was responsible for their reappearance.

Ingegneri composed "O Bone Jesu," and "Tenebrae Factae Sunt."

Francisco Soto de Langa was one of the Roman group of Spanish musicians.

Antonio Valente, a ricercare composer, was active at this time.

Italian architecture:
Giacomo Della Porta, Il Gesu, an early Baroque church in Rome (facade, 115' x 114' high).

French painting:
François Quesnel, Portrait of Henry III.

Italian painting: Veronese decorated the Sala del Collegio in the Palazzo Ducale.

(and 1610) The title "Cantiones

c.1575(cont.)

Sacrae" was given to several collections of Latin motets published in London during this period.

(to c.1695) The English school of chamber music for stings flourished brilliantly and lasted from the last quarter of the sixteenth century until the end of the seventeenth. The major names associated with the field were Byrd, Dering, Gibbons, Jenkins, Peerson, Purcell, Sympson, Tomkins, and Ward.

(to c.1699) During this period the Violin and the tenor were replacing the higher viols. The Bass Viol, however, maintained its position and afforded a wide opportunity for a large group of players and composers, especially in England, Franch and the Netherlands.

(to 1710) The most conspicuous feature of instrumental music during this period was the profusion of dance tunes that appeared.

1576

(August 15 or 22)
Valentin Bakfark, lutenist and composer, died in Padua, a victim of the plague (born 1507).

(August 15) Palestrina's son Iginio married
Virginia Guarnecci on the Feast of the Assumption at the church of San Lorenzo (in the Trojan Forum).

(October 25) The Pope issued a brief to the effect that the Directorium Chori was to be revised.

Nicolas Du Chemin, a French (cont.) music publisher, died (born c.1510).

Girolamo Cardano, a writer on music, died (born 1501).

Daniel Hitzler, a theorist of some repute, was born (died 1635). He based a system of "Bebisation" on La, Be, Ce, De, Me, Fe, Ge.

Gregor Meyer, a composer who contributed to the "Dodecachordon," died (birthdate unknown).

Daniel Norcome, an English madrigal composer and lay-clerk at St. George's Chapel, Windsor, was born at Windsor (date of death unknown).

Angelo Palestrina's second child, a son named after his father, was born (died 1576).

The most famous of all Meistersinger is Hans Sachs, the cobbler, poet-composer of Nürnberg, died (born 1494). His musical output was great as was his contribution to the historical importance of the Meistersinger.

San Onofrio A Capuana founded in this year by private benefactions was named the "confraternity of the Bianchi."

Joan Brudieu, a madrigal composer of some note, went to Balaguer.

Thomas Este was engaged in printing as early as this time.

Giovanni Gabrieli went to Munich with Lassus and joined the ducal court.

1576(cont.)

Hautin was still actively publishing and printing at this time.

George de la Hèle was a prize-winner in a musical contest held by the Confraternity of St. Cecilia at Evreux. He won a silver harp as well as a silver lute.

Lassus ceased composing musical settings for madrigals.

Da Monte directed his choir after this date under two emperors, Maximilian II in Vienna and Rudolf II in Prague.

Morley's date of birth was established as 1557 by the title of a "Domine, non est," preserved in the Bodleian Library. It read "Thomae Morley, aetatis suae 19 Anno Domini 1576."

Monteverdi's father entrusted the son's musical education to Ingegneri, who was prefect of music at the Cremona Cathedral at this time and the leading musician in the area.

Pope Gregory XIII ordered Palestrina to exert his maximum effort toward restoring the entire system of Plain Song to its original purity. He was among other things to revise the "Graduale" and the "Antifonario." Palestrina was to be assisted in this by his pupil, Guidetti.

Lord Petre of Writtle was granted knighthood.

The name of Christof II, father of Heinrich Schütz, appeared for the first time in a petition by his father, Christof I, to the (cont.) Chemnitz Council for a grant of assistance from the foundation established by Ulrich Schütz, I.

A harpsichord with three stops was referred to in an inventory of the Fugger collection, Augsburg, at this time. It was said to have a strong tone and was made by Franco Ungaro in Venice.

Understandably archaic in spots, Victoria's mass based on plainsong, the "Missa Ave maris stella," and probably his earliest, was published this year.

Adam Berg's fifth volume of the "Patrocinium musices" was published.

The "Chansons, Odes, et Sonetz de Pierre Ronsard" set for four, five, and eight voices by Jean de Castro, appeared at this time.

A collection of vaux-de-vire, a particular type of monophonic chansons, was published by Chardavoine during this year.

The last composition specifically for the vihuela was by Esteban Daza and was published during this year at Valladolid. Its title was "El Parnaso."

A collection from this year by Andrea Gabrieli includes "Filiae Jerusalem" for four voices.

"Liber primus, qui Missas, Psalmos, Magnificat, ad Virginem Dei Salutationes, aliaque complectitur 4,5,6,8 voc. Venetiis, apud Angelum Gardanum 1576." was published.

1576(cont.)

Some of Lassus' German lieder were published in a collection at this date (See also 1572, 1573, 1583 and 1590).

Lassus finished the first series of his "Patrocinium Musices" and the third part of the "Teutsche lieder" which included twenty -two compositions. He also completed and published "Thresor de musique" a collection of 103 chansons.

Lassus' series of the "Patrocinium Musices" stopped short at this time.

Luzzasco Luzzaschi's second book of madrigals (for five voices) appeared.

Giovanni Macque's first madrigal book was issued.

Petrarch's "Hor che'l ciel e la terra" was set by da Monte.

Regnart's villanella, "Ich hab vermeint," was composed.

Susannen frumb was published in Spain.

Antonio Valente's "Intavolatura de cimbalo" containing written -out fantasie was published.

Victoria published his second collection of compositions.

Gascoigne's "The Steele Glasse" a satirical work was written.

Edmund Spenser received the degree of M.A. from Cambridge University.

The earliest playhouse in London was built this year and called simply "the Theatre." (cont.) It provided the first permanent home for English actors.

Richard Edwards was the compiler of and main contributor to a collection of poems, "The Paradise of Dainty Devices." It was not, however, published until this year, ten years after his death.

Paolo Giordano Orsini, the Duke of Bracciano, purportedly strangled his wife in the Castello Cerreto Guidi near Empoli because of his love for Vittoria Accoramboni. The Orsini name was destroyed by this event.

Spanish painting: Antonio Moro, Portrait of Hubert Golzius, Chronicler of Philip II.

Tiziano Vecellio, renowned Italian painter, known as Titian, died (born c.1485).

A Dominican Gradual published this year had pages decorated with woodcuts in two colors.

(and 1577, 1579) Regnart's "Kurtzweilige teutsche Lieder zu dreyen stimmen nach art der Neapolitanen oder Welschen Villanellen" was published in three parts in these years respectively.

(and 1581) Six of Victoria's magnificat settings were published by 1576 and the balance by 1581.

(to 1582) Palestrina and Guidetti worked throughout the first five years of this period on the revision of the services in the Roman Church. The former was chosen because of his knowl-

1576(cont.)

ledge of all the manuscripts at St. Peters as well as the other important churches in Rome. Palestrina described the work as "opus nullins ingenii, multarum tamen vigiliarum." The work was finally published in 1582 under the title "Directorium chori . . . Opera Joannis Guidetti Boneniensis, etc." Guidetti held the rights for the sale of the volume for a ten-year period.

(and 1583) Du Caurroy was a prize-winner in musical contests held by the Confraternity of St. Cecilia at Evreux at these dates.

(to 1586) Ferretti composed two books of "Canzoni" for six voices, published in Venice during this period.

(to 1586) The tradition of maintaining court music at Cracow at a high level continued, after the Jagiello dynasty disappeared.
King Stephen Bathori was the leader in this effort.

(to 1587) Orazio Colombani published five collections of psalms set for five, six and nine voices as well as two madrigals during this period. In the Portugal Royal Library at Lisbon several other works by Colombani were preserved including a "Te Deum" in Lindner's "Corollario cantionum sacrarum," two magnificats and several madrigals.

(and 1589) Two books of six voiced madrigals by Giovanni Macque were published at these dates.

(to 1606) Lodovico Balbi, a composer of madrigals, masses and motets, was in Venice and active during this period.

c.1576

Thomas Byrd, son of William Byrd, was born (date of death unknown).

Stephan Zirler, a pupil of Lorenz Lemlin and a lied composer, died (birthdate unknown).

1577

(October 4) An extract from the Aberdeen Burgh records transcribed by the editors of the Spalding Club publications stated, "The said day the counsell grantit the soume of four poundis to the support of James Symsonne, doctour of thair sang scuill, to help to buy him cloythis.

(October 27) Nanino was elected a member of the Pontifical Choir in which he sang tenor.

(October 28) In a papal brief Pope Gregory decreed that plainchant was to be "purged of many barbarisms, obscurities, contradictions, superfluities and wrong notes (mali suoni)."

(November 29) Cuthbert Mayne, a priest and steward to the Tregian family, was convicted of high treason, hanged, drawn, and quartered at Launceston.

(June) Sir Francis Drake, during his journey around the world, arrived in California at this time when his ship lay in harbor for five weeks.

(June) The house of Golden was entered and searched, and Cuthbert Mayne, a priest of

1577(cont.)

Douay, steward to Francis Tregian, was arrested and imprisoned, with several other of the Tregian servants, "all gentlemen saving one," says a contemporary account, in Launceston Gaol.

Matthäus Le Maistre, sacred composer and doppelmeister, died (birthdate unknown).

Jacob Meiland, a Protestant composer, died (born c.1542).

Anerio was a contralto in the Julian Chapel, under Palestrina's direction, at this time.

Baltazarini (Baltagerini), an Italian musician and the best violinist of his day, was brought to Catherine de' Medicis from Piedmont during this year by Marshall de Brissac. He was made intendant of her music and her first valet de chambre. Baltazarini adopted the name of M. de Beau, oyeulx.

Byrd was first heard of at Harlington, west of Middlesex, in this year when his wife's name appeared in the list of recusants living at the village.

The Reverand Richard Carlton was at Clare College, Cambridge and received the degree of Bachelor of Arts this year.

Giles was appointed clerk at the chapel of Magdalen College, Oxford.

Pope Gregory XIII commissioned Palestrina and Annibale Zoilo to examine the chant-books that had been issued after the publication of the Breviary and Missal ordered by the Council of (cont.) Trent. Their job was to eliminate barbarisms and other defects that had occured through errors by "composers, scribes, and printers."

A Spinet carrying the name of Rosso of Milan as its maker, in this year, was purportedly ornamented with nearly 2,000 precious and semi-precious stones.

The serious illness of the Archbishop Giulio Feltrio della Rovero served as a reminder to Porta to fulfill his promise to publish some new works.

The saltarello-like "Courante du roi" was preserved in tablature by Bernhard Schmid the Elder.

Sweelinck was in Holland from this date forward.

The Tregian family was apparently suspect because of their wealth as well as their religion, and at least one source claimed that a conspiracy took place to ruin the group.

Vecchi travelled in the northern parts of Lombardy with Count Baldassarre Rangoni, a member of an illustrious noble family from Modena.

The Church of St. Maria della Salute was founded this year in memory of the plague which had felled the venerable and respected Titian. Zarlino was commissioned to compose a mass for the occasion.

The third Roman book of laude was issued this year at the behest of the Fathers of the Congregazione dell'Oratorio. The music was for three voices and was easier than the first two books "so that it can be sung by all" as was stated in the preface.

A setting of Psalm CXXXIII for six voices was written by Anton Jung of Kolozsvár (=Cluj), minister in Szászorbó. It survived in the Brassó Library.

Twelve pieces for two voices with no texts were composed and published by Lassus in this year. Twelve other two-voiced pieces without texts also appeared and these were probably to be used as etudes for young members of the Bavarian chapel. The entire group of compositions were called "cantiones."

Le Maistre's "Schöne und auserlesene teutsche und lateinische geistliche Gesänge zu 3 Stimmen" was published.

Marenzio's first publication was a madrigal "Donna bella e crudele." It was included in a Venetian anthology edited by Mosto and Merulo, "Il primo fiore della ghirlanda musicale," and published this year.

Regnart's "Kurtzweilige teutsche Lieder zu dreyen stimmen nach art der Neapolitanen oder Welschen Villanellen" was published in three parts, one part this year (see also 1576 and 1579).

Teodoro Riccio of Brescia's "Primo libro delle canzone alla napolitana" appeared.

Gardano published de Rore's "madrigals spartiti," or literally, de-parted in score-form with bar-lines, at Venice.

(cont.) They were for four voices.

Salinas' theoretical work, the "De musica libri septem" restated in Latin many of the theories that Zarlino had voiced in Italian. The work was published at Salamanca.

Schmid the Elder's "Zwey Bücher einer neuen Künstlichen Tabulatur . . ." was published this year. It contained many simple dance tunes, Hungarian by nationality. The publication was issued at Strassbourg.

Tansillo's "se quel dolor che va innanzi al morire" was set to music by de Wert.

Utendal published three books of motets, one this year (see also 1571 and 1573).

Jan Willemszoon Lossy was given an increase in pay this year for assisting by doubling the lower voices on his bass shawm (see 1568).

The Lutherans protected themselves against the Reformed with the Formula of Concord, made official in Saxony this year.

Burton, the English author, was born (date of death unknown).

George Gascoigne, Elizabethan dramatist, died (born c.1525).

Holinshed's Chronicles were published in England.

George Peele, English author and actor, was graduated from Oxford.

Peter Paul Rubens, renowned Flemish painter, was born at

1577(cont.)

Siegen, Westphalia (died 1640).

(to 1580) Drake circumnavigated the globe during these years.

(to 1581) Sweelinck was appointed to the position of organist previously held by his father at the Old Church of Amsterdam.

(and 1596) Johannes Eccard composed "Crepundia sacra" that were published at Mühlhausen at these dates.

c.1577

A lute-book by Fabritio Caroso was published.

The "Pastor fido" by G.F. Guarini combined with Tasso's pastoral play, Aminta, provided a great source of pastoral atmosphere for Monteverdi, the leading lyrical madrigalist.

De Rore's madrigals were published in the form of a "study score." This was a new procedure of interest to students.

The renowned theoretician Salinas was active in Salamanca.

1578

(January 13) Hans Ruckers was baptized at Antwerp.

(July 5) Christoforo died at the Villa d'Este outside Rome.

(November 1) Palestrina wrote to the Duke of Mantua concerning some revisions made by the Duke in some Chant melodies. He described the melodies as, "well-purged of barbarisms and wrong notes" and suggested that the amended versions be included in the new edition of the (cont.) Graduale which was to be published.

(December 2) Agostino Agazzari, a composer of motets and a cadet from a noble family in Siena, was born (died c.1640). He also produced several theoretical works.

The Archduke Ferdinand of Styria later Emperor Ferdinand II was born (died 1637).

Asola was appointed maestro di cappella of Treviso Cathedral.

Joan Brudieu served as maestro and organist at Barcelona.

Byrd was still living at Harlington, Middlesex.

Giulio Caccini went to Florence.

Alfonso Ferrabosco I broke his pledge to Queen Elizabeth and left his two children with a court musician while he returned to Italy.

De la Hèle received a demi -prebendary at Tournai.

Ingegneri became a singer at Cremona Cathedral.

Lassus returned to Italy (also in 1562, 1567, 1574, 1585, and 1587).

Victoria remained at the Collegium Germanicum until this year.

Claudio Merulo started to compose madrigals and motets.

Tarquinia Molza was a widow.

Duke Guglielmo Gonzaga asked Palestrina for a set of masses

1578(cont.)

to be composed on particular plainchant themes selected by the Duke himself.

Porta stated in the preface to a mass collection that he had attempted to make the text as intelligible as possible in order to conform with the requirements of the Council of Trent. The volume was dedicated to the Archbishop of Ravenna.

Palestrina was seriously ill and in a letter to Duke Guglielmo he mentioned "many days in bed." The illness was an influenza -type which created great problems for him two years later.

A papal brief of this year confirmed Palestrina's appointment as "Master of the Music at the Vatican Basilica" for life, with a salary increase that had been granted three years earlier. This amounted to fifteen scudi which was almost double that paid to Animuccia. His pension had also been increased because of his various compositions for the choir.

Pevernage left Courtrai to go to Antwerp.

Albrecht Schütz was a highly respected member of the town council of Weissenfels. He was the grandfather of the renowned composer.

When Victoria resigned from the German seminary in this year he became a resident priest at the Church of San Girolamo della Carità.

Tasso's "Gelo hà Madonna il seno, e fiamma il volto" was set to music by Bellasio.

Anthoine de Bertrand's two volumes of four-part chanson settings of Ronsard's Amours, published this year, included some compositions in both chromatic and enharmonic modes.

Cabezón was the composer of a very important organ tablature, the "Obras de música para tecla, arpa y vihuela," published this year at Madrid by his son Hernando. The composer had died twelve years previously.

Eccard composed twenty-four Deutsche Lieder which were published at Mühlhausen during this year.

The play, "Panthea and Abradatas, was written this year. It was often attributed to Richard Farrant of Windsor, but he probably only wrote the music.

The Oratorio di S. Gio Battista and a manuscript of an opera "La Forza dell' Amor paterno" were preserved, the latter bearing this date and the location of Genoa.

F. Haemus' "Poemata" published this year at Antwerp included an elegy, "in obitum Iacobi Vasii, Caesaris Maximiliani archiphonasci." This was quoted by M. van der Straeten.

Ingegneri published a book of madrigals for four voices.

Leroy's short and easy instruction book for the "Guiterne" (guitar) appeared.

Nanino's "Madrigali" Volume I was published.

Nanino's "Motetti, à 3 voci" was

1578(cont.)

published at Venice.

Nanino's "Motetti, à 5 voci" was published probably also at Venice.

All the masses printed by Plantin at Antwerp in this year were parody masses. The models were shown in the table of contents and the collections were fine technical products.

Thomas Szadek composed a mass based on "Dies est laetitiae." It survived only in an incomplete copy.

Gardano published a book of Valenzuela's madrigals at Venice this year. The composer was a lesser known Spanish madrigalist.

"The Gude and Godly Ballates," a collection of ballads by John and Robert Wedderburn of Dundee, appeared.

Heinrich von Friesen of Rotha was born (date of death unknown).

Although the Alteration which established the Reformed Church was accomplished by reasonably peaceful means at Amsterdam, it still created a violent period of change.

The fate of Amsterdam from this date forward was entrusted to the Protestant rebels. Their leader, Prince William of Orange was known as "the Silent."

During the war, the Protestants captured Courtrai and persecution of Catholics followed immediately.

"A Gorgeous Gallery of Gallant (cont.) Inventions," a work by an anonymous poet, appeared.

John Lyly's "Euphues the Anatomy of Wit" appeared. This was the first of a two volume "prose romance."

Edmund Spenser belonged to an informal group called the "Areopagus." The members promoted the use of classical meters in English verse.

Edmund Spenser met Sir Philip Sidney in London as well as the latter's uncle, the Earl of Leicester, who was a favorite of Queen Elizabeth. Gabriel Harvey arranged the meeting.

Lescot, the French architect responsible for the "Lescot" wing of the Louvre, died (born c.1510).

Italian painting: Tintoretto, Mercury and the Three Graces.

Veronese decorated the Sala del Maggior Consiglio in the Ducal Palace. He painted the "Triumph of Venice" there during this year.

(to 1579) Scotto published four collections by Infantas at Venice during this period.

(to 1580) There were no publications by Lassus during these years.

(and 1589) Eccard published two collections of volkslieder in four and five parts at Mülhausen and Königsberg, at these two dates respectively. An imperfect copy of the latter one was preserved at the British Museum.

c.1578

Christof Schütz II (the Younger) married Euphrosyne, the daughter of a future Gera burgomaster, Bieger.

Vecchi's first book of canzonette appeared.

1579

(January 8) Clara Massimilia Monteverdi was born (date of death unknown).

(February 28) A letter preserved in the British Museum (Lansd. 29, No. 38) from the Earl of Northumberland to Lord Burghley provided interesting background material on Byrd.

(August 1) Marenzio entered the service of Cardinal Luigi d'Este, Duke Alfonso's brother.

(August 30) Andries Ruckers was baptized at Antwerp.

(November 21) Sir Thomas Gresham, founder of Gresham College, London, died (birthdate unknown). His will made provision for fellowships in astronomy, divinity, geometry, law, medicine, music and rhetoric.

(April) Duke Albert V guaranteed Lassus his salary of 400 florins for life.

(October) Duke Albert V of Bavaria died (born 1527).

George Barcrofte was vicar-choral and organist at Ely Cathedral at this time.

The Trionfo di musica of this year was dedicated to the Grand Duchess of Tuscany, Bianca Cappello. It included compositions performed at her (cont.) wedding to the Grand Duke Francesco de' Medici.

During the carnival of this year Mantuan musicians accompanied Guglielmo's heir, Vincenzo, to the marriage of his sister, Margherita Gonzaga, and Alfonso II. This marriage was a disappointment to the d'Estes in their hopes for an heir.

Phalèse continued to issue lute collections as late as this date.

Hans Ruckers was admitted to the Lucas guild as Hans Ruyckers, "clavisinbalmakerne," during this year.

From this date until his death Verdonck was in the service of various wealthy landowners in the Netherlands.

Byrd wrote music for "Ricardus Tertius," a Latin play by Thomas Legge. It was produced at St. John's College this year.

Costeley wrote a treatise "Musique" published at Paris this year.

"The Psalmes of David in English meter with notes of foure partes set unto them by Guilielmo Damon, for John Bull, to the use of the godly Christians for recreatyng themselves, instede of fond and unseemly Ballades. Anno 1579 at London Printed by John Daye. Cum privilegio." appeared.

The Windsor or Eton Tune was not included in Damon's collection of this year.

A collection of hymns was published by William Damon. This was probably a reference to his

1579(cont.)

psalter, but not necessarily.

Didier le Blanc's "Airs de plusieurs musiciens . . . " appeared.

Infantas' "Plura modulatione genera," a collection of one hundred contrapuntal compositions based on the plainsong "Laudate Dominum" and composed for two to eight voices, appeared this year.

Ingegneri published a book of madrigals for four voices.

L. Lossius' "Psalmodia" was published at Wittenbach at this time.

Giovanni Macque's book of madrigals for four voices appeared.

A second madrigal book by Macque appeared.

Merulo set Tasso's "Gelo hà Madonna il seno, e fiamma il volto" to music.

Palestrina composed a Madrigal "O felice ore" for the marriage of Francesco de' Medici and Bianca Capello, in this year.

Regnart's "Kurtzweilige teutsche Lieder zu dreyen stimmen nach art der Neapolitanen oder Welschen Villanellen" was published in three parts, one part in this year (see also 1576 and 1577).

Lechner published five part arrangements of twenty-one of Regnart's pieces for three voices. Regnart's chordal settings were changed into polished songs, madrigalian in style.

Striggio also contributed music for the marriage of Francesco Medici and Bianca Capello, "daughter of the Republic" at Venice.

Vecchi collaborated with Andrea Gabrieli, Vincenzo Bel'hauer, Claudio Merulo, Baldisserra Donato, and Tiburtio Massaino on the composition of a sestina in honor of the wedding of the Duke Francesco. The sestina was published by Scotto in a collection with other festive pieces titled "Trionfo di musica" and dedicated to the "vera et particulare figliuola" of the Venetian Republic.

Della Viola's motets in five parts were published this year at Venice.

Alfonso d'Este's third wife, Margherita Gonzaga, arrived in Ferrara.

Laura Peperara arrived at the court of Ferrara.

John Fletcher, Elizabethan poet, was born (died 1625).

Sir Walter Raleigh went to America on an unsuccessful voyage with his half-brother, Sir Humphrey Gilbert.

North's Plutarch was written.

Spenser wrote and published the twelve ecologues of "The Shepherd's Calendar," dedicated to Sidney. Originally this work was anonymous. The work which added much to the popularity of pastoral poetry was illustrated with twelve wood-

1579(cont.)

cuts, one for each month.

Franz Snyders, Flemish painter, was born (died 1657).

Spanish painting:
Alonso Sanchez Coello, The Infanta Isabella, Daughter of Philip II.

(to 1580) Anerio was a contralto at San Luigi de' Francesi under Soriano's direction.

(to 1580) A fine folio of Antiphonarium was published at Venice by Peter Liechtenstein of Cologne.

(to 1580) An ornate folio Graduale was published at Venice by Liechtenstein.

(to 1583) Italian sculpture:
Giovanni Bologna, Rape of the Sabines.

(to 1586) During these years Marenzio served Cardinal Luigi d'Este at Rome, and later served Cardinal Cinzio Aldobrandini, a patron of the arts and protector of Tasso.

(and 1588, 1598) Nanino's "Madrigali, a 5 voci," Lib. I was published at Venice on these dates.

(to 1612) Benedetto Pallavicino, a composer of madrigals, wrote one book for four voices, one for six voices, and eight books for five voices between these years.

(and 1651) Four members of the Ruckers family were living at Antwerp and built harpsichords. They achieved great reputations for their craftsmanship.

c.1579

Byrd wrote a three-part song for Legge's Latin play "Richardus III." This was apparently one of very few, if not his only, composition for the stage.

1580

(January 18) Antonio Scandello, an Italian composer of Protestant church music, died (born 1517). He came from Bergamo.

(April 1) Alonso Mudarra, a Spanish composer of instrumental and secular vocal music, died at Seville (born c.1506).

(July 6) Johann Stobaeus, pupil of Eccard and composer of "Preussische Festlieder" was born (died 1646).

(July 23) Lucrezia, Palestrina's wife, died and was buried in the Cappella Nuova of St. Peter's (birthdate unknown).

(August 8) Luca Marenzio's "Primo libro de Madrigali a 5 voci" was published at Venice by Gardano. It was an immediate success and was dedicated to the Cardinal. Marenzio's relationship with Tasso and Guarini was already established by this time.

(September 20) Da Monte was in Prague at this time.

(September 20) The dedication of Da Monte's fourth book of six -voiced madrigals in Venice and that of his ninth book of five -voiced madrigals in Prague were signed on the same day. It was obvious, however, that da Monte was in Prague at this time.

(November 6) When he left Loreto Porta went back to Ravenna. This was indicated by

1580(cont.)

Pomponius Spretus, who described Cardinal Sforza's arrival in that city on this date and mentioned the performance of "a delightful piece of music composed by. M. Costanzo Porta of Cremona, the first musician of the time, and chapel-master of our cathedral."

(November 20) Da Monte's ninth book of madrigals was issued.

(November 30) Richard Farrant, English organist and singer, died (born c.1525 or c.1533).

(September) The ballad, "A new Northerne dittye of the Ladye Greene Sleeves," was entered in the Stationers' Register for this date, but the tune was probably from the reign of King Henry VIII.

Vincenzo Borghini, an Italian author on musical subjects, died (birthdate unknown).

Pierre Haultin, music printer and publisher, died (birthdate unknown).

Juan Navarro, Spanish composer, died at Palencia (born c.1530).

Andres Torrentes, Spanish composer who worked and lived in Italy, died (birthdate unknown).

A "Maria pieters de Zuster van de organist" was buried.

Animuccia's music did not adhere to the syllabic, chordal style adopted by Ruffo in his masses composed this year.

An oblong clavecin made in Antwerp and signed "Martinus Vander Biest" carrying this (cont.) date was preserved in the Nürnberg Museum. It included an octave spinet.

Gioseppe Caimo was organist at the Milan Cathedral from this date forward.

Calvisius was made music director at Pauliner Church in Leipzig.

De Castro was chapelmaster to the Prince of Juliers.

Heinrich Colander, an organist from Schwabach, received a church appointment at Weissenfels. He was twenty-three years of age at the time.

John Dowland went to Paris as a page for the English ambassador, Sir Henry Cobham. While there he converted to Catholocism.

Eccard became vice-kappelmeister at Königsberg.

Richard Farrant was attached to the Chapel Royal during much of the reign of King Edward VI until his death in this year (see November 30).

Giovanni Gabrieli remained at the ducal court at Munich at this time.

The Italian madrigal entered its final and most advanced stage under the leadership of Marenzio.

Marenzio found a patron to support him.

Del Mel arrived in Rome.

Montaigne heard a mass with violins at Verona some time this year.

1580(cont.)

Otto applied for a position as cantor at the Dresden court and was rejected.

The loss of Palestrina's patron, Ippolito d'Este, was to a degree compensated for through the kindness of Giacomo Buoncompagni, nephew of Gregory XIII, to the composer. The latter came to Rome in this year and was awarded nobility by a relative.

Ruffo was at Sacile, near Treviso.

Soriano from this date forward was intermittently maestro di cappella at San Luigi de' Francesi, Santa Maria Maggiore, St. John Lateran, Tivoli Cathedral, and St. Peter's.

Sweelinck was organist at Amsterdam at this time.

The earliest date of a true violin-type instrument reported by one source was a tenor instrument made by Peregrino Zanetto the younger of Brescia during this year.

Conversi's "Canzoni a 5 voci" was reprinted by Scotto in a four part edition during this year.

Andrea Gabrieli's second book of six-voiced madrigals published this year acted as a manifesto.

Galilei composed a setting of Count Ugolino's lament in the Divine Comedy for five voices, specifically tenor voice and viols.

Gallus wrote nineteen masses, sixteen of which were published (cont.) in Prague this year. The majority of them were parody masses.

The original edition of Gomólka's works published at Cracow in this year included 150 psalms. Each part was printed across two pages as in a score but there were no measure lines.

Colo Nardo di Monte of Bari, an Apulian musician, composed four -voiced madrigals based on villanelle texts.

Beginning with his ninth book of madrigals for five voices this year da Monte had very few works reprinted.

Palestrina wrote the motets "Surge Sancte Dei de habitatione tua" and "Ambula Sancte Dei ad locum predestinatum" this year. They were composed for certain solemn festivities in connection with the transferring of the relics of St. Gregory Nazianzen.

In England Peeter Philips' pavanne composed this year was widely known as a consort piece. It was instrumentated for treble viol, flute, bass viol, lute, cittern, and pandora, typical of the times.

Porta issued a book of fifty-two motets, which included the antiphon "Diffusa est gratia" for seven voices.

Ruffo's "novamente composte seconda la forma del Concilio Tridentino" appeared.

Szadek composed a mass that used the melody "Pis ne me peult venir," the same one on which Crecquillon had composed a mass.

1580(cont.)

Michele Varotto's five to ten -voiced magnificats were composed.

Vecchi had published a collection of canzonette by this time. He explained in his dedication to Count Bevilacqua that most of the compositions were already distributed all over Italy in manuscript form and under the names of other composers.

Pietro Vinci wrote nine madrigal books as well as a book of settings of "sonetti spirituali" by Vittoria Colonna, Marchioness of Pescara. She was a friend of Michelangelo and Cardinal Bembo.

A single part-book from this date was preserved in the Bodleian Library.

The body of St. Gregory Nazianzen was transferred to the chapel of S. Maria del Soccorso.

Philipp II inherited the entire Portuguese empire.

A Puritan Pamphlet which stated "Let cathedral churches be utterly destroyed" was published.

William Shelley, who owned Stondon Place through his wife, was committed to the Fleet prison this year for being involved in a Jesuit plot.

John Lyly's "Euphues and his England" appeared. It was the second in a two-volume series. The first, "Euphues, the Anatomy of Wit," was published in 1578.

Andrea Palladio, Italian architect, died (born 1518). He had included a permanent scenic (cont.) background in the Teatro Olympico at Vicenza.

English architecture: Montacute House (160' x 85').

(to 1582) Ferretti was supposed to have been the choirmaster at the Santa Casa in Loreto during these years.

(and 1582, 1587, 1605) Nanino's "Madrigali," Lib. II was published and reprinted at these times.

(to c.1583) Guarini's dramatic poem, "Il Pastor Fido," was started in 1580 and completed about three years later.

(to 1584) Sir Philip Sidney met Lady Rich and wrote a sonnet sequence to her called "Astrophel and Stella." This cycle was the first collection of love sonnets of this quality. The form was important in the development of English poetry in the Elizabethan period.

(to 1588) Caimo was organist at the Milan Cathedral during these years.

(and 1588) Palestrina's second volume of motets was reprinted by Scotto, in Venice, at both of these dates.

(to 1588) English architecture: Wollaton Hall (190' wide).

(to 1589) The canzonetta was a simple three-or four-part setting of an unpretentious poem and first appeared as a form during this period.

(to 1589) Collectors of anthologies with names such as Nervi d'Orfeo or "Lieblicher,

1580(cont.)

Welscher Madrigalien auss den berühmtester Musicis Italicis" used Marenzio's music. His works of this period were their choices.

(to 1589) Marenzio produced nine books of madrigals for five voices during this period.

(to 1589) De Wert became interested in academic ideas during these years.

(to 1590) Monteverdi studied with Ingegneri during these years.

(to 1590, 1611) Vecchi's four books of Canzonette for four voices written between 1580 and 1590 were later collected with additions by Phalesius (1611).

(to 1600) A manuscript book carrying these dates and including twenty-two ricercari and fugues in four and five parts, as well as other popular songs, was preserved in a private collection in England.

c.1580

Gregorio Allegri, a priest and composer, was born at Rome (died 1652, February 18).

Hans Bach, son of Veit, was born (died 1626). He was described as "the player," a professional musician.

Jacques Cordier, known also as Bocan, was born at Lorraine (date of death unknown). He was a violinist as well as a dancing master.

Alfonso Ferrabosco, II the younger was born at Greenwich (died 1628).

Thomas Ford, an English composer, was born (died 1648).

John Farmer, "practitioner in the art of Musique," was active at this time.

Farnaby, Mus. Bac., started his musical studies.

Jacob Gallus (Handl), a native of Krain, was active at this time. He was kapellmeister first to Stanislas Pawlowski, Bishop of Olmütz, and later at the imperial chapel in Prague.

Da Monte was a serious composer and became more conservative in his last two books of four-part madrigals. Although in many respects quite "modern," he would not compose canzonettas, which had by this time already been very influential on the style of madrigals.

Szadek was Chaplain of the Rorantists.

The art of composing for concerted voices in strict diatonic style reached its highest point of excellence at about this time.

Experiments proved the expediency of placing soundholes front to front as demonstrated in an early Italian violin from this time. Using this system the soundhole attained the familiar shape which is distinctive of the violin family.

Lassus published a new set of "Vigiliae Mortuorum."

Adam Puschman, a pupil of Hans Sachs, wrote "Songbook and A thorough Description of the German Meistergesang."

c.1580(cont.)

John Webster, English playwright, was born (died 1625).

Tarquinia Molza arrived at the court of Ferrara.

Cycles of mystery and miracle plays existed in England as late as this date.

Franz Hals, Dutch portrait painter, was born (died 1666).

Juan Montañes, a great Spanish sculptor, was born (died 1649).

French painting: Antoine Caron, Augustus and the Sibyl.

Italian painting: Veronese, Rape of Europa.

Italian painting: Veronese, Venus and Adonis (83½" x 75¼").

(to 1581) Franz Hals, painter, was christened.

(to c.1599) At about this time songs for one voice began to be well-received and to push airs for three, four, five and six voices out of the forefront.

(to c.1599) The Cancionero in Turin preserved canciones and villancicos from this period.

(to c.1599) During this period a great deal of "entertainment" music, with quasi-dramatic texts was composed. However, it was not intended for actual staged productions.

(to c.1599) This period produced the finest music ever written for the services of the Catholic church, music of both aesthetic and liturgical perfection never since surpassed, (cont.) perhaps not even equalled.

(to c.1599) Italian music came strongly to the forefront during these years.

(to c.1599) At this time the trend was to move the melody from the tenor to the soprano, a beginning of "polarity of voices."

(to c.1599) Peter Philipps was canon at Bethune in French Flanders during these years.

(to c.1599) During these years sacred music was greatly influenced by the rising tide of Protestantism and the Counter -Reformation movement.

(to c.1599) Within a period of a few years two or three great composers came from Saxony.

(to c.1599) The Tenbury manuscript was from this period.

(to c.1600) John Dowland's almans, galliards, and toys, included clear harmonies that supported dance tunes. Occasional sudden changes in tonality indicated that the composer went to Italy during this period.

(to c.1600) Most English composers apparently became fascinated by the knowledge displayed by Italian composers in their music.

(to 1600) Italy took the lead in European music for a period of more than two centuries. Her musical supremacy did not really assert itself until fairly late, with the Italian madrigalists. The imagination and courage

c.1580(cont.)
displayed by the pioneers of Florentine opera helped put Italy in its commanding position.

(to 1640) Gaspar di Salo, Giovita Rodiani Zanetto and Maggini Zanetto were all making instruments in Brescia during these years.

1581

(February 7) Luca Monteverdi was born (date of death unknown).

(February 24) Notice of an intended marriage between Palestrina and Virginia Dormuli was given.

(March 20) Palestrina had been admitted to minor orders of the priest hood. This was indeed strange in view of his projected marriage.

(March 28) Palestrina married Virginia Dormuli.

(April 10) Luca Marenzio was in Venice and dedicated his first book of madrigals for six voices to Alfonso d'Este, Duke of Ferrara.

(May 1) Sweelinck was city organist at the Protestant "Oude Kerk in Amsterdam.

(June 26) Da Monte's tenth book of madrigals appeared.

(June 28 and 1582, January 19, April 2; 1583, January 18, April 15, December 4; 1584, March 27, May 4, October 5; 1585, March 31, July 2; 1586, October 7; 1592, April 7) The Sessions Rolls of the County of Middlesex showed that true bills "for not going to church, chapel or any usual place of common (cont.) prayer" were found against "Juliana Birde wife of William Byrde" of Harlington. A servant of Byrd's, John Reason, was included in all these indictments, and Byrd himself was included in the one on October 7, 1586. Also Byrd appeared without his wife or servant in a true bill found against him on April 7, 1592.

(July 2) Michel de Montaigne went from Florence to Empoli.

(August 14) Urbani provided a description of a musical evening at the court of Mantua.

(October 15, Sunday) Baltazarini produced "Circe" at the marriage of the Duc de Joyeuse and Mlle. de Vaudemont on this date. It bore the title "Ballet comique de la royne" and was a genuine ballet de cour as well as the first ballet music that was preserved. Baif, Jodelle, Ronsard and other poets were in charge of court entertainment and their joint efforts provided a sense of unity that contibuted to the ballet. Dance tunes, choruses, musical dialogues, and ritornelli were composed by Beaulieu and Salmon. The ballet was acted at the Chateau de Moutiers and attended by King Henri III (Petit Bourbon Palace, Paris). The cost of production was said to be between three and four million francs.

(October 17) Byrd's interest in Michael Tempest's wife, Dorothy, was shown by an incident revealed in a holograph letter preserved at the Record Office and bearing this date.

(January) The papal bull in

1581 (cont.)

which Palestrina was designated a "clericus" carried this date.

(February) Urbani mentioned Laura Peperara ("La Mantovana") as performing duets with Giulio Cesare Brancaccio, in a report of this date.

(June) The first authorized edition of the "Gerusalemme liberata" appeared at Ferrara at this time.

Giulio Cesare Colonna died (birthdate unknown).

G.P. Maggini, a violin maker and pupil of Gasparo da Salo, was born (died 1632).

Johann Staden, a German lieder composer, was born (died 1634).

Alexander Utendal, a Netherlandish kapellmeister at Innsbruck, died (birthdate unknown).

Asola was appointed maestro di cappella at the Vicenza Cathedral.

A list of places frequented by certain recusants in and about London on this date included the following entry: "Wyll'm Byred of the Chappele, at his house in p'rshe of Harlington, in com. Midds."

The Christ Church manuscripts (984-8) were started in this year.

Severin Cornet, a Netherlandish composer was "maitre des enfants de choeur" at the Cathedral of our Lady at Antwerp.

The "Robert Dow" set of manu- (cont.) script part-books were started this year.

Giovanni Andrea Dragoni became choirmaster at the church of St. Giovanni in Laterano.

Vicentio Galileo stated in his "Dissertation on Ancient and Modern Music," published at Florence this year, that the double harp (harp with two rows of strings) was common in Italy at the time.

Galilei at this time and Kircher at a later date, described the practice of leaving the Spaces vacant and indicating the Notes by Points placed upon the Lines only, the actual degrees of the scale being determined by Greek letters at the end of the staff.

Gumpelzhaimer assumed the position of Cantor at Augsburg, where he remained until his death in 1625.

De la Hèle left for Madrid.

Ingegneri married Margherita de Soresina, a Cremonese noblewoman.

Le Jeune attended the wedding of the Duc de Joyeuse, and commented on the magical effect of his own music.

Marenzio began to publish.

Mauduit won a prize at a musical contest held by the Confraternity of St. Cecilia at Evreux.

Da Monte dedicated his tenth madrigal book to the Emperor this year. He spoke openly of his attempts to alter his style in order to please those who were dissatisfied with his earlier works.

Palestrina married again.

Three of Palestrina's grandchildren, the two orphans left by Angelo, whose widow remarried, and an infant son of Iginio all died before the year was over. They stayed with their maternal grandfather but Palestrina paid for their maintenance.

Palestrina was involved with the young Duke of Sora, a son born to Pope Gregory XIII before he entered the priesthood.

Francesco Soriano was Maestro di cappella at St. Ludovico dei Francesi.

Byrd's "Song of Pietie," "Why do I use my paper, ink and pen?" was composed to words by Henry Walpole. It served as "An Epitaph of the Life and Death of the most famous Clerk and virtuous Priest Edmund Campion," who was executed this year.

Marco Fabritio Caroso's "Il Ballerino . . . con intavolatura di liuto, e il soprano della musica nella sonata di ciascun ballo" was published at Venice. It was actually a dance manual.

Giovanni Cavaccio's "Magnificat omnitonum, pars I" was published at Venice.

Severin Cornet's "Chansons françoises" were published at Antwerp.

Mateo Flecha the Elder composed ensaladas which were collected by Mateo Flecha the Younger who published them at Prague this (cont.) year. He included ensaladas by himself and by "otros authores" in the volume.

Galilei's "Diálogo della musica antica e della moderna" was published at Florence. It was the first volume to include the so-called Hymns of Mesomedes, early Grecian pagan music. The book dealt with the abuses of "modern music" and was particularly critical about the technique of "tone painting."

Galilei's "Discorso intorno alle opere di messer Gioseffe Zarlino di Chioggia" was published at Florence.

Lassus' "Liber Missarum" was published by Gerlach.

Lassus published a "Libro de Villanelle, Moresche, et altre Canzoni, a 4, 5, 6 et 8 voci, in Paris. The collection was dedicated to his patron, Duke William V.

Lassus" "Libro De Villanelle, Moresche, et altre Canzoni" for four, five and eight voices was published in Paris. It included twenty-three selections, some of them well-known and unmistakeably late compositions of derivative or "relative" character.

Marenzio's "Il 1° libro de Madrigali a 6 voci" was published by Gardano at Venice.

Marenzio's second madrigal book for six voices was dedicated to Duke Alfonso.

Marenzio's "Il 2° libro de Madrigali a 5 voci" was published by Gardano at Venice.

1581(cont.)

Marenzio's third madrigal book for five voices was dedicated to Lucrezia, the Duchess of Urbino.

Palestrina's Book I for five voices was published.

Palestrina published a series of "Canzoni spirituali" including twenty-six pieces. Settings of Petrarch's mystical stanzas to the Blessed Virgin "Vergine bella che di sol vestita" comprised the first eight numbers in the collection. The Petrarch settings were dedicated to Giacomo Boncompagni.

Palestrina's fourth book of masses was published.

Palestrina's collection of twenty-one motets was published.

Palestrina's motets "super flumina Babylonis" and "Sicut cervus" were published.

Palestrina's third volume of motets was reprinted by Scotto and Gardano at Venice (see also 1575, 1589 and 1594).

Pallavicino published his first book of five-voiced madrigals.

Francesco Soriano published a book of madrigals for five voices. This was his first work.

Vittoria's book of hymns for four voices including four Psalms for eight voices, was published at Rome this year. The full title was "Hymni totius anni secundum S. Rom. Eccl. consvetudinem qui quatuor concinuntur vocibus, una cum quatuor Psalmis pro praecipuis festivitatibus, qui Octo (cont.) vocibus modulantur." All the hymns for the liturgical year were included.

Additional magnificat settings by Victoria were published (see also 1576). The original title was "Cantica B.V. vulgo Magnificat 4 voc. cum 4 Antiphones B.V. per annum 5 and 8 voc."

Two of Victoria's collections were published at Rome.

Wert's first settings of texts by Tasso were included in his seventh madrigal book published this year. Also included was a setting of Guarinis "Tirsi morir volea."

The trend toward dramatic treatment started with the Ballet Comique de la Royne and continued in the rejuvenated ballet now known as the "ballet de cour."

Queen Elizabeth's orchestra at this time included flutes, sackbuts, trumpets and violins, as well as musicians whose instruments were not distinctly specified.

John Lyly's "Campaspe" was written.

Merbecke published "A Book of Notes and Common Places," and "The Ripping up of the Pope's Fardel," the latter a theological work.

A collection of sonnets by Thomas Watson titled, "Hecatompathia, or Passionate Centurie of Love," was licensed during this year.

Marc Duval, a French painter,

1581(cont.)

died (born c.1530).

(and 1582) Lassus' special privilege for the publication of his works, granted to him by King Henry III, was renewed in both of these years.

(and 1582) Giovanni Macque's books of six-voiced "madrigaletti e napolitane" appeared during these years.

(and 1583) The Reverendo Monsignore Lodovico Agostini of Ferrara was certainly an admirer and follower of Striggio, whose "Nasce la pena mia" he parodied in a canzone of his own this year and whose style he used as a model in other madrigals, "Dolce Lucrezia," 1583, "Ad imitazione del S. Al. Striggio."

(to 1584) Guerrero was in Rome during these years.

(to 1584) Pietro Vinci was maestro di cappella at the Nicosia Cathedral during this period.

(to 1585) The historical value of Byrd's songs lay in the fact that at least some of them were written many years before the publication of Dowland's "First Book of Songs or Ayres." Several were included in the Christ Church manuscripts (984-8) which dated from these years.

(and 1585) Warton referred to a small publication, "VII Steppes to heaven, alias the vij (penitential) Psalms reduced into meter by Will Hunnys." He stated that this book was published by Henry Denham in this year and also that "Seven sobs (cont.) of a sorrowfull soule for sinne," published in 1585, was a second edition of the same work but with a new title.

(to 1586) Guglielmo I employed Palestrina's pupil Soriano at Mantua during these years.

(and 1586) Wert's music for Tasso's "Gerusalemme" appeared at these dates.

(to 1587) Christopher Marlowe was educated at the King's School, Canterbury and at Corpus Christi (then Bene't College, Cambridge) where he held a scholarship during this period.

(to 1590) Guarini's "Il Pastor fido" written during this period ranked with the poetical works of Tasso whose pastoral comedy "Aminta" had already inspired many madrigalists. The Guarini work was a major poetical source for Monteverdi's most emotional madrigals.

(and 1594) Palestrina's so-called "Madrigali Spirituali," in two volumes, published in these years respectively, were composed for the members of Neri's congregations.

(to 1594) From 1581 to his death Palestrina published three books of madrigals, three of motets and four collections of masses. He also published two each of litanies and offertories and one each of hymns and magnificats. He used money earned in the fur business to finance these publications.

(to 1600) Complete instructions for dancing of the Passamezzo were included in Caroso's "Il

1581(cont.)

Ballarino" published at Venice in 1581 and also in "Nobiltà di Dame" published in 1600, also at Venice.

(to 1611) Giovanni Cavaccio's works included madrigals, magnificats, and Psalms, all composed during this period.

c.1581

Leroy published five volumes of chansons for four voices. Thirty-nine were by Le Jeune, and valued highly by Leroy, a musician himself who issued them with works by Lassus. The last two volumes were devoted exclusively to those two composers.

Soriano became choirmaster at St. Luigi dei Francesi.

Soriano while in service at Mantua was maestro of the duke's private chapel for sometime.

(to 1585) Robert Dow, who wrote a set of part-books at Christ Church, Oxford during this period, added a more elaborate note than usual at the end of one of Byrd's compositions.

(to 1588) Soriano while in the service of the Duke of Mantua dedicated a book of five-part madrigals to each employer.

1582

(January 19) See Byrd entry 1581, June 28.

(February 1) Lassus' "jampridem summâ diligentiâ compositum," 26 sacrae cantiones à 5 appeared.

(April 2) See Byrd entry 1581, June 28.

(October 23) A letter was written to Lord Burghley, on this date, by T. Norton. It summed up the complaints by stating that "Bird and Tallys have musike bookes with note which the complainantes confesse they wold not print nor be furnished to print though there were no privilege. They have also ruled paper for musike."

(November 28) A marriage license was issued to William Shakespeare and Anne Hathaway.

(December 1) Marenzio was at Rome.

(December 24) John Bull was appointed organist of Hereford Cathedral and later master of the children.

(January) Lassus dedicated a book containing the second set of "Lectiones ex libris Hiob," and eleven new motets to the Bishop of Würtzburg.

(March) Lassus' set of Motets in six parts "singulari authoris industriâ," was composed for voices or instruments.

(August) Monteverdi described himself for the first time as "discepolo di Ingegneri" on the title-page of his publication, the "Cantiunculae Sacrae" at this time.

Jean de Clève, Netherlandish composer, died (born 1529).

Severin Cornet, a composer referred to in a Rossignol composition, died (born c.1540).

Pedro Alberch Vila (Vich), Spanish composer, died at

1582(cont.)

Barcelona (born 1517).

Robert Brown and Richard Jones were already associated by this date as members of the Earl of Worcester's troupe.

An attempt to attract Gioseppe Caimo to Munich was made but negotiations were unsuccessful.

Calvisius became Cantor at Schulpforte.

John Day was Master of the Stationers' Company.

Gastoldi was appointed successor to the ailing de Wert as choirmaster at St. Barbara.

Gastoldi was director of church music at Mantua after 1582.

Granjon was at Rome at this time.

The later Directorium corresponded to the work prepared by Guidetti at this time, with the assistance of his teacher Palestrina.

Lassus had no fixed method of writing his name, in the "Lectiones Hiob" of this year he signed it "Orlando de Lasso."

Marenzio composed a few things for the ladies of Ferrara on order of the Cardinal.

Nenna, a native of Bari, dedicated his first madrigal book to Fabrizio Carafa, Duke of Andria.

Pallavicino was at Mantua from this date forward.

Wert became seriously ill and had to turn his duties at St. Barbara over to Gastoldi.

Zarlino was elected a Canon of Chioggia.

Giulio Cesare Barbetta's "Novae tabulae musicae testudinariae hexachordae et heptachordae . . ." was published at Strassbourg.

Didier le Blanc's "Airs de plusieurs musiciens . . ." was reprinted.

Calvisius' treatise "Melopeia . . ." was published this year at Erfurt.

Giovanni Caraccio's "Magnificat omnitonum pars 2" was published at Venice.

The Finnish collection "Piae Cantiones" appeared.

Galilei composed a setting of Ugolino's monologue from Dante's "Inferno."

Guerrero dedicated the second volume of his masses published this year to the Virgin.

"Directorium chori . . . Opera Joannis Guidetti Boneniensis, etc." was published. Guidetti held the rights for the sale of the volume for a ten-year period (see entry for 1576).

Kerle's "Missa de Beata Virgine" appeared in a revision with the tropes removed.

Lassus authorized a "Christianized" German edition of his works to be issued at Ratisbon this year.

Motetta by di Lassus were pub-

1582(cont.)

lished at Monaco by A. Berg.

Leonhard Lechner's "Neue teutsche Lieder" appeared.

Macque's third madrigal book appeared.

Marenzio's Il 1° libro de Madrigali a 5 voci was reprinted by Gardano at Venice.

Two of Marenzio's madrigals were included in "Dolci Affetti Madrigali a cinque voci, Venice, herede di Scotto."

Two of Marenzio's madrigals were included in "Il Lauro Secco, Ferrara, Baldini."

One of Marenzio's madrigals, arranged for lute, was included in "Novae tabulae musicae Strasbourg, Jobin."

Marenzio's "Il 3° libro de Madrigali a 5 voci" was published by Gardano at Venice. It was dedicated to the Accademici Filarmonici at Verona which was under the patronage of Mario Bevilacqua.

Da Monte's first and only book of three-voiced madrigals was commissioned by the publisher Gardano, who dedicated it to Maddalena Casulana, a composer.

Monteverdi's "Liber Primus" of the "Cantiunculae Sacrae" was published. The contents were three-part motets composed to scripture texts from the "Breviarum Romanum." The composer was only fifteen years old but the work established him immediately as a child genius.

Nanino's "Madrigali," Lib. II was reprinted (see also 1580, 1587, 1605).

Nenna's first book of madrigals appeared.

The first publication of the following occurred: "Eripeme," "L'Homme armé," "Jesu nostra redemptio," "Lauda Sion," "O magnum mysterium," "Primi toni," and "Secunda."

Palestrina's Missa quarta of this year was based on "L'homme armé."

The "Piae Cantiones" was published by Theodoricus Petri at Greifswald in western Pomerania (then part of Sweden). The volume was a collection of anonymous school and religious songs in one to four parts. The introduction described the work as much used in Finland and Sweden.

Peeter Philips' "Fantasia" for virginal appeared.

The "Dolci affetti" was a collection of five-voiced madrigals published this year by the heirs to Scotto in Venice. The collection was dedicated to Monsignor Ottavio Bandini.

A German psalter with one-line melodies by Caspar Ulenberg was published.

St. Theresa of Jesus died (born 1515).

Lawrence and William Hollingsworth acquired a twenty-one year lease on Stondon Place from Shelley.

The Jubilate was added to the

1582(cont.)

Benedictus in this year thus eliminating repetition when the Benedictus occurred in the gospel or second lesson.

Some of the earliest examples of orchestral scores still in existence were those from Baltazarini's "Ballet comique de la royne" published in Paris this year.

(to 1584) Monteverdi's early works from these years came into existence at the peak of the Renaissance.

(to 1584) Details of Palestrina's life during these years were scarce.

(to 1587) Monteverdi dedicated his works published during these years to Cremonese clergy and noblemen including Pater Caninio Valcarengo, Count Marco Verità, and the patricians Pietro Ambrosini and Alless. Fraganesco, who probably helped the rising young musician.

(to 1591) Kerle was imperial court chaplain to Rudolph II in Prague.

(to 1595) Del Mel published five books of motets and fifteen books of madrigals during these years. He also contributed to several collections which brought his name to Antwerp, Munich, Nürnberg, Rome, and Venice.

c.1582

Thomas Ravenscroft, Mus. Bac., English composer, was born (died c.1630).

Dowland returned to England.

Edmond Hooper became connected with the choir at Westminster Abbey.

Alfonso I entered the service of Duke Charles Emmanuel I of Savoy at Turin.

1583

(January 18) See Byrd entry 1581, June 28.

(January 27) A raid was made upon "the house of M[ris] Hampden of Stocke (?Stoke) in the County of Bucks" and an inventory was made "of suche things as were found and caryed away from there by Mr Pawle Wentworth."

(February 16) Vecchi was appointed choirmaster at Modena cathedral.

(April 15) See Byrd entry 1581, June 28.

(September 9) An article by F.X. Haberl in "Kirchenmusikalisches Jahrbuch für das Jahr (Regensburg)" provided documentary evidence which showed that Frescobaldi was born in 1583. The register of his baptism at the Cathedral of Ferrara was the source of the evidence.

(September 9) Giróolamo Frescobaldi, Italian composer and quite possibly the greatest organist of his time, was born at Ferrara (died 1643). He became organist at St. Peter's in Rome.

(December 4) See Byrd entry 1581, June 28).

(April) Tarquinia Molza entered the service of Lucrezia Duchess of Ferrara as a "dama d'onore"

1583(cont.)

and was immediately in the center of musical life at the d'Este court.

(April) Porta went to the court of Ferrara from Ravenna.

(May) Shakespeare's first child, Susanna, was baptized.

Girolamo Belli was born as a subject of Duke Alfonso of Ferrara and dedicated his first work, a book of six-voiced madrigals, to him.

Manuel Rodrigues Coelho, a Portuguese composer of Flores de Musica, a collection of tientes, was born (died c.1623). He was also a harpist and organist.

Orlando Gibbons, English composer, organist, and virginalist, was born, probably at Cambridge (died 1625, June 5). He was a pre-eminent madrigalist and later in life was awarded a Doctorate in music from Oxford.

The Reverend Monsignore Lodovico Agostini of Ferrara dedicated a madrigal to the singer Laura Peperara, "De l'odorate spoglie," this year.

Ammerbach and Schmid the Younger extended the upper limit of the range to c'''.

Giulio Cesare Brancaccio lived at Alfonso's court. His excellent bass voice was praised by both Guarini and Tasso.

Du Caurroy was a prize-winner in musical contests held by the Confraternity of St. Cecilia at Evreux, one this year and an earlier one in 1576.

Eccard was made vice-capellmeister at Königsberg.

A private library in Vienna preserved Hadrianus, "Pratum Musicum," one of the earliest lute tablatures known, carrying this date.

There was a twenty-seven year interval between the publication of the "Madrigali Spirituali" in this year and Monteverdi's next piece of sacred music.

Palestrina was offered another opportunity to leave Rome. He was offered the position of musical director at the court of his patron, the Duke of Mantua, but his salary demands were again excessive.

Cardinal-prince, Andrea Bathory was sent as ambassador to the Papacy by King Stephen of Poland, his uncle, in this year. Since he loved music, he sought out Pierluigi, who was enjoying the peak of the fame and acclamation brought on by his motets on the Song of Solomon.

Peri was Maestro to Ferdinand I.

La Pietà de'Turchini was founded.

Heinrich Posthumus von Reuss while he was a student at the University of Strassburg may have participated in some of the musical activities of the Argentina.

San Onofrio was founded.

Torquato Tasso's "Aminta" was performed at Ferrara. It was a fine example of pastorale drama.

De Wert initiated his visits to Ferrara.

1583(cont.)

Duke William sent a set of madrigals to the press.

Duke William sent a copy of published madrigals to the d'Este Court.

After the death of Marco de' Medici, Bishop of Chioggia in this year, Zarlino was selected to fill the vacant See.

The Reverend Monsignore Lodovico Agostini of Ferrara used Striggio's style as a model in the madrigals, "Dolce Lucrezia," 1583, "Ad imitazione del S. Al. Striggio" (see also 1581).

Ammerbach's tablature appeared.

"Li amorosi ardori di diversi eccellentissimi musici," a secular collection, appeared.

The "Quomodo cantabimus" by Byrd was found in a manuscript that was placed at this date.

Giovanni Caraccio's "Madrigali a 5 voci, lib. I" was published at Venice.

The "Dallis Pupil's Lute Book" appeared this year.

Some selections from Ferretti's canzoni publications appeared in reprints issued at Antwerp around this time.

One of Andrea Gabrieli's finest works was "Psalmi Davidici poenitentiales, tum omnis generis instrumentorum, tum ad vocis modulationum accomodati, sex vocum" published at Venice this year.

Gabrieli's book of Salmi (cont.) Davidici referred to instruments on the title page.

Galilei, father of the astronomer, was the author of a dialogue on the lute, "Il Fronimo," published this year at Venice.

The "Villotte mantovane" of this year was published at Venice by Gardano.

Lassus wrote thirty-three original chansons to sacred and secular German words "Neue teutsche Lieder, geistlich und weltlich," short pieces in four-part counterpoint.

Lassus' Teutsche Lieder mit fünff Stimmen was published at Nürnberg.

Some of Lassus' German lieder were published in a collection at this date (see also 1572, 1573, 1576 and 1590).

Marenzio's "Il 2° libro de Madrigali a 5 voci" was reprinted at Venice by Gardano.

One of Marenzio's madrigals was included in "Li Amorosi Ardori di Diversi Eccellentissimi Musici" published by Gardano at Venice.

One of Marenzio's madrigals was included in "De Floridi Virtuosi d'Italia" published at Venice by Vincenti and Amadino.

Four madrigals by Marenzio were included in "Harmonia Celeste di diversi eccellentissimi musici" published by Phalèse and Bellère at Antwerp.

One madrigal by Marenzio was included in "Il Lauro Verde" published by Baldini at Ferrara.

1583(cont.)

One madrigal by Marenzio was included in "Musica divina di XIX autori illustri" published by Phalèse and Bellère at Antwerp.

Da Monte's first book of "madrigali spirituali" for six voices appeared.

Da Monte set the opening verses of the Psalm "Quomodo cantabimus" for eight voices and sent the motet to Byrd in this year.

Monteverdi's "Madrigali Spirituali" appeared.

An Italian madrigal collection, "Musica divina," was published at Antwerp.

Otto's "Cantiones sacrae" for five to six voices was published.

Jacob Paix's "Tabulatura Nova" appeared.

An Italian madrigal collection, "Harmonia celeste . . . raccolta per Andrea Pevernage," was published at Antwerp.

A Pass'e mezzo d'Italia included in the Phalèse book of this year showed a striking example of an augmented sixth chord.

Phalèse's "Chorearum molliorum collectanea" appeared.

A collection of motets published at Nürnberg this year contained three motets by Porta, one of them being the six-part "Oravi Dominum Deum."

A complete edition of sixty-seven lieder by Regnart, "Kurtzweilige teutsche Lieder zu dreyen stimmen nach art der Neapolitanen order Welschen (cont.) Villanellen" was published.

Book II of a series edited by Soto de Langa was published. It included twenty-eight three-part laude and nineteen for four voices. Four were carried over from the 1577 book and six had Spanish texts.

The third Roman book of laude was reprinted, with alterations. This was the beginning of a new series of five collections, edited by Soto de Langa.

Another edition of Bartolommeo Spontone sets of madrigals for five voices was published at Venice. There had been an earlier edition in 1567 and another was issued in 1585.

Vecchi's book of madrigals for six voices appeared.

Victoria published a four-voice Missa pro defunctis which included the Responsory for the Absolution, Libera me. The plainsong was in the superius.

Vittoria's "A First Book of Masses" was published at Rome in this year. The volume was dedicated to King Philip II of Spain, and included nine masses, five for four voices, two for five voices, and two for six voices.

Vittoria published a new book of motets for four, five, six, eight and twelve voices at Rome during this year.

Vittoria's first book of motets for four to eight voices was reprinted with additions during this year.

1583(cont.)

De Wert along with other madrigalists payed tribute to Laura Peperara in a collection, "Il Lauro verde . . . a sei voci" published this year.

Italy's musical development throughout this century and up to the time of Monteverdi's first publication this year followed the polyphonic principle in sacred composition and in chamber music that had been inspired by the Flemish and French Masters.

Hugo Grotius, Dutch humorist and jurist, was born (died 1645).

Wallenstein, a born Lutheran, however, Jesuit-trained general, was born (died 1634).

Laura Peperara married Count Annibale Turco.

The Company of Rome was started as a society apparently for the purpose of ousting foreigners from Rome.

Several poems by Nevill were included in Bentley's "Monument of Matrons" published this year.

Sir Philip Sidney wrote his "Defense of Poesy."

The term "tan-ta-ra" appeared in Stanyhurst at this time.

(to 1584) Da Monte and Byrd initiated a friendly exchange of compositions during this period.

(and 1584) The poets who contributed the texts for Monteverdi's early "Canzonette a 3" (1584) and the fragmentary (cont.) "Madrigali Spirituali" (1583) were anonymous.

(and 1586) De Wert's service as maestro di cappella at Mantua was interrupted by illness. When this occurred his place was temporarily taken by Gastoldi, who may well have been de Wert's assistant. Gastoldi apparently did not, however, succeed de Wert in the position.

(to 1587) Every antholigist from this period wanted one of Marenzio's works, either a new one or an older one in reprint, such as a madrigal from Marenzio's own collections.

(to 1587) Marenzio was in touch with the Tuscan Court at this time. This was made obvious by his dedication of an earlier book of five-part madrigals to the Grand Duchess Bianca Capello.

(to 1587) Italian painting: Tintoretto, St. Mary of Egypt (13'11" x 6'11").

(to 1589) Nine volumes of de Wert's works from this period were collected at a Glascow library.

(and 1590) Cristofano Malvezzi of Lucca composed two books of madrigals for five voices in these two years respectively. The last one was dedicated to Emilio de' Cavalieri.

(to 1591) Ruggiero Giovanelli was maestro di cappella at San Luigi de' Francesi during these years.

(to 1598) Le Roy served as maestro at the Viceroyal Chapel during this period.

c.1583

Michael Altenburg, the first of a musical family of some repute, was born at Tröchtel in Thuringia (date of death unknown).

Robert Johnson II, composer and lutenist, was born (died 1634).

William Lawes, composer of music for masques, was born (died 1645).

1584

(March 27) See Byrd entry 1581, June 28.

(April 15) Marenzio dedicated his second book of six-voiced madrigals to "Cardinal di Guisa."

(April 24) Marenzio was in Rome on this date.

(April 29) Marenzio dedicated his "madrigali spirituali a cinque" to Lodovico Bianchetti, Chamberlain to Pope Gregory XIII.

(May 4) See Byrd entry 1581, June 28.

(May 5) Marenzio dedicated his fourth book of five-voiced madrigals to a Signor Girolamo Ruis. It was one of four publications by Marenzio whose dedications were executed at Venice.

(July 23) John Day, English music printer and publisher, died (birthdate unknown).

(August 27) Palestrina wrote a letter on this date to the Duke of Mantua which started, "The boundless obligations I have towards your Highness," and continued by Palestrina's offering the Duke a copy of the (cont.) "new book of motets on the Song of Solomon."

(October 5) See Byrd entry, 1581, June 28.

(October 31) Pietro Tini published Caimo's second book of "canzonette a quattro. He described the composer as no longer among the living and mentioned that he had died a "bitter and unexpected death."

(November 6) On this date Vincenzo Gonzaga wrote to de Wert from Poggio.

(November 20) Pietro Tini published a book of five-voiced madrigals by Caimo, "nobile milanese." The book included a dedication signed by the composer himself on this date, three weeks after his supposed death.

(December 15) Marenzio was in Rome on this date.

(December 22) De Wert was more often in Ferrara visiting Tarquinia Molza than he was in Mantua. On this date Duke Guglielmo demanded in sharp language that his choirmaster return at once.

John Taverner of Norfolk, later a professor of music at Gresham College, was born (died 1638, August).

Nathaniel Tomkins, chorister at Magdalen College, Oxford from 1596 to 1604, was born (date of death unknown).

Pietro Vinci, Italian madrigalist, died (born c.1530).

Girolamo Belli dedicated his second madrigal book for six

1584(cont.)

voices to Duke Guglielmo.

Kroyer stated that Caimo of Milan was already under the influence of Marenzio by this date.

The "Compagnia dei Musici di Roma" was instituted.

Conversi was in the service of Cardinal Granvella, Viceroy of Naples, at this time and perhaps even earlier.

The Della Pietà de' Turchini was instituted by the confraternity of St. Maria della Incoronatella. During the year they made their house an asylum for both the homeless orphans of Naples and those whose parents were unable to support them.

Dowland visited France and Germany and later went to Italy.

Antonio Dueto, a canon of the cathedral in Genoa, dedicated a book of madrigals to Nicolo Pallavicino, a nobleman from Genoa.

The French began to change to Italian tablature at this time.

Shortly after Merulo left his position at St. Mark's to go to Parma, Andrea Gabrieli was appointed first organist and the position of second organist went to his nephew Giovanni.

Giovanni Gabrieli filled the vacancy as first organist at St. Mark's after Merulo departed and prior to Andrea's appointment. He was, however, never officially appointed as first organist.

Some gipsies captured as they were leaving the residence of a Turkish official in occupied Hungary were greatly admired for their singing as well as their instruments. They had a two-stringed rebec and a psaltery plucked with the fingers, "with which the students make music at the Mass."

Hasler went to Venice to study with Andrea Gabrieli.

John Hilton was a lay-clerk as well as a member of the choir at Lincoln Cathedral.

Marenzio was chapel-master to Cardinal d'Este.

Raugel asserted that a certain Canon Marino had founded a "Congregazione di S. Cecilia" at the end of this year.

Palestrina was still hoping for the coveted position of "maestro" of the Papal Choir.

Palestrina's early madrigals were certainly not sensual. He was aware of this and in this year included an apology for them in the preface of a book of motets.

Palestrina publicly disavowed madrigals at this time.

In the dedication of the motets on the "Song of Solomon" to Pope Gregory XIII Palestrina berated the sins of his youth, which included the composition of madrigals.

Palestrina sent a copy of the "Song of Solomon" settings to the Duke as soon as they were published this year.

1584(cont.)

Pevernage apparently lived in Antwerp until this year.

Pevernage was permitted to resume his position at Courtrai at this time but only stayed there briefly.

Pinello was discharged from his position as court Kapellmeister in Dresden because he had allegedly threatened one of the choir boys with a dagger.

A group of copper engravers, led by Johannes Sadeler, began engraving copperplate reproductions of existing art works. Many of these included complete musical compositions.

Alessandro Striggio spied upon the singing of the "tre dame" at the d'Este court in Ferrara. He tried to exploit his discoveries in his own compositions.

A body calling itself the "Vertuosa Compagnia dei musici" was founded. Its members undertook mutual assistance and apparently felt there was religious significance to their work, possibly in the obligation to see that members had proper burial with a sung requiem.

Victoria entered the service of Empress Maria, sister of Philip II and widow of Maximilian II. He went with her to Madrid and in this year she and her daughter Margaret entered the convent of Descalzas Reales.

Pieces for two, three, and four lutes were included in the "Novum pratum musicum" by Emanuel Adriansen (Hadrianus) of Antwerp.

D'Antiquis' "Il primo libro di canzonette a due voci, da diversi autori di Bari" was published at Venice this year.

A highly imitative fantasia composed by de Antiquis carried this date.

Asola's Madrigali . . . of this year were peculiar in that canons for two voices were included.

William Bathe published "A Brief Introduction to the true arte of Musicke" this year.

Byrd composed "Quomodo cantabimus" for eight voices and sent a copy to da Monte at the above date.

Conversi's "Madrigali a 6 voci, lib. 1" were published in Venice at this time.

A lute-book by Gabriele Fallamero was published at this time.

Galilei's settings of five of Palestrina's secular madrigals for lute, including a collection of similar compositions published under the title of "Fronimo" by Scotto of Venice, was reissued. It had been originally published in 1568.

Twenty-nine two-part Contrapunti in ricercare style by Galilei appeared.

A third enlarged edition of "Geistliche Lieder und Psalmen" was published.

Girolamo dalla Casa's "Il vero modo di diminuir" appeared at this time. It was essentially a work on ornamentation.

Lassus' "Psalmi Davidis

1584(cont.)

poenitentiales" was published.

Cristofano Malvezzi of Lucca composed a book of madrigals for six voices during this year.

A reprint of Marenzio's Il 1° libro de Madrigali a 6 was issued by Gardano at Venice.

Marenzio's four madrigals arranged for lute in "Il 1° libro de intavolatura da liuto" were published by Gardano at Venice.

Marenzio's "Madrigali spirituali . . . a 5" was published at Rome by Gardano.

Marenzio's "Il 2° libro de Madrigali a 6" was published by Gardano at Venice.

Two madrigals by Marenzio were included in "Spoglia Amorosa" published at Venice by Scotto.

Marenzio's "Il 4° libro de Madrigali a 5" was published by Vincenti and Amadino at Venice.

Marenzio's "Il 1° libro delle Villanelle a 3, raccolte de Ferrante Franchi" was published by Vincenti and Amadino at Venice.

Florenzio Maschera's "Canzoni francesi" was published at Brescia.

Monteverdi's first secular publication, a collection of twenty-one canzonette for three voices, appeared this year. It was issued as opus 3 and published at Venice. The pieces were of high quality and had the same intricacies and complexities that had pervaded his madrigals. This volume with his "tricinium" (cont.) movements of the "Cantiunculae Sacrae" and the "Madrigali Spirituale" made his position as a leading composer significant.

Nanino's "Madrigali" Id., Lib. III" was published.

Palestrina's series of motets to texts selected from the Song of Solomon was published by Gardano. They were for five voices and there were twenty-nine selections included in the book which was dedicated to Pope Gregory XIII.

Palestrina published his fifth book of motets for five voices and dedicated it to Andrea Battore, nephew of Stephen, King of Poland. The latter had been appointed a Cardinal.

Sweelinck's pieces as well as several by Verdonck were included in a volume of chansons a 5 for instruments or voices issued this year.

Pietro Vinci's setting of "Quivi sospiri" appeared.

John Lyly's "Sappho and Phao" was written.

Christopher Marlowe received his B.A. degree from Corpus Christi (then Bene't) College, Cambridge.

George Peele's "The Arraignment of Paris" was published.

Sir Walter Raleigh headed the expedition which founded the American colony named "Virginia" by Raleigh in honor of Elizabeth, the virgin queen.

1584(cont.)

The "Nobil Accademia delli Pittori," an organization for painters, was founded.

Italian architecture: Palladio Vicenzo, Teatro Olimpico was completed (stage 230' wide).

(and 1586, 1588) Performances of Guarini's "Pastor Fido" in Ferrara (1584), Turin (1586) and Florence (1588) have been claimed but the facts have not been documented.

(to 1587) Villanellas by Marenzio were composed during this period.

(and 1588, 1591) Paolo Virchi's three madrigal books appeared at these years respectively.

(to 1590) Johannes Wanning's gospels for the year appeared during this period.

(to 1593) B.A. Wallner mentioned "conceiled music" in connection with the Stuttgart Lusthaus ("Art of Stone Engraving").

(to 1594) Spanish painting: El Greco, Unknown Man.

(to 1598) The reign of Czar Theodore I over Russia.

(to 1599) Monteverdi composed canzonettas and madrigals during this period.

(to 1638) Monteverdi's works in the idiom of the madrigal embraced the period from his earliest youth to his old age (Eighth Book of Madrigals, 1638).

(to 1652) A series of performances in Italian by Italian artists in France began in 1584 and continued with little or no interruption until 1652.

c.1584

Francis Beaumont, Elizabethan poet and playwright, was born (died 1616).

Hassler was appointed organist to Octavian Fugger II, a member of the Augsburg family of bankers.

Tasso wrote a dialogue "La Cavaletta."

Many texts by Tasso were set to music by Gesualdo, Marenzio, Monteverdi and de Wert. This competition was well documented in a series of valuable letters written about this time by Striggio (from Ferrara) to the Florentine court, particularly to the Grand Duke Francesco and his Secretary Belisario Vinta.

Nicholas Yonge's wife's name was Jane and they were probably married at about this time.

1585

(January 1) Giovanni Gabrieli actually succeeded Claudio Merulo as first organist of St. Mark's on this date.

(February 9) Marenzio dedicated his book of motets to Scipione Gonzaga.

(February 12) Marenzio's connection with Medici's was strengthened by his dedication of the third book of six-voiced madrigals to the Grand Duchess on this date.

(March 31) See Byrd entry 1581,

1585(cont.)

June 28.

(June 26) Nathaniel Giles received the degree of Bachelor of Music from Oxford.

(July 2) See Byrd entry 1581, June 28.

(July 15) Marenzio dedicated his only book of madrigals for four voices to his patron at the papal court "Monsignore Marc' Antonio Serlupi."

(July 15) Marenzio was still in Rome at this time.

(August 15) Palestrina's mass "Assumpta est Maria," according to some sources, was hurriedly composed for the Feast of the Assumption on this date and performed on that day at Santa Maria Maggiore.

(October 8) Heinrich Schütz, renowned German composer, was born at Köstritz, Saxony at 7:00 pm, according to the biography that was heard at his funeral (died 1672). His name was indissolubly associated with that of Monteverdi and the two must be considered as the major predecessors of Bach and Handel. Schütz received his formal education at the University of Marburg.

(October 9) Schütz was baptized on this date, according to the church record.

(November 23) Thomas Tallis, "father of English cathedral music," died at Greenwich (born c.1505). He was a great organist as well as composer and, in collaboration with Byrd, publisher.

(January) John Bull was elected to the Chapel Royal.

(February) Shakespeare's twin children, Hamnet and Judith, were baptized.

(October) Lassus was in Ferrara at this time.

Fernando Franco, first polyphonic composer in the New World, died at Mexico City (birthdate unknown).

Luigi Gesualdo, elder brother of the composer, died (birthdate unknown).

Johann Grabbe, early member of the musical family, was born (date of death unknown).

Pope Gregory died and was succeeded by Sixtus V.

Hans Heugel, German composer, died at Kassel (birthdate unknown).

The Rev. Giulio Cesare Martinengo was born in Verona (date of death unknown). He was maestro at St. Mark's for a period between Croce and Monteverdi.

Osbert Parsley, English composer, died (born 1511).

The registers of St. Giles, Cripplegate, confirmed the existence of a contemporary John Wilson, a musician, son of a minstrel, who was baptized this year.

Ancina in an epigram included in the 1585 motet collection stated that Victoria was known "even to the Indies." This statement was more than strik-

1585(cont.)

ing rhetoric since it was true.

Anerio was appointed maestro at the Collegium Anglicum.

Giovanni Bassano called himself "Musico dell' Illustr. Signoria di Venetia" in a publication of this year.

Bull was elected to the Chapel Royal.

When Tallis died the benefit of the monopoly in music-printing fell to Byrd and became his sole property. During the next few years he was very prolific in composition.

Byrd now owned the monopoly on music printing. At a later date he assigned his license for music -printing to Thomas East (Este).

Baron Giuliano Cesarini, a Roman, was made Duke of Cività Castellana by Pope Sixtus V in this year.

Croce dedicated his Opus I to the great Venetian families, the Bembos, the Morosini, the Priuli and the Sanudos.

Andrea Gabrieli became first organist at St. Mark's.

Giovanni Gabrielli became second organist at St. Mark's.

Carlo Gesulado, the composer, fell heir to the house of Gesualdo upon the death of his elder brother. He was forced to marry in order to produce an heir.

Lassus returned to Italy (also in 1562, 1567, 1574, 1578 and 1587).

Lechner went to Stuttgart.

In a dedication from Marenzio to Bianca Capello, Grand Duchess of Tuscany, he indicated that he was annoyed by the miserable salary his patron was paying him. The volume containing the dedication was the third book for six voices.

At the opening of the parliament of Medgyes this year a kettledrum player and eight trumpeters were stationed in front of the city hall. They alternated with the city trombonist who was stationed on the church steeple. The Prince was on his way to a "Te Deum" at the time.

A strange affair occurred which concerned the Papal Choir and involved Palestrina's name.

Palestrina wrote to the Duke of Mantua and included some compositions, the names of which were not specified. Palestrina made reference to himself as "quasi senili," "getting old," a reminder to the Duke that he was then fifty-nine years old.

Peri was attached to Grand Ducal Court at Florence.

A set of motets for six voices was dedicated to Pope Sixtus V by Porta. The title-page indicated that the composer had returned to Padua as chapel -master at the cathedral.

Primavera was an author as well as a prolific madrigalist. His madrigals were often settings of his poetry. He came from Barletta in Apulia and was on good terms with Gesualdo, to whom he dedicated his seventh

1585(cont.)

madrigal book this year.

Roy received the title of maestro di cappella from the Viceroy of Naples.

David Scheidemann was organist at St. Michael's church in Hamburg at this time.

Lord Lumley served on the commission that indicted William Shelley for high treason in this year. This fact created another link with Byrd's personal history.

Tallis remained a Gentleman of the Chapel Royal until his death this year.

Anerio's three books of "Sacred Madrigals" for five voices were published this year by Gardano at Rome.

Giovanni Bassano's seven "Fantasie a tre voci per cantar e sonar con ogni sorte d'Istrumenti" appeared.

The works of Joan Brudieu were published in Spanish.

The "Sadler" manuscript of this date included some motets by Byrd, but none were published during the composer's lifetime.

Cesare Caporali's "Le piacevoli rime" was published this year at Milan.

Giovanni Caraccio's "Musica a 5 voci da sonare" was published at Venice.

Tasso's "Gelo hà Madonna il seno e fiamma il volto" was set to music by Cavalieri.

Benjamin Cosyn, probably a son of John Cosyn, published sixty psalms in six parts in plain counterpoint this year.

"Musicke of six and five parts made upon the common tunes used in singing of the Psalmes by John Cosyn" was published in London by John Wolfe this year. The tunes had first been published by Daye.

Andrea Gabrieli wrote the music for a performance of "Edipo tiranno" performed at the opening of Palladio's Teatro Olimpico in Vicenza.

Andrea Gabrieli finished choral music for Giustiniani's translation of "Oedipus Rex" by Sophocles. This was produced at Vicenza.

Guerrero's dramatic-type Passions according to St. Matthew and St. John were essentially chordal settings for various combinations, from two to six voices. They were published this year.

"Seven sobs of a sorrowfull soule for sinne" was published this year. It was apparently a second edition of "VII steps to heaven . . ." published in 1581 and reduced into meter by Will Hunnys.

Le Jeune's Melanges included eight Italian madrigals and twenty-eight other Italian compositions.

The complete set of nine Lamentations were among Lassus' best works. The set was published this year.

Lassus set Petrarch's "Trionfo

1585(cont.)

della fama" to music, apparently for a special occasion. The work was included in his madrigals published this year.

In his madrigal book of this year, dedicated to Count Bevilacqua of Verona, Lassus ended with a composition for six voices in a canon. In the work the second cantus followed the first at the unison and gave an echo effect.

Lassus published a new set of madrigals for five voices and a book of motets which also included the "Hieremiae prophetae Lamentationes."

A tablature by Löffelholtz, in a manuscript bearing this date, contained forty-eight compositions, mostly dances.

The so-called Polish dance was included in Löffelholtz's Klavierbuch published this year.

Marenzio set Girolamo Casone's text "Quell' ombra esser vorrei" to music during this year.

Marenzio's "Il 2° libro delle Canzonette alla Napoletana a 3" was published by Vincenti and Amadino during this year.

Two of Marenzio's madrigals were included in "Canzonette Spirituali de Diversi, a tre voci libro primo" published by Gardano at Rome this year.

Four of Marenzio's madrigals were included in "Symphonia Angelica" published by Phalèse and Bellère at Antwerp during this year.

One of Marenzio's madrigals was (cont.) included in "Moscaglia, Il secondo libro de Madrigali a quattro voc" published by Vincenti and Amadino at Venice at this time.

Two of Marenzio's madrigals appeared in "Spoglia Amorosa Madrigali a cinque" published this year by Scotto at Venice.

Marenzio's "Il 3° libro delle Villanelle a 3" was published this year by Gardano at Rome.

A reprint of Marenzio's "Il 1° libro delle Villanelle a 3" appeared at Venice, issued by Vincenti.

Marenzio composed two more madrigal books, a book of motets and two collections of villanelle during this year.

Marenzio's "Motectorum pro festis totius anni" was published this year by Gardano and Amadino at Venice.

Giovanni Battista Moscaglia published a book of madrigals during this year.

Francesco Landoni printed Palestrina's madrigals "vestiva i colli" and "Cosi le chiome mie" in a miscellaneous volume. The title was "Spoglia Amorosa" and the publication was released through Scotto of Venice this year.

Four more masses by Palestrina appeared this year (though only in manuscript form for use by the Papal Choir).

This year marked the first publication of Palestrina's Mass #28, "Confitebor tibi."

1585(cont.)

Nicolaus Selneccer published seven penitential psalms.

A book of motets for six voices dedicated to Pope Sixtus V appeared. "Ecce sacerdos magnus" was included and was possibly written as a special tribute to the Pope.

Another edition of Bartolommeo Spontone's set of madrigals for five voices was published at Venice. There had been earlier editions in 1567 and 1583.

Luigi Tansillo's "Le Lagrime di San Pietro" was published but apparently not completed.

Two collections of Victoria's works were published at Rome.

A collection of Victoria's works published this year, "Motecta festorum totius anni," contained two compositions by Guerrero and one by Soriano.

Victoria's "Officium Hebdomadae Sanctae" was published this year at Rome.

Victoria set some portions of the Passion according to St. Matthew and they were included in the publication "Officium Hebdomadae Sanctae" published this year. The dramatic expressiveness shown in the work was unsurpassed in choral Literature. The parts chosen by Victoria were the parts of the text spoken by the crowd. Gardano published the composition at Rome.

An Italian madrigal collection by Waelrant, "Symphonia angelica . . .," was published at (cont.) Antwerp.

The "Trihoris" was mentioned by Rabelais ("Pantagruel," bk. iv. ch. xxxviii.) and by his imitator, Noël du Fail, Seigneur de la Herrisaye, in chapter xix. of his "Contes et Discours d'Eutrapel" which appeared this year.

Cardinal Richelieu, defender of the crown of France and patron of music, was born (died 1642).

Shortly after the assassination of William the Silent, Queen Elizabeth granted requests for support and in this year sent six thousand troops to the Netherland's under the leadership of Robert Dudley, Earl of Leicester.

Alexander Farnese recaptured Antwerp and restored Catholicism.

The academicians were stopped from activity because of the religious as well as civil fighting that eventually led to King Henry III's death and the group disappeared after this year.

(to 1586) Andrea Gabrieli was first organist at St. Mark's during these years.

(to 1586) William Kemp, a famous Shakespearian comedian and dancer of jigs, was in the Earl of Leicester's company and went with him to the Netherlands during these years.

(to 1586) De Wert was ill during these years.

(and 1589) Ruggiero Giovanelli published two books of music on the "sdruccioli" of the "Arcadia"

1585(cont.)
one in each of these years.

(and 1589) Palestrina dedicated a volume of hymns from 1589 to Pope Sixtus V. Probably, the dedication was executed since one of the hymns was associated with a memorable occasion in this year when the Pope had presided at a ceremony in the piazza of St. Peter's when the great obelisk, first brought from Egypt by Caligula, was erected there.

(to 1589) The Papal reign of St. Sixtus V (born in Grottammare). During his reign the Baroque period started to form.

(to 1590) Palestrina's 6-part mass written for feast of All Saints, "Ecce ego Joannes" was probably completed during the Pontificate of Sixtus V.

(to 1591) Balbi was maestro di cappella at San Antonio in Padua during this period.

(to 1591) Stefano Ugeri's name appeared in the Papal Choir lists during these years.

(to 1610) Eccard, Hassler, Lechner, and Schröter, the German-Venetian motettists, were all active during this period.

(to 1610) Cornelius Verdonck's compositions consisted mainly of madrigals for four, six, and up to as many as nine voices. Many of them were included in miscellaneous collections published at Antwerp by Waelrant and Phalèse during this period.

(to 1612) Giovanni Gabrieli was second organist at St. Mark's (cont.) during this period.

(and 1613) Gesualdo's compositions were contained in a single volume of madrigals published at Genoa, in parts, (1585) and in score (1613).

(and 1619) Psalms which used Horatian meters were set to music by Statius Olthoff and published on these two dates.

c.1585

Antoine Boesset, composer of lute tablature, was born (died 1643).

Gallus Dressler, a Lutheran composer, died (born 1533).

John Merbecke, who wrote "The Booke of Common Praier Noted," died at Windsor (born 1523 or c.1510).

Pietro Francesco Valentini, contrapuntist and pupil of Nanino, was born (died 1654).

John Mundy succeeded John Merbecke as one of the organists of St. George's Chapel, Windsor.

The British Museum preserved additional manuscripts (17802-5) which were dated about this time.

Guarini's "Pastor fido," a pastoral, was written.

Palestrina's "Assumpta est Maria" was probably composed later than this date, but perhaps begun earlier. It was completed and revised several years later.

1586

(January 1) Orazio Vecchi was poorly paid as choirmaster of the Modena Cathedral and he

1586(cont.)

found it necessary to appeal for help from his local admirers in order that he might help his impoverished, ailing father. On this date he resigned at Modena to become choirmaster at Reggio Cathedral.

(January 20)
Johann Hermann Schein was born at Grünhain in Meissen (died 1630). Schein was a major predecessor of Bach and held the position of cantor at St. Thomas in Leipzig. He was the first major songwriter of the early Baroque. One source placed his birthdate at January 29 rather than January 20.

(April 23) Quite possibly it was William Kemp who was involved in a banquet at Utrecht held this year on St. George's Day. There was "dancing, vaulting, and tumbling, with the forces of Hercules, which entertained the strangers who had not previously seen this type of performance.

(July 7) Henry Garnett and Robert Southwell, two noted Jesuit priests, landed in England where they were met by Weston.

(July 9) John Bull was awarded the degree of Mus. Bac. from Oxford, "having practised in that faculty fourteen years."

(July 9) John Mundy received the degree of Mus. Bac. from Oxford.

(August 21) A list of houses to be searched, drawn up on this date, included "Mr Birdes house at Harmansworth or Craneford."

(September 1) Pope Sixtus V in a Papal Bull ("In suprema") conferred upon the College the right to elect, from among their own body, an officer to whom would be committed the duty of governing the Choir, for three, six, or twelve months, or in perpetuity, according to the pleasure of the Electors.

(September 29) Francis Tregian the younger was educated at Eu, and entered Douay on this date.

(October 7) See Byrd entry 1581, June 28.

(December 30) Cardinal Luigi d'Este died (birthdate unknown).

(May) Merulo went to Parma to be organist of the Steccata (ducal chapel). His salary there was to be double that he had received at Venice.

(July) Tasso arrived at Mantua.

Andrea Gabrieli, first organist at St. Mark's and eminent Italian composer, died (born 1510 or c.1520).

Paul Sieffert, an organist and pupil of Sweelinck, was born (date of death unknown).

Lodovico Balbi used the designation capriccio in a publication from this year.

Vincenzo Bel'aver was second organist at St. Mark's, Venice.

Music printing from engraved copper plates supposedly started at Rome with a collection of Canzone "Diletto spirituale." The collection was engraved by Martin van Buyten, and pub-

1586(cont.)

lished by Simone Verovio this year.

Apparently Juliana Byrd died shortly after this date and Ellen became Byrd's second wife.

Alfonso d'Este considered the Florentine competition harmless and sent three of his ladies to Florence for the wedding of Cesare d'Este and Virginia Medici.

Ferretti made a contribution in honor of Giovanni Bardi's bride.

Filippo, Duc of Flanders dedicated his last published work to Johann Jacob and Karl Kisl, both sons of the treasurer, to Archduke Carl of Graz.

Giovanni Gabrieli succeeded Mérulo as first organist at St. Mark's in Venice.

Gallus surely lived in Prague at this time since the preface to Book I of his "Opus musicum" was executed in Prague this year.

Gesualdo married Donna Maria d'Avalos.

Performances of Guarini's "Pastor Fido" in Ferrara (1584), Turin (1586) and Florence (1588) have been claimed but the facts have not been documented.

Pope Sixtus V convinced Guidetti to publish at Rome this year.

William Kemp, the Shakespearean actor and jig dancer was at Lüneburg.

This year warnings of Lassus' failing strength started to become obvious.

Giovanni Macque came to Naples and entered the service of Fabrizio Gesualdo.

Da Monte's eleventh book of five-voiced madrigals, published this year, completed the great change in style that had started the last period of his work as a madrigalist. He dedicated the book to Count Mario Bevilacqua in Verona, a great music patron of the most famous of the "accademie." Da Monte made it clear that he hoped this latest work might give singers as much pleasure as it had provided him with amusement while writing it in as animated and gay a style as possible.

Nanino proved his mastery of contrapuntal writing in his thirty different canon settings for three, four, and five voices of a single cantus firmus in his "Motecta" published this year.

Performances by children from the orphanage were enjoyed by Florentine nobility, according to the records of this year. They played "cornetto, traversa, viola o trombone."

Osiander shifted the melody to the treble (soprano) from the tenor as previously written in Luther's "Ein' feste Burg."

The Egyptian obelisk which had been brought to Rome by Caligula was moved by order of Sixtus V this year. Palestrina's setting of the hymn "Vexilla Regis" was sung at the ceremony.

Sixtus V took over the handling of the choir and his actions were not those of a man who wished to appoint Palestrina to

1586(cont.)
the position.

Palestrina paid homage to Cesare Colonna, Prince of Palestrina, by dedicating his second volume of madrigals for four voices to him.

Palestrina's second book of four-part madrigals indicated that he had assimilated the principles of pictorialism and verbal expression. Quite obviously pastoral atmosphere did not interest him.

Palestrina wrote three new masses this year.

Mateo Romero went to Spain.

Sweelinck's starting salary of one hundred guilders for being organist at Amsterdam was doubled.

Francis Tregian, fourteen years old at the time, arrived at Douai.

Vecchi entered holy orders and was appointed canon at Correggio Cathedral this year. Five years later he became archdeacon.

De Wert's eighth book of madrigals this year indicated his close attachment to the court at Ferrara. Whether he was in its service was dubious since it was fairly certain that he remained connected with the Mantuan court.

A secular collection, "Armonia di scelti autori," appeared.

The "Dies irae" was included in a "Missa pro Defunctis," for four voices, by Asola, published this year at Venice.

John Case, a Fellow of St. John's College, Oxford published a treatise titled "The Praise of Musicke." He was a doctor of medicine.

A collection of canzonette with religious texts for three and four voices, some in Latin and some in Italian, appeared at Rome this year. Two editions were published by Simone Verovio at Rome under the title, "Diletto spirituale," and were particularly fine examples of engraved music.

The anthology "Dolci affetti, madrigali a cinque voci de diversi eccellenti musici di Roma" was published this year.

Giovanni's "Sacro tempio d'honor" was included this year in a collection of twelve settings of inferior sonnets by Zuccarini. They were written in honor of Bianca Cappello, Grand Duchess of Tuscany.

During this year Pope Sixtus V had Guidetti publish "Cantus ecclesiasticus Passionis Domini nostri Jesu Christi secundum Matthaeum, Marcum, Lucam, et Joannem," St. Matthew's version to be used for the mass on Palm Sunday, St. Mark's to be used on Tuesday of Holy Week, St. Luke's for Wednesday, and St. John's for Good Friday. The work was published at Rome.

Ingegneri's collection "Madrigali a sei voci" was published.

Lute tablatures by Sixt Kargel were published at Strassbourg.

Giovampier Manenti of Bologna,

1586(cont.)

a court musician to Grand Duke Francesco, published a book of "Madrigali ariosi" this year.

One of Marenzio's madrigals was included In "Corona di dodici sonetti di Gio. Battista Zuccarini," published this year by Gardano at Venice.

Two of Marenzio's madrigals were included in "Diletto Spirituale . . . con l'intavolatura del cimbalo et liuto," published during this year by Verovio at Rome with plates engraved by van Buyten.

One of Marenzio's madrigals was included in "De Floridi Virtuosi d'Italia, il primo libro de Madrigali a cinque voci," published this year by Vincenti and Amadino at Venice.

One madrigal by Marenzio was included in "I Lieti Amanti," published this year by Vincenti and Amadino at Venice.

One madrigal by Marenzio was included in "Musica spirituale," published this year by Gardano at Venice.

Marenzio's "Il 1° libro de Madrigali a 5" was reprinted at Venice by Vincenti and Amadino this year.

Marenzio's "Il 1° libro delle Villanelle a 3" was reprinted at Venice this year by Vincenti.

Da Monte included a setting of "Anima dolorosa" (a love lament of a shepherdess) in his eleventh madrigal book for five voices.

Da Monte's first book of four-voiced madrigals was reprinted this year.

Nanino's "Madrigali" Id., Lib. IV." was published.

Nanino published "Motecta" a collection of canon settings in fine counterpoint this year.

Osiander's "Geistliche Lieder und Psalmen mit 4 Stimmen auf Contrapunkts weiss . . . also gesetzt, dass ein christliche Gemein durchauss mit singen kann" was published this year.

Palestrina's second book of secular madrigals was published this year. This book was considered to include some of his best madrigals including the "La cruda mia nemica" and "Alla riva del tebro."

Palestrina's "Morì quasi il mio core" appeared.

Verovio published the "Melodie spirituali" by Jacopo Peetrino (Jacob Pieters) of Malines.

Porta contributed one of the twenty-eight settings of Guarini's "Ardo sì ma non t'amo" which comprised the collection "Sdegnosi ardori" published this year.

Striggio wrote the first, second, and fifth intermezzi of Bardi's "Amico fido." The pieces were performed on the occasion of the wedding of Don Cesare d'Este and Virginia de' Medici this year. Bardi was the patron of the Florentine Camerata.

Vecchi set a sonnet written for him by Zuccarini of Feltre. The sonnets, "Corona di dodici

1586(cont.)

Sonetti" were a tribute to Bianca Capello.

Wert's eighth book of five -voiced madrigals appeared.

The Diary of the Canon Pepin at the Ste. Chapel in Dijon included this year.

Sir Christopher Hatton was a member of the Commission at the Trial of Mary Queen of Scots.

In the summer of this year Jesuits were under special observation.

Sir Philip Sidney, Elizabethan poet mortally wounded at the battle of Zutphen this year, died (born 1554).

It was assumed that Shakespeare went to London.

Sidney's death affected Edmund Spenser deeply. He wrote "Astrophel" this year, in memory of his friend.

Lucas Cranach the Younger, German painter, died (born 1515).

Luis de Morales, Spanish painter, died (born c.1500).

Spanish painting: El Greco, Burial of Count Orgaz.

(and 1587) Le Jeune's Melanges were reprinted in both these years.

(and 1587, 1591) Gallus had a privilege from the Emperor to publish "Handl Jac. Musici operis, harmoniarum 4,5,6,8 et plurium vocum" at Prague in four volumes during these years. It was a collection of great (cont.) value and included motets for the entire liturgical year.

(and 1589) Artusi's "Arte del contrapunto ridotto in tavole" was published in a German translation by Frost at these dates.

(to 1592) Ruggiero Giovanelli published five books of madrigals, and two volumes of canzonette and vilanelle, during this period.

(to 1595) Verovio's publications of vocal compositions with keyboard and lute transcriptions in tablature during this period were important in the development of Italian keyboard music.

(and 1600) Two editions of Palestrina's first regular volume of motets were published by Scotto at Venice.

(to 1608) Verovio collected the secular and spiritual examples of music-engravings and some of the Roman musicians' canzonette for three and four voices. He published these in their original vocal form as well as in arrangements for clavier and lute.

(to 1610) Three principal styles in German music competed with one another during these years.

(and 1610) Macque's madrigal books for four voices appeared at these dates.

(to 1611) Victoria served at various times as choirmaster, organist, and priest at the Descalzas Reales convent where he stayed during this period which ended with his death.

c.1586

Fiesco is said to have died (birthdate unknown).

Cornelis de Vos, Flemish painter, was born (died 1651).

Juan Carlos Armat's treatise "Guitarra española" was published this year at Barcelona.

Tasso's dialogue "La Cavaletta" was published.

(to 1587) Byrd's "A Printed Broadside" for six voices was composed during these years.

1587

(February 9) Vicenzo Ruffo, madrigal, mass and motet composer, died at Sacile (near Treviso), birthdate unknown.

(April 15) Lassus dedicated twenty-three new madrigals to the court physician, Dr. Mermann.

(June 15) Pinello di Gherardi, a Genoese musician, died (born c.1540)

(July 6) Palestrina wrote to Duke William to introduce a certain Stefano Ugeri, a Cremonese.

(September 22) Alessandro Striggio the Elder, organist, lutenist and composer of noble birth, died at Mantua (born c.1535 or 1535).

(October 10) Da Monte was in Prague at this time.

(December 10) Marenzio's new madrigal book "Madrigali a quattro, cinque, et sei voci libro primo" was signed "Venice, December 10, 1587" and dedicated (cont.) to Count Bevilacqua in Verona.

(July) Sometime after this date de Mel became director of the episcopal chapel at Liége.

(August) Lassus' new volume of the "Patrocinium Musices" appeared. It included thirteen magnificats and two masses, "Locutus Sum" and "Beatus qui intelligit." The masses bear the same date.

Samuel Hafenreffer, author on music, was born (died 1660).

George de la Hèle, madrigal composer, died at Madrid (born 1547).

John Heywood, court virginalist to King Henry VIII of England, died (born 1497).

Gregor Lange, a motet composer, died (birthdate unknown).

Melchor Robledo, Spanish choirmaster, died (birthdate unknown).

Salomone Rossi, a Jewish composer known as Hebrao, was born (died 1628). Other sources gave his birthdate as c.1570.

Samuel Scheidt, a German organist often called "the father of German organ music," was born at Halle. He held the position of organist at St. Moritz in Halle and also contributed a major work in the "Tabulatura Nova." (died 1654).

Asola composed an eight-part "Nova Vespertina . . . Psalmodia" this year. In the "Nisi Dominus" he balanced the simplicity of some of the sec-

1587(cont.)

tions by clashes between the macrorhythm and microrhythm as well as by contrasts in timbre.

Burney stated that the word "Concerto" was used for the first time in Scipione Bargaglia's "Trattenimenti . . . da suonare" published at Venice this year.

Bertrand apparently realized the problems in singing quarter -tones, since he discarded them in his edition of chansons issued this year.

Carpentrasso's "Lamentations" were sung each year in the Sistine Chapel, until this date when they were replaced to make room for the compositions of Palestrina.

Pope Sixtus V ordained, that the first Lamentation for each day should be set into polyphonic music more fitting for the expression of the sad character of the words. He stated further, that the second and third Lessons should be sung, by a soprano soloist, using the Plainchant melody as revised by Guidetti.

Thomas East's first publication as assignee was entered at Stationers Hall.

Elizabeth's band included a bagpipe, harps, lutes, nine minstrels, two rebecs, six sackbuts, eight viols, three virginal players, and sixteen brasses, probably ten trumpets and six trombones.

Matteo Foresto was at the Cathedral of Mantua.

A seven voice concert piece was composed by Andrea Gabrieli, "Angelus ad Pastores ait."

Andrea Gabrieli's Concerti of this year were the first work in concerted style.

The earliest indication of a part specifically for "Violino" appeared in "Concerti di Andrea e Giovanni Gabrieli - per voci e stromenti musicali" published at Venice this year.

Concerti composed this year by Andrea and Giovanni Gabrieli were dedicated to Jakob Fugger.

Giovanni Gabrieli dedicated his "Song of Homage" for single chorus to the Fuggers.

Ruggiero Giovanelli was maestro di capella to San Luigi de' Francesi on the Corso in Rome.

Guglielmo Gonzaga was succeeded by his son Vincenzo late in this year.

Duke William gave Lassus a country house at Geising on the Ammer for "occasional retirment."

Lassus begged for rest from his arduous duties as chapel-master.

Lassus' four-, five-, and six -voiced madrigals of this year were dedicated to his Munich friend, Dr. Thomas Mermann, a physician to the Duke. Included in the collections were occasional "secular" pieces. The works were strongly influenced by Marenzio and Lassus consistently emphasized the key words, "venti" and "corso" in Fiamma's "Per aspro mar." He varied his treatment of the words according

1587(cont.)

to his illustrative reasons.

Lasus returned to Italy (also in 1562, 1567, 1574, 1578 and 1585).

Marenzio's earlier patrons must have included Scipione Gonzaga, Tasso's friend, as well as a cardinal in this year. The composer dedicated his four-voiced "Motecta festorum totius anni" to Gonzaga this year.

Del Mel was at Liége this year and several members of his family were in the service of Ernest, Duke of Bavaria.

Giovanni Antonio Merlo was Maestro della Cappella Pontificia.

Francisco de Montanos wrote a treatise "Arte de música teórica y práctica." In Spain it was regarded as the best and only complete work on composition.

Monteverdi composed the greater portion of his best music as the last in the line of great madrigalists. He was the exponent of an art-form which reached its peak when he published his "First Book of Madrigals" this year.

Monteverdi was still working under the guidance of Ingegneri when he wrote his first madrigal book. He progressed from the balanced sonority of chamber-music typical of the motet-like madrigals of Ingegneri and Porta as well as their Flemish colleagues, Arcadelt, da Monte, de Rore, Verdelot and Willaert.

By the time Monteverdi was (cont.) twenty he had already published four works of diverse types, tricinia, sacred madrigals, canzonettas and secular madrigals. They revealed a composer strikingly mature in technique and fertile in imagination.

Palestrina's affiliation with the House of Gonzaga came to an end when the Duke died this year.

The last letter from Palestrina to the duke was about a month before the latter's death. In it he mentioned that he was sending a singer to the duke for his choir. The man in question was a bass, formerly one of the papal singers.

Plantin even demanded that da Monte pay 135 florins toward the cost of printing his first book of masses this year.

Francesco Soriano was Maestro di cappella at St. Maria Maggiore.

In his canzonette for six voices composed this year Vecchi exceeded Ferretti in his sense of sonority, animated dialogue, and delicate workmanship.

Wert wrote the festive mass for the coronation of Duke Vincenzo this year.

Two madrigal books for five voices by Alfonso I appeared at Venice. One was dedicated to the Duke and the other to the Duchess. The Duke was Charles Emmanuel I of Savoy.

Scipione Bargaglia wrote "Trattenimenti, dove da vaghe donne e giovani vomini sono rappresentati onesti e

1587(cont.)

dilettevoli giuochi, narrate novelle et cantate alcune amorose canzoni" published this year at Venice.

A third collection of Bertrand's chansons, with texts by several poets, appeared.

The four-voiced madrigals by Antonio Buonavita appeared.

Byrd published "Psalmes, Sonets and Songs of Sadnes and Pietie, made into musicke of five parts."

Gardano in this year published a collection of madrigals and motets by the two Gabrielis which included Andrea Gabrieli's eight-voice setting of Petrarch's sonnet "I' vo piangendo, A le guancie, and tirsi."

Andrea Gabrieli's "Canti concerti a 6,7,8,10 e 16 voci" appeared. The work was edited by Giovanni Gabrieli.

"Sacri di Giove augei" and "Lieto godea" were included in the Andrea Giovanni collection.

Galilei's madrigal book for four and five voices appeared.

Guidetti's "Cantus ecclesiasticus officii majoris hebdomadae" was published at Rome this year by the composer.

A second book of masses by Ingegneri appeared.

Macque set Tasso's "Gelo hà Madonna il seno, e fiamma il volto" to music.

Marenzio's "Il 2º libro delle Canzonette alla Napoletana a3 (cont.) was reprinted at Venice by Vincenti.

Four of Marenzio's madrigals were included in "Primus liber suavissimus praestantissimorum" published by Baumann at Erfurt.

Marenzio's "Il 1º libro da Madrigali a 5" was reprinted by Vincenti and Amadino at Venice.

Marenzio's "Il 2º libro de Madrigali a 5" was reprinted by Vincenti at Venice.

Marenzio's "Il 4º libro de Madrigali a 6" was reprinted by Vincenti and Amadino at Venice.

Marenzio's "Motectorum pro festis . . . " was reprinted by Amadino at Venice.

Luca Marenzio's second through fifth books of villanelle had been issued by this time.

Marenzio's "Il 3º libro delle Villanelle a 3" was reprinted by Vincenti at Rome.

Marenzio's "Il 4º libro delle villanelle a 3" was published by Vincenti at Venice.

Marenzio's "Il 5º libro delle villanelle a 3" was published by Scotto at Venice.

In Comin Ventura's "Rime di diversi celebri poeti dell'età nostra" was published at Bergamo this year. Celiano was included along with several poets who were significant in Marenzio's work such as Goselini, Guarini, Grillo, and Tasso.

Monteverdi published a book of madrigals for five voices.

1587(cont.)

By this year Monteverdi had composed music for Guarini's "Ardo si" as well as Tasso's "risposta" and "contrarisposta" "Ardi e gela" and "Arsi e alsi."

Nanino's "Canzonetti, à 3 voci" was published.

Nanino's "Madrigali" Lib. II was reprinted (see also 1580, 1582, 1605).

Jakob Paix, the German composer, wrote a mass based on Crecquillon's "Domine, da nobis" this year.

Leonard Schroeter's most important work, "Hymni Sacri," was published this year at Erfurt.

During this year Nicolaus Selneccer published "Christliche Lieder und Kirchen -gesänge" at Leipzig.

Striggio's "Ecce beatam lucem" was in a manuscript dating from this time.

Vecchi's "Canzonette a 6 voci" appeared.

Vecchi's "Lamentations" appeared.

John Foxe, English author of Actes and Monuments, died (born 1516).

Guglielmo I of Mantua, a patron of the arts, died (born 1538).

Mary Queen of Scots was executed.

Sir Christopher Hatton was made Lord Chancellor.

Christopher Marlowe received the degree of M.A. at Corpus (cont.) Christi (then Bene't) College, Cambridge.

Christopher Marlowe had finished the first part of "Tamburlaine" by this time.

(to 1588) Palestrina composed a series of three Lamentations to replace those of Carpentrasso after urging by Pope Sixtus V.

(to 1596) Adriano Banchieri was organist at San Michele in Bosco, an Olivetan monastery which he joined in 1587.

(and 1597, 1599, 1613) Macque's madrigal books for five voices appeared at these years.

(to 1605) Six prints published during these years contained thirty-three ricercari by Andrea Gabrieli.

(to 1605) Monteverdi was greatly influenced by the work of Gesualdo and Marenzio during these years.

(to 1612) Monteverdi worked under Vincenzo I during the final reign of the Gonzagas at Mantua including these years.

(to 1612) Vincenzo I surely recognized Monteverdi's significance but he preferred the works of Striggio, the Elder, Rovigo and Pallavicino.

(to 1614) Polyphonic madrigals of which Monteverdi was the main creative genius brought the great Flemish-Italian era of the madrigal to its close. The period had embraced just under thirty years.

(to 1617) During this period Chevalier composed all or parts

1587(cont.)

of thirty four court ballets, according to a list left by Michel Henry, one of Louis XIII's twenty-four violins. The list was preserved in the Paris Bibliothéque.

(to 1632) The reign of King Sigismund III over Poland.

(to 1638) Monteverde's published works included eight books of madrigals from this period.

c.1587

The Passepied (English Paspy) was a dance which originated amongst the sailors of Basse Bretagne, and was probably first danced in Paris by street -dancers during this year.

1588

(July 8) Thomas Morley received the degree of Mus. Bac. from Oxford.

(September 8) Marin Mersennus, Le Père Mersenne, theorist and composer, was in the village of Oizé, in Maine (died 1648, September 1).

(October 1) Musica Transalpina was published. It was the first printed collection of Italian madrigals with English words and was issued this year in London. The dedication carried this date.

(November 22) This date appeared in the Privilegium of an edition of Arbeau's "Orchésographie."

(December 3) Edmond Hooper was appointed Master of the Children.

(December 25) Louis, Cardinal de Guise was murdered at Blois at the command of King Henri III. (cont.) The day before his brother Henri, Duc de Guise had been similarly dispatched.

(January) Palestrina produced a volume this month which contained a complete set of the nine Lamentations, three for each of the three days. This book was published the same year by Gardano under the title "Lamentationum liber primus."

Alfonso Ferrabosco I, an English composer, although born in Italy, died at Turin (born 1543).

Johann A. Herbst, author on music, was born (died 1666).

Nicholas Laniere, masque composer, scenic designer, and painter, was born (died c.1665). He was also Master of the King's Music.

Giovanni Battista Spaccini, a compatriot of Orazio Vecchi, was born (died 1636).

The Orchésographie, a manual by Thoinot Arbeau (Jehan Tabourot), at this date provided detailed descriptions and pictorial illustrations. These gave the choreography of the French versions of various dances so thoroughly that the steps could be reconstructed. The book also gave an interesting account of the Mantassins. The volume was published at Langres.

In the "Orchésographie," Arbeau asserted that when he was young the Morisco was frequently danced by boys in blackface, wearing bells on their legs.

The "Orchesographie" referred to the use of musical instruments in war. It mentioned "les

1588(cont.)

buccines et trompettes, litues et clerons, cors et cornets, tibies, fifres, arigots, tambours, et aultres semblables."

The "Sink-A-Pace," five steps, or combinations of steps, were thoroughly described in "Orchésographie."

This year the Spanish Armada was defeated, and possibly the prosperity which subsequently came to England coupled with the new sense of security, also affected Byrd's fortunes and brought new opportunities to him.

Byrd addressed a warning to the "Benigne Reader" in his first publication this year. He asserted that they would discover unexpected features in his work which might be difficult to explain.

Byrd gave early evidence of the use of unprepared dominant seventh chords before Monteverdi. The latter has frequently been credited with this innovation.

Byrd was forty-five and already a highly respected English composer when the Musica Transalpina stimulated the vogue for madrigals.

Parish records indicated that Byrd had a house at Harlington in Middlesex as late as this date and that he probably remained there until he moved to Stondon, in Essex.

The preface to Byrd's Psalmes, Sonets, and Songs of sadnes and pietie proved that ayres were being composed as early as this (cont.) date.

The publication of Yonge's collection and Byrd's "Psalmes, Sonets, & Songs" was a prelude to the impressive output of English madrigals that occurred during the next twenty-five years.

Muoni in his chronicles still listed Caimo as cathedral organist.

Manuel Cardoso entered the Carmelite order at Lisbon.

Cavalieri took charge of entertainments at the court of Tuscany.

John Dowland received the degree of Mus. Bac. from Oxford, along with Morley. He possibly received the same degree from Cambridge.

Many of Alfonso Ferrabosco's madrigals were included in Musica Transalpina.

The "Gelati" academy in Bologna was founded. It encompassed all arts and sciences and flourished throughout the century.

Gesualdo was certainly influenced by Marenzio, whose book of "mesta gravità" had been available since this year.

Tasso had come to Naples early this year and had met Gesualdo.

Comparatively little interest attended either the Edinburgh or Glasgow schools. Minutes of the Town Council of Glasgow indicated that the institution collapsed this year, "the scuile sumtyme callit the sang

1588(cont.)

scuile" was sold to defray the expenses brought on by the occurrence of the heavy plague.

Gioseffo Guami became Giovanni Gabrieli's colleague by succeeding Bell'Haver as first organist at St. Mark's this year.

Performances of Guarini's "Pastor Fido" in Ferrara (1584), Turin (1586) and Florence (1588) have been claimed but the facts have not been documented.

Guerrero fulfilled his desire to visit the Holy Land.

Le Jeune attempted to flee the siege of Paris.

The Counter Reformation was responsible for the "Teutsche geistliche Psalmen" this year. This was a collection of fifty settings for three voices of a German Psalter, half by Lassus and half by his son Rudolph. The one-line melodies were published by Caspar Ulenberg and the psalter was written to combat the popular Lutheran psalm-lieder.

The English madrigal school began to assume a serious note and flourished from this date forward.

Marenzio entered the service of the Medici. However, first he made vain efforts, after the Cardinal's death, to obtain appointment at St. Barbara in Mantua. A malicious opinion expressed by Palestrina defeated his hopes.

Thomas Morley, Byrd's most famous pupil, received the degree (cont.) of Mus. Bac. From Oxford this year, probably while he held the position of organist at St. Giles, Cripplegate, London.

Yonge published the Musica Transalpina in England this year. The book launched Italian musical domination of the madrigal in England.

In England it became profitable to publish a large anthology of Italian madrigals with good translations, as evidenced by the success of the Musica Transalpina.

Otto succeeded Heugel as head of the court choir at Kassel.

At this time Palestrina was about sixty-three years old and had experienced much sorrow. He was also dissatisfied with his musical career.

Soriano became choirmaster at St. Maria Maggiore.

Barre of Milan published several of Animuccia's motets in a miscellaneous volume this year.

Thoinot Arbeau's treatise "Orchésographie" was the earliest book in which percussion parts were written out. The book was essentially a manual on the dance.

Barrè published "Liber Primus Musarum cum quatuor vocibus, seu sacrae cantiones quas vulgo Mottetta appellant" this year at Milan.

Byrd's "Seven Penitential Psalms" set for three voices were included in his "Songs of sundrie natures." They were not up to

1588(cont.)

his standards, nor were the ten five-part psalms in this year's collection .

William Byrd published his first book of "Psalmes, Sonets, and Songs of sadnes and pietie." In the collection he showed his predilection for legal phrases and ideas. The collection was for five voice parts and included the following compositions:

"All as a sea," No. 28.

"Although the heathen poets," No. 21.

"Ambitious Love," No. 18.

"As I beheld I saw a herdman," No. 20.

"Blessed is he that fears the Lord," No. 8.

"Care for thy soul," No. 31.

"Come to me, grief, for ever," No. 34.

"Constant Penelope," No. 23.

"Even from the depth," No. 10.

"Farewell, false love," No. 25.

"Help, Lord, for wasted are those men," No. 7.

"How shall a young man?" No. 4.

"If that a sinner's sighs," No. 30.

"If women could be fair," No. 17.

(cont.)

"I joy not in no earthly bliss," No. 11.

"In fields abroad," No. 22.

"La Virginella," No. 24.

"Lord, in thy wrath," No. 9.

"Lullaby, my sweet little Baby," No. 32.

"Mine eyes with fervency," No. 2.

"My mind to me a kingdom is," No. 14.

"My soul oppressed with care," No. 3.

"O God, give ear," No. 1.

"O Lord, how long wilt thou forget me?" No. 5.

"O Lord, who in thy sacred tent," No. 6.

"O that most rare breast," No. 35.

"O you that hear this voice," No. 16.

"Prostrate, O Lord, I lie," No. 27.

"Susanna fair," No. 29.

"The match that's made," No. 26.

"Though Amaryllis dance," No. 12.

"What pleasure have great princes?" No. 19.

"Where fancy fond," No. 15.

1588(cont.)

"Why do I use my paper?" No. 33.

"Who likes to love," No. 13.

Byrd's two masses were probably published (without title-pages) this year. The type for the mass for five voices was like that which Easte used when he began to publish music as Byrd's assignee this year.

Byrd was a contributor to: Musica Transalpina, Madrigales translated, of foure, five and six parts, published this year.

Caraccio's Dialogo à 7 voci nel, lib. I, di Madrigali di Claudio da Correggio, was published this year at Milan.

John Case, M.D., published "Apologia Musices tam vocalis tam instrumentalis et mixtae" at this time.

The "Psalter of Henrie Denham" was apparently published in England this year. Canon Havergal gave the volume its name.

One of Este's first published works which was known was Byrd's "Psalmes, Sonets and Songs of sadnes and pietie."

Some compositions from Ferretti's canzoni publications appeared in reprints in London from this date forward.

Ferretti's book of 5-part madrigals was published this year at Venice.

Andrea Gabrieli's "Ecco vinegia bella" was included in (cont.) the "Gemma Musicalis" published this year by Gardano at Venice.

Andrea Gabrieli's music composed for a performance of "Edipo tiranno" was published.

Bartholomäus Gese composed a version of the Passion in which the Lord's words were set for four voices, those of the Crowd for five voices, and those of St. Peter and Pontius Pilate for three voices, and those of the Maid Servant for two voices.

Ruggiero Giovanelli's twenty-three "Villanelle et Arie alla Napolitana" appeared this year.

Guidetti published a volume of "Praefationes in Cantu firmo" this year at Rome.

Ingegneri published his most significant work, "Responsoria Hebdomadae Sanctae." For many years the work was attributed to Palestrina.

Ingegneri's publications during this year included a set of twenty-seven "Responses for Holy Week."

Lassus, in conjunction with his son Rodolfo published fifty "Teutsche Psalmen." Commer published the twenty-five compositions composed by the father.

One of Marenzio's madrigals was included in L'Amorosa Eto rappresentata da' piu celebri musici d'Italia, published by Sabbio at Brescia.

Thirteen madrigals by Marenzio were included in "Gemma Musicalis" published by Gerlach at Nürnberg.

1588(cont.)

Marenzio's "Il 1º libro de Madrigali a 5 voci" was reprinted by Vincenti at Venice.

Marenzio's "Madrigali a 4,5, e 6, lib. I" was published by Vincenti at Venice.

Marenzio's "Il 5º libro de Madrigali a 5" was published by Scotto at Venice.

Marenzio's "Madrigali Spírituali . . . a 5" was reprinted by Scotto at Venice.

Seven of Marenzio's madrigals were included in Musica Transalpina, published by East at London.

Three of Marenzio's motets were included in "Continuatio cantionum sacrarum" published by Gerlach at Nürnberg.

Marenzio's work was first introduced in England this year in the "Musica Transalpina" collection.

Marenzio's "Il 1º libro della villanelle a 3" was reprinted by Vincenti and Amadino at Venice.

Da Monte's thirteenth book of madrigals appeared.

The "Musica Transalpina" included madrigals by Byrd, Lassus, Marenzio, da Monte, and Palestrina among others.

Nanino's "Madrigali, a 5 voci, Lib. I was published at Venice this year (see also 1579 and 1598).

Otto's "Gesange Martin Luther" for five to six voices was published and dedicated to Moritz in Torgau.

Palestrina's second volume of motets was reprinted by Scotto in Venice (see also 1580).

The first publication in England of Palestrina's music was represented by five of his madrigals included in "Musica Transalpina."

This year saw the publication of four books of masses, including twenty-seven works, seven books of motets representing over two hundred compositions and three collections of madrigals. All told these collections probably represented more than half of Palestrina's creative output up to this date.

Pietro Ponzio's "Raggionamento di musica" appeared.

A collection by Andreas Raselius, German composer, was published this year.

Book III of the series edited by Soto de Langa was issued. It included twenty-three three -part laude as well as twelve for four parts. Two were in Spanish. Some of the works included were unacknowledged but of the highest quality.

Tallis' "Discomfit them. O Lord" was adapted from "Absterge Domine" in a manuscript preserved at Christ Church Library.

One of Verdonck's madrigals was included in "Musica Transalpina."

Victoria published a book of Motets for eleven voices to be used for the feasts of the year. The volume was published at Rome.

1588(cont.)

One of Paolo Virchi's three madrigal books appeared this year. The others were issued in 1584 and 1591 respectively.

In his ninth book de Wert apparently returned to a more conventional choice of texts. This volume included a sonnet by Sannazaro and several poems by Petrarch.

Nicholas Yonge published "Musica Transalpina" in London (see 1588, October 1).

Zarlino's "Sopplimenti musicali" was published this year at Venice.

The Saraband was introduced at the French court this year. Richelieu, wearing green velvet knee-breeches, with bells on his feet, and castanets in his hands, danced it in a ballet before Anne of Austria.

The Spanish crusade in the North collapsed with the destruction of the "Armada Católica."

Sir Walter Raleigh took an active part in the defeat of the Spanish Armada.

Alonso Sanchez Coello, Spanish painter, died (born c.1531).

Hendrik Terbrugghen, Netherlandish painter, was born (died 1629).

Paolo Caliari, known as Veronese, great Italian painter, died (born 1526).

Italian painting: Tintoretto, Paradise (in the Sala del Maggior Consiglio).

(to 1589) Guerrero made his pilgrimage to the Holy Land during these years.

(to 1589) Byrd's madrigals during this period included: "Though Amaryliss Dance In Green," "Come To Me Grief, Forever," "Come, Woeful Orpheus," "I Thought That Love Had Been A Boy," "In Winter Cold," and "Who Made Thee, Hob, Forsake The Plough."

(and 1589) Byrd contributed two madrigals to Book I of "Musica Transalpina." A year later Byrd published two more works.

(and 1589, 1611) Byrd's strength in the English anthem lay in the spirit of praise and joyfulness, rather than in penitence and solemnity. This fact was in sharp contrast with the style of his Latin motets. It was strange that while so little of value in this year was evident in the publications of 1588 and 1589, there were several fine examples of the typical English anthem in the set published in 1611.

(to 1591) Byrd's output during this period was quite remarkable.

(and 1591) Soto published the third and fourth books of Laudi Spirituali at these dates respectively. They were a continuation of the two edited by Animuccia.

(to 1596) Fifty-two German Songs and Psalmes for 8 voices were published by Weber.

(and 1597) Este printed Yonge's "Musica Transalpina" at both of these dates.

1588(cont.)

(and 1597) Many of Ferrabosco's madrigals were included in the two books of "Musica Transalpina" published at these dates respectively.

(to 1598) The reign of Prince Sigismund Báthori over Hungary.

(and 1601) Croce's canzonette for three and four voices appeared at these dates.

c.1588

Edward "the Deafe" who married, as his second wife, Grisold, daughter of Thomas Hughes of Uxbridge, died about this year at Uxbridge (birthdate unknown).

English musical taste definitely moved toward the native madrigal.

Christopher Marlowe finished the second part of "Tamburlaine" as well as "Faustus" at this time.

English painting:
Nicholas Hilliard, Unknown Youth Leaning against a Tree of Roses (5 3/8" x 2 3/4").

1589

(May 2, 6 and 13)
Cristofano Malvezzi of Lucca was the primary author of the famous "Intermedii e concerti" written for the wedding of Ferdinando de' Medici and Cristina of Lorraine and performed three times this year, on May 2 in connection with Girolamo Bargagli's "La Pellegrina," on May 6 in connection with the "Zingara" played by the Comici Gelosi, and on May 13 in connection with Isabella Adreini's "La Pazzia."

(June 3) Hawkins maintained that it was on Tallis' recommendation that Elway Bevin was admitted a gentleman extraordinary of the Chapel Royal on this date. This was an error, he was not admitted until June 3, 1605, by which time Tallis had been dead almost twenty years.

(October 25) Byrd's "Liber Primus Sacrarum Cantionum quinque vocum," dedicated to the Earl of Worcester, was published by Easte.

(March) The Hollingsworths divided the property of Stondon Place, each taking an equal part.

(May) Bargagli's comedy "La Pellegrina" was performed at Florence.

(May) When he was Cardinal Medici, the new Grand Duke, Ferdinand, undoubtedly knew Marenzio in Rome. He apparently brought him to Florence and to use him for the festivities at his marriage to Christina of Lorraine. The famous "Intermedii et Concerti" comprised the program.

(October) Tarquinia Molza was forced to leave the court of Ferrara to return to Modena under close surveillance by the ducal "governatore." Also there were to be no further communications with de Wert.

(November) Marenzio was relieved of his duties to Cardinal Medici and returned to Rome.

(December) Palestrina held great admiration for many of his contemporaries. This was made evident by the records of the

1589(cont.)

Julian Choir of St. Peter's in which, under this date, an entry was found relating to payment for copies of Morales' works made on Palestrina's order.

M. Baif, musician and friend of Ronsard, died (born 1532).

Tommaso Garzoni, an Italian madrigalist and author, died (born 1549).

Marcin Lwowczyk, Martin of Lwów (Leopolita), a Polish composer, died (born 1540).

Anerio directed the musicians of the Compagnia.

According to Wood, Elway Bevin was organist of Bristol Cathedral this year.

The younger Boxe sold all his property to Sir Henry Unton and during this year Unton resold it to Basil Fettiplace.

Robert Brown and Richard Jones were associated again this year. Jones transferred his share in a stock of theatrical goods, including musical instruments, to another actor-musician of later fame, Edward Alleyn.

Giovanmaria Cecchi's play "Esaltazione della Croce" was performed at Florence.

Eccard purportedly wrote music describing the hubbub of the Piazza San Marco at Venice. Details of this accomplishment are lacking.

Some of Ferretti's canzoni appeared in reprints issued at Nürnberg this year.

Some of the greatest musicians of the time were on hand for the wedding festivities of Ferdinando de' Medici and Christine de Lorraine. Among them were Cavalieri, Malvezzi, Marenzio and Peri, all of whom were invited to write the music for the festival play that was to be performed.

After the wedding of the new Grand Duke this year Marenzio's duties in Florence probably were anything but time-consuming.

The Florentine interest in solo singing was like that of Ferrara. A richer coloratura was found in the prologue of "Armonia" which opened the "Intermedii e concerti" at the wedding of Ferdinand and Christina.

The Intermezzi now assumed grander proportions at Florence, since they were to be used at the marriage of the Grand Duke Ferdinand and Christine de Lorraine.

Leroy's name disappeared from publications of the firm and it may be assumed that he died.

Marenzio had been active in Florence to this time.

Tarquinia Molza left the court of Ferrara.

Palestrina dedicated a volume of hymns from this year to Pope Sixtus V. Probably the dedication was executed because one of the hymns was associated with a memorable occasion in 1585 when the Pope had presided at a ceremony in the piazza of St. Peter's when the great obelisk first brought from

1589(cont.)

Egypt by Caligula was erected there.

Palestrina and Gagliardi's fur business prospered. The partnership deed stipulated that 200 scudi must be put away in reserve yearly and 1,300 scudi of the money accumulated was invested this year in the purchase of land in the Borgo Sant' Angelo, close to the city walls. Two houses were built by the partners on the land and leased at a good profit.

A textless piece in four parts probably intended for instrumental ensemble (at least the three lower lines gave the music a somewhat instrumental character) had a superius that was quite vocal. It was found in a Polish manuscript of this year which otherwise consisted of anonymous compositions with Latin texts.

An interlude written by Rinuccini for a comedy was produced at Florence this year at the marriage of Ferdinand de' Medici and Christine of Lorraine. Its subject was the fight between Apollo and the dragon.

Franciscus Sale became a tenor in the Imperial Chapel under da Monte.

Orazio Vecchi began his association at Mantua by dedicating a book of five-voiced madrigals to Duke Vincenzo Gonzaga.

Victoria apparently held the position of choir-master at St. Apollinaris until this year.

The Archives of the Royal Chapel (cont.) at Madrid indicated that during this year Victoria was appointed vice-master of the Chapel (newly established by Philip II) under the Flemish musician Philip Rogier.

Anerio published "Le Gioie," a collection of madrigals for five voices by several members of the Compagnia including Marenzio and Palestrina.

The Compagnia, in the collection of madrigals edited by Anerio, described him as Master of the Choir, and included among the compositions, works by Pelestino (sic), Dragoni, Soriano, Marenzio, Stabile, Giovanelli, Bernardino Nanino, as well as works by three members of the Pontifical Choir.

Thoinot Arbeau's book "Orchésographie et Traité en forme de dialogue par lequel toutes personnes peuvent facilement apprendre et pratiquer L'honnête exercise des danses" was published by Jean de Preys at Langres this year.

Luca Bati was credited with the composition this year of the intermezzi for "L'esaltazione della croce" a sacred representation.

The sixth volume of the "Patrocinium musices" by Berg was published this year.

The seventh volume of the "Patrocinium musices" by Berg was published this year.

Byrd's "Liber Primus Sacrarum Cantionum Quinque Vocum" was published this year. It included the following:

1589(cont.)

"Aspice, Domine, de sede." 1 pars. "Respice Domine." 2 pars. 5 voc. No. 18 and 19.

"Defecit in dolore." 1 pars. "Sed tu, Domine, refugium." 2 pars. 5 voices. No. 1 and 2.

"Deus, venerunt gentes." 1 pars. "Posuerunt morticinia." 2 pars. "Effuderunt sanguinem." 3 pars. "Facti sumus opprobrium." 4 pars. 5 voc. No. 11, 12, 13, 14.

"Domine, praestolamur." 1 pars. "Veni, Domine." 2 pars. 5 voc. No. 3 and 4.

"Domine, secundum multitudinem." 5 voc. No. 27.

"Domine, tu iurasti." 5 voc. No. 15.

"In resurrexione tua." 5 voc. No. 17.

"Laetentur coeli." 1 pars. "Orietur in diebus." 2 pars. 5 voc. No. 28 and 29.

"Memento, Domine." 5 voc. No. 8.

"Ne irascaris." 1 pars. "Civitas sancti tui." 2 pars. 5 voc. No. 20 and 21.

"O Domine, adiuva me." No. 5. 5 voc.

"O quam gloriosum." 1 pars. "Benedictio et claritas." 2 pars. 5 voc. No. 22 and 23.

"Tribulationes civitatum." 1 pars. "Timor et hebetudo." 2 pars. "Nos enim pro

(cont.)

peccatis." 3 pars. 5 voc. No. 24, 25, 26.

"Tristitia et anxietas." 1 pars. "Sed tu, Domine, qui non." 2 pars. 5 voc. No. 6 and 7.

"Vide, Domine, affictionem." 1 pars. "Sed veni, Domine." 2 pars. 5 voc. No. 9 and 10.

"Vigilate, nescitis enim." 5 voc. No. 16.

Byrd's "Songs of Sundrie Natures, some of gravitie, and others of mirth, fit for all companies and voyces," dedicated to Sir Henry Cary, Lord Hunsdon, was published by Thomas Easte. The work was for three, four, five and six voices and included:

"And think ye, nymphs?" "Love is a fit of pleasure" (2nd part) No. 42 and 43.

"An earthly tree." "Cast off all doubtful care." (Chorus). No. 40 and 25.

"Attend mine humble prayer."

"Behold, how good a thing." "And as the pleasant morning dew." (2nd part) No. 38 and 39.

"Christ rising again." "Christ is risen again." (2nd part) No. 46 and 47.

"Compel the hawk to sit." No. 28.

"From Citheron." "There careless thoughts." (2nd part) "If love be just." (3rd part.) No. 19, 20 and 21.

1589(cont.)

"From depth of sin." No. 6.

"From Virgin's womb." "Rejoice, rejoice." (Chorus). No. 35 and 24.

"If in thine heart." No. 44.

"Is love a boy?" "Boy, pity me." (2nd part.) No. 15 and 16.

"I thought that love." No. 32.

"Lord, hear my prayer." No. 5.

"Lord, in thy rage." No. 1.

"Lord, in thy wrath." No. 3.

"O dear life." No. 33.

"Of gold all burnished." "Her breath is more sweet." (2nd part) No. 36 and 37.

"O God, which art most merciful." No. 4.

"O Lord, My God." No. 22.

"Penelope that longed." No. 27.

"Right blest are they." No. 2.

"See those sweet eyes." "Love would discharge." (2nd part). No. 29 and 34.

"Susanna fair." No. 8.

"The greedy hawk." No. 14.

"The nightingale so pleasant." No. 9.

"Upon a summer's day."

(cont.)

"Then for a boat." (2nd part). No. 12 and 13.

"Unto the hills." No. 45.

"Weeping full sore." No. 26.

"When first by force." No. 31.

"When I was otherwise." No. 30.

"When younglings first." "But when by proof." (2nd part). No. 10 and 11.

"While that the sun." No. 23.

"Who made thee, Hob?" No. 41.

"Wounded I am." "Yet of us twain." (2nd part). No. 17 and 18.

Caraccio's Madrigali a 5 voci, lib. 2; was published at Venice.

Girolamo Conversi's book of five -voiced "canzoni alla napoletana" had by this time been reprinted seven times in quick succession.

Songs and madrigals by Gaspard Coste were preserved in "Ghirlanda di Fioretti musicale" published this year at Rome.

Eccard published two collections of volkslieder in four and five parts at Mülhausen and Königsberg, the latter at this date. An imperfect copy of this one was preserved at the British Museum (see also 1578).

Eccard composed Newe Deutsche Lieder, published at

1589(cont.)

Königsberg, this year.

Eccard included a "Zanni e Magnifico" in his "Newe Deutsche Lieder."

An interesting work titled "Litanioe Catholicoe ad Christum, Beatam Virginem, et Sanctos" was published by Wolfgang Eder at Ingolstadt this year.

Este (Easte) published Byrd's "Songes of sundry natures . . ."

It was probable that Andrea Gabrieli sang for the members of the Accademia Filarmonica in the Petrarch sestina. The work was published by Bonagionta in 1568, then reprinted as the first selection in his posthumous "Madrigali e Ricercari" for four voices published this year. It must have been intended as chamber music.

Andrea Gabrieli's third book of five-voiced madrigals was published.

Galilei's "Dialogo della musica e della antica moderna" was published this year at Florence.

Galilei's "Discorso intorno alle opere di messer Gioseffo Zarlino di Chioggia" was published this year.

Ruggiero Giovanelli published two books of music on the "sdruccioli" of the "Arcadia," the second this year, the first in 1585.

Guarini's dramatic poem, "Il Pastor Fido, was first printed late this year.

Guerrero published a collection (cont.) of "Canciones y villanescas espirituales" with Spanish texts. Some of the texts were, according to the preface, religious parodies.

Guerrero published a motet book.

Guerrero's "Trahe me post te, Virgo Maria" was published this year.

A book by Guidetti was published by Coattinum.

A book of six voiced madrigals by Macque was published this year. A previous one had been issued in 1576.

C. Malvezzi published a volume titled "Florentine Intermedia."

Marenzio's "Il 4° libro de Madrigali a 5" was reprinted by Vincenti and Amadino at Venice.

Sixteen of Marenzio's madrigals were included in "Liber secundus Gemmae Musicalis" published by Gerlach at Nürnberg.

One of Marenzio's madrigals was included in "Ghirlanda di Fioretti Musicali" published by Verovio at Rome.

One of Marenzio's madrigals was included in "Le Gioie Madrigali a cinque voci" published by Amadino at Venice.

One of Marenzio's madrigals was included in "Musicale Essercitio di Ludovico Balbi" published by Gardano at Venice.

Marenzio's "Il 1° libro de Villanelle a 3" was reprinted by Vincenti and Amadino at Venice.

1589(cont.)

Marenzio was hired to compose considerable music for the celebration connected with the wedding of Grand Duke Ferdinand I and Christina of Lorraine this year.

Palestrina's "Hymni Titius Anni," a collection of hymns for every Festival throughout the Ecclesiastical Year of the Roman Church, was published by Coattinus at Rome.

Palestrina's "Lamentationum, liber primus" was reprinted in eight volumes by Scotto at Venice.

Palestrina's name appeared in a volume of madrigals, "Le gioje," published this year.

Palestrina's third volume of motets was reprinted by Scotto and Gardano at Venice (see also 1575, 1581, and 1594).

Palestrina's polyphonic setting of the "Veni Creator Spiritus" included in the "Hymni totius anni" was one of the finest of the many versions of this chant.

A copy of Riccio's Introitus published this year at Venice was preserved in a private library in Boston.

The three books of laude edited by Soto de Langa were combined in one in a reprint this year. Several changes and additions were made, including a reduction of all the compositions to three voice arrangements. The latter was dedicated to the Dutchess of Aquasparta.

Vecchi's book of madrigals for five voices appeared.

"Il bianco e dolce cigno," a madrigal comedy, was composed by Vecchi.

Verovio's "Ghirlanda di Fioretti Musicali" appeared.

De Wert published the "Canzonette Villanelle" at Venice. The book was dedicated to Leonora, Duchess of Mantua.

A classical Greek text was used for a "villanella greca" included in de Wert's "Primo Libro delle Canzonette Vilanelle a cinque voci" published this year.

Zarlino reprinted his "Supplimenti musicali," preceded by the "Istitutioni," and the "Dimostrationi," in a complete edition of his works. He also issued a fourth volume which contained a "Trattato della pazienzia," ("Discourse on the true date of the Crucifixion of our Lord,") a treatise on "The Origin of the Capuchins," and the "Resolution of some doubts concerning the correctness of the Julian Calendar." The complete publication was issued at Venice.

Zarlino's complete works in four volumes were preserved at Trinity College in England.

Czar Theodore II of Russia was born (died 1605).

De' Poveri di Gesù Cristo was established this year by a Franciscan, Marcello Foscataro di Nicotera. It was for foundlings in Naples.

John Lyly was involved in the "Marprelate" controversy and wrote a pamphlet "Pappe with an

1589(cont.)

Hatchet" this year in support of the Bishops.

Hercules Seghers, Dutch etcher, was born (died 1638).

Italian illustration: Buontalenti's drawings of the intermedi (1589) showed Luca Marenzio as Saturn with a scythe, and Gio. del Minugiaio as Mars with a helmet.

(to 1590) In the second series of the "Patrocinium Musices" only the first volume was contributed by Lassus.

(to 1590) In a letter written later, Monteverdi mentioned his nineteen years of unbroken court service which proved that he must have started at Mantua during the winter of this year at the latest.

(to 1590) Palestrina composed his "Stabat Mater" during these years.

(and 1591) Byrd's two books of "Cantiones sacrae" were published at these two dates by Este.

(and 1591) Lyly was a member of four Parliaments.

(to 1591) Pevernage's approximately eighty chansons were published in four collections during this period.

(to 1591) Vecchi's madrigals for five and six voices, five parts in all, were composed during these years.

(to 1602) Victoria was at the Royal Chapel in Madrid during these years.

(to 1610) The reign of King Henry IV of Navarre (House of Bourbon) over France.

c.1589

Elias Herlitz, an organist from Stralsund and follower of Duke Heinrich Julius of Bruns Brunswick in the dramatic field, wrote a satirical comedy at this time called "Musicomastix," on the subject of the despiser of music.

Christopher Marlowe's "The Jew of Malta" appeared.

Italian painting: Caravaggio, Bacchus.

Italian painting: Caravaggio, The Lute Player.

1590

(January 1) Monteverdi's second madrigal book was published with a dedication bearing this date.

(February 4) Zarlino performed the duties of Maestro di Cappella at St. Mark's until his death on this date (born 1517).

(September 20) The Reverend Monsignore Ludovico Agostini of Ferrara died at the age of fifty-six and was buried at Santo Spirito in Ferrara (born 1534).

(October 8) Magister Zacharius Hestius was born in Unckersdorf near Dresden (date of death unknown).

(October 26) Gesualdo's wife and her lover, Don Fabrizio, were murdered.

(May) Giovanni Macque was second organist at the Annunziata.

(October) Robert Brown was in

1590(cont.)

Lieden.

After the catastrophe on October 26 of this year, Gesualdo's life of ease came to an end and he fled to the d'Este court at Ferrara. A child that he suspected was not his own was also purportedly murdered at the same time as Gesualdo's wife and her lover.

Melchior Newsidler, German lutenist, died (born 1507).

Jacob Regnart, Netherlandish composer, died (born c.1540).

Francisco de Salinas, Spanish composer and author, died at Burgos (born 1513).

Bernard Schmid the elder, a coloristic school composer, died (born c.1520), see c.1596.

J. Schop, a musician from Hamburg, was born (date of death unknown).

Albrecht Schütz, a member of the famous musical family, died (birthdate unknown).

Ulrich Steigleder, a Swabian musician, was born (date of death unknown).

Francesco Turini, a noted contrapuntist, was born at Prague (died 1656).

Ippolito Baccusi was Maestro di Cappella at Verona Cathedral.

William Byrd contributed to: Watson's "First Sett of Italian Madrigals Englished, 1590."

Byrd apparently considered the (cont.) Italian style too frivolous although he proved he was capable of writing in the style with the selection "after the Italian vaine" for Watson's book. "This sweet and merry month of May" for six voices, his contribution, was one of the greatest of all English madrigals, yet quite Italian in style.

A production of "Aminta" with music by Cavalieri was done at Florence.

Cavalieri's saecular pieces, "Il Satiro," and "La Disperazione di Fileno," were privately performed.

Donato succeeded Zarlino as maestro di cappella at St. Mark's in Venice.

Este printed the Watson Madrigal collection.

Lyly managed a group of boy actors at Blackfriars for several years up to this date.

Macque was appointed second organist at the Church of the Annunciation in Naples.

Malvezzi composed two books of madrigals for five voices, the second this year was dedicated to Cavalieri, the first was written in 1583.

Del Mel probably lived mainly in Rome.

In Vienna and Prague, da Monte dedicated his fourteenth book of madrigals to the Duke of Ferrara this year.

Monteverdi continued to acknowledge his indebtedness to

1590(cont.)

Ingegneri.

Monteverdi became a viol player and singer at the court of Mantua ruled by Duke Vincenzo Gonzaga I.

Monteverdi went to Milan prior to this year.

Morley moved to London and became Byrd's pupil.

Claude Nyon's "Roi des ménestrels" appeared.

A clavicembalo made by Domenico di Pesaro, bearing this date, was acquired by South Kensington Museum. The octave strings had two stops.

The dedication date of a collection of madrigals by Peter Philips indicated that he was established at Antwerp at this time.

The earliest of Hans Ruckers the elders' clavecins were from this time. Three different instruments all bore this date.

The serpent was usually considered as an invention by a canon of Auxerre, Edmé Guillaume.

Sweelinck's name was internationally known by this time.

Sweelinck's salary as organist at Amsterdam was raised to 300 guilders and he was simultaneously offered the option of an additional 100 guilders as a wedding present or free rent, the choice to be his.

Vecchi dedicated his first book of motets to Duke Wilhelm V of Bavaria.

An early instance of the appearance of the Ochetus as an aid to expression appeared in Vecchi's Motet, "Velocitur exaudi me" published this year at Venice. It was used with great pathos, at the words "defecit spiritus meus."

Thomas Watson edited a "Sett of Italian Madrigalls Englished, not to the sense of the originall dittie, but after the affection of the Noate."

Although Watson's "First Sett of Italian Madrigals Englished" was published this year, it could not be assured that Byrd's four-part setting published twenty years later was written after the six-part version which used much of the same melodic material.

Weissenfels Kantorei was transformed into a "Patrician Collegium Musicum."

After Zarlino died (four years before the deaths of Palestrina and Lassus) the "golden age of Venetian church music" apparently waned. It had flourished for more than sixty years.

Aichinger's "Sacrae Cantiones" were published this year at Venice.

Byrd's "The Woods so Wild" appeared.

Byrd contributed two settings of "This sweet and merry month of May" to Watson's "First Sett of Italian Madrigalls Englished."

"Il Satiro" and "La Disperazione di Fileno," both secular pieces, were set to mu-

1590(cont.)

sic by Cavalieri.

A vocal version of Conversi's "Sola soletta" was included in Watson's collection of this year.

Croce's "Mascarate piacevoli e ridicolose per il Carnevale" for four, five, six, seven, and eight voices, appeared.

Gallus finished his collection of simple madrigals for four voices, titled, "Moralia." The collection was executed in order to appease his critics.

Hassler's "xxiv Canzonetti a 4 voci" was published this year at Nürnberg. This was his first work.

Some of Lassus' German lieder were published in a collection of this date (see also 1572, 1573, 1576 and 1583).

Watson's book was one to which Marenzio contributed over twenty of twenty-eight selections.

Two of Marenzio's madrigals were included in "Dialoghi Musicali" published by Gardano at Venice.

One of Marenzio's madrigals was included in "Selva di varia ricreatione di Horatio Vecchi" published by Gardano at Venice.

Five of Marenzio's madrigals were included in "Symphonia Angelica" published by Phalèse and Bellère at Antwerp.

Tasso's "Gelo hà Madonna il seno, e fiamma il volto" was set to music by da Monte.

Monteverdi's five-voiced "Second Book of Madrigals" was published this year about the time of his appointment as "suonatore di Vivuola" at the Mantuan court. They were far less conventional than those in the earlier volumes. Nine of Tasso's poems were included, one of which was the "Ecco mormorar l'onde."

The madrigal "Quell'ombra esser vorrei" by Girolamo Casone was set to music by Monteverdi.

Ockeghem's "Prennez sur moi" was used by theorists in treatises as late as this time.

This year marked the first publication of the following masses by Palestrina: "Aeterna Christi munera," "Jam Christus astra ascenderat," "Panis quem ego dabo," "Iste confessor," "Nigra sum," "Sicut lilium inter spinas," "Nasce la gioia mia," and "Sine nomine."

Palestrina's "Missarum . . . Liber Quintus" was published this year by Coattino at Rome and dedicated to Duke William of Bavaria, Lassus' patron.

Palestrina composed a "Stabat Mater" for a double choir of eight voices.

A collection, "Bicinia . . ." was published by Phalesius and Bellerus at Antwerp this year. It was probably the one by Calvisius.

Michele Varotto's five-voiced hymns appeared.

A lute-book by Vecchi was published.

1590(cont.)

One of Vecchi's major madrigal collections, "the Selva di varia ricreatione," appeared.

Whythorne's "Duos or Songs" of this year constituted the earliest printed collection of instrumental music in England.

Etienne Tabouret, a French poet, died (born 1549).

Loge's "Rosalind," written this year, provided Shakespeare with the principal story thread of "As You Like It."

Sir Philip Sidney wrote "The Arcadia" as an imitation of the Greek romances of the Alexandrian period. After its publication this year a style in prose more elaborate than that of "Eupheus" was set.

Sidney's "Arcadia" was published this year.

Edmund Spenser published the first three books of "The Faerie Queene."

Spenser went to London with Sir Walter Raleigh.

Le Mercier, a French architect, was born (died 1660).

(to 1590) The Papal reign of St. Urban VII (born in Rome).

(to 1591) Perhaps Monteverdi worked "on probation" at Mantua during 1590 and later obtained a permanent position (probably at the beginning of 1591) as "suonatore di Vivuola" in the Cappella of Duke Vincenzo Gonzaga I, of Mantua.

(to 1591) Shakespeare's (cont.) "Henry VI" part I appeared during this period.

(to 1591) The Papal reign of St. Gregory XIV (born in Cremona).

(to 1592) Marlowe probably had a share in the second and third parts of Shakespeare's "Henry VI" written during this period.

(and 1597, 1604) Vecchi's Motets, and Sacrae Cantiones appeared at these dates.

(to 1599) Marenzio discarded the lighter poetry of Sannazaro in favor of the more contemporary Guarini, whose Pastor Fido provided him with the laments and overblown lyrics which were typical of all the madrigalists at the time.

(to 1599) The verse from Petrarch's "sestina" fit the mood of those chosen by Marenzio so aptly that it was not surprising that he also provided a setting of it.

(to 1603) Baldassare Donati was Maestro di Cappella at St. Mark's in Venice during this period.

(to 1603, 1603 to 1609, and 1609 to 1613) During the régime of Zarlino's successors at St. Mark's Donati (1590 to 1603) and della Croce (1603 to 1609) the standards of the choir decreased and decadence in style and performing technique was speeded under Martinengo (1609 to 1613).

(to 1605) There were several risky chromatic harmonies in Monteverdi's second to fifth

1590(cont.)

books of madrigals, written during these years. These culminated in the unprepared ninth chords in "O Mirtillo," (the fifth book), the dominant seventh chord in "Era L'anima mia" (fifth book) and the excessive chromaticism of the madrigal version of the "Arianna Lamento" (contained in the sixth book).

(to 1610) As Byrd grew older during these years he became more in sympathy with the English version of the Scriptures.

(to 1612) Seth Calvisius' music, original and edited, made up "Biciniorum libri duo . . . " collected during these years.

(to 1612) Monteverdi served the Mantuan court during this period.

(to 1620) Since a large number of evangelical church orders provided for a double reading of the Gospel, polyphonic settings which (in Lutheran style) used church language almost entirely until about 1590 and at least half the time until 1620, were intended for Latin rites.

(to 1620) In the body of contemporary literature written during these years there were no theoretical books on music which better demonstrated Monteverdi's intellectual capacity than his discussion contained in the Syntagma III.

c.1590

Aguilera de Heredia, a monk and Spanish composer, was born (date of death unknown).

Artus Auxcousteaux, a master of church music, was born (died 1658).

Daniell Batcheler, English lutenist and composer, was born (date of death unknown).

Gabriel Diaz, Spanish madrigalist, was born (died 1631).

Steffano Landi, an eminent operatic composer of the period, was born (died c.1655). He was a member of the papal choir and choirmaster at the cathedral in Padua. He became one of the leading representatives of Roman Opera.

Francesco della Porta, organist and church composer, was born in Milan (died 1666).

Luigi Rossi, a cantata composer and contemporary of Carissimi's, was born at Naples (date of death unknown).

Thomas Whythorne, an English composer of madrigals and villanellas, died (born 1528).

Thoinot Arbeau (Tabourot), French priest and musician, was active at this time.

Byrd lived at St. Helen's parish in Bishopsgate.

Monteverdi's "crisis of style" began at the same time as when Marenzio was evolving a new idiom.

Morley was appointed organist at St. Paul's in London.

Nathaniel Patrick was appointed Master of the Children.

Roy added strings and reed in-

c.1590(cont.)
struments to the choir at the Viceroyal Chapel.

Vecchi was maestro di cappella at Santa Maria della Scala in Milan. The opera house was named after the church.

Barbetta's "Intavolatura de Liuto . . ." was published.

A composition for virginal by Byrd was preserved at Christ Church, Oxford. It was referred to as "Mr. Birds Battel" and was probably composed around this time.

Some of Maudit's compositions as, for example, "Vous me tuez si doucement," possessed considerable charm.

Pevernage's "Nata et grata polo" was on the title page of the "Encomium musices," published this year.

Intemporance, pride and vanity were so strong at this time that a quiet citizen, concerned with the behavior of his generation, wrote to the Council of Brunswick at this time, "O Germany, Germany, I fear that a great punishment will overwhelm Germany!"

The national chorale had already started to play an important part in Germany's intimate life.

Italian, French, and Belgian composers were all referred to as "Galli" and no attempt was made to distinguish between them until the end of the century.

Instruments were not specified for particular parts in composi- (cont.) tions of this time.

The lute reached the zenith of its popularity and artistry at this time.

On the strength of Luther's statement that: "A schoolmaster must be able to sing; otherwise I will regard him as of no value" unmusical teachers in the upper Palatinate were driven from their positions at this time.

The musical ornament dated from this time but was named the trill at a later date.

At this time composers were almost always singers in the choirs for which they composed. The composer's relations with his fellow choristers were closer than those existing between modern composers and an orchestra.

Until the end of the century singing as an independent art (solo singing) was held in little respect and was almost exclusively the vocation of troubadours and popular music composers.

Italian drawing: Zuccari, The "Mannerist" artist's day-dream, Taddeo Zuccari at work on the scaffolding of a palace is being watched with admiration by the Aged Michelangelo. The goddess of Fame trumpets his triumph all over the world.

(to c.1600) Ellis Gibbons was organist at Salisbury Cathedral.

(to 1602) Monteverdi was in the service of the Duke of Mantua as violist and cantor until 1602 and after that as

c.1590(cont.)
"Maestro della Musica."

(to 1606) Caravaggio was in Rome during this period.

(to c.1615) William Cobbold, English composer of psalm-tunes and madrigals, was active during this period.

(to c.1620) Antonio Naldi Bardella, called "Il Bardello," a chamber-musician to the Duke of Tuscany, was active during this period.

(to c.1620) Leoni was maestro di cappella at Vicenza.

(to c.1620) Gasparo di Salo, a famous violin-maker in Brescia, quite possibly born at Salo, was active during this period.

(to 1620) The famous "Thysius Lute Book" was compiled during these years.

(to c.1620) Trabaci was an Italian unlike his predecessors and was an important figure in Neopolitan music of this period.

1591

(July 4 or July 18) Jacob Gallus (Handl), German sacred composer of masses and motets, died at Prague (born 1550).

(August 14) On this date the Bishop of Piacenza was present on a visit. Francis Tregian the younger was chosen to deliver an address of welcome in Latin.

(August 31 to 1592, March 31) At Harlington, a true bill was found against Byrd for being a recusant, for the period stated above.

(September 10) The tenth and final volume of Wert's madrigals was published on this date at Venice. This was very close to his death.

(September 11) A very carefully, beautifully written virginal manuscript was copied by John Baldwin and carried this date. The work was Byrd's "My Ladye Nevell's Booke."

(October 12) Anthony Anderson became a Gentleman of the Chapel Royal.

(October 15) Pope Gregory XIV died (birthdate unknown).

(November 4) Byrd published the "Liber Secundus Sacrarum Cantionum, Quinque Vocum." The volume, dedicated to Lord Lumley, included:

"Afflicti pro peccatis." 1 pars. "Et eruas nos a malis." 2 pars. 6 voc. No. 27 and 28.

"Apparebit in finem." 5 voc. No. 12.

"Cantate Domino." 6 voc. No. 29.

"Circumdederunt me." 5 voc. No. 15.

"Cunctis diebus." 6 voc. No. 30.

"Descendit de coelis." 1 pars. "Et exivit per auream portam." 2 pars. 6 voc. No. 21 and 22.

"Domine, exaudi orationem." 1 pars. "Et non intres in iudicium." 2 pars. 5 voc. No. 10 and 11.

1591(cont.)

"Domine, non sum dignus." 6 voc. No. 23.

"Domine, salva nos." 6 voc. No. 31.

"Exsurge, Domine." 5 voc. No. 19.

"Fac cum servo tuo." 5 voc. No. 5.

"Haec dicit Dominus." 1 pars. "Haec dicit Dominus." 2 pars. 5 voc. No. 13 and 14.

"Haec dies." 6 voc. No. 32.

"Infelix ego omnium." 1 pars. "Quid igitur faciam." 2 pars. "Ad te igitur." 3 pars. 6 voc. No. 24, 25, 26.

"Laudibus in sanctis." 1 pars. "Magnificum Domini." 2 pars." "Hunc arguta." 3 pars. 5 voc. No. 1 and 2.

"Levemus corda nostra." 5 voc. No. 16.

"Miserere mei, Deus." 5 voc. No. 20.

"Quis est homo." 1 pars. "Diverte a malo." 2 pars. 5 voc. No. 3 and 4.

"Recordare, Domine." 1 pars. "Requiescat, Domine." 2 pars. 5 voc. No. 17 and 18.

"Salve Regina." 1 pars. "Et Jesum benedictum." 2 pars. 5 voc. No. 6 and 7.

"Tribulatio proxima." 1 pars. "Contumelias et terrores." 2 pars. 5 voc. No. 8 and 9.

(February) Lord Admiral Howard wrote a passport for his "Joueurs et serviteurs" Robert Brown, John Bradstreet, Thomas Sackville, and Richard Jones on this date. Howard announced that they would tour Friesland, Holland, and Zeeland, and meanwhile "d'exercer leurs qualitez en faict de musique, agilitez, et joeuz de commedies, tragedies et histoires, pour s'entretenir et fournir à leurs despenses en leur dict voyage."

(September) Byrd was at Harlington, when the famous "My Ladye Nevells Booke," which included forty-two examples of his keyboard works, was completed by John Baldwin of Windsor.

When William Blitheman died on Whitsunday of this year he was buried at the church of St. Nicholas Olave, Queenhithe. A brass plate was installed which carried a metrical epitaph that recorded his skill as an organist and musician as well as the fact that he was John Bull's teacher.

Joan Brudieu, eminent madrigalist, died (birthdate unknown).

William Daman, English psalmist, and Walloon composer, died in London (born c.1540).

Vincenzo Galilei, Italian madrigal composer, died at Florence (born c.1520).

Vespasiano Gonzaga, a member of the noble family, died (born 1531).

Sir Christopher Hatton, an early member of the family of composers and dramatists, died (birth-

1591(cont.)

date unknown).

Robert Herrick, English Cavalier poet, was born (died 1674).

Jacobus de Kerle, Netherlandish composer, died at Prague (born c.1531).

William Mundy, vicar choral of St. Paul's and father of John Mundy, was active until his death.

Jacob Paix, German intabulator, died (born 1556).

Andries Pevernage, French composer, died at Antwerp and was buried in the cathedral there (born 1543).

In a manuscript carrying this date John Baldwin "singing man of Windsor" wrote on the principal composers of his time as follows, "I will begin with White, Shepperd, Tye and Tallis, Parsons, Gyles, Mundie, th'oulde one of the Queen's pallis."

Bassano in his "Motetti, Madrigali et Canzoni francese . . . diminuti," published this year at Venice, included a Lassus chanson as one of his examples.

In an "In nomine" by Blitheman, written prior to this date, an early example of triplet figuration in virginal music was found throughout the entire composition.

John Bull succeeded Blitheman as organist of the Chapel Royal.

The earliest marches, per se, were included in "My Ladye (cont.) Nevells Booke" for harpsichord.

Giovanni Luca Conforti was admitted to the Papal Choir.

The Windsor or Eton Tune was first found in Damon's music for the Psalms, published this year. It was harmonised in four parts and set to Psalm cxvi.

The present University of Dublin was founded by Queen Elizabeth and, at the same time, the "College of the Holy and Undivided Trinity," near Dublin.

Robert Flud became a student of St. John's College, Oxford. He studied physics there.

Matteo Foresto was in Cologne at this time.

Gastoldi's "Balletti" and Vecchi's semi-dramatic madrigal comedies prepared the way for Monteverdi's "Scherzi Musicali" as well as for madrigalian opera-ballets.

Gastoldi composed dance-songs called "Balletti." They brought him recognition as one of the leading composers of this light type of madrigal, which was an outgrowth of the frottola and the villanella.

Galilei, prior to his death this year, planned to publish a treatise on counterpoint.

Jacob Händl, the old German master, had his name latinised into Gallus. This was in line with the fashionable custom of "punning" in vogue at this time.

The title-page of Lindner's "Bicinia Sacra," published this

1591(cont.)

year, used both German and Latin.

Lord Lumley entertained Queen Elizabeth at Lewes this year when Byrd's second book of "Cantiones" was published. The volume was dedicated to him by the noted composer.

Starting at this time Marenzio received the patronage of Cinzio Aldobrandini (later Cardinal Aldobrandini). The latter was one of the two influential nephews of Pope Clement VIII, Tasso's patron and literary heir. Pope Clement reserved two rooms in the Vatican for Marenzio's use.

Del Mel was appointed to the cathedral and the new college at Magliano.

Gian Domenico Montella entered the Viceroyal Chapel as a lute -player.

Morley apparently was organist at St. Paul's but shortly after this year resigned from the position.

John Mundy, as well as his father, William, was mentioned in verses at the end of a manuscript collection of madrigals and motets transcribed by Baldwin to honor the most famous musicians of the period.

Lord Northampton lived in a little cell at Greenwich through the courtesy and generosity of the Lord Admiral.

When the diocese of Sabina was put in Gabriel Paleotto's charge this year he founded a college there, improved the (cont.) cathedral at Magliano, and made various changes in the internal government of the diocese.

Palestrina sent his fifth volume of masses to Duke William V of Bavaria.

Hans Ruckers the elder became tuner of the organ at the Virgin's chapel of the Cathedral.

Schütz' father and grandfather held a good social position at Weissenfels. His father had moved there from Köstritz with his family when the grandfather died this year.

In Van der Straetern's "La Musique aux Pays-Bas" a portrait of des Prés was reprinted from a book published by Peter Opmeere at Antwerp this year.

The Rev. Thomas Tomkins, chanter and minor canon at Gloucester cathedral, and father of the famous composer, died (birthdate unknown).

Vecchi was appointed archdeacon at Coreggio Cathedral.

All the composers except Verovio who were included in the "Diletto" were quoted in a purely secular canzonetta collection published by the same firm this year.

At Weissenfels Christoph Schütz, II employed a tutor, Hofmeister Michael N. for his five children.

Adriano Banchieri's first work, "Conclusioni per organo" appeared at Lucca.

1591(cont.)

The eighth volume of the "Patrocinium musices" by Berg was published this year.

Byrd's "Hughe Ashton's Grownde" appeared prior to this date.

Byrd wrote "My Ladye-Nevells Booke" which included forty-two compositions (see 1591, September).

Byrd's "Walsingham variations" appeared prior to this date.

The first book of five-voiced madrigals by Serafino Cantone appeared.

Caraccio's "Salmi di compieta con le antifone della Vergine, ed otto falsi bordoni a 5 voci" was published at Venice.

This year marked the issuance of Damon's "The former Booke of the Musicke of M. William Damon, late one of her Majesties Musitions, containing all the tunes of David's Psalms, as they are ordinarily soung in the Church: most excellently by him composed into 4 partes. In which sett the Tenor singeth the Church tune. Published for the recreation of such as delight in Musicke by W. Swayne, Gent. Printed by T. Este, the assignè of W. Byrd, 1591."

Two psalters by William Daman appeared this year in England.

John Farmer this year published a short tract titled "Divers and sundrie waies of two Parts in one, to the number of fortie upon one playn song; sometimes placing the Ground above and the parts benethe, and otherwise the Ground benethe and the parts (cont.) above."

Stefano Felis, a Neapolitan composer, published a setting of a madrigal for five high voices written by Tasso in honor of Tarquinia Molza.

Gallus had a special privilege, granted by the Emperor, to publish "Hańdl Jac. Musici operis, harmoniarum 4,5,6,8 et plurium vocum" at Prague in four volumes. It was a collection of great value and included motets for the entire liturgical year (see also 1586).

One hundred and seventy out of three hundred and fifty titles listed in a surviving catalogue published by Gardano were madrigal collections.

Gastoldi's "Balletti per cantare, sonare & ballare" was first published.

The success of Gastoldi's five-voiced balletti of this year overshadowed that of Ferretti's canzoni, published at Venice, was quickly followed by others at Antwerp, Paris and Rotterdam. In Paris opposition to Italian music was usually quite strong.

"Bicinia Sacra, ex variis autoribus . . . edita etc. was published this year by Gerlach at Nürnberg.

Hassler's "Cantiones sacrae de festis praecipuis totius anni 4,5,8 et plurium vocum" was published this year at Augsburg. The volume contained twenty-eight motets.

Hawkins printed a Latin motet for three voices by King Henry VIII that was from a

1591(cont.)

manuscript collection of anthems, motets, etc. by John Baldwin. Baldwin subsequently became a Gentleman of the Chapel Royal where he also held the position of "clerk of the checkque."

The collection "Intermedii e concerti" with fourteen part-books was published. The bulk of the contents was by Malvezzi.

Eight compositions by Marenzio were included in "Intermedii et concerti," published by Vincenti at Venice.

Marenzio's "Leggiadre ninfe" was first published this year.

Marenzio's "Il 3º libro de Madrigali a 5" was reprinted by Vincenti at Venice.

Marenzio's "Il 5º libro de Madrigali a 6" was published by Gardano at Venice. The volume was dedicated to Virginio Orsini, Duke of Bracciano.

One of Marenzio's madrigals was included in "Canzonette per cantar et sonar di liuto libro terzo" published by Vincenti at Venice.

One of Marenzio's madrigals was included in "Canzonette Spirituali a 3" published by Verovio at Rome.

One of Marenzio's madrigals was included in "Canzonette a quattro voci" published by Verovio at Rome.

One of Marenzio's madrigals was included in "Il Lauro Verde" published by Phalèse and Bellère at Antwerp.

Five of Marenzio's madrigals were included in "Melodia Olympica" published by Phalèse and Bellère at Antwerp.

One of Marenzio's madrigals was included in "La Ruzina" published by Gardano at Venice.

Marenzio's "Il 5º libro delle Villanelle a 3" was reprinted by Gardano at Venice as "Villanelle et Arie."

An Italian madrigal collection: "Melodia Olympica" was published at Antwerp.

Georg Otto's setting for Lobwasser's Psalter appeared in manuscript form.

Palestrina's "Benedicta sit" was composed.

A third edition of Palestrina's Volume I of masses was published by Gardano at Rome.

Palestrina published a volume this year which included two settings of the magnificat in each of the first eight modes. The book was dedicated to Pope Gregory XIV.

Palestrina's magnificat on the eighth tone was considered to be one of the best in the collection published this year.

Palestrina's "Missa pro Defunctis," for five voices, was first published at Rome.

The "Dies irae," missing in Palestrina's "Missa pro Defunctis," was included at the end of the third edition of Volume I of his masses.

A canzone, "La Serpentina," by

1591(cont.)

Vincenzo Pellegrini appeared.

Soto published the fourth book of Laudi Spirituali at this date. It was a continuation of two edited by Animuccia, and one published by Soto in 1588.

"Tancred and Gismunda" was published.

A cataloge issued by Vincenti named approximately two hundred and twenty-five items and madrigal collections accounted for about one hundred of them.

One of Virchi's third madrigal books appeared this year. The others were issued in 1584 and 1588 respectively.

A book of tablatures by Matthäus Waissel (Waisselius) was published at Frankfurt an der Oder this year (see also 1573 and 1592).

Harrington's "Orlando Furioso" of Ariosto appeared in England.

John Lyly's "Endymion" was published in England.

Shakespeare's "Comedy of Errors" was completed.

Shakespeare's "Love's Labour's Lost" was completed.

Sir Philip Sidney set the fashion for writing sonnets in series to a single person in his "Astrophel and Stella" published this year.

Guercino, an Italian painter, was born (died 1666).

José de Ribera, known as Lo Spagnoletto, a Spanish painter, was born (died 1652).

Valentin de Boullongne, an Italian painter, was born (died 1634).

(to 1591) The Papal reign of St. Innocent IX (born in Bologna).

(and 1592) Literary historians maintained that during this period a performance of Guarini's "Pastor Fido" was in preparation at the court of Mantua and that de Wert and Francesco Rovigo were assigned the composition of the choruses. This work did not qualify as a genuine opera.

(to 1592) Shakespeare's "Two Gentlemen of Verona" was written during these years.

(1594, and 1611) Peter Philipp's "Melodia Olympica di diversi Excellentissimi Musici a IV, V, VI, et VIII voci" was published in 1591 and then reprinted in 1594 and 1611.

(to 1595) Marenzio was employed by Cardinal Aldobrandini in Rome during this period.

(to 1595, 1596) Gastoldi composed "Balletti da suonare, cantare, e ballare" published at Venice (1591-1595) and at Antwerp (1596). These apparently served as models for Morley in his "Ballets or Fal las."

(and 1598) Two further laude collections by Soto de Langa followed in these years respectively.

(1603 to 1612) The Carman's Whistle, an old English tune, appeared in the Virginal books

1591(cont.)

of Lady Nevill in 1591 and Queen Elizabeth 1603-1612. The versions were both with harmony and variations by Byrd.

(and 1605) Byrd published little or nothing during this period.

c.1591

William Mundy, English motet composer, died (born c.1530).

Compositions by Gastoldi appeared at this time.

1592

(April 7) The latest record of Byrd's residence at Harlington is that of 7 April 1592, when a true bill was found against him for being a recusant (see also 1581, June 28).

(July 1) Marc' Antonio Ingegneri, composer and teacher of Monteverdi, died at Cremona (born 1545).

(July 7) John Bull was incorporated Mus. Doc. at Oxford.

(July 7) Giles Farnaby graduated at Christ Church and was awarded the degree of Mus. Bac.

(July 7) The Rev. Edward Gibbons was awarded the degree of Bachelor of Music at Cambridge, and on July 7, 1592, was incorporated at Oxford.

(July 9) Giles Farnaby was awarded the degree of Bachelor of Music at Oxford.

(July 11) Francis Tregian the Younger left Douay.

(July 24) Thomas Morley became a Gentleman of the Chapel Royal.

(September 15) A letter written on this date and signed by Asola accompanied a musical offering, dedicated in glowing terms to Palestrina, compared the latter to "an ocean of knowledge" whereas it described other composers as "rivers whose life is bound up with the sea, into which they shed their tribute."

(November 8) Domenico Mazzocchi, oratorio composer and a member of the musical family, was born at Civita Castellana near Rome (died 1665).

(November 18) Thomas Morley was promoted to Gospeller of the Chapel Royal.

(November 30) Giovanni Guidetti, Italian composer and a pupil of Palestrina, died at Rome (born 1532).

(February to April) Tasso and Gesualdo became better acquainted when the poet visited Naples for the second time during this period.

John Jenkins, English musician and composer, was born at Maidstone (died 1678).

Annibale Zoilo, choirmaster of the Lateran, died (birthdate unknown).

Richard Allison's name first appeared when listed as a contributor to Este's "The Whole Booke of Psalms" published this year.

A collection of "Psalmodia vespertina" appeared this year and included a dedication to Palestrina, written by Asola. The collection was prepared as an act of homage and contribu-

1592(cont.)

tors included Asola himself, Croce, Gastoldi, Leoni and Porta.

Palestrina was considered to be the most important figure in the Roman School by Asola who described him as "the Ocean towards which all streams flow."

Count Bardi was brought to Rome this year to act as Maestro di camera to Pope Clement VIII.

Bassano was appointed maestro at the Seminary of St. Mark's to succeed Donato. The Seminary had been moved this year to a new location further from the cathedral,Bassano was born 1510.

Edward Blancks was one of the ten composers who contributed to "The Whole Booke of Psalmes" published by Este this year and reprinted by the Musical Antiquarian Society.

John Bull was awarded the degree of Mus. Doc. from Oxford.

Byrd may not have left Harlington immediately after the spring of this year as was supposed.

Cavaccio contributed to the collection of Psalms, dedicated to Palestrina this year.

Michael Cavendish was one of the ten composers who contributed to "The Whole Booke of Psalmes" published by Este this year.

Domenico Pietro Cerone went to Spain.

Cerone was admitted to the chapel of King Philip II.

Orazio Colombani joined other musicians in dedicating the collection of Psalms to Palestrina this year.

Dowland contributed to Leighton's Teares, to East's psalter and to Ravenscroft's psalter. Other than that his output of sacred music included a set of seven psalms written for the funeral of Henry Noel, an Elizabethan courtier.

Dowland was one of the musicians who contributed to "The Whole Booke of Psalms" published by Este this year.

Edward, Earl of Worcester, received the degree of M.A. from Oxford this year.

The Windsor or Eton Tune appeared in "The Whole Booke of Psalmes" which included the Church Tunes as well as "other short tunes usually sung in London and most places of the Realme."

John Farmer was one of the ten composers who contributed to "The Whole Book of Psalms" published this year by Este.

Giles Farnaby was one of the ten composers who contributed to "The Whole Book of Psalms" published by Este this year.

Gastoldi was maestro di capella at Milan at this time.

Gastoldi was invited to contribute to one of the most distinguished collections of the time, the "Trionfo di Dori" (1592) for which he composed one of his most successful pieces, "Al mormorar de'liquidi cristalli," as well as "Gloria musicale,"

1592(cont.)

dedicated to Count Bevilacqua.

Monteverdi's M.B. III (1592) included seven poems which have been identified as by Guarini, two of them from the "Pastor fido."

Edmond Hooper was one of the ten composers who contributed to "The Whole Booke of Psalms" published by Este this year.

Lord Admiral Howard's "Joueurs et serviteurs" were travelling in the Netherlands.

Edward Johnson was one of the ten composers who contributed to "The Whole Booke of Psalms" published by Este this year.

George Kirbye was one of the ten composers who contributed to "The Whole Booke of Psalmes" published by Este this year.

Macque became strongly idenfified with Naples this year when he married a "damigella" whose parents stipulated, in the marriage contract, that he might not leave the city without the lady's written consent, or he would have to pay a penalty of one thousand ducats, the lady in question was Isabella Tonto, a Neapolitan.

Monteverdi was rapidly promoted from the position of simple "violist" to that of "cantore." He had described himself as the former in the dedication of his "Second Book of Madrigals" this year.

Monteverdi's M.B. III (1592) included a trilogy which included stanzas 59,60 and 63 from Canto XVI, giving expression to (cont.) Armida's grief after she has been abandoned by Rinaldo. The result was a fore-runner to the "Lamento" in Rinuccini's "Arianna" libretto.

Landgrave Moritz began his reign this year at the age of twenty.

The "Old Hundredth" appeared in Este's Psalter this year.

Palestrina was probably anxious concerning his pension from the Papal Choir since there had been four popes during a period of less than two years following the death of Pope Sixtus V in August of 1590.

Pope Clement VIII increased Palestrina's stipend from the Papal Choir to sixteen scudi a month. This was done as a gesture of appreciation because of the composer's excellent work.

Palestrina and Marenzio were both represented in "Il Trionfo di Dori" this year. This collection served as a model for the "Triumphes of Oriana" published in England.

Ottavia Rinuccini began the composition of "Dafne," one of the earliest if not the earliest opera.

Striggio was a contributor to the "Trionfo di Dori." The collection was written on the order of Leonardo Sanudo.

Zacconi inserted Palestrina's "L'homme armé" in his "Practica Musicale."

One motet was included in Conforti, Psalmi, Motecta, Magnificat et antiphona, pub-

1592(cont.)

lished by Coattino at Rome.

Christoph Demantius' "Forma musices, gründlicher . . . Bericht der Singekunst" appeared this year.

Este edited and published "The Whole Book of Psalms, with their wonted tunes, in four parts." The quality of music contained therein was distinguished.

Gardano published a collection of madrigals titled "Il Trionfo di Dori" at Venice.

Gastoldi published his first book of three-voiced canzonette.

Marenzio's "Il 2° libro delle Canzonette alla Napoletana a 3" was reprinted by Vincenti at Venice.

One of Marenzio's madrigals was included in "Il Devoto Pianto della Gloriosa Vergine" published by Verovio at Rome.

One of Marenzio's madrigals was included in "Il Trionfo di Dori" published by Gardano at Venice.

One of Marenzio's madrigals was included in "La Gloria Musicale" published by Amadino at Venice.

One of Marenzio's madrigals was included in "Spoglia Amorosa a 5" published by Gardano at Venice.

Marenzio's Motectorum lib. secundus was issued but has been lost.

Marenzio's "Motectorum pro festis totius anni" was published by Amadino at Venice.

Six of Marenzio's pieces were included in "Novum pratum musicum" published by Phalèse and Bellère at Antwerp.

Marenzio's "Il 3° libro delle Villanelle a 3" was published by Gardano at Rome.

"Marenzio's "Il 4° libro delle Villanelle a 3" was published by Vincenti at Venice.

Merulo's "Canzoni d'intavolatura d'Organo . . . Lib. 1" was composed.

Monteverdi's third madrigal book appeared.

Included in Monteverdi's third book of madrigals was a setting of "O come è gran martire," a poem by Guarini.

Palestrina's 6-part secular madrigal "Quando dal terzo cielo" was included in the "Il Trionfo di Dori" collection published this year at Venice.

This year marked the first publication of Palestrina's Mass "Dominicalis."

Peter Philips' "Galiarda Passamezzo" appeared.

On page 142 of Queen Elizabeth's Virginal Book there was a "Passamezzo Pavana" carrying this date. It was by Peter Philips and composed in an elaborate style, followed by a "Galiarda Passamezzo."

Giovanni Maria Radino's "Balli per sonar di liuto," composed this year, contained dance pieces which had frequent modulations. It was titled, "Il primo libro di Balli

1592(cont.)

d'Arpicordo."

Richardo Rogniono wrote a manual on ornamentation.

Ruffo's collection of Masses "Missae Borromeae" appeared.

Salinas' "De Musica" was chiefly a theoretical work.

Soriano published his second work.

Sweelinck's first published works were a set of "Chansons" from this year. They have since been lost.

A collection of Victoria's works was published at Rome.

Vittoria's second book of masses appeared.

A book of tablatures by Matthäus Waissel (Waisselius) was published at Frankfurt an der Oder this year (see also 1573 and 1591). This volume contained forty-eight Polish dances.

Lodovico Zacconi's "Prattica di musica" was published this year.

The transformation of the "Kantorei" into the "Patrician Collegium musicum" was confirmed by the town council of Weissenfels.

Robert Greene, Elizabethan poet, died (born c.1560).

Shakespeare had by this time established a reputation as a dramatist.

Ammanati, Italian architect (cont.) (Pitti Palace), died (born 1511).

Jacques Callot, French painter, was born (died 1634).

Italian architecture: Zuccari, Window from the Palazzo Zuccari in Rome. (This window was designed in the form of a face.)

(to 1594) Sweelinck's "Chansons françaises" were actually issued in three parts at Antwerp during this period.

(to 1594) Italian painting: Tintoretto, The Last Supper (12' x 18'8"). This work was dated as 1547 by another source.

(and 1603, 1605) Monteverdi's next three Books, III, 1592, IV, 1603 and V, 1605, were published at Mantua and showed the evolution in his style up to the period immediately preceding the era of the figured bass.

(to 1605) The Papal reign of St. Clement VIII (born in Florence).

(and 1622) Lodovico Zacconi wrote the "Musica Prattica" during this period.

c.1592

Thomas Watson, a poet, died at London. It was not certain whether this was the same man who published the Italian madrigal collection.

The Rev. Edward Gibbons was appointed organist at Bristol Cathedral as well as priest-vicar, subchanter, and master of the choristers at the same location.

In many of the madrigals pub-

c.1592(cont.)
lished after this date it became evident that Marenzio was becoming an "advanced" composer.

Ben Jonson married.

Christopher Marlowe's "Edward II" appeared.

1593
(January 9) Trinity College, Dublin, was opened for the reception of students.

Paolo Agostini, Italian composer, was born at Vallerano (died 1629).

Pieter Cornet, organist to the Infanta Clara Eugenia at Brussels, was born (died 1626).

Severin Cornet, composer of chansons, madrigals, and motets, died at Antwerp (born c.1540).

Johann Klemme was born in Oderan near Freiberg, Saxony (date of death unknown).

William Hollingsworth mortgaged his lease to William Chambers and in this year he and Chambers assigned the whole property of Stondon Place to Byrd. It included about two hundred acres and all of their interest in it. The price was £300.

Byrd moved to Stondon, Essex.

Thomas Campion had already achieved recognition as a poet by this time.

Domenico Pietro Cerone was a member of the chapel of King Philip II.

Giovanni Croce was appointed teacher of the choirboys at (cont.) St. Mark's in Venice.

Edward, Earl of Worcester, was made a Knight of the Garter this year.

When the fantasia emerged with Gabrieli and, this year, with Vecchi, it was a highly developed style based on one theme, modified by inversion, ornamentation, and other compositional devices.

Gesualdo arrived at Ferrara.

The Grouwels family of harpsichord and virginal makers were by this time settled at Middelburg.

Francesco Guami was maestro di cappella at San Marciliano in Venice.

Alfonso Lobo was elected maestro at Lisbon, Toledo.

The two sets of offertories in five parts, covering the entire ecclesiastical year, were not published by Palestrina until this year, shortly before his death. They contained several pieces that were probably composed many years earlier, since their texts did not conform with the revised missal issued in 1570 by Pope Pius V.

Palestrina apparently contemplated retirement so that he might complete the publication of many of his works which were still in manuscript.

Peter Philips was among those who came to visit Sweelinck in Amsterdam as early as this time.

Hans Ruckers the Elder added fourteen or fifteen stops to the

1593(cont.)

large organ at the Virgin's chapel of the Cathedral.

Schütz started a friendship with the sister of Moritz the Learned.

The masses of Stadelmayr were a novelty at this time.

Sweelinck and Philips met when Philips went "into Holland onely to sie and heare an excellent man of his faculties in Amsterdam."

Vecchi returned to Modena to direct the singers at the Cathedral.

Andrés de Villalar was maestro at Zamora.

Zacconi was invited to Vienna by the Archduke Charles, who appointed him as his Kapellmeister.

Caraccio's "Salmi a cinque per tutti i vesperi dell' anno, con alcuni hymni, mottetti, e falsi bordoni accommodati ancora a voci di donne" was published at Venice.

Conforto's "Breve . . . maniera . . . a far passaggi" appeared this year.

Part I of Diruta's "Il Transilvano" appeared.

A volume containing intonazioni appeared. Eight of them were attributed to Andrea Gabrieli, eleven to Giovanni Gabrieli.

"Intonazioni For Organ" by Giovanni Gabrieli was published. This may, however, have been identical with the collection mentioned above.

Marenzio's "Il 1,2,3,4 e 5 lib. de Madrigali a 5, ridotti in un corpo" were published by Phalèse at Antwerp.

Marenzio's "Il 2° libro de Madrigali a 5" was reprinted by Gardano at Venice.

Marenzio's "Il 4° libro de Madrigali a 6" was reprinted by Gardano at Venice.

One of Marenzio's madrigals was included in "Florindo e Armilla" published by Amadino at Venice.

Eight of Marenzio's madrigals were included in "Harmonia Celeste" published by Phalèse and Bellère at Antwerp.

Two of Marenzio's madrigals were included in "Nuova Spoglia Amorosa" published by Vincenti at Venice.

One of Marenzio's madrigals arranged for lute was included in "Terzi, Intavolatura di liutto" published by Amadino at Venice.

Among the earliest settings not purely vocal in character were the "Canzoni da sonare" by Maschera of this year. They were, perhaps, originally composed for the organ, but printed in separate parts, and evidently therefore intended for performance by various instruments.

This year marked the publication of a collection by Rogier Michael, a German composer.

Morley's first publication, "Canzonets, or Little Short Songs to three voyces" appeared this year. They were actually

1593(cont.)

short madrigals rather than canzonets. The publisher was Este.

Nanino, a fine canzonetta composer, included madrigalian melismas and occasional imitation in his "Primo Libro delle canzonette a tre voci" published this year.

Palestrina published a volume of "Litanies" for four voices and his sixth volume of masses for four and five voices. The latter was dedicated to Cardinal Aldobrandini who had appointed him director of his concerts.

Palestrina, who was especially devoted to the Litaniae Lauretanae, published a volume including, in two books, ten different settings of great beauty this year. He composed the works for the use of the "Confraternity of the Holy Rosary."

Palestrina's sixty-eight Offertories for the whole year, for five voices, was published in two books this year. The title was "Offertoria Totius Anni" and the books, of great historical importance, were dedicated to a French Benedictine monk of noble birth, Abbé de la Baume Saint-Amour.

The "Exultako Te Domine" was included in Palestrina's offertories.

Peeter Philips' "Pauana Dolorosa. Treg." appeared this year.

Sebastiano Raval, a Spaniard, (cont.) in the dedication of his first book of madrigals for five voices, of this year, provided a picture of the society in which Marenzio moved.

Giovanni Antonio Terzi's "Ballo Tedesco Novo de L'Autore" (for guitar) appeared.

Terzi published "Intavolatura di Liutto" for a seven-string lute in Italian tablature at Venice. Eight transcriptions of chansons and madrigals for two lutes were included in the collection.

Christopher Marlowe, Elizabethan playwright, died (born 1564).

Because of his views, a warrant was issued for Christopher Marlowe's arrest this year.

Christopher Marlowe collaborated to some extent in "Titus Andronicus" published this year.

Shakespeare's "John" was completed.

Shakespeare's "Richard III" was completed.

Shakespeare's "Venus and Adonis" were entered at Stationers' Hall.

Georges de la Tour, French painter, was born (died 1652).

Jacob Jordaens, Flemish painter, was born (died 1678).

Dutch drawing: Gerritt Pietersz. Sweelinck, Open air musical party.

1593(cont.)

Dutch etching: Gerrit Pietersz. Sweelinck, St. Cecilia.

(to 1594) Shakespeare's "Titus Andronicus" was written during these years.

(and 1594) Pietro Paolo Tozzi, a Paduan publisher, had Vincenti print some of Torelli's canzonette at Venice.

(to 1595) Morley produced two books of Canzonets, one, of "Madrigals to foure Voyces," and one of Ballets during these years.

(to 1599) Lute books by Terzi were published during these years.

c.1593

When Gesualdo left for Ferrara for his second wedding Tasso wished to go with him.

This year marked the first publication of the following Palestrina Masses, "Dies sanctificatus," "In te Domine speravi," "Je suis desheritée," "Quam pulchra es" and "Dilexi quoniam."

Christopher Marlowe's "The Massacre at Paris" and "The Tragedy of Dido" were probably written at this time with Nash participating in the latter.

Shakespeare's "Comedy of Errors" appeared at this time.

Louis Le Nain, French painter, was born (died 1648).

1594

(January 13) Richard Verstegan provided interesting material on Peter Philips in a letter to (cont.) Father Persons, on this date.

(January 26) Palestrina suffered an attack of pleurisy on this date which proved to be terminal.

(February 2) Giovanni Pierluigi da Palestrina, Italian composer, died at Rome (born c.1524, December 17). Many of his greatest works had not yet been published at the time of his death on the Feast of the Purification. Palestrina's position in the field of polyphony was unparalleled and, as a Roman Catholic composer, his work helped that church to combat the reformation and the various threats to its very existence. Palestrina, as a composer, has remained a major figure in the overall history of music.

(February 5) Vecchi (in Modena) was attacked by an unknown assassin but fortunately escaped unharmed.

(February 14) A Requiem Mass was performed in Palestrina's memory. It was sung in the chapel of St. Maria del Soccorso in the basilica nuova.

(March 1) Palestrina's son Igino informed the Pope that his father had, during the last moments of his life, charged him with the responsibility for publication of all the composer's remaining manuscripts. He further stated that it was his intention to fulfill this charge as his means provided him the opportunity. In performing this filial duty he humbly hoped for the assistance of the Holy Father.

1594(cont.)

(March 12) Ruggiero Giovanelli was appointed to succeed Palestrina at St. Peter's and assumed his duties three days later.

(April 3) Anerio was named "Compositore" to the Papal Chapel.

(April 5) John Wilson, Mus. Doc., was born at Feversham, Kent (died 1673, February 22).

(May 24) Lassus' "Lagrime di S. Pietro" signed on this date and "Cantiones Sacrae," Feast of St. Michael, were published.

(May 28) A letter carrying this date mentioned a brother of William Byrd in connexion with certain people who as Catholics were under the observation of the authorities.

(June 14) Orlando di Lassus, monumental polyphonic composer and contemporary of Palestrina, died at Munich (born 1532). He had remained in the service of the Bavarian dukes until his death, see also 1530.

(September 10) Luzzasco Luzzaschi, the head of the d'Este court music, dedicated his fourth book of madrigals to Gesualdo on this date.

(September 29) In the records of the City of London a letter (#16) was found from the Lord Keeper, Sir John Puckering, to the Lord Mayor, requesting him to see that "William Warren, lately chosen Master of the Musicians' Company, but prevented from the peaceful exercise of his office by some of the members of the company, be not further in-

(cont.) terfered with."

(January) Palestrina issued his last publication this month, a collection of "Madrigali spirituali," for five voices, in honor of the Virgin and dedicated to the Grand-Duchess of Tuscany, wife of Ferdinand de' Medici.

(September) On recommendation of Roy, Macque was appointed successor to the Spanish organist at the Royal Chapel, one Cristóbal Obregón.

King Gustavus Adolfus of Sweden was born (died 1632). He was greatly concerned with the threat of Catholicism to the religious and commercial independence of Sweden and was active in defending this position.

Valentin Balassi, a Hungarian lyric poet, died (born 1551).

Giovanni Battista Doni, jurist, classical scholar, professor and writer on musical subjects, was born (died 1647).

Giovanni Andrea Dragoni, sacred polyphonic composer, died (born 1540).

Cardinal Ippolito d'Este died (birthdate unknown), see 1572.

John Johnson, English lute composer, died (birthdate unknown).

Hofmeister Michael N, tutor to the Schütz family, died (birthdate unknown).

An extract from the records of Aberdeen Burgh as faithfully transcribed by the editors of

1594(cont.)

the Spalding Club publications stated: "Item to the Maister of the sang schoile xiij."

Pope Clement VIII summoned Felice Anerio to officially assume the position of composer to the Papal Chapel, which Palestrina had held de facto.

Madrigals by Antonio Bicci were found among the works this year of Luca Bati.

Bolt was arrested as a papist this year and later went to Brussels. He spent the balance of his life abroad.

Byrd's music may have been written for a play, printed this year and titled "The Warres of Cyrus King of Persia, against Antiochus King of Assyria, with the Tragicall ende of Panthaea."

Seth Calvisius became Cantor and Schulcollege at the Thomasschule and music director at the St. Thomas church of Leipzig.

With the death of Palestrina and Lassus the same year the members of the Florentine "Camerata" started work on the first opera, "Dafne," by Peri-Corsi and Rinuccini. Vecchi's madrigal-comedy "L'Amfiparnasso" had already been published by this time.

Zarlino appointed Croce a member of the Choir at San Marco, where he became vice-choirmaster under the aging Donati.

John Dowland's application for a court post in England was refused because of his faith. He then went to Germany, first to the Duke of Brunswick, then to (cont.) the Landgrave of Hesse, where he became acquainted with Alexander Orologio.

Gesualdo married Eleonora d'Este and settled down for some time at the court of Ferrara.

The Gesualdo who left his mark for the following generation and for posterity did not appear until after this date.

Ruggiero Giovanelli succeeded Palestrina as maestro at St. Peter's in Rome.

John Hilton was assistant organist at Lincoln Cathedral until this year when he left to become organist at Trinity College, Cambridge.

Edward Johnson, Mus. Bac., was graduated from Cambridge this year.

Richard Jones returned to England this year and became a singer for Court performances by Lord Admiral's company.

A few days before his death Lasso signed the dedication of a madrigal publication "Lagrime di San Pietro," dedicated to the Pope.

Joseph Lupo, quite possibly a relative of Thomas Lupo, was a composer of fancies, and author of the verses prefixed to John Mundy's "Songs and Psalms" of this year.

Marenzio was admitted to the Papal Choir.

Tiburzio Massaino was maestro di capella of the Cremona Cathedral after this date.

1594(cont.)

Palestrina was taken ill while preparing to leave Rome, and in the midst of superintending the publication of his seventh book of masses.

Soon after Palestrina's death this year the "Homophonic School" became noticeable.

The libretto for "Dafne" was set by Peri and later by Marco da Gagliano and Schütz also provided music for the same story.

Ottavio Rinuccini wrote Dafne, probably performed this year for the first time at Jacopo Corsi's home. The libretto was written in Florence.

Mateo Romero was appointed a cantor of the capilla flamenca.

A harpsichord built by Hans Ruckers the Elder and carrying this date was preserved in a private museum in Berlin.

When Count Philip Ludwig II of Hanau-Münzenberg visited Amsterdam this year he made notations on the most important events and places. Hearing the city's organist, Sweelinck, was one such event.

Tomkins went to London to study with Byrd.

Francis Tregian the Younger was chamberlain to Cardinal Allen for two years. When the latter died this year Tregian delivered a funeral oration in the church of the English College at Rome.

Vecchi's "Amfiparnasso, commedia harmonica" was produced at Modena this year.

Vitoria returned to Spain at this time.

Simone Balsamino, the Venetian choirmaster, published a setting of a scene and an entire dialogue from Tasso's "Aminta." It had been written several years earlier for an "accademia" in Urbino, his birthplace. The work was referred to as "Aminta Musicale."

The ninth volume of Berg's "Patrocinium musices" was published this year.

Hércole Bottrigari's dialogue "Il Desiderio overo (or) de' concerti di varij strumenti musicali" was published this year at Venice.

Giovanni B. Bovicelli's "Madrigali e motetti passeggiati" appeared this year.

Early writers had made no mention of St. Cecilia's skill in music, even up to this time. A long Italian poem by Castelletti, "La Trionfatrice Cecilia, Vergine e Martire Romana," was published at Florence this year, but did not allude to it either.

Seth Calvisius' treatise "Compendium musicae practicae . . ." was published this year at Leipzig.

Caraccio's "Madrigali a 5 voci, lib. 4" was published this year at Venice.

Caraccio's "Salmi a cinque" was published this year at Venice.

A collection of double-chorus motets by Croce was published

1594(cont.)

this year and included one of the earliest known examples of a printed organ bass.

Dragoni's fourth book of madrigals appeared at this time.

The complete Psalter was published by Este this year.

Gastoldi published his second book of three-voiced canzonette this year.

This year marked the publication of a collection by Bartholomäus Gesius, a German composer.

Gesualdo's first and second books of madrigals for five voices appeared this year.

Johannes Heroldt's Passion after Matthew appeared this year.

Lechner's "St. John's Passion" appeared this year.

Leroy published Le Jeune's "Recueil de plusieurs chansons et airs nouveaux" at Paris.

A treatment of the Psalter in Lobwasser's version by Samuel Marschal appeared this year.

Marenzio's "Il 4º libro de Madrigali a 5" was reprinted by Gardano at Venice.

Marenzio's "Il 5º libro de Madrigali a 5" was reprinted by Gardano at Venice.

A collected edition of Marenzio's "Madrigali a sei voci in un corpo ridotti" was published by Phalèse and Bellère at Antwerp.

Marenzio's "Il 6º libro de Madrigali a 5" was published by Gardano at Venice.

Three of Marenzio's madrigals were included in "Florilegium omnis fere generis cantionum" published by Greuenbruch at Cologne.

Samuel Marschal's "Der ganze Psalter Ambrosii Lobwassers mit 4 Stimmen" was published this year at Leipzig.

Monteverdi's "Third Book of Madrigals" appeared.

Monteverdi's "Madrigal, Stracciami pur il core" was included in his Third Book of Madrigals.

Este published Morley's madrigals, "Madrigalls to foure Voyces" this year.

John Mundy this year published "Songs and Psalmes, composed into 3,4, and 5 parts, for the use and delight of such as either love or learne Musicke."

Johann von Münster's "Traktat vom ungottseligen Tanz" appeared this year.

Palestrina's Book II for five voices was actually a canzone in thirty sections, each forming a madrigale spirituale. It appeared this year.

Palestrina's "Liber sextus . . . Missae Quinque 4 ac 5 vocibus concinatus" was dedicated to Cardinal Pietro Aldobrandini and published by Coattino at Rome this year.

Palestrina's "Liber Septimus . . . Missae Quinque" (4 ac 5

1594(cont.)
vocibus) was published by Coattino at Rome this year.

This year marked the first publication of the following masses by Palestrina: "Ave Maria," "Sanctorum meritis," "Emendemus in melius," "Sacerdos et pontifex," and "Tu es pastor ovium."

Palestrina's six-part "Ave Maria" appears in print for the first time this year.

Palestrina's second volume of motets was reprinted by Gardano at Venice this year.

Palestrina's third volume of motets was reprinted by Scotto and Gardano at Venice (see also 1575, 1581 and 1589).

Volumes eight and nine of Palestrina's works were published this year.

Peter Philipp's "Melodia Olympica di diversi Excellentissimi Musici a IV, V, VI, et VIII voci" was published in 1591 and reprinted this year (see also 1611).

Some madrigals by Bartolommeo Spontone were included in collections of Waelrant's works this year.

Sweelinck's five-part "chansons" appeared this year.

After Cardinal Allen's death this year, Charles Tregian wrote a "Planctus de Morte Cardinalis Alani."

Vecchi's "L'Amfiparnasso" was performed at Mantua this year and published soon afterwards (cont.) at Venice.

Waelrant's "Symphonia Angelica" was published this year at Antwerp.

Edmund Spenser married Elizabeth Boyle.

Kyd's "Spanish Tragedy" was published this year.

Thomas Nash's "The Unfortunate Traveller, or, The Life of Jack Wilton" appeared this year.

Shakespeare enjoyed a good reputation as an actor by this time.

Shakespeare's "Lucrece" was entered at Stationers' Hall at this time.

William Claesz, Dutch painter, was born (died c.1680).

Nicolas Poussin, French painter, was born (died 1665). He exerted great influence on European art.

Jacopo Robusti, Italian painter known as Tintoretto, died (born 1518).

During this period and with express permission from the Duke, Monteverdi married Claudia Cattaneo, the daughter of a violist colleague. She herself was a professional singer.

(to 1595) Landgrave Moritz became acquainted with Alessandro Orologio and John Dowland, the English lutenist, during this year.

(to 1595) Raselius - gospels for the year in German appeared during this period.

1594(cont.)

(to 1595) Shakespeare's "Romeo and Juliet" was completed at this time.

(to 1595) Shakespeare's "Midsummer-Night's Dream" was completed during this period.

(and 1598) Luca Bati's two madrigal books appeared at these two dates respectively.

(to 1598) The reign of Prince Sigismund of Poland over Sweden. He was most interested in music.

(and 1600) A pastoral drama, "Dafne," written by Rinuccini with music by Caccini and Peri, was completed this year. "Euridice, Tragedia per Musica" by the same poet and musicians (1600) was to be the actual beginning of modern opera.

(to 1601) Iginio, the composer's son, disposed of some of Palestrina's masses and madrigals to several people who published them during this period. Six books of masses resulted from this situation.

(and 1604) Two other editions of "The Whole Book of Psalms, with their wonted tunes, in four parts" were printed by Este at these years respectively.

(to 1607) Lodovico Grossi da Viadana was Maestro di Capella at Mantua Cathedral during these years.

(to 1612) In the years between the deaths of Palestrina and Giovanni Gabrieli (1612) the patterns of musical thought underwent great changes as a (cont.) result of Italian innovations.

(to 1613) After Polycarp Leyser's tenure during these years a difficult and problematical figure, an Australian nobleman, Mathias Hoe von Hoenegg emerged.

(to 1615) Calvisius was the Cantor at the Thomasschule in Leipzig for this entire period.

(and 1750) Palestrina's music, unique in its technical purity as well as its self-imposed limitations, carried over from Flemish polyphony, was as much an artistic anachronism at this time as was Bach's "Art of Fugue" in 1750.

c.1594

Juan Blas de Castro became músico privado to the Duke of Alba at Salamanca around this time.